THE JOURNAL OF INDUSTRIAL ECONOMICS

VOLUME XXXIII
1984–85

ISSN 0022-1821

BASIL BLACKWELL
OXFORD

CONTENTS

VOLUME XXXIII

Number 1, September 1984

RONALD R. BRAEUTIGAM, ANDREW F. DAUGHETY and MARK A. TURNQUIST
A Firm Specific Analysis of Economies of Density in the US Railroad Industry 3

G. THOMAS SAV
The Engineering Approach to Economic Production Functions Revisited: An Application to Solar Processes 21

BRUNO L. DE BORGER
Cost and Productivity in Regional Bus Transportation: The Belgian Case 37

DAVID E. MILLS
Demand Fluctuations and Endogenous Firm Flexibility 55

C. Y. BALDWIN, J. J. TRIBENDIS and J. P. CLARK
The Evolution of Market Risk in the US Steel Industry and Implications for Required Rates of Return 73

Short Articles and Notes

ROBERT M. FEINBERG
Paralegals and Substitution Among Labor Inputs in the Law Firm 99

STEPHEN FARBER
Pareto-Optimal Effluent Taxation and Market Structure in the Presence of Uncertain Demand and Detection 105

BERNHARD WANIK
The Development of Wages of German Industrial Corporations 113

STEVEN S. WILDMAN
A Note on Measuring Surplus Attributable to Differentiated Products 123

F. M. SCHERER
Measuring Surplus Attributable to Differentiated Products: Reply 133

ARVIND MAHAJAN
Profitability Measures as Indicators of Post-Merger Efficiency Revisited 135

G. MEEKS and J. G. MEEKS
Profitability Measures as Indicators of Post-Merger Efficiency: Reply 139

Number 2, December 1984

PANKAJ GHEMAWAT
Capacity Expansion in the Titanium Dioxide Industry 145

DAVID M. BARTON and ROGER SHERMAN
The Price and Profit Effects of Horizontal Merger: A Case Study 165

DONALD J. LECRAW
Diversification Strategy and Performance 179

THOMAS E. GETZEN
A "Brand Name Firm" Theory of Medical Group Practice 199

M. E. BEESLEY and R. T. HAMILTON
Small Firms' Seedbed Role and the Concept of Turbulence 217

Short Articles and Notes

JOHN C. HILKE
Excess Capacity and Entry: Some Empirical Evidence 233

R. S. THOMPSON
Structure and Conduct in Local Advertising Markets: The Case of Irish Provincial Newspapers 241

BRUCE L. BENSON
On the Ability of Spatial Competitors to Price Discriminate 251

Number 3, March 1985

ROBERT A. TAGGART, Jr.
Effects of Regulation on Utility Financing: Theory and Evidence 257

JAMES A. BRANDER and BARBARA J. SPENCER
Tacit Collusion, Free Entry and Welfare 277

DOUGLAS TODD
Productive Performance in West German Manufacturing Industry 1970–80: A Farrell Frontier Characterisation 295

DAMIEN NEVEN
Two Stage (Perfect) Equilibrium in Hotelling's Model 317

M. S. KUMAR
Growth, Acquisition Activity and Firm Size: Evidence from the United Kingdom 327

Short Articles and Notes

GEIR GRIPSRUD and KJELL GRØNHAUG
Structure and Strategy in Grocery Retailing: a Sociometric Approach 339

M. S. SILVER
On the Measurement of Changes in Aggregate Concentration, Market Concentration and Diversification 349

ALAN J. DASKIN
Dynamics of Canadian Deposit-Taking Institutions: Comment 353

ARUN K. MUKHOPADHYAY
Returns to Scale in R &D and the Schumpeterian Hypothesis: a Comment 359

MEIR KOHN and JOHN T. SCOTT
Scale Economies in Research and Development: a Reply 363

Number 4, June 1985

P. A. GEROSKI, L. PHLIPS and A. ULPH
Oligopoly, Competition and Welfare: Some Recent Developments 369

RAY REES
Cheating in a Duopoly Supergame 387

KEVIN ROBERTS
Cartel Behaviour and Adverse Selection 401

ROBERT H. PORTER
On the Incidence and Duration of Price Wars 415

JONATHAN B. BAKER and TIMOTHY F. BRESNAHAN
The Gains from Merger or Collusion in Product-Differentiated Industries 427

DAVID EASLEY, ROBERT T. MASSON and ROBERT J. REYNOLDS
Preying for Time 445

CHRISTOPHER HARRIS and JOHN VICKERS
Patent Races and the Persistence of Monopoly 461

HUW DIXON
Strategic Investment in an Industry with a Competitive Product Market 483

NORMAN J. IRELAND
Product Diversity and Monopolistic Competition under Uncertainty 501

G. K. YARROW
Welfare Losses in Oligopoly and Monopolistic Competition 515

THOMAS von UNGERN-STERNBERG and CARL CHRISTIAN von WEIZSÄCKER
The Supply of Quality on a Market for "Experience Goods" 531

Bibliography 541

THE JOURNAL OF INDUSTRIAL ECONOMICS

Volume XXXIII SEPTEMBER 1984 No. 1

RONALD R. BRAEUTIGAM, ANDREW F. DAUGHETY AND MARK A. TURNQUIST
A Firm Specific Analysis of Economies of Density in the U.S. Railroad Industry 3

G. THOMAS SAV
The Engineering Approach to Economic Production Functions Revisited: An Application to Solar Processes 21

BRUNO L. DE BORGER
Cost and Productivity in Regional Bus Transportation: The Belgian Case 37

DAVID E. MILLS
Demand Fluctuations and Endogenous Firm Flexibility 55

C. Y. BALDWIN, J. J. TRIBENDIS AND J. P. CLARK
The Evolution of Market Risk in the U.S. Steel Industry and Implications for Required Rates of Return 73

Short Articles and Notes

ROBERT M. FEINBERG
Paralegals and Substitution Among Labor Inputs in the Law Firm 99

STEPHEN FARBER
Pareto-Optimal Effluent Taxation and Market Structure in the Presence of Uncertain Demand and Detection 105

BERNHARD WANIK
The Development of Wages of German Industrial Corporations 113

STEVEN S. WILDMAN
A Note on Measuring Surplus Attributable to Differentiated Products 123

F. M. SCHERER
Measuring Surplus Attributable to Differentiated Products: Reply 133

ARVIND MAHAJAN
Profitability Measures as Indicators of Post-Merger Efficiency Revisited 135

G. MEEKS and J. G. MEEKS
Profitability Measures as Indicators of Post-Merger Efficiency: Reply 139

ISSN 0022-1821
BASIL BLACKWELL OXFORD ENGLAND

CHANGE IN THE NORTH AMERICAN EDITOR

AS FROM 1st September 1984, Professor Lawrence J. White of the Graduate School of Business Administration, New York University, will succeed Professor H. Michael Mann as North American Editor of the Journal. Professor White is the author of numerous books and journal articles in the field of industrial organisation. He previously taught at Princeton University, and was Chief Economist in the Economic Policy Office of the Antitrust Division of the U.S. Department of Justice 1982–83.

Submissions *from North America* should in future be sent to Professor L. White, The Journal of Industrial Economics, Graduate School of Business Administration, New York University, 100 Trinity Place, New York, NY 10006, U.S.A. Submissions from all countries outside North America should continue to be sent to the General Editor in the U.K.

Many readers of the Journal will wish to know of the circumstances that led to Professor Mann's resignation. In January of this year he suffered a severe heart attack, as a result of which he is permanently disabled. Members of the Editorial Board wish to put on record their appreciation of his conscientious execution of his editorial responsibilities for the eight years in which he held the post of North American Editor. They also wish to express their sympthy to his wife and family.

THE ELIZABETH BRUNNER MEMORIAL FUND

The University of Lancaster is setting up a fund to commemorate the outstanding contribution of the late Professor Elizabeth Brunner. The fund will be used to finance Elizabeth Brunner Prize(s), awards to be made annually to the most outstanding undergraduate student(s) in the Department of Economics.

If you wish to contribute to The Elizabeth Brunner Memorial Fund, please send donations to:

Miss Stephanie Arkwright
Department of Economics
University of Lancaster,
Gillow House
Lancaster LA1 4YX

or

The University Finance Officer
University of Lancaster
University House,
Lancaster LA1 4YW

Cheques to be made payable to The University of Lancaster.

THE JOURNAL OF INDUSTRIAL ECONOMICS 0022–1821 $2.00
Volume XXXIII September 1984 No. 1

A FIRM SPECIFIC ANALYSIS OF ECONOMIES OF DENSITY IN THE U.S. RAILROAD INDUSTRY*

RONALD R. BRAEUTIGAM, ANDREW F. DAUGHETY AND MARK A. TURNQUIST

I. INTRODUCTION

AN UNDERSTANDING of the nature of costs of production is important in every regulated industry, both for policy makers and firms. Policy makers may be interested in whether there are economies of scale in production, and in whether there are technological aspects of an industry that will pose difficult problems if an industry is regulated. Regulators and firms may be interested in costs for ratemaking purposes, and in decisions about the effects of introducing new services or discontinuing existing services.

Historically most cost studies in regulated industries have used data drawn from a cross section of firms, or from a combination of cross section and time series data. These studies typically assume that there is a single production structure common amongst the firms in the industry. However, the formal representation of the cost function sometimes includes a set of parameters designed to capture elements of the environment, such as weather or terrain, that may affect the underlying production process.

Though the inclusion of such parameters may improve specification of the model, it fails to capture many basic differences among firms. As Mundlak [1961] has shown, in time series-cross section studies, the failure to capture firm-specific effects can lead to biases in estimated coefficients important to policy prescriptions. This is further emphasized in the recent work of Caves, Christensen, and Tretheway [1981]. These authors found that the introduction of dummy variables to distinguish each firm in their sample of airlines resulted in a finding of increasing returns to scale, while the estimated model without the dummy variables indicated constant returns to scale.

There is, therefore, an important role for econometric analysis of cost at the level of a single firm, using time series data. That role is to provide an opportunity to examine the existence and extent of such biases in studies relying on cross sectional data.

This brings us to the point of the present paper. We formulate and estimate a long run cost function for a single, large railroad firm, using time series data. In a previous paper (Braeutigam, Daughety, and Turnquist [1982], hereafter referred to as BDT), we performed a similar study to estimate a short run

* The authors thank Steve Lanning and the executives and staffs of the railroads studied herein. This research was supported by a contract DOT-OS-70061, between the United States Department of Transportation and Northwestern University.

variable cost function for a smaller sized railroad. Each study has the advantage of avoiding the effects of mixing technology, and therefore the kinds of biases described by Mundlak. Each has also relied on data obtained directly from the firm, thereby avoiding the rather arbitrary transformations and allocations of cost often found in the data reported by the Interstate Commerce Commission.[1] Further, each study has included a measure of quality of service (the speed of service through the system) to improve model specification.

One of the important operating characteristics we investigate in both of our studies is economies of density. As Keeler [1974] has observed, one can distinguish at least two types of scale economies in the railroad industry. If the network configuration is held fixed, then economies of scale resulting from increased traffic volume is referred to as *economies of density*. On the other hand, one might ask whether there are scale economies when the size of the network (in terms of the numbers of network nodes and arcs) can also change as output varies and the traffic volume along each arc is adjusted optimally. We define this broader notion of economies of scale as *economies of size*.

The distinction between economies of density and economies of size can be crucial for certain types of policy questions. For example suppose that in determining whether to allow a parallel merger, policy makers are concerned about the potential effects on railroad costs as more traffic moves over a given network. Then economies of density would be of particular interest. On the other hand, in assessing the cost effects of end-to-end mergers, then economies of size would also be relevant. Of course, combinations of the two could also be important.

The important point is this. The distinction between the two is crucial since economies of density neither imply, nor are implied by, economies of size. Unfortunately most of the cross section studies of railroad costs fail to make this distinction; railroads reflecting different sizes and configurations are mixed together in the estimations.

As an example of the difficulties one may encounter when firm-specific effects are omitted, consider the recent study of Caves, Christensen and Swanson [1980]. Using a combination of cross section and time series data, these authors were unable to reject the hypothesis of constant returns to scale in the railroad industry. However, since the authors do not control for firm-specific differences, the test cannot distinguish between economies of size and economies of density. Moreover, sub-groups of firms may experience economies (or diseconomies) of density or size, while others do not. Relying on a single aggregate measure masks these differences.

In our own work, we have taken advantage of the opportunity to identify clearly and distinctively the economies of density. In the present study as well as the earlier one, the size of the network was essentially unchanged in both

[1] For a discussion of the kinds of problems arising from the use of ICC data, see, for example, Friedlaender [1969], particularly Appendix A.

cases. Thus, the two studies are able to test for, and in fact do find, substantial economies of density.

Further, these studies provide a strong indication that quality of service is important in a properly specified cost model. In addition, the omission of such a variable can alter substantially the coefficients on other terms in a cost function. Among the other consequences of such an omission might well be incorrect inferences about the existence and extent of economies of size and density.

The paper proceeds by developing the model to be estimated and discussing the firm selection and data development in section two and providing the results of the short-run variable cost function estimation in section three. Section three also contains the estimate of the long-run function and the analysis of returns-to-density as well as the tests of the model with respect to: 1) inclusion of quality of service variables, and 2) separability of inputs from outputs in the description of the firm's technology. Section four provides conclusions and a summary of major implications of our research on firm-level cost functions.

II. THE MODEL AND DATA

The Model

Our approach will be to specify short-run variable costs as a function of a vector of outputs (flow, y, and quality (average speed) of service, s), a fixed factor, k, and an n-vector of exogeneously determined variable factor prices, p^v, which is expressed as follows:

$$(1) \qquad c^v(y, s, p^v, k).$$

A functional form will be assumed for (1) and estimated, yielding the short-run variable cost function. The long-run cost function will be found by appending a fixed cost term to (1) and solving for the optimal level of fixed factor k^*:

$$(2) \qquad c(y, s, p) = \min_k [c^v(y, s, p^v, k) + p^f \cdot k]$$

where $p = (p^v, p^f)$ is the vector of factor prices in the long run function. As in BDT we assume that the flow variable, y, is determined exogeneously since the firm operates as a common carrier and is required to provide service to any shipper requesting service at the tariff in force. This assumption has been made implicitly (or explicitly) by all previous railroad cost studies and reflects the institutional setting that has existed for almost one hundred years. We will not assume presently that average speed of service, s, is exogenous; we will return to this point shortly.

In order to estimate (1) a functional form was assumed; we will use the transcendental logarithmic (translog) form developed by Christensen, Jorgenson and Lau [1973]. The translog representation of (1) will be the following:

$$C^v = \sum_{i=1}^{m} \alpha_{io} X_i + 1/2 \sum_{i=1}^{m} \sum_{j=1}^{m} \alpha_{ij} X_i X_j \tag{3}$$

where $m = n + 3$ is the number of variables in (1) and

C^v = ln(short-run variable cost/average of short-run variable costs),

X_i = ln(variable i/average of observations for variable i).

Thus, X_1 and X_2 correspond to flow and speed respectively, X_3 to X_{n+2} correspond to the variable factor prices and X_m to the fixed factor. The above transformation of the variables accomplishes two things. First, it centers the estimation at the "point-of-means", placing the tightest part of the model's prediction confidence interval in the middle of the data base. Second, it protects the proprietary nature of the data; by not providing the sample means we can still provide a complete analysis of the cost function without revealing proprietary information on *absolute* levels of cost.

Following Christensen and Greene [1976] we append $n - 1$ factor share equations to (3) which are of the form

$$h_i = \alpha_{io} + \sum_{j=1}^{m} \alpha_{ij} X_j \qquad i = 3, \ldots, m - 2. \tag{4}$$

Note that only $n - 1$ equations are needed since total factor shares sum to one. The factor share equations are derived using Shephard's Lemma (see Shephard [1970]) as:

$$h_i = \frac{\partial C^v}{\partial X_i} = \frac{p_i}{c^v} \frac{\partial c^v}{\partial p_i} = \frac{p_i x_i}{c^v} \qquad i = 2, \ldots, m - 2$$

where x_i is the quantity of variable factor i used by the firm.

From economic theory (see, for example, Varian [1978]) we know that the cost function should be: 1) monotonically non-decreasing in outputs and 2) homogeneous of degree one and concave in prices. Homogeneity is enforced by restricting the parameter estimates as follows:

$$\begin{aligned} &\sum_{i=3}^{m-1} \alpha_{io} = 1 \\ &\sum_{j=3}^{m-1} \alpha_{ij} = 0 \qquad i = 1, \ldots, m. \end{aligned} \tag{5}$$

Since the cost function and marginal cost function will be assumed to be continuous functions of their arguments, the cross-partials should satisfy symmetry restrictions:

$$(6) \qquad \alpha_{ij} = \alpha_{ji} \qquad i, j = 1, \ldots, m.$$

Concavity and monotonicity will not be enforced in the estimation. We shall see that the resulting estimated cost function satisfies these properties.

In BDT we assumed that the average speed of service, s, was exogenous. This made sense for the railroad studied therein since it was a firm that functioned as a bridge line between two major carriers. The railroad under study had to meet the schedules of the major carriers, since alternative routes existed for the major firms. Thus s was set exogenously to the firm.

The railroad under study in this paper is not a bridge line; it is, in fact, a major carrier. Thus, the discussion above is not applicable. Certainly, in the long run, one would expect s to be set endogenously so as to maximize profit (presumably s is important to shippers). It may also be true that s is endogenous in the short-run, thereby requiring an additional equation (that the marginal revenue with respect to speed, MR_s, is equal to the short-run marginal cost with respect to speed, $MC_s^v = \partial c^v/\partial s$). Such a restriction is not linear in the parameters of (3). However, a slight manipulation is, namely:

$$MC_s^v \frac{s}{c^v} = \frac{\partial C^v}{\partial X_2}$$

$$= \alpha_{20} + \sum_{j=1}^{m} \alpha_{2j} X_j .$$

Thus, if there is evidence that the firm sets the speed of service endogenously in the short run, we will append the following equation:

$$(7) \qquad MR_s \frac{s}{c^v} = \alpha_{20} + \sum_{j=1}^{m} \alpha_{2j} X_j .$$

Finally, we will assume jointly distributed, additive error terms for (3), (4) and (7). Furthermore, since we will employ monthly data for a specific firm, we allow first-order autocorrelated error terms. A representation of this is the following:

$$(8) \qquad \varepsilon_i^t = \sum_{j=1}^{4} \rho_{ij} \varepsilon_j^{t-1} + u_i^t \qquad i = 1, \ldots, m-2$$

where ε_i^t is the additive error term in equation i for month t, the u_i^t are independent, normally distributed random variables and the ρ_{ij} are the autocorrelation coefficients. Note that the translog cost function (3) is represented by $i = 1$, the MC_s^v equation (7) by $i = 2$, and the $n - 1$ factor share equations (4) by $i = 3$ to $i = m - 2$.

Therefore our model to be estimated is the cost function (1) the speed equation (7) (if there is evidence of short-run endogeneity of s), and $(n - 1)$ factor share equations (4), subject to price homogeneity (5), symmetry (6) and autocorrelation (8).

Firm Selection and Data Development

Several criteria were used in considering potential railroad candidates for this study. We desired a large Class I railroad with a management willing to work with us in providing the data required for analysis. While the firm in question completed some merger activity during the period studied, the companies were already owned and operated as subsidiaries, so that data would be added across the firms to maintain a consistent reporting base.

One obvious requirement for the analysis was that we obtain a complete set of data, reported on a consistent basis, for all of the variables discussed in the theoretical section. We were able to obtain such a set of data on a monthly basis for the 35 months between January, 1976 and November, 1978.

One of the additional points we considered in our development was the possibility of including explicitly a variable to represent technological change in the system. However, because the time horizon was only 35 months, the issue of technological change did not emerge as a major point to be included in the model.

Costs and Revenues

We obtained operating cost data directly from company records. Since these data do not include implicit capital costs on cars and locomotives, an estimate of these additional costs was made using the car and locomotive prices and the number of cars and locomotives. The additional costs plus operating costs yield the short run variable cost data required for our estimation. Thus, the short-run variable cost includes maintenance, fuel, labor, cars, locomotives, staff and supplies. Operating revenues were also obtained directly from company records. Both cost and revenue data were reported on a monthly basis.

Prices of Variable Factors

At the beginning of our study, we intended to include two kinds of labor in the analysis—crew labor and noncrew (i.e., all other) labor. We computed a factor price for noncrew labor by dividing the total number of noncrew hours actually worked into the sum of the noncrew wage bill, payroll taxes, and medical insurance paid by the firm. We also computed a crew labor price by dividing the straight time actually worked for crews into the sum of total wage payments to crews, payroll taxes for crew labor, and medical insurance payments.

We found that the prices for crew and noncrew labor had a correlation coefficient in excess of 0.95. Therefore, we merged the information to get a single price of labor, calculated by taking the total wage bill, payroll tax and insurance payments for both crew and noncrew labor, and then dividing that sum by the total hours worked in the two categories. We also generated a labor share by dividing the total wage, payroll tax and medical insurance payments by the total short-run variable cost of the firm.

We also investigated whether labor should be treated as a variable or fixed factor, and found overwhelming institutional evidence that it should be treated as variable. The basis for this is the existence of "extra boards" which allow the firm to redistribute labor where needed in the firm. This spatial and temporal redistribution mechanism leads to great flexibility in the use of labor. Further, if the labor requirements of the firm are reduced to such a level that redistribution of labor by extra boards cannot fully employ the labor, then the firm can (and often does) furlough unneeded laborers.

We obtained data for each time period on the number of cars owned and leased, by type of car. We also found the number of locomotives, by type, both owned and leased. We obtained data on the prices of cars and locomotives from *Economic ABZ's of the Railroad Industry* [1980] and Welty [1978]. These prices for physical units of capital were converted to equivalent rental prices using the interest rate on equipment obligations of the firm and depreciation rates from Swanson [1968].

We then found that the factor prices for locomotives and cars over the 35 month period had a correlation coefficient in excess of 0.95. Therefore, we used the locomotive factor price to represent the two categories. We will refer to this price as the price of equipment. Also, the omitted share equation (as discussed earlier) was the one for locomotives and cars. Thus we did not compute a factor share for these inputs; the share attributed implicitly to the locomotives and cars is the equipment share.

Flow and Speed

To measure the volume of traffic moved we obtained company data on all movements in the system, by origin-destination and by two-digit Standard Transportation Commodity Code, on a monthly basis. The flow output is measured in total carloads moved for each month.

Data enabling us to calculate average speed on the system also were obtained directly from operating records. We gathered data on the total loaded car-miles during each month for the whole system, and then divided this by the total loaded car-days-on-line for that month. This calculation yielded a monthly average velocity, in terms of miles per day for loaded cars on the system. This approach provides a convenient way to estimate average speed of service.

Fixed Factor

It is not an easy task to characterize the fixed factors of a system as complex as a railroad. The fixed factors include track, switches, land and buildings, to name the most obvious of the elements. We have employed a measure of miles of track to represent the level of the fixed factor in our analysis. We have done so because track represents the largest component of the system that can be regarded as fixed within a monthly horizon but which can be varied (at least to some extent) over a 35 month horizon. Moreover, investment in track appeared to be the main component of a general vector of fixed factors that was adjusting during the period studied.

In our study we observed that the total track-miles in place did not vary significantly over the 35 month period. However, the firm was investing in track in amounts significantly greater than would be required to maintain a constant quality of track in the face of normal depreciation. Thus, it was apparent that the firm was varying not the quantity of track in place over the three year period, but rather was improving track quality through track investment.

Thus, we constructed a measure of "effective" track as follows. Consider the disposition of investment in track during period t. The amount of gross investment (in miles) is I_t. I_t is considered to have three possible uses: (1) expansion or contraction of the system (generally small in our case), (2) coverage of physical depreciation of existing track, and (3) changes in the amount of effective track through quality improvements in the existing system. Thus, we define:

T_t = the actual number of miles of track at the end of period t;

δ = depreciation rate of existing track;

Δk_t = changes in effective track during period t.

Then the uses of I_t (gross investment) are summarized as:

$$I_t = (T_t - T_{t-1}) + \delta T_{t-1} + \Delta k_t. \tag{9}$$

The first term on the right hand side of the equation indicates the amount by which actual track-miles change during period t. The second term shows how much investment (in track-miles) would be required to offset normal depreciation (wear and tear) on existing track. The last term represents improvement in track quality above normal requirements to cover depreciation during period t.

We observe that the above equation can be rewritten, using the fact that $k_t - k_{t-1} = \Delta k_t$. Then the following relationship can be stated:

(10) $k_t = k_{t-1} + I_t(T_{t-1} - T_t) - \delta T_{t-1}.$

(We re-emphasize that the parenthetical term on the right hand side is essentially negligible in our actual case study.) Because this is a difference equation one of the k_t must be chosen arbitrarily. The equation then defines the remaining effective track values relative to this one. This was done by letting $k_t = T_t$ at the end of 1976.

The Price of the Fixed Factor

An extensive study of track costs was undertaken by Danzig, *et al.* [1976]. The net cost per mile of track is in the range of about $58,000 per mile, assuming 25% tie replacement and some ballast replacement. Ballast cost includes labor expenditures which in principle we would exclude because we desire capital costs, exclusive of labor. However, since total ballast costs are minimal, we view this as a minor problem, especially since we have examined a broad range of track costs in our derivations of long-run cost functions for the estimated short-run cost function.

Implicit Exogeneity of Speed-of-Service

Our statistical evidence suggests that average speed-of-service is exogenously determined in the short-run. This was discovered when we calculated the marginal revenue with respect to speed-of-service and discovered that it was often negative (in many cases substantially negative). Our procedure for imputing the marginal revenue with respect to speed-of-service was to assume that total revenue (TR) is a function of speed (s) and flow (y). Differentiating totally we have that $dTR = MR_s\,ds + MR_y\,dy$ where MR_s is the marginal revenue with respect to speed, MR_y is the marginal revenue with respect to flow and ds and dy are the infinitesimals of speed and flow. Solving for MR_s we have:

$$MR_s = \frac{dTR - MR_y\,dy}{ds}.$$

Let dTR be approximated by the change in operating revenues from month to month:

$$dTR^t = OR^t - OR^{t-1}$$

where OR^t is the operating revenue for the firm in month t. Furthermore, let $dy^t = y^t - y^{t-1}$ and $ds^t = s^t - s^{t-1}$. Finally, since this firm is regulated in terms of tariffs charged, marginal and average revenue with respect to y are the same; i.e., $MR_y = AR_y$. Let us approximate AR_y^t as:

$$AR_y^t = \frac{OR^t}{y^t}.$$

Thus, our approximation for MR_s^t becomes:

$$(11) \qquad MR_s^t = \frac{(OR^t - OR^{t-1}) - \dfrac{OR^t}{y^t}(y^t - y^{t-1})}{s^t - s^{t-1}}.$$

MR_s^t was computed via (11) using the monthly data described above. Sixty-five percent of the computed values were negative. If s were endogenous to the firm this should not happen; marginal revenue should exceed zero since otherwise reducing s would contribute to revenues and presumably reduce costs, thereby increasing profits.

The implication of this is that speed is not endogenous to the firm in the short-run. This reflects the intense competition the railroad faces with respect to speed-of-service: this railroad competes with other railroads and with trucks. Thus, competition has acted to make speed implicitly *exogenous* to the firm in the short-run. The exogeneity of speed-of-service implies that the speed equation (7) should be dropped from the system. The resulting system to be estimated has three equations and twenty-seven coefficients.

III. ESTIMATION RESULTS

Given the discussion above, we repose the system to be estimated as follows:

$$(12) \qquad C^{vt} = \sum_{i=1}^{6} \alpha_{io} X_i^t + 1/2 \sum_{i=1}^{6} \sum_{j=1}^{6} \alpha_{ij} X_i^t X_j^t + \varepsilon_1^t$$

$$(13) \qquad h_i^t = \alpha_{io} + \sum_{j=1}^{6} \alpha_{ij} X_j^t + \varepsilon_{i-1}^t \quad i = 3, 4$$

$$\sum_{i=3}^{5} \alpha_{io} = 1$$

$$(14) \qquad \sum_{j=3}^{5} \alpha_{ij} = 0 \qquad i = 1, \ldots, 6$$

$$(15) \qquad \alpha_{ij} = \alpha_{ji} \qquad i, j = 1, \ldots, 6$$

with the following correspondences:

i	X_i^t
1	Flow (in carloads)
2	Speed (in miles/day)
3	Fuel Price (in dollars/gallon)
4	Wage rate (in dollars/hour)
5	Equipment price (in dollars/month)
6	Fixed Factor (miles of effective track)

and allowing for autocorrelation:

$$(16) \qquad \varepsilon_k^t = \sum_{l=1}^{3} \rho_{kl}\, \varepsilon_l^{t-1} + u_k^t$$

where $k = 1$, 2 and 3 correspond to the cost, fuel share and labor share equations, respectively.

The above system was estimated via full information maximum likelihood using the WYMER program, on Northwestern's CDC/Cyber computer. The homogeneity restrictions were incorporated by normalizing the cost variable and all prices to the price of equipment. Thus, values of coefficients associated with price of equipment are implied by the regression and the standard errors of these coefficients are computed by approximation. Table I provides the estimated coefficients for the cost function and the standard errors. Mnemonics for the prices have been used (i.e., PFUEL is the price of fuel, etc.).

The first-order coefficient estimates for flow, capital and the three price terms are significant (at the 0.001 level) and of the correct sign. Thus, the cost function is non-decreasing in outputs as required, and is homogeneous of

TABLE I
TRANSLOG SHORT-RUN VARIABLE COST FUNCTION

Variable	*Coefficient*	*Estimate*	*Standard Error*
Y	α_{10}	0.3984	0.0694
S	α_{20}	−0.0659	0.0746
PFUEL	α_{30}	0.1902	0.0600
PLABOR	α_{40}	0.5253	0.0547
PEQUIP	α_{50}	0.2845	0.0248
K	α_{60}	−0.2771	0.0887
Y · Y	α_{11}	4.1260	1.5776
Y · S	α_{12}	−2.6510	1.3848
Y · PFUEL	α_{13}	−0.0167	0.0069
Y · PLABOR	α_{14}	0.0090	0.0258
Y · PEQUIP	α_{15}	0.0077	0.0264
Y · K	α_{16}	−2.8813	1.0598
S · S	α_{22}	−0.3681	1.8906
S · PFUEL	α_{23}	0.0404	0.0069
S · PLABOR	α_{24}	0.0067	0.0298
S · PEQUIP	α_{25}	−0.0471	0.0306
S · K	α_{26}	2.9855	1.2109
PFUEL · PFUEL	α_{33}	0.0623	0.0104
PFUEL · PLABOR	α_{34}	−0.0489	0.0083
PFUEL · PEQUIP	α_{35}	−0.0134	0.0061
PFUEL · K	α_{36}	0.0668	0.1557
PLABOR · PLABOR	α_{44}	0.0860	0.0176
PLABOR · PEQUIP	α_{45}	−0.0371	0.0165
PLABOR · K	α_{46}	0.1166	0.2213
PEQUIP · PEQUIP	α_{55}	0.0505	0.0189
PEQUIP · K	α_{56}	−0.1834	0.3739
K · K	α_{66}	2.5447	3.0202

degree one in prices. Computation at the point-of-means reveals that the cost function is concave in prices (this is in spite of the fact that the translog cost function is not concave in prices).[2]

The first-order price terms are the elasticities of cost with respect to price at the point of means. Thus, for example, a one percent change in the wage rate will increase costs by slightly over 0.5 percent. The coefficient on the price of equipment represents the impact of both locomotives and cars. Increases in the amount of effective track reduces short-run variable costs at the point of means; a one percent increase in effective track miles implies a 0.2771 percent reduction in short-run variable costs, which is reasonable since the cost of the improvement is not included in short-run variable costs.

The first-order speed-of-service parameter (α_{20}) is insignificant but a test[3] of the hypothesis that the speed variables should be dropped is soundly rejected (at the 0.005 level). Thus, even though the first-order speed term is insignificant, the speed variable itself is very important for proper model specification.

The first-order flow term is significant, positive and indicates that a one percent change in flow will generate a 0.3984 percent increase in short-run variable costs. Thus,

$$\frac{\partial \ln c^v}{\partial \ln y} = \left(\frac{y}{c^v}\right)\left(\frac{\partial c^v}{\partial y}\right) = \frac{MC_y}{AVC_y} = 0.3984;$$

i.e., short-run marginal costs are below short-run average variable costs at the point of means. Thus at the point of approximation, short-run average variable costs are falling with respect to flow.

Since we wiew output as reflecting both a physical flow of goods y and a quality measure s, (average speed-of-service), simplification of the cost function would result if y and s were jointly separable from the inputs (represented by p and k). The hypothesis that y and s are separable from the inputs was tested and rejected at the 0.005 level.[4]

[2] Note that the estimated translog function is not concave in prices (second-order own price coefficients are all positive). The price Hessian of the cost function (at the point-of-means) is computed via the following:

$$\frac{\partial^2 c^v}{\partial p_i \, \partial p_j} = \frac{c^v}{p_i p_j}\left[\alpha_{ij} + \alpha_{jo} - \alpha_{io}\,\delta_{ij}\right]$$

where

$$\delta_{ij} = \begin{cases} 1, & i = j. \\ 0, & \text{otherwise.} \end{cases}$$

Using this expression we find the cost function is concave in prices at the point-of-means.

[3] Log-likelihood ratio tests (see Theil [1971]) were employed in both this test and the test of separability to be discussed below.

[4] One should bear in mind that Blackorby, Primont and Russell [1978] and Denny and Fuss [1977] have shown that the imposition of separability restrictions on a translog system implicitly imposes significant structure on certain aggregate functions used in the test. Thus, a rejection of the test may only reflect rejection of the aggregation functions, and not necessarily rejection of separability itself.

Construction of the Long-Run Cost Function

Let p_k be the price of a mile of effective track (see Section II). At the point of means for all the variables *except* k we have the following equation for short-run *total* costs (i.e., variable plus fixed):

$$c^v(\bar{y}, \bar{s}, \bar{p}; k) = \bar{c}^v \exp(\alpha_{60} \ln(k/\bar{k}) + \alpha_{66}(\ln(k/\bar{k}))^2) + p_k k \qquad (17)$$

where a (—) over the variable represents the mean of the observations for the variable. A golden section technique (Wilde [1964]) was used to find k^*, the optimal level of the fixed factor. As suggested in Section II, there is considerable uncertainty concerning the proper cost of a mile of effective track. Moreover, the appropriate depreciation rate and cost of capital are also uncertain. We chose to vary the cost of a mile of track from \$40,000 to \$130,000, the depreciation rate from 3 percent to 9 percent and the cost of capital from 8 percent to 12 percent. The results are very encouraging: k^* is reasonably insensitive to such changes. In what follows we will use the assumed values of track cost of \$58,000/effective track-mile, depreciation of 3 percent and cost of capital of 10 percent since these values appear to be reasonable estimates of the appropriate numbers.

Under these conditions we find that $k^* = 1.079\,\bar{k}$. At the point of means the optimal plant size (level of fixed factor) is 1.079 times the average for the period studied. Since the configuration is fixed this implies that the firm should increase the quality of the existing track by approximately 8 percent. Using this value of k^*, we can substitute into the short-run cost function and derive the long-run cost which is presented in Table II. Notice that the first order terms have new coefficients, which are:

$$\tilde{\alpha}_{i0} = \alpha_{i0} + \alpha_{i6} \ln(k^*/\bar{k}) \qquad i = 1, 5.$$

Moreover, a constant term $\tilde{\alpha}_{00} = \alpha_{i0} + \alpha_{i6} \ln(k^*/\bar{k}) + \alpha_{66}(\ln(k^*/\bar{k}))^2$ now appears. It should also be noted that since we are simply substituting k^* into $c^v(y, s, p, k)$, the resulting function is net of fixed costs. This will not affect any of the derivatives of the cost function, and thus Table II contains all the relevant information associated with the long-run cost function.

As indicated in the table, the first order coefficient on flow ($\tilde{\alpha}_{10}$) is insignificant. This appears to be a direct result of the large negative coefficient on the flow/capital cross-term in the short-run function (α_{16} in Table I) coupled with a substantial covariance between α_{16} and the main determinants of k^* (α_{60} and α_{66}). Since the estimate of returns-to-scale (or in this case, density) at the point of means depends on this coefficient, this is a somewhat disappointing result. We will return to this later, after discussing some of the other terms in the function.

The other first-order terms have the expected signs, including speed-of-service which is now significant at approximately the 0.06 level. The coefficient on the first-order speed variable is positive as would be expected since higher quality service should incur higher costs.

TABLE II
TRANSLOG LONG-RUN COST FUNCTION

Variable	*Coefficient*	*Estimate*	*Standard Error*
Y	$\tilde{\alpha}_{10}$	0.1793	0.2852
S	$\tilde{\alpha}_{20}$	0.1611	0.1051
PFUEL	$\tilde{\alpha}_{30}$	0.1953	0.0574
PLABOR	$\tilde{\alpha}_{40}$	0.5342	0.0669
PEQUIP	$\tilde{\alpha}_{50}$	0.2705	0.0698
Y · Y	α_{11}	4.1260	1.5776
Y · S	α_{12}	−2.6510	1.3848
Y · PFUEL	α_{13}	−0.0167	0.0069
Y · PLABOR	α_{14}	0.0090	0.0258
Y · PEQUIP	α_{15}	0.0077	0.0264
S · S	α_{22}	−0.3681	1.8906
S · PFUEL	α_{23}	0.0404	0.0069
S · PLABOR	α_{24}	0.0067	0.0298
S · PEQUIP	α_{25}	−0.0471	0.0306
PFUEL · PFUEL	α_{33}	0.0623	0.0104
PFUEL · PLABOR	α_{34}	−0.0489	0.0083
PFUEL · PEQUIP	α_{35}	−0.0234	0.0061
PLABOR · PLABOR	α_{44}	0.0860	0.0176
PLABOR · PEQUIP	α_{45}	−0.0371	0.0165
PEQUIP · PEQUIP	α_{55}	0.0505	0.0189
CONSTANT	$\tilde{\alpha}_{00}$	−0.0064	0.2283

Table III displays estimates of the factor demand and Allen substitution elasticities. Thus, for example, the own price elasticity of labor is −0.3048, meaning that a one percent increase in the wage rate generates a 0.3048 percent decrease in demand for labor by the firm. The substitution elasticities indicate that fuel, labor and equipment are weak substitutes for one another. Thus, for example, a rise in the price of labor (for output and fuel fixed) will encourage increased use of equipment (e.g., longer trains) relative to labor.

As indicated above, the standard error on the first-order flow term is high, and thus prediction of economies of density using such a number is question-

TABLE III
FACTOR DEMAND AND ALLEN SUBSTITUTION ELASTICITIES AT THE POINT-OF-MEANS

	Elasticity (ε_{ij})	*Allen Elasticities of Substitution* (σ_{ij})		
		Fuel	Labor	Equipment
Fuel	−0.4857	—	0.5312	0.7463
Labor	−0.3048		—	0.7433
Equipment	−0.5428			—

$$\varepsilon_{ij} = \frac{\alpha_{ii}}{\alpha_i} + \alpha_i - 1$$

$$\sigma_{ij} = \frac{\alpha_{ij}}{\alpha_i \alpha_j} + 1$$

able. Let economies of scale be measured as $[\partial \ln c/\partial \ln y]^{-1}$. Friedlaender and Spady [1981] show that one can use the short-run variable cost function to compute long run returns to density at the point-of-means as follows:

$$\left[\frac{\partial \ln c}{\partial \ln y}\right]^{-1} = \frac{1 - [\alpha_{60} + \alpha_{66} \ln(k^*/\bar{k})]}{\alpha_{10}} = 2.71 \tag{18}$$

When coupled with an estimate of the standard error of (18) we can reject the hypothesis of constant returns-to-density at the 0.01 level.

To see the extent of the density economies one would compute the average cost function and find the minimum point. This is accomplished by forming the family of short-run average cost functions as a function of flow and capital:

$$AC(y, \bar{s}, \bar{p}; k) = \frac{1}{y}\left[\bar{c} \exp(\alpha_{10} \ln(y/\bar{y})) + \frac{\alpha_{11}}{2}(\ln(y/y))^2 + \alpha_{60} \ln(k/\bar{k}) + \frac{\alpha_{66}}{2}(\ln(k/\bar{k}))^2 + p_k k\right]$$

and find values y^{**} and k^{**} that simultaneously minimize $AC(y, \bar{s}, \bar{p}; k)$: i.e., find the bottom of the average cost curve. Figure 1 displays the result of this exercise (the dotted lines are approximate extrapolations). The horizontal axis represents flow on the fixed configuration in units of 0.1 MES (minimum efficient scale). Computations show that $\bar{y}$ is approximately 0.4 MES. The range over which the average cost function is at its minimum is from MES to 1.1 MES. Extrapolition indicates that for $y > 1.1$ MES, average cost rises rapidly.

Three short-run average cost curves have been drawn at $k^* = 1.079$, 3.0 and 3.6 $\bar{k}$ respectively. The last two are not overly realistic, since it is hard to

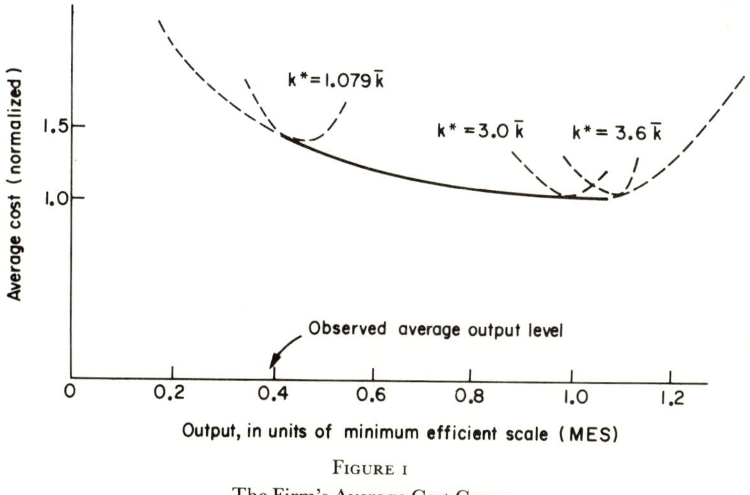

FIGURE 1
The Firm's Average Cost Curve

imagine the present network being improved to three times its present quality. Rather, the point of the figure is to illustrate the fact that the firm does face significant economies-of-density over a wide range of output: average cost at $y = \bar{y}$ is 1.5 times the average cost at y = MES. This result is consistent with Friedlaender and Spady's work on rail cost functions where they found that exhausting economies-of-scale was not "just around the corner" (Friedlaender and Spady [1981, p. 156]). These results do appear to conflict with those of Caves, Christensen and Swanson [1980] in that they could not reject constant returns to scale.

A second reason for the difference between this study and the cross-section results mentioned above is the inclusion in this model of the quality-of-service variable, s. Caves, Christensen and Swanson [1980] did not include a quality-of-service variable; Friedlaender and Spady introduce technological variables, but these would at best be surrogates for a quality-of-service measure. This is an advantage of firm-level analysis: such data are generally not available at the aggregate level which cross-section studies must use.

The effect of omitting this measure is very interesting. As mentioned above, omitting s as a variable is a specification error; the χ^2-value on the hypothesis test of setting the speed-related coefficients to zero was over twice the table value at the 0.005 level. However, if we were to use the model without the speed variable, it would imply a value for k^* in excess of the one computed above, slightly higher average costs and a lower estimate of returns-to-density. Thus, failing to include a properly constructed quality-of-service measure alters the estimated cost function in the direction of constant return-to-scale (i.e., density).

IV. CONCLUSION

In this paper we have formulated and estimated a long run cost function for a large railroad firm, using time series data. This paper, along with our earlier paper which analyzed a smaller sized firm, has presented an opportunity to work with data obtained directly from a firm. This has enabled us to avoid the kinds of problems often encountered in the use of the transformed data reported by the ICC. It has also allowed us to work with individual technologies rather than from the usual assumption of cross sectional analysis that all firms operate with a single underlying technology.

While our findings are numerous, in this section we state those that appear to be most important. First, these studies indicate strongly that the quality of service is important in a properly specified cost model. In both our studies, we have measured quality of service by the speed at which shipments move through the system. Omission of a service quality variable affects the coefficients on other terms in a cost function. In particular, our studies have indicated that omission leads to an understatement of the extent of economies of density in the system.

Both of our studies have indicated that there are strong economies of density. Since the two railroads are of significantly different sizes our findings suggest that density economies exist for a significant portion of the railroad industry.

Finally, our own time series work at the level of the firm has enabled us to assess the structure of railroad costs while avoiding the kinds of biases that can arise in cross section or time series-cross section analyses that fail to capture firm-specific effects. (Again, see Mundlak [1961] and Caves, Christensen and Tretheway [1981].) Studies at the level of the firm unavoidably require substantial time and money. Nevertheless, they have a most important role in serving to test the validity of studies that rely on cross section data. This is particularly significant since those cross section studies are often advanced to support particular policy conclusions. Our work indicates that aggregate studies may not, in fact, provide sufficient support for such conclusions.

Ronald R. Braeutigam,
Department of Economics,
Northwestern University,
Evanston,
Illinois 60201

ACCEPTED JUNE 1983

REFERENCES

BLACKORBY, C, D. PRIMONT and R. RUSSELL, 1978, *Duality, Separability, and Functional Structure: Theory and Economic Applications* (North-Holland, New York).

R. BRAEUTIGAM, A. DAUGHETY and M. TURNQUIST, 1982, "The Estimation of a Hybrid Cost Function for a Railroad Firm," *Review of Economics and Statistics*, **64**, No. 3, (August), pp. 394–404.

D. CAVES, L. CHRISTENSEN and J. SWANSON, 1980, "Productivity in U.S. Railroads, 1951–1974," *The Bell Journal of Economics*, **11**, No. 1, (Spring), pp. 166–81.

D. W. CAVES, L. R. CHRISTENSEN and M. TRETHEWAY, 1981, "A Reexamination of Scale Economies for U.S. Trunk Airlines," Working Paper, Department of Economics, University of Wisconsin.

L. CHRISTENSEN, D. JORGENSON and L. LAU, 1973, "Transcendental Logarithmic Production Functions," *Review of Economics and Statistics*, **55**, No. 1, (February), pp. 28–45.

L. CHRISTENSEN and W. H. GREENE, 1976, "Economies of Scale in U.S. Electric Power Generation," *Journal of Political Economy*, **84**, No. 4, pt. 1, pp. 655–76.

J. DANZIG, J. RUGG, J. WILLIAMS and W. HAY, 1976, *Procedures for Analyzing the Economic Costs of Railroad Roadway for Pricing Purposes*, report prepared for the U.S. Department of Transportation.

M. DENNY and M. FUSS, 1977, "The Use of Approximation Analysis to Test for Separability and the Existence of Consistent Aggregates," *American Economic Review*, **67**, No. 3, (June), pp. 404–18.

Economic ABZ's of the Railroad Industry, 1980, (Association of American Railroads, Washington, D.C.).

FRIEDLAENDER, A. F., 1969, *The Dilemma of Freight Transport Regulation*, (Brookings Institution, Washington, D.C.).

Friedlaender, A. F. and R. Spady, 1981, *Freight Transport Regulation*, (MIT Press, Cambridge).

T. Keeler, 1974, "Railroad Costs, Returns to Scale and Excess Capacity," *Review of Economics and Statistics*, **56**, No. 2, (May), pp. 201–208.

Y. Mundlak, 1961, "Empirical Production Function Free of Management Bias," *Journal of Farm Economics*, **43**, No. 1, (February), pp. 44–56.

Shephard, R., 1970, *Theory of Cost and Production Functions*, (Princeton University Press, New Jersey).

J. A. Swanson, 1968, "Railroad Investment Demand, 1948–1965: A Neoclassical Model," (Unpublished Ph.D. dissertation, University of Wisconsin).

Theil, H., 1971, *Principles of Econometrics*, (John Wiley & Sons, New York).

Varian, H., 1978, *Microeconomic Analysis*, (W. W. Norton, New York).

G. Welty, 1978, "Budget Planning 1979," *Railway Age*, (November 17), pp. 26–32.

Wilde, D. J., 1964, *Optimum Seeking Methods*, (Prentice-Hall, Englewood Cliffs, New Jersey).

THE JOURNAL OF INDUSTRIAL ECONOMICS 0022-1821 $2.00
Volume XXXIII September 1984 No. 1

THE ENGINEERING APPROACH TO ECONOMIC PRODUCTION FUNCTIONS REVISITED: AN APPLICATION TO SOLAR PROCESSES

G. THOMAS SAV*

I. INTRODUCTION

DESPITE the renewed and increasing interest in substituting solar produced energy for conventional nonrenewable resources, very little of general interest has been done in the way of empirically characterizing technological substitution possibilities via economic production functions. The absence of econometric approximations can be attributed to the lack of adequate statistical data. On the other hand, we have largely ignored the possibility of deriving meaningful production functions from physical laws and engineering models. The idea of deriving economically useful production functions from engineering data is an intriguing one albeit not new. Chenery's seminal work [1949, 1953] and later extensions by Ferguson [1950], Grosse [1953], Smith [1957, 1959, 1961], and Cowing [1974], among others, evidence the successfulness of the general approach in a wide variety of applications. Moreover, the recent literature has witnessed a resurgence of interest in the use of engineering models via Hoffman and Jorgenson [1977], Hausman [1979], and Griffin [1972, 1977(a), 1977 (b), 1978, 1979].[1]

The purpose of this paper is to continue along this vein of interest and investigate the usefulness of engineering models in deriving an economic production function which describes interprocess substitution possibilities between solar produced energy and conventionally produced energy. Advantages offered by the engineering approach are well documented in the literature cited above as well as the more broadly concerned studies by Walters [1963], Brown [1967], and Johansen [1972]. The chief explanation for relying on this approach rather than a statistical approach in the present inquiry is that the latter was precluded by the absence of historically observed data. Solar produced energy is a relatively new technology or at least it has not been adopted for use on a wide scale. The most technologically feasible application appears to be within the residential and commercial building sectors for the purpose of producing domestic hot water (DHW) services. Other applications that are not as technologically mature include space

* The paper has benefitted from the useful suggestions of James Griffin, Raymond Kopp, Anthony Yezer, and an anonymous referee.

[1] The approaches developed in these later studies differ considerably from the pure engineering approach of Chenery, *et al.* Most recently, Griffin employs what he has dubbed the pseudo data approach.

heating, space cooling, and industrial process heat. Although each of these present interesting challenges in terms of production modeling, this paper concentrates on interprocess substitution possibilities in the production of DHW. Yet the approach provides the foundations necessary for an inquiry into these other applications of solar energy processes.

In Section II, the notion of an aggregate utilized energy service is established. Unlike the Berndt and Wood [1979] utilized capital service, this energy service represents the energy output required to satisfy an end use (e.g., DHW, space heat, etc.). Functional separability is postulated as a means of deriving the aggregate. Section III concentrates on deriving a general form for the utilized DHW energy service production function. This analysis culminates in a stock-flow type production function. Section IV employs engineering models to derive an economically useful production function of the stock-flow type. Empirical estimates of the production coefficients are provided in Section V. Due to the dependence of solar output on climatic conditions, a regional approach is undertaken in this section. Coefficients are estimated for four broad U.S. geographical regions. In addition, interprocess substitution possibilities are estimated for three alternative conventional fuels: electricity, oil, and natural gas. Section VI summarizes the principal findings.

II. THEORETICAL FRAMEWORK

We set out by considering a producer (firm, household, or individual) facing a positive, twice differentiable exante production function relating the maximum output, Y, obtainable from a set of n elementary inputs:[2]

$$(1) \qquad Y = G(x_1, x_2, \ldots, x_n).$$

Some of the n inputs are flows per unit of time (current inputs), others are stocks of durable capital embodied in the production technique. The fundamental advantage underlying the exante stock-flow formulation is that it allows one to choose factor proportions prior to the investment in equipment or in new production techniques (Johansen [1972]; Sato [1975]). In the latter context it is also useful to account for the possibility that $Y > 0$ for some $x_i = 0$; i.e., some x_i (e.g., new technology or auxiliary capital) are nonessential inputs.[3]

In both theoretical and empirical work, we generally collapse the production function (1) by constructing aggregate quantity indices from mutually exclusive subsets of elementary inputs. The necessary and sufficient conditions for collapsibility are the well known functional separability conditions.[4] Weak separability is postulated here for the purpose of grouping ele-

[2] The terminology "elementary inputs" is adopted from Green [1964]. Chenery [1949] earlier referred to such inputs as engineering variables.

[3] In the two input case, $Y = F(x_1, x_2)$, $x_1 \geq 0$, $x_2 > 0$, the isoquants intersect the x_1 axis.

[4] For a historical development of functional separability see Diewert [1974].

mentary inputs into two mutually exclusive subsets. The first subset consists of k elementary inputs entering the production of an aggregate utilized energy service, E. The remaining $n - k$ elementary inputs define the second subset used to produce an aggregate composite index, Z. Consequently,

$$Y = G((x_1, \ldots, x_k), (x_{k+1}, \ldots, x_n)) = G(E, Z) \tag{2}$$

In this sense, $G(\quad)$ is weakly separable in that

$$\frac{\partial(G_i/G_j)}{\partial x_h} = 0 \qquad ij \in E, h \in Z. \tag{3}$$

That is, the marginal rate of technical substitution between elementary inputs in the production of the utilized energy service, E, is independent of elementary inputs outside of E.[5]

The production process is now two-level. On the first level, the micro functions are

$$E = F(x_1, \ldots, x_k) \tag{4}$$

and

$$Z = G(x_{k+1}, \ldots, x_n). \tag{5}$$

On the second level, the aggregates E and Z combine to produce Y. The direct implication of the two-level formulation is that functional separability enables one to examine technical substitution possibilities among elementary inputs in producing energy services in (4) in the absence of considering other inputs outside of (4) (Berndt and Wood [1979]).[6]

III. DHW SPECIFICATION

Many types of energy services consumed within the firm or household are produced on-site rather than purchased directly in the market. DHW, space heating, space cooling, and industrial process heat are prime examples. Production is usually accomplished by means of a conventional energy process in which conventional, nonrenewable fuels (electricity, oil, natural gas) are combined with durable capital (furnaces, air conditioners, and DHW heaters). However, the advent of the 1973–74 Arab oil embargo has accelerated the

[5] Berndt and Wood [1979] have recently applied functional separability in deriving their KLEM function in which (1) is collapsed into the aggregates capital (K), labor, (L), energy (E), and materials (M).

[6] Functional separability also carries important implications with respect to cost minimization. Green [1964] demonstrates that weak separability insures that sequential cost minimization within two groupings of a collapsed function is equivalent to global cost minimization in the uncollapsed function. The equivalence also holds with respect to more than two groupings, but only under the more restrictive conditions of strong separability and weak homogeneous separability.

development of technologically feasible alternatives to these conventional processes. One of the most promising alternatives is solar DHW processes.

In the context of DHW, the aggregate utilized energy service may be defined as the energy output from a production process as follows:

$$(6) \qquad E = F(E_c, E_s)$$

where E_c and E_s are energy aggregates representing the quantity of energy produced by a conventional process and a solar process, respectively. Here the aggregates E_c and E_s arise from lower level production functions containing elementary inputs. In particular, (6) may be expressed as an energy balance as follows:

$$(7) \qquad E = E_c + E_s.$$

Although in (7) the elasticity of substitution between energy aggregates is infinite (a BTU is a BTU regardless of its source), it does not follow that interprocess substitutions among elementary inputs are as fluid. Durable solar capital is substitutable for conventional fuel inputs, but is generally nonsubstitutable for conventional capital inputs in the DHW process. This limitation is invoked by the fact that solar technology makes it prohibitively costly to rely completely on solar produced DHW (e.g., during extended periods of inclement weather). Thus, solar DHW processes are primarily marketed as auxiliary processes which require a full capacity conventional process as backup. As a result, conventional energy capital is an essential input in the lower level production function, while solar process capital is auxiliary and therefore nonessential.

Considering the conventional process capacity constraint imposed by solar storage technology, the E_c aggregate may be viewed as being produced with one variable elementary input—viz., conventional, nonrenewable fuel, F. On the other hand, solar processes are highly capital intensive. For the purpose of specifying the structure of such processes we may, for convenience, lump solar capital into the two major process components—solar collector surface area, A, and solar storage volume, V. Employing the energy balance (7), we obtain the following block additive form for the utilized DHW energy service, E, in terms of the two lower level production functions:[7]

$$(8) \qquad E = E_c(F) + E_s(A, V).$$

Elementary inputs now define a stock-flow production structure in which new technology in the form of durable solar process capital is substitutable for a current flow input.

[7] The separability conditions imply that F, A, and V in (8) do not enter other lower-level micro functions. Although this is a rather stringent assumption, it is invoked, as Griffin [1979] points out, not only because of convenience, but because data limitations make it necessary.

IV. THE ENGINEERING APPROACH

Several engineering process models are currently available for the purpose of predicting the performance of solar DHW processes in residential and commercial building applications. Most commonly we encounter computer simulation models which predict the hourly and/or monthly proportion of a given total DHW energy requirement supplied by a solar process. The remaining proportion is supplied by a back-up conventional DHW process. One of the most well documented and widely accepted engineering models is referred to as F-CHART.[8]

F-CHART predicts the monthly proportion, P_j, of DHW energy requirements, E_j, supplied by a solar process. A general expression for the technique may be stated as follows:[9]

$$P_j = E_{sj}(A, V, E_j) \cdot E_j^{-1}, \tag{9}$$

where $E_{sj}(\quad)$ is the solar process function and the subscript j is used to denote a monthly index. The monthly quantity of energy, E_j, required to meet a desired level of DHW service (including DHW temperature and volume) is defined for a particular building structure.[10]

A synthesis of the F-CHART documentation reveals that the simulation model can be expressed in the following more deterministic form:

$$P_j = (\beta_{1j} A - \beta_{2j} A^{1.25} V^{-0.25} - \beta_{3j} A^2 E_j^{-1} + \beta_{4j} A^{2.5} V^{-0.5} E_j^{-1} + \beta_{5j} A^3 E_j^{-2}) E_j^{-1}, \tag{10}$$

where the parameters $\beta_{ij} > 0$ depend upon monthly climatic conditions at the particular geographical location and engineering design characteristics of the solar process.[11] A somethat puzzling, but nevertheless present, constraint imposed in the F-CHART model is that storage volume, V, must vary linearly

[8] F-CHART is currently marketed by the Solar Energy Laboratory, University of Wisconsin, in a Fortran IV program. It is also well documented in Beckman, Klein, and Duffie [1977].

[9] The notation used here differs considerably from the notation found in the F-CHART documentation, since the latter was found to be quite cumbersome.

[10] F-CHART determines E_j as follows:

$$E_j = sdpv(t_0 - t_i)n_j, \tag{10}$$

where s = specific heat of water; d = density of water; p = number of persons occupying building; v = volume of DHW required per person per day; t_0 = DHW output temperature; t_i = cold water mains input temperature; and n_j = number of days per month. For present purposes, E_j is assumed to be exogenous.

[11] Perhaps one of the major obstructions to the engineering approach is that it requires the use of detailed engineering data which economists are rarely equipped to evaluate. In fact, a major effort underlying the present study but not reflected in this paper involved the interpretation of the theory of thermal processes and a reconstruction of a rather complicated engineering simulation model. For example, equation (11) was obtained by sifting through computer documentation and engineering calculations related to the F-CHART model. However, it seems the better part of wisdom to limit the scope of this presentation to as little engineering and as much economic content as possible. Therefore, an Appendix which shows the derivation of (11) and the engineering calculations underlying the coefficients is available from the author upon request.

with solar collector area, A; $V = \alpha A$. Although it will become useful to initially impose this constraint, the empirical analysis presented in the next section indicates that it may be valid only over a small range of production.

The engineering model presented above is useful for predicting the monthly performance of solar DHW process. However, economists are ordinarily interested in time horizons extending beyond monthly values. Moreover, unlike the present engineering model, an economic production function expresses output as a function of inputs. By defining E_s as the annual energy output from a solar process, the above model can be transformed into an expression more akin to our notion of a production function. Summing over the twelve monthly values in (11) produces the following:[12]

$$(12) \qquad E_s = \Sigma_j P_j E_j = A\Sigma\beta_{1j} - A^{1.25}V^{-0.25}\Sigma\beta_{2j} - A^2\Sigma\beta_{3j}E_j^{-1} + A^{2.5}V^{-0.5}\Sigma\beta_{4j}E_j^{-1} + A^3\Sigma\beta_{5j}E_j^{-2}.$$

Still an awkward expression, we may further simplify by recognizing that, within the bulk of the building sector, energy usage related to DHW services is relatively stable on a monthly basis. This is especially evident when compared to the seasonal variability observed in energy usage related to space heating and cooling services.[13] A rather innocuous assumption, therefore, involves the substitution of an average monthly DHW energy service, $E/12$, for E_j in (12), where E is the annual energy service. Proceeding, we obtain

$$(13) \qquad E_s(A, V, E) = \delta_1 A - \delta_2 A^{1.25}V^{-0.25} - \delta_3 A^2 E^{-1} + \delta_4 A^{2.5}V^{-0.5}E^{-1} + \delta_5 A^3 E^{-2},$$

where,

$$\delta_1 = \Sigma\beta_{1j} > 0$$

$$\delta_2 = \Sigma\beta_{2j} > 0$$

$$\delta_3 = 12\Sigma\beta_{3j} > 0$$

$$\delta_4 = 12\Sigma\beta_{4j} > 0$$

$$\delta_5 = 144\Sigma\beta_{5j} > 0$$

Equation (13) is the solar process production function contained in (8) above with the exception that E_s now depends upon the desired level of aggregate DHW service, E, in addition to the inputs A and V. This is due to the physical laws by which solar DHW is produced. Specifically, the instantaneous proportion of energy supplied by a solar process is dependent upon the energy requirement placed on the process and the rate at which energy is drawn out

[12] There is, of course, an implicit aggregation problem involved in summing over monthly values, as opposed to integrating over hourly or even daily values. The magnitude of error is unknown at this time and would probably differ among climatic conditions and according to various solar process design configurations.

[13] In the present analysis, E_j varies only with respect to n_j in (10).

of the solar storage unit. Integrating over a given time interval (presently a year) the proportion depends upon the total energy requirement, E, for that time interval.

Unlike the above derivation, an expression for the conventional energy process production function, E_c in (8), is straightforward and best accomplished by reference to the following flow diagram:

Energy Input (hF) ⟶ Conventional DHW Equipment: Efficiency Level $= \beta_0$ ⟶ Energy Output $E_c = \beta_0 hF$

⟶ Conversion Loss $(1 - \beta_0)hF$

Here, conventional fuel, F, containing a given heating value, h, is combusted in conventional DHW equipment with an efficiency level, $0 < \beta_0 \leq 1$, (e.g., electric resistance heaters are 100% efficient, $\beta_0 = 1$, oil and gas fired heaters are generally 60% to 75% efficient, $\beta_0 = 0.6$ to 0.75). After accounting for conversion losses

$$E_c = \delta_0 F \tag{14}$$

where $\delta_0 = \beta_0 h$ and both F and E_c are defined as annual input and output quantities, respectively.

The utilized energy service stock-flow production function is now complete. Substituting (13) and (14) into (8), we obtain

$$E = \delta_0 F + \delta_1 A - \delta_2 A^{1.25} V^{-0.25} - \delta_3 A^2 E^{-1} + \delta_4 A^{2.5} V^{-0.5} E^{-1} + \delta_5 A^3 E^{-2}, \tag{15}$$

where $\delta_i > 0$. Alternatively, imposing the fixed proportions constraint $V = \alpha A$

$$E = \xi_0 F + \xi_1 A - \xi_2 A^2 E^{-1} + \xi_3 A^3 E^{-2}, \tag{16}$$

where,

$$\xi_1 = \delta_1 - \delta_2 \alpha^{-0.25}$$

$$\xi_2 = \delta_3 - \delta_4 \alpha^{-0.5}$$

and as a matter of notational convenience $\xi_0 = \delta_0$ and $\xi_3 = \delta_5$, where $\xi_i > 0$.

The production functions (15) and (16) are unique in that they have been derived from engineering models and underlying physical laws representing the technology of DHW production via conventional and solar energy processes. To some, such functions may appear disordered since their implicit form does not conform well to our standard notion of an economic production function. That is, output appears on both sides of the expressions. However, as previously discussed this is an engineering performance feature of solar DHW processes. Also, this implicit form is prevalent within that portion of the literature where empirically derived economic production functions have their roots in physical and engineering laws (e.g., Chenery [1949] [1953] and Smith, [1961]).

Perhaps even more significant is the fact that the production function is relatively well behaved, possessing the required concavity over at least some range of positive inputs. Given (16), strict convexity of the isoquants is insured under the condition

$$\frac{\partial^2 F}{\partial A^2} = \xi_0^{-1}(-2\xi_2 E^{-1} - 6\xi_3 A E^{-2}) > 0. \tag{17}$$

Rearranging terms, convexity requires

$$E > 3\xi_2^{-1}\xi_3 A. \tag{18}$$

The relevant region of production is therefore defined by the interval $F > 0$, $0 \leq A < \xi_2\xi_3^{-1}E/3$. Substituting (18) into the production function (16) and solving for F we obtain

$$F = \xi_0(3\xi_2^{-1}\xi_3 - \xi_1 + 2\xi_2^2\xi_3^{-1}/9)A. \tag{19}$$

Along this ray in input space, isoquants change from convex to concave. Figure 1 illustrates a typical isoquant, the ray $F = h(A)$ corresponding to

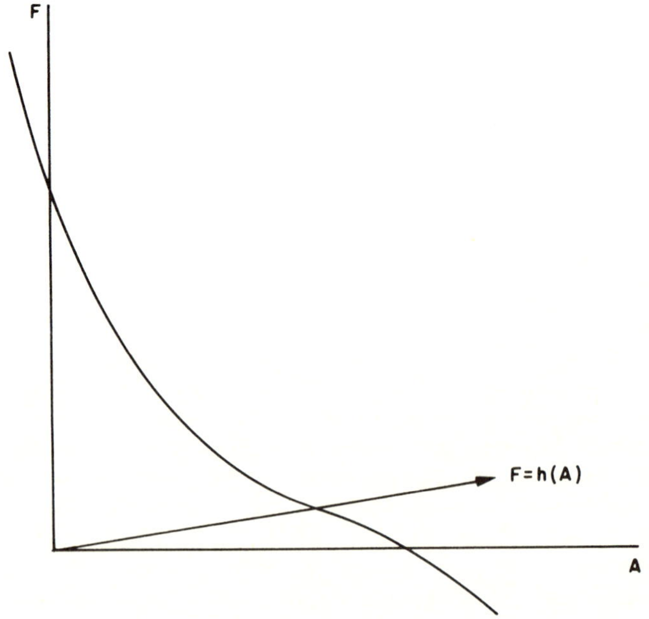

FIGURE 1.
Typical Isoquant for Production of DHW Energy Serivice

condition (19). In the next section, it is shown empirically that the uneconomic region of production is a trivial subset of the nonnegative input space.

The production function (16) fits into the broad class of homothetic production functions possessing a variable elasticity of substitution (VES). While the energy aggregates E_c and E_s in (7) are perfectly substitutable, σ is constant for a given ratio of elementary inputs F/A but varies for movements along an isoquant generated from (16). If we implicitly differentiate (16) and define $S = f_A/f_S$, then σ reads

$$\sigma = \frac{S}{AF} \frac{AS + F}{S\dfrac{\partial S}{\partial F} - \dfrac{\partial S}{\partial A}}. \tag{20}$$

Performing the required differentiation,

$$\sigma = \frac{\xi_1 - 2\xi_2 AE^{-1} + 3\xi_3 A^2E^{-2} \dfrac{(A(\xi_1 - 2\xi_2 AE^{-1} + 3\xi_3 A^2E^{-2}) + \xi_0 F)}{}}{2\xi_0(-\xi_2 - 3\xi_3 AE^{-1})AFE^{-1}}, \tag{21}$$

which can be shown to decrease as the input ratio F/A decreases and asymptotically approaches zero as F/A approaches the concave region given by (19).

V. EMPIRICAL ANALYSIS

This section presents empirical estimates of interprocess substitution possibilities between conventional fuels and durable solar capital in the production of DHW services. In order to capture the effect of climate (solar radiation) a regional approach is undertaken. Four broadly defined U.S. geographical regions are examined: Northeast (NE), Southeast (SE), Northwest (NW) and Southwest (SW). Climatic data are available at the city level for a select number of cities. Thus, a specific location in each region is selected so as to best represent average climatic conditions in the respective regions: Boston, MA, Atlanta, GA, Portland, OR, and Phoenix, AZ.

A typical solar DHW process configuration is selected on the basis of present installations and marketing reports. It is comprised of flat-plate liquid collectors having a transparent glass cover and a flat-black absorber surface. A heat exchanger separates the main collector flow loop from the storage unit. A water-antifreeze solution is used as the heat transfer fluid between the collectors and the storage unit. The latter uses water as the storage medium. Solar collectors are oriented to face due south at a tilt of geographical latitude plus fifteen degrees.

All data are measured in the International System of Units (SI). Annual energy quantities are expressed in joules per annum, J. Solar collector surface and storage volume are expressed in square meters, M^2, and liters, L, respectively. Conventional fuel quantities are expressed as follows: kilowatt hours, KWH, of electricity, liters of oil, and square meters of natural gas.[14]

Table I presents an interfuel and interregional comparison of the estimated coefficients for the fixed proportions production function (16). Initially, storage volume is constrained at 75 L/M^2 of collector surface. This value is selected as the mean of engineering recommendations that storage is optimal in the range of $\alpha = 50$ to 100 L/M^2 of collector surface (Beckman, Klein, and Duffie [1977]). Generally this capacity provides at least one day of DHW requirements for a four-member residential household.

TABLE I.
PRODUCTION COEFFICIENTS: FIXED PROPORTIONS[a]

		Electric		Gas[b]		Oil[b]	
$\xi_0(\times 10^8)$		0.036		0.234		0.246	
	NE		SE		NW		SW
$\xi_1(\times 10^{10})$	0.257		0.323		0.230		0.482
$\xi_2(\times 10^{19})$	0.245		0.380		0.225		0.741
$\xi_3(\times 10^{28})$	0.852		0.158		0.819		0.399

[a] Based on $V = 75A$.
[b] Based on $\beta_0 = 0.6$.

Figure 2 depicts interregional substitution possibilities using electricity as the conventional fuel source. Isoquants for each region are derived for an annual DHW service of 25×10^9 J. This level of service is typical for a four-member household consuming 100 L of DHW per person per day at 60°C. In the absence of a solar process this level of service requires 7000 KWH's of electricity. As expected, a given size solar process contributes more to the reduction of conventional fuel consumption in southern, relative to northern, regions of the U.S. For example, a 50% reduction in the NW relative to the SW requires a system $2\frac{1}{2}$ times as large.

Using the SE as an intermediate climate, Figure 3 illustrates the homothetic and VES properties of the production function. Isoquants are derived for a typical residential structure and small commercial structure ($E = 25 \times 10^9$ J), a medium size commercial structure ($E = 50 \times 10^9$ J), and a large commercial structure ($E = 100 \times 10^9$ J). Estimates of σ are reported for three alternative input ratios (as previously noted σ approaches zero as the input ratio approaches the convexity constraint). *Inter alia*, the homogeneity of the function implies that for a constant input ratio, the annual proportion , P, of energy output contributed by the solar process is also constant. That is, proportional changes in F and A do not alter P,

$$P = 1 - \frac{E_c}{E} = 1 - \frac{\xi_0 F}{E},$$

[14] Climatic data and data related to the engineering specifications of the solar equipment are part of the Appendix referred to in Footnote 11 and available upon request from the author.

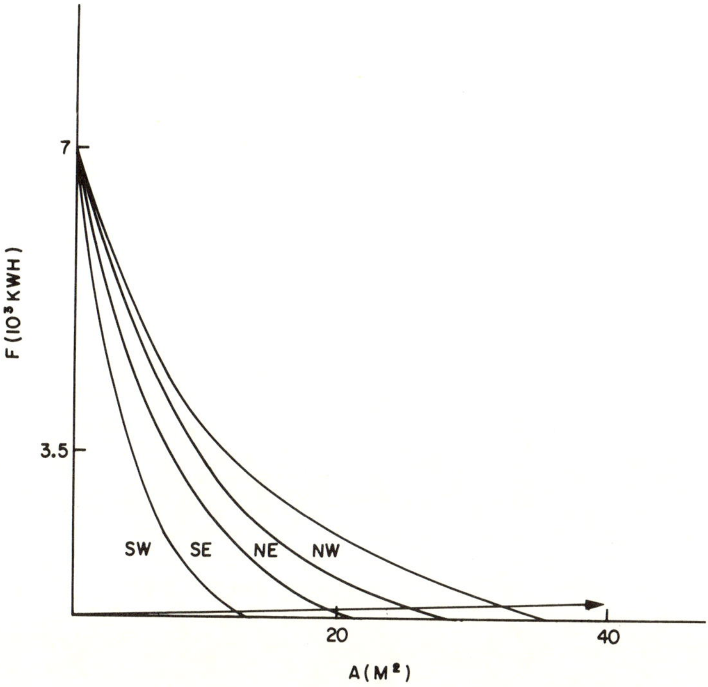

FIGURE 2.
Regional Isoquants for $E = 25 \times 10^9$ J

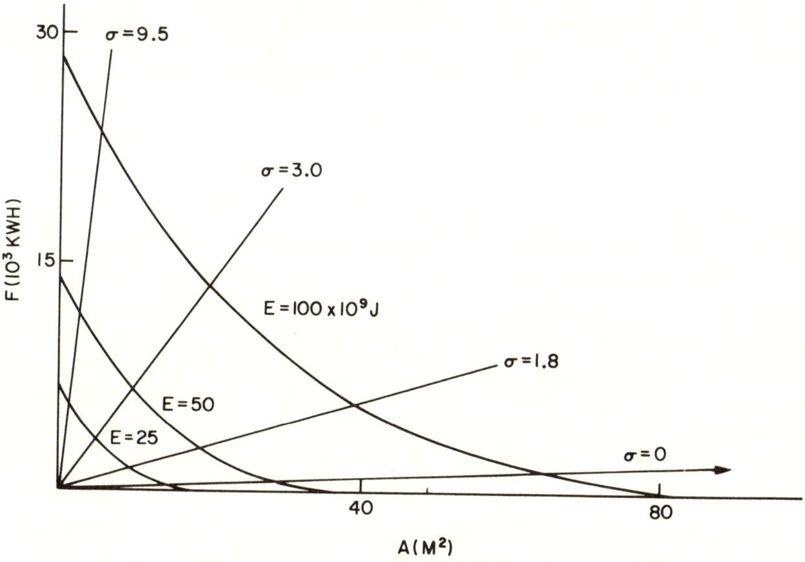

FIGURE 3.
Isoquants: SE Region

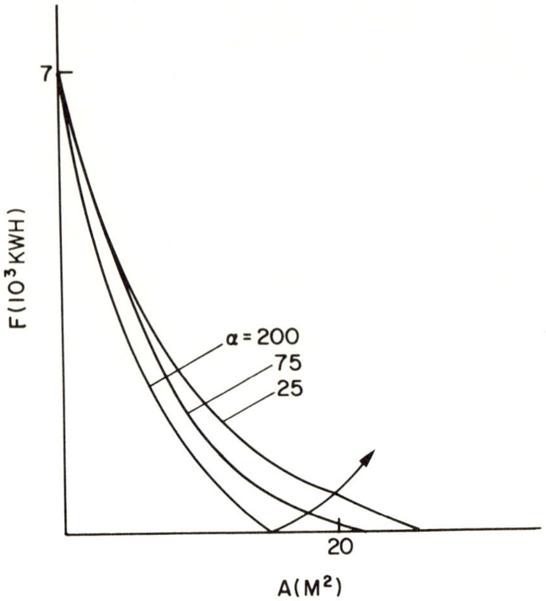

FIGURE 4.
Effect of Alternative α on SE Region Isoquants

since E is linearly homogeneous in F and A. Thus, given relative input prices sufficient to induce interprocess substitutions, energy-intensive users and conservation-minded users are predicted to reduce fuel consumption by the same proportion.

Thus far the analysis has been based upon the fixed proportions constraint that $V = 75\ A$. We now examine the effects of varying proportions using the SE region and electricity as the conventional fuel. Figure 4 illustrates the isoquant shifts ($E = 25 \times 10^9$ J) occasioned by variations in α between 25 L and 200 L per M^2 of collector surface. These are considerable extremes compared to engineering recommendations that α is optimal between 50 and 100

TABLE II
PRODUCTION COEFFICIENTS: VARIABLE PROPORTIONS

		Electric		Gas[a]		Oil[a]	
$\delta_0(\times 10^8)$		0.036		0.234		0.246	
	NE		SE		NW		SW
$\delta_1(\times 10^{10})$	0.326		0.413		0.306		0.568
$\delta_2(\times 10^{10})$	0.202		0.264		0.224		0.253
$\delta_3(\times 10^{19})$	0.266		0.413		0.250		0.773
$\delta_4(\times 10^{19})$	0.181		0.295		0.218		0.279
$\delta_5(\times 10^{28})$	0.852		0.158		0.819		0.399

[a] Based on $\beta_0 = 0.6$

L/M^2. As indicated, the substitution possibilities between storage volume and collector surface are relatively small for small solar installations but increase with installation size. This suggests that perhaps a nonlinear specification between V and A in the solar process function may be more appropriate. For this reason, the coefficients of the variable proportions DHW function (15) are derived and reported in Table II.

VI. CONCLUDING REMARKS

The purpose of this paper has been to derive a production function for solar process applications by utilizing physical laws and engineering models. Above all, the approach has proved to be both feasible and fruitful.

Although an obvious empirical approach to establishing production functions is to use technological information and engineering data, the approach has not been widely employed. With the exceptions of a few early excursions and a recent resurgence of interest, the engineering approach has not been cultivated very far beyond the point at which Walters [1963] noted it to be when he commented "the use of engineering and technical data for production functions is still in its infancy." Perhaps the most evident reasons for the current validity of this statement are that (1) economists are rarely equipped to evaluate the physical and engineering laws describing the underlying technology of a particular process and, (2) the engineering approach is generally applicable to the very micro level of production while empirical production analyses have been primarily at the macro level.

As Griffin [1977(a)] suggests, the successfulness of the engineering approach rests upon the quality of the engineering model. However, the present inquiry indicates that economists may be able to provide a potentially useful function in helping with the specification of engineering process models. Regarding the second statement, Johansen (1972) suggests that the engineering approach is relevant at the macro level, since the macro function can be established from the *ex ante* micro level functions. This perhaps merits additional attention and research.

The empirical analysis presented here should be of interest to policy makers currently advocating tax incentives for the purchase and utilization of solar energy processes. The analysis indicates that consideration should be given to scaling tax incentives to the energy intensity of users and that they should differ by fuel and region, since substitution possibilities vary accordingly.

G. Thomas Sav,
Department of Economics,
West Georgia College,
Carrollton,
Georgia 30118.

ACCEPTED JUNE 1983

REFERENCES

BECKMAN, W. A., KLEIN, S. A. and DUFFIE, J. A. 1977, *Solar Heating Design by the F-CHART Method* (John Wiley & Sons, New York).

BERNDT, E. R. and WOOD, D. O. 1979, "Engineering and Econometric Interpretations of Energy-Capital Complementarity", *American Economic Review* **69** (June), pp. 342–54.

BROWN, M. (ed.), 1967, *The Theory and Empirical Analysis of Production* (Columbia University Press, New York).

CHENERY, H. B., 1949, "Engineering Production Functions", *Quarterly Journal of Economics* **63** (November), pp. 507–31.

——— , 1953, "Process and Production Functions from Engineering Data", in W. Leontief, *et al.* (eds.), *Studies in the Structure of the American Economy* (Oxford University Press, New York), pp. 297–325.

COWING, T. G., 1974, "Technical Change and Scale Economies in an Engineering Production Function: The Case of Steam Electric Power", *Journal of Industrial Economics 23* (December) pp. 135–52.

DIEWERT, E. E., 1974, "Applications of Duality Theory", in Michael D. Intriligator and David A. Kendrick (eds.) *Frontiers of Quantitative Economics* (North-Holland Publishing Co., Amsterdam).

FERGUSON, A. R., 1950, "Empirical Determination of a Multidimensional Marginal Cost Function", *Econometrica* **18** (July), pp. 217–35.

GREEN, J. A. J., 1964, *Aggregation in Economic Analysis* (Princeton University Press, Princeton).

GRIFFIN, J. M., 1972, "The Process Analysis Alternative to Statistical Cost Functions: An Application to Petroleum Refining", *American Economic Review* **63** (March), pp. 46–56.

——— , 1977(a), "Long-run Production Modeling with Pseudo Data: Electric Power Generation", *Bell Journal of Economics* **8** (Spring), pp. 112–27(a).

——— , 1977(b), "The Econometrics of Joint Production: Another Approach", *Review of Economics and Statistics* **59** (November), pp. 389–97(b).

——— , 1978, "Joint Production Technology: The Case of Petro-Chemicals", *Econometrica* **46** (March), pp. 379–97.

——— , 1979, "Statistical Cost Analysis Revisited", *Quarterly Journal of Economics* **93** (February), pp. 107–28.

GROSSE, A. P., 1953, "The Technological Structure of the Cotton Textile Industry", in W. Leontief, *et al.* (eds.) *Studies in the Structure of the American Economy* (Oxford University Press, New York), pp. 360–420.

HAUSMAN, J. A., 1979, "Individual Discount Rates and the Purchase and Utilization of Energy-Using Durables", *Bell Journal of Economics* **10** (Spring), pp. 33–54.

HOFFMAN, K. C. and JORGENSON, D. W. 1977, "Economic and Technological Models for Evaluation of Energy Policy", *Bell Journal of Economics* **8** (Autumn), pp. 444–66.

JOHANSEN, L., 1972, *Production Functions* (North-Holland Publishing Co., Amsterdam).

KURZ, M. and MANNE, A. S., 1963, "Engineering Estimates of Capital-Labor Substitution in Metal Machinery", *American Economic Review* **53** (September), pp. 662–79.

SATO, K., 1975, *Production Functions and Aggregation* (North-Holland Publishing Co., Amsterdam).

SMITH, V. L., 1957, "Engineering Data and Statistical Techniques in the Analysis of Production and Technological Change: Fuel Requirements of the Trucking Industry", *Econometrica* **25** (April), pp. 281–301.

———, 1959, "The Theory of Investment and Production", *Quarterly Journal of Economics* **73** (February), pp. 61–87.
———, 1961, *Investment and Production* (Harvard University Press, Cambridge).
WALTERS, A. A., 1963, "Production and Cost Functions: An Econometric Survey", *Econometrica* **31** (January–April), pp. 1–66.

THE JOURNAL OF INDUSTRIAL ECONOMICS 0022–1821 $2.00
Volume XXXIII September 1984 No. 1

COST AND PRODUCTIVITY IN REGIONAL BUS TRANSPORTATION: THE BELGIAN CASE*

BRUNO L. DE BORGER

INTRODUCTION

ALTHOUGH productivity in large public transport firms is often a main issue in public policy discussions, little time and research effort has been devoted to develop reliable indices to measure this crucial concept. This apparent inconsistency is easily explained in terms of the difficulties involved in properly defining productivity. Unfortunately, many firms and economic studies in the past have used definitions of productivity growth that are unacceptable from an economic point of view.

In this paper, we apply the methodology recently proposed by Caves, Christensen and Swanson [1981] to study technological change in regional bus transportation in Belgium. The method correctly accounts for factor substitution over time and does not *a priori* restrict the nature of technological improvements. It is based upon a very general production structure and involves the estimation of a flexible cost function to describe the underlying technology. The resulting productivity indices give a much more reliable picture of productivity growth over time than other more naive methods that previously have been used.

The paper is organized as follows: in a first section we briefly review some of the important approaches to productivity measurement that have appeared in the literature, with special emphasis on the transportation industries. In the next section we present the methodology used to calculate productivity indices for regional bus transportation on the basis of a flexible variable cost function. We discuss the properties of the translog variable cost function in Section III. The estimation results and a detailed explanation of their implications are presented in Section IV. Calculated productivity indices for regional bus transportation are derived and carefully interpreted in Section V. A comparison is also made between our proposed indices and the index used by the firm responsible for regional bus transportation. A final section contains a summary of the main conclusions.

* The final version of this paper was written while the author was at the University of Wisconsin-Madison. Financial support from the Interuniversity College for Doctoral Studies in Management is gratefully acknowledged. Comments by G. Blauwens, D. Harmatuck, W. Nonneman and a referee are greatly appreciated. Excellent computational assistance was provided by M. Weverbergh. The usual caveat applies.

I. PRODUCTIVITY MEASUREMENT IN THE TRANSPORTATION INDUSTRIES

Productivity measurement is a difficult exercise. This is especially true for the transportation industries where the heterogeneity of services provided causes substantial problems in properly defining output. Moreover, factor substitution over time makes construction of indices of productivity growth a complicated task. It is not surprising, therefore, that only very recently have acceptable methods been developed to measure changes in total factor productivity.[1]

Most early studies have used output per unit of input as a measure of factor productivity, see e.g. Abramovitz [1962]. This type of productivity concept is at this moment still widely used by transportation firms in many countries. Many railroads e.g. use the number of passenger-miles per man-hour as an indicator of productivity in the production of passenger transport.[2] Economists have been aware of the weakness of this approach for quite some time. Productivity growth was more formally defined as the shift in the production function over time as distinguished from movements along the production function [Solow (1957)]. It measures the improvement over time in the efficiency with which a firm or industry transforms its factors of production into output. It is clear that indicators of the type "output per unit input" are poor approximations of productivity as they do not properly account for factor substitution over time. Indeed, many public transportation firms show substantial increases in passenger-miles per man-hour precisely because of capital-labor substitution. Use of the simplistic indicator of labor productivity to measure total factor productivity leads to overestimating productivity growth.

A significant improvement was made by Jorgenson and Griliches [1967]. They measured the shift in the production function over time and constructed productivity indices. However, they used the assumption of constant returns to scale prevailing in the industry under investigation. Moreover, it was assumed that output was priced at marginal cost. These competitive conditions might be valid approximations for many industries but they cannot be accepted for the transport sector which is characterized by extensive regulation.

More recently, Meyer and Morton [1975] calculated productivity growth rates for the U.S. railroad industry using index procedures to represent aggregate output and input. Instead of measuring labor and capital productivity separately they used the input cost shares as weights to determine an aggregate input index. This was combined with an output index in order to calculate total factor productivity. However, the procedures they developed to

[1] The difficulties involved in calculating the growth in productivity over time leads Meyer and Morton [1975, p. 497] to conclude: "At best, productivity measures incorporate an element of art as well as of science."

[2] This apparently simplistic productivity index is used by many firms responsible for passenger transportation in Belgium, including the firm we study in this paper.

characterize output and input implied very restrictive assumptions on the underlying technology.[3] Therefore, their proposed methods may not give very reliable results.

A powerful alternative was proposed recently by Caves, Christensen and Swanson [1980, 1981]. Although their methodology is related to the work of Jorgenson and Griliches, it provides substantial improvements by relaxing several restrictive assumptions. They propose productivity indices based upon the specification of a flexible functional form to describe the underlying production and cost structure. The authors choose the translog function as the appropriate description of technology. This specification implies no *a priori* restrictions concerning the nature of returns to scale, the elasticity of substitution between inputs, separability between outputs and inputs, etc. Moreover, productivity indices calculated from the translog function are compatible with nonneutral technological change. A further advantage is that it is possible to derive productivity indices both from the variable and the total cost function.

II. PRODUCTIVITY MEASUREMENT: METHODOLOGY

In this section we derive productivity indices for regional bus transportation in Belgium on the basis of a variable cost function to be estimated. The bus company is assumed to produce a single output (Y), and use three distinct inputs in the production process, viz., labor (L), energy (E), and capital services (T). Under these circumstances the transformation function can be written as

$$F(Y, L, E, T, t) = 0 \tag{1}$$

where t is time. This variable is included to account for technological shifts in the production function and is an essential factor in calculating productivity growth. Differentiating (1) yields

$$F_{\bar{Y}}\, d\bar{Y} + F_{\bar{L}}\, d\bar{L} + F_{\bar{E}}\, d\bar{E} + F_{\bar{T}}\, d\bar{T} + F_t\, dt = 0 \tag{2}$$

where F_X is the partial derivative of the transformation function with respect to X and $\bar{X} = \ln X$.

Following Caves, Christensen and Swanson [1981] we use two alternative definitions of productivity growth. The first one (P_1) is defined as the rate at which output can grow over time with all inputs held at a constant level. Using (2) it follows

$$P_1 = -\frac{F_t}{F_{\bar{Y}}} \tag{3}$$

[3] It has been shown that index numbers to represent input and output can be derived from particular aggregator functions describing the production process (Samuelson and Swamy [1974]). As a consequence a more satisfying approach would be to choose first a suitable function to describe the underlying technology and then to derive input, output and productivity indices.

An alternative, though less natural, definition would be the common rate at which all inputs can be reduced over time with output held at a fixed level (P_2). Applying the definition we find

$$(4) \qquad P_2 = \frac{F_t}{F_{\bar{L}} + F_{\bar{E}} + F_{\bar{T}}}$$

There is no *a priori* reason to expect these two productivity measures to be equal. It turns out that $P_1 = P_2$ only if the production process is characterized by constant returns to scale.[4]

Previous research has indicated that the transportation industries in general and passenger transportation in particular are typically operating with considerable excess capacity.[5] Therefore, imposing the assumption of total cost minimization would be quite unrealistic. We allow the firm to be operating at a less than optimal level for its capital stock and assume that the firm's main objective is to minimize variable costs. Although this is still a strong assumption to make, we believe it is not unreasonable. This approach has still another practical advantage. Given the non-uniform treatment of capital costs in the firm's annual accounts over time, it is much easier to obtain accurate variable cost figures than to find reliable indicators of total costs. We are convinced, therefore, that estimation of a variable cost function and using the resulting estimates to construct productivity indices will lead to more reliable results.

Taking into account previous remarks, we assume that the firm minimized variable costs subject to a well-behaved technology, i.e. it is required that the production function be twice continuously differentiable and strictly quasi-concave in inputs. Under these conditions a unique variable cost function exists giving the minimum variable costs needed to produce a specified output level at observed factor prices for the variable inputs.[6] If we assume the capital stock to be fixed in the short-run, we can write the variable cost function

$$C_V(Y, p_L, p_E, T, t)$$

where p_L and p_E are the input prices of labor and energy, respectively.

It is possible to relate the defined productivity growth measures P_1 and P_2 to the variable cost function. Noting that C_V is the result of minimizing

[4] The degree of returns to scale (R) has been defined in the literature as the proportional growth in output due to a proportional increase in all inputs. Holding time fixed in order to distinguish between returns to scale and productivity growth we find, using (2),

$$R = -\frac{(F_{\bar{L}} + F_{\bar{E}} + F_{\bar{T}})}{F_{\bar{Y}}}$$

It is obvious that $P_1 = RP_2$ so that $P_1 = P_2$ only if $R = 1$.

[5] See e.g. Keeler [1974], Meyer, Kain and Wohl [1965], Viton [1980].

[6] See e.g. Diewert [1974], McFadden [1978].

$(p_L L + p_E E)$ subject to (1) and using the envelope theorem it is straightforward to prove the following relations:

$$(5) \qquad \frac{\partial \ln C_V}{\partial \ln Y} = - \frac{F_{\bar{Y}}}{F_{\bar{L}} + F_{\bar{E}}}$$

$$(6) \qquad \frac{\partial \ln C_V}{\partial \ln T} = - \frac{F_{\bar{T}}}{F_{\bar{L}} + F_{\bar{E}}}$$

$$(7) \qquad \frac{\partial \ln C_V}{\partial t} = - \frac{F_t}{F_{\bar{L}} + F_{\bar{E}}}$$

These expressions allow us to write the productivity measures P_1 and P_2 in function of the cost elasticities defined in (5), (6) and (7). Manipulation of (3)–(7) yields:

$$(8) \qquad P_1 = \frac{-\dfrac{\partial \ln C_V}{\partial t}}{\dfrac{\partial \ln C_V}{\partial \ln Y}}$$

$$(9) \qquad P_2 = \frac{-\dfrac{\partial \ln C_V}{\partial t}}{1 - \dfrac{\partial \ln C_V}{\partial \ln T}}$$

These relations will be used to calculate productivity growth on the basis of an estimated variable cost function. Note that the indices would be different if calculated from a total cost function. Caves, Christensen, and Swanson [1981, p. 996] have shown that the two procedures only lead to the same result if the firm is actually minimizing total costs.

III. A VARIABLE COST FUNCTION FOR REGIONAL BUS TRANSPORTATION

In this section we present a variable cost function for regional bus transportation in Belgium. Regional bus transport services are provided by a single firm, the "Nationale Maatschappij voor Buurtspoorwegen" (NMVB). The firm is regulated in the sense that the government is largely responsible for the prices charged. Moreover, government is involved in determining which routes should be served at which frequency, i.e. in the determination of the firm's vehicle-kilometers. Demand factors determine the ultimate number of passenger-kilometers produced by the firm. This implies that output is no choice variable for the company and that its only flexibility is to be found at the input side: the firm is assumed to provide the transportation services at the lowest possible variable cost. These remarks also justify estimation of the cost function rather than the production function[7] in order to derive information on the underlying technology.

A substantial amount of research on the cost structure in the transport sector has been undertaken in the past two decades. Whereas many early studies specified linear (e.g. Meyer *et al.* [1959]) or Cobb-Douglas (e.g. Keeler [1974]) cost functions, most recent studies have used the translog specification which provides a second-order approximation to an arbitrary cost function. It contains all necessary information concerning the production structure such as economies of scale, price elasticities of input demands, elasticies of substitution, etc.

Although the translog cost function has been used more extensively in the railroad and trucking industries[8] several recent papers have applied the methodology to the bus industry. Viton [1981] analyzes the short and long-run cost behavior of the sector using a sample of U.S. firms. A small sample of Illinois bus companies is used by Williams and Dalal [1981] in order to investigate the possibilities of factor substitution in urban bus transport. A study by Berechman [1983] produces evidence on the cost structure of the industry in Israel.

As the translog form provides a second-order approximation of the true cost function at a point, we have to specify this point. Following current practice we used the sample means as the relevant approximation points in this paper. Moreover, the cost function should be linear homogeneous of degree one in factor prices in order to correspond to a well-behaved technology. Imposing the relevant restrictions the translog variable cost function may be written as:[9]

$$\begin{aligned}\ln C_V - \ln p_E^* = {} & \alpha_0 + \alpha_Y \ln Y^* + \tfrac{1}{2}\alpha_{YY}(\ln Y^*)^2 \\ & + \alpha_L(\ln p_L^* - \ln p_E^*) + \tfrac{1}{2}\alpha_{LL}(\ln p_L^* - \ln p_E^*)^2 \\ & + \alpha_{YL} \ln Y^*(\ln p_L^* - \ln p_E^*) + \alpha_T \ln T^* \\ & + \tfrac{1}{2}\alpha_{TT}(\ln T^*)^2 + \alpha_{TL} \ln T^*(\ln p_L^* - \ln p_E^*) \\ & + \alpha_{YT} \ln Y^* \ln T^* + \alpha_t t^* + \alpha_{tY} t^* \ln Y^* \\ & + \alpha_{tL} t^*(\ln p_L^* - \ln p_E^*) + \alpha_{tT} t^* \ln T^* + \mu\end{aligned}$$

where all starred variables were obtained after dividing by their sample mean (e.g. $Y^* = Y/Y'$ with Y': sample mean) and μ is a stochastic disturbance term. Note that this specification allows the time variable to interact with output,

[7] Estimation of the production function will in general suffer from simultaneous equations bias due to the dependence of factor demands on output. A better procedure is, therefore, to focus on the cost function which contains only exogenous variables.

[8] Railroad cost functions have been estimated by e.g. Caves, Christensen, and Tretheway [1980], Harmatuck [1979] and Viton [1980]. The cost structure in the trucking industry has been analyzed by Friedlaender [1978], Harmatuck [1981] and Klem [1978].

[9] Also see Viton [1981]. The appropriate restrictions are derived in Christensen and Greene [1976].

input prices and capital stock in order to impose no *a priori* restrictions on the nature of productivity growth.

To make estimation of the cost function feasible some adjustments have to be made. Without additional information it is likely to obtain inefficient parameter estimates due to the high correlation between many of the cross-products among explanatory variables. In order to reduce this problem and to use additional information without introducing new parameters we consider estimating the cost function jointly with the factor share equations. These are derived using Shephard's lemma:

$$\frac{\partial C_V}{\partial p_L^*}\frac{p_L^*}{C_V} = s_L = \alpha_L + \alpha_{YL} \ln Y^* + \alpha_{LL}(\ln p_L^* - \ln p_E^*) + \alpha_{TL} \ln T^* + \alpha_{tL} t^*$$

$$\frac{\partial C_V}{\partial p_E^*}\frac{p_E^*}{C_V} = s_E = (1 - \alpha_L) - \alpha_{YL} \ln Y^* - \alpha_{LL}(\ln p_L^* - \ln p_E^*) - \alpha_{TL} \ln T^* - \alpha_{tL} t^*$$

Since the factor shares sum to unity use of both shares would introduce linear dependency in the data so that the variance-covariance matrix of the error terms would be singular. Moreover, it is quite probable that the error terms of the cost function and the share equations correlate due to the large number of common explanatory variables. To account for these problems a correct procedure is to use a modification of the Zellner technique for seemingly unrelated regressions. The method assumes that the disturbances in each equation are homoscedastic and non-autocorrelated and that there is zero correlation between non-contemporaneous disturbances of different equations.[10] It allows, however, the contemporaneous covariance between error terms in different equations to be nonzero. In order to avoid the singularity of the variance-covariance matrix one of the factor share equations is deleted before carrying out the second stage of the Zellner procedure. It has been shown that the resulting parameter estimates have the same asymptotic properties as maximum likelihood estimates (Berndt *et al.* [1974]). Moreover if the assumption of zero autocorrelation holds, the results of the procedure are insensitive to which factor share equation is deleted prior to the second stage.

The economic properties of the translog cost function are easily reviewed. The partial elasticity of substitution between labor and energy is given by:[11]

$$\sigma_{LE} = \frac{-\alpha_{LL} + s_E s_L}{s_E s_L}$$

[10] The assumption of lack of autocorrelation is not trivial given the use of time-series data. On the basis of the respective first-order auto correlation coefficients and the DW statistics (all calculated using the estimated residuals in the cost and factor share equation) reported in Table I below, we decided not to correct for first-order serial correlation along the lines suggested by Berndt and Savin [1975].

[11] See e.g. Uzawa [1962].

The input price elasticities for energy and labor are:

$$k_E = \frac{\alpha_{LL} + s_E(s_E - 1)}{s_E}$$

$$k_L = \frac{\alpha_{LL} + s_L(s_L - 1)}{s_L}$$

Finally, estimation of the translog cost model allows us to test whether the cost structure satisfies certain economic properties. The underlying technology is homothetic if and only if the cost function is separable in output. The results would be compatible with a homothetic technology only if $\alpha_{YL} = 0$. A more severe restriction is homogeneity, which implies $\alpha_{YL} = \alpha_{YY} = \alpha_{YT} = \alpha_{Yt} = 0$. It can further be tested whether the elasticity of substitution equals one. This will be the case if $\alpha_{LL} = 0$.

Before turning to the estimation results it is useful to point out two problems that might be associated with estimating cost functions. These might lead to biased parameters. A first source of possible bias results from the classical "regression fallacy", as noted by Borts [1960]. If costs are based upon a planned output level and differences between actual and planned output occur in practice, the firm might be unable to adapt completely to these unforeseen circumstances. The regression fallacy implies overestimated marginal costs.

A second difficulty concerns the assumptions of the methodology involved. Although the firm is allowed to be in disequilibrium with respect to the fixed capital stock, it is assumed that minimization of variable costs is the main objective. If this is not the appropriate goal of the firm's management, inefficiencies might bias the choice of inputs away from the cost minimizing mix and the firm might be operating off its cost curve. As a consequence the parameters and hence the technological characteristics estimated from econometric cost relations will be subject to specification bias due to misspecification of the behavioral model. Moreover, the classical duality principles are no longer generally valid. Under these circumstances the estimated cost relation will reflect the firm's behavior rather than its technology.[12]

IV. DATA AND ESTIMATION RESULTS

The variable cost function previously discussed was estimated using time series data on output, input prices for labor and energy, a measure for the fixed capital stock and a time trend. The sample covers the period 1951–79.

[12] The methodology for correcting this type of possible bias is in its infancy. In an admirable foray Fuss and Waverman [1978] suggest how to estimate cost functions for the Averch-Johnson type firm operating under rate of return regulation. However, as this behavioral assumption is more unrealistic for the firm under investigation in this paper than the cost minimization hypothesis, their methods do not seem very useful for our purposes. We therefore accepted cost minimization as a working hypothesis.

It has become quite common in recent studies (see e.g. Caves, Christensen and Tretheway [1980]) to consider passenger transportation as yielding several distinct outputs, e.g. passenger-miles and average trip length. This approach has the advantage of distinguishing between the cost effects of increases in passengers and changes in distance traveled. However, data limitations precluded this type of analysis in this paper. Indeed, the only reliable output measure available was the number of seat-kilometers provided.[13] Although this is not a very common variable in transport studies it has the advantage of being a pure supply measure which suggests a close relationship to costs. As a consequence, significant estimates of marginal costs may be expected. This is far less likely if we used e.g. passenger-kilometers which is determined by both supply and demand factors. Once the routes to be served and the departure schedules have been fixed, passenger-killometers are almost exclusively determined by demand factors. As long as we are unable to distinguish between peak and off-peak travel in our cost analysis the overall marginal cost of additional passenger kilometers is likely to be very low. A strong relation between costs and this output measure is not to be expected and accurate estimates of marginal costs are doubtful. A further advantage of using seat-kilometers is the fact that this variable is probably subject to less measurement errors than demand determined output measures. A disadvantage of our output measure is that it is not straightforward to use the resulting marginal costs in the analysis of pricing policies. Precisely because seat-kilometers is supply determined there is no obvious relation between this variable, the price paid by users of the bus system and the demand for bus transportation. Thus a price rise for example may be matched by no reduction in seat-kilometers and costs at all, which makes the analysis of pricing policies rather complicated. However, as the main emphasis of this study is on the development of productivity indices we do not consider our output measure as a major disadvantage.

The prices for energy and labor were derived from the NMVB annual reports by dividing total expenditures on these inputs by the quantities used.[14] Our variable cost figures were taken from these reports as well. In order to obtain a cost variable consistent with the theoretical analysis previously described only labor and energy costs were included. All cost and price variables were deflated using the wholesale price index.

As a measure for the capital stock we used the size of the bus fleet. Contrac-

[13] The bus company published passenger-kilometers and the number of passengers in its annual reports. However, these figures include output produced by private companies to whom the NMVB subleases some of its services. Of course the costs of this transport do not enter the NMVB's accounts. This implies that using the published data on passenger-kilometers or the number of passengers would give misleading cost-output relations.

[14] By using aggregate inputs labor and energy we implicitly assume input separability. This implies that we are assuming e.g. that the marginal rate of substitution between "line-haul" labor and "line-haul" energy is the same as between "line-haul" labor and "maintenance" energy. Data limitations precluded the use of more disaggregated inputs or activities to relax these assumptions.

TABLE I
PARAMETERS OF THE VARIABLE COST FUNCTION (*)

Parameters	*Estimate*	*Standard Error*	*t-Value*
α_Y	−1.388	0.029	−47.86
α_{YY}	−3.463	1.231	−2.82
α_L	0.892	0.074	12.04
α_{LL}	0.046	0.015	3.07
α_{YL}	−0.004	0.007	−0.54
α_T	−0.769	0.343	−2.24
α_{TT}	0.001	0.001	0.96
α_{TL}	0.168	0.083	2.04
α_{TY}	0.003	0.001	3.14
α_t	−0.018	0.008	−2.22
α_{tY}	−0.170	0.053	−3.22
α_{tL}	−0.0005	0.0003	−1.53
α_{tT}	−0.007	0.02	−0.32

R^2 cost relation = 0.95 DW cost relation = 1.78
R^2 factor share = 0.96 DW factor share = 1.49
$\rho_{CC} = 0.14$ $\rho_{CL} = 0.08$
$\rho_{LL} = 0.29$ $\rho_{LC} = 0.23$

* Note: ρ_{ij}: first-order serial correlation coefficient of the residuals of equations i and j.

tual arrangements between the firm and the producer of the vehicles suggests that in the short-run the stock of buses can indeed be assumed to be fixed. The lags between order and delivery are often quite long; over the period 1950–79 these lags were between two and five years. Although the bus company has the possibility of changing its fleet size even in the short-run by a flexible policy of selling and buying on the second-hand market and by changing its depreciation behavior, this is not very common practice. Therefore, following Williams [1979], we assume fleet size to be the fixed factor in the variable cost model.

We applied the modified Zellner procedure discussed in the previous section. The results in Table I indicate that most parameters exceed their standard error by a factor larger than two.[15] The explanatory power of the translog function appears to be satisfactory as well. Several interesting features emerge from the results. First of all the hypothesis of homotheticity is not contradicted as α_{YL} is not significantly different from zero. However, the assumption of a constant cost elasticity with respect to output appears to be unreasonable as both α_{YY} and α_{tY} are highly significant. These results imply that the output cost elasticity varies with changes in output but not with variations in factor prices. The variability of the cost elasticity will be discussed in greater detail below. It further follows from the estimates that the hypothesis of unitary elasticity of substitution is not supported by the data, i.e. $\alpha_{LL} \neq 0$. This rules out the use of the Cobb-Douglas cost function as a reasonable description of the cost behavior of the firm.

[15] Note that first-order serial correlation did not seem to be a major problem.

Apart from the previous observations the parameters of the cost function have no clear direct interpretation. Their importance lies in their being estimates of the gradients and the Hessian of the true underlying cost function. This allows us to derive a set of relevant implications concerning the economic structure of the firm. Table II summarizes the main results. It contains an annual evaluation of the elasticity of substitution, the price elasticities of the firm's demand for labor and energy, the estimated marginal and average variable costs and the parameter D which is an indicator of the degree of economics of density. This measure was defined by Christensen and Greene [1976] as

$$D = 1 - \frac{\partial \ln C_V}{\partial \ln Y}.$$

A positive value (or an elasticity of costs with respect to output below unity) indicates economics of density, i.e. variable costs increase less than proportion-

TABLE II

Year	*Elasticity of Substitution* σ_{LE}	*Price elasticity of labor demand* k_L	*Price elasticity of energy demand* k_E	*Marginal Cost*	*Average variable cost*	*Economics of Density* D
1951	0.696	−0.129	−0.567	0.197	0.156	−0.262
52	0.701	−0.133	−0.568	0.224	0.174	−0.291
53	0.703	−0.135	−0.568	0.225	0.176	−0.447
54	0.700	−0.133	−0.568	0.218	0.164	−0.332
55	0.686	−0.122	−0.564	0.146	0.150	0.024
56	0.679	−0.117	−0.561	0.061	0.138	0.556
57	0.680	−0.118	−0.561	0.046	0.138	0.666
58	0.660	−0.107	−0.554	0.031	0.141	0.779
59	0.654	−0.104	−0.551	0.051	0.137	0.625
1960	0.627	−0.090	−0.537	0.032	0.127	0.746
61	0.606	−0.082	−0.524	0.049	0.126	0.608
62	0.555	−0.065	−0.490	0.033	0.123	0.732
63	0.541	−0.061	−0.480	0.023	0.124	0.811
64	0.517	−0.055	−P.462	0.029	0.123	0.767
65	0.496	−0.050	−0.455	0.061	0.130	0.531
66	0.490	−0.049	−0.441	0.103	0.141	0.271
67	0.483	−0.048	−0.436	0.165	0.149	−0.107
68	0.482	−0.047	−0.435	0.224	0.154	−0.456
69	0.462	−0.044	−0.419	0.269	0.156	−0.720
1970	0.420	−0.036	−0.385	0.308	0.163	−0.892
71	0.413	−0.035	−0.378	0.400	0.196	−1.046
72	0.351	−0.027	−0.324	0.451	0.209	−1.156
73	0.326	−0.024	−0.302	0.473	0.207	−1.281
74	0.401	−0.034	−0.368	0.499	0.210	−1.378
75	0.420	−0.036	−0.384	0.602	0.247	−1.441
76	0.374	−0.030	−0.344	0.612	0.242	−1.517
77	0.373	−0.029	−0.343	0.779	0.286	−1.725
78	0.316	−0.023	−0.293	0.870	0.314	−1.771
79	0.409	−0.035	−0.374	0.929	0.319	−1.916

ately with increases in output, given a fixed capital stock. In this sense economics of density are the short-run analogue of scale economics.[16]

The most striking result is certainly the volatile evolution of marginal costs and economics of density over time. However, taking into account the firm's policy over the period 1951–79 these results are not at all implausible. The firm reduced substantially the size of its bus fleet in the early fifties and seemed to be unable to increase output without incurring important additional costs. However, during the period 1954–65 the firm gradually adopted the one-man-car (OMC) exploitation system. This resulted in excess labor which could be used to expand output without much additional cost. The firm exploited the extremely low marginal cost over this period and the resulting strong economics of density to increase output substantially. New routes were served and on many existing routes frequencies were augmented. In the late sixties, however, the evolution towards OMC exploitation was completed. The resulting increase in marginal costs was reinforced by rising inflation in labor and especially energy input prices during the last decade. From Table II we observe highly increasing marginal costs over this period with diseconomies of density growing very strong in most recent years.

Many previous studies have analyzed the existence of economies of scale in the bus industry. There seems to be no agreement on this issue in the literature: Koshal [1972] and Lee and Steedman [1970] find no significant scale economics using U.S. and British data, respectively. The paper by Wabe and Coles [1975] produces evidence of diseconomies of scale. Most recent studies, using more appropriate cost models, seem to indicate the existence of economies of scale, although both the magnitude of the effect and the output range over which it holds depend on the particular sample analyzed. Williams [1979] found long-run scale economies using a cross-section of U.S. firms. Whereas Williams and Dalal [1981] suggest positive scale effects for the larger operators in their sample, Viton [1981] concludes that there are short-run economies of density and long-run scale economies for the smaller firms only. Using Israeli data, Berechman estimates economies of scale with respect to the number of passenger trips.

All of these studies used cross-section data so that is not straightforward to compare their results with those derived in this paper. Our analysis does indicate, however, that not only the level of output but also the shift in technology over time itself has a strong effect on the existence and the magnitude of scale and density economies. This at least provides a partial explanation for the wildly varying results found in the literature, where samples at different points in time and containing firms operating in a different environment (e.g. urban versus regional bus transport) have been analyzed.

[16] It is not surprising, therefore, to find a relation between D and the measure R of returns to scale. It's easy to show

$$R = \left(1 - \frac{\partial \ln C_V}{\partial \ln T}\right) \Big/ (1 - D).$$

A second piece of useful information concerns the price elasticities of the firm's demand for labor and energy and the associated elasticity of substitution between these inputs.[17] The figures in Table II are plausible. The elasticity of substitution appears to be substantially below unity in all years, confirming the inappropriateness of the Cobb-Douglas specification.[18] The demand for energy and especially for labor is very inelastic. These finding are not inconsistent with previous research[19] and may be explained by the firm's contractual obligations. The higher elasticity for energy demand probably reflects the firm's greater flexibility in negotiating its energy contracts. Whereas labor contracts are usually negotiated over periods of several years, changes in energy contracts can be accomplished within a much shorter time period. A lower elasticity for the demand for labor is also suggested by the fact that downward changes in the labor force are usually achieved by not replacing retiring workers rather than by direct lay-offs. This creates adjustment lags in the demand which may be reflected in low price elasticities.

V. PRODUCTIVITY INDICES FOR REGIONAL BUS TRANSPORTATION IN BELGIUM

In this section we present productivity indices for regional bus transportation in Belgium, calculated on the basis of the cost function analyzed in the previous paragraph. For each year in our sample we evaluated the expressions (8) and (9). The calculated productivity growth rates are presented in the first two columns of Table IIIa. We mentioned before that the firm constructs its own productivity indicator in its annual reports. In order to compare our indices with the NMVB productivity index, this is presented in the third column as well. It is of the classical type output per unit of input as it is defined as the number of seat-kilometers provided per man-hour labor used.

Consider the calculated productivity indicators. Recall that these would have given the same results only if the firm had exhibited constant returns to scale over the whole sample period. It follows from our analysis of the economics of density parameter D and the relation between the returns to scale

[17] All series are slightly trended over time. This is due to the fact that the elasticities depend upon the factor shares, a special feature of the translog form.

[18] We used simple t-test and found the elasticity of substitution to be significantly different from one over the complete sample period. Assuming that the cost shares of the inputs are nonstochastic (i.e. using observed rather than predicted shares) the standard error of the estimated elasticity of substitution can be calculated to be

$$\frac{1}{s_L s_E} \sigma_{\alpha_{LL}}, \text{ where } \sigma_{\alpha_{LL}} \text{ is the standard error of } \alpha_{LL}.$$

[19] Only Viton [1981] presents significant elasticities of substitution between labor and energy. His estimates range from 0.22 to 0.56. The estimates of Williams and Dalal [1981] are insignificant, whereas other authors did not include energy prices in the cost function (e.g. Berechman [1983]). Our findings with respect to the price elasticities are again consistent with those in Viton [1981]. The labor demand elasticities presented by Berechman [1983] are close to zero and insignificant.

TABLE IIIa

Year	Annual Productivity growth according to index P_1	Annual Productivity growth according to index P_2	Annual Productivity growth according to index *NMVB*
1951	6.0	3.9	4.5
52	5.3	3.6	4.6
53	4.5	3.4	4.6
54	3.8	2.9	4.5
55	3.5	2.3	8.4
56	4.4	1.6	6.4
57	5.2	1.2	3.3
58	5.7	0.93	2.4
59	4.5	0.77	3.5
1960	2.9	0.60	7.0
61	2.1	0.42	0.7
62	0.76	0.20	1.3
63	−0.44	−0.05	5.2
64	−1.14	−0.17	3.8
65	−0.72	−0.14	1.6
66	−0.08	−0.02	1.5
67	0.25	0.18	1.6
68	0.39	0.37	2.8
69	0.41	0.48	1.8
1970	0.38	0.51	−0.4
71	0.33	0.49	−0.3
72	0.28	0.44	3.0
73	0.22	0.38	2.8
74	0.16	0.28	1.3
75	0.09	0.16	0.9
76	0.05	0.09	0.8
77	0.03	0.05	0.0
78	−0.01	−0.01	−1.6
79	−0.03	−0.06	−1.5

measure R and D that this was not the case. As a consequence, large differences in absolute value between both indices should not be surprising. However, as far as the evolution over time is concerned both series show the same consistent pattern of productivity growth. They indicate a remarkable increase in productivity over the complete period 1951–60 followed by a long period of very modest growth. The conclusion is obvious: nearly all productivity increases of the sample period 1951–79 occurred during the first decennium. During the sixties and seventies no substantial growth was achieved. Both indices even show periods of slight productivity decline.

The indicator used by the bus company implies quite a different time pattern. Although it indicates substantial productivity growth over the period 1951–60, it shows large further increases during the next decennia except for most recent years, where the index slightly declines.

The differences in time pattern and absolute productivity growth as given by our three alternative indicators can more clearly be observed by considering the information summarized in Table IIIb. This table contains the average growth rate for successive five year periods and for the complete period 1951–79. The overall growth rate as measured by the firm largely exceeds that implied by the calculated indices. This confirms our main findings: the two alternative definitions of productivity growth lead to substantially different results in absolute terms (especially over the period 1955–65 characterized by strong economies of density), but they show approximately the same evolution over time. The index given by the NMVB indicates a completely different time path and substantially overestimated productivity growth over the period 1951–75.

Table IIIb

Period	*Average growth rates according to*		
	P_1	P_2	*NMVB*
1951–54	4.90	3.45	4.55
1955–59	4.66	1.13	4.80
1960–64	0.84	0.20	3.60
1965–69	0.05	0.17	1.86
1970–74	0.27	0.42	1.28
1975–79	0.03	0.05	0.28
1951–79	1.68	0.84	2.54

The public policy implications of our findings are easily summarized. We believe that our results are interesting in view of the importance of productivity growth in transport policy discussions. The argument of productivity increases is often used by transportation officials to shift the responsibility of financial losses to the government. The latter has a major impact on the determination of the firm's output in terms of vehicle-miles. Therefore, it is often argued that given the transport services the government imposes the firm to offer to the public, productivity growth is an indication of efficient operation. Increased productivity in the provision of transportation facilities might in turn weaken the public opposition against subsidy payments to compensate deficits. Moreover, productivity growth is a major issue in the wage negotiation process. The use of biased estimates of productivity shifts may affect the relative strength of the participating parties and even influence the final outcome of the negotiations. Therefore, policy makers are likely to consider reliable productivity estimators as very useful. We consider the development of reliable indicators on the basis of readily available statistical data as the main contribution of this paper. If we assume the parameters of the variable cost function to remain stable at least in the near future, the estimated function and the simple formulas derived in the text can be used to calculate better productivity growth rates than those previously used. I am convinced, therefore, that the development of productivity indices was not an irrelevant academic exercise.

VI. SUMMARY AND CONCLUSIONS

In this paper we applied the methodology recently developed by Caves, Christensen and Swanson [1981] to calculate productivity indices for regional bus transportation in Belgium. The procedure involved two steps: first we estimated a flexible variable cost function to describe the cost and production structure. In a second step the estimation results were used to calculate two different indicators of productivity growth over the period 1951–79.

The translog variable cost function was the flexible functional form chosen in this paper. Our main findings concerning the cost structure were the volatile evolutions of both the economies of density parameter and the associated marginal cost. These were explained in terms of the NMVB's policy towards one-man-car exploitation during the period 1951–65 and the rapidly increasing factor prices for labor and energy in recent years. Our results further indicated the elasticity of substitution to be significantly below unity, ruling out the use of simpler functional forms such as Cobb-Douglas to describe the cost and production structure in regional bus transportation. The price elasticities for energy and especially labor were found to be low, reflecting contractual obligations of the bus company.

In the second part of the paper we used two alternative definitions of productivity growth to calculate indices based upon our estimated variable cost function. The resulting productivity indices showed substantial growth over the period 1951–60. However, no significant productivity increases were observed in later periods i.e. the growth in productivity over the period 1951–79 is almost exclusively due to the increases in the first decennium. The calculated indices were compared with a more naive indicator of productivity used by the bus company. The latter implies average growth rates which largely exceeded those implicit in our proposed indices. Moreover, the NMVB index showed a completely different time pattern, indicating quite large productivity increases during the sixties and the early seventies.

Finally we discussed the importance of reliable productivity indicators for public policy. In view of the role of productivity growth rates in policy discussions we would strongly argue for the construction of indices according to the method described in this paper. These can be used as alternatives to the rather loosely defined productivity index presented in the firm's annual report.

ACCEPTED DECEMBER 1983

Bruno De Borger,
UFSIA-SESO,
University of Antwerp,
Prinsstraat 13,
B-2000 Antwerpen, Belgium.

REFERENCES

ABRAMOVITZ, M. 1962, 'Economic Growth in the United States', *The American Economic Review*, Vol. 52, 4 (September), pp. 762–82.

BERECHMAN, T., 1983, 'Costs, Economies of Scale and Factor Demands in Bus Transport', *The Journal of Transport Economics and Policy*, Vol. XVII, 1 (January), pp. 7–24.

BERNDT, E. K., HALL, B. E., HALL, R. E. and HAUSMAN, J. A., 1974, 'Estimation and Inference in Nonlinear Structural Models', *The Annals of Economic and Social Measurement*, Vol. 3, 4 (October), pp. 653–65.

BERNDT, E. K. and N. E. SAVIN, 1975, 'Estimation and Hypothesis Testing in Singular Equation Systems with Autoregressive Disturbances', *Econometrica*, Vol. 43, 5–6 (September–November), pp. 937–57.

BORTS, G. H., 1960, 'The Estimation of Rail Cost Functions', *Econometrica*, Vol. 28, 1 (January), pp. 108–31.

CAVES, D. W., CHRISTENSEN, L. R. and SWANSON, J. A., 1980, 'Productivity in U.S. Railroads 1951–1974', *The Bell Journal of Economics*, Vol. 11, 1 (Spring), pp. 166–81.

CAVES, D. W., CHRISTENSEN, L. R. and SWANSON, L. R., 1981, 'Productivity Growth Scale Economics and Capacity Utilization in U.S. Railroads 1955–1974', *The American Ecovomic Review*, Vol. 71, 5 (December), pp. 994–1002.

CAVES, D. W., CHRISTENSEN, L. R. and TRETHEWAY, M. W. 1980, 'Flexible Cost Functions for Multiproduct Firms', *The Review of Economics and Statistics*, Vol. LXII, 3 (August), pp. 477–81.

CHRISTENSEN, L. R. and GREENE, W. H., 1976, 'Economies of Scale in U.S. Electric Power Generation', *Journal of Political Economy*, Vol. 84, 4 (August), pp. 655–76.

DIEWERT E. W., 1974, 'Applications of Duality Theory', in: Intriligator and Kendrick, *Frontiers of Quantitative Economics, Vol. 2*, (North-Holland, Amsterdam), pp. 106–71.

FRIEDLAENDER, A. F., 1978, 'Hedonic Costs and Economies of Scale in the Regulated Trucking Industry', in: *Motor Carrier Economic Regulation*, (National Academy of Sciences, Washington, D.C.), pp. 33–56.

FUSS, M. and WAVERMAN, L., 1978, 'Multi-Product Multi-Input Cost Functions for a Regulated Utility: The Case of Telecommunications in Canada', *Institute for Policy Analysis Report 7810*, University of Toronto.

HARMATUCK, D. J., 1979, 'A Policy-Sensitive Railway Cost Function', *The Logistics and Transportation Review*, Vol. 5, 2 (April), pp. 277–315.

HARMATUCK, D. J., 1981, 'A Motor Carrier Joint Cost Function', *The Journal of Transport Economics and Policy*, Vol. XV, 2 (May), pp. 135–53.

JORGENSON, D. W. and GRILICHES, Z., 1967, 'The Explanation of Productivity Change', *The Review of Economic Studies*, Vol. XXXIV, 3 (July), pp. 249–83.

KEELER, T. E., 1974, 'Railroad Costs, Returns to Scale and Excess Capacity', *The Review of Economics and Statistics*, Vol. LVI, 2 (May), pp. 201–208.

KENDRICK, J. W., 1973, *Postwar Productivity Trends in the U.S.*, (NBER, New York).

KLEM, R., 1978, 'The Cost Structure of the Regulated Trucking Industry', in *Motor Carrier Economic Regulation*, (National Academy of Sciences, Washington, D.C.), pp. 141–62.

KOSHAL, R. K., 1972, 'Economies of Scale in Bus Transport: Some U.S. Experience', *The Journal of Transport Economics and Policy*, Vol. VI, 2 (May), pp. 151–53.

LEE, N. and STEEDMAN, I., 1970, 'Economies of Scale in Bus Transport', *The Journal of Transport Economics and Policy*, Vol. IV, 1 (January), pp. 15–28.

MCFADDEN, D., 1978, 'Cost, Revenue and Profit Functions', in: Fuss, M. and McFadden, D., *Production Economics: A Dual Approach to Theory and Applications*, (North-Holland, Amsterdam).

MEYER, J. R. and MORTON, A. L., 1975, 'The U.S. Railroad Industry in the Post World War II Period: A Profile', *Explorations in Economic Research*, Vol. 2, 4 (Fall), pp. 449–501.

MEYER, J. R., KAIN, J. and WOHL, M., 1965, *The Urban Transportation Problem*, (Harvard University Press, Cambridge, MA).

MEYER, J. R., PECK, M. H., STENASON, J. and ZWICK, C., 1959, *The Economics of Competition in the Transportation Industries*, (Harvard University Press, Cambridge, MA).

SAMUELSON, P. and SWAMY, P., 1974, 'Invariant Economic Index Numbers and Canonical Duality: Survey and Synthesis', *The American Economic Review*, Vol. 64, 3 (June), pp. 566–93.

SOLOW, R. A., 1957, 'Technical Change and the Aggregate Production Function', *The Review of Economics and Statistics*, Vol. XXXIX, 3 (August), pp. 312–20.

SPADY, R. H. and FRIEDLANDER, A. F., 1978, 'Hedonic Cost Functions for the Regulated Trucking Industry', *The Bell Journal of Economics*, Vol. 9, 1 (Spring), pp. 159–79.

UZAWA, H., 1962, 'Production Functions with Constant Elasticity of Substitution', *The Review of Economic Studies*, Vol. XXIX, 1 (January), pp. 291–99.

VITON, P. A., 1980, 'On the Economics of Rapid-Transit Operations', *Transportation Research*, Vol. 14, Series A, 4 (August), pp. 247–53.

VITON, P. A., 1981, 'A Translog Cost Function for Urban Bus Transit', *The Journal of Industrial Economics*', Vol. XXIX, 3 (March), pp. 287–304.

WABE, S. and COLES, O., 1975, 'The Short and Long Run Cost of Bus Transport in Urban Areas', *The Journal of Transport Economics and Policy*, Vol. IX, 2 (May), pp. 127–40.

WILLIAMS, M. 1979, 'Firm Size and Operating Costs in Urban Bus Transportation', *The Journal of Industrial Economics*, Vol. XXVIII, 2 (December), pp. 209–18.

WILLIAMS, M. and DALAL, A., 1981, 'Estimation of the Elasticities of Substitution in Urban Bus Transportation: A Cost Function Approach', *The Journal of Regional Science*, Vol. II, 2 (May), pp. 263–77.

ZELLNER, A., 1962, 'An Efficient Method for Estimating Seemingly Unrelated Regressions and Tests for Aggregation Bias', *Journal of the American Statistical Association*, Vol. 57, 298 (June), pp. 348–65.

THE JOURNAL OF INDUSTRIAL ECONOMICS 00–1821 $2.00
Volume XXXIII September 1984 No. 1

DEMAND FLUCTUATIONS AND ENDOGENOUS FIRM FLEXIBILITY*

DAVID E. MILLS

I. INTRODUCTION

IF a firm faces demand-induced price fluctuations in its output market with stationary and positively inclined marginal costs, it will earn greater expected profit the greater is the variability of price around its mean. Or at least this is so if the firm can adjust output from one market period to the next to maintain equality between marginal cost and price. This was demonstrated by W. Oi [5]. J. H. Drèze and J. J. Gabszewicz [1] explored the implication of Oi's finding that a demand-induced increase in price fluctuations will attract entry because it increases expected profit among firms in what previously was a competitive equilibrium. The entry of new competitors will continue until expected profits decline to their normal level and a new equilibrium is established.

E. Sheshinski and Drèze [6] reconstructed, generalized and extended the results of Drèze and Gabszewicz, and established the essential characteristics of competitive equilibrium with fluctuating demand. This equilibrium is stationary insofar as the number and identity of firms is concerned (there is no entry/exit from one market period to the next), but nonstationary where price and output are concerned. As market demand rises and falls, so do price and firms' output. Properties of this equilibrium include the following: (1) firms produce at a level that is less on average than "capacity" output—the average cost minimizing output level achieved in every market period with stationary demand; (2) the number of firms sustained by competition is greater than with stationary demand; (3) the expected cost per unit of output produced is greater than with stationary demand.

In exploring the comparative static properties of this equilibrium with respect to changes in the structure of market demand, Sheshinski and Drèze confine the response pattern of firms to two modes: entry/exit and changing the mean and variance of output. This overlooks some other avenues of adjustment. In particular it overlooks the myriad of ways in which the internal organization of firms might be adjusted to accommodate more or less output fluctuation. These adjustments are both technological (e.g. changing the mix of production factors) and organizational (e.g. altering the lines of

* I would like to thank Roger Sherman, participants in the Microeconomics Workshop at Vanderbilt University and an anonymous referee for thoughtful comments on an earlier version. The Earhart Foundation provided financial support for this research.

administrative control). In this paper I will extend previous models of competitive markets with demand fluctuations by injecting elements of internal organization into firms' choice sets. This allows a more elaborate and realistic response pattern of firms to long-run changes in the structure of market demand than has been described by previous research.

The aspects of firms' internal organization relevant to markets with demand fluctuations are those that facilitate routine output adjustments. As seen by competitive firms, these adjustments are made in response to price fluctuations and their extent is gauged by supply elasticity. This suggests that the relevant aspects of firms' internal organization are embodied in their cost structure and that the relevant range of choice is represented by a feasible set of cost curves. A long-run change in market demand alters the price distribution, and this induces firms to alter their choice of a cost curve.

That firms' choice of cost structure depends on the extent of anticipated output fluctuation over the period the firm is bound to that structure was recognized by G. J. Stigler [7] and A. G. Hart [2]. Stigler's discussion of this choice is especially helpful. He refers to the attribute of cost curves that determines how responsive output decisions are to price fluctuations as "flexibility". This discussion of flexibility is not formal but T. Marschak and R. Nelson [3] persuasively argue that Stigler's notion of flexibility is one that varies inversely with the curvature of the total cost curve, or the slope of the marginal cost curve. Flexibility is least when marginal costs are steep and average costs rise precipitously around their minimum; flexibility decreases as average costs are flatter and marginal costs less steep. Figure I (corresponding to the relevant figure in Stigler) shows two average cost curves and their corresponding marginal cost curves. The "one" pair of curves shows greater flexibility than those indexed "two".

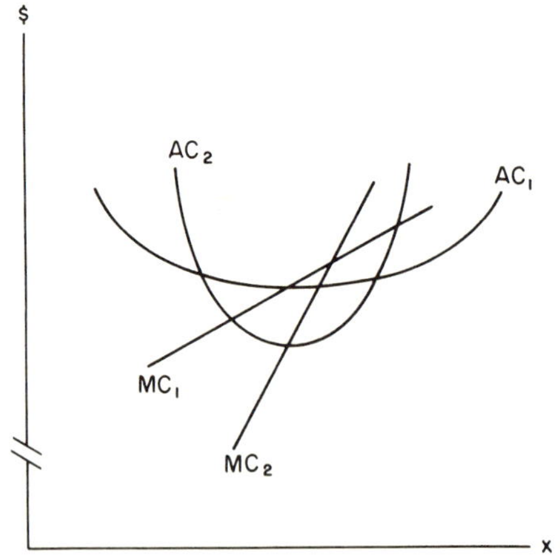

FIGURE I
Flexibility and Cost Curves

Notice that minimum average costs are shown to vary inversely with flexibility. (The fact that both average cost curves are minimized at the same output level is inessential and merely facilitates comparisons.) This means that the attributes of internal organization that increase flexibility also inflate unit costs when output is near capacity. As Stigler put it, "flexibility will not be a 'free good': A plant certain to operate x units of output per week will surely have lower costs at that output than will a plant designed to be passably efficient from $x/2$ to $2x$ units per week" [7, p. 311]. This tradeoff among feasible cost structures, each of which corresponds to a different internal organization, is theoretically plausible and plays a fundamental role in this paper's analysis of market structure determination.

The paper is organized as follows. Section II highlights some of the incentives of firms facing price fluctuations with a choice among more and less flexible cost structures. Section III goes beyond this by showing how endogenous flexibility is determined in competitive markets with demand fluctuations. Section IV presents some of the important properties of the resulting competitive equilibrium, and section V presents some comparative statics results. Conclusions and comparisons with previous research are drawn in the final section.

To fully characterize firms' choices among cost structures it is necessary to lay out an explicit set of options. The approach taken here is to make that set as simple as practically possible while preserving the fundamental tradeoff between flexibility and static-efficiency. This is achieved by modeling options as a family of quadratic total cost curves with an endogenous "flexibility" variable. This approach has the usual drawbacks of confining analysis to specific functional forms, but the major results produced are broadly indicative of more general and less tractable cases. Also, the analysis is sufficiently general to accommodate several interpretations of demand fluctuations. It applies equally to stochastic fluctuations and fluctuations that follow a well-established and forseeable cyclical pattern (e.g. ordinary seasonality).

II. FLEXIBILITY AND THE FIRM

Consider a competitive, risk-neutral firm in a market where demand fluctuations make price p fluctuate among market periods. Let the mean and variance of p be $\bar{p}$ and σ_p^2. Let the firm's output, chosen to maximize expected profits, be x and let its total cost curve be stationary (that is, not fluctuating) and quadratic:

$$c(x) = \alpha + \beta x + \frac{x^2}{2\gamma} \qquad (1)$$

α, β and γ are positive constants, so marginal costs are positive and increasing:

$$c_x = \beta + x/\gamma \qquad (2a)$$

$$c_{xx} = 1/\gamma \qquad (2b)$$

From (2b) we see that γ varies inversely with the curvature of total costs, or the slope of marginal costs. Following Stigler's line of reasoning, Marschak and Nelson refer to the reciprocal of c_{xx} as a flexibility indicator. This associates flexibility with flatter marginal costs and output adjustments highly responsive to price fluctuations. In keeping with this convention, γ is a measure of flexibility for cost function (1).

Since it is a competitor the firm chooses x in every market period to equate marginal cost to price. From this we obtain the decision rule:

$$x(p) = \gamma(p - \beta) \tag{3}$$

Also, firm profit y is a function of p:

$$y(p) = px(p) - c[x(p)] \tag{4}$$

Differentiating (4), we obtain

$$y_p = x(p) + px_p - c_x x_p,$$

which by substituting (2a) and (3) becomes

$$y_p = \gamma(p - \beta).$$

This of course equals (3). Differentiating, we get

$$y_{pp} = \gamma. \tag{5}$$

Since total costs are quadratic, (4) may be written as a second order expansion around $p = \bar{p}$:

$$y(p) = y(\bar{p}) + y_p(p - \bar{p}) + \frac{y_{pp}}{2}(p - \bar{p})^2 \tag{6}$$

Taking the expectation of (6) and substituting (5) we have

$$E[y(p)] = y(\bar{p}) + \frac{\sigma_p^2 \gamma}{2} \tag{7}$$

From (7) we immediately obtain Oi's proposition that the firm's expected profit will increase with a mean-preserving increase in price variability:

$$\partial E[y(p)]/\partial\sigma_p^2 = \gamma/2 > 0.$$

We also see that

$$\partial E[y(p)]/\partial\gamma = (\bar{p} - \beta)^2/2 + \sigma_p^2/2 > 0. \tag{8}$$

This implies that expected profit will increase with greater flexibility ceteris paribus. In addition, (8) implies that the marginal gain from increased flexibility is greater the more variable is price. This observation was made by Marschak and Nelson and seems to have been central to Stigler's early discussion of flexibility.

Stigler's major point had to do not so much with the output adjustments a firm makes from one period to the next in response to price fluctuations, but rather with the prior commitment it makes to the cost structure that defines those adjustments. Given a choice among technological and organizational options and their associated cost curves, and given that such a choice once made cannot be changed except in the long run, it is obvious from (8) that more flexibility is preferred to less, other things the same. It is unlikely, however, that the field of choice is one that leaves all other things the same. What is more likely, as Stigler argued and as is depicted in Figure 1, is that cost structures is one faced by all competitors. As all firms exercise this choice means the firm's choice of cost structure must resolve a tradeoff between flexibility and static-efficiency. Faced with much price variability it will prefer greater flexibility even at the expense of a loss in static-efficiency. With little or no price variability the firm will opt for a cost curve that is less flexible and more static-efficient.

Actually things are more complicated than this insight suggests. Since the firm in question is a competitor, it is plausible that the choice it faces among cost structures is one faced by all competitors. As all firms exercise this choice they have a collective, endogenous effect on the price distribution. The price distribution upheld by competitive equilibrium depends not only on fluctuating market demand and the output decisions of all firms, but also on their choice of *flexibility*. If entry/exit is free, this equilibrium will let all firms earn zero expected profit. A characterization of this kind of competitive equilibrium is presented below.

III. MARKET EQUILIBRIUM WITH ENDOGENOUS FLEXIBILITY

In order to take explicit account of the tradeoff between flexibility and static-efficiency, let us suppose that firms may choose from a continuum of total cost curves of the type:

$$(9) \qquad c(x, \gamma) = \alpha(\gamma) + \beta(\gamma)x + \frac{x^2}{2\gamma}.$$

Once chosen the cost curve dictates the supply response of firms to demand-induced price fluctuation. These curves and their associated production technologies are identified by a level of flexibility γ, and the continuum is bounded by $\gamma \in [\Gamma_0, \Gamma_1]$. The only assumptions imposed on this class of cost curves other than the previous requirements that α, β and γ are positive are

$$(10a) \qquad \beta_\gamma > -\frac{d\sqrt{2\alpha/\gamma}}{d\gamma} > 0,$$

$$(10b) \qquad \beta_{\gamma\gamma} > \frac{d^2\sqrt{2\alpha/\gamma}}{d\gamma^2} > 0.$$

(Henceforth we streamline notation by suppressing γ as an argument of α and β except where necessary.)

Assumption (10a) endows this class of cost curves with the previously mentioned characteristic that minimum average costs vary inversely with flexibility. To see this let $x^0(\gamma)$ be the average-cost-minimizing (or "capacity") output level. From (9) we get

$$x^0(\gamma) = \sqrt{2\alpha\gamma} \tag{11}$$

Then from (9) and (11) we get

$$c[x^0(\gamma), \gamma]/x^0(\gamma) = \beta + \sqrt{2\alpha/\gamma} \tag{12}$$

Assumption (10a) implies that minimum average costs (12) are increasing in flexibility γ. Assumption (10b) upholds a second-order condition for firms' optimal choice of flexibility. Also, with (10a) it provides assurance that all sustained firms share a unique and common choice of γ.[1]

Following Sheshinski and Drèze we assume (with no serious loss of generality) that fluctuating market demand Q is totally price inelastic. The mean quantity demanded per market period if $\bar{Q}$ and the variance is constant at σ_Q^2. With free entry and a continuum of firms competitive equilibrium is identified by the market structure that minimizes the total expected costs of producing (fluctuating) Q. We proceed by solving for the (expected) cost-minimizing market structure conditional on all firms being identical. After this it is shown that this equilibrium is immune to entry by firms who choose a different γ. This establishes that no market structure with heterogeneous firms can supplant the homogeneous-firm equilibrium.

A market structure with identical firms is fully specified by some number of firms n and the level of flexibility γ chosen. The market structure that sustains competitive equilibrium is identified by n^*, γ^* which together

$$\min_{\gamma} G(\gamma),$$

where

$$G(\gamma) \equiv \min_{n} \{E[nc(Q/n, \gamma)]\} \tag{13}$$

Interpreting, $G(\gamma)$ is the expected total cost of producing Q conditional on all firms having chosen γ. γ^* is the level of flexibility that minimizes $G(\gamma)$ over γ, and n^* is the number of such firms sustained.[2]

[1] It is possible that competitive equilibrium with demand fluctuations sustains a set of heterogeneous firms where some choose flexible cost structures and absorb a disporportionately large share of industry-wide output fluctuations while others chose cost structures more static efficient and maintain relatively stable output levels. To get heterogeneous firms, however, requires a discrete set of cost options. I describe the properties of this kind of equilibrium elsewhere [4].

[2] This is as good a point as any to observe that with quadratic costs, marginal costs $(\beta + x/\gamma)$ are linear in output and always exceed average variable costs $(\beta + x/2\gamma)$ when $x > 0$. Since Q is always positive, so must be x for all firms. Firms never face a price so low that they discontinue production due to a failure of revenues to cover variable costs.

Observe from (9) that

$$(14) \qquad E[nc(Q/n, \gamma)] = n\alpha + \beta\bar{Q} + (\bar{Q}^2 + \sigma_Q^2)/2\gamma n.$$

$G(\gamma)$ is the minimum of (14) over all n. Minimizing over n yields

$$(15) \qquad n = \frac{\sqrt{\bar{Q}^2 + \sigma_Q^2}}{\sqrt{2\alpha\gamma}}$$

(15) designates a global minimum over n since the second derivative of the r.h.s. of (14) with respect to n is positive. Substituting (15) into (14) we get

$$(16) \qquad G(\gamma) = \sqrt{2\alpha/\gamma}\sqrt{\bar{Q}^2 + \sigma_Q^2} + \beta\bar{Q}.$$

The optimal level of flexibility γ^* is determined by minimizing (16) over γ; then n^* is found by evaluating (15) at $\gamma = \gamma^*$.

Take first the most interesting case—that of an interior solution $\gamma^* \in (\Gamma_0, \Gamma_1)$. Assumption (10b) is sufficient to insure $G_{\gamma\gamma} > 0$ so for this case γ^* is solved by equating G_γ to zero. Differentiate (16) with respect to γ and rearrange terms to get

$$(17) \qquad \frac{\sqrt{\bar{Q}^2 + \sigma_Q^2}}{\bar{Q}} \frac{d\sqrt{2\alpha(\gamma^*)/\gamma^*}}{d\gamma} + \beta_\gamma(\gamma^*) = 0$$

Now define

$$(18) \qquad K(\gamma) \equiv -\beta_\gamma \Bigg/ \frac{d\sqrt{2\alpha/\gamma}}{d\gamma}$$

$K(\gamma)$ must exceed 1 because of assumption (10a). Also

$$K_\gamma = -\frac{\beta_{\gamma\gamma}}{\dfrac{d\sqrt{2\alpha/\gamma}}{d\gamma}} + \frac{\beta_\gamma \dfrac{d^2\sqrt{2\alpha/\gamma}}{d\gamma^2}}{\left(\dfrac{d\sqrt{2\alpha/\gamma}}{d\gamma}\right)^2} > 0$$

follows from assumptions (10a, b). (17) and (18) yield

$$(19) \qquad \sqrt{\bar{Q}^2 + \sigma_Q^2}/\bar{Q} = K(\gamma^*)$$

which can be solved for an interior solution to the flexibility choice of firms γ^*.

For values of $\bar{Q}$ and σ_Q^2 where $G(\gamma)$ has no interior solution, the following rule applies:

$$(20a) \qquad \gamma^* = \Gamma_0 \quad \text{if} \quad G'(\Gamma_0) > 0$$

$$(20b) \qquad \gamma^* = \Gamma_1 \quad \text{if} \quad G'(\Gamma_1) < 0$$

Both interior and boundary solutions are depicted by the solid line in Figure 2. Consider first the case where

$$K(\Gamma_0) < \sqrt{\bar{Q}^2 + \sigma_Q^2}/\bar{Q} < K(\Gamma_1).$$

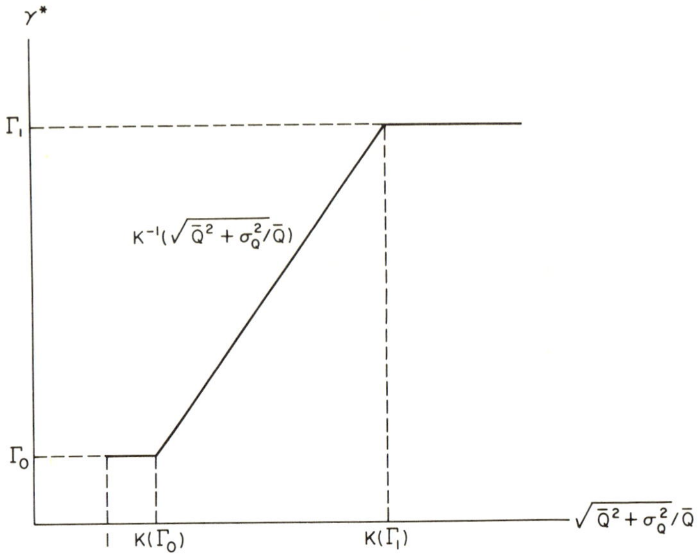

FIGURE 2
Optimal Flexibility

Using (19) γ^* is determined by the inverse of the K-function. Clearly γ^* rises with $\sqrt{\bar{Q}^2 + \sigma_Q^2}/\bar{Q}$. For values of $\sqrt{\bar{Q}^2 + \sigma_Q^2}/\bar{Q}$ greater than or equal to $K(\Gamma_1)$, γ^* is Γ_1; for values less than or equal to $K(\Gamma_0)$, but obviously no less than one, γ^* is Γ_0.

In competitive equilibrium, all firms achieve zero expected profit $E[y]$. To see this substitute (1) and (3) into (4) and evaluate at $p = \bar{p}$:

$$y(\bar{p}) = (\bar{p} - \beta)^2\gamma/2 - \alpha.$$

Substitute this into (7) to get

$$E[y] = [(\bar{p} - \beta)^2 + \sigma_p^2]\gamma/2 - \alpha. \tag{21}$$

For any market structure n, γ, the market supply curve is

$$p = \beta + Q/n\gamma,$$

from which it follows that

$$\bar{p} = \beta + \bar{Q}/n\gamma, \tag{22a}$$

$$\sigma_p^2 = \sigma_Q^2/(n\gamma)^2. \tag{22b}$$

Substituting (22a, b) into (21) yields

$$E[y] = \frac{\bar{Q}^2 + \sigma_Q^2}{2n^2\gamma} - \alpha.$$

When (15) is substituted into this equation, we obtain $E[y] = 0$. This is true for any market structure n, γ that satisfies (15) and is thus true for the competitive market structure n^*, γ^*.

To show that the cost-minimizing industry structure with identical firms (n^*, γ^*) cannot be supplanted by an alternative market structure with heterogeneous firms, it is sufficient to show that no firm with $\gamma \neq \gamma^*$ can make nonnegative profit with the price distribution it sustains. From (21) note that for the equilibrium values of $\bar{p}, \sigma_p^2$,

$$E[y]\left\{\begin{matrix} = \\ < \end{matrix}\right\}0 \langle = \rangle \beta + \sqrt{2\alpha/\gamma - \sigma_p^2}\left\{\begin{matrix} = \\ > \end{matrix}\right\}\bar{p} \tag{23}$$

holds for any feasible γ. Equality holds for γ^*. To show that $E[y] < 0$ for any $\gamma \neq \gamma^*$ with this price distribution, it is shown that $\beta + \sqrt{2\alpha/\gamma - \sigma_p^2}$ is convex and minimized at γ^*. With (23) this means that

$$\beta + \sqrt{2\alpha/\gamma - \sigma_p^2} > \bar{p}$$

and thus that $E[y] < 0$ for all $\gamma \neq \gamma^*$.

Assumptions (10a, b) provide assurance that $\beta + \sqrt{2\alpha/\gamma - \sigma_p^2}$ is convex. To find the value of γ that minimizes this expression, differentiate with respect to γ and equate to zero. This with definition (18) implies that $\beta + \sqrt{2\alpha/\gamma - \sigma_p^2}$ is minimized where

$$K(\gamma) = \sqrt{2\alpha/\gamma}/\sqrt{2\alpha/\gamma - \sigma_p^2}. \tag{24}$$

We know from (23) that

$$\bar{p} - \beta(\gamma^*) = \sqrt{2\alpha(\gamma^*)/\gamma^* - \sigma_p^2}. \tag{25}$$

And from (22a) we know that

$$\bar{p} - \beta(\gamma^*) = \bar{Q}/n^*\gamma^*$$

or using (15):

$$\bar{p} - \beta(\gamma^*) = \frac{\bar{Q}\sqrt{2\alpha/\gamma}}{\sqrt{\bar{Q}^2 + \sigma_Q^2}}. \tag{26}$$

Together, (25) and (26) yield

$$\sqrt{2\alpha/\gamma}/\sqrt{2\alpha/\gamma - \sigma_p^2} = \sqrt{\bar{Q}^2 + \sigma_Q^2}/\bar{Q}.$$

This equation and (19) imply that (24) holds for γ^*, which establishes the desired result; profits are negative for any potential entrant who might choose $\gamma \neq \gamma^*$. No heterogeneous-firm market structure can supplant the cost-minimizing identical firm market structure, so competitive equilibrium has identical firms.

IV. SOME CHARACTERISTICS OF EQUILIBRIUM WITH ENDOGENOUS FLEXIBILITY

The special case where market demand is stationary, $\sigma_Q^2 = 0$, provides a convenient benchmark for comparison with fluctuating-demand equilibria with endogenous flexibility. With stationary demand equal to $\bar{Q}$, firms face a constant price p^s and share a common, constant level of output x^s. As seen in Figure 2, the level of flexibility chosen by firms in this case is Γ_0, the lowest feasible level. Flexibility is of no value when firm output is constant, and since flexibility varies inversely with static efficiency Γ_0 achieves the lowest feasible level of average costs.

Without fluctuations each firm produces

$$x^s = x^0(\Gamma_0) = \sqrt{2\alpha(\Gamma_0)\Gamma_0}. \tag{27}$$

(Recall (11).) The stationary price is the minimum minimorum of average costs, or from (12):

$$p^s = \beta(\Gamma_0) + \sqrt{2\alpha(\Gamma_0)/\Gamma_0}. \tag{28}$$

The number of firms sustained with stationary demand $\bar{Q}$ is

$$n^s = \bar{Q}/x^s = \bar{Q}/\sqrt{2\alpha(\Gamma_0)\Gamma_0} \tag{29}$$

utilizing (27). The total cost of producing $\bar{Q}$ is designated G^s. Since firm profit is zero and p^s equals average cost,

$$G^s = p^s\bar{Q} \tag{30}$$

Combining (30) and (28) gives

$$G^s = [\beta(\Gamma_0) + \sqrt{2\alpha(\Gamma_0)/\Gamma_0}]\bar{Q} \tag{31}$$

All the parameters x^s, p^s, n^s and G^s may be compared to their correspondents in fluctuating-demand equilibria where $\sigma_Q^2 > 0$. The most interesting cases for comparison are where non-extreme values of γ are optimal. The following proposition concerns these cases. (Its *Proof* and that of subsequent *Propositions* are in the Appendix).

Proposition 1: If $\gamma^* \in (\Gamma_0, \Gamma_1)$, then

(a) $E[x] < x^0(\gamma^*)$
(b) $G(\gamma^*) > G^s$

Part (a) states that with fluctuating demand firms produce less on average than where they are static-efficient. Borrowing an interpretation from Sheshinski and Drèze, firms maintain excess capacity on average.

A corollary of this result has to do with the relationship between the mean price $\bar{p}$ and average costs. Since firms' marginal costs (and indeed the market supply curve) are linear, $\bar{p}$ corresponds exactly to mean output:

$$x(\bar{p}) = E[x].$$

This with *Proposition 1a* implies that $\bar{p}$ is less than marginal cost at $x^0(\gamma^*)$

$$(32) \qquad \bar{p} < \beta(\gamma^*) + \sqrt{2\alpha(\gamma^*)/\gamma^*}.$$

And since marginal cost equals average cost at $x^0(\gamma^*)$, (32) states that the mean price is less than firms' minimum level of average costs. This might seem to imply that firms earn negative expected profit, but this is refuted by the previous finding that $E[y] = 0$ with n^*, γ^*. The reconciliation is provided by observing that while $\bar{p}$ is the mean of the price distribution, it is not the mean price at which transactions occur. Output is greater when price is greater and conversely, so the mean price weighted by output is greater than unweighted $\bar{p}$. The mean price weighted by units of x sold equals the mean level of average costs incurred in their production.

Part (b) of *Proposition 1* states that the expected total cost of producing Q with fluctuating demand exceeds the cost when demand is stationary. The resource cost of serving demanders of Q is greater with fluctuating demand than otherwise. Since firm profit is zero the mean price weighted by units sold is just $G(\gamma^*)/\bar{Q}$. Comparing this to (30) in light of *Proposition 1b* implies that this weighted mean price is greater than p^s, the constant price with stationary demand. The expected price at which units are sold is greater with fluctuations than without.

In general it cannot be said whether firms' mean output level with fluctuating demand is more or less than their constant output level with stationary demand. Or what amounts to the same thing, it is not possible to say whether the competitive regime with demand fluctuations has more or fewer firms than with stationary demand. This is contrary to Sheshinski and Drèze who show that without endogenous cost-structure adjustments there are always more firms with demand fluctuations than without.

It is possible, however, to add another cost-structure assumption to (10a, b) that is sufficient for maintaining the Sheshinski and Drèze result. This assumption is:

$$(33) \qquad \frac{d[\alpha(\gamma)\gamma]}{d\gamma} \leq 0$$

The chief implication of (33) falls out of (11). It is

$$\frac{dx^0(\gamma)}{d\gamma} \leq 0,$$

which states that the average-cost-minimizing level of firm output does not increase when flexibility does. Assumption (33) means flexible firms have capacity levels no greater than inflexible firms. Whether this is so is an empirical question open to investigation.[3]

[3] I have argued elsewhere [4] that an inverse relationship between firm-size and flexibility is plausible on theoretical and empirical grounds. But the notion of flexibility employed in that study is less restrictive than the one used here and so the conclusions do not carry over without qualification.

Proposition 2: If $\gamma^* \in (\Gamma_0, \Gamma_1)$ and if (33) holds, then

(a) $E[x] < x^s$

(b) $n^* > n^s$

With fluctuating demand, competition sustains more firms each of which produces less on average than those sustained with demand stationary at the mean. If assumption (33) does not hold, as where larger firms are more flexible than small ones, it does not follow from *Proposition 2* that demand fluctuations necessarily decrease the sustainable number of firms. The effect of fluctuations on market concentration is indeterminate without (33).

V. COMPARATIVE STATICS

As condition (19), Figure 2 and previous discussion suggest, γ^*, n^* and the mean and variance of firms' output (and of market price) all depend on the ratio $\sqrt{\bar{Q}^2 + \sigma_Q^2}/\bar{Q}$. Where cv_Q is the coefficient of variation of Q, we have

$$\sqrt{\bar{Q}^2 + \sigma_Q^2}/\bar{Q} = \sqrt{1 + cv_Q^2} \tag{34}$$

which means all the equilibrium variables are functions of cv_Q. In this section some comparative static results are presented that depict how key equilibrium variables change with cv_Q (or σ_Q^2, $\bar{Q}$). Only interior solutions are considered.

We begin with

Proposition 3:

(a) If cv_Q increases, then γ^* increases and conversely.

(b) If cv_Q increases, then $G(\gamma^*)/\bar{Q}$ increases and conversely.

(c) If (33) holds and cv_Q increases, then $E[z]$ decreases and conversely.

Part (a) indicates that the equilibrium level of flexibility is greater the greater are demand fluctuations in relative terms. This establishes as a property of competitive equilibrium the observation Stigler made of isolated firms, that greater output variability favors more flexible cost structures. Since an increase in cv_Q can be produced by an increase in σ_Q^2 or a decrease in $\bar{Q}$, either a mean-preserving spread in the distribution of Q or a decrease in mean demand leads to more flexible firms in the long run.

Part (b) of *Proposition 3* indicates that the resource cost of serving demanders of Q is an increasing function of relative demand variability. Part (c) concerns the effect of a change in demand variability on firms' mean output. With assumption (33), where flexible firms have no greater capacity than inflexible ones, mean output varies inversely with demand variability.

With this last result it might seem that the reduction in average output would be accompanied by an increase in n^* since, as a rule, the number and average output of firms are inversely related. But this does not follow here. For instance if cv_Q increases due to a decrease in $\bar{Q}$ (σ_Q^2 remaining unchanged), n^*

may fall even though $E[x]$ falls too! Again contrary to Sheshinski and Drèze's analysis nothing general may be said of how a change in $\bar{Q}$ affects $\bar{n}$. The case of a mean-preserving change in the Q-distribution is another matter however.

Proposition 4: If (33) holds and σ_Q^2 increases, then n^* increases and conversely.

As previously with *Proposition 2*, waiving assumption (33) forcloses the possibility of making conclusive statements about the effect of a change in cv_Q on the number and average size of firms.

VI. CONCLUSIONS

The impetus for this paper is the insight of Stigler and Hart that a firm's choice among technological and organizational options likely depends on the extent of anticipated output fluctuations. For purposes of economic analysis this choice can be represented as a choice among cost curves that embody a tradeoff between flexibility and static efficiency. (If there is no tradeoff, there is no economic problem and fluctuations have no bearing on firms' choices). The contribution of this paper is to establish some of the properties of long-run competitive equilibrium when this choice is endogenous.

Because of the assumed cost tradeoff between flexibility and static efficiency, firms choose the least flexible option when demand and price are stationary. If demand fluctuates and if the relative magnitude of fluctuations is sufficiently large (e.g. if $\sqrt{\bar{Q}^2 + \sigma_Q^2}/\bar{Q} > K(\Gamma_0)$), then firms choose greater flexibility in spite of having to accept a reduction in static efficiency. What they lose by having higher costs when output is near its mean is more than offset by gains from lower costs with extreme levels of output.

In competitive equilibrium with fluctuating demand, firms produce less on average than they would if demand and price were stationary (*Proposition 1a*). They carry what looks to be excess production capacity on average. Also the resource cost of producing Q is greater than with stationary demand (*Proposition 1b*). These results are in complete accord with Sheshinski and Drèze's where firms have no choice of cost structure. But other results here are different. For instance Sheshinski and Drèze are able to establish conclusively that competition sustains more and smaller firms with demand fluctuations than without. With endogenous cost structure this may or may not hold. *Proposition 2* provides a sufficient condition for their result: flexible firms must have no greater capacity levels than inflexible firms. Without this condition the non-stationary equilibrium described in this paper actually may sustain fewer firms than with stationary demand. That is, demand fluctuations actually might decrease the number (and increase the size) of firms sustained.

Comparative static analysis demonstrates how firms' long-run flexibility choice, the number and size of firms sustained, and the resource cost of production change with relative demand variability. An increase in the coefficient of demand variation (and by inference an increase in the variance or decrease in the mean of demand) increases both the level of flexibility firms choose and the expected cost of each unit produced (*Proposition 3a, b*). If the previous condition holds—that capacity levels do not increase with flexibility—an increase in the relative demand variability makes firms' average output fall (*Proposition 3c*). The effect of changes in demand variability on the number of firms supported by competitive equilibrium is even more problematical. Unlike Sheshinski and Drèze's conclusion, it is not always the case that increased demand variability increases the number of firms. The opposite may hold. The one conclusive case is where capacity levels do not increase with flexibility. With this a mean-preserving increase in demand variability will always increase the number of firms (*Proposition 4*).[4]

In conclusion, demand fluctuations are certain to alter firms' choice of cost structure—greater variability always favors greater flexibility—and to increase the resource cost of production. Still the resource cost is less (or surely no greater) than if there was no room for choice among cost structures. (The market will not impose a change in cost structure unless such a change is cost-saving.) The effect of demand fluctuations on industry structure is less certain than previous research has indicated. Without imposing stricter assumptions on the feasible set of firms' cost structure it is not possible to say whether fluctuations, or an increase in their amplitude, cause more or fewer firms to be sustained by competition. A strong sufficient condition for more firms to be sustained is that flexibility is inversely related to the level of output where average costs are least.

ACCEPTED APRIL 1983

David E. Mills,
University of Virginia,
Department of Economics,
Rouss Hall,
Charlottesville, VA 22901

APPENDIX

Proof of Proposition 1

(a) Since x is identically Q/n, we have

$$\text{(A1)} \qquad E[x] = \bar{Q}/n^*$$

Evaluating (15) at γ^* yields n^*, and substituting this into (A1) produces

$$\text{(A2)} \qquad E[x] = \frac{\bar{Q}\sqrt{2\alpha(\gamma^*)\gamma^*}}{\sqrt{\bar{Q}^2 + \sigma_Q^2}}.$$

[4] Sheshinski and Drèze's conclusion that a *ceteris paribus* increase in $\bar{Q}$ will increase n^* does not carry over to the present case with endogenous cost structure either. The effect of a change in Q on n^* here is ambiguous even with assumption (33).

Substituting (11) evaluated at γ^* into (A2) then produces

$$E[x] = \frac{\bar{Q}x^0(\gamma^*)}{\sqrt{\bar{Q}^2 + \sigma_Q^2}}$$

which establishes the inequality.

(b) Combining (16) with (19), the necessary condition for optimal flexibility choice, we get

$$\text{(A3)} \qquad G(\gamma^*) + [\sqrt{2\alpha(\gamma^*)/\gamma^*}\,K(\gamma^*) + \beta(\gamma^*)]\bar{Q}$$

To get the desired result, we must establish that (A3) exceeds (31), or equivalently, that

$$[\sqrt{2\alpha(\gamma^*)/\gamma^*}\,K(\gamma^*) + \beta(\gamma^*)] > [\sqrt{2\alpha(\Gamma_0)/\Gamma_0} + \beta(\Gamma_0)].$$

Since $K(\Gamma_0) > 1$, demonstration that

$$[\sqrt{2\alpha(\gamma^*)/\gamma^*}\,K(\gamma^*) + \beta(\gamma^*)] > [\sqrt{2\alpha(\Gamma_0)/\Gamma_0}\,K(\Gamma_0) + \beta(\Gamma_0)]$$

will suffice. Since $\gamma^* > \Gamma_0$, the above inequality holds if

$$\frac{d[\sqrt{2\alpha/\gamma}\,K(\gamma) + \beta]}{d\gamma} > 0,$$

or if

$$K(\gamma)\,\frac{d\sqrt{2\alpha/\gamma}}{d\gamma} + \sqrt{2\alpha/\gamma}\,K_\gamma + \beta_\gamma > 0.$$

Using (18), this reduces to

$$\sqrt{2\alpha/\gamma}\,K_\gamma > 0$$

which holds since both l.h.s. components are positive.

Proof of Proposition 2

(a) We know from the proposition's hypothesis that

$$\text{(A4)} \qquad \sqrt{2\alpha(\gamma^*)\gamma^*} < \sqrt{2\alpha(\Gamma_0)\Gamma_0}.$$

This, (A2) and (27) establishes the inequality.

(b) Evaluating (15) at γ^* produces

$$n^* = \frac{\sqrt{\bar{Q}^2 + \sigma_Q^2}}{\sqrt{2\alpha(\gamma^*)\gamma^*}}.$$

Comparing this to (29), recalling (A4), produces the desired inequality.

Proof of Proposition 3

(a) From (34), we see that

$$\frac{d(\sqrt{\bar{Q}^2 + \sigma_Q^2}/\bar{Q})}{dcv_Q} > 0.$$

This, with equilibrium condition (19), implies

$$\frac{dK(\gamma^*)}{dcv_Q} > 0.$$

Since $K(\gamma)$ is strictly increasing, the above inequality means

$$\text{(A5)} \qquad \frac{d\gamma^*}{dcv_Q} > 0.$$

(b) Repeating the line of reasoning followed in the proof of *Proposition 1b*, we get

$$\frac{d[\sqrt{2\alpha/\gamma}\,K(\gamma) + \beta]}{d\gamma} > 0$$

This, with (16) and (A5), implies that

$$\frac{dG(\gamma^*)/\bar{Q}}{dcv_Q} > 0$$

(c) From (A2) and the definition of cv_Q, we get

$$\text{(A6)} \qquad E[x] = \frac{\sqrt{2\alpha(\gamma^*)\gamma^*}}{\sqrt{1 + cv_Q^2}}$$

(33) implies that the numerator of (A6) decreases when γ^* increases; with (A5), this means the numerator of (A6) decreases with an increase in cv_Q. Obviously, the denominator of (A6) increases with an increase in cv_Q. Together, these imply

$$\text{(A7)} \qquad \frac{dE[x]}{dcv_Q} < 0.$$

Proof of Proposition 4

If σ_Q^2 increases, then so does cv_Q. From (A7), which we obtained assuming (33), this means $E[x]$ decreases. This and the identity (A1) establish the desired result.

REFERENCES

[1] Drèze, J. H. and J. J. Gabszewicz, "Demand Fluctuations, Capacity Utilization and Prices", *Operations Research Verfahren*, **3** (1967), pp. 119–41.
[2] Hart, A. G., *Anticipations, Uncertainty and Dynamic Planning* (Kelley, New York), 1951).
[3] Marschak, T. and R. Nelson, "Flexibility, Uncertainty and Economic Theory", *Metroeconomica*, 14, **1** (August 1962), pp. 42–60.
[4] Mills, D. E., "Demand Fluctuations and Sustainable Firm Diversity", manuscript, University of Virginia, 1983.
[5] Oi, W., "The Desirability of Price Instability under Perfect Competition", *Econometrica*, 29, **1** (January 1961), pp. 58–64.
[6] Sheshinski, E. and J. H. Drèze, "Demand Fluctuations, Capacity Utilization and Costs", *American Economic Review*, 66, **5** (December 1976), pp. 731–42.
[7] Stigler, G. J., "Production and Distribution in the Short Run", *Journal of Political Economy*, 47, (June 1939), pp. 305–27.

THE JOURNAL OF INDUSTRIAL ECONOMICS 0022-1821 $2.00
Volume XXXIII September 1984 No. 1

THE EVOLUTION OF MARKET RISK IN THE U.S. STEEL INDUSTRY AND IMPLICATIONS FOR REQUIRED RATES OF RETURN

C. Y. Baldwin, J. J. Tribendis, and J. P. Clark*

I. INTRODUCTION

The steel industry of the United States, as well as those of many other countries, is in dire financial straits. Much has been written about the low profitability of the domestic steel industry compared to other manufacturing industries and the inability of domestic firms to finance future capacity expansion through internally generated funds. A number of prescriptions have been offered ranging from reduction of the regulatory burden to imposition of import controls.

All of these proposed changes are intended to enable domestic firms to improve their financial performance. Improved financial performance is vital to the industry as, in the long term, only efficient and least cost facilities can survive given free trade and the expansion policies of the developing world. However, before implementing measures aimed at industry revitalization, federal policymakers should have an understanding of the incentives necessary to attract private capital to the U.S. industry.

The purpose of this analysis is to consider the performance of the U.S. steel industry from a capital market perspective, and to estimate the market-risk-adjusted required rate of return on new investment in steel-making capacity. It is assumed that the past performance of steel companies' securities provides useful information on required rates of return for steel investment. Whenever possible, adjustments have been made for changes in industry practice (e.g. changing debt policies) but the forecasts do not encompass changes in market structure or technology, which could make the future radically different from the past. The approach taken is based on modern capital theory, where the financial performance of steelmaking firms is assessed in the context of a broadly diversified portfolio of marketable securities. The Capital Asset Pricing Model is used to estimate the required rate of return for three homoge-

* The authors wish to thank Professors Donald R. Lessard and Richard S. Ruback of the Sloan School of Management at M.I.T., and Professor John F. Elliott of the Department of Materials Science and Engineering, M.I.T. for helpful discussions in early stages of this work. We thank the referee, John Lintner, for his constructive comments which resulted in a significant sharpening and improvement of the analysis. We are also grateful to Tania Zouikin for providing an independent replication of a portion of our results and to Stuart Bryan and Patrick O'Connor for capable assistance in data analysis and computer programming. The work reported in this paper was supported at M.I.T. under contract No. JOI-88010 by the U.S. Bureau of Mines. Any mistakes are of course our own.

neous groups of steel firms—integrated producers, scrap based producers and specialty firms—and for the industry as a whole.

II. EVALUATION OF PAST MARKET PERFORMANCE

A. *Modern Financial Theory*

The Capital Asset Pricing Model (CAPM), used in the following analysis, is a theory of the equilibrium relationship between risk and single period return in a capital market. Underlying this model are assumptions about both the investor and the capital market. It is assumed that investors: act rationally in their investment decisions; are numerous, so no one investor manipulates the market; are non-collusive; are risk averse; are wealth maximizers; have homogeneous beliefs about future cash flow outcomes; and have identical investment horizons. The capital market is assumed to be competitive, perfect or frictionless, and accessible to all investors.

According to the premise of the CAPM, investors must be compensated for bearing risk. Therefore, the required rate of return on any security is equal to a risk free rate of return (e.g., the 90 day U.S. Treasury bill rate) plus a premium for the risk borne:

$$(1) \qquad \begin{matrix}\text{Required rate of}\\ \text{return on security } i\end{matrix} = \begin{matrix}\text{Riskless rate}\\ \text{of return}\end{matrix} + \begin{matrix}\text{Risk}\\ \text{premium}\end{matrix}$$

The risk assumed by the investor is divided into segments of systematic and unsystematic risk. Unsystematic risk is that portion of the total risk which can be reduced by diversification of one's portfolio. In contrast, systematic risk cannot be diversified away. Systematic risk is determined by the comovement of returns, that is, the degree to which returns move in conjunction with one another and with the general capital market. Only systematic risk is relevant for a well diversified investor, thus only systematic risk is reflected in the risk premium. (For a discussion of the relevance of systematic vs. unsystematic risk to investors' portfolio decisions see Sharpe [37].)

Systematic risk is measured by a coefficient (beta or β) defined as the covariance between the security and market rates of return, divided by the variance on the market's rate of return. The coefficient beta can be estimated by assuming that the rate of return on asset i is a linear function of the market and risk free rates of return. The form of this relation is:

$$(2) \qquad R_i - R_f = \alpha_i + \beta_i(R_m - R_f) + \tilde{\varepsilon}$$

where

R_i = rate of return on asset i,
R_f = rate of return on the risk asset,
R_m = rate of return on the market portfolio,
α_i = excess return coefficient pertaining to asset i,
β_i = systematic risk coefficient pertaining to asset i,
$\hat{\varepsilon}$ = residual term.

Utilizing time series data for R_i, R_f, and R_m, α_i and β_i can be estimated for any asset. However, the estimated coefficients, α_i and β_i, can and do change over time. This non-stationary behavior makes the precision of estimates questionable for a long time series of data. Furthermore, α_i, β_i and ε are affected by changes in industry structure, resource mobility and cyclicality in ways we do not fully understand. Empirical tests have indicated that betas are positively associated with business cyclicality (covariance with general economic indicators), with financial leverage and with the variance of earnings, but our detailed knowledge of the real determinants of systematic risk is still incomplete.[1]

The validity of beta as the measure of a security's risk and the equilibrium risk-return relationship predicted by the CAPM have been tested extensively. Major empirical tests have been conducted by Miller and Scholes [27], Black, Jensen and Scholes [5], Blume and Friend [6], Fama and MacBeth [14], Gibbons [17], and others. The tests have generally confirmed that beta is an appropriate measure of risk for a portfolio or security, and that the risk-return relationship is upward-sloping and linear in beta. The empirically estimated market line generally exhibits a higher intercept than predicted by the theoretical CAPM; however, most tests are unable to reject the CAPM hypothesis at statistically significant levels.[2] This finding does not affect our statistical analysis (Section II) but does have implications for our forecasts of required rates return (Section III).[3]

The methodology used to forecast required rates of return has previously been used to estimate required rates of return in regulated industries such as electric power, natural gas transmission, telecommunications and insurance (Pogue [34], Myers [29]).[4] We first forecast the risk-free rate and the average excess return on the market from time series data. Using the CAPM, these forecasts are combined with estimates of beta to obtain a forecast of the required rate of return.

The Capital Asset Pricing Model has recently come under criticism on both

[1] Myers [31], Galai and Masulis [16], Myers and Turnbull [32], Subrahmanyam and Thomadakis [39] and Bowman [7] have investigated the real determinants of systematic risk from a theoretical standpoint. Beaver, Kettler and Scholes [3] pioneered the empirical work in this field; they are followed by Rosenberg and McKibben [36], Beaver and Manegold [4] and others. Myers [31] provides an excellent survey and synthesis of early work in this field.

[2] See Fama [14] for a discussion of tests of the CAPM. Most recently Gibbons [17] uses multivariate methods to improve the statistical power of his estimates. He confirms that the risk-return relationship is positive, upward-sloping and linear in beta, but rejects the CAPM's intercept hypothesis in five out of ten subperiods and in the sample as a whole. Gibbons suggests that the deviations of the empirical from the theoretical line may be due to an unidentified risk against which investors attempt to hedge (Merton [23]).

[3] The statistical analysis measures risk (beta) and excess return over time for various sectors of the steel industry. The section focuses on beta as the appropriate risk measure for assets held in a broadly diversified portfolio, but does not require a specific assumption about the capital market's risk-return tradeoff. In contrast, the forecasts of Section III require an assumption about the equilibrium relationship between risk and return expected to prevail over the forecast period. Our estimates are based on the theoretical Capital Asset Pricing Model, rather than on an empirically estimated market line. However a comparison of our CAPM slope and intercept with the empirical market line parameters reported in Fama [14] indicates that using the empirical line would not materially alter the forecast.

[4] Besides these references, testimony from numerous law cases and regulatory hearings could be cited. Chartoff *et al.* [9] reviews legal applications and findings on the CAPM.

theoretical and empirical grounds. Roll [35] has crititized tests of the CAPM because of their dependence on a market proxy (usually common stocks traded on the New York Exchange). He claims that statistical inferences might be reversed if omitted assets (including residential real estate, consumer durables, bonds, etc.) were included in the market portfolio. However, investigating this proposition, Stambaugh [38] found that including other assets in the market portfolio did not change inferences drawn from the standard stock-only portfolio in a significant way.

More fundamentally, contemporaneous market related risk may not be the only determinant of required rates of return on specific assets. In a dynamic setting, consumers may seek to hedge against consumption risks (e.g. inflation) or against changes in investment opportunities over time. These "hedge demands" will have an impact on required rates of return (Merton [23, 24]). In addition, in the corporate sector, certain events or states may impose excess costs on a firm or industry: if the probability of such events is correlated with externally observable firm characteristics then these will also have an impact on required rates of return. For example financial distress[5] may cause some firms to lose market share (because of customers' doubts about the quality of the product or its availability in the future) or to operate inefficiently (because of restrictions on credit or product flows). The probability of a firm becoming financially distressed is related to its total, as opposed to systematic risk. Thus for industries with high costs of financial distress, unsystematic as well as systematic risk would be predicted to influence required rates of return.[6]

In sum, criticisms of the CAPM are concerned mainly with extensions or refinements of the basic theory, or improved statistical procedures. Such criticisms do not detract from the model's fundamental validity nor from its value as an approximately true description of equilibrium in the U.S. capital market. An analysis of the systematic risk of the steel industry thus provides valuable information about the relative riskiness of steel assets in the general economy, and can serve as the basis of estimates of required rates of return for steel investments in the future.

B. *Empirical Tests*

i. *Procedures and Data*

We intend to use beta as a measure of risk and ultimately as a determinant of the required rate of return for investment in and by the U.S. steel industry.

[5] A firm is said to be in financial distress when there is perceived to be a substantial probability that the firm will be unable to meet its financial commitments. The so-called state of financial distress is actually a continuum whose boundary is not well-defined, thus the classification of particular firms as "in" or "not in" financial distress can be debated. The lack of a clearcut boundary is inconvenient, but it captures the important fact that the costs and consequences of *potential* failure may be felt by a firm long before a formal default or bankruptcy occurs.

[6] Lintner [21] argues that a number of capital market imperfections, including the costs of monitoring debt contracts, the costs of financial distress and the transaction and information costs that lead investors to hold undiversified portfolios, will cause unsystematic risk to have an impact on corporate required rates of return.

Since steel is a heterogeneous industry composed of large integrated firms as well as small mini-mills, and with products ranging from low cost carbon steel to high cost specialty alloys, we need to know if risks and required returns differ across these sectors. Three subsectors were identified within the U.S. steel industry and corresponding securities portfolios were formed. These subsectors were:

1. Large integrated steel producers characterized by having blast furnaces to produce pig iron; utilizing a mix of three main types of steelmaking furnaces (open hearth, electric arc and basic oxygen); having high capital investment requirements and producing a wide variety of finished steel products in large quantities.
2. Small non-integrated steel producers using only electric arc furnaces and utilizing primarily scrap and some direct reduced iron as raw materials. These so-called "minimills" generally produce a limited range of carbon steel products.
3. Specialty steel producers that manufacture primarily alloy or stainless steel products in small tonnages.

Monthly securities return data for 22 steel firms were taken from the CRSP tapes (Center for Research in Security Prices, Graduate School of Business, University of Chicago). Only firms whose principal business was steel manufacture were included in the study: diversified firms with more than 30% of sales in non-steel related areas were omitted from the sample. Because of mergers, acquisitions and the birth of new companies, a complete time series on the security returns of each firm was not available for the period 1955–80. Companies were included in a portfolio until their data terminated, or excluded from a portfolio until their data became available. Therefore, actual portfolios may include only a subset of the originally intended group of firms for a given time period.[7]

Using monthly data on security prices, rates of return (adjusted for dividends) and number of shares for each security, a value weighted monthly

[7] Steel firms included in the sample were: Integrated companies (11): Armco, Inc., Bethlehem Steel Corp., Colorado Fuel and Iron Corp., Inland Steel Co., Jones and Laughlin Steel Corp., McLouth Steel Corp., National Steel Corp., Sharon Steel Co., U.S. Steel Corp., Wheeling Steel Co., Youngstown Sheet and Tube Co.; Scrap-based companies (3): Florida Steel Co., Keystone Consolidated Ind. Corp., Northwestern Steel & Wire Co.; Specialty companies (6); Carpenter Technology Co., Copperweld Corp., Crucible Steel Co., Lukens Steel Co., Simmonds Steel Co., Washington Steel Company. A list of firms included in each subportfolio by sector and over time is available from the authors. One scrap-based producer, Nucor Corp., was excluded from the sample because of its extraordinarily high rate of growth. The betas of companies with substantial growth opportunities are biased upward relative to the beta of the underlying business (Myers and Turnball [32]). Because of this effect, including Nucor without a compensating adjustment for its growth would have biased estimates of the risk of scrap-based steel-making and led to potentially misleading results. Except for Nucor, steelmaking firms generally experienced low (or negative) rates of growth from 1955–80.

return for each portfolio was calculated.[8] The calculated monthly portfolio returns together with the monthly rate of return for 90 day U.S. Treasury bills (R_f = the risk free rate) and the monthly market rate of return taken from the CRSP tapes for the period January 1955-December 1980 were substituted into equation (2) and values α_i and β_i for each portfolio were estimated using ordinary least squares. The regressions were performed on four years of monthly data, updating the estimation every two years. In this way overlapping and disjoint estimates of α and β over time were produced.[9]

ii. *A-Priori Hypothesis*

Our first hypothesis was that the intercept terms α_i measuring excess returns would exhibit no consistency of sign, and would be insignificantly different from zero in most sub-periods. This hypothesis is consistent with the Capital Asset Pricing Model's prediction that the expected rate of return of a security with $\beta = 0$ is the risk-free rate.

We further believed that the β_i's measuring systematic risk would differ across industry sectors and probably over time. It was hypothesized that in absolute value, the scrap based producers would exhibit lower betas than the integrated producers and that the specialty producers would show relatively higher beta values than integrated steel companies.

Scrap based producers have as their main raw material ferrous scrap. During periods of high steel demand the price of scrap is usually high, while in periods of slack steel demand, scrap prices tend to be depressed. Thus scrap based producers are thought to perform less well financially than integrated producers in periods of high steel demand, but relatively better in times of low demand. Steel demand is correlated with the business cycle, thus the counter-cyclical tendencies of scrap-based companies should result in lower relative betas.

Specialty producers, on the other hand, are more vulnerable to swings in the business cycle because of the nature of their products and behavior of the specialty steel market. Specialty steel production entails a high degree of "operating leverage", that is, fixed costs are relatively high and costs and profits are thus very sensitive to capacity utilization at the mill. In order to

[8] The formula for portfolio return is:

$$R_{pt} = \frac{\sum_{i=1}^{n} N_{i,t-1} \times P_{i,t-1} \times R_{i,t}}{\sum_{i=1}^{n} N_{i,t-1} \times P_{i,t-1}}$$

where R_p is the portfolio rate of return; N_i the number of shares outstanding of security i; P_i the price per share of security i; and R_i the rate of return of security i (adjusted for dividends). The subscripts $t-1$ and t denote prices etc. as of the beginning and end of month respectively.

[9] When the initial tests were run, security prices for 1979 and 1980 were not available. The final time period (1977–80) was added to the second, supplementary series in 1982.

keep capacity utilization up, steel producers may set prices below average cost when the economy is soft and import competition stiff, then raise prices to take advantage of recovery. This type of pricing with attendant profit variability appears to be particularly characteristic of stainless steel production: a recent study conducted for the U.S. Bureau of Mines [10] indicates that domestic stainless steel producers may sustain losses (sell below total cost) for 2 to 4 years, with the expectation of realizing above average returns when demand rebounds. Theory suggests, and past empirical studies (e.g. Beaver, Kettler and Scholes [3]) have tended to confirm that cyclicality and higher operating leverage are associated with higher systematic risk. Thus we believed that the specialty sector within the steel industry would exhibit higher betas than the integrated sector or the industry taken as a whole.

The hypothesis that steel betas would have changed over time was motivated by the fact that from 1955–80, the structure and prominence of the U.S. steel industry both nationally and internationally changed dramatically. In 1955 the U.S. was a net exporter of steel; during the 1960s and 1970s, it became a major net importer of steel. A concomitant development has been the tremendous growth of raw steel production elsewhere in the world: the U.S. share of global production dropped from 39.4% in 1955 to 17.5% in 1978. Steel has also become a less important contributor to the domestic economy. The value of steel industry shipments as a percentage of GNP declined from 3.5% in 1955 to 2.5% in 1978.

We felt that such far-reaching structural changes would not be neutral in their effect on systematic risk and therefore, that betas would change over time. However, the direction of change, as well as its consistency across portfolios, was not certain. One clue as to the possible direction of change in beta was the change in the capital structure of the industry. Since the mid-fifties, the U.S. steel industry, particularly the integrated sector, has steadily increased the share of debt in its total capitalization. Financial leverage is known to be positively associated with beta, thus, one might expect an upward shift in steel betas over the sample period, assuming everything else about the industry had stayed the same.

iii. *Results*

Summaries of the regression results for all portfolios are presented in Tables I–IV. The tables show estimated coefficients for α and β with their corresponding t-statistics for the primary time series (1955–78) and for the overlapping, supplementary time series (1957–80). Also exhibited are R^2, the multiple correlation coefficient; σ_{st}, the standard error of the estimate; and DW, the Durbin-Watson statistic.

Analysis of Excess Returns. Examining the estimates of excess returns (α) in Tables I-IV, it can be seen that, as theory predicts, the majority of values are not significantly different from zero. In the few subperiods where α's are

TABLE I
REGRESSION RESULTS FOR INTEGRATED STEEL PRODUCERS

Time Period		*Estimated Coefficients (t – statistics)*		*Test Statistics*		
Primary Series	*Supple-mentary Series*	α	β	R^2	σ_{st}	*DW*
1955–58		0.003	1.42	0.65	0.035	2.09
		(0.76)	(9.41)			
	1957–60	−0.006	1.33	0.63	0.33	1.79
		(−1.28)	(9.06)			
1959–62		−0.014	1.26	0.69	0.033	1.97
		(−2.93)	(10.33)			
	1961–64	−0.012	1.39	0.65	0.036	2.25
		(−2.16)	(9.47)			
1963–66		−0.006	1.14	0.42	0.035	2.46
		(1.14)	(5.89)			
	1965–68	−0.005	0.99	0.41	0.040	2.56
		(−0.84)	(5.76)			
1967–70		−0.003	0.92	0.51	0.041	1.96
		(−0.56)	(7.06)			
	1969–72	−0.005	1.12	0.54	0.045	2.22
		(−0.76)	(7.47)			
1971–74		0.012	0.94	0.43	0.053	2.02
		(1.53)	(6.01)			
	1973–76	0.016	0.88	0.42	0.057	1.85
		(1.92)	(5.95)			
1975–78		−0.008	1.12	0.42	0.058	2.02
		(−0.98)	(5.95)			
	1977–80	−0.012	1.01	0.44	0.050	2.34
		(−1.63)	(6.20)			

significantly different from zero, exogenous shocks to the steel industry may have contributed to the phenomenon. The significant negative excess return exhibited by all except scrap based producers in the time period 1957–64 is possibly the result of the 116 day industry wide strike in 1959 and the corresponding sharp increase in steel imports. During this time the U.S. became a net importer of steel for the first time since the beginning of the twentieth century. The significant positive excess returns observed in 1971–74 may have been a result of record high steel demand in 1973–74 plus the initiation of the Experimental Negotiating Agreement (ENA) in 1973. (The ENA is an agreement between ten major steel companies and United Steel Workers that prohibits an industry-wide strike and imposes binding arbitration on unsettled contracts).

The period 1975–78 represented hard times for the steel industry in general. In this period, specialty producers alone showed almost significant, *positive*

TABLE II
REGRESSION RESULTS FOR SCRAP BASED STEEL PRODUCERS

Time Period		*Estimated Coefficients (t – statistics)*		*Test Statistics*		
Primary Series	*Supplementary Series*	α	β	R^2	σ_{st}	*DW*
1955–58		0.003 (0.38)	0.79 (3.38)	0.18	0.55	1.38
	1956–60	−0.003 (−0.47)	0.67 (2.98)	0.14	0.051	1.99
1959–62		−0.004 (−0.52)	0.79 (4.31)	0.27	0.050	2.49
	1961–64	−0.005 (−0.87)	0.97 (6.39)	0.46	0.037	2.54
1963–66		−0.0015 (−0.39)	0.94 (6.45)	0.46	0.027	2.10
	1965–68	0.006 (0.96)	1.00 (5.33)	0.37	0.044	1.88
1967–70		0.009 (1.13)	0.76 (4.35)	0.28	0.054	1.38
	1969–72	0.008 (1.03)	0.86 (4.74)	0.31	0.054	1.85
1971–74		0.016 (1.63)	1.05 (5.20)	0.36	0.068	1.85
	1973–76	0.002 (0.17)	0.79 (3.86)	0.23	0.079	1.96
1975–78		−0.009 (−0.99)	0.81 (4.21)	0.26	0.059	2.12
	1977–80	−0.005 (−0.71)	1.00 (6.69)	0.48	0.046	2.09

excess returns. A reason for this behavior might be found in the import protection given to the specialty steel producers at this time. In January of 1976 the U.S. International Trade Commission reported to President Ford that certain specialty steel products were being imported into the U.S. in such large quantities as to cause a threat of serious injury to the domestic specialty steel industry. After failure to establish orderly marketing agreements with the nations involved, import quotas were established effective June 14, 1976 for a period of three years.[10] The quotas were based on the annual average quantity or value of specialty steel imported during the period 1971–75. This protection was granted to improve the profitability and productivity of the specialty steel industry and may have resulted in a positive shock to the sector's returns.

[10] The quotas were extended from June 14, 1979 to February 13, 1980.

Table III
Regression Results for Specialty Steel Producers

Time Period: Primary Series	Time Period: Supplementary Series	Estimated Coefficients (t – statistics): α	Estimated Coefficients (t – statistics): β	Test Statistics: R^2	Test Statistics: σ_{st}	Test Statistics: DW
1955–58		0.003 (0.35)	1.70 (8.03)	0.57	0.050	1.78
	1957–60	−0.012 (−1.66)	1.54 (7.01)	0.51	0.049	2.04
1959–62		−0.008 (−1.12)	1.30 (7.41)	0.53	0.047	1.96
	1961–64	−0.005 (−0.71)	1.48 (8.56)	0.61	0.043	2.26
1963–66		0.006 (0.88)	1.22 (4.60)	0.30	0.048	2.37
	1965–68	0.008 (1.11)	1.09 (5.00)	0.34	0.050	2.37
1967–70		−0.006 (−0.96)	1.01 (7.10)	0.51	0.045	2.33
	1969–72	−9.004 (−0.44)	1.27 (6.47)	0.47	0.058	2.28
1971–74		0.014 (1.35)	1.36 (6.40)	0.46	0.071	2.34
	1973–76	0.012 (1.25)	1.08 (6.36)	0.46	0.066	2.30
1975–78		0.012 (1.67)	0.82 (5.06)	0.34	0.061	2.15
	1977–80	0.006 (0.88)	0.99 (6.76)	0.49	0.045	2.28

Table IV
Regression Results for All Steel Producers

Time Period		Estimated Coefficients (t – Statistics)		Test Statistics		
Primary Series	Supplementary Series	α	β	R^2	σ_{st}	DW
1955–58		0.004 (0.75)	1.43 (9.57)	0.66	0.035	2.08
	1957–60	−0.006 (−1.33)	1.33 (9.20)	0.65	0.033	1.79
1959–62		−0.014 (−2.89)	1.25 (10.38)	0.69	0.032	1.97
	1961–64	−0.011 (−2.14)	1.38 (9.57)	0.66	0.036	2.26
1963–66		−0.005 (−1.03)	1.14 (5.95)	0.42	0.035	2.48
	1965–68	−0.004 (−0.74)	1.00 (5.96)	0.42	0.039	2.54
1967–70		−0.003 (−0.55)	0.92 (7.32)	0.53	0.039	1.94
	1969–72	−0.004 (−0.71)	1.11 (7.57)	0.55	0.044	2.22
1971–74		0.012 (1.57)	0.96 (6.22)	0.45	0.052	2.00
	1973–76	0.015 (1.85)	0.88 (6.09)	0.43	0.056	1.86
1975–78		−0.007 (−0.92)	1.01 (6.11)	0.44	0.055	2.00
	1977–80	−0.011 (−0.59)	1.01 (6.63)	0.48	0.047	2.30

Analysis of Beta Coefficients. We first consider the sectoral differences in the beta series and then examine the trend in beta over time. On first examination, it appears that the hypotheses presented earlier concerning sectoral differences in beta are all correct. Results of both the primary and supplementary series show betas increasing from scrap based to integrated to specialty steel producers. In fact, the hypothesized relationships are violated only twice in primary series and twice in the secondary series.[11]

To validate this conclusion, an analysis of variance (ANOVA) was performed on the values of beta for the primary and supplementary series of each portfolio. The results indicated that the three groups were indeed statistically different from each other at the 95% level of significance. Carrying the analysis one step further, a pairwise analysis of variance was used to see which portfolio groups were actually different from each other. This test was performed for each sector pair and for each sector against the industry as a whole. The results indicated that scrap-based producers do indeed exhibit significantly lower values of beta than either integrated or specialty producers.[12] However, we could not reject the hypothesis that integrated and specialty steel producers have similar betas. Also, integrated and specialty betas do not differ significantly from the beta of the industry taken as a whole: this is not surprising, since integrated and specialty producers together make up the bulk of the steel industry.

Trends in betas over time also provide evidence of the similarity of integrated and specialty companies and their difference from scrap-based companies. Betas of the integrated and specialty sectors and of the industry as a whole decreased between 1955 and 1980. Most of the observed decline took place in the first part of the sample period (1955–70 roughly); in the second half of the sample betas in these sectors may have leveled off. In contrast there appears to have been no significant trend in the beta of the scrap based sector.

One potential explanation of a change in stock market betas is a change in industry capital structure. Hamada [18] has shown that "asset betas" can be estimated by unlevering the equity, i.e., stock market, betas utilizing the capital structure of the firm or industry in the following manner:[13]

$$\text{(3)} \qquad \beta \text{ asset} = \beta \text{ equity} \frac{\sum_{i=1}^{n} N_i P_i}{\sum_{i=1}^{n} [N_i P_i + (1 - t_i) D_i]}$$

[11] The maximum number of potential violations of hypotheses in each series was eighteen.

[12] The differences between scrap-based and integrated and specialty betas were significant at the 1% level. Tukey's test was also performed and tended to confirm the result that scrap-based companies had significantly lower betas. (See Nickerson and Nickerson [33] pp. 264–65).

[13] This formula is valid for firms whose debt relative to total capital is low enough so that the probability of default on the debt is small. Most companies conform to this requirement. The formula is invalid for firms with highly levered capital structures who are in or approaching financial distress.

TABLE V
CALCULATED ASSET BETAS FOR EACH PORTFOLIO

Time Period		*Portfolio*							
Primary Series	*Supplementary Series*	*Integrated*		*Scrap Based*		*Specialty*		*Industry*	
1955–58		1.34		0.71		1.54		1.34	
	1957–60		1.22		0.56		1.33		1.22
1969–62		1.08		0.66		1.15		1.08	
	1961–64		1.23		0.83		1.31		1.23
1963–66		0.93		0.84		1.08		0.94	
	1965–68		0.81		0.88		1.02		0.82
1967–70		0.67		0.64		0.87		0.67	
	1969–72		0.82		0.78		1.15		0.83
1971–74		0.70		0.95		1.15		0.72	
	1973–76		0.66		0.69		0.95		0.68
1975–78		0.69		0.70		0.75		0.71	
	1977–80		0.67		0.87		0.90		0.70

Note: Asset betas are calculated from observed equity betas using the formula

$$\beta_{\text{asset}} = \beta_{\text{equity}} \frac{\sum N_i P_i}{\sum (N_i P_i + (1 - t) D_i)}$$

where $N_i P_i$ is the market value (no. of shares × price per share) of the ith firm, D_i is the ith firm's outstanding debt and t is the current marginal tax rate. For example, for 1975–78, β equity for the integrated portfolio was measured at 1.12 (Table I). As of 1978, the market value of equity for companies in the portfolio was $5.3 billion; their outstanding debt was $6.3 billion and the marginal corporate tax rate was 48%. Substituting these figures into the formula, we obtain the estimated β_{asset}, 0.69. (We have used the book value of debt as a proxy for the market value of debt in the formula. We have also "unlevered" the beta using end-of-period market value weights: other possibilities would be mid-period weights, or an average over the sample period. Alternate weighting procedures do not significantly change the asset betas.)

where N_i = number of shares outstanding of ith firm; P_i = price per share of the ith firm's stock; t_i = marginal tax rate of ith firm; and D_i = long term debt outstanding of ith firm.

Asset betas for each portfolio were calculated from the portfolio equity betas and are presented in Table V. The unlevered asset betas are lower than the equity betas, and also exhibit a downward trend over time. From 1955–80, the proportion of debt in the industry's capital structure increased. Thus, if the asset beta series had been constant, observed equity betas should have increased. Instead, we observe rising debt and decreasing beta, therefore, the declining trend of asset betas is even stronger than the trend in equity betas.

The results of the statistical analysis are summarized as follows:

1. Integrated and specialty producers exhibit similar values of beta. Specialty betas appear somewhat higher, but the hypothesis that both sets of betas

were drawn from the same distribution could not be rejected at the 95% confidence level. Since these producers comprise most of the steel industry, their betas are also close to the industry's.

2. Both equity and asset betas of integrated and specialty producers declined significantly from 1955 to around 1968–70. Since 1970, betas of these sectors appear to have leveled off. Recent asset betas for the integrated sector are in the range of 0.65 to 0.85; for the specialty sector, the range of asset betas is 0.75–1.15.
3. The beta of scrap based producers is significantly lower than the beta's of other industry sectors. Unlike integrated and specialty betas, scrap-based betas do not appear to have declined from 1955 to 1980. Most recently, scrap-based asset betas have been observed to be in the same range as integrated and specialty betas.
4. Alphas, or excess returns, show no consistent positive or negative value and are generally not statistically different from zero. Significant positive and negative values were observed in some time periods for some portfolios, but appear to be related to large external shocks which affected industry performance.

iv. *Why Are Steel Betas So Low?*

Steel is a cyclical industry with a volatile earnings stream. Previous studies have shown that cyclicality and earnings volatility are positively correlated with beta. Within this study, there is weak evidence that the more cyclical specialty steel companies have higher betas than integrated or scrap-based producers. However, the integrated producers show only average levered equity betas in the range of 0.88–1.12 (where, by definition the market average of levered equity betas is one). Furthermore, in the most recent time periods unlevered asset betas for integrated steel companies and the industry as a whole have fallen below unlevered asset betas of most other industries.[14]

Unlevered asset betas for a cross-section of industries including steel were estimated by Pogue [34] for a period covering the mid-seventies. These results are summarized in Table VI. Although the portfolios and time periods are not strictly comparable, Pogue's estimates provide independent confirmation of our results. Pogue reports a steel unlevered asset beta of 0.66; our industry wide unlevered asset beta over comparable periods ranges from 0.68–0.72. (The unlevered asset beta of the integrated sector ranges from 0.66–0.70). These figures are below the asset betas reported for every other manufac-

[14] An unlevered asset beta for the market can be estimated by applying Hamada's adjustment (Equation (3)) to the market's equity beta, (which is one by construction). As a rough calculation, debt makes up approximately 21% of the aggregate capital of public corporations: using this figure and a marginal tax rate of 46%, one obtains 0.89 as the estimated asset beta of the market (all industries weighted by market values). Comparison with Table VI confirms that this is close to the median unlevered asset beta for Pogue's representative sample of industries.

TABLE VI
INDUSTRY BETAS

Industry	*Beta*
Electronic components	1.49
Crude petroleum and natural gas	1.07
Retail department stores	0.95
Petroleum refining	0.95
Motor vehicle parts	0.89
Chemicals	0.88
Metal mining	0.87
Food	0.84
Trucking	0.83
Textile mill products	0.82
Paper and allied products	0.82
Retail grocery stores	0.76
Airlines	0.75
Steel	0.66
Railroads	0.61
Natural gas transmission	0.52
Telephone	0.50
Electric utilities	0.46

Source: U.S. Federal Energy Regulatory Commission, Testimony of Gerald A. Pogue, Williams Pipe Line Co., Docket Nos. OR79–1, *et al.*, p. 74.

Note 1: These are *asset* betas. The effect of financial leverage on beta has been removed.

Note 2: These betas are consistent with the ones calculated in this study. However, they are not to be directly compared because of different portfolios considered and differing time spans.

turing industry in Pogue's sample, and are close to the reported asset betas of regulated industries such as airlines[15] and railroads.

The amplitude of fluctuations in steel profits and production has not changed substantially over the sample period. Furthermore, analysis of securities returns indicates that the total variability[16] of steel returns did not fall and, if anything, may have increased over the sample period. Nevertheless, betas of steel companies fell significantly. This suggests that during the fifties and sixties, the steel industry cycle became less linked than before to the general business cycle.

The decline in systematic risk might in part be related to structural changes in the industry over the past two-and-a-half decades. In particular there is evidence that from 1959 (the year of the strike) to 1974 (when the ENA was introduced) or 1977 (when its efficacy was demonstrated), variations in domestic steel demand were in part driven by the exogenous timing of labor

[15] Airline deregulation took place after the sample period.
[16] Measured by the variance of the portfolio returns.

negotiations. Before the ENA's adoption, customers would hedge against the possibility of a long, disruptive strike by building up steel inventories, thereby creating unsustainably high demand. When in every case, a strike did not materialize, the same customers would work off their swollen inventories, creating abnormally low demand in the post-settlement period. To the extent that this contract demand cycle was independent of the business cycle, it would have increased the total variability of the industry's performance, and reduced the association between steel industry returns and the market as a whole. These effects would be consistent with a lower observed industry beta and no change, or an increase, in the total variability of steel industry returns.

III. USING BETA TO ESTIMATE THE REQUIRED RATE OF RETURN

In this section, betas derived from the preceding statistical analysis are combined with data on past market performance to obtain estimates of the cost of capital for each of the three major sectors (integrated, specialty, scrap based) of the steel industry. We present, first, estimates of the *real* cost of capital for the steel industry: these discount rates should be applied to after-tax cash flows expressed in constant (not inflated) dollar amounts. We then show how a *nominal* cost of capital may be obtained by combining an inflation premium with the real rate of return. The nominal cost of capital estimate is mainly illustrative in that it is based on inflationary expectations imbedded in long-term interest rates as of March 1983. As inflation expectations change and bring corresponding changes in long-term rates, our estimates of the nominal cost of capital would be altered.

A. *Leverage, Tax Shields and the Required Rate of Return*

The real and nominal cost of capital estimates we present are "unlevered", that is, they are based on unlevered asset beta's and thus represent appropriate discount rates for after-tax operating cash flows, without regard to the allocation of capital between debt and equity. It is generally believed that, for companies with positive net taxable income, interest tax shields on debt constitute an additional component of value. Using a simple model Miller [26] has lately argued that in equilibrium incremental tax shields are of zero value. However, in a more general and realistic model, deAngelo and Masulis [12], [13] show that in most cases individual firms will gain from using debt finance, but that the value of incremental tax shields will be a function of firm-specific factors.[17]

[17] In particular the value of incremental tax shields depends on whether the firm is above or below its optimal debt level, and on the tax shields from investment credits and depreciation allowances it already has available. In a study of corporate exchange offers, Masulis [22] found, for the firms in his sample, that the average incremental tax shield from debt was between 10% and 20%.

Recent theoretical and empirical work on the value of corporate debt tax shields has thus yielded mixed results. Our method of resolving the controversy is as follows. First, at the industry level, we assume that aggregate debt tax shields exist and that they affect the relative magnitudes of equity and asset betas. Following Hamada, we then calculate asset from equity betas using the statutory corporate tax rate in each time period. The statutory rate is an upper bound on the industry's effective marginal tax rate. Use of lower rates in the asset beta calculation (see Equation (3)) would tend to decrease asset betas and thus lower the estimates of the required rate of return.

At the level of the firm or individual project, the value of incremental tax shields is less certain. Thus a sound capital budgeting practice is to estimate separately the present values of operating cash flows (after corporate tax) and interest tax shields for a given project.[18] The unlevered cost of capital estimates presented here may be used to discount after tax operating cash flows to obtain the "operating" component of a project's present value. The value of interest tax shields would then be separately estimated, taking account of the firm's marginal tax rate as well as any project financing opportunities.[19] The value of tax shields would then be added to the value of operating cash flows, and the construction cost subtracted, to obtain the net present value of the project.

Alternatively a weighted average cost of capital for a levered firm or project may be calculated as:

$$\text{Weighted Average Cost of Capital} = R(1 - t_i\theta_i) + g(\theta_i) \qquad (4)$$

where R is the required rate of return on the unlevered assets (the rate estimated in this paper); t_i is the firm's marginal tax rate; θ_i is the optimal fraction of assets to be financed by debt and $g(\theta_i)$ is the added return required to compensate for costs of higher leverage or financial distress.[20]

B. *Forecasts of the Real Risk-Free Rate, the Market Risk Premium and Expected Inflation.*

Recall that the Capital Asset Pricing Model relates the expected rate of return $\bar{R}_i$ (cost of capital) of a risky asset to (1) the risk free rate (R_f), (2) the expected return on the market ($\bar{R}_m$), and (3) a risk measure (β_i) according to the following formula:

$$\bar{R}_i = R_f + \beta_i(\bar{R}_m - R_f) \qquad (5)$$

[18] This procedure, known as present value by components or adjusted present value, was first developed by Myers [30]. See Brealey and Myers [8, Chapters 11 and 12] for an explanation.

[19] Such as government guaranteed debt.

[20] Lintner [20], [21] discusses this method of capital budgeting and in particular, categorizes the costs of excessive leverage and financial distress. Empirical estimates of some of the costs of financial distress are found in Warner [40], Baldwin and Mason [2] and White [41].

All elements in equation (5) refer to rates and covariance relations *expected to prevail* over the lifetime of the proposed investments. Therefore, to estimate the current real cost of capital for the steel industry, we must forecast:

1. the real risk-free rate (R_f),
2. the market risk premium ($\bar{R}_m - R_f$); and
3. individual sector β's which are expected to prevail over the lifetime of the assets.

To estimate a nominal cost of capital (which is comparable to a bond yield), we must also forecast the rate of inflation expected over the lifetime of the assets.

In a longitudinal study of stock, bill, and bond market returns from 1926–81, Ibbotson and Sinquefield [19] found that:

1. Adjusted for inflation, U.S. Treasury bills returned on average 0.1% annually over the entire period.
2. Adjusted for inflation, the arithmetic mean of the maturity premium on U.S. government bonds was 0.2%. However, this outcome entailed a large capital loss on bond portfolios: adjustment for this historical anomaly leads to an estimate of the expected maturity premium of 1.3% annually.
3. Over the same period, the arithmetic mean of the annual risk premium on common stocks, adjusted for inflation, was 8.3%.

In an exploratory study, Merton [25] criticized the standard methodology which uses the sample mean of long time series of returns to estimate expected risk premiums. He presents three alternative models of the determination of excess returns, which, when applied to data from 1926–78, yield estimates of the annual risk premium of 8.3% 10.4% and 12.0% respectively. In our forecast, we shall use the first and second of these estimates as lower and upper bounds on the market risk premium. (The third estimate is based on less attractive assumptions and therefore excluded.) Assuming that basic market risk/return relationships are stationary, the following forecast ranges for the real risk-free rate and the market risk premium were estimated:

TABLE VII
FORECAST RANGE OF R_f AND $R_m - R_f$

	Low	*Midpoint*	*High*
Real Risk Free Rate (R_f)	0.0%	0.1%	0.2%
Market Risk Premium ($R_m - R_f$)	8.3%	9.4%	10.4%

The expected rate of inflation over the lifetime of an investment can be estimated by subtracting an average maturity premium from the current longterm interest rate.[21] In March 1983, yields on long-term (10–30 year) Treasury bonds were in the range of 10.7%. Subtracting Ibbotson-Sinquefield's estimated maturity premium of 1.3% from this figure, we obtain an estimate of the expected annual inflation rate of 9.4%. This forecast may be combined with estimates of the real cost of capital from the CAPM (see below) to obtain current estimates of nominal rates of return required on investments in risky steel assets.

C. *Forecasting Beta*

Betas for the steel industry by sector were estimated in Section II of this paper. In the integrated and specialty sectors, a significant downward trend in beta was noted. However, the trend appears to have stabilized during the seventies. In estimating the required rate of return now for investments lasting over the next 10–30 years, it is important to judge if the past trend will be resumed, or if betas are expected to be stable at their current levels.[22]

i. *Integrated and Specialty Sectors*

As shown in Table V, in recent years, unlevered asset betas for integrated steel companies have ranged from 0.66 (1973–76) to 0.70 (1971–74). In the future, it seems reasonable to project that betas for integrated steel companies will not fall substantially below this level. We base this prediction, first, on the fact that only regulated industries have betas as low as steel (see Table VI), and second, on evidence from cross-industry studies indicating that more cyclical firms tend to have higher betas [31, 3, 4].

The future path of steel betas will depend in part on how a number of regulatory and foreign trade issues are resolved over the next several years. The inroads of foreign steel producers into the domestic market have caused industry participants (including companies, labor unions, and municipal officials in areas where steel plants are located) to lobby for tariffs, quotas, and other protectionist measures. In addition, the record import levels of August 1981, coupled with the depressed conditions in the U.S. market, precipitated several anti-dumping suits by domestic producers against foreign industries. But, even if these suits are successfully prosecuted, the industry will still be subject to strong cyclical market fluctuations, and thus, it is not likely that unlevered asset betas for integrated steel producers would fall below the current 0.66–0.70 range. (Currently, among major industries only heavily regulated and non-cyclical industries such as railroads, gas pipelines, tele-

[21] A more refined version of this procedure using the full term structure of interest rates is described in Ibbotson-Sinquefield [19]. Essentially, the method assumes that the term structure of real interest rates is stationary and independent of the inflation rate.

[22] A further interesting issue is the potential cyclicality of beta, which might cause required returns on steel assets to be higher in some periods than in others. Unfortunately, the identification of a cycle is beyond the power of our statistical tests.

phone and electric utilities exhibit unlevered asset betas below 0.65: see Table VI).

In fact, there is reason to believe that betas of integrated steel companies might rise in the future. Because of problems in labor contract negotiations, some would argue that during the sixties and seventies, the integrated steel companies were exposed to substantial non-market-related risk and constrained to adopt inefficient, overly conservative investment strategies [1]. Such policies would have resulted in higher-than-optimal variable costs for the industry implying lower-than-optimal operating leverage: this in turn, could cause the industry's observed beta to be lower than under the optimal productive configuration. If the rationalization of productive capacity which appears to be taking place currently causes integrated producers to reduce variable costs and increase capital intensity, then we would predict a corresponding rise in the beta of that sector. A technological trend toward lower operating costs (particularly lower labor costs) seems to be already underway, thus our mean forecast beta for the integrated sector is slightly higher than unlevered betas actually observed in the recent past. We estimate unlevered asset betas for integrated producers will be in the range of 0.65 to 0.85 with a most likely value of 0.75.

Specialty steel companies are more difficult to analyze. In the past, betas of the specialty sector have exhibited more radical period-to-period fluctuations than the integrated companies'. However, these fluctuations could be statistical in origin: that is, they might be due to the small number of specialty steel companies in the sample and to the changing composition of the specialty steel portfolio. Statistical tests applied to the regression results could not reject the hypothesis that betas for specialty and integrated steel companies were equal to one another. Because of the problems of small sample size and changing composition of the specialty portfolio, we elected to base our estimate of the specialty steel unlevered asset beta in part on the integrated steel results. The estimated range of beta for the specialty sector is therefore 0.75 to 1.0. The range takes into account the fact that in every sample sub-period, the specialty steel asset beta was above the integrated companies' asset beta, but that the hypothesis that specialty and integrated betas were the same could not be rejected. The wider bounds of the forecast also reflects our reduced confidence in the estimate.[23]

ii. *Scrap Based Sector*

Scrap based betas have recently ranged from 0.64 (1967–70) to 0.95 (1971–74). Scrap based betas have been much more stable over time than integrated or specialty betas and statistical tests tend to support the hypothesis that scrap based betas are significantly different from and lower than betas of the other

[23] On their own data, specialty steel betas would have been estimated to range from 0.75 to 1.15.

two sectors. This result is unsurprising since the economics of scrap based companies are quite different from those of integrated and specialty companies.

In general, a lower beta for scrap-based firm is consistent with the countercyclical performance of this sector: these companies generally benefit from low scrap prices that usually occur during periods of slack economic activity. Thus, it is projected that asset betas for scrap based companies will continue to be lower than betas of integrated and specialty companies (implying commensurately lower required rates of return for this sector). We forecast scrap betas to range from 0.6 to 0.8. (The most recent observation (1977–80) lies outside this range. This could have been a statistical fluke: however careful monitoring of future trends in this sector is warranted).

Table VIII summarizes forecast ranges for steel industry betas by sector:

TABLE VIII
FORECAST RANGES FOR UNLEVERED ASSET BETAS BY SECTOR

	Low	*Midpoint*	*High*
Integrated Companies	0.65	0.75	0.85
Specialty Companies	0.75	0.88	1.00
Scrap Based Companies	0.60	0.70	0.80

D. *Estimation of Required Rates of Return by Sector*

The estimates of Table VIII were combined via the Capital Asset Pricing Model with forecasts of the real risk free rate and market risk premium (Table VII) to obtain estimates of real required rates of return by sector. These estimates are displayed in Table IX. The midpoint estimates shown in this Table represent our best current estimate of the required *real* rate of return on new steel company investments by sector.

TABLE IX
FORECAST RANGES OF REQUIRED REAL RATES OF RETURN[24]

	Low	*Midpoint*	*High*
Integrated Companies	5.40%	7.15%	9.04%
Specialty Companies	6.23%	8.33%	10.60%
Scrap Based Companies	4.98%	6.68%	8.52%

[24] The "low" column combines low estimates of R_f and $R_m - R_f$ (Table VII) with the low estimate of the relevant β (Table VIII). The "midpoint" and "high" columns were computed in similar fashion.

In capital budgeting applications, the real rates shown in Table IX can only be applied to cash flows expressed in terms of constant dollars. However, real rates can be converted into nominal rates by means of the Fisher relation:

$$\text{(6)} \qquad \text{Nominal Rate} = (1 + \text{Real Rate})(1 + \text{Inflation Rate}) - 1$$

Above, we estimated the expected long-term inflation rate imbedded in March 1983 yields on long-term Treasury-backed securities to be 9.4%. Combining this estimate with the real rates in Table IX, Table X displays corresponding estimates of required *nominal* rates of return on steel assets by sector. These nominal rates can be used to discount cash flows expressed in terms of nominal (inflated) dollars.[25]

TABLE X

FORECAST RANGES OF REQUIRED NOMINAL RATES OF RETURN

	Low	*Midpoint*	*High*
Integrated Companies	15.30%	17.22%	19.29%
Specialty Companies	16.21%	18.51%	21.00%
Scrap Based Companies	14.85%	16.71%	18.72%

IV. CONCLUSIONS

This paper examined the market risk and required rate of return for three sectors of the U.S. steel industry, from 1955 to 1980. Values of systematic risk (beta) were estimated for portfolios of integrated, specialty, and scrap based companies over discrete and overlapping time periods. Statistical tests showed that (1) integrated and specialty companies and the industry as a whole exhibit similar values of beta (with specialty betas marginally higher in most time periods); (2) betas of integrated and specialty companies decreased significantly over the sample period; and (3) scrap based firms exhibit lower market risk than other sectors (although in recent years the betas of scrap-based and other sectors have tended to overlap).

The Capital Asset Pricing Model was then used to forecast the real after-tax rate of return required on investments in each sector of the industry. After adjustment for inflation and taxes, these rates are: integrated companies 5.4–9.0%; specialty steel companies 6.2–10.6%; and scrap based companies 5.0–8.5%. Combining these with an estimated average inflation rate of 9.4%, we obtain corresponding estimates of nominal required rates of return as follows: integrated companies 15.3–19.3%; specialty companies 16.2–21.0%; and scrap based companies 14.8–18.7%.

The estimates of required rates of return on steel assets reported in this paper are not precisely comparable to estimates found in other studies. Most

[25] However, caution must be exercised in application of these estimates. The inflation assumptions underlying projected cash flows *must be consistent* with the inflation premium in the discount rate. Otherwise serious valuation errors will occur. (See Modigliani and Cohn [28].)

previous estimates (for example, [11]) have been based on accounting data and may be subject to biases on that account. Accounting data are likely to be especially distortive when inflation is present in the economy. A second difference is that most previous studies have not explicitly considered the risk of steel relative to other industries. In general they have assumed that the steel industry is as risky as the average manufacturing industry and, hence, requires a similar rate of return. This paper, however, has shown that unlevered steel assets are less risky, in terms of systematic or market-related risk, than most other unlevered manufacturing assets (see Table VI). Based on this result, we conclude that (except for specialty steel) the required rate of return on steel investments as determined by the Capital Asset Pricing Model, may be lower than the average of manufacturing industries. But the study also shows that low betas and commensurately low required rates of return are a new and possibly transitory phenomenon in the steel industry. A cost of capital estimated fifteen years ago by the methodology used here would have been significantly higher than that estimated today.[26]

In estimating required rates of return for the steel industry we used the Capital Asset Pricing Model to characterize an expected equilibrium relationship between risk and return. The CAPM rests on the assumptions of homogeneous investor beliefs, costless information and frictionless markets. However, these assumptions hold only as an approximation in actual securities markets. In reality, capital markets are not perfect, and investors do not necessarily hold well diversified portfolios. Furthermore, the costs and risks of debt finance depend on the unsystematic as well as systematic risk of a particular enterprise. Hence some adjustment of estimates derived from the theoretical CAPM is probably desirable to reflect aspects of real capital markets and real contractual relationships that are not incorporated in the theory. In particular, as we indicated in Section IIA, costs of monitoring debts and the (related) costs incurred by firms in financial distress make total, as well as systematic, risk relevant to the determination of the required rate of return.

The total risk of the steel industry is relatively high as evidenced by its volatile earnings stream, and the high residual variance of returns. High residual variances are probably correlated with high costs of incremental debt finance, and high implicit costs of financial distress. Thus steel firms can be expected to face somewhat higher costs of capital than firms with equal systematic risk but lower total and residual risk. On the basis of this observation, we conjecture that the impact of adjusting for market imperfections would be to raise our estimates of the steel industry's cost of capital toward the high values in the forecast ranges we report (in Tables IX and X). However, more evidence relating the effects of market imperfections to specific firms and

[26] This is strictly true for the *real* after-tax cost of capital. In nominal terms, the risk premium would have been higher fifteen years ago. However, bond rates were lower then and might have led to lower absolute estimates of the nominal cost of capital.

industries is clearly necessary and thus the analysis of firm and industry costs of capital under conditions of costly information and costly contracting is a promising line of future research in industrial economics.

Carliss Y. Baldwin,
Harvard University,
Graduate School of Business Administration
Soldiers Field,
Dillon 22,
Boston, MA, 02163

ACCEPTED FEBRUARY 1983

REFERENCES

[1] Baldwin, Carliss Y., "Labor Unions and Productivity: An Application of the Theory of Self-Enforcing Contracts", *Journal of Business*, LVI, **2** (April 1983), pp. 155–85.

[2] Baldwin, Carliss, Y., and Scott P. Mason, "The Resolution of Claims in Financial Distress: The Case of Massey Ferguson" *Journal of Finance*, XXXVIII, **3** (May 1983), pp. 505–16.

[3] Beaver, W., P. Kettler and M. Scholes, "The Association between Market-Determined and Accounting-Determined Measures of Systematic Risk", *Accounting Review*, XLV, **3** (October 1970), pp. 654–82.

[4] Beaver, W. and J. Manegold, "The Association Between Market-Determined Risk and Accounting-Determined Measures of Systematic Risk: Some Further Evidence", *Journal of Financial and Quantitative Analysis*, X, **3** (June 1975), pp. 231–84.

[5] Black, F., M. C. Jensen and M. Scholes, "The Capital Asset Pricing Model: Some Empirical Tests", in *Studies in the Theory of Capital Markets*, Jensen, ed. (Praeger, New York, 1972), pp. 79–124.

[6] Blume, Marshall and Irwin Friend, "A New Look at the Capital Asset Pricing Model, "*The Journal of Finance*, XXVIII, **1** (March 1973), pp. 19–34.

[7] Bowman, R. G., "The Theoretical Relationship between Systematic Risk and Financial (Accounting) Variables", *Journal of Finance*, XXIV, **3** (June 1979), pp. 617–30.

[8] Brealey, Richard and Stewart Myers, *Principles of Corporate Finance*, (McGraw Hill, New York, 1981).

[9] Chartoff, J., G. W. Mayo, Jr. and W. A. Smith, Jr., "The Case Against The Use of The Capital Asset Pricing Model in Public Utility Rate Making", *Energy Law Journal*, III, **1** (1982), pp. 67–91.

[10] Clark, J. P., F. Katrak and T. B. King, "An Analysis of Stainless Steel Supply and Demand in the United States", Final Report to the U.S. Bureau of Mines under Contract No. J0166169, February 1979.

[11] Council on Wage and Price Stability, "Prices and Costs in the United States Steel Industry", (Executive Office of the President, October 1977).

[12] DeAngelo, Harry and Ronald W. Masulis, "Optimal Capital Structure under Corporate and Personal Taxation", *Journal of Financial Economics*, VIII, **1** (March 1980), pp. 3–30.

[13] DeAngelo, Harry and Ronald W. Masulis, "Leverage and Dividend Irrelevancy under Corporate and Personal Taxation", *The Journal of Finance*, XXXV, **2** (May 1980), pp. 453–64.

[14] Fama, Eugene F., *Foundations of Finance* Chap. 9 (Basic Books, Inc., New York, 1976).

[15] Fama, Eugene F. and James D. Macbeth, "Risk, Return and Equilibrium: Empirical Tests", *Journal of Political Economy,* LXXI, **3** (May/June 1973) pp. 607–36.

[16] Galai, Dan and Ronald W. Masulis, "The Option Pricing Model and The Risk Factor of Stock", *Journal of Financial Economics* Vol. III, I, (March 1976), pp. 53–81.

[17] Gibbons, Michael, R., "Multivariate Tests of Financial Models—A New Approach" *Journal of Financial Economics,* X, **1** (March 1982), pp. 1–27.

[18] Hamada, Robert S., "The Effect of the Firm's Structure on the Systematic Risk of Common Stocks", *Journal of Finance,* XXVII, **2** (May 1972), pp. 435–58.

[19] Ibbotson, Roger G., and Rex A. Sinquefield, *Stocks, Bonds, Bills and Inflation: The Past and the Future* 1982 Edition, (The Financial Analysts Research Foundation, University of Virginia, 1982).

[20] Lintner, John, "Allowable Rates of Return of Public Utility Equities: The Theory of Optimal Rate of Return Regulation of Utilities and the Double Leverage Controversy", Harvard Business School Working Paper 81–82, 1981.

[21] Lintner, John, "Some New Perspectives on Tests on CAPM and Other Capital Asset Pricing Models and Issues of Market Efficiency", in *Economic Activity and Finance*—Blume, Crockett and Taubman, eds. (Ballinger, Cambridge, Mass. 1982).

[22] Masulis, Ronald W., "The Effects of Capital Structure Change on Security Prices: A Study of Exchange Offers", *Journal of Financial Economics,* VIII, **2** (June 1980), pp. 139–78.

[23] Merton, Robert C., "An Intertemporal Capital Asset Pricing Model" *Econometrica* XLI, **5** (September 1973) pp. 867–87.

[24] Merton, Robert C., "The Theory of Finance in the Framework of Continuous Time" *Journal of Financial and Quantitative Analysis,* X, **3** (November 1975), pp. 659–74.

[25] Merton, Robert C., "On Estimating the Expected Return on the Market: An Exploratory Investigation", *Journal of Financial Economics,* VIII, **4** (December, 1980), pp. 323–62.

[26] Miller, Merton H., "Debt and Taxes", *The Journal of Finance,* XXXII, **2** (May 1977), pp. 261–75.

[27] Miller, Merton H. and Myron Scholes, "Rates of Return in Relation to Risk: A Re-examination of Some Recent Findings", in *Studies in the Theory of Capital Markets,* Jensen, ed. (Praeger, New York, 1972), pp. 47–78.

[28] Modigliani, Franco, and Richard A. Cohn, "Inflation, Rational Valuation and the Market, *Financial Analysts Journal,* XXXV, 2, (March 1979), pp. 24–44.

[29] Myers, Stewart C., "The Application of Finance Theory of Public Utility Rate Cases", *Bell Journal of Economics and Management Science,* I, **1** (Spring 1972), pp. 58–97.

[30] Myers, Stewart C., "Interactions of Corporate Financing and Investment Decisions—Implications for Capital Budgeting", The Journal of Finance XXIX, **1** (March 1974), pp. 1–25.

[31] Myers, Stewart C., "The Relation Between Real and Financial Measures of Risk and Return" in *Risk and Return in Finances* Friend, Bicksler, eds., (Ballinger, Cambridge, Mass., 1977).

[32] Myers, Stewart C., and Stuart Turnbull, "Capital Budgeting and the Capital Asset Pricing Model: Good News and Bad News", *Journal of Finance,* XXXII, **2** (May 1977), pp. 321–33.

[33] NICKERSON, C. A. and I. A. NICKERSON, *Statistical Analysis for Decision Making*, (Petrocelli Books, New York, 1978).

[34] POGUE, GERALD A., Testimony before the U.S. Federal Energy Regulatory Commission, Williams Pipe Line Co., Docket No. OR79–1, *et al.*

[35] ROLL, RICHARD, "A Critique of the Asset Pricing Theory's Tests. Part 1", *Journal of Financial Economics*, IV, **2** (March 1977), pp. 129–76.

[36] ROSENBERG, B. and W. MCKIBBEN, "The Prediction of Systematic and Specific Risk in Common Stocks", *Journal of Financial and Quantitative Analysis*, VIII, **1** (March 1973), pp. 317–33.

[37] SHARPE, WILLIAM S., *Investments*, (Prentice Hall, Inc., Englewood Cliffs, N.J., 1978).

[38] STAMBAUGH, ROBERT F., "On the Exclusion of Assets from Tests of the Two Parameter Model: A Sensitivity Analysis", *Journal of Financial Economics* X, **3** (November 1982), pp. 237–68.

[39] SUBRAHMANYAM, M. G., and S. B. THOMADAKIS, "Systematic Risk and the Theory of the Firm" Working Paper No. 170, NYU Salmon Bros. Center for the Study of Financial Institutions, March 1978.

[40] WARNER, JEROLD B., "Bankruptcy, Absolute Priority and the Pricing of Risky Debt Claims", *Journal of Financial Economics*, IV, **3** (May 1977), pp. 239–76.

[41] WHITE, MICHELLE J., "Bankruptcy and the New Bankruptcy Code", *Journal of Finance*, XXXVIII, **3** (May 1983), pp. 477–88.

THE JOURNAL OF INDUSTRIAL ECONOMICS 0022–1821 $2.00
Volume XXXIII September 1984 No. 1

PARALEGALS AND SUBSTITUTION AMONG LABOR INPUTS IN THE LAW FIRM

ROBERT M. FEINBERG*

I. INTRODUCTION

DESPITE the recent interest in economic analysis of the law firm and the market for legal services,[1] little attention has been given by economists to a phenomenon of increasing importance in the markets for inputs to the production of legal services—the rise of the "paralegal". To illustrate, between 1972 and 1977 the number of practicing attorneys in the U.S. increased by 41 percent but the number of "paraprofessionals" in legal services increased by 135 percent. If we look at all law firms in the U.S., we find the share of labor cost paid to paralegals almost doubled in those five years, increasing from 3.7 percent to 6.7 percent. On the other hand, the cost share of salaried associate lawyers was stable over the same period. This raises the questions of how easily substitutable the various labor inputs are for one another.

In this paper we examine this issue by using a short-run labor substitution model, estimating cost-share equations derived from a translog labor price function. Data from the 1977 Census of Service Industries are used to derive quantity and price measures for three types of labor inputs—associate lawyers, paraprofessionals, and all others—for law partnerships in 65 Standard Metropolitan Statistical Areas. The primary result is that paralegals seem more closely substitutable with other workers (secretarial, clerical, messengers) than with associate lawyers, suggesting that wages and employment of lawyers are unlikely to have been significantly affected by the influx of paralegals.

II. THE TRANSLOG COST MODEL

The translog function, first presented by Christensen, Jorgenson and Lau [1973], is a flexible form which allows the elasticities of substitution between each pair of inputs to vary for each sample observation. Either cost or production functions can be estimated to investigate substitution possibilities, however Hamermesh and Grant [1979] point out that each type of estimation requires certain assumptions to be made. Cost function estimation assumes exogenous factor prices and cost-minimizing behavior, while estimation of factor demands or cost shares derived from the production function requires assuming that factor quantities are exogenous, and that profits are maxi-

* The author is grateful to Mark Roberts for his many suggestions and to a referee of this *Journal* without implicating them in any errors or omissions which remain.

[1] See, for example, Pashigian [1977], Kwon [1978], Cox *et al.* [1982].

mized. In the context of a law firm, the assumption of cost-minimizing behavior seems more plausible than that of profit-maximization; furthermore, Hamermesh and Grant argue that wages can be appropriately regarded as exogenous if labor is disaggregated by occupational category, as is done here.

The discussion above points to the desirability of estimating a translog *cost* function. If we assume both a separability of labor cost from capital (K) and materials (M), and homotheticity, the cost function can be written[2]

$$(1) \qquad C = f(W(W_1, \ldots, W_N), P_K, P_M, Q)$$

where W is an index of labor costs and W_j is the (relative) price of labor input j. W is the cost per unit of labor to the law firm, and we can estimate this labor cost function, assuming the firm minimizes expenditures on labor given fixed amounts of other inputs.

If we write W in the translog form, cost-minimizing behavior implies that factor demand functions for the individual labor types (as shares of cost of the labor aggregate) have the following form:

$$(2) \qquad \alpha_i = V_i + \sum_j \gamma_{ij} \ln(W_j)$$

where α_i is the share of labor input i in total payroll. We are ignoring scale (or output) effects in estimating a short-run model (although we do include a dummy variable to distinguish different technologies associated with large vs. small law firms). The separability of labor expenses from capital and materials implies that the elasticity of substitution between different types of labor is assumed to be independent of capital and materials, and that the elasticities of substitution of capital for the various types of labor be identical. The exclusion of capital and materials from the analysis was dictated by the lack of good data on these inputs in the Census of Service Industries legal services report.[3] We do control in the estimation for partners per law firm, which can be regarded as a more fixed labor input for which a relative price is not available.

The following symmetry constraint is imposed on the estimated translog functions:

$$(3) \qquad \gamma_{ij} = \gamma_{ji} \qquad \text{for all } i, j;\ i \neq j$$

In addition, the cost function must be linearly homogeneous in input prices implying[4]

$$(4) \qquad \sum_i \gamma_{ij} = 0 = \sum_j \gamma_{ij}$$

[2] For a discussion of the assumptions required in estimating translog factor price functions, see Fuss [1977].

[3] The 1967 Census of Business did report that, for the U.S. as a whole, capital expenditures for legal partnerships were equal to seven percent of their total payroll costs. Non-payroll operating expenses are roughly equal to payroll costs.

[4] See Binswanger [1974].

From equations (2) we can estimate[5] partial elasticities of substitution

$$\sigma_{ij} = \frac{\gamma_{ij}}{\alpha_i \alpha_j} + 1 \quad (5)$$

and (constant output) price elasticities of derived demand

$$\eta_i = \frac{\gamma_{ii}}{\alpha_i} + \alpha_i - 1. \quad (6)$$

Since the sum of cost shares must equal one we will only be able to estimate two of the three cost-share equations. However, by (4), we can impute the γ, σ, and η values for the "missing" share equation.

III. DATA AND EMPIRICAL RESULTS

The following variables were constructed for 65 SMSAs from the 1977 Census of Service Industries:

α_L = fraction of partnership payrolls paid to associate lawyers;

α_p = fraction of partnership payrolls paid to paraprofessionals;

W_L = annual wages of associate lawyers;

W_p = annual wages of paraprofessionals;

W_0 = annual wages of others;

N = partners per law firm;

Q = receipts per law firm, adjusted by a cost-of-living index[6]

SMALL = 1 if $Q <$ sample mean,
= 0 otherwise.

Descriptive statistics on these variables are given in Table I.

The cost-share equations for associate lawyers and paraprofessionals were estimated jointly using Zellner's seemingly unrelated regression technique with linear homogeneity and symmetry restrictions imposed. (As is standard,

[5] These results are given in Binswanger [1974], and Freeman and Medoff [1982]. Hamermesh and Grant [1979] point out that the estimates of η_i may be biased towards zero when capital is excluded (since substitution towards capital when any wage rises is not allowed for).

[6] An index "of comparative costs based on an intermediate budget for a 4-person family, autumn 1976" (U.S. urban average costs = 100) is available in the 1978 Handbook of Labor Statistics for 38 of the 65 SMSAs. A regression equation was run explaining the index for those 38 SMSAs by 1980 population, growth in population (1970 to 1980), and region of the country; this equation (with an R^2 of 0.62) was used to impute a cost-of-living index for the other 27 SMSAs.

TABLE I
DESCRIPTIVE STATISTICS

	Mean	Standard Deviation
α_L	0.366	0.069
α_P	0.067	0.020
W_L	\$20,083	\$3,777
W_P	\$8,732	\$2,822
W_0	\$8,854	\$1,105
N	3.60	0.66
Q	\$375,265	\$129,565
SMALL	0.55	0.50

all independent variables were scaled by their mean values.) The weighted R^2 for the system[7] was 0.30, and the estimated equations follow (with standard errors in parentheses):

$$\hat{\alpha}_L = \underset{(0.011)}{0.398} + \underset{(0.042)}{0.181} \ln(W_L/W_0) - \underset{(0.013)}{0.021} \ln(W_P/W_0)$$

$$- \underset{(0.016)}{0.055}\ \text{SMALL} - \underset{(0.043)}{0.019} \ln N \qquad \text{sample size} = 65$$

$$\hat{\alpha}_P = \underset{(0.004)}{0.070} - \underset{(0.013)}{0.021} \ln(W_L/W_0) + \underset{(0.009)}{0.024} \ln(W_p/W_0)$$

$$- \underset{(0.006)}{0.004}\ \text{SMALL} + \underset{(0.017)}{0.014} \ln N$$

One apparent result is that cost-shares are not significantly affected by the average number of partners per firm; however there is evidence that relatively small firms devote a smaller share of cost to salaried associate lawyers and a correspondingly higher share to other employees (but not to paralegals).

From equation (4) we can impute

$$\gamma_{LO} = \gamma_{OL} = -0.160,\ \gamma_{PO} = \gamma_{OP} = -0.003, \text{ and } \gamma_{OO} = +0.163.$$

From these estimates, we can calculate elasticities of substitution[8] and demand elasticities as in equations (5) and (6), with the following results at the mean values of the cost shares (with standard errors[9] in parentheses below the parameter estimates):

$$\sigma_{PL} = \sigma_{LP} = \underset{(0.53)}{+0.15}, \quad \sigma_{OL} = \sigma_{LO} = \underset{(0.20)}{+0.23}, \quad \sigma_{OP} = \sigma_{PO} = \underset{(0.47)}{+0.92}$$

$$\eta_L = \underset{(0.11)}{-0.14}, \quad \eta_P = \underset{(0.13)}{-0.58}, \quad \eta_O = \underset{(0.08)}{-0.15}$$

[7] This is the R^2 that corresponds to the F-test on all non-intercept parameters in the system.
[8] The monotonicity and concavity conditions were satisfied at all data points.
[9] These are calculated using formulas given in Toevs [1982]. In addition, to calculate standard errors (and covariances) for the demand elasticities, the assumption, made by Binswanger [1974], of non-stochastic cost share is required.

Using a one-tailed test at 5% we fail to reject the hypotheses that σ_{PL}, σ_{OL}, and η_L are equal to zero. However, σ_{OP}, η_P and η_O *are* significantly different from zero. These estimated elasticities suggest that paralegals are substitutable for the residual "others" category of workers, but that there is no significant substitutability between associate lawyers and any other category of labor input within the law firm.[10] The (constant output) price elasticities of demand are all low (in absolute value); this may reflect the bias toward zero noted earlier due to the exclusion of capital inputs from the analysis. On the other hand, the finding that demand for paralegals is more elastic than is demand for associate lawyers[11] is consistent with the result noted in Hamermesh and Grant [1979] that own-price demand elasticities tend to fall in absolute value as the amount of human capital embodied in an occupational category rises.

IV. CONCLUSION

This paper has provided some evidence that the recent growth in numbers of paralegals has posed more of a threat to legal secretaries and clerical workers than it has to salaried attorneys, in terms of possibilities for substitution. Derived demand for all types of labor inputs was found to be price-inelastic, with demand for salaried associate lawyers particularly insensitive to price. The fact that the substitution elasticities estimated here seem to conflict with the stated claims of paralegal training schools regarding the skills their graduates possess could perhaps be explained by overt or tacit restraints placed by the legal profession.[12] The question deserves further study.

Robert M. Feinberg,
Department of Economics,
The Pennsylvania State University,
613 Kern Graduate Building,
University Park, PA, 16802

ACCEPTED SEPTEMBER 1983

REFERENCES

BINSWANGER, H. P., 1974, 'The Measurement of Technical Change Biases with Many Factors of Production', *American Economic Review*, LXIV, 5 (December), pp. 964–76.

CHRISTENSEN, L., JORGENSON, D. and LAU, L., 1973, 'Transcendental Logarithmic Production Frontiers', *Review of Economics and Statistics*, LV, 1 (February), pp. 28–45.

[10] However, we also find that σ_{OP} and σ_{LP} are not significantly different from each other at conventional levels, using the standard errors reported above and an estimated cov(σ_{OP}, σ_{LP}) of -0.165.

[11] This difference is significant at 5%, using the standard errors reported above and an estimated cov(η_P, η_L) of 0.000314.

[12] Pollock [1983] discusses the tremendous variance in how paralegals are used in large New York firms and notes that "lawyers in firms of all sizes seem reluctant to delegate even the most routine legal tasks, so many paralegals spend much of their time on clerical work that can't be billed to clients". [1983, p. 7].

Cox, S. R., Deserpa, A. C. and Canby, W. C., 1982, 'Consumer Information and the Pricing of Legal Services', *Journal of Industrial Economics*, XXX, 3 (March), pp. 305–18.

Freeman, R. B. and Medoff, J. L., 1982, 'Substitution Between Production Labor and Other Inputs in Unionized and Nonunionized Manufacturing', *Review of Economics and Statistics*, LXIV, 2 (May), pp. 220–33.

Fuss, M. A., 1977, 'The Demand for Energy in Canadian Manufacturing', *Journal of Econometrics*, V, 1 (January), pp. 89–116.

Hamermesh, D. S. and Grant, J. H., 1979, 'Econometric Studies of Labor-Labor Substitution and their Implications for Policy', *Journal of Human Resources*, XIV, 4 (Fall), pp. 518–42.

Kwon, J. K. 1978, 'A Model of the Law Firm', *Southern Economic Journal*, VL, 1 (July), pp. 63–74.

Pashigian, B. P., 1977, 'The Market for Lawyers', *Journal of Law and Economics*, XX, 1 (April), pp. 53–85.

Pollock, E. J., 1983, 'How Paralegals Pay Off Big', *American Lawyer*, (March), pp. 7–9.

Toevs, A., 1982, 'Approximate Variance Formulas for the Elasticities of Substitution Obtained from Translog Cost Functions *Economics Letters*, X, 1–2, pp. 107–13.

U.S. Dept. of Commerce, Bureau of the Census, *1977 Census of Service Industries*.

U.S. Dept. of Labor, Bureau of Labor Statistics, *1978 Handbook of Labor Statistics*.

THE JOURNAL OF INDUSTRIAL ECONOMICS 0022–1821 $2.00
Volume XXXIII September 1984 No. 1

PARETO-OPTIMAL EFFLUENT TAXATION AND MARKET STRUCTURE IN THE PRESENCE OF UNCERTAIN DEMAND AND DETECTION

STEPHEN FARBER

I. INTRODUCTION

The analysis of the effect of market structure on optimal effluent taxation under certainty was initiated by Buchanan [1969]. He showed that equal effluent taxes, reflecting marginal damages, imposed on monopolistic and competitive industries alike would result in sub-optimal output by the monopolist. This has provided a caveat to the argument that equal effluent taxes on all firms will lead to Pareto-optimal effluent control when marginal damages are identical across firms. This argument has been further refined by Dnes [1981], Endres [1978], and Lee [1975], who present models in which the Pareto-optimal tax, or subsidy, is determined as a function of market structure. All these models have been deterministic and conclude that the monopolistic firm should pay a lower tax than competitive firms.

The purpose of this paper is to investigate the effects of uncertainty in firm demand and uncertainty of effluent detection on the Pareto-optimal effluent tax. It will be shown that in an uncertain world it is not implausible that optimal taxes for more competitive firms may be less than optimal taxes for less competitive firms. Section II derives the optimal tax in the presence of uncertain demand, while Section III derives the optimal tax when detection is uncertain. Section IV summarizes these results.

II. STOCHASTIC FIRM DEMAND

Suppose that a regulator has the duty of administering a fixed total effluent standard at minimum social cost. This standard may or may not be socially optimal. The regulator can meet this goal by taxing effluent of polluting firms in such a way as to equate the marginal social cost of abatement across firms. Assuming this is the regulator's goal, it is shown below that this Pareto-optimal tax will vary across firms according to market structure, degree of risk aversion, and degree of market demand uncertainty.

Suppose that a single firm faces an additively stochastic demand $P(Q) = \mu(Q) + \rho$, $P' \leq 0$, where ρ is random and symmetric with zero mean and $\mu(Q)$ is the certainly equivalent demand. Assume that $\mu(Q)$ is iso-elastic with elasticity η throughout. In this case, marginal revenue along the certainty equivalent demand is $MR = \mu(1 - 1/\eta)$, and $MR' = \mu'(1 - 1/\eta) \leq 0$. The firm is subject to a concave, well-behaved production function,

$Q = Q(L, E)$, where L is a productive input and E represents an environmental input, i.e., effluence.[1] If L is purchasable at price w, and E at price t, the effluent tax rate, profits are a concave function:

$$(1) \qquad \pi(L, E) = (\mu(Q) + \rho)Q(L, E) - wL - tE,$$

when price is randomly determined ex post and output *ex ante*.[2] The firm has a concave von Neumann-Morgenstern utility function, $U(\pi)$, with absolute risk aversion, $R(\pi) = -U''(\pi)/U'(\pi)$, which may increase or decrease over π. The firm seeks levels of L and E which maximize expected utility, $\xi[U(\pi)]$, where ξ represents the expectations operator.

First order conditions for maximizing expected utility require that:

$$(2) \qquad \partial\xi[\cdot]/\partial L = \xi[U' \cdot (Q_L(\mu(1 - 1/\eta) + \rho) - w)] = 0$$

and

$$(3) \qquad \partial\xi[\cdot]/\partial E = \xi[U' \cdot (Q_E(\mu(1 - 1/\eta) + \rho) - t)] = 0.$$

Second order conditions require concavity of $\xi[\cdot]$. Since $U(\cdot)$ and $\pi(\cdot)$ are concave and ξ is a linear operator, $\xi(\cdot)$ is concave, and solutions to (2) and (3) are unique. In particular, $E^* = h(w, t)$. Separating first order condition (3) and dividing by $\xi[U']$, condition (3) becomes:

$$(4) \qquad t = \mu Q_E(1 - 1/\eta) + Q_E \xi[U' \cdot \rho]/\xi[U'].$$

Since $\xi[U' \cdot \rho] = \xi[U'] \cdot \xi[\rho] + \mathrm{cov}(U', \rho)$, and $\xi[\rho] = 0$, $\xi[U' \cdot \rho] = \mathrm{cov}(U', \rho)$, which is negative when $U'' < 0$; i.e., firms are risk averse. Condition (4) can be illustrated in Figure 1. A tax rate of $\bar{t}$ results in E^* chosen by the firm.

In the case of demand certainty and perfect competition, $\rho \equiv 0$ and $\eta = \infty$, so condition (4) becomes $t = \mu Q_E$. The firm selects $\bar{E}$ in Figure 1 in response to $\bar{t}$ set by the regulator. However, in general, i.e., $\eta \neq \infty$ and $\rho \neq 0$, the r.h.s. of (4) is less than μQ_E, as Figure 1 illustrates. The firm's response to tax $\bar{t}$ is to use E^* environmental inputs, where $E^* < \bar{E}$.

If the goal of the regulator is to minimize the social cost of a given pollution level across firms, it would seek a level of effluent, $\bar{E}$, for a firm such that the marginal value of effluent, μQ_E, is identical across firms. Letting $\bar{t}$ represent the optimal tax on a competitive firm with certain demand, $\bar{t} = \mu Q_E$ at $\bar{E}$, the optimal tax on any firm, t^*, is obtainable from (4):

$$(5) \qquad t^* = \bar{t}(1 - 1/\eta) + Q_E \xi[U' \cdot \rho]/\xi[U'],$$

[1] This production function approach has been used by Lee [1975], Russell [1972], Burrows [1977] and others. $E = Q^{-1}(L, Q)$ represents total effluence if Q is produced with L productive inputs.

[2] $\pi_{LL} = MR' \cdot Q_L^2 + MR \cdot Q_{LL} < 0$; $\pi_{EE} = MR' \cdot Q_E^2 + MR \cdot Q_{EE} < 0$; $\pi_{LL}\pi_{EE} - \pi_{EL}^2 = MR \cdot {}^2 \cdot (Q_{EE}Q_{LL} - Q_{EL}^2) + MR \cdot MR'(Q_L^2 Q_{EE} + Q_E^2 Q_{LL} - \partial Q_E Q_L Q_{EL}) > 0$.

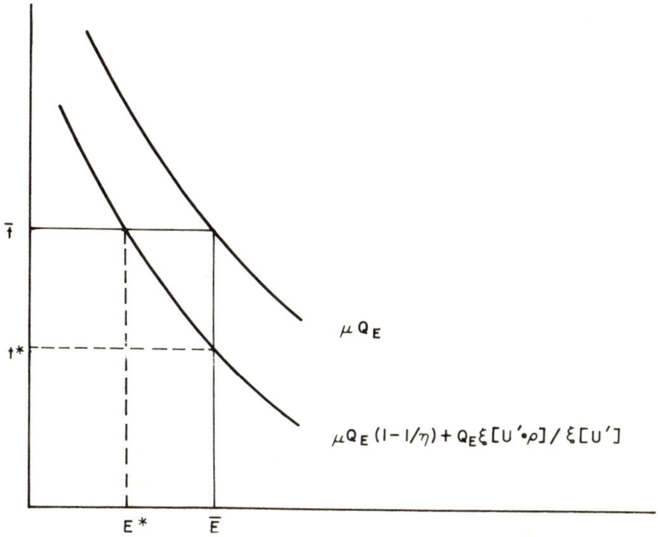

FIGURE 1
Optimal Effluent Tax, t^*, with Uncertain Demand

and is represented in Figure 1, where $t^* < \bar{t}$. In the extreme a subsidy may be necessary. The effect of uncertain demand is to reduce the optimal tax below what it would be under certainty.[3] For example, the regulator may seek a μQ_E that requires some output restriction by firms. A risk averse firm will restrict output in response to demand uncertainty. Further output restriction may be unnecessary; i.e., $t^* = 0$.

From (5) we can derive $\partial t^*/\partial\eta = \bar{t}\eta^{-2} > 0$. As other studies have shown (Lee [1975]), an increase in demand elasticity will increase the optimal tax rate under certainty. This can be loosely interpreted as follows. In order to raise μ sufficiently to equate μQ_E across firms, output must be restricted more in firms facing more elastic demands. This requires higher taxes on firms with more elastic demands. This is also true under uncertainty.

The marginal effects of increases in risk aversion and risk on the optimal tax rate, t^*, can be determined. Using a Taylor's second order approximation of $U(\cdot)$ and $U'(\cdot)$ around $\bar{\pi}$, the mean profit level for any E:

(6) $$U(\bar{\pi} + \rho Q) = U(\bar{\pi}) + U'(\bar{\pi})\rho Q + U''(\bar{\pi})\rho^2 Q^2/2$$

and

(7) $$U'(\bar{\pi} + \rho Q) = U'(\bar{\pi}) + U''(\bar{\pi})\rho Q + U'''(\bar{\pi})\rho^2 Q^2/2.$$

[3] Under risk neutrality, $U'' = 0$. In this case, $\xi[U' \cdot \rho] = 0$, so $t^* = \bar{t}(1 - 1/\eta)$ in (5). Uncertain demand has no effect on the optimal tax.

From 7:

(8) $$\xi[U'] = U'(\bar{\pi}) + Q^2U'''(\bar{\pi})\sigma_\rho^2/2\sigma_\rho^2$$

and

(9) $$\xi[U' \cdot \rho] = QU''(\bar{\pi})\sigma_\rho^2 + Q^2U'''(\bar{\pi})\xi[\rho^3].$$

Symmetry of ρ implies $\xi[\rho^3] = 0$, and recognizing that $\xi[U' \cdot \rho]/\xi[U'] = (\xi[U' \cdot \rho]/U'(\bar{\pi}))/(\xi[U']/U'(\bar{\pi}))$, substituting from (8) and (9):

(10) $$\xi[U' \cdot \rho]/\xi[U'] = (Q\sigma_\rho^2 U''(\bar{\pi})/U'(\bar{\pi}))/(1 + Q^2\sigma_\rho^2U'''(\bar{\pi})/2U'(\bar{\pi})).$$

Absolute risk aversion, $R = -U''/U'$ [6]; therefore, $dR/d\pi = R^2 - U'''U'$. Constant risk aversion then implies $R^2 = U'''/U'$. Substituting into (10) under the assumption of constant risk aversion:

(11) $$\xi[U' \cdot \rho]/\xi[U'] = -RQ\sigma_\rho^2/(1 + (Q\sigma_\rho R)^2/2)$$

Differentiating (11) with respect to R and σ_ρ^2:

(12) $$\partial(\xi[U' \cdot \rho]/\xi(U'])\partial R = -Q\sigma_\rho^2(1 - (Q\sigma_\rho R)^2)/2)/((1 + (Q\sigma_\rho R)^2/2)^2.$$

and

(13) $$\partial(\xi[U' \cdot \rho]/\xi[U'])/\partial\sigma_\rho^2 = -RQ((1 + (\sigma_\rho QR)^2)^{-2}$$

The sign of (12) is ambiguous. The sign of (13) is negative. From (5) it can be seen that since $\partial t^*/\partial\sigma_\rho^2 = Q_E\, \partial(\xi[U' \cdot \rho]/\xi[U'])/\partial\sigma_\rho^2$, t^* decreases as risk increases for firms with constant risk aversion. Risk averse firms automatically reduce output in response to uncertainty.[4] This result implies that increased uncertainty will further stimulate firms to restrict output; hence, reducing the need to levy high taxes on firms facing highly uncertain demand.

It has been shown that in a certain world the optimal tax increases with demand elasticity. This is nothing new. However, this relation also holds when demand is uncertain, although demand uncertainty, by itself, reduces the optimal tax. It was also shown that increased risk reduces the optimal tax, *ceteris paribus*, under constant risk aversion. If more competitive markets are more risky, the positive effect of increeased demand elasticity on the optimal tax could be offset by the negative effect of increased uncertainty when competitive markets are more risky.

III. UNCERTAIN DETECTION

Suppose now that the firm faces a probability, $F(E)$, of being taxed at rate $t > 0$ for the use of environmental input E. Let $F' > 0$, $F'' > 0$. Profits without

[4] Under risk neutrality, $R \equiv 0$; therefore (12) is not meaningful, and (13) implies no effect of increased risk on the optimal tax.

the tax are $\pi^0 = PQ - wL$ and with the tax, $\pi^1 = PQ - wL - tE$. Expected utility is:

$$\xi[U] = F(E)U(PQ - wL - tE) + (1 - F(E))U(PQ - wL) \tag{14}$$

First order conditions for expected utility maximization with respect to E require that:

$$\partial\xi[U]/\partial E = F'(U(\pi^1) - U(\pi^0)) + FU'(\pi^1)(MR \cdot Q_E - t) + (1 - F)U'(\pi^0)MR \cdot Q_E = 0 \tag{15}$$

where $MR = P'Q + P = (1 - 1/\eta)P$.[5] Substituting for MR in (15), recognizing that $\bar{t} = PQ_E$ at $\bar{E}$, and solving (15) for t^*, the optimal tax rate:

$$t^* = F'(U(\pi^1) - U(\pi^0))/FU'(\pi^1) + \bar{t}(1 - 1/\eta)(1 + (1 - F)U'(\pi^0)/FU'(\pi^1)). \tag{16}$$

Figure 2 shows the optimal tax, $\bar{t} = PQ_E$, under perfect competition and certainty, necessary to induce the firm to use $\bar{E}$, the regulator's equalizing marginal social cost goal for this firm. When $F \equiv 1$, $t^* \rightarrow \bar{t}$ as $\eta \rightarrow \infty$, as expected. When $0 < F < 1$, $F' = 0$ and $\eta = \infty$, $t^* = \bar{t}(1 + (1 - F)U'(\pi^0)/FU(\pi^1)) > \bar{t}$.[6] This case is illustrated in Figure 2. When $F' > 0$, since $U(\pi^1) - U(\pi^0) < 0$, the optimal tax may or may not be greater than $\bar{t}$. However, as in the previous model, it is clear from (16) that t^* increases as demand elasticity increases. When $F' = 0$, $\partial t^*/\partial F = -\bar{t}(1 - 1/\eta)U'(\pi^0)/FU'(\pi^1)$, which is negative, as expected. Increased probability of detection reduces the requisite effluent tax.

Using Taylor's expansion of $U(\cdot)$ around π^1, $U(\pi^0) - U(\pi^1) = U'(\pi^1)(\pi^0 - \pi^1) + U''(\pi^1)(\pi^0 - \pi^1)^2$. Dividing through by $-U'(\pi^1)$, $(U(\pi^1) - U(\pi^0))/U'(\pi^1) = (\pi^1 - \pi^0) + R(\pi^0 - \pi^1)^2$ since $R = -U''/U'$. Also using Taylor's expansion for $U'(\pi^0)$ around π^1,

[5] Second order conditions require that $\partial^2\xi[U]/\partial E^2 < 0$. Since $F(E)$ is convex and $U(\cdot)$ is concave, $\xi[U]$ is not necessarily concave. In fact,

$$\begin{aligned}\partial^2\xi/\partial E^2 = {} & \pi_E^1(2F'U'(\pi') + FU''(\pi^1)\pi_E^1) \\ & + \pi_E^0(-2F'U'(\pi^0) + (1 - F)U''(\pi^0)\pi_E^0) \\ & + F''(U(\pi^1) - U(\pi^0)) \\ & + FU'(\pi^1)\pi_{EE}^1 + (1 - F)U'(\pi^0)\pi_{EE}^0\end{aligned}$$

where $\pi_E^1 = \partial\pi'/\partial E$, $\pi_{EE}^1 = \partial^2\pi^1/\partial E^2$, etc. All but the first term are negative. Rewriting the first term: $\pi_E^1(2F'U'(\pi^1) + FU''(\pi^1)\pi_E^1)U'(\pi^1)\pi_E^1)[2F' + F\pi_E^1 U''(\pi^1)/U'(\pi^1)]$. This term is negative under two conditions:
(a) $F' = 0$
(b) $R(\pi^1) = -U''(\pi^1)/U'(\pi^1) \geq 2F'/F\pi_E^1$.
Consequently $\partial^2\xi/\partial E^2 < 0$ when either (a) or (b) holds. When second order conditions do not hold the firm maximizes E for any t.

[6] Even under risk neutrality, $t^* > \bar{t}$.

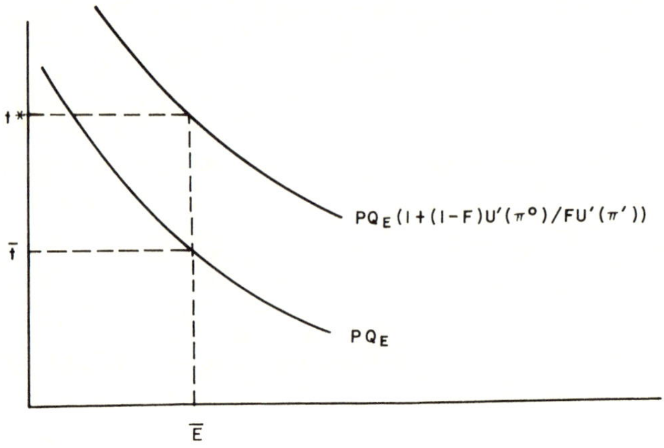

FIGURE 2
Optimal Effluent Tax, t^*, with Uncertain Detection

$U'(\pi^0) = U'(\pi^1) + U''(\pi^1)(\pi^0 - \pi^1)$. Dividing through by $U'(\pi^1)$, $U'(\pi^0)/U'(\pi^1) = 1 - R(\pi^0 - \pi^1)$. Substituting each of these expressions into (16):

$$(17) \qquad t^* = (F'/F)[(\pi^0 - \pi^1) + R(\pi^0 - \pi^1)^2] + (1 - 1/\eta)\bar{t}[1 + ((1 - F)/F)(1 - R(\pi^0 - \pi^1))].$$

Differentiating (17) with respect to R:

$$(18) \qquad \partial t^*/\partial R = (F'/F)(\pi^0 - \pi^1)^2 - (1 - 1/\eta)\bar{t}((1 - F)/F)(\pi^0 - \pi^1).$$

The first term of (18) is positive while the second term is non-negative since $\pi^0 \geq \pi^1$; therefore, the sign of (18) is indeterminate. Increased risk aversion will not necessarily lower the optimal tax. However, when $F' = 0$, the optimal tax does decrease with risk aversion. In this case where $F' = 0$, risk aversion is itself causing output restriction, reducing the need to tax in order to create this output restriction. When $F' > 0$, risk aversion reduces both the output and the detection probability. Reduced detection probabilities may be sufficient to motivate less effluent control; hence increasing the need to raise the penalty of polluting if detected.

This section has shown that when detection is uncertain the optimal tax necessary to stimulate the firm to use the optimal environmental input will be different from the case when detection is certain. Only in the limited case in which increased environmental input use does not result in the increased probability of taxation will the optimal tax rate exceed the certainty tax rate. When increased environmental input use does not increase taxation probabilities, $F' = 0$, increased detection probability and increased risk aversion lower the optimal tax rate. Demand elasticity always increases the optimal tax rate, *ceteris paribus*. If $F' = 0$ and risk aversion was greater in more competitive markets, the optimal tax may be lower in more competitive markets.

IV. SUMMARY

Other studies have concluded that the Pareto-optimal effluent tax rate should increase with market demand elasticity when the regulator has a minimum social cost level of effluence goal. This study has shown that the presence of market demand uncertainty does not alter this relation. First, it has shown that market risk reduces the optimal effluent tax when firms are risk averse. Second, it has shown that there is a positive relation between demand elasticity and the optimal tax even in the presence of uncertainty. If market demand is more uncertain in competitive than monopolistic markets, the effect of risk and demand elasticity may be offsetting and the tax may not have to vary with market structure. When detection is uncertain, the optimal tax may be greater or less than the certainty tax. In any case, it was shown that increased demand elasticity is positively correlated with the optimal tax, *ceteris paribus*.

Stephen Farber,
Department of Economics,
Louisiana State University,
Baton Rouge, LA, 70803–6303.

ACCEPTED SEPTEMBER 1983

REFERENCES

BUCHANAN, J. M., 1969, "External Diseconomies, Corrective Taxes, and Market Structure", *American Economic Review*, LIX, **1**, (March), pp. 174–77.

BURROWS, PAUL, 1977, "Pollution Control with Variable Production Processes", *Journal of Public Economics*, **8**, 3 (December), pp. 357–67.

DNES, A. W., 1981, "The Case of Monopoly and Pollution", *Journal of Industrial Economics*, XXX, **2**, (December), pp. 213–16.

ENDRES, A., 1978, "Monopoly Power as a Means to Pollution Control", *Journal of Industrial Economics*, XXVII, **2**, (December), pp. 185–87.

LEE, D. R., 1975, "Efficiency of Pollution Taxation and Market Structure", *Journal of Environmental Economics and Management*, **2**, pp. 69–72.

PRATT, JOHN W., 1964, "Risk Aversion in the Small and in the Large", *Econometrica*, **32**, 1–2, (January–April), pp. 122–37.

RUSSELL, CLIFFORD, S., 1972, *Residuals Management in Industry: A Case Study of Petroleum Refining*, (Johns Hopkins, Baltimore).

THE JOURNAL OF INDUSTRIAL ECONOMICS 0022-1821 $2.00
Volume XXXIII September 1984 No. 1

THE DEVELOPMENT OF WAGES OF GERMAN INDUSTRIAL CORPORATIONS*

BERNHARD WANIK

I. INTRODUCTION

FROM THE point of view of the firm wages are costs whereas from the workers' point of view wages are income. Hitherto results on the development of primary and secondary distribution of firm income have been published [1]. The aim of this article is to explain endogeneously the development of wages at the firm level. Whilst a considerable amount of work has been done on the explanation of wages at the level of the economy or certain industries, only very little has been done on explaining wages at the level of the firm using firm data. Horwitz and Shabahang [8] point out that in many arbitration cases in the U.S. the concept of financial ability to pay is frequently mentioned. They select seven variables concerning productivity, liquidity, and profitability, which are assumed to represent aspects of ability to pay. The (single) coefficient of correlation between these variables in period $t-1$ and the wage increases in period t is, however, significant in only two cases. Foley and Maunders [5, pp. 75–78] regress wage increases against a set of variables similar to that used by Horwitz and Shabahang. In their cross sectional analysis only three variables come out as apparently significant; R^2 is extremely low at 10%. In a cross sectional study of German Corporations Neumann *et al.* [12] show that wages and concentration are negatively correlated, whereas wages and profitability, capital intensity, or degree of unionization are positively correlated. Including further variables their R^2 is at 45%. If one judges these contributions using firm data for the explanation of wages, the statistical results are not very strong.

II. DATA

The results given in this paper are derived from published financial data (balance sheet, profit and loss account) of 151 German Industrial Corporations for the years 1960 to 1978. All these corporations are registered on the stock exchange. The main advantages of the sample may be summarized as follows: (1) the figures given in the financial statements are standardized in that they are in accordance with generally accepted accounting principles and the German Corporation Law (Aktiengesetz 1965); (2) data are firm specific and (3) data are available for "long" time periods.

* This paper is a revised version of the paper presented to the 8th Conference on Industrial Structure of EARIE in Basle, September 16–18th, 1981.

III. RESULTS

Wages are measured as the total sum of wages and salaries, social expenditures, and pension expenditures and voluntary payments divided by the number of employees, i.e. wages equal total expenditure for labour per employee. Average wages rose from DM 8,693 in 1960 to DM 41,043 in 1978 which corresponds to an average annual rate of change of wages of 9.01%. Of course wages and average rate of change of wages differ between industries (Table I). Cross sectional analyses show a significantly positive correlation between average industry wages and average productivity (value added per employee).

TABLE I
INTERINDUSTRY WAGE STRUCTURE AND AVERAGE ANNUAL RATE OF CHANGE OF WAGES

	Interindustry Wage Structure		*Average Annual Rate of Change of Wages*
	1960	*1978*	*1960–1978*
ALL FIRMS	100.0	100.0	9.01
Textiles	77.8	73.3	8.65
Building Materials	82.4	85.8	9.25
Electrical Engineering	87.4	85.8	8.90
Iron-, Tin-, and Metal-working	90.0	93.6	9.24
Machinery	93.7	96.3	9.17
Vehicles	98.2	103.4	9.32
Iron and Steel	98.4	94.5	8.76
Constructional Steel	99.5	107.5	9.47
Brewing and Malting	107.9	102.5	8.69
Chemicals	109.6	103.1	8.64
Cement	114.7	110.9	8.80
Electricity	115.7	126.2	9.53

From 1960 to 1978 the interindustry wage structure has been remarkably stable. The development of the interindustry wage structure can be measured by the development of the coefficient of variation of the average wages in every industry. The results (Table II) show that since 1967 the downward trend in the coefficient of variation has changed, i.e. there have been growing differences between the average wages in every industry. The development of the interindustry wage structure corresponds to the development of the unemployment rate. There is a significantly positive relation between the coefficient of variation of wages and the unemployment rate as long as it is prohibited by law to hire workers from abroad [18, p. 101].

A survey of microeconomic models for the explanation of absolute wages shows that there is no comprehensive theory of wages [17]. Hypotheses derived from these models are tested by pooling cross section and time-series data of 151 German Industrial Corporations from 1960 to 1978. The corporations are classified into twelve industries (of at least 5 firms) and seven special

TABLE II
THE DEVELOPMENT OF THE INTERINDUSTRY WAGE STRUCTURE

Year	*Interindustry Wage Structure*[a]
1960	12.604
1961	12.814
1962	13.686
1963	12.993
1964	13.359
1965	12.644
1966	11.093
1967	13.604
1968	13.494
1969	13.306
1970	14.133
1971	13.947
1972	13.875
1973	13.687
1974	13.470
1975	14.798
1976	13.693
1977	13.446
1978	13.889

[a] coefficient of variation of wages in the 12 industries

groups of 18 firms each with respect to growth (average rate of growth of sales from 1960 to 1978 with and without merger), factor intensity (total expenditure for labour divided by sales 1970), and size (sales 1970). The regressions are run using firm specific intercepts but regression coefficients which are assumed to be the same for all firms (ordinary least squares with dummy variables (OLSDV)). An F-test to answer the question whether these assumptions are generally admissible is not carried through. Instead we stick to Wallace's [16] trade-off argument that in empirical investigations the assumption of homogeneous regression coefficients very often cannot be confirmed, but that the combination of time series and cross sectional data results in a reduction of the variance of the estimated regression coefficients large enough to justify this assumption.

The level of real wages W (total expenditure for labour per employee in constant prices) is explained by the productivity of labour PROD (value added per employee in constant prices), the rate of return on total capital ROR (profit after taxes plus interest paid divided by total capital), and the degree of unionization UNION, which is the same for all firms (i = number of the firm, t = 1960, . . . 1978)

$$(1) \qquad W_{it} = a_{oi} + a_1 \mathrm{PROD}_{it} + a_2 \mathrm{ROR}_{it} + a_3 \mathrm{UNION}_t + u_{it}.$$

TABLE III
REAL WAGES; REGRESSION RESULTS FOR EQUATION (1)

	Firmspecific Intercept	PROD	UNION	ROR	SEE $\bar{R}^2$
Growing firms		0.549	0.906	−52.982	2.106
		(21.08)	(9.44)	(−9.35)	0.989
Growing firms (without merger)		0.616	0.637	−33.364	1.586
		(30.96)	(9.10)	(−11.19)	0.994
Shrinking firms		0.436	1.030	−35.871	2.061
		(16.88)	(11.95)	(−9.74)	0.988
Labour intensive firms		0.826	0.234	−32.547	0.843
		(59.04)	(5.76)	(−23.58)	0.998
Capital intensive firms		0.441	1.008	−58.122	2.187
		(20.44)	(11.20)	(−9.69)	0.989
Large firms		0.485	0.866	−45.617	2.024
		(21.02)	(9.94)	(−7.93)	0.990
Small firms		0.678	0.568	−19.960	1.480
		(30.83)	(9.18)	(−10.64)	0.994
All firms (OLS)	−39.998	0.276	1.538	−11.688	2.989
	(−36.09)	(59.74)	(46.30)	(−7.02)	0.775
All firms (average)	(−11.62)	0.636	0.507	−48.838	

t-statistics in parentheses.

The results for regression (1) are shown in Table III.[1] In all cases we find strongly significant positive relationships between wages and productivity as well as between wages and the degree of unionization.

Neoclassical theory stresses the fact that in equilibrium real wages equal marginal productivity of labour. Though we do not have any possibility to measure marginal productivity, but can only measure average productivity,[2] average productivity should have major influence on wages. Nevertheless, it has to be mentioned that other variables may influence wages via the productivity of labour:

— According to the basic assumption of the human capital model higher qualified workers are more productive than lower qualified workers. Therefore higher qualified workers should earn higher wages.
— Changes in labour productivity may be interpreted as proxy for technical progress. Further regression results that are not presented here show that labour productivity explains wages better than capital intensity or investment intensity (total investment per employee). We can therefore conclude that induced technical progress does not influence wages equally strongly as (direct) technical progress.
— As the average productivity of labour is larger in large firms the positive correlation between wages and the productivity of labour is an indirect confirmation of the hypothesis that large firms pay higher wages [11] [3] [4].

[1] The detailed regression results for the industries are given in Wanik [18].
[2] In the case of a Cobb-Douglas production function marginal productivity is even strictly proportional to average productivity.

The relationship between wages and the rate of return on total capital is significantly negative. The estimated coefficient for the rate of return on total capital becomes the lower the more capital intensive the industries are. According to management science theories of wages the absolute conflict of distribution is expressed by this negative regression coefficient; higher rates of return on total capital are supported by less demanding wage claims. The rate of return on total capital therefore is no proxy for "ability to pay" [9]. High rates of return on capital will not immediately be passed to wage earners.

The UNION variable is included in regression equation (1) to represent short run institutional influences on wages. Since the estimated coefficients show a rather important influence of the Union-variable (see also Table IV), one can assume that some other variables influence wages via the degree of unionization, e.g. the rate of change of prices or the unemployment rate [7, especially p. 233ff.] [13, especially p. 4ff. and 17ff.]. Further investigations need to be done in this area.

As the capacity of the regression programme is limited, the regression over all firms cannot run with firm specific intercepts (OLSDV). By using ordinary least squares (OLS) it seems to be that the estimated coefficients are biased in the direction of the estimated coefficients in capital intensive industries. More generally, the coefficients of firm specific determinants seem to be biased towards zero. We therefore prefer the result for "all firms (average)" which is calculated from the regression results for the industries by using the percentages of employees in an industry as weights. From this result we can calculate the elasticities of wages given in Table IV.

TABLE IV
ELASTICITIES OF WAGES

	Elasticity of Real Wages with respect to . . .
Productivity of labour	0.9131
Degree of unionization	0.8911
Rate of return on total capital	−0.1164

Table IV shows that increases in labour productivity result in almost equal increases in wages. The important influence of productivity on the development of wages is supported by some further results [18, p. 162ff.]:

— The estimated coefficient of labour productivity does not significantly differ for different time periods.

— The estimated coefficient of labour productivity is significantly larger in those industries where the average rate of growth of labour productivity has been above average. Workers in these industries participate above average in technical progress by receiving higher wages. *Only* these industries improved their relative position in the interindustry wage structure during 1960 to 1978. This fact seems important, because the interindustry wage structure on the whole remained rather stable.

We now turn to an explanation of the rate of change of money wages. Because of our working hypothesis that economic determinants of wages are far more important than institutional ones, a regression equation of the Phillips curve-type seems to be appropriate.

In the Walrasian model the market clearing real wage rate is determined by labour supply and labour demand. In disequilibrium, i.e. if labour supply does not equal labour demand, the wage rate will change so as to equate labour supply and labour demand. The rate of change of wages is an increasing function of the excess demand for labour through the origin.

A static stability condition cannot be a dynamic theory on the adjustment of wages in the case of a disequilibrium on the labour market. Furthermore employers and workers influence only nominal wages. As Friedman [6] and Phelps [14] argue it is real wages and not money wages which will respond to excess demand. Money wages will respond both to excess demand and expected changes in prices. To the extent that workers correctly anticipate changes in prices the adjustment coefficient for changes in prices equals unity. An adjustment coefficient smaller than unity indicates money illusion of the workers. It may, however, also show that expected changes in prices could not be carried through in the negotiation of wages.

Finally we have to consider those forces which cause changes in money wages if the labour market is in equilibrium, i.e. if excess demand equals zero. Tobin [15, p. 10f.] assumes that the rate of change of money wages in equilibrium depends on the development of money wages for labour of comparable quality on the external market. "A 'competitive wage' . . . is what employers will offer if they wish to maintain their share of the volume of employment. This will happen where the rate of growth of marginal revenue product—the compound of productivity increase and price inflation—is the same as the trend in wages".

We will therefore explain the rate of change of money wages GRW by the rate of change of prices GRP, the rate of change of labour productivity GRPROD, and the unemployment rate U

$$\text{GRW}_{it} = a_{oi} + a_1\,\text{GRP}_t + a_2\,\text{GRPROD}_{it} + a_3 U_t + u_{it}\,. \tag{2}$$

Equation (2) assumes that the anticipated rate of change of prices resp. the excess demand for labour can be adequately measured by the actual rate of change of prices resp. the actual unemployment rate.

Kühl [10] has shown that for the economy capacity utilization and vacancies are highly correlated. It is therefore obvious to try the firm specific utilization of labour force as an indicator for the firm's need to recruit workers on the external labour market (as well as an indicator of the business cycle of the firm). The utilization of labour force becomes a proxy for the firm specific excess demand for labour without having to assume any constraints on labour mobility; it shows the influence of certain short qualities of labour which may exist even if there is unemployment on the external labour market. As pay relativities within a firm have great significance, changes in the wage rates for some short qualities of labour will induce changes in the wage rates of all other qualities of labour to restore the old pay relativities.

As the utilization of labour force is measured by comparing actual and trend productivity of labour [2], both variables should not enter a regression equation together. Equation (2) therefore becomes

$$(3) \qquad \mathrm{GRW}_{it} = a_{oi} + a_1 \mathrm{GRP}_t + a_2 \mathrm{DELANS}_{it} + u_{it},$$

where DELANS is the absolute change in the utilization of labour force.

The regression results for equations (2) and (3) are given in Tables V and VI. All estimated coefficients significantly show the expected signs. The relationship between the rate of change of money wages and the rate of change of labour productivity is strongly positive.

TABLE V
RATE OF CHANGE OF MONEY WAGES; REGRESSION RESULTS FOR EQUATION (2)

	Firmspecific Intercept	*GRP*	*GRPROD*	*U*	*SEE* $\bar{R}^2$
Growing firms		1.576	0.294	−0.00534	0.066
		(6.69)	(9.78)	(−3.34)	0.706
Growing firms		1.136	0.267	−0.00450	0.059
(without merger)		(5.46)	(9.28)	(−3.11)	0.744
Shrinking firms		1.087	0.191	−0.00410	0.068
		(4.49)	(7.66)	(−2.34)	0.652
Labour intensive firms		1.078	0.212	−0.00572	0.076
		(3.94)	(6.76)	(−2.99)	0.641
Capital intensive firms		1.286	0.221	−0.00529	0.071
		(5.16)	(7.85)	(−3.00)	0.632
Large firms		1.520	0.338	−0.00580	0.066
		(6.63)	(12.02)	(−3.56)	0.714
Small firms		1.033	0.213	−0.00689	0.076
		(3.84)	(7.54)	(−3.61)	0.619
All firms (OLS)	0.0284	1.323	0.248	−0.00581	0.066
	(8.52)	(16.41)	(24.61)	(−10.30)	0.261
All firms (average)	(0.0235)	1.388	0.310	−0.00604	

The estimated coefficients for those variables not specific to a single firm (rate of change of prices, unemployment rate) are not significantly different between the industries and the special groups. The hypothesis that adjustment for changes in these variables is the same for all industries (special groups) thus cannot be falsified.

In particular the coefficient of the rate of change of prices is not significantly different from unity for equations (2) and (3). So the Friedman–Phelps–Hypothesis is confirmed by our data. As the weighted average of the coefficients is larger than unity (cf. "all firms (average)"), one can even say that the expected changes in prices were more than compensated by changes in money wages.

TABLE VI

RATE OF CHANGE OF MONEY WAGES; REGRESSION RESULTS FOR EQUATION (3)

	Firmspecific Intercept	*GRP*	*DELANS*	*SEE $\bar{R}^2$*
Growing firms		1.310	0.458	0.066
		(5.78)	(10.37)	0.704
Growing firms (without merger)		0.953	0.461	0.057
		(4.89)	(11.20)	0.760
Shrinking firms		0.964	0.412	0.064
		(4.40)	(10.59)	0.692
Labour intensive firms		0.982	0.599	0.068
		(4.19)	(12.44)	0.718
Capital intensive firms		1.076	0.387	0.071
		(4.45)	(8.37)	0.626
Large firms		1.246	0.550	0.065
		(5.70)	(13.28)	0.721
Small firms		0.885	0.437	0.073
		(3.53)	(10.21)	0.649
All firms (OLS)	0.0503	1.117	0.455	0.065
	(16.22)	(14.57)	(29.20)	0.283
All firms (average)	(0.0496)	1.164	0.493	

The regression results for equation (3) show that the rate of change of money wages strongly responds to changes in utilization of labour force: An absolute change of the utilization of labour force by 0.05 (e.g. from 0.9 to 0.95 or 0.85) corresponds with a change of 2.47 percentage points in the rate of change of money wages. Only labour intensive vs. capital intensive firms differ significantly in their reaction to changes in the business cycle of the firm; as expected, labour intensive firms reaction is stronger.

This strong reaction of money wages to changes in the business cycle of the firm is mainly due to the high flexibility of those parts of wages which are not standard wages. There is a strongly significant positive correlation between the wage drift and changes in the utilization of labour force; money wages adjust very fast, i.e. with lags shorter than one year, to changes in the business cycle of the firm [18].

IV. CONCLUSION

Our results may be summarized as follows:

- There is a strongly positive relationship between excess demand for labour or anticipated changes in prices and the development of wages.
- Wages will respond quickly to changes in the productivity of labour or changes in the business cycle of the firm.
- Only permanent increases in the productivity of labour will improve the relative position of an industry within the interindustry wage structure.

Since permanent increases in the productivity of labour cannot be reached in the short-run, our results may be one reason for the observed stability of the interindustry wage structure. It will last some time until economic influences will become effective, but in the long-run they cannot be dominated by institutional forces.

Bernhard Wanik,
Peat, Marwick, Mitchell & Co.,
Königsallee 21–23,
D 4000 Düsseldorf 1,
Germany.

ACCEPTED DECEMBER 1982

REFERENCES

[1] Albach, H., Fues, T. and Geisen, B., Approaches to a Theory of Income Distribution in the Firm. In: Griliches, Z., Krelle, W., Krupp, H.-J. and Kyn, O. (Ed.), *Income Distribution and Economic Inequality* (Frankfurt 1978), pp. 133–54.

[2] Boness, A., Das Arbeitsplatzpotential, die Besetzung mit Arbeitskräften und deren Anpassung im Konjunkturverlauf, DIW Beiträge zur Strukturforschung 53 (Berlin 1979).

[3] Calvo, G. and Wellisz, S., Hierarchy, Ability, and Income Distribution, *Journal of Political Economy* 87 (1979), pp. 991–1010.

[4] Dackman, H. and Ohlsson, , J., *Wages and Plant Size in the Swedish Engineering Industry*, Working Paper Series no. 2-1979, University of Uppsala, Department of Economics.

[5] Foley, B. and Maunders, K., *Accounting Information Disclosure and Collective Bargaining* (London 1977).

[6] Friedman, M., The Role of Monetary Policy, *American Economic Review* 58 (1968), pp. 1–17.

[7] Hines, A., Trade Unions and Wage Inflation in the United Kingdom 1893–1961, *Review of Economic Studies* 31 (1964), pp. 221–52.

[8] Horwitz, B. and Shabahang, R., Published Corporate Accounting Data and General Wage Increases of the Firm, *The Accounting Review* 46 (1971), pp. 243–252.

[9] Kaldor, N., Economic Growth and the Problem of Inflation, *Economica N.S.* 26 (1959), pp. 212–26 and 287–98.

[10] Kühl, J., Zum Aussagewert der Statistik der Offenen Stellen, Mitteilungen aus der Arbeitsmarkt- und Berufsforschung 3 (1970), pp. 250–76.

[11] Masters, S., An Interindustry Analysis of Wages and Plant Size, *Review of Economics and Statistics* 51 (1969), pp. 341–45.

[12] Neumann, M., Böbel, I. and Haid, A., Marktmacht, Gewerkschaften und Lohnhöhe in der Industrie der Bundesrepublik Deutschland, *Kyklos* 33 (1980), pp. 230–45.

[13] Parsley, C., Labor Unions and Wages: A Survey, *Journal of Economic Literature* 18 (1980), pp. 1–31.

[14] Phelps, E., Phillips Curves, Expectations of Inflation, and Optimal Unemployment Over Time, *Economica N.S.* 34 (1967), pp. 254–81.

[15] Tobin, J., Inflation and Unemployment, *American Economic Review* 62 (1972), pp. 1–18.

[16] Wallace, T., Weaker Criteria and Tests for Linear Restrictions in Regressions, *Econometrica* 40 (1972), pp. 689–98.

[17] Wanik, B., Ansätze einer betriebswirtschaftlichen Lohntheorie, Zeitschrift für Betriebswirtschaft 51 (1981), pp. 496–522.

[18] Wanik, B., Die Lohnentwicklung deutscher Industrieaktiengesellschaften, Bonner Betriebswirtschaftliche Schriften Vol. 10 (Bonn 1981).

THE JOURNAL OF INDUSTRIAL ECONOMICS 0022-1821 $2.00
Volume XXXIII September 1984 No. 1

A NOTE ON MEASURING SURPLUS ATTRIBUTABLE TO DIFFERENTIATED PRODUCTS*

STEVEN S. WILDMAN

I. INTRODUCTION

IN A RECENT article in this journal, F. M. Scherer [1] presented a study, both analytical and empirical, of the welfare economics of brand proliferation in the ready-to-eat cereal industry. Comparing estimates of contributions to surplus for new products with launching costs, Scherer concluded that during the period 1958–70 most new cereal products were introduced at a net cost to society.

Scherer's measure of a product's contribution to surplus is the consumer's surplus portion of the area under what he calls a *ceteris paribus* demand function (hereafter abbreviated as *c.p.*), the demand function for a single product holding the availability and prices of other products constant. Explicitly ignored in the calculation was the effect of price increases that generally accompanied the introduction of new products. Since consumers' surplus is reduced by an increase in price, Scherer felt that his estimates probably overstated new product benefits.

Using a spatial model like the one employed by Scherer in the analytical portion of his paper, I show in Section II that while Scherer's measure does ignore lost consumer surplus due to price increases, and thus overstates the benefits to consumers, also ignored in Scherer's measure is an increase in producer surplus due to higher prices coupled with the appearance of new product variants. The net effect of the two omissions is ambiguous, leaving open the possibility that Scherer's measure of surplus is actually biased downward instead of upward as he supposes. An algebraic exercise reported in Section III shows that Scherer's measure underestimates a product's contribution to surplus if individual demand functions are linear in price and a spatial measure of product differences. Possible uses of *c.p.* demand functions for estimating the marginal benefits of differentiated products are discussed in Section IV.

II. ACTUAL AND MEASURED CHANGES IN SURPLUS

Figure 1 corresponds to Scherer's Figures 2 and 3. The range of product variation in some changeable characteristic is measured along the horizontal

* This paper benefitted from correspondence with Professor Scherer, especially the material on welfare measures in Section IV. The author would also like to acknowledge the helpful suggestions of an anonymous referee.

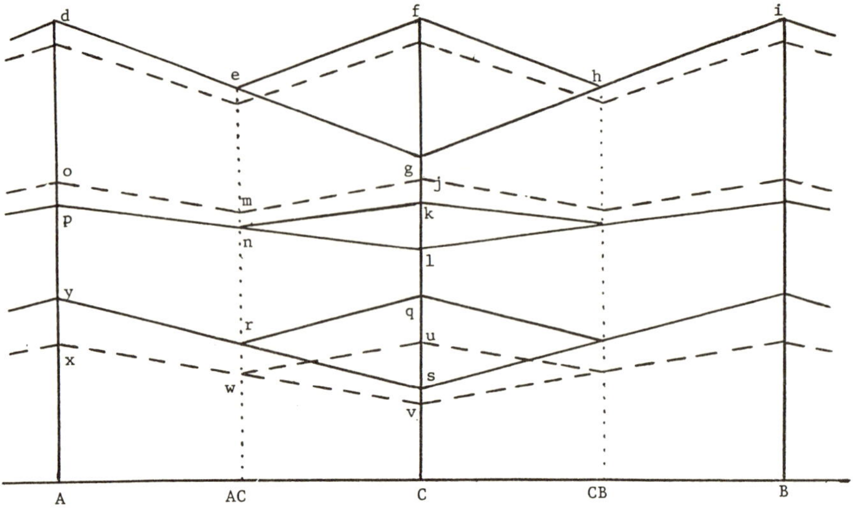

FIGURE 1.
Surplus Before and After a New Product

axis. Both consumers and products are described by their locations along this spectrum of product variation. A consumer's location identifies his preferred variant of the product while a product's location tells how much of the characteristic it provides. A, B, and C identify the locations of three products in the portion of the product spectrum shown in Figure 1. The products at A and B were in the market originally and the product at C is the new product whose net contribution to surplus we want to measure. The analysis is simplified by the assumption that consumers are uniformly distributed across the product spectrum and that, due to the symmetry of their situations, all products sell at the same price in equilibrium. In this case consumers always buy the nearest product and the midpoint on the spectrum between adjacent products separates their clientele.

The area under the solid line deghi is the total of consumers' and producers' surplus in the segment AB when only the products at A and B are in the market. The height of this line above any point is the sum of the areas under the inverse demand functions for all of the consumers at that location minus the variable costs attributable to their purchases. If price did not change with the entry of a new product surplus would increase by the area of quadrangle efhg as consumers between AC and CB switched to the product at C. The division of total surplus between producers and consumers is indicated by the two lower sets of solid lines. Here the middle set of solid lines measures producer surplus while the lowest set of solid lines measures consumer surplus.[1] For example, with a product at C and the original price, total

[1] Consumers' surplus could also be represented by the distance between the total surplus and producers' surplus lines, as Professor Scherer does in Figures 1–3 in his article. The difference in the figures reflects different expositional objectives and has no effect on the conclusions.

surplus due to the consumption of individuals at C is Cf, producer surplus is Ck, and consumer surplus is Cq. Prior to the appearance of the new product total surplus due to consumption at C was Cg, producer surplus was Cl and consumer surplus was Cs.

Surplus after the price increase is measured by the dashed lines; the upper, middle, and lower dashed lines showing total, producers', and consumers' surplus respectively. If, as Scherer claims, prices rise with the introduction of new products, consumption, total surplus, and consumer surplus must fall; therefore the dashed consumer surplus and total surplus lines are drawn below the corresponding solid lines. On the other hand, the post-price increase producer surplus line is above the pre-price increase line, reflecting the fact that, while prices went up as new products were introduced, *per capita* cereal consumption remained nearly constant during the period examined by Scherer.[2]

Since Scherer estimated "average consumer surplus on a typical 11 oz. package" in 1970, the price underlying his estimates is the price prevailing at the end of the period of observation, the higher price following the introduction of new products. Therefore we use the dashed set of consumer surplus lines to represent Scherer's measure of surplus. In Figure 1 consumers' surplus under the *c.p.* demand function for the product at C is twice the area of triangle wuv. (The portion of the figure to the right of the line Cf is the mirror image of the part on the left.) This is Scherer's measure of the benefits of a new product.[3]

To determine the actual change in surplus we must compare total surplus at the old price with just the products at A and B with total surplus after the introduction of the new product and the increase in price. When only the products at A and B were in the market consumer surplus in the segment AB

[2] If prices increase and *per capita* consumption remains constant following the introduction of new products, then producers' surplus must increase if marginal cost is relatively constant. This does not require that surplus realized by producers exceed its earlier value on the purchases of each consumer as is suggested by Figure 1, only when averaged over all consumers. Figure 1 is drawn as it is to simplify the exposition. However, if firms always set price to maximize joint profits over all products, a possibility suggested by Scherer, then each buyer's contribution to producer surplus will increase as new products are introduced since the effect is the same as if firms were instituting a finer division of the market for purposes of price discrimination.

[3] Consumers' surplus under the *c.p.* demand function for the product at C does not include the area under line wv and the corresponding area on the other side of Cf as one might expect. This follows the distinction between a normal demand function and a *c.p.* demand function. The *c.p.* demand function is the schedule of prices and quantities for a single product when the prices for all other products in the market are held constant. As a result, the *c.p.* demand function has a lower price intercept than the regular demand function. For example, the price intercept of the individual *c.p.* demand function for a buyer of the product at C will be at the price at which this individual is just indifferent between the product at C and a more distant product at a lower price. With any further increase in price this individual will switch to either the product at A or the product at B, depending on whehter he is to the right or left of C. This consumer will still realize some surplus on the purchase of the more distant product and it is the consumer surplus available on purchases of close substitutes that is measured by the area under line wv. Thus the sum of individual products' contributions to surplus, the areas under their *c.p.* demand functions, is less than total surplus, a relationship proved algebraically by Spence [2].

was twice the area under line yrs. With the product at C consumer surplus is twice the area under xwu. So Scherer's estimate does overstate the increase in consumer surplus as claimed; his measure exceeds the actual increase by twice the area of quadrangle yrsvwx.

The increase in producers' surplus left out of Scherer's measure is twice the area between the dashed line omj and the solid line pnl. Since the change in consumers' surplus is inflated and producers' surplus gains are omitted, the actual relationship between Scherer's measure and the true change in surplus depends on the structure of consumer demand and the size of price increases. In the next section I show that if individual demand functions are linear Scherer's measure understates the true gains in surplus due to new products.

III. AN EXAMPLE

Here we follow convention in the use of spatial models for the analysis of nongeographic differentiation. Transport costs are interpreted as the utility loss per unit distance attributed by a consumer to the distance in characteristic space between his location and the location of a product elsewhere. Individual demand functions are assumed to be linear in both price and transport cost. The demand of a consumer purchasing a product distance α from himself at price P (mill price) with unit transport cost of c is given by (1), while (2) is the associated inverse demand function.

$$q(P;\ \alpha) = a - b(P + c\alpha). \tag{1}$$

$$p(q;\ \alpha) = a/b - q/b - c\alpha. \tag{2}$$

In addition we assume that consumers are uniformly distributed across the product space with density of 1 and the distance between A and B in Figure 1 is 2. Thus the distance from A to C and from C to B is 1. The analysis is further simplified by restricting ourselves to cases in which all consumers purchase positive amounts of the product both before and after the appearance of the new product at C. This corresponds to the situations portrayed in Scherer's figures.

A final assumption of convenience is that the marginal cost of production is zero for all products. As long as marginal cost is constant the assumption that it is zero involves no additional loss of generality while reducing algebraic complexity considerably. Alternatively, and equivalently, we could let P stand for mill price net of a constant marginal cost.

Using (1) and (2), we can derive expressions for quantities useful for comparing Scherer's measure of a new product's contribution to surplus with the actual benefits of the new product. Define $Q_0(P)$ to be total consumption of cereal for consumers between A and B when there are just two products in the market and price is P and let $Q_1(P)$ be total consumption for the same consumers at price P after the addition of a new product at C.

$$Q_0(P) = 2\int_0^1 [a - b(P + c\alpha)]\,d\alpha$$

$$= 2a - 2bP - bc.$$

$$Q_1(P) = 4\int_0^{1/2} [a - b(P + c\alpha)]\,d\alpha$$

$$= 2a - 2bP - bc/2.$$

It will prove useful to have an expression for the area under a consumer's inverse demand function. Denote this expression $v(P; \alpha)$ for a consumer distance α from the product he purchases when the price is P.

$$v(P; \alpha) = \int_0^{q(P;\,\alpha)} p(q; \alpha)\,dq$$

$$= a^2/2b - bP^2/2 + bc^2\alpha^2/2 - ac\alpha.$$

Subtracting out his expenditure for the product, consumer surplus for the same individual is

$$s(P; \alpha) = v(P; \alpha) - Pq(P; \alpha)$$

$$= a^2/2b + bP^2/2 + bc^2\alpha^2/2 - ac\alpha - aP + bcP\alpha.$$

When only the products at A and B are in the market, the total of the areas under the inverse demand functions, that is, total surplus, over all consumers between A and B is

$$V_0(P) = 2\int_0^1 v(P; \alpha)\,d\alpha$$

$$= a^2/b + bc^2/3 - bP^2 - ac.$$

With the addition of the product at C total surplus becomes

$$V_1(P) = 4\int_0^{1/2} v(P; \alpha)\,d\alpha$$

$$= a^2/b + bc^2/12 - bP^2 - ac/2.$$

Both Scherer's measure of the change in surplus due to the addition of the third product and the true change in surplus may be expressed in terms of the quantities just defined. Let P_0 be the price prevailing when there were only the two products at A and B, P_1 be the new higher price following the introduction of the product at C, and define $\delta = P_1 - P_0$. Then Scherer's measure is

$$(3) \qquad SM = 2\int_0^{1/2} s(P_1;\, \alpha)\, d\alpha - 2\int_{1/2}^{1} s(P_1;\, \alpha)\, d\alpha$$
$$= ac/2 - bc^2/4 - bcP_1/2,$$

and the true change in surplus is given by

$$(4) \qquad TC = V_1(P_1) - V_0(P_0)$$
$$= ac/2 - bc^2/4 - 2bP_1\delta + b\delta^2.$$

Subtracting (3) from (4) we have the difference, D, between the true change in surplus and Scherer's measure.

$$(5) \qquad D = bcP_1/2 - 2bP_1\delta + b\delta^2.$$

In all cases but one it is necessary to know the values of P_1 and δ to evaluate D. The single exception occurs when consumption prior to the introduction of the new product is equal to consumption afterward. This case is of interest because Scherer's data show that *per capita* cereal consumption varied little during the period examined, and because, at least for this model, holding total consumption constant produces smaller values of D than are determined by more plausible scenarios for determining price increases.

Equating $Q_0(P_0)$ to $Q_1(P_1)$ and solving for δ gives $\delta = c/4$. Substituting for δ in (5), the terms with P_1 cancel; so $D = bc^2/16$, which is positive. In fact, D is positive for all smaller values of δ, including negative values, and for a significant range of larger values as well.

Scherer also suggests the possibility that cereal companies set price to maximize joint profits over all products. We will use this case for illustrative purposes and indicate the corresponding values of P_0, P_1, and δ with a superscript j. $P_0^j = a/2b - c/4$, $P_1^j = a/2b - c/8$, and $\delta^j = c/8$. Since δ^j is less than the price change required to keep total consumption constant, we know that D is positive in this case as well. With price competition δ should be smaller yet; so D should be positive in a more competitive environment too.

Substituting P_1^j and δ^j into (3) and (4) we have

$$SM^j = ac/4 - 3bc^2/16, \quad \text{and} \quad TC^j = 3ac/8 - 13bc^2/64.$$

If applied in this case, Scherer's measure would at best capture two thirds of the actual increase in surplus. This is the limiting value of SM^j/TC^j as b approaches zero. In this case consumption is completely unresponsive to changes in price or transport costs. A larger fraction of total surplus gains is missed if b is positive. This is not to say that Scherer underestimated the benefits of new cereal products by at least a third. Without knowledge of the underlying demand functions and the history of price increases over the period examined by Scherer, the exact relationship between Scherer's estimates and the actual changes in surplus cannot be determined. The point is that the magnitude of the error due to the omission of producers' surplus changes in Scherer's estimates is potentially quite large.

While the exercise reported in this section is based on explicit functional forms, a couple of generalizations relating to the size of the error in Scherer's measure appear warranted. One is that the importance of producers' surplus omitted from Scherer's measure is larger the more consumers value the differences between products. This is obvious in the comparison of *TC* and *SM*. The difference between the two is an increasing function of c. Consumers benefit the most from new products when the utility loss associated with using less than ideal variants of a product is high. Sellers capture a part of what would otherwise be consumer surplus gains by raising price. Therefore, one would expect the producers' surplus gains left out in Scherer's measure to be greatest when estimated consumers' surplus gains are large.

A similar argument suggests that omitted gains in producers' surplus will be larger the more sensitive are consumers to changes in price. This is because the increase in surplus due to a price decrease will be greater if demand functions are flat than if they are steep. Consumers treat reductions in transport costs like reductions in price. Therefore the increase in total surplus to be distributed between consumers and producers following the introduction of a new product is larger if individual demand functions are flat. This is reflected in the linear model worked out above. For a range of values of δ that would seem to include all plausible possibilities, D is an increasing function of b. A comparison of the expressions for SM^j and TC^j tells the same story if firms are joint profit maximizers.

IV. A FINAL OBSERVATION ON USES FOR *Ceteris Paribus* DEMAND FUNCTIONS

For reasons that will be clear shortly, it is generally not possible to construct the expression for the total change in surplus given in equation (4) from estimable areas under *ceteris paribus* demand functions. The exception, discussed below, is a new product whose introduction does not precipitate a price change. Thus, in most cases, production of a measure of benefits with exact correspondence to *TC* requires that one estimate the complete demand structure for a set of related products, both with and without the new product. Surplus at the initial price for the original product set could then be compared with surplus at the final price with the new product. The data required for these estimates would be considerable and one would have to exercise care in specifying the form for cross product effects. However, *c.p.* demand functions can be used to estimate bounds within which the true change in surplus must fall and, if changes in consumption due to new products can be estimated, a close approximation to the actual change in surplus is possible.

Making use of the definitions of $V_1(P)$, $V_0(P)$, and $v(P;\alpha)$, the general form of the expression for TC in equation (4) may be written as

$$\begin{aligned} TC &= 4\int_0^{1/2}\int_0^{q(P_1;\alpha)} p(q;\alpha)\,dq\,d\alpha - 2\int_0^1\int_0^{q(P_0;\alpha)} p(q;\alpha)\,dq\,d\alpha \\ &= 4\int_0^{1/2}\int_0^{q(P_1;\alpha)} p(q;\alpha)\,dq\,d\alpha - 2\int_0^1\int_0^{q(P_1;\alpha)} p(q;\alpha)\,dq\,d\alpha \\ &\quad - 2\int_0^1\int_{q(P_1;\alpha)}^{q(P_0;\alpha)} p(q;\alpha)\,dq\,d\alpha \\ &= 2\left[\int_0^{1/2}\int_0^{q(P_1;\alpha)} p(q;\alpha)\,dq\,d\alpha - \int_{1/2}^1\int_0^{q(P_1;\alpha)} p(q;\alpha)\,dq\,d\alpha \right. \\ &\quad \left. - \int_0^1\int_{q(P_1;\alpha)}^{q(P_0;\alpha)} p(q;\alpha)\,dq\,d\alpha\right]. \end{aligned}$$

Separating $p(q;\alpha)$ into its consumer surplus and producer surplus components and integrating over q for the first two terms we get

$$\begin{aligned} TC = 2\Bigg[&\int_0^{1/2} s(P_1;\alpha)\,d\alpha - \int_{1/2}^1 s(P_1;\alpha)\,d\alpha \\ &+ P_1\int_0^{1/2} q(P_1;\alpha)\,d\alpha - P_1\int_{1/2}^1 q(P_1;\alpha)\,d\alpha \\ &- \int_0^1\int_{q(P_1;\alpha)}^{q(P_0;\alpha)} p(q;\alpha)\,dq\,d\alpha\Bigg]. \end{aligned}$$

Substituting from (3) we have

$$(4') \qquad \begin{aligned} TC = SM + 2P_1\int_0^{1/2} q(P_1;\alpha)\,d\alpha - 2P_1\int_{1/2}^1 q(P_1;\alpha)\,d\alpha \\ - 2\int_0^1\int_{q(P_1;\alpha)}^{q(P_0;\alpha)} p(q;\alpha)\,dq\,d\alpha, \end{aligned}$$

a very intuitively appealing form of TC.

SM is consumers' surplus under the *c.p.* demand function while $2P_1\int_0^{1/2}q(P_1;\alpha)\,d\alpha$ is producers' surplus realized on sales of the new product. So the sum of the first two terms on the right side of (4′) is the total surplus under a *c.p.* demand function. From this is subtracted surplus producers would have earned on sales to the same consumers without the new product, $2P_1\int_{1/2}^1 q(P_1;\alpha)\,d\alpha$, and the change in dead weight loss on sales to all consumers due to the change in price from P_0 to P_1, $2\int_0^1\int_{q(P_1;\alpha)}^{q(P_0;\alpha)} p(q;\alpha)\,dq\,d\alpha$. Clearly, as long as $P_1 > P_0$, the total benefits of the new product cannot exceed total surplus under the *c.p.* demand function. So the total surplus under its *c.p.* demand function is an upper bound on the benefits of a new product.

$2P_1 \int_{1/2}^{1} q(P_1; \alpha)\, d\alpha$ corresponds to what Scherer called cannibalization, producers' surplus transferred from old products to new. At most the reallocated surplus can equal the producers' surplus of the new product. Thus *SM* minus the change in dead weight loss is a lower bound for new product benefits.

Unfortunately no measurable area under a *c.p.* demand curve corresponds exactly with the change in dead weight loss; so, in addition to the usual sources of statistical error, estimates of this quantity will be flawed by the inexactness of the measure employed. Of course this problem disappears if price is unchanged. Otherwise, since the change in dead weight loss is likely to be small in comparison to the other surplus magnitudes being estimated, one might choose to ignore dead weight loss, as Scherer did in constructing his measure of benefits; recognizing as he does that the measure errs in overstating benefits, or, in this case, the lower bound on possible benefits. For what is probably a liberal measure of the change in dead weight loss, one might use the change in dead weight loss for the same price change under the estimated *c.p.* demand function for the new product multiplied by the inverse of the ratio of the new product's sales to the sales of the group of related products whose prices were affected by its introduction.[4]

Evidence reported by Scherer indicates that the cereal companies try to determine the extent to which new products cannibalize the old. If the extent of cannibalization can be estimated, we do not have to be content with estimates of the bounds on new product benefits. The change in total surplus is the minimum bound on benefits described above plus uncannibalized producers' surplus, and both could be estimated.

In his footnote 50, Scherer states that, for an assumed marginal cost of 32 cents per pound, the inverse demand function $P = 1 - 0.001Q^3$ gives rise to "profit maximizing price-cost margins (that) appear representative of 1970 experience for relatively new RTE products." Profit maximizing price would be 83 cents a pound in this case and output about 5.54 million pounds for a new product. Using this example to illustrate the benefit measures described above, producers' surplus under the *c.p.* demand function is approximately \$2.83 mil. and consumers' surplus, which is also *SM*, about \$0.71 mil. Assuming price rose by eight cents, or about ten percent, following entry, the

[4] $2 \int_0^1 \int_{q(P_1;\, \alpha)}^{q(P_0;\, \alpha)} p(q; \alpha)\, dq\, d\alpha$ is the change in dead weight loss under the general demand function from which the *c.p.* demand function is derived, assuming the price change applies to all products. Since they hold other prices constant, *c.p.* demand functions must be more elastic. Substituting changes in dead weight loss under *c.p.* demand functions for the change under the general demand function biases the measure of the change in dead weight loss upward. But even if this source of bias is ignored, the measure suggested still probably overstates changes in dead weight loss. The measure assumes that the ratio of dead weight loss to consumption is the same for the consumers of all products and that the price increase would have caused the same loss of surplus on sales to buyers of the new product even if they were still consuming their original brands. If buyers of new products increase consumption after they switch, this second assumption implies an overstatement of the change in dead weight loss on their purchases. However, the possibility that the shape of their demand functions may change with the switch could work in the opposite direction.

increase in dead weight loss under this demand function is about \$0.03 mil. If the new product has one fourth of the sales for its segment of the market and all products in this market segment experience similar price increases, our measure of the increase in dead weight loss would be \$0.12 mil.

In this example, with producers' surplus so large relative to consumers' surplus and the change in dead weight loss, the bounds on the true change in surplus are quite far apart. The benefits of a new product cannot exceed \$3.54 mil. and are probably no less than \$0.59 mil. Letting β stand for the proportion of the new product's sales attributable to cannibalization, the addition to surplus should be between $(1-\beta)$ (\$2.83 mil.) + \$0.59 mil. and $(1-\beta)$ (\$2.83 mil.) + \$0.71 mil.

The importance of cannibalization to the accuracy of Professor Scherer's measure of benefits is obvious. If β is near one, his measure is close to the mark. Otherwise, the error can be significant, especially when producers' surplus accounts for such a large percentage of total surplus under the *c.p.* demand function as in this example. In this case, if just 15 percent of the new product's sales were due to enhanced demand, the error in Scherer's measure would be on the order of fifty percent.[5]

Steven S. Wildman,
Economists Incorporated,
Suite 1250, 1750 K Street N.W.,
Washington, D.C., 20006,
U.S.A.

ACCEPTED APRIL 1983

REFERENCES

[1] Scherer, F. M., "The Welfare Economics of Product Variety: An Application to the Ready-to-Eat Cereals Industry," *The Journal of Industrial Economics*, XXVII, 1 (December 1979), pp. 113–34.

[2] Spence, Michael, "Product Selection, Fixed Costs and Monopolistic Competition," *Review of Economic Studies*, XLIII, 2 (June 1976), pp. 217–35.

[5] Unless individual inverse demand functions are vertical, the fact that *SM* is positive is evidence that new products are responsible for some increase in consumption. This is evident upon inspection of the linear demand expressions for the individual demand function and *SM*.

$$q(P;\alpha) = a - b(P + c\alpha).$$

$$SM = ac/2 - bc^2/4 - bcP_1/2.$$

SM is positive only if c is positive, that is only if consumers value product variety. Nonvertical inverse demand functions imply $b > 0$. But if $b > 0$ buyers of new products will increase their purchases since for them the new product reduces $c\alpha$.

THE JOURNAL OF INDUSTRIAL ECONOMICS 0022-1821 $2.00
Volume XXXIII September 1984 No. 1

MEASURING SURPLUS ATTRIBUTABLE TO DIFFERENTIATED PRODUCTS: REPLY

F. M. Scherer

Professor Wildman's paper performs a double service for which I must express personal and professional appreciation. It correctly identifies an error I made in attempting to estimate the surplus attributable to new cereal products. In effect, I confused how total welfare was affected *ex ante* by price changes with what one could actually observe *ex post*. And it greatly extends the theory relevant to measuring new products' welfare contribution. It is disappointing that the measurement problem turns out to be so difficult—much more so than I assumed in my article. Nevertheless, Wildman's comment also helps identify and place bounds upon the cases in which tolerably accurate measurements can be made—notably, those in which the resulting price changes are zero or small (to which cereals did not conform) and those in which the fraction of producer's surplus cannibalized is high (to which cereals did conform, although not perfectly).

It seems clear from Wildman's analysis that I understated the net benefits from new cereal products and hence underestimated the number of new products with positive net welfare contributions. I doubt, however, that the latter estimate was seriously askew, since I found that the (under)estimated benefits from new products tailed off rapidly as one added to the list products with smaller market shares. A sensitivity analysis revealed that raising the surplus estimate by 46 percent increased the number of net welfare-enhancing brands by only 29 percent (from 17 to 22).

F. M. Scherer,
Swarthmore College,
Department of Economics,
Swarthmore,
PA., 19081,
U.S.A.

ACCEPTED APRIL 1983

THE JOURNAL OF INDUSTRIAL ECONOMICS 0022–1821 $2.00
Volume XXXIII September 1984 No. 1

PROFITABILITY MEASURES AS INDICATORS OF POST-MERGER EFFICIENCY REVISITED

ARVIND MAHAJAN

RECENTLY in this journal, Meeks and Meeks [3] (MM hereon) described the pitfalls of using common measures of profitability to infer operational efficiency changes resulting from mergers. This article (a) points out an error in Meeks and Meeks discussion of the "gearing bias", (b) suggests a method of purging this bias, and (c) identifies another bias inherent in the common measures of profitability.

MM concentrated on three common profitability measures, viz.,

(a) profit-sales ratio,
(b) ratio of shareholders' income to shareholders' assets, i.e., rate of return on equity capital, and
(c) rate of return on total net assets.

They analyzed the distortions created in these due to:

Bias 1. Influence of change in bargaining power due to a merger on profitability.
Bias 2. Distortion created in profit-sales ratio as the post-merger sales figures used do not reflect any pre-merger interfirm sales.
Bias 3. Distortion due to accounting convention regarding timing in treating profit and total net assets in computation of return on total net assets for the merger year.
Bias 4. Influence of change in gearing ratio on return to equity.
Bias 5. "Goodwill Bias" in computing amalgamation's return on total net assets due to the acquirer paying more than the book value for the acquired firm's assets.

As MM note, Bias 1 is common to all profitability measures and exists due to the difficulty of separating the influences of changes in bargaining power and efficiency from the profitability measures (due to a lack of observable proxies).[1] To discern efficiency changes from profitability measures empirically, a researcher has to assume the influence of a merger on profitability due

[1] Meeks and Meeks [3, p. 342] suggest that adjustment to changes in input and output prices associated with the merger could be attempted for this purpose (e.g. Cowling *et al.* [2]) but they note that "even where such data can be obtained, this is a very costly exercise normally feasible only for small samples and in any case subject to various qualifications".

to a change in bargaining power. Therefore, we would like to emphasize that *any* empirical test of efficiency using profitability measures is a simultaneous test of two hypotheses, viz., (i) the assumed change in bargaining power and thus profitability due to a merger and (ii) the stated null hypothesis regarding the influence of a merger on efficiency and thus profitability.

Regarding Biases 2 and 3, MM aptly conclude the inappropriateness of using profit-sales ratio as a measure whose alleviation requires data which are not published, and justifiably suggest ignoring the year of merger from analysis. Therefore, we will limit our discussion to the influence of Biases 4 and 5 on the remaining two profitability measures, viz., return on equity and return on total net assets. MM conclude by strongly recommending return on total net assets over return on equity "since e (return on equity) is afflicted with all the problems of r (return on total net assets) and the gearing bias besides"[2] (parentheses added). MM arrive at this conclusion by utilizing equations which ignore the fact that interest payments on debt are tax deductible. If this fact is explicitly incorporated in the analysis, one would find the gearing bias to afflict both profitability measures. However, as we show, this bias can be adjusted for in both the measures. We repeat MM's equation (4):

$$(1) \qquad e = r + [g/(1 - g)](r - i)$$

where e is return on equity, g is the gearing ratio, i is the interest rate on long-term bonds and r is the return on net assets of an identical firm which uses no debt. MM's equation (4) (i.e., our equation (1)) was originally derived by Modigliani and Miller [4] under the assumption of no tax deductibility of interest payments. Later, as Modigliani and Miller [5] recognized the existence of tax deductibility of interest payments, they corrected their original return on equity equation to:

$$(1') \qquad e = r + [g/(1 - g)](r - i)(1 - t)$$

where t is the marginal corporate tax rate. The second term in equation (1′) can be decomposed into two parts—$[g/(1 - g)](r - i)$ and $-t[g/(1 - g)](r - i)$. While the former term is the gearing risk premium, the latter, ignored by MM, captures the advantage of gearing due to tax deductibility of interest. Clearly, equation (1′) is the proper measure of return on equity in our world of tax deductibility of interest. In this world, Modigliani and Miller further showed that the return on total net assets (cost of capital in equilibrium) for a geared firm (r_g) would be

$$(2) \qquad r_g = r - g(r - i)t.$$

[2] Meeks and Meeks [3, p. 342].

Note that the return on total net assets, with tax deductibility of interest, is a decreasing function of gearing, hence subject to the gearing Bias 2.[3]

To the extent mergers result in a change in gearing (as MM observe), comparing pre-merger and post-merger profitability (using either e or r_g) will not provide meaningful inference regarding change in profitability due to a merger, because the observed change could be due to a change in gearing. However, such a bias can be easily purged if one knows the change in gearing ratio due to the merger. Letting subscripts 0 and 1 on variables represent their values before and after the merger respectively, and defining $\Delta\{g/(1-g)\} = \{g_1/(1-g_1)\} - \{g_0/(1-g_0)\}$ and $\Delta g = g_1 - g_0$, a change in gearing would change e by $\Delta\{g/(1-g)\}(r-i)(1-t)$ and r_g by $-\Delta g(r-i)t$. Therefore, in comparing post-merger and pre-merger profitability, the gearing bias can be purged if the post-merger measure is appropriately adjusted (denoted by *) for comparison with the pre-merger observation as follows:

$$(1'') \qquad e_1^* = e_1 + \Delta\{g/(1-g)\}(r-i)(1-t)$$

and

$$(2') \qquad r_{g1}^* = r_{g1} - \Delta g(r-i)t.$$

The "goodwill" Bias 5 in both the traditional profitability measures under discussion occurs "because acquirers often pay more (and rarely less) for victims, and record the subsidiary's assets in their own book at a higher valuation, than the figure at which they appeared before takeover".[4] The disparity between book and market valuation of the assets is a well recognized cause of this bias. To the extent market values of debt and equity are better indicators of a firm's real asset value than their book values (and it seems that they are), the influence of this bias can be largely mitigated by using market values rather than accounting values. As publicly traded firms' equity prices are widely published and thus easily observable (as compared to their debt and other liabilities' values), this should favor (contra to MM) recommending the use of return to equity over return on total net assets.

Finally, caution needs to be exercised in discerning efficiency changes due to a risk bias. If the operating, and, therefore, risk characteristics of a firm

[3] r_g in equation (2) is the post-tax return on total net assets and we consider it a superior profitability measure than its pre-tax counterpart in a world of tax deductibility of interest. To show this, let X be the operating profit of two firms A and B, identical in all respects except that A is geared and B uses no gearing. Letting I be the interest paid by A on its long term bonds, the cash flow to A's equity owners is $(X-I)(1-t)$ and to its bond holders is I. The total cash flow to all capital suppliers of firm A, therefore, is $(X-I)(1-t)+I = X(1-t)+tI$. However, the total cash flow to all capital suppliers of firm B is only $X(1-t)$. Clearly, geared firm A generates tI more than firm B. It can afford to (and will) reduce its output prices, thus seemingly reducing its pre-tax return on total net assets—a reduction attributable to gearing and definitely not to an efficiency decline. Thus, the use of pre-tax return can be hazardous if not erroneous. Given the objective of discerning efficiency changes due to mergers, our adjusted post-tax measure of equation (2′) is free of the gearing bias as well as the hazards associated with using pre-tax returns.

[4] Meeks and Meeks [3, p. 341].

change due to the merger,[5] comparing post-merger and pre-merger profitability (using conventional measures) can lead to biased inferences. Though controlling for this bias is more complicated than for the gearing bias due to a lack of good observable proxy for risk, attempts heretofore for such purpose have in general favored the use of return on equity over return on total assets.

Arvind Mahajan,
Department of Finance,
Texas A & M University,
College of Business Administration,
College Station,
Texas 77843–4218

ACCEPTED APRIL 1983

REFERENCES

[1] AMIHUD, Y. and LEV, B., "Risk Reduction as a Managerial Motive for Conglomerate Mergers", *The Bell Journal of Economics*, 12, No. 2 (Autumn 1981), pp. 605–17.

[2] COWLING, K. *et al.*, *Mergers and Economic Performance* (Cambridge University Press, Cambridge, 1980).

[3] MEEKS, G. and MEEKS, J. G., "Profitability Measures As Indicators of Post-Merger Efficiency", *Journal of Industrial Economics*, XXIX (4) (June 1981), pp. 335–44.

[4] MODIGLIANI, F. and MILLER, M. H., "The Cost of Capital, Corporation Finance and the Theory of Investment", *The American Economic Review*, XLVIII, No. 3, (June 1958), pp. 261–97.

[5] MODIGLIANI, F. and MILLER, M. H., "Corporate Income Taxes and the Cost of Capital: A Correction", *The American Economic Review*, LIII, No. 3, (June 1963), pp. 433–43.

[5] We are not alluding to risk change due to diversification *à la* Capital Asset Pricing Model but instead due to operating decisions and real asset structure changes. One instigator for such changes through mergers, for example, could be the "managerial motive" proposed and tested by Amihud and Lev [1].

THE JOURNAL OF INDUSTRIAL ECONOMICS 0022–1821 $2.00
Volume XXXIII September 1984 No. 1

PROFITABILITY MEASURES AS INDICATORS OF POST-MERGER EFFICIENCY: REPLY

G. MEEKS AND J. G. MEEKS

THE error is Mahajan's: the discussion of the gearing bias in our earlier paper [5] still stands. Mahajan has been misled by an entirely superficial resemblance between some of the *ex post* accounting relationships we used and the conditions for capital market equilibrium derived in the two famous papers by Modigliani and Miller [6], [7].

According to Mahajan, our equation (4)

$$e = r + \frac{g}{1 - g}(r - i)$$

is simply a rehash of Modigliani and Miller [6] equation (8): dropping subscripts,

$$i = \rho + (\rho - r)\frac{D}{S}$$

But this is false unless the terms in these expressions are defined identically; and Modigliani and Miller would surely agree with us that they are not.

Consider the definitions of r in our (4) and ρ in their (8):

$$r = \frac{P}{A} \text{ (see our equation (3))}$$

where

P = actual profit (before interest and tax)

and

A = historic cost of the firm's net assets,
i.e. book value of the firm

whereas in contrast,

$$\rho = \frac{\bar{X}}{V} \text{ (see their equation (4))}$$

where

$\bar{X}$ = expected profit (before interest and tax)—
a hypothetical income stream

and

V = market value of the firm, capable of adjusting in their model to ensure equilibrium.

Or again, the debt-equity ratio in our equation (4), $g/1 - g$, refers to fixed book values, whereas it is the essence of the Modigliani-Miller model that its debt-equity ratio, D/S, involves market values that are assumed to adjust through arbitrage to bring about market equilibrium. So in merging Meeks and Meeks [4] with Modigliani and Miller [6] (8), Mahajan is mistaken.

This mistake over the nature of the variables we were discussing matters all the more in Mahajan's subsequent argument. Equations (11.c and 12.c) of Modigliani and Miller's 1963 note [7] correct the relationships presented in their 1958 paper [6] (11 and 12) for the profit rate and the rate of earnings on equity in equilibrium under a system of tax-deductibility of interest. These new relations depend both on the market discounting stock for added leverage (as in their original model) and on it capitalizing the additional earnings due to the tax concession at a more favourable rate than that used for uncertain streams (the 1963 correction). Plainly neither of these equilibrating mechanisms could possibly affect the variables we discussed, whose denominator incorporates the fixed A, not the shifting V. Yet Mahajan simply rewrites Modigliani and Miller's revised equations (11.c and 12.c) using our book value terms (and failing to follow Modigliani and Miller in distinguishing pre- and post-tax terms into the bargain). The resulting expressions for the post-tax yield on shareholders' assets at book value (post-tax e) and on total net assets at book value (post-tax r) (Mahajan's equations (1′ and 2)) are quite incorrect.[1] He has not understood that our paper and theirs not only differ in notation but also relate to entirely different variables which, not surprisingly, in general behave differently too.

Mahajan's muddled equations apart, what remains of his Comment? He might perhaps have argued—and at one point does seem to fall into arguing—that the use of (actual) market value measures is to be preferred to

[1] Our original argument concerned pre-tax measures of r and e, where only e is subject to a gearing bias; and the pre-tax discussion still seems to us to be appropriate. It relates to the measures actually reported in several key empirical studies. It is also more directly relevant to the policy issue we were concerned with. In evaluating mergers' social benefits for policy purposes, a key question is whether mergers typically enhance efficiency (as distinct from whether they make shareholders better off); and, taken as an efficiency proxy, the pre-tax surplus of revenue over cost has the advantage of abstracting from mere changes in the distribution of the surplus between shareholders, debtholders and the government.

In a footnote, Mahajan attempts to show that even our pre-tax r is affected by gearing and concludes that the post-tax measure, adjusted for gearing in the light of his equations (2 and 2′), is to be preferred in the policy context. But the adjustment proposed on the basis of these equations would make nonsense of post-tax r. And this suggestion that pre-tax r is biased is in any case unconvincing. This suggestion derives from the contention that a newly-merged firm which achieves higher gearing, and enjoys an extra subsidy from the tax authorities in consequence, will undertake full forward shifting. But the literature would suggest that in the case at issue, where only one member of an industry finds its tax position altered, such forward shifting is a most unlikely outcome; and Mahajan provides no theoretical or empirical support for the contrary view.

that of book value ones in discussion of the efficiency effects of merger. Book values are not of course perfect indicators. But one reason for adopting them in the context of the debate on merger policy—as the main empirical studies do—is that well-known imperfections in the capital market give rise to biased assessments of the performance of merged firms if market values are used instead. As Prais [8] and Lynch [2] have shown, larger firms are given an undue preference in actual stock market valuations; and thus, with efficiency and profitability unchanged as a result of merger, an amalgamation may well be more highly valued by the market, solely on grounds of size, than its constituent parts were beforehand. Moreover, relevant though market values are to shareholders' gains from merger, their well-known volatility (Keynes would say capriciousness) makes them in practice an unreliable component of profitability measures used to assess the benefits of merger to the whole economy. And since one of us has explained elsewhere [4] how to remedy the potential goodwill bias in studies using book values—the bias which Mahajan proposes to eliminate by use of market values—his case for changing the basis on which efficiency gains from merger might be assessed collapses.[2]

G. Meeks,
Faculty of Economics and Politics
and
J. G. Meeks,
Department of Applied Economics,
Unversity of Cambridge, England.

ACCEPTED NOVEMBER 1983

REFERENCES

[1] Amihud, Y. and Lev, B, 'Risk Reduction as a Managerial Motive for Conglomerate Mergers', *Bell Journal of Economics* 12, No. 2 (Autumn 1981), pp' 605–17.
[2] Lynch, H. H., *Financial Performance of Conglomerates* (Harvard University Press, 1971).
[3] Mahajan, A., 'Profitability Measures as Indicators of Post-Merger Efficiency: A Comment', *Journal of Industrial Economics*, XXXII, No. 3, (June 1984), pp. .
[4] Meeks, G., *Disappointing Marriage: A Study of the Gains from Merger* (Cambridge University Press, Cambridge 1977).
[5] Meeks, G. and Meeks, J. G., 'Profitability Measures as Indicators of Post-Merger Efficiency', *Journal of Industrial Economics*, XXIX, No. 4, (June 1981), pp. 335–44.
[6] Modigliani, F. and Miller, M. H., 'The Cost of Capital, Corporation Finance and the Theory of Investment', *American Economic Review*, XLVIII, No. 3, (June 1958), pp. 261–97.

[2] Mahajan's final point—that allowing for his new 'bias', changes in risk on merger (where the changes are said not to be due to diversification), favours the use of e rather than r—is opaque. He, puzzlingly in the context, mentions Amihud and Lev's thesis [1] that reduction of managerial employment risk may be a motive for conglomerate (diversified) mergers. This may help to explain why such mergers are undertaken even when profitability is unlikely to rise, but it appears to have no bearing on the concern of our paper—the efficiency implications of recorded profitability levels. And the link with e in preference to r is left obscure.

[7] Modigliani, F. and Miller, M. H., 'Corporate Income Taxes and the Cost of Capital: A Correction', *American Economic Review*, LIII, No. 3, (June 1963), pp. 433–43.

[8] Prais, S. J., *The Evolution of Giant Firms in Britain* (Cambridge University Press, Cambridge, 1976).

We are grateful to the following, in addition to our Associate Editors, for acting as referees over the past year:

Ana Aizcorbe,
Boston College
Robert L. Avinger, Jr.,
Sterling Management Co.,
Charlotte
V. N. Balasubramanyam,
University of Lancaster
Randall Bartlett,
Smith College, Northampton
J. I. Bernstein,
Carleton University, Ottawa
Ralph M. Bradburd,
Williams College, Williamstown
Thomas G. Cowing,
SUNY at Binghamton
J. Cubbin,
Queen Mary College, London
M. G. S. Denny,
University of Toronto
V. A. Dickson,
University of New Brunswick
N. Dorward,
The Polytechnic of North London
D. Elliott,
Monopolies and Mergers Commission
J. R. Franks,
London Graduate School of
Business Studies
Steven Globerman,
Simon Fraser University, Burnaby
Christopher Green,
McGill University
Jeffrey E. Harris,
M.I.T., Cambridge
Patrick Hess,
Ohio State University
Ignatius Horstmann,
Western Ontario University
Sharan Jagpal,
Rutgers, The State University
of New Jersey
Stephen Karlson,
Wayne State University, Detroit
Michael L. Katz,
Princeton University
John Kwoka, Jr.,
The George Washington University
Dwight R. Lee,
Virginia Polytechnic Institute
Marvin Lieberman,
Stanford University
A. J. Marcus,
Boston University
Karen McCormick,
University of Lowell
Francis M. McLaughlin,
Boston College
James W. Meehan,
Colby College
Michael Naughton,
Boston College
Philip B. Nelson,
Federal Trade Commission
Sharon Oster,
Yale University
Harold Petersen,
Boston College
Robert H. Porter,
University of Minnesota
Thomas Pugel,
New York University
Joseph F. Quinn,
Boston College
Peter C. Reiss,
Stanford University
Mark Roberts,
Pennsylvania State University
David S. Salkever,
John Hopkins University
David Sappington,
University of Pennsylvania
John R. Schroeter,
Iowa State University
R. Shaw,
University of Stirling
Wayne Simpson,
University of Manitoba
M. D. E. Slater,
St. Edmund Hall, Oxford
Robert S. Stillman,
Lexecon Inc., Chicago
Michael J. Stutzer,
Federal Reserve Bank of MN
Sheridan Titman,
University of California
William Tye,
Putnam, Hayes & Bartlett,
Cambridge

John Vernon,
Duke University, Durham
Philip A. Viton,
University of Pennsylvania
Ingo Vogelsang,
Boston University
C. W. R. Ward,
University of Lancaster
Frederick R. Warren-Boulton,
Department of Justice, Washington
M. Waterson,
University of Newcastle
Steven S. Wildman,
Economists Incorporated,
Washington

Journal of Business Finance & Accounting

Editors: Richard Briston & John Perrin

Autumn 1984 Vol. 11 No. 3

Contents

The Relationship Between Duration and Economic Depreciation: A Note *Richard P. Brief*

A Microeconomic Analysis of the Amey/Solomons Debate *R. K. Ashton*

Joint Product Decisions, The Fixed Proportions Case: A Note *Lloyd R. Amey*

Accounting Ratios to Locate Take-Over Targets *Udayan P. Rege*

LIFO-FIFO, Accounting Ratios and Market Risk: A Re-Assessment *Pieter T. Elgers and Dennis Murray*

The Effect of Presentation Form on Judgement Confidence in Performance Evaluation *Jan Bell*

Valuation and Risk-Adjusted Discount Rates *Charles W. Haley*

An Algorithm for Determining Unique Nonnegative Inernal Rates of Return *Allen M. Russell and John A. Rickard*

Timeliness of Accounting Reports and their Informational Content on the Capital Market *Daniel Zeghal*

Forecasting Corporate Revenue and Profit: Time-Series Models versus Management and Analysts *David A. Kodde and Hein Schreuder*

An Expanded Commercial Paper Rating Scale: Classification of Industrial Issuers *John W. Peavy and S. Michael Edgar*

Autocorrelation in Market Model Residuals *Ronald E. Copley, Philip L. Cooley and Rodney L. Roenfeldt*

An Economic Analysis of Value to the Owner: A Comment *F.K. Wright*

An Economic Analysis of Value to the Owner: A Reply *R.K. Ashton*

1984 subscription £31.50 in UK and £38.60 elsewhere (or US $77.50 or Can $95) to library and business subscribers, or £16.95 in UK and £20.75 elsewhere (or US $41.70 or Can $51) to individual teachers and students. Order from Journals Dept., Basil Blackwell Publishers, 108 Cowley Road, Oxford, OX4 1JF, UK. Editorial communications to JBFA/CRIBA, University of Warwick, Coventry CV4 7AL, UK. Students and teachers in the UK and members of the E.A.A. and E.F.A. may qualify for a specially reduced subscription price; details may be obtained on request from the editors.

THE JOURNAL OF INDUSTRIAL ECONOMICS

Published first in October 1952, the Journal has a very wide international circulation, and has established itself as the leading journal in the field of industrial economics. It was founded to promote the analysis of modern industry, particularly the behaviour of firms, and the functioning of markets. More specifically it seeks to bring the tools of modern economic analysis to bear on the analysis of real problems of industrial economies.

Contributions are welcomed covering all the major areas of industrial economics. One such area is the relationship between market structure and market behaviour in the areas of pricing, product differentiation, advertising and the dissemination of information and R and D. Another area focuses more directly on the firm, its objectives, finance, investment and growth. A third area comprises the background environment within which industrial firms operate: the changing structure of industry, public policy on monopoly and restrictive trade practices, regulation, fiscal and monetary policy as they affect firms, and underlying changes in productivity and international competitiveness.

The Journal has a tradition of publishing a blend of theory and evidence. Theoretical discussion is welcomed provided that the more abstract theory includes sufficient introduction and other explanation to convey the significance of the material to the general reader who wants to decide whether to follow the analysis through. Empirical analysis, and especially econometric analysis, should include an explanation of the data sources used, of the methods applied and of the underlying theoretical basis of the study. The Journal has a particular tradition of case studies of firms and industries, which the Editors would wish to continue. However contributors of such studies are asked to remember that a study will be of interest to the international readership of the Journal only if it makes a particular contribution to the methodology of such studies, or if the empirical results are exceptionally interesting.

Alongside articles of more normal length, the Editors are ready to publish shorter notes, especially where these give interim results of important research studies, or where they report significant new empirical results. Books are not reviewed, although books received will be listed, sometimes with a short note: but substantial review articles will be considered.

Information for Contributors

Submissions (*three* copies are required) should be in typescript, double-spaced, and conform to the style of the Journal. Detailed Information for Contributors is available from the General Editor. The submission should include an Abstract, not exceeding 100 words.

Typescripts from North America should be sent to the North American Editor, Journal of Industrial Economics, Graduate School of Economics and Business Administration, New York University, 100 Trinity Place, New York, NY 10006, U.S.A.

Typescripts from *all* other countries should be sent to the General Editor, Journal of Industrial Economics, Institute of Economics and Statistics, University of Oxford, St. Cross Building, Manor Road, Oxford OX1 3UL, U.K.

Information for subscribers

The journal is published four times a year, in September, December, March and June, by Basil Blackwell Publisher Ltd., 108 Cowley Road, Oxford OX4 1JF, England. Prices are as follows:

	UK	Overseas	USA	Canada
Institutions	£26.50	£33.50	$65.75	$80.50
Individuals	£16.25	£20.35	$38.00	$47.00
Single issue prices for:				
Institutions	£7.20	£8.80	$17.70	$21.50
Individuals	£5.20	£6.40	$12.00	$14.70

CONTRIBUTORS TO THIS NUMBER

RONALD R. BRAEUTIGAM: Associate Professor of Economics, Northwestern University, and Associate Editor of this Journal.

ANDREW F. DAUGHETY: Associate Professor of Management Sciences and Economics, College of Business Administration, The University of Iowa.

MARK A. TURNQUIST: Professor of Civil and Environmental Engineering, Cornell University, Ithaca, New York.

G. THOMAS SAV: Associate Professor of Economics, West Georgia College, Carrollton.

BRUNO L. DE BORGER: Research Associate, Department of Economics, University of Antwerp, UFSIA, Belgium, and C.I.M. Research Fellow, Department of Economics, University of Wisconsin, Madison.

DAVID E. MILLS: Associate Professor of Economics, University of Virginia, Charlottesville.

C. Y. BALDWIN: Associate Professor of Finance, Graduate School of Business, Harvard University, Boston.

J. J. TRIBENDIS: Formerly Research Associate, Department of Materials Science and Engineering, M.I.T., Cambridge, and currently Planning Analyst, Technology Forecasting, ALCOA, Pittsburgh.

J. P. CLARK: Associate Professor of Materials Systems, Department of Materials Science and Engineering, M.I.T., Cambridge.

ROBERT M. FEINBERG: Associate Professor of Economics, The Pennsylvania State University, University Park.

STEPHEN FARBER: Professor, Department of Economics, Louisiana State University, Baton Rouge, LA.

BERNHARD WANIK: Accountant, Peat, Marwick, Mitchell & Co., Dusseldorf, formerly Member of the Sonderforschungsbereich 21, University of Bonn.

STEVEN S. WILDMAN: Senior Economist, Economists Incorporated, Washington DC.

F. M. SCHERER: Professor of Economics, Swarthmore College, and Editor of this Journal.

ARVIND MAHAJAN: Assistant Professor, Department of Finance, Texas A & M University.

G. MEEKS: Assistant Director of Research, Faculty of Economics and Politics, University of Cambridge, and Associate Editor of this Journal.

J. G. MEEKS: Research Associate, Department of Applied Economics, University of Cambridge.

US Mailing: Second class postage paid at New York. Postmaster: Send address corrections to: Journal of Industrial Economics, c/o Expediters of the Printed Word Ltd., 515 Madison Avenue, New York, NY 10022 (US Mailing Agent).

Reprints of Back Volumes: Volumes 1–28 of the journal are available (in complete volumes only) from the Kraus Reprint Corporation, Route 100, Millwood, New York 10546, USA. More recent back issues are available from the publisher at the current single issue price.

Microfilm: An agreement for the supply of microfilm copies from Volume 1 onwards has been made with University Microfilms International, Department PR, 30–32 Mortimer Street, London W1N 7RA, England, or 300 North Zeeb Road, Ann Arbor, Michigan 48106, USA.

Set by Santype International Ltd., Salisbury, Wilts.
Printed and bound by Whitstable Litho Ltd., Whitstable, Kent.

THE JOURNAL OF INDUSTRIAL ECONOMICS

Volume XXXIII DECEMBER 1984 No. 2

PANKAJ GHEMAWAT
Capacity Expansion in the Titanium Dioxide Industry 145

DAVID M. BARTON and ROGER SHERMAN
The Price and Profit Effects of Horizontal Merger: A Case Study 165

DONALD J. LECRAW
Diversification Strategy and Performance 179

THOMAS E. GETZEN
A "Brand Name Firm" Theory of Medical Group Practice 199

M. E. BEESLEY and R. T. HAMILTON
Small Firms' Seedbed Role and the Concept of Turbulence 217

Short Articles and Notes

JOHN C. HILKE
Excess Capacity and Entry: Some Empirical Evidence 233

R. S. THOMPSON
Structure and Conduct in Local Advertising Markets: The Case of Irish Provincial Newspapers 241

BRUCE L. BENSON
On the Ability of Spatial Competitors to Price Discriminate 251

ISSN 0022-1821
BASIL BLACKWELL OXFORD ENGLAND

THE JOURNAL OF INDUSTRIAL ECONOMICS 0022-1821 $2.00
Volume XXXIII December 1984 No. 2

CAPACITY EXPANSION IN THE TITANIUM DIOXIDE INDUSTRY

PANKAJ GHEMAWAT*

RECENT attempts to apply industrial organization to the analysis and shaping of competitive strategy suggest that the approach of focussing on the static determination of prices in homogeneous industries is inadequate in explaining many competitive interactions. More fruitful is a combination of industrial organization and the industry history approach taken at business schools. In other words, micro-economic analysis has to be wedded to detailed consideration of strategic moves and countermoves, sufficiently broad coverage of firms' interactions along a number of different dimensions and recognition that firms' resource endowments can frequently be varied only in the medium to long-term—and even then, only at a cost.[1]

In this paper, I use a hybrid approach to study the capacity expansion process in capital-intensive industries. In Part I, I develop a theoretical model that leads to the conclusion that where costs differ significantly across firms, the lowest cost producer will tend to preempt the others in adding new capacity. But two factors can reverse this outcome: resource constraints, which are likely to occur during periods of very heavy investment, and uncertainty about demand. Conversely, concern about supply coordination failures and most sorts of informational asymmetries among firms are likely to favor preemption by the lowest cost producer, as is a desire to dominate the industry in order to restrict output.

The model also suggests that if the less efficient producers are financially constrained or suffer from informational asymmetries, the lowest cost producer has an incentive to price strategically by holding prices artificially low until new capacity comes on-stream and then raising them. Another prediction of the model is that licensing is unlikely to be profitable if preemption occurs. Therefore, we expect the lowest cost producer to show more interest in licensing its technology overseas than to domestic competitors.

Part II examines capacity expansion in the U.S. titanium dioxide industry in the context of these theoretical predictions. Du Pont's strategy in titanium dioxide over 1972–77 accords with the predictions from Part I but also highlights some of the risks of preemption.

* The author is indebted to Richard E. Caves, Stacy Dick, Marvin B. Lieberman, Michael E Porter, A. Michael Spence and two referees for their comments and to the Division of Research a the Harvard Graduate School of Business Administration for financial support.

[1] For a more detailed exposition, see Poeter [1980].

I. THEORY

A. *The Basic Model*

For our purposes, two types of cost differences among firms are of interest: absolute cost disparities and dynamic scale economies; the latter are familiar to economists as "learning by doing" (Arrow [1962]). Their effects can most readily be discerned in a market served by two firms. Assume that at time 0, firm 1 (the "leader") operates K_1 units of capacity and firm 2 (the "laggard") K_2 units. The plants can be operated forever at zero variable cost so that firm i's costs of producing at the rate K_i are entirely sunk.[2]

Capacity is added in increments of one unit. The cost disparity between the two firms comes into play here. We assume that as the *net* result of learning and absolute cost differences, firm 1's total costs of constructing a new plant are lower than firm 2's.[3] Symbolically,

$$C_1(K_1 + 1) < C_2(K_2 + 1). \tag{1}$$

Finally, let the market be expanding so that given total capacity, K,

$$\frac{\partial p(K, t)}{\partial t} > 0, \tag{2}$$

where p stands for the real price of the product and t denotes time.[4] In particular, assume demand is such that over the planning period (time 0 to T), only one unit of capacity will be added. With noncooperative behavior, which firm will build it?

To find the answer, recast the problem as an auction in which the firms alternate in making public "bids" about the dates at which they are willing to add capacity. The bidding continues until one firm makes a bid that its rival is unwilling to match. That bid takes effect and the firm that made it adds the new unit of capacity at the promised date. (In view of the bidding process, this outcome is the rational expectations equilibrium.)

Let firm j start the bidding. Denote the first bid as t_j^*. If firm i lets this bid stand, its total profits are

$$\int_0^{t_j^*} K_i p(K, t) e^{-rt} dt + \int_{t_j^*}^{T} K_i p(K + 1, t) e^{-rt} dt, \tag{3}$$

[2] This assumption, although somewhat unattractive, lets us avoid getting bogged down in the mechanics of price and output determination in the short run.

[3] Although it is more usual to explain learning on the basis of cumulated output, convenience dictates that the model focus on cumulated gross investment—for which there is also some empirical support. See Sheshinski [1967].

[4] Without demand growth, p would hold steady for any given level of capacity, K, because cost reductions are assumed to occur only through new investment.

where r is the discount rate. The alternative of undercutting firm j's bid by s leads to profits of

$$(4)\qquad \int_0^{t_j^*-s} K_i p(K,t)e^{-rt}dt + \int_{t_j^*-s}^{T} (K_i+1)p(K+1,t)e^{-rt}dt - C_i(K_i+1)e^{-r(t_j^*-s)}.$$

Since firm i can make s arbitrarily small, the limiting profits from undercutting are

$$(5)\qquad \int_0^{t_j^*} K_i p(K,t)e^{-rt}dt + \int_{t_j^*}^{T} (K_i+1)p(K+1,t)e^{-rt}dt - C_i(K_i+1)e^{-rt_j^*}.$$

Comparing equations (3) and (5), we can see that firm i will undercut any bid t_j by firm j as long as

$$(6)\qquad \int_{t_j}^{T} p(K+1,t)e^{-rt}dt > C_i(K_i+1)e^{-rt_j}.$$

From equation (6), the laggard, which has higher capacity costs, will be the first to stop bidding and the leader will find preemption profitable.

Three points about the model are worth noting. First, the preemption result is robust vis-à-vis the cost function assumed. It can allow for exogenous technical progress so long as the leader's capacity costs are lower than the laggard's and accommodate spillovers of learning across firms if the leakage is less than total.[5] Second, the analysis can be extended to allow for any number of firms and for demand profiles requiring the construction of more than one unit of capacity (Gilbert and Harris [1981]). Finally, non-zero variable costs can provide another rationale for preemption by the leader if they make operation below capacity profitable, since the leader augments its ability to restrict output by adding capacity itself rather than farming it out to competitors.

B. *Uncertainty*

Uncertainty varies in its impact on the preemption result depending on the form that it takes. The most obvious sort, demand uncertainty, tends to blur cost differences among firms. To demonstrate this point, I modify the basic model by letting the market price be a nondeterministic function of capacity and time; the indeterminacy, in this context, is a consequence of uncertain

[5] However, spillovers are likely to decelerate the pace of capacity expansion. See Ghemawat and Spence [1982].

demand. Then the net present value of revenue per unit of capacity from time t^* onwards, assuming that total capacity remains K, is

$$(7) \qquad \int_{t'}^{T} \tilde{p}(K, t)e^{-rt}dt,$$

with a variance of σ_t^{*2}.[6]

Replicating our earlier analysis (see equation (6)), we find that the incremental expected revenue from adding a unit of capacity at time t^* is the same for both firms and can be ignored. Assuming, as a descriptive matter, that managers care about variance rather than covariance with the market, the incremental risk-adjusted cost of a new unit to firm i is

$$(8) \qquad C_i(K_i + 1)e^{-rt^*} + \phi(K_i + 1)^2\sigma_{t^*}^2 - \phi K_i^2\sigma_{t^*}^2$$
$$= C_i(K_i + 1)e^{-rt^*} + \phi(2K_i + 1)\sigma_{t^*}^2,$$

where ϕ is the risk-aversion coefficient.

The implication is that demand uncertainty acts as the great leveller in tending to equalize firms' costs, and therefore their market shares.[7] More exactly, demand uncertainty is likely to overturn the preemption result when the laggard has much less capacity than the leader but only a slight learning-related cost disadvantage and when the risk aversion of the two firms and the variance of the revenue stream are high.

Another form of uncertainty that may rule out preemption by the leader is the legal sort. U.S. courts have never resolved whether cost-based preemption is a legitimate business practice (Beckenstein and Gabel [1981]). Since the costs of legal conflict can be high, such uncertainty should blunt the incentive for the leader to preempt.

On the other hand, some uncertainties favor the leader at the expense of the laggard. Consider a situation in which the leader, by virtue of its greater experience, has better information than the laggard about a cost or demand characteristic relevant to post-expansion profits—as may well happen when the laggard has less experience than the leader with the technology that the new plant is to use, or is highly diversified and thus faces considerable costs in gathering information about a particular market.[8] In both cases, the leader's ability to preempt is likely to be enhanced.

Another impetus to the leader to preempt relates to what Smith [1981] has called supply coordination failure. Smaller firms are likely to have less accurate forecasts about each other's expansion plans than about the leader's since the latter is the obvious candidate for adding capacity. Consequently, if the leader fails to exercise its dominance and abandons the field to smaller rivals,

[6] To simplify the argument, let this variance be independent of K.

[7] This result is far from new. Chandler [1980] reports that such considerations had begun to influence Du Pont's strategy as early as 1903.

[8] The latter sort of situation seems quite frequent given the prevalence of portfolio planning in large companies. See Haspeslagh [1982].

the probability of miscalculations in capacity expansion will increase. In the form of overcapacity, these can hurt each firm's profitability.

C. *Resource Constraints*

Students of business policy have long recognized that a firm's strategy is constrained by the resources available to it. Such constraints can make a multiplicity of forms: organizational, managerial, financial. Although I shall focus on the effects of limited financial resources, the conclusions concerning the pattern and pace of capacity expansion (although not those about margins) can easily be shown also to hold in the presence of organizational and managerial limitations as well.

To elucidate the effect of imperfect financial markets, I modify the basic model in several ways. First, I assume that capacity expansion has to be entirely self-financed.[9] Second, the leader is now allowed to choose a non-negative level of variable costs, a, that the laggard must match to stay competitive.[10] Finally, convenience dictates the restriction that a be small enough in relation to marginal revenue for the two firms to keep operating at capacity.

Now, the earliest date, $t_{i'}$, at which firm i has the capital to build a new plant is given by

$$(9) \qquad I_i + \int_0^{t_i} K_i(p(K, t) - a)e^{-rt}dt = C_i(K_i + 1)e^{-rt_i'},$$

where I_i is its initial resource endowment. Replicating our earlier analysis (and remembering that a will always be set to zero after expansion), the earliest date at which firm i would be willing to build, t_i, is given by

$$(10) \qquad \int_{t_i}^{T} p(K + 1, t)e^{-rt}dt = C_i(K_i + 1)e^{-rt_i}.$$

Then with financial constraints, firm i's earliest bid will be

$$(11) \qquad t_i'' = \max(t_i, t_i').$$

The new unit will be added by the firm with the lowest t_i''.

[9] A similar analysis holds in the presence of debt as long as there is an upper bound on leveraging.

[10] This somewhat artificial device, introduced as an analytically convenient way of letting the leader strategically set margins, calls for some elucidation. First, a is an expense incurred at the leader's discretion. Second, it plays no role in expanding demand for the product; instead its role is purely rivalrous in requiring matching commitments (per unit sold) by each firm if it is to sell its output. (Competitive advertising that would cause buyers to shift from one seller to another without increasing aggregate demand is one possible example.) Third, a could be assumed to be subject to learning by doing. This complicates the notation but does not reduce the incentive to preempt. Fourth, after the capacity expansion has been completed, the leader will always set a to zero, i.e., minimize costs. It is only prior to the expansion that the leader *might* choose to set a greater than zero in order to affect other firms' ability to expand.

Several points emerge from this way of setting up the problem. First, financial constraints may retard capacity expansion, but they never accelerate it. Second, the leader will not always be able to preempt. For instance, during periods of rapid demand growth or technological obsolescence, the magnitude of capacity expansion required makes it likely that the laggard will be able to add at least some of the capacity that needs to be brought on-stream. Third, although we cannot, at this level of generality, derive sufficient conditions for the leader to choose, prior to expansion, to set a greater than zero, it is likely that this would require inelastic demand (which gives the leader an incentive to delay construction) and capacity costs that are large compared to the laggard's initial resource endowment and earning streams (which make it likely that the laggard is financially constrained).[11]

If, as mentioned in the last section, the laggard has much less information about the industry than the leader, the latter will have yet another reason to manipulate margins. In some circumstances, the leader will then find it worthwhile to invest in sending costly signals (i.e., setting a at a positive level) to make the laggard unwarrantedly pessimistic about the expansion that it would otherwise like to undertake.[12]

Finally, when a is set greater than zero, perverse changes in the margins may be observed at the date at which the new capacity goes on-stream. At that instant, the margin changes from

$$p(K, t) - a \tag{12}$$

to

$$p(K + 1, t). \tag{13}$$

Hence margins may actually increase as quantity supplied goes up.

D. *Licensing*

When a market is structurally disposed to preemption by the leader, licensing will not occur.[13] To see this, recall that the revenue term that the leader and the laggard factor into their construction decision is the same. With licensing in the form of equalization of efficiency, the costs of adding capacity are also equal. The licensor (firm 1—the leader) and licensee (firm 2—the laggard) are then equally matched and will compete the incremental profits from a new plant down to zero. So the maximal royalty that firm 2 can afford to pay firm

[11] In the context of capital market imperfections, the Kuhn-Tucker conditions can be used to show that for a to be set greater than zero, it is necessary that firm 2 be financially constrained.

[12] Although it seems counterintuitive to think that strategic pricing (setting a greater than zero) can succeed in deterring expansion by laggards who know that the leader is contemplating such strategic behavior, rigorous analysis of competitive interactions as games of incomplete information shows that such deterrence *can* work (Milgrom and Roberts [1980]).

[13] Market failures in the arm's-length transfer of knowledge reinforce this conclusion.

1 is zero. As a result, with licensing, firm 1's incremental profits, gross of revenue losses on existing plants but net of royalties received, are also zero. This is clearly dominated by the no-licensing equilibrium at which the corresponding profit term for firm 1 is positive. Therefore, firm 1 will forego licensing and add the new plant itself.[14]

However, uncertainty and financial constraints can, as we have seen, invalidate the predicted preemption result. In this case, licensing may be to the leader's advantage.

These considerations lead us to predict that less licensing will occur among firms in the same country than across national boundaries, since the latter situation typically involves greater uncertainty and resource constraints.[15]

II. EMPIRICAL EVIDENCE[16]

Titanium dioxide is a commodity chemical used in paints, paper and plastics. The analysis here treats the United States as the relevant geographic market; international linkages seem inconsequential because imports from Europe would face cost disadvantages amounting to 12–20% of the U.S. selling price [CX 209] while the U.S. market itself is unified by compelling scale economies and relatively low transport costs.[17]

The first three parts of this section of the paper provide background material on the events that, in 1972, conferred a substantial cost advantage on Du Pont over other U.S. titanium dioxide producers. The next three parts trace the implications for Du Pont's titanium dioxide strategy over the 5 succeeding years.

A. *Technology*

There are two ways to manufacture titanium dioxide: batch process sulfate technology which uses ilmenite feedstock, and continuous process chloride technology, which can be adapted to handle either ilmenite or rutile.[18] The second process exhibits much stronger static scale economies than the first; engineering average cost estimates given by equations (1) and (2) in Table IA

[14] For a more detailed discussion, see Ghemawat [1982].

[15] Available empirical evidence (Caves [1981]) supports this hypothesis.

[16] This analysis draws on publicly available data from FTC Docket No. 9108. The abbreviations used to refer to sources are:

CX Complaint Counsel's Exhibit
RX Respondent's Exhibit
AB Complaint Counsel's Appeal Brief

Other discussions of the industry can be found in Gilbert [1978], Shephard [1979], [1980a] [1980b] and "E. I. du Pont de Nemours & Co.—Titanium Dioxide" [1981]. The footnotes will indicate that Gilbert's is the only account of which I have made some use.

[17] Transport costs amounted to only 1.3% of product value over 350 mile hauls (CX 21)— a modest figure compared to Scherer *et al.*'s [1975] calculations for 12 other products. Scale economies are the focus of the next section.

[18] Ilmenite ore contains less titanium dioxide than rutile ore and therefore requires more complex processing.

TABLE IA
STATIC AND DYNAMIC SCALE ECONOMIES

Equation	(1) *Sulfate plants*	(2) *Chloride plants*	(3) *All Du Pont plants*	(4) *New Johnsonville*
Time Period	—	—	*1955–70*	*1959–70*
Dependent Variable	*LSULFA*	*LCHLOR*	*LDPCOS*	*LJVCOS*
Independent Variables				
Constant	5.609[a]	5.837[a]	6.499[a]	5.277[a]
	(0.033)	(0.056)	(0.372)	(1.826)
LEXP			−0.329[a]	−0.287[b]
			(0.068)	(0.162)
LCAP	−0.110[a]	−0.223[a]	−0.243	0.095
	(0.008)	(0.013)	(0.206)	(0.396)
LCU			−0.304[b]	−0.408[b]
			(0.084)	(0.266)
R^2	0.93	0.93	0.95	0.96
F	210	302	82	65
D-W	—	—	1.50	2.37
D.F.	16	23	12	8

Note: Standard errors are given in parentheses. Levels of statistical significance (one-tailed test) are a = 1 per cent, b = 10 per cent.

TABLE IB
VARIABLE DEFINITIONS AND SOURCES

Variable	*Definition*	*Sources*
LSULFA	Logarithm of deflated average manufacturing costs for the sulfate process at capacity operation.	CX 38I
LCHLOR	Logarithm of deflated average manufacturing costs for the chloride process at capacity operation.	CX 40Z
LDPCOS	Logarithm of Du Pont's average cost of sales (current figures deflated by the wholesale price index).	CX 109Z14
LJVCOS	Logarithm of average labor costs at Du Pont's new Johnsonville plant (current figures deflated by the wholesale price index).	CX 109Z12
LEXP	Logarithm of cumulated titanium dioxide tonnage at all Du Pont plants (regression 3) and at New Johnsonville (regression 4).	Ghemawat [1982]
LCAP	Logarithm of capacity at the relevant plant (regresions 1, 2, and 4) and of weighted average capacity at all Du Pont plants (regression 3).	Ghemawat [1982]
LCU	Logarithm of capacity utilization at all Du Pont plants (regression 3) and at New Johnsonville (regression 4).	Ghemawat [1982]

indicate that each doubling of plant size cuts manufacturing costs for the sulfate process by 7.5% and for the chloride process by 14.3%.[19]

Industry sources also indicate that learning effects are present. Du Pont's calculations, based on data from 1950–70, indicate a learning rate (i.e., elasticity of average costs with respect to cumulated output) of 0.322, or a slope of 80% [CX 109Z14]. My estimates, based on the 1955–70 period because of reports of disequilibrium until the mid-1950s, are presented in equation (3). The learning rate turns out to be 0.329, which is very close to the Du Pont figure. The aggregate static scale economy coefficient of 0.243—corresponding to a slope of 84.5%—meshes well with the estimate in equation (2) (as it should, because all of Du Pont's expansion over this period was chloride-based) but is not statistically significant. Finally, for given levels of experience and capacity, greater capacity use lowers costs.

To alleviate anxiety about the level of aggregation used in equation (3), I also calculated a learning rate for labor costs at Du Pont's New Johnsonville plant. The coefficient of 0.287 in equation (4) corresponds to a slope at 82.0% and indicates, I think, the adequacy of an 80–85% learning curve as a ballpark figure.[20]

The absolute cost positions of titanium dioxide plants depend not just on scale economies but also on such process-related factors as investment required per ton of capacity and the costs of ingredients and waste disposal. Table II presents some rough pre-1970 estimates for 50,000 ton per year

TABLE II
COSTS IN 1972 CENTS/LB.

	Chloride-Ilmenite	*Chloride-Rutile*	*Sulfate*
Ore	2.5	3.5	2.5
Other ingredients	3.9	2.9	3.7
Energy	1.5	1.5	2.9
Labor	1.9	2.9	3.7
Miscellaneous	4.6	4.6	4.1
Capital	3.0	2.5	4.0
Waste disposal	0.2	0.1	0.3
	17.6	18.0	21.2

Sources: [CX 23], [CX 28] and various other documents.

[19] Two points should be made here. First, Du Pont had operating experience with both processes over a wide range of scales so that these particular engineering cost estimates are probably more reliable than most. Second, although the regressions present estimates of the elasticity of cost with respect to output, it aids the intuition to talk in terms of the slope, which is defined by

$$S \equiv 2^{-m}$$

where S is the slope and m the elasticity. The figures cited above in the text are equal to $1 - S$.

[20] A referee also voiced misgivings that equations (3) and (4) might be misspecified. In testing for first order autocorrelation, the Durbin-Watson statistic tended to fall into the inconclusive region (which tends to be large for small sample sizes). This leaves open the possibility that cost reductions were based on exogenous technical progress—although sustained interfirm differences in production efficiency then become quite difficult to explain.

plants operating at capacity and drawing on similar pools of learning but using different technologies.[21] The data indicate that at that scale and date, the rutile and ilmenite chloride processes were at rough cost parity but enjoyed a 15–17% cost advantage over the sulfate process.

B. *Industry History*

National Lead began production of titanium dioxide in the United States in 1918. Du Pont entered the industry through acquisition in 1931. By 1955, American Cyanamid and Glidden (to be acquired later by SCM) had joined their ranks.

Until the mid-1960s, all firms with the exception of Du Pont used the sulfate process. While expanding its sulfate units in the 1930s, Du Pont had become aware of problems with the process [AB, p. 6] and in 1941 it began work on a manufacturing process using chloride technology. (The decision to chlorinate ilmenite rather than rutile was made simply because little rutile was available at the time whereas Du Pont had captive stocks of high-quality ilmenite [CX 16].) A process of learning by doing at progressively larger scales culminated in the successful operation of the 35,000 ton chloride unit at Edge Moor in 1951. This was followed by the 1958 start-up of a plant at New Johnsonville, Tennessee, that had an initial capacity of 45,000 tons but was expanded to 100,000 tons by the end of the 1960s.

The low costs and superior product of the New Johnsonville plant inspired the other producers (who now included New Jersey Zinc, subsequently to be acquired by Gulf & Western) to undertake their own experiments with chloride technology. These differed from Du Pont's early essays in one important respect. By the late 1950s, rutile ore had been discovered in large quantities in Australia. The ore's low price combined with the lower investment costs of the rutile process and its relative simplicity and cleanliness to make rutile the economically preferred route for any plant built between 1961 and 1969 [RX 20A]. Thus all firms, including Du Pont, based their new units in the 1960s on the rutile chloride technology. That Du Pont entered the 1970s with a substantial amount of ilmenite chloride capacity was simply an historical accident.

C. *Disequilibrium*

1970 and 1971 saw a jump in ore prices and the introduction of new pollution control legislation that sharply increased waste disposal costs. These developments undercut the positions of the rutile chloride and sulfate producers respectively (Table III).[22] As the only producer using ilmenite chloride tech-

[21] I have tried to eliminate accounting distortions.

[22] Table III understates the cost advantage of the ilmenite chloride process for several reasons, including the fact that over 1972–76, Du Pont incurred heavy start-up expenditures that were expensed unduly rapidly [CX 680, P].

Table III
Relative Mill Costs

	1972	*1973*	*1974*	*1975*	*1976*
Ilmenite Chloride vs. Rutile	0.69	0.74	0.69	0.88	0.81
Ilmenite Chloride vs. Sulfate	0.70	0.67	0.69	0.88	0.80

Sources: [CX 182T, U].

nology (which accounted for 70% of its total capacity in 1972), Du Pont profited from these events. Combined with its greater average scale per plant and learning, they gave it total costs 21–23% lower than its competitors'.

Du Pont reacted in the way section I predicted. In a May 1972 report to Du Pont's Executive Committee that was based on analysis of competitors, the head of the Pigments Department observed that Du Pont was "in a unique position to increase its share of the market by a substantial amount. Sulfate producers, with the exception of NL Industries (National Lead) will be unable to cope with waste disposal problems and will shut down. (Rutile) chloride process operators probably will continue operations but it is difficult to see how they can cope with waste disposal and generate sufficient funds for major expansion" [CX 26C].

Du Pont's internal discussions indicate that the growth strategy, as the programme for preemption was called, was decided upon for the reasons discussed in section I.A.: Du Pont was the lowest cost producer and it thought that margins would be higher in the long run if it preempted and then exercised its market power to restrict output.

Du Pont did not perceive the uncertainties that might work against preemption as being very significant. Demand had grown steadily since 1955 so that major fluctuations were not expected [CX 182L]. And the shutdown of three of the competitors' sulfate units did appear inevitable; the 1972 ROI on each was under 1% and the parents seemed to lack either the debt capacity or the inclination to make the heavy anti-pollution investments necessary for continued operation [CX 23, 28, 246].

In contrast, uncertainties that encouraged preemption were very much in evidence. Du Pont thought that the dominant share resulting from preemption would reduce the long-term risk of supply coordination failures—of no small importance in an industry where efficient scale was very high (at least 12% of 1972 U.S. demand) and 35% of total costs were fixed even at capacity operation [CX 2Z23, 114].

At a more immediate level, the technology that competitors would have had to use to expand (rutile chloride) was more sensitive to ore prices than Du Pont's ilmenite technology; in 1972, ore accounted for 30% of total cost for the former but only 18% for the latter [CX 23]. So the uncertainty attending ore prices cast less of a burden on Du Pont than on other firms.[23] In fact, there

[23] I owe this observation to Gilbert [1978].

is evidence that over 1972–74, competitors postponed expansions and tried to resolve the uncertainty about ore prices by developing artificial rutile with costs similar to those of natural rutile [CX 16B].

Financial constraints also seemed to weigh more heavily on its competitors than on Du Pont. The sulfate plants required especially large investments—approximately $60 per ton of capacity at 1972 prices—to meet the new pollution controls [CX 51]. Since the sulfate process accounted for a smaller fraction of total capacity for Du Pont than for any other producer except Kerr-McGee (Table IV), its major competitors suffered more from lack of capital for expansion.

TABLE IV
1972 CAPACITIES

Firm	*Total Capacity* (*Kilotons*)	*Sulfate Process* (%)
Du Pont	265	21
National Lead	180	100
American Cyanamid	110	64
SCM	75	67
Gulf & Western	65	62
Kerr-McGee	45	0

Source: [CX 23, 26].

For all these reasons, the perceived profitability of the growth (i.e., preemption) strategy was high [CX 29K, O]. The following sections describe its original objectives and implementation over 1972–77.

D. *Investment Policy*

The growth strategy originally called for total preemption. In 1972, Du Pont estimated that by the end of the 13-year planning period, demand for titanium dioxide would have risen by 377,000 tons. It also assumed that apart from National Lead, all competitors would have closed their sulfate units by then, eliminating 160,000 tons of existing capacity. These developments were expected to create room for 537,000 tons of new capacity, of which Du Pont intended to add 94%. The target market share for 1985 was 65% [CX 26].

Du Pont paid little attention to adverse uncertainties in devising this plan. Since the revised investment program called for a tenfold increase in investment over 1972–79 compared to the earlier business plan [CX 259X], rather more attention was focused on possible capital constraints. Simulations indicated that the largest (undiscounted) cumulative cash flow shortfall of the titanium dioxide business would occur in 1978 as the second line of a new plant went on-stream, and would amount to roughly $55 million [CX 322]. This seemed a small enough part of the $410 million budgeted investment expenditure for Du Pont to feel that financing it would present no special problem [CX 23, 259].

But there was one practical barrier to total preemption, and that related to physical constraints on the rate of investment. For a plant with an annual capacity of 150,000 tons, there is a lag of at least four years between the decision to construct and the date on which the plant can be started up [CX 40I,178F]. Existing plants can be expanded more quickly. Therefore in 1972, Du Pont decided to expand in two phases. Until 1975, incremental capacity was to be obtained by expanding ("reaming out") existing facilities to their practicable limits. Construction work on a large new plant was projected to begin in 1975.

These plans first began to go awry when shortages of titanium dioxide developed in 1973–74 and looked set to persist until 1977. In response, Kerr-McGee announced in mid-1974 that it would build a 50,000 ton plant at Mobile [CX 178L]. Du Pont could do little to thwart this move since it was in no position to increase the amount of capacity that it planned to add over the next four years. However, to dissuade other firms from emulating Kerr-McGee, it issued a press release that referred to the magnitude of the expansions at existing Du Pont plants and announced (falsely) that it had decided to begin construction of the 130,000 ton first line of a new plant at DeLisle, Mississippi [CX 54A, 159F].

Because of the economic downturn and unexpectedly high price sensitivity, the demand-supply imbalance for titanium dioxide began to reverse itself in 1974.[24] By early 1975, a number of factors dictated revision of the capacity plans that Du Pont had made in 1972. First, demand was expected to lag the 1972 forecasts at least through 1980 [CX 178C]. Second, the uncertainty now perceived to surround demand projections made attempts at total preemption seem very risky [CX 182D]. Third, unexpected leniency in the enforcement of pollution controls had let competitors' sulfate units continue to operate [CX 182E]. Fourth, low capacity utilization and sharp increases in chlorine and construction costs led planners to realize that the cash flow from the titanium dioxide business over 1975–78 would be at least $100 million below 1974 predictions [CX 54K, 75S, 254]. Since there was a corporate shortage of capital ("E.I. du Pont de Nemours & Co.—Titanium Dioxide" [1981]), financial constraints were beginning to pinch.

Consequently, a number of major decisions were taken in February 1975. The second line at DeLisle and a 110,000 ton plant in Europe were postponed indefinitely, and expansions of existing plants that were to have been completed by 1975 were staggered until 1977 [CX 26, 172, 178E, F].

The major strategic question that Du Pont continued to wrestle with concerned the timing of the 130,000 ton first line at DeLisle. Because of reduced

[24] Du Pont estimated that the price elasticity of demand for titanium dioxide lay between −0.22 and −0.44 [CX 99]. My simultaneous equations model of supply and demand over 1955–70 suggests a price elasticity of −1.399. Details will be provided on request.

demand projections and capital constraints, start-up in 1977 was no longer attractive. Key managers of the Pigments Department spent five months in 1975 simulating the effects of the three scenarios listed in Table V. They knew that delaying DeLisle would reduce the cash outflow over the critical 1975–78 period but would also let competitors raise prices. Using estimates of these short-term price rises, competitors' costs, and the rates of return that their respective parents were known to demand on new investment projects, Du Pont calculated the amount of capacity that competitors were likely to add. Feeding the effects of these expansions back into the long-run prices (see Table V), it found that start-up in the third quarter of 1978 would be the most profitable choice *if* demand recovered as expected.

TABLE V
THE IMPLICATIONS OF DIFFERENT DELISLE START-UPS

Strategy	*Start-up Date*	*Du Pont's 1985 Share*	*Others' Expansions: 1975–81*	*Du Pont Discounted Cash Flow: 1975–84**
Maintain	Postponed	43%	160,000 tons	$14 million
Growth: A	1979 Q3	<55%	110,000 tons	$53 million
Growth: B	1978 Q4	55%	50,000 tons	$73 million

* The cash flow is discounted at the rate of 10%. Higher discount rates do not affect the rankings of the three strategies.
Sources: [CX 755, 109F, 111B, 213B, C, D].

However, demand continued to trail forecasts. By October 1977, it was clear that Kerr-McGee had deferred its expansion plans indefinitely, so that no major competitive expansion would occur before 1982 [CX 178]. The need for capacity expansion no longer dictated the immediate start-up of DeLisle. But numerous factors—prior commitment of 77% of the project cost and apprehensions about cost escalation, the ability to renew environmental permits and future credibility [CX 188T, 1969]—ensured that further delay was not advantageous so the DeLisle plant was started up in 1979.

E. *Pricing Policy*

In 1972, Du Pont had decided "to maintain prices at a point to provide cash for Du Pont expansion but limit competition's ability to expand" [CX 76D]. The price in the first half of 1972, 26 cents/lb., seemed satisfactory on both counts. Escalated to cover inflation, it appeared adequate to let the Pigments Department self-finance all but $55 million of $410 million of investment budgeted for 1972–79 [CX 26I, 290]. By contrast, Table VI shows that the higher cost competitors would be unable to pay for an efficient 50,000–100,000 ton chloride unit (at an investment cost of at least $1,000 per ton of capacity) out of their titanium dioxide operations [CX 98, 175E]. Because of this and lack of favorable operating experience with the chloride process, immediate expansion by National Lead and Gulf & Western seemed unlikely. American Cyanamid had the requisite debt capacity, but given the low ROI on its existing titanium dioxide operations, apparently did not wish to commit more resources to that industry [CX 246H]. Du Pont considered Kerr-McGee and SCM (in that order) the competitors most likely to expand [CX 213B].

TABLE VI
1972 RETURNS AT ALTERNATIVE PRICES

	26¢/lb.		*28¢/lb.*		
	Net Income ($ million)	*ROI %*	*Net Income ($ million)*	*ROI %*	*Debt Capacity*
Du Pont	17.9	13	23.2	16	Ample
National Lead	4.4	4	8.0	8	Marginal
American Cyanamid	1.6	2	3.8	5	Ample
SCM	0.6	1	2.1	4	Marginal
Kerr-McGee	1.3	4	2.2	7	Ample
Gulf & Western	0.0	0	0.8	3	Marginal

Sources: [CX 23, 28E, 246A, D, C].

Kerr-McGee moved first by initiating a 2 cents/lb. price increase in July 1972. Despite the prospect of a $10 million annualized increase in operating earnings, Du Pont refused to acquiesce because both Kerr-McGee and SCM had told major customers (who had promptly relayed the message to Du Pont) that the price increase was needed to justify their expansion plans [CX 28A]. This refusal did not immediately force competitors to back down; in 1972 Du Pont's excess capacity amounted to only 3% of total industry demand so that it lacked the leverage to force a price cut.[25] As a result, an unusual two-tier price structure prevailed in the industry for nearly a year.

In 1973 and (especially) 1974, widespread shortages and rapid increases in costs led to a steep climb in price (Table VII). Since it was operating at capacity, Du Pont had to accept these increases even though they led Kerr-McGee to announce plans to build a 50,000 ton plant.

TABLE VII
DU PONT'S TITANIUM DIOXIDE COST AND PRICE INDICES

	1972	*1973*	*1974*	*1975*	*1976*	*1977*
Ingredient, Fuel and Waste Disposal Costs	100	116	169	209	197	208
Price	100	108	140	163	178	184

Source: [CX 182P].

[25] Gilbert [1978] also makes this point.

The weakening of demand in early 1975 initially led Du Pont to adopt a tougher stance. In January, it used its excess capacity (which now accounted for 12% of industry demand) to force Kerr-McGee to roll back a 5 cents/lb. increase that it feared would encourage other competitors, especially SCM, to expand [CX 178O].

But as the full impact of the recession became clear, Du Pont realized, as we saw in the section on investment policy, that preemption was a risky and perhaps unattractive strategy. Accordingly, it analyzed the effects on price of the three capacity strategies listed in Table V. The results are depicted in Figure 1.

Consider first the implications of the maintain strategy. In phase A, the announcement that DeLisle was being abandoned was expected to let com-

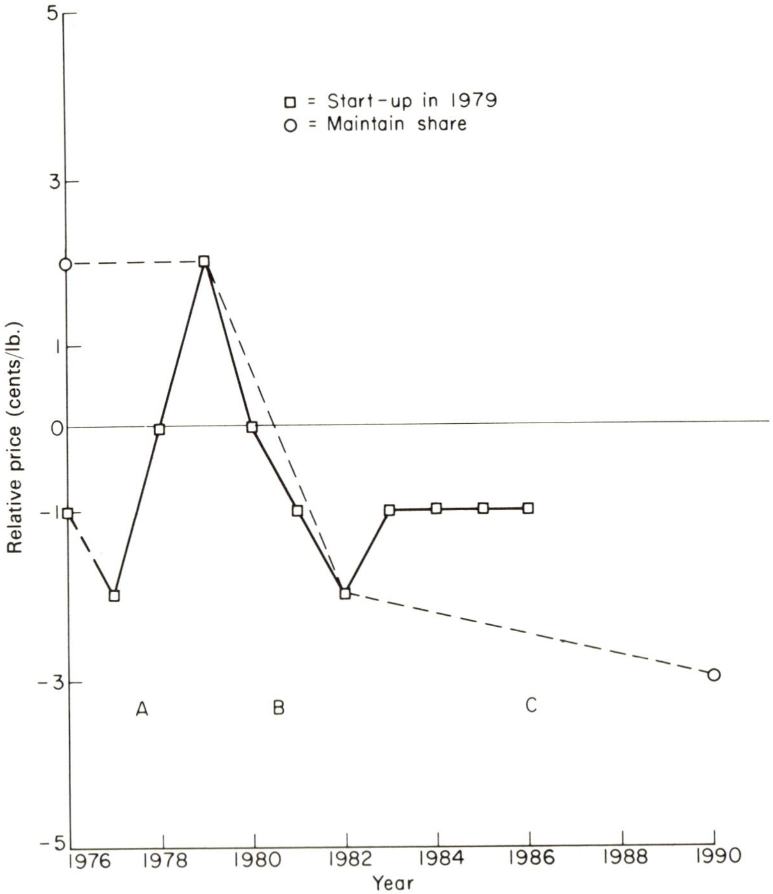

FIGURE 1

Price relative to the base case of start-up in the third quarter of 1978 petitors take advantage of tight supply to raise the price by 2 cents/lb. In phase B, temporary oversupply would erode prices until in 1982 they stood at 2 cents/lb. lower than in the base case. In phase C, competitors would descend their 80% chloride learning curve with the result that in 1990, their costs would be 4–5% lower than in the base case. This cost reduction was expected to translate into a price differential of −3 cents/lb. [CX 109Z14].

Second, examine the perceived effects of delaying the DeLisle start-up to 1979. In phase A, Du Pont would initially have to hold prices low in order to "protect" the market for DeLisle, but prices would climb in 1979 as Du Pont began operating at capacity and lost control. In phase B, competitors would scramble to fill their new capacity, leading to drops in price. Finally, in phase C, the industry would return to equilibrium but competitors would have reduced their costs by learning so that the industry price would be 1 cent/lb. lower than in the base case [CX 213C].

These price projections were, as we noted above, used to calculate the discounted cash flow from the three strategies over 1975–84. Thus they were instrumental in the end-1975 decision to bring DeLisle onstream in 1978 if demand recovered—which it did not [CX 178R].

F. *Licensing Policy*

Beginning in 1972, Du Pont received a "large number" of enquiries about licensing, particularly from National Lead [CX 33C]. But Du Pont seemed to be aware of the implications of licensing for the pattern of capacity expansion in the industry (section I.D.) and rejected domestic requests without even calculating the royalties that might be generated.

As predicted, overseas licensing presented a different picture. No requests for licenses from European producers were entertained, presumably because of Du Pont's interest in competing directly in the West European titanium dioxide market. But Du Pont carefully explored license applications from countries outside its zone of interest—Brazil, China, Japan, and the U.S.S.R. The Japanese proposal advanced to the negotiating stage but was shelved in autumn 1977 because of weak demand [CX 180E].

The remedy proposed by the FTC in the antitrust case that it brought against Du Pont in 1978 also agrees with our analysis. The FTC's appeal brief [p. 65] notes that:

> Royalty-free licensing would "break the chain" of this preemptive process by immediately placing competitors in a position of cost parity with Du Pont. . . . Licensing with royalty fees would not be nearly as effective in upsetting the Du Pont "growth strategy", since the effect of requiring royalty payments would be to maintain the Du Pont cost advantage over time. Competitors would continue to be at a cost disadvantage by the amount of royalty payment.

III. CONCLUSION

Du Pont's formulation of its growth strategy agrees well with our discussion of preemption driven by cost asymmetries. The results are of general interest because the same process appears to drive capacity expansion in many other industries. For instance, petrochemical producers in oil-rich countries enjoy significant cost advantages based on cheap feedstock and subsidized access to capital.[26] They are expected to use their lower costs to increase their share of installed global capacity.

Also thought-provoking, though, are the results of Du Pont's strategy. They suggest that preemption is a hazardous process in which miscalculations can depress profitability—for the entire industry—for years to come. The moral is perhaps "caveat preemptor".

Pankaj Ghemawat,
Harvard University,
Graduate School of Business Administration,
Soldiers Field, Boston, MA, 02163.

ACCEPTED NOVEMBER 1983

REFERENCES

ARROW, K. J., 1962, "The Economic Implications of Learning by Doing", *Review of Economic Studies*, XXIX (June), pp. 155–73.

BECKENSTEIN, A. R. and GABEL, H. L., 1981, "Experience Curve Pricing and the Antitrust Laws", University of Virginia.

CAVES, R. E., 1981, "Multinational Enterprises and Technology Transfer", Harvard University.

CHANDLER, A. D., JR., 1980, *The Visible Hand: The Managerial Revolution in American Business* (Cambridge, MA.: Belknap Press).

"E. I. DU PONT DE NEMOURS & CO.—Titanium Dioxide", 1981, Harvard Case Services.

"Federal Trade Commission vs. E. I. Du Pont de Nemours Company", FTC Docket No. 9108, Washington, D.C.

GHEMAWAT, P., 1982, "The Experience Curve and Corporate Strategy", Ph.D. dissertation, Harvard University.

——— and SPENCE, A. M., 1982, "Learning Curve Spillovers, Shared Experience and Market Performance", Harvard University.

GILBERT, R. J., 1978, "Pre-emptive Competition in the Titanium Dioxide Industry", University of California at Berkeley.

——— and HARRIS, R. G., 1981, "Investment Decisions with Economies of Scale and Learning", *American Economic Review*, LXXI (May), pp. 172–77.

HASPESLAGH, P., 1982, "Portfolio Planning: Uses and Limits", *Harvard Business Review*, 60 (January–February), pp. 58–73.

MILGROM, P. and ROBERTS, J. 1980, "Limit Pricing and Entry Under Incomplete Information: An Equilibrium Analysis", Northwestern University.

PORTER, M. E., 1980, "Strategic Interaction: Some Lessons from Industry Histories for Theory and Antitrust Policy", Harvard University.

[26] For a useful but dated discussion, see Turner and Bedore [1977].

SCHERER, F. M., *et al.*, 1975, *The Economics of Multi-Plant Operation: An International Comparisons Study*, Cambridge, MA: Harvard University Press.

SHEPHERD, W. G., 1979, "Anatomy of a Monopoly (1): Excess Capacity and the Control of Price", *Antitrust Law and Economics Review*, XI, Number 4, pp. 103–16.

———, 1980a, "Anatomy of a Monopoly (II): The Power to Control Prices", *Antitrust Law and Economics Review*, XII, Number 1, pp. 73–92.

———, 1980b, "Anatomy of a Monopoly (III): Costs, Prices, and Innovation", *Antitrust Law and Economics Review*, XII, Number 2, pp. 93–106.

SHESHINSKI, E., 1967, "Tests of the 'Learning by Doing' Hypothesis", *Review of Economics and Statistics*, XLIX (November), pp. 568–78.

SMITH, R. L., II, 1981, "Efficiency Gains from Strategic Investment", *Journal of Industrial Economics*, XXX (September), p. 1–23.

TURNER, L. and BEDORE, J. 1977, "Saudi and Iranian Petrochemicals and Refining: Trade Warfare in the 1980s?", *International Affairs*, LIII (October), pp. 572–86.

THE JOURNAL OF INDUSTRIAL ECONOMICS 0022-1821 $2.00
Volume XXXIII December 1984 No. 2

THE PRICE AND PROFIT EFFECTS OF HORIZONTAL MERGER: A CASE STUDY

DAVID M. BARTON and ROGER SHERMAN*

I. INTRODUCTION

THE economic rationale behind antitrust concern for horizontal mergers rests primarily on the familiar structure-performance paradigm that links market concentration with supra-competitive profits and, implicitly, with higher prices. A vast empirical literature has demonstrated a positive statistical relationship between measures of industry structure, such as entry barriers and concentration, and average industry profit using cross section data. A small number of cross section studies, most dealing with banking services, have claimed to find a positive relationship between concentrated market structure and price measures (Aspinwall [1970], Bell and Murphy [1969], Heggestak and Mingo [1976], Hester [1979], Lamm [1981], Landon [1971], Marion *et al.* [1979] and Marvel [1978]), but we are unaware of any study that traces the effect of an actual *change* in market structure on prices or profits. In this paper we exploit an unusual opportunity to test for price effects and estimate profit consequences of two acquisitions that resulted in substantial increases in the market share of the acquiring firm.

The evidence we examine arises from a recent Federal Trade Commission antitrust suit against Xidex corporation, the world's largest producer of duplicating microfilm. The Xidex case is unusual in three respects. (1) Although the size of the market is small (sales under $100 million), the acquisitions involved greater changes in market shares than are usual in antitrust actions. (2) The suit was brought five years after the first acquisition and two years after the second; so a post-acquisition record of price behavior exists for this example. Furthermore, the price data used in this study are actual transaction prices. (3) Special characteristics of the products allow a relatively straightforward test for price effects of the acquisitions.

The next section provides background information concerning the firms and products involved. Following that, we describe the data and methodology used to estimate the price effects of the acquisitions, and present results which indicate significant price increases traceable to the acquisitions. We then offer estimates of the incremental profits attributable to those price increases. A final section provides a summary.

* The analysis and conclusions set forth in this study are those of the authors and do not necessarily reflect the views of Federal Trade Commission Staff or the Commission itself. All data and other information used in the study are in the public domain This includes information obtained by the Commission which has become part of the public record. For helpful comments we thank Allan Fisher, Ron Lafferty, Paul Pautler and Rich Sciacca of the Bureau of Economics, Federal Trade Commission.

II. BACKGROUND

The Federal Trade Commission brought an antitrust suit against Xidex Corporation in 1981 for its earlier acquision of two competitors. The acquisitions, in 1976 and 1979, had eliminated a major rival of Xidex in each of its two main product lines, two types of "non-silver" duplicating microfilm known as "diazo" and "vesicular". These two types of microfilm employ photo-imaging processes that can only be used for making duplicate copies from "silver" (halide) originals.[1] They have a significant cost advantage compared to the alternative of using silver duplicating film (an advantage estimated at one-fourth to one-half the cost of using silver film) and are much simpler to handle and process.[2] Diazo and vesicular are used to make about 95% of all duplicate microfilm copies and an even larger percentage of microfilm copies of active business files.[3] Diazo and vesicular are closely competing alternatives for making duplicate copies, but not perfect substitutes.[4]

In 1976 Xidex acquired the diazo business of Scott Graphics, Inc., increasing its U.S. market share in diazo microfilm from 40% to 55%. In 1979 it acquired the assets of Kalvar Corporation, increasing its U.S. market share in vesicular microfilm from 67% to 93%. Combining the two products, the 1976 acquisition increased Xidex's share of U.S. "non-silver duplicating microfilm" sales from 46% to 55%, and the 1979 acquisition raised it from 61% to 70% (Xidex Corporation, [1981, pp. 28, 32–33]). Judging from market-share

[1] The duplicating process starts with a master negative (of a paper document or an image on a CRT screen) made using silver halide "original" microfilm. Diazo and vesicular cannot be used for this step because they lack the light sensitivity needed to form an image from reflected light. From the original, duplicate copies are made—using diazo, vesicular, or silver duplicating film—by directing a high intensity light source through the original (which serves as a template) onto the duplicate film. In the case of vesicular, the latent image is created by a photochemical reaction which releases minute amounts of nitrogen gas which is trapped in the film coating. When heat is applied, the gas expands creating microscopic bubbles (vesicules). These bubbles diffract light to create a dark image where the film was exposed to light. Thus vesicular copies reverse the photographic sign of the document (the film preserves the sign of the negative). In the case of diazo, the image is created by a different photochemical reaction which in the presence of heat and ammonia prevents the formation of a dye where the diazo film has been exposed to light; the unexposed areas develop dark. This film preserves the sign of the original document (reverses the sign of the negative) (Xidex Corporation, [1981, p. 13 ff]).

[2] The cost advantage of non-silver films is due to both the lower cost of the film itself and the simplicity of processing. Silver films require a series of chemical baths to develop the latent image. In contrast vesicular film requires only the application of heat while diazo requires heat and ammonia (Xidex Corporation [1981, p. 14]).

[3] Diazo and vesicular have almost entirely displaced silver duplicating film in uses other than making copies for archival storage. The continuing use of silver film in this application is influenced by official archival certification of silver film (Xidex Corporation [1981, p. 16]).

[4] The most important factor limiting short-run substitutability between the two is that duplicating equipment is specialized to accommodate one or the other. In addition to price, the choice of diazo vs. vesicular is influenced by differences in film characteristics and the developing process. Other things equal a microfilm copy with a dark background and light text is preferred because it reduces eye fatigue; so the photographic sign of source material is a consideration. Vesicular reverses the photographic sign of the original document, while diazo preserves the sign (see foot note 1). Diazo requires heat and ammonia to develop the image while vesicular requires only heat. Vesicular thus has the advantage of not requiring special venting and other precautions necessary when working with and storing ammonia. On the other hand, the resolution of diazo is less affected by dust particles (Xidex Corporation [1981, pp. 18–23]).

statistics, these acquisitions would appear to have had a significant impact on market structure. The issue we examine next is whether there were discernible effects on the prices of diazo and vesicular duplicating microfilm as a result of Xidex's extension of "market power" in the two product lines.

III. PRICE EFFECTS

Methodology and Data.

Our study uses data covering a ten year period. In order to identify and measure price effects due to the acquisitions, we have to control for the influence during that period of general inflation and changes in the costs of inputs specific to the production of diazo and vesicular microfilm. For example, the cost of plastic film base increased due to the increase in petroleum prices, which also affected the cost of coatings since the coatings for both films use petroleum based resins. For both types of film, the cost of the film base and chemicals used for the coatings are estimated to account for 50% to 70% of price (Xidex Corporation [1983(b) p. 58]). Offsetting increases in materials cost and the effect of inflation on non-microfilm specific costs were gains in productivity as the result of increased coating line speeds and quality control improvements which improved yields (Xidex Corporation [1983(b), pp. 60–61] and Xidex Corporation [1979]).

To control for the influence of these factors on the level of absolute prices and thereby isolate price effects of the acquisitions, we use price *ratios* of vesicular and diazo microfilm in given product "configurations". A product configuration is defined by physical dimensions of the film (width, thickness and length) and whether or not it has a special edge stripe for marking. Because of the similarity in materials and processes, the vesicular-to-diazo price ratio for a given configuration should not be much affected by changes in petroleum prices, productivity, or general inflation. In making diazo or vesicular microfilm a coating is applied to a roll of plastic film base, which is the same for both types of microfilm. The coated film base is then cut into strips of various widths and lengths in the case of roll microfilm or into small sheets for aperture cards or microfiche. The difference between the production of the two film types is that a different coating is applied, but even these have many basic ingredients in common and the processes used to coat the films are very similar.[5] We shall examine whether there is a change in the relative price

[5] The same coating equipment can be used to coat either type of film (Xidex Corporation [1983(b), pp. 233, 252, 363, 635, and 1150]). Although the manufacturing processes are very similar, production substitution is hampered by the web of patents and trade secrets surrounding vesicular coating formulations (Xidex Corporation [1983(b), pp. 344–51]). There are three such formulations in use. With its acquisition of Kalvar, Xidex controlled two. The third has yet to capture any significant portion of the market. Patent protection on diazo coating formulations expired before the time period examined in our study. However, even absent patent protection on coatings, entry into film coating, whether diazo or vesicular, appears to be difficult due to learning curve effects. Production on a commercial scale requires skills acquired by trial and error and is not easily transferable. Several potential entrants into film coating gave up in frustration following unsuccessful attempts to product microfilm using methods which seemed promising in the laboratory (Xidex Corporation [1983(b), pp. 714–23]).

ratio following the acquisition affecting each product line. We should note that our method of using price ratios to identify price effects from the acquisitions is biased against finding such effects to the extent that the two products are good substitutes. If they were perfect substitutes, increases in absolute prices might have no effect on the price ratio.

The price data used for this study are U.S. General Services Administration (GSA) contract prices for eighteen configurations of diazo and vesicular microfilm for contract years (ending June 30) 1973 to 1982. The prices are actual transaction prices determined by competitive bidding which takes place during the first quarter of each calendar year (for the contract year beginning July 1). Product specifications remained unchanged during this period.

The GSA purchase schedule for microfilm lists well over two hundred separate microfilm product "items" (General Services Administration, Federal Supply Schedule). A number of the product distinctions (film color and film speed, for example) are irrelevant for our purposes since the bid prices (for a given firm) did not vary by these distinctions (General Services Administration, Abstract of Bids). We therefore collapsed the product classifications for each film type into a smaller group of relevant configurations. The price data used here are the average GSA contract prices (i.e., winning bid prices) of diazo and vesicular in the eighteen configurations that were common to both.[6] All of the matching configurations were for roll microfilm.

Because of the large volume of film purchased by the Federal Government, GSA prices are probably lower than average market prices (Xidex Corporation [1983(b), p. 233]). However, our methodology for estimating the price effects of the acquisitions only assumes that GSA prices reflect the general trend in market prices. We believe this assumption is justified since marketing documents and testimony reveal that firms used these prices as reliable indices of market prices (Xidex Corporation [1983(b), pp. 198, 508–9]).

Price Comparisons

We adopt the convention of computing the price ratios for each of the eighteen matching configurations as the price of vesicular divided by the price of diazo, i.e., V_i/D_i ($i = 1, \ldots, 18$). Post acquisition prices will be denoted by V'_i and D'_i. Unprimed, V_i and D_i denote "competitive benchmark" prices, this term serving as shorthand for "the prices that would have obtained in the absence of the acquisitions". (As discussed later these benchmark prices may have been above true competitive prices.) For each configuration, we use the time series data on GSA contract prices to calculate the average price ratio for three subsperiods.

$$R_{ci} = \text{the average value of } V_i/D_i$$

[6] Each configuration may contain more than one GSA product "item"; so there may be more than one low bid in that configuration.

(the competitive benchmark price ratio). The average price ratio prior to either acquisition, computed using prices for contract years 1972–73 through 1976–77.

R_{si} = the average value of V_i/D'_i.

The average price ratio following the Scott acquisition, but before the Kalvar acquisition, computed using prices for contract years 1977–78 and 1978–79.

R_{ki} = the average value of V'_i/D'_i.

The average price ratio following the Kalvar acquisition, computed using prices for contract years 1979–80 through 1981–82.[7]

Suppose we expect the Scott acquisition to result in an increase in diazo prices above their competitive benchmark level. Our hypothesis then can be stated as

$$(1) \qquad D'_i = D_i(1 + d), \quad d > 0,$$

were d denotes proportional increase in diazo prices above their competitive benchmark levels. Divide (1) through by V_i and take the reciprocal to get an expression in terms of the V/D price ratios,

$$(2) \qquad V_i/D'_i = V_i/D_i(1 + d)$$

Thus, if $d > 0$ the V/D price ratio following the Scott acquisition will fall relative to the competitive benchmark price ratio. On substitution of the observed average price ratios, we have

$$(2') \qquad R_{si} = R_{ci}/(1 + d)$$

Our estimate of d is calculated by solving for d in (2′) as $d = R_{ci}/R_{si} - 1$.

In the case of the Kalvar acquisition, we are concerned about the effects on vesicular prices. The analogue to equation (2) is

$$(3) \qquad V'_i/D_i = (V_i/D_i)(1 + v),$$

where v is the proportional increase in vesicular prices above their competitive benchmark level. In this case, however, we do not have data corresponding to the price ratio appearing on the left-hand side since the Kalvar (vesicular)

[7] Bids for contract year 1979–80 were submitted on February 26, 1979. The purchase agreement between Xidex and Kalvar was reached on February 14, 1979 (effective March 22) (Xidex Corporation [1981, p. 8]). The reason why we treat the prices for this year as post acquisition prices is due to the unusual circumstances surrounding the contract awards. Kalvar was the low bidder on most vesicular products. Xidex was typically the next to the lowest bidder, but with prices that were substantially higher than those bid by Kalvar. One would think that, in acquiring Kalvar, Xidex would have incurred the obligation to fulfil Kalvar's contracts at the prices tendered by Kalvar. (Apparently GSA contract officers were of this opinion as there is a series of legal memoranda in GSA files concerning a dispute on this issue, but no record regarding its final disposition.) However, when the 1979–80 supply schedule was published, Xidex was listed as the supplier on all contracts on which Kalvar had been the low bidder, and the final contract prices were those that had been tendered by Xidex.

acquisition occurred after the Scott (diazo) acquisition. We have two alternatives. The first is to use R_{si} and R_{ki} to estimate v. If we divide through (3) by $(1 + d)$ and use (1), we have

$$(4) \qquad (V'/D')_i = (V/D')_i(1 + v),$$

an equation containing price ratios corresponding to average price ratios, R_{ki} and R_{si}. Therefore one method of estimating v would be to use

$$(4') \qquad R_{ki} = R_{si}(1 + v),$$

which yields an estimate of v calculated as $v = R_{ji}/R_{si} - 1$. The problem with this approach is that it implicitly assumes any effect of the Scott acquisition on diazo prices persisted during the period following the Kalver acquisition. Suppose the Scott acquisition had a positive but more brief effect on diazo prices. Since this effect is embedded in R_{si}, using (4′) would result in an estimate of v that would be biased upward. We have adopted the more conservative approach of assuming that $d = 0$ at the time of the Kalvar acquisition. We use R_{ki} as defined above but compare it with R_{ci} rather than R_{si}. The estimate of v that we use is therefore given by $v = R_{ki}/R_{ci} - 1$.[8]

Results

Statistical tests are given in Table I. The values of R_{ci}, R_{si}, and R_{ki} for each of the eighteen matching configurations are given in the first three columns of Table I, followed by the calculated values of d_i and v_i. We use the sample values of d_i and v_i to estimate d and v. The estimates are 0.111 and 0.228, respectively. The null hypotheses, $d = 0$ and $v = 0$, are each rejected in favor of the alternatives, $d > 0$ and $v > 0$, at the 0.01 level of significance or better.

A picture is useful in conveying the circumstances behind the statistical results. In Figure 1 we have plotted the value of the average price ratio across all configurations for each contract year. The solid lines give the average values of R_{ci}, R_{si}, and R_{ki} from Table I.[9] The hypothesis that the changes in market structure had a positive impact on prices implies that the average

[8] Let $\bar{v}$ be the true value of v. If $d > 0$ then

$$R_k = \frac{V(1 + \bar{v})}{D(1 + d)}.$$

So using $(R_k/R_c) - 1$ to estimate v as we have done yields

$$v = \frac{\bar{v} - d}{1 + d}$$

which is clearly less than $\bar{v}$ if $d > 0$.

[9] The average values of R_{ci}, R_{si}, and R_{ki} do not correspond exactly to the unweighted mean of the average annual values of (V/D) in the corresponding subperiod. In some contract years, the price ratio for some configurations could not be calculated because there was no contract award for one of the two products.

TABLE I
ESTIMATES OF PROPORTIONAL PRICE INCREASES

Configuration	R_{ci}	R_{si}	R_{ki}	d_i	v_i
1	1.012	1.133	1.374	−0.1072	0.3576
2	1.019	1.089	1.323	−0.0637	0.2975
3	1.065	0.926	1.257	0.1502	0.1799
4	1.083	0.924	1.260	0.1723	0.1631
5	1.019	0.910	1.161	0.1186	0.1398
6	1.051	0.934	1.187	0.1245	0.1224
7	1.069	0.949	1.372	0.1270	0.2838
8	1.071	0.915	1.323	0.1705	0.2335
9	1.079	0.940	1.276	0.1481	0.1827
10	1.106	0.936	1.285	0.1817	0.1620
11	1.010	0.914	1.158	0.1061	0.1463
12	1.054	0.920	1.197	0.1457	0.1361
13	0.912	0.773	1.112	0.1785	0.2197
14	0.937	0.953	1.365	−0.0170	0.4560
15	0.999	0.776	1.104	0.2873	0.1057
16	0.975	0.954	1.363	0.0218	0.3974
17	1.037	0.789	1.136	0.3137	0.0958
18	0.897	0.957	1.283	−0.0632	0.4315
mean	1.022	0.927	1.252	0.1108*	0.2283†

* $d > 0$ significant at 0.01 level with $t_{17} = 2.72$
† $v > 0$ significant at 0.001 level with $t_{17} = 8.40$

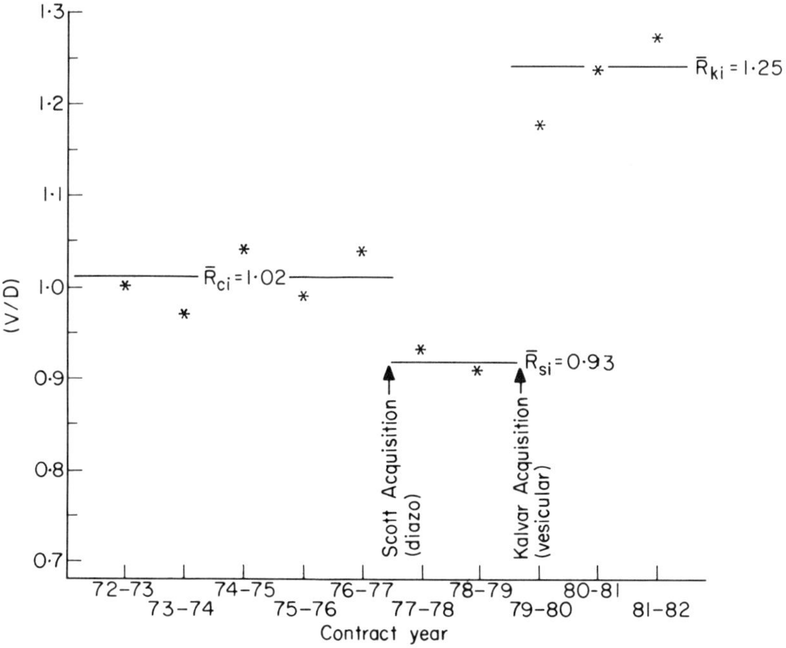

FIGURE 1
Behavior of average price ratio

price ratio, measured as V/D, would fall following the Scott (diazo) acquisition and then rise following the Kalvar (vesicular) acquisition. This pattern is clearly evident in Figure 1. In addition, since the Kalvar acquisition gave Xidex a near monopoly in vesicular, one would expect the price effect of this acquisition to be greater than that of the Scott acquisition, as it appears to be. Note also that the average value of V/D has a rising trend following the Kalvar acquisition. This is consistent with (but, of course, does not confirm) the possibility that the price impact of the Scott acquisition was being dissipated, since a decline in d from its initial value would be reflected in a rising value for the V/D price ratio.

IV. ESTIMATES OF THE SHORT-RUN EFFECTS ON PROFITS

We now turn to estimating the impact of the acquisitions on Xidex's profits. The acquisitions may have increased profits through economies of scale in production and distribution or from Xidex's superior management skill.[10] Our interest, however, is with the increase in profits due to the elevation of prices above their competitive benchmark levels. We denote these "supra-competitive" profits as π' (with subscripts d and v where appropriate).

Methodology

To estimate supra-competitive profits we take Xidex sales revenue for each product line separately following the acquisition affecting that product line and then subtract the estimate of sales at competitive benchmark prices. In Figure 2 let DD represent Xidex's (annual) demand curve for one of the two products in a particular post-acquisition year. P' and Q' are post acquisition price and quantity; P denotes the benchmark competitive price and Q the quantity that Xidex would sell at that price. Total sales revenue, $S = P'Q'$, is the sum of areas A, B, and C. Our estimate of supra-competitive profit due to the price effect of the acquisition is given by area A. Using the relationship

$$P' = P(1 + j), \quad j = d \text{ or } v, \tag{5}$$

the dollar value of areas $B + C$ is given by

$$PQ' = \frac{P'Q'}{(1 + j)} = \frac{S}{(1 + j)}. \tag{6}$$

So the value of π' (area A) is given by

$$\pi' = P'Q' - PQ' = S\frac{j}{(1 + j)}. \tag{7}$$

[10] See Williamson [1968]. At least in the case of the Kalvar acquisition, there is a strong presumption that there was no efficiency gain from the merger. Two months after the acquisition, the plant was closed and the employees were fired (Xidex Corporation [1981, p. 9]).

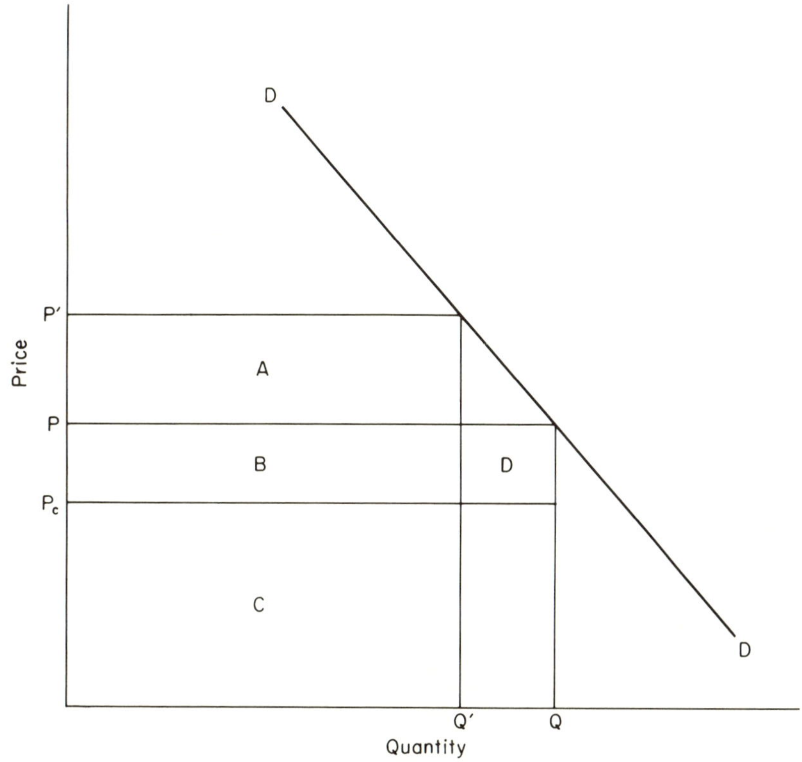

FIGURE 2
Profit effects of price changes

The estimates of supra-competitive profits on diazo and vesicular microfilm for post acquisition years are calculated from (7) using annual sales revenue for the product in question and our estimates of d or v substituted for j. These estimates are given in last two columns of Table II.

Qualifications

Before discussing them further, we need to discuss a source of possible upward bias in these profit estimates and to point out sources of offsetting downward bias that are due to our conservative assumptions. In Figure 2, area A measures the gain in profits due to the price effects of the acquisition correctly only if P is the "true" competitive price yielding no excess profits. Recall, however, that P is an estimate of the price that would have obtained had the acquisition not taken place. Since the sales for both diazo and vesicular were highly concentrated in few sellers before the acquisitions, prices might have been above competitive levels due to oligopolistic behavior. If P actually is above the true competitive price, P_c, then the value of the profit gain due to price

TABLE II
ESTIMATES OF EFFECTS ON PROFITS

Fiscal Year (Ending 6/30)	Xidex Duplicate Microfilm Sales (000)			Estimates of "Supra-Competitive" Profits (000)	
	Total	Diazo	Vesicular	π'_d	π'_v
1978*	29,282	18,194	11,088	1,818	
1979*	39,736	23,605	16,131	2,358	
1980†	49,596	(29,462)	(20,134)		3,738
1981†	54,802	(32,554)	(22,247)		4,131
Total				4,176	7,869

* Sales data for FY 1978 and 1979 taken from Xidex Corporation [1979]. data separately for diazo and vesicular for FY's 1974–8.
† Combined sales of diazo and vesicular for FY 1980 and 1981 were taken from Xidex's annual reports (microfilm sales are not broken down by film type). For FY1980 and 1981 total microfilm sales were allocated between diazo and vesicular using proportions for FY 1979 sales.

increases is A minus D rather than A alone. Our procedure for estimating π' thus assumes Xidex was earning only a competitive rate of return at price P; in other words it implicitly assumes $P = P_c$. If $P > P_c$, then our procedure overstates the gain in profits attributable to the price increases.

To get a feel for the magnitude of the bias assume that marginal costs are constant over the interval $Q'Q$. The dollar values of areas A and D are given by

$$A = (P' - P)Q' \quad \text{and}$$
$$D = (P - P_c)(Q - Q').$$

The relative size of the bias is, therefore, given by

$$\frac{D}{A} = \frac{P - P_c}{P' - P}\left(\frac{Q - Q'}{Q'}\right). \tag{8}$$

Let m represent the proportional difference between P and P_c, as $m = (P - P_c)/P$, or $P(1 - m) = P_c$. Using this definition of m we can restate (8) as

$$\frac{D}{A} = \frac{mP}{P' - P}\left(\frac{Q - Q'}{Q'}\right). \tag{9}$$

Now a reasonable definition of arc elasticity of demand, with primes denoting new prices and quantities, is

$$E = \frac{P}{Q'}\frac{Q' - Q}{P' - P}. \tag{10}$$

Instead of P and Q or P' and Q', the reference point is an average over the arc obtained by using P and Q' which is closer to the middle of the arc.[11] From equations (9) and (10) it is clear that the size of D/A depends on how much P exceeds P_c, captured by m, and on the absolute value of price elasticity of demand:

$$\frac{D}{A} = m|E|. \tag{11}$$

Thus, as long as demand is not very elastic over the interval $P'P$ and m is quite small, area A in Figure 2 will be a good estimate of the gain in profits due to the price effects of the acquisition.

The net bias from our procedure for estimating the gain in profits is likely to be small (and may be negative) because of three instances in which we took the conservative option in estimating magnitudes that affect our estimates of π'. First, in estimating v, recall that we assumed d was zero, i.e., the price effect of the Scott acquisition vanished at the time of the Kalvar acquisition. If the price effect of the Scott (diazo) acquisition was not entirely eroded by then, the average value of v_i would be larger than 0.228; thus our estimate of π'_v based on $v = 0.228$ would be biased downward.

Second, consistent with using $d = 0$ in calculating v, we have assumed that $\pi'_d = 0$ following the Kalvar acquisition; no supra-competitive profit from the Scott (diazo) acquisition is included after fiscal year 1979 (see Table II). Notice we also ignore the possibility of any supra-competitive profit on diazo for fiscal year 1977 even though the Scott acquisition took place in June 1976. We do this because we use the bidding on GSA contracts to date price increases. The bidding on GSA contracts for fiscal year 1977 took place in early 1976, four or five months before the acquisition, so we conservatively date the price increase in diazo at the time of the bidding for the 1977–78 contract year which took place in early 1977 (the first round of GSA bidding following the Scott acquisition). However, it is surely possible that price increases in diazo were reflected in sales to non-GSA customers during fiscal year 1977.

The third instance of conservatism concerns our method of calculating total sales for each product line following the Kalvar acquisition. For this period sales data for diazo and vesicular are not separately available. To separate sales by product line we used the proportions from the last fiscal year in which separate sales data were available, 1979. This almost certainly understates the proportion of vesicular sales in later years, since the Kalvar acquisition removed Xidex's only real competition in vesicular. Of course, if we have understated the proportion of total film sales that were vesicular, we have understated the sales base used to calculate the supra-competitive profit on vesicular and thus understated the amount of such profits.

[11] If P and Q were used the result obtained below in (11) would have to be multiplied by Q'/Q, which would make the estimate of D/A smaller. Using P' and Q' has the opposite effect on D/A.

Lastly we reiterate the point made earlier concerning our methodology for estimating price effects. Since diazo and vesicular are substitutes, an increase in the price of one will have, if anything, a positive effect on the price of the other. Thus our procedure of using changes in relative price ratios to estimate the increase in prices due to the acquisitions is conservative to begin with.

Results.

Our estimate of supra-competitive profit for diazo is $4,176,000 in fiscal years 1978 and 1979 and for vesicular is $7,869,000 in fiscal years 1980 and 1981. To put these figures in perspective, the purchase price of Scott was $4,225,000 and that of Kalvar was about $6 million.[12] In each case the estimated gain from raising prices (relative to competitive benchmark levels) was sufficient to recoup the cost of the acquisition in two years. Even if our estimates of supra-competitive profit contain some upward bias, which we have attempted to avoid, the acquisitions would appear to be handsome investments.

V. SUMMARY

A Federal Trade Commission suit against Xidex Corporation, challenging its acquisitions of Scott Graphics in 1976 and Kalvar Corporation in 1979, has yielded an unusual opportunity to observe price behavior before and after the acquisitions. Each acquisition involved a substantial gain for Xidex in its share of a well defined microfilm product line. The materials and processes used in producing the two products are so similar that a ratio of prices can be used to control for input price or productivity changes which would affect the level of absolute prices over the time period covered by our study. Prices in each affected product line were found to increase after the acquisition occurred. It was also possible to estimate the profit gain due to the price increases. The price increases yielded substantial profit gains, in each case sufficient to recover the cost of the acquisition in about two years.

Litigation in the Federal Trade Commission antitrust suit against Xidex began in December 1981 and ended in March 1982 when Xidex agreed to settlement by consent. The consent allows Xidex to retain the acquisitions with the exception of Kalvar's vesicular technology and knowhow which it is required to divest. In addition, the consent requires licensing of Xidex's property vesicular technology at below market-rates and royalty-free licensing of

[12] Xidex acquired the duplicate microfilm business of Scott Graphics (including a production facility) for $4,225,000 in cash and notes. Xidex paid Kalvar $1,776,000 in cash and assumed, or agreed to reimburse Kalvar for, virtually all of its liabilities, totaling $4,253,892. Xidex received Kalvar's physical assets, accounts receivable, patents and trade secrets, copyrights and trade names, and an agreement not to compete in the duplicate microfilm business for five years. Kalvar retained its corporate identity, cash and tax loss carry-forwards (Xidex Corporation [1981, pp. 7–9]).

diazo technology. After an extended period for public comment, the final order became effective on July 7, 1983 (Xidex Corporation, [1983(a)]).

David M. Barton,
Bureau of Economics,
U.S. Federal Trade Commission,
Washington, DC, 20580.

ACCEPTED FEBRUARY 1984

Roger Sherman,
Department of Economics,
University of Virginia,
Charlottesville, VA, 22901.

REFERENCES

ASPINWALL, R. C., 1970, 'Market Structure and Commercial Bank Mortgage Interest Rates', *Southern Economic Journal*, **36** (April), pp. 376–84.

BELL, F. W. and MURPHY, N. B., 1969, 'Impact of Market Structure on the Price of a Commercial Banking Service', *Review of Economics and Statistics*, **51** (May), pp. 210–13.

GENERAL SERVICES ADMINISTRATION, Federal Supply Service, *Abstract of Bids* (FSC 67 Part IV, Section A).

———, Federal Supply Service, *Federal Supply Schedule FSC 67 Part IV, Section A* (Micrographic Supplies).

HEGGESTAK, A. A. and MINGO, J. J., 1976, 'Prices, Nonprices, and Concentration in Banking', *Journal of Money Credit and Banking*, **8** (February), pp. 107–17.

HESTER, D., 1979, 'Customer Relationships and Terms of Loans: Evidence from a Pilot Survey', *Journal of Money Credit and Banking*, **11** (August), pp. 349–57.

LAMM, R. M. JR., 1981, 'Prices and Concentration in the Food Retailing Industry', *Journal of Industrial Economics*, **30** (September), pp. 67–78.

LANDON, J. H., 1971, 'The Relation of Market Concentration to Advertising Rates: The Newspaper Industry', *Antitrust Bulletin* **16** (Spring), pp. 53–100.

MARION, B., MUELLER, W., COTTERILL, R. W., GEITHMAN, F., and SMELZER, J., 1979, 'The Price and Profit Performance of Leading Food Chains', *American Journal of Agricultural Economics*, **61** (August), pp. 420–33.

MARVEL, H. P., 1978, 'Competition and Price Levels in the Retail Gasoline Market', *Review of Economics and Statistics*, **60** (May), pp. 252–58.

WILLIAMSON, O. E., 1968, 'Economies as an Antitrust Defense: The Welfare Tradeoffs', *American Economic Review*, **58** (March), pp. 18–36.

XIDEX CORPORATION, 1979, 'Xidex: Corporate Update', October.

———, 1981, Doc. No. 9146, Complaint Counsel's Trial Brief, May 4.

———, 1983(a), Doc. No. 9146, *Federal Trade Commission Decision and Order*, July 7.

———, 1983(b), Doc. No. 9146, Trial Transcript.

THE JOURNAL OF INDUSTRIAL ECONOMICS 0022–1821 $2.00
Volume XXXIII December 1984 No. 2

DIVERSIFICATION STRATEGY AND PERFORMANCE

DONALD J. LECRAW

I. INTRODUCTION

THE MOTIVATION and consequences of diversification by firms out of their base industries has been studied extensively by both economists and business researchers. Until recently, however, each group has approached the phenomenon quite differently. Economists have treated the extent of a firm's diversification as determined by structural variables in the industries in which the firm operated and the economics of the organization of activity within the firm compared to via the market.[1] Business researchers have focused on the human and physical assets of the firm (its internal strengths and weaknesses) in relation to the goals of the firm as the major determinants of its diversification strategy.[2] This latter group of researchers has often used discrete categories of strategies, while the former group has emphasized the continuous nature of diversification.[3] Recently, research by Caves *et al.* [1980] has joined these two approaches in analyzing the performance of samples of 125 and 67 large firms in Canada. This study yielded significant insights on the causes and effects of diversification by firms.[4]

The research in this paper was designed to expand and extend the work of Caves *et al.*, [1980] by: 1) using a larger data base covering more firms, i.e., the 200 largest publicly-held, non-financial firms in Canada instead of 67 firms; 2) using more theoretically sound definitions of the four diversification strategies followed by the firms in the sample, 3) using multiple discriminant analysis to classify the firms into *four* (not three) strategic groups; 4) testing for the effects of the choice of diversification strategy and the extent of diversification on firm profitability. This last feature is permitted by the expanded sample, whereas Caves *et al.*, [1980] had to drop one group for statistical reasons. Nevertheless, the work of Caves *et al.*, [1980] remains the touchstone of this study.

This paper seeks to provide answers for two questions concerning the diversification strategies of large firms in Canada: 1) To what extent did the structural characteristics of the base industry of a firm and the firm's own characteristics influence the diversification strategy it followed? 2) What were

[1] See, for example, Alchian and Demsetz [1972] Berry [1975] Gort [1962], Caves [1975] Williamson [1975] and, on a more fundamental level, Penrose [1959] and Coase [1937].

[2] See, for example, Andrews [1971] Chandler [1977] and Lawrence and Lorsch [1967].

[3] See Rumelt [1974] and Wrigley [1970] for an analysis using discrete strategies for the United States, and Lecraw and Thompson [1978] for Canada.

[4] In most of their analyses Caves *et al.*, [1980] used a sample of 125 firms, but for the analysis of the determinants of a firm's choice of strategy and the effect of this strategic choice on performance, their sample was reduced to 67.

the effects on a firm's performance of the appropriateness of its diversification strategy (given firm and industry characteristics), the generic strategy it chose, and the *extent* to which it followed a given strategy?

The model developed to analyze these questions walks the middle ground between the fields industrial organization and business policy. On the one hand, it depends heavily on the findings of industrial organization that industry structural variables influence the diversification strategy and the profitability of the firms within the industry. On the other hand, it allows for the possibility that different firms in the same industry may follow different diversification strategies based on management's formulation of the firm's goals and assessment of its strengths and weaknesses (i.e., the analysis allows for *intra*-industry variation of firm diversification strategy and performance), and that the success (profitability) of a firm may depend on the strategy it chooses, the appropriateness of this strategy, and the extent to which it follows this strategy, as well as the profitability of the industries in which it is operating.

II. THEORY

In this paper a firm's "strategy" will have a quite restricted meaning. A "strategy" will be defined as the distribution of the firm's resources, and hence the distribution of its output, among industries, i.e., its diversification strategy. The analysis follows in the tradition of Wrigley [1970] and Rumelt [1974] in that it identifies *discrete* diversification strategies based on the relationship in production and marketing between the industries in which the firm operated and the proportion of its activities that were located in each industry.

The firms in the sample were the 200 largest firms in terms of sales in the manufacturing sector in Canada in 1975. These firms were placed into four strategic groups based on the type and extent of their diversification: Single Business (SB), Vertically Integrated Business (VIB), Related Business (RB), and Unrelated Business (UB) depending on the relationship between the industries in which the firm operated and the distribution of its operations among those industries. (The operational definition of the characteristics of the firm by which they were assigned to each strategic group is described in the next section.)[5]

The "Dominant Business" category of Wrigley-Rumelt and Caves *et al.* was not used. Instead, firms that might have been placed in this category were classified into VIB, RB or UB categories depending on the type and extent of their diversification. The Dominant Business strategy (i.e., a strategy of a dominant share of a firm's output in one industry with a minor amount in vertically integrated, related, or unrelated industries) was taken to be a transition stage from an SB to one of the other strategies that was motivated by the

[5] See Lecraw and Thompson [1978] for a list of the 200 firms and the strategic diversification groups to which they were assigned.

same base industry conditions and that would have had the same effects on performance as did membership in one of the strategic groups: SB, VIB, RB, UB.[6] This definition of the strategies followed by the firms in the sample is a significant departure from previous work.

Assuming that firms and their managers had goals of maximizing risk adjusted profitability and growth, each firm was faced with a set of opportunities by which it could achieve its goals and threats to their achievement. These opportunities and threats arise partly from the structure of the base industry in which the firm operated and partly from the characteristics of the firm itself including the skills of its employees. This framework of analysis is similar to that developed by Chandler [1977].

The hypotheses in this section concerning the characteristics of the firm and its base industry that influence its choice of diversification strategy have been well developed in the literature. (See Chandler [1977], Wrigley, [1970], Rumelt, [1974], and especially Caves *et al.* [1980]. Caves *et al.* devote two chapters (Chapter 8 and 12, especially pp. 300–24) to this subject. The analysis in this section will simply summarize the influences on diversification strategy that have already been identified (rather than once more describing their underlying theoretical basis) except in the case of the effect of foreign ownership for which this paper makes a departure from most previous work.

If a firm were in a fast growing industry with above average profitability and below average risk, it may have been able to satisfy its profit and growth goals without diversifying out of its base industry. Even in slow growth industries, relatively small firms with small market shares may have been able to satisfy their goals by above average growth in sales through internal growth or acquisitions to gain market share without precipitating strong competitive reaction or government intervention. SB firms might also be found in industries relatively insulated from the threats and challenges of international trade. On the opportunities side, SB firms might not have diversified because they had not generated intangible assets arising from high levels of R & D (that yielded expertise in other products), high levels of advertising (that could have produced transferable brand names, expertise at branding products, or underutilized capacity in the distribution system), or a high percentage of managers to workers (to generate transferable intangible assets in management) in their base industries.

In concentrated industries whose production technology was capital intensive and required a large proportion of raw materials inputs, firms may have had the incentive to integrate backward to secure a stable source raw materials supplies under their control in order to prevent capacity underutilization due to raw materials shortages and lack of coordination of supply with demand, and in order to erect barriers to entry by other non-integrated

[6] The close relationship between many of the financial performance characteristics of the firms in Rumelt's [1974, p. 92] sample that had followed "related" and "unrelated" diversification strategies supports this point.

firms. The base industries of vertically integrated business (VIB) firms may have presented few opportunities for the R & D or advertising that would have generated intangible assets and led them to diversify into other industries to increase their returns on these assets. Given Canada's comparative advantage in many raw materials, VIB firms should have required low tariff barriers in the base industries to survive and should have exported a large percentage of their output. On the other hand, growth of VIB firms should have been low compared to other firms given the income inelastic nature of resource intensive basic industries and the relatively concentrated structure of their base industries. The profits of industries populated by VIB firms may have either been higher or lower than average. On the one hand, high concentration and barriers to entry might have led to above average profits. On the other, VIB firms may have been both exposed to import competition and have had to engage in competition on export markets which may have lowered profitability. Moreover, since these firms should have tended to be more capital intensive, their profits would have been more sensitive to swings in demand and possibly more vulnerable to price wars. VIB firms should have had a higher ratio of managers to other employees than did SB firms in their base industries reflecting the relatively greater need for intangible assets in management to coordinate vertically integration.

Firms may have followed a strategy of diversification into related businesses (RB) for several reasons related to characteristics in their base industries. Firms in industries with high levels of R & D for product or process technology may have developed intangible assets that could be transferred to new, but related, industries. Similarly, high advertising expenditures may have allowed a firm to develop a brand name as well as skills in marketing and distribution that could have been transferred to new products in a related industry at low cost. These firms should also be in base industries with a higher proportion of managers to other employees than SB or VIB firms to generate transferable intangible assets in management needed to manage the firm's more diverse operations. These firms might also have had the incentive to diversify into related industries if their base industries were threatened, i.e., if the industry were unconcentrated with relatively low barriers to entry and openness to foreign trade.

Finally, firms may have followed a strategy of diversification into unrelated industries for several reasons. If their base industries were concentrated and their market share were high, but industry growth were low, firms would have had to diversify into other industries if they desired to increase their growth rate above the industry average. If R & D or advertising intensities were low, there might not have been an opportunity for diversification into products related by a common product or process technology or related marketing techniques. If profits were high, instead of remitting the cash flow generated from their operations to their stockholders, the firms might have followed a strategy of unrelated diversification in order to earn a return on their underutilized intangible managerial assets and possibly to earn their investors a higher return via more valued capital gains rather than dividends. The proportion of managers to total employees should be higher in the base industries of UB than for firms in the other three groups.

There has been considerable controversy over the effect of foreign ownership on the diversity of output of firms and plants in Canada. Caves [1975, p. 28] found that "a firm's diversity in the U.S. is not a very good predictor of its diversity in Canada", although they were positively related. Caves *et al.*, [1980] in their analysis of diversification of firms in Canada (Chapter 8, Table 9.4, and Chapter 11, Table 11.4) and strategic choice of diversification strategy (Chapter 12, Tables 12.2 and 13.2) did not differentiate between foreign-owned and domestically-owned firms in Canada in their statistical analyses. Gorecki [1980] has taken exception to this procedure on theoretical grounds and supported his conclusions with statistical analysis based on data from the food processing industry. Gorecki [1980, p. 338] concluded:

> . . . the pattern of enterprise diversification in the Canadian food-processing sector depends importantly upon origin of ownership. Domestic enterprise diversification, in contrast to foreign, is related to local Canadian market conditions . . . in future research on the determinants of the diversified enterprise in Canada, the distinction between foreign and domestic ownership should be made.

The effect of foreign ownership on diversification strategy was therefore incorporated into the analysis. Foreign-owned firms may have had lower cost access to the product and process technology and brand names developed by their parents and might be expected to have followed strategies of related and unrelated diversification to a greater extent than did Canadian-owned firms

TABLE I
BASE INDUSTRY AND FIRM CHARACTERISTICS OF FIRMS FOLLOWING DIFFERENT DIVERSIFICATION STRATEGIES

Base Industry Characteristics	*SB*	*VIB*	*RB*	*UB*
Concentration	low	high	low	high
Growth	high	low	average	low
Profits	high	average	average	high
Risk	low	high	average	high
Exposure to trade	low	high	average	high
R & D intensity	average	low	high	low
Advertising intensity	low	low	high	low
Use of raw materials	average	high	average	average
Managers/employees	low	average	high	high
Market Share	low	high	average	high
Foreign Ownership	low	low	high	high

SB = single business, VIB = vertically integrated business,
RB = related business, UB = unrelated business.

and followed a strategy of single business operations (and possible vertically integrated business operations) to a lesser extent. If the hypothesis that a firm's diversification strategy is influenced by characteristics of the firm and its base industry is correct, then using data on *Canadian* base industry and firm characteristics may not be appropriate for foreign-owned firms.

Table I displays the hypotheses about the characteristics of the firm and its base industry that may have influenced each of the diversification strategies.

III. DATA AND METHODOLOGY

The data used to test the hypotheses presented in the previous section came from a wide variety of sources. The majority of the data came from data tapes assembled by Caves *et al.* in their work for the Canadian Royal Commission on Corporate Concentration (1975–78) augmented by more recent data. Some data were assembled by the author as part of his research activities for the same Royal Commission. Other data, particularly those used to classify the firms in the sample to one of the four diversification strategies and the market share data were obtained directly from the firms themselves.

The firms in the sample comprised the two hundred largest publicly-owned manufacturing firms in Canada. The sample included firms that were wholly-owned and partly-owned subsidiaries of foreign firms. Caves *et al.* used two samples: a sample of 125 firms data for which were on the FRI data tapes and a subsample of 67 firms for which more complete data were available. Their full sample included at least 26 firms with some degree of foreign ownership. Eightyseven of the 125 firms in their study are included in the 200 firms in this study. The composition of their smaller sample was not published.

The basis of the classification of a firm into a strategic group has already been described. Operationally a firm was classified as a single business (SB) if 95% of the firm's revenues came from sales in a single three digit SIC industry. A firm was classified as a vertically integrated business (VIB) if less than 95% of its revenues came from a single industry but more than 70% of its revenues arose from by-products, intermediate products, and end products of a vertically integrated sequence of processing activities. A firm was classified as following a strategy of related business (RB) diversification if less than 95% of its revenues came from a single industry, but greater than 70% of its revenues came from businesses related via their product or process technology or their marketing characteristics. Finally, a firm was classified as following a strategy of unrelated business (UB) diversification if less than 70% of its revenues came from businesses related by their product or process technology or their marketing characteristics.[7] Firms were classified as foreign-owned if 50% or more of their equity was held outside Canada. The distribution of the

[7] Compare this classification with that of Rumelt [1974, pp. 9–46]. Rumelt also discusses the methodological problems in classifying firms to strategic categories on both a theoretical and operation grounds.

TABLE II
NUMBER OF FIRMS FOLLOWING THE FOUR DIVERSIFICATION STRATEGIES IN THE LARGEST 200 FIRMS, 1978.

	Total	*Foreign*[a] *Owned*	*Canadian Owned*
Single Business	32	18	18
Vertically Integrated Business	42	24	18
Related Business	72	39	27
Unrelated Business	54	41	15
TOTAL	200	122	78

[a] Foreign equity ownership greater than 50%.

200 firms in this study among the four strategic groups in 1978 is shown in Table II. (A list of these firms with their strategy in 1975 is in Lecraw and Thompson [1978, Appendix B].)

Multiple discriminant analysis was used to uncover the interrelationships between the characteristics of the base industries and the firms for firms in the four strategic categories. Use of multiple dicriminant analysis allowed tests for the significance of differences among the profiles of the base industries and firm-specific variables of firms that were in the four strategic categories, determination of the linear combinations of independent variables that discriminated best among the four categories, and determination of which variables accounted for most of the observed intergroup differences.[8] Essentially the multiple discriminant analysis assigned each firm to one of the four strategic groups based on the characteristics of the firm and its base industry so as to minimize the probability that the firm was assigned by the discriminant function to a category to which it in fact did not belong. (The discriminant analysis also generated the probability of the firm belonging to each of the other three strategic groups.) The more powerful the discriminant function, the lower the number of misclassified firms.

In order to account for the (possible) effect of foreign ownership on the diversification strategy of the firm, the firms in the sample were divided into foreign owned (foreign ownership greater than 50%) and Canadian-owned firms. For the Canadian-owned firms, the base industry and firm variables (as listed in Table I) were entered in the discriminant function as independent variables. For the foreign-owned firms, two different sets of variables were used. The first set was simply the same set as for the Canadian-owned firms. This analysis tests whether the diversification strategies of foreign-owned firms were affected by the same variables as those of Canadian firms. The second set of variables used included all the former variables with the addition of dummy variables representing the diversification strategy followed by their parent firm in its home country. This analysis tests whether the diversification strategy of foreign-owned firms followed that of their parents.

[8] See Green [1978, Ch. 4 and 7] for a description of discriminant analysis.

Table III

Strategic Group Discriminant Analysis—Canadian-Owned Firms

Base Industry Variable	Canadian-Owned Firms Mean Scores (centroids)					Foreign Subsidiaries Mean Scores (centroids)					Foreign Subsidiaries -Parent Strategy Mean Scores (centroids)				
	SB	*VIB*	*RB*	*UB*	*V**	*SB*	*VIB*	*RB*	*UB*	*V*	*SB*	*VIB*	*RB*	*UB*	*V*
Concentration	27.3	71.2	43.0	72.1	ac	47.3	52.5	49.5	61.4	c	43.5	51.2	47.5	54.4	—
Growth	12.3	8.2	10.1	6.0	a	10.3	8.2	8.3	9.7	c	13.2	8.7	11.1	7.9	c
Profits	12.8	9.8	13.2	8.7	a	9.4	8.3	13.2	9.5	b	14.2	10.3	13.5	9.0	c
Risk	0.43	0.51	0.30	0.54	a	0.47	0.58	0.31	0.53	c	14.3	9.2	11.3	10.7	c
Trade Exposure	0.50	0.86	0.36	0.29	c	0.63	0.72	0.48	0.37	c	0.52	0.73	0.42	0.38	—
R & D Intensity	1.75	0.85	2.42	0.53	b	1.73	0.93	2.23	1.73	c	1.53	1.24	1.93	0.85	—
Advertising/Intensity	1.20	0.75	3.23	0.90	b	1.35	0.93	2.93	1.24	—	1.10	0.74	2.12	1.21	—
Use of Raw Materials	7.2	35.5	8.5	4.8	a	18.7	31.2	15.3	9.4	—	10.5	31.4	12.7	17.1	—
Managers/employee	15.7	9.1	16.9	19.3	b	15.5	9.3	16.1	17.4	—	15.4	10.1	16.2	18.1	c
Firm Variables															
Market Share	19.8	29.2	25.0	27.1	a	11.1	37.1	19.7	32.8	c	17.5	25.0	17.3	22.1	a
SB											0.73	0.07	0.12	0.13	a
VIB											0.07	0.86	0.13	0.12	a
RB											0.13	0.04	0.65	0.14	a
UB											0.07	0.03	0.10	0.61	a

* V = Bartlet's V statistic which tests for equality of the group means.
It is distributed as the Chi statistic with $n(G - 1)$ degrees of freedom.

a = significant at the 0.01 level, b = significant at the 0.05 level, c = significant at the 0.01 level.

Concentration = C_4, the percentage of shipments accounted for by the largest four firms.

Growth = Average industry growth 1961–75.

Profits = Net profit after taxes divided by total equity.

Risk = Standard deviation of profitability about the average 1961–75.

Trade Exposure = Imports divided by value of shipments.

R & D Intensity = Sum of internal and external R & D divided by total industry sales.

Advertising Intensity = Ratio of reported total advertising costs to industry shipments.

Use of Raw Materials = Percent of industry inputs spent on raw materials.

Market Share = Market Share of the firm in its base industry.

Managers/employees = nonproduction workers/total employees.

The results of these discriminant analyses are reported in Table III. For the subsample of Canadian-owned firms the means for the base industry and firm specific variables differed among the strategic groups in the hypothesized direction and these differences were significant, usually at the 0.01 level as shown by the Bartlet V statistic. Three discriminant functions were estimated, the first accounting for 71% of the variation explained. All three discriminant functions were statistically significant at the 0.01 level as indicated by a Wilk's lambda of 0.65, 0.83 and 0.99 respectively.

The "confusion matrix" generated by using these discriminant functions to predict the diversification strategy of the firms given the characteristics of their base industry and firms (Table IV) indicates that the discriminant functions were successful in correctly classifying 73% of the firms to the strategic categories they in fact chose. This figure compares with 25% and 27% correctly classified if the firms had been classified randomly to each group or were

TABLE IV
"CONFUSION MATRIX" FOR THE NINE VARIABLES USED IN CLASSIFYING FIRMS TO THE STRATEGIC GROUPS

Actual Group Membership	*Predicted Group Membership*[a] *Canadian Firms*				
	SB	*VIB*	*RB*	*UB*	*Total*
SB	13	1	2	2	18
VIB	2	12	1	3	18
RB	2	3	21	1	27
UB	3	1	0	11	15
TOTAL	20	17	24	17	78

[a] Canadian ownership greater than 50%.

FOREIGN SUBSIDIARIES (CANADIAN VARIABLES)

Actual Group Membership	*Predicted Group Membership*				
	SB	*VIB*	*RB*	*UB*	*Total*
SB	9	3	4	2	8
VIB	4	10	3	7	24
RB	3	5	26	5	39
UB	5	8	12	16	41
TOTAL	21	26	45	30	122

FOREIGN SUBSIDIARIES—CANADIAN VARIABLES PLUS PARENT STRATEGY

Actual Group Membership	*Predicted Group Membership*				
	SB	*VIB*	*RB*	*UB*	*Total*
SB	16	0	1	1	18
VIB	1	20	2	1	24
RB	2	1	32	4	39
UB	2	0	2	37	41
TOTAL	21	21	37	43	122

all classified to the most populous group, the related business group. The 73% correctly classified is significantly different at the 0.01 level from the percentage correct if the maximum chance criterion had been selected.

When the same analysis was performed on foreign-owned firms using discriminant analysis, the results were not as good as those for Canadian-owned firms (Table III). Several of the variables were not significant, and the number of misclassifications rose, although the number correctly classified was significantly above the percentage correct if the maximum chance criterion had been selected (Table IV).

When the diversification strategies of the parents of the foreign-owned firms were entered, the predictive power of the discriminant function was high (Table III). In general the significance of the Canadian industry variables and firm characteristics were lower than in either of the two previous cases.[9]

These results lend support to two of the hypotheses of this paper: the characteristics of the base industry of *Canadian-owned* firms and their firm characteristics had a strong influence on the strategy followed by these firms, but this influence was not deterministic in that firms could and did follow diversification strategies that differed from the one predicted using a linear combination of the characteristics of their base industries and the firms themselves to construct the discriminant functions. This analysis goes beyond that reported in Caves *et al.* since it explicitly shows not only which variables were significant in discriminating between strategic groups, but also how well these variables could be used to discriminate between the four strategic groups.

The results of the discriminant analysis of foreign-owned firms support two hypotheses: 1) foreign-owned firms were less responsive in their diversification strategy to industry and firm conditions in Canada than were Canadian-owned firms and 2) these firms tended to follow the diversification strategy of their parent although their strategy also was influenced by conditions in Canada. These conclusions, especially the second one, however, must be treated with caution. As suggested by Caves [1982] the parents of these subsidiaries could have followed a diversification strategy in relation to industry conditions in their home markets. As shown by Globerman [1977] and Marfels [1976] there is a high correlation between industry variables in the United States (and to a lesser extent in other countries) and in Canada. In the relationship between the diversification strategy of foreign-owned subsidiaries to Canadian industry variables, the Canadian industry variables may have simply been proxies for industry conditions in the home market. This hypothesis could best be tested by using industry variables for the *home countries* of the foreign-owned subsidiaries. Such a test, however, was beyond the scope of this study.

Based on the discriminant analysis, 17% of the Canadian-owned firms and (when parent firm strategy was used) 23% of the foreign-owned subsidiaries

[9] Canadian subsidiaries followed the same diversification strategy as their parents 63% of the time.

were classified to strategic categories which were not the ones they had followed, i.e., the misclassified firms may have followed an "inappropriate" strategy based on the predictions of the discriminant analysis. In what sense, however, were the strategies of the firms that did not follow their predicted strategy "inappropriate"? In fact, they may not have been inappropriate at all, but rather the problem could well be that the variables in the discriminant functions, the method of linear estimation, and the definition of the four strategic categories themselves may be inappropriate or misspecified. Moreover, unless a firm were penalized in terms of lower profits for following an "inappropriate" strategy, an inappropriate strategy might not be an "incorrect" one from the firm's point of view.

This question was partially resolved by testing to determine whether firms that had followed diversification strategies other than those predicted by the model were penalized for this decision in terms of lower profits in relation to firms that had followed the predicted strategy. Two comparisons can be made that speak to this question. The profitability of firms that did not follow the predicted strategy could be compared to firms within the strategic group they *actually* occupied or to firms within the strategic group *predicted* by the discriminant functions. To clarify this distinction with an example, if a firm were predicted to be in the UB strategic group but actually followed a VIB strategy, its profitability could be compared to both firms that actually followed a VIB strategy and to firms that were predicted to follow an UB strategy and did in fact follow that strategy.

There are three possible bases for assigning a foreign-owned subsidiary to a strategic group and two different bases of comparison between the profitability of firms that followed the predicted strategy and those that did not, i.e., there are six possible combinations in all. Since the analysis is of *foreign-owned* subsidiaries operating *in Canada*, it would seem that the best argument could be made for using the predictions based on Canadian industry variables and the strategy of the parent and for making profitability comparisons using the full sample of Canadian and foreign-owned firms. The subsequent analysis reported here will follow this procedure. Our confidence in the conclusions of this analysis is strengthened somewhat by the fact that when the two other classification methods and the other basis of comparison were used the results were generally the same, i.e., the differences in profitability between firms that followed the predicted strategy and those that did not were in the same direction as the comparisons reported here.

As shown in Table V, within common strategic groups, among the four strategic groups for both Canadian-owned and foreign firms, the mean profit for the firms that followed the strategy predicted by the discriminant analysis was significantly higher than that of the firms that did not follow the predicted strategy. For Example, as shown in Table V, column 1, for Canadian-owned firms which *actually* followed a single business strategy, the profits (as a percent return on equity) of firms that were *predicted* to follow that strategy were 2.3%

Table V
Profitability for Firms that Followed the Strategy Predicted by the Discriminant Analysis and Compared to Firms that Did Not

	Differences in return on equity between Canadian-owned firms[a]		*Differences in return on equity between foreign-owned subsidiaries*	
	1	*2*	*3*	4
Single Business	0.017[b]	0.021[b]	0.012[b]	0.024[b]
Vertically Integrated Business	0.015[b]	0.027[b]	0.008[b]	0.020[b]
Related Business	0.022[a]	0.053[a]	0.019[b]	0.042[a]
Unrelated Business	0.026[a]	0.010[c]	0.027[a]	0.008[c]
TOTAL	0.020[b]	0.031[a]	0.019[b]	0.024[a]

[a] differences in profitability were significant at the 0.01 level.
[b] the differences in profitability were significant at the 0.05 level.
[c] the differences in profitability were significant at the 0.10 level.
Comparisons 1 and 3 are between the firms *actually* in the same strategic group that were or were not *predicted* to be within that group.
Comparisons 2 and 4 are between the firms that were *predicted* to be within a strategic group that were or were not *actually* within that group.

higher than for firms that were predicted to follow some other strategy. The second comparison, i.e., of firms that were *predicted* to be within the same strategic group but were or were not *actually* within that group, (column 2) yielded somewhat different results. Firms that were predicted to follow a UB strategy but followed some other strategy did not have significantly lower profits than firms that were predicted to follow a UB strategy and actually did follow that strategy. On the other hand, firms that were predicted to follow an RB strategy but did not, had significantly lower profits than firms that were predicted to follow a RB strategy and followed that strategy. For firms that did not follow VIB and SB strategies as was predicted, profits were slightly lower than for firms that did follow the predicted VIB or SB strategy (but the difference was still significant).

These results indicate that although a UB strategy was not attractive for Canadian-owned firms in terms of return on equity, those firms whose base industry structure and firm characteristics indicated such a strategy were not able to avoid those low returns by following another strategy. Firms whose base industry structure and firm characteristics indicated that they would follow an RB strategy (a relatively profitable strategy) but did not, paid for that choice by significantly lower profits. A similar conclusion was supported, but with less force, for firms classified in SB and VIB strategic groups but which followed other diversification strategies. For these three groups of Canadian-owned firms, (but perhaps not for UB firms) it would then seem to be correct to speak of "appropriate" and "inappropriate" strategies since Canadian-owned firms that did not follow the predicted strategy were penalized in terms of lower profitability. As can be seen in columns 3 and 4 in

Table V similar results occurred for foreign-owned subsidiaries although the differences in profitability, while still significant, were smaller.

So far it has been established that discriminant analysis based on the characteristics of the firm's base industry and firm characteristics could be used to predict the diversification strategy followed by the firms in the sample and that if a firm followed a strategy that differed from the one predicted, an "inappropriate" strategy, it was often penalized for this decision. There would then seem to have been a latitude in the choice of diversification strategy, although an inappropriate choice may have led to a penalty of lower return on equity depending on the opportunities open to the firm and the choice it made.

These conclusions may need to be qualified further, however. It would be interesting to discover whether the firm's diversification strategy itself had influenced the firm's profits or whether its profits were simply a function of the profitability of the industries in which it operated (i.e., profits in its base industry and the industries into which it had diversified).

The business units that composed a diversified business could have been related through marketing, production, R & D, etc. The more closely they were related, the greater might the opportunity have been for the firm to have realized economies of scale in production, marketing, R & D, and management. Diversification into unrelated industries, conglomerate diversification, may have led to increased firm efficiency and increased profits via economies of scale in management, information and data processing and control. For unrelated diversification however, these effects may have been smaller than if the firm had engaged in related diversification. At the same time, for unrelated diversification, the potential negative effects might have been more pronounced—loss of performance incentives for management, loss of control and unfamiliarity of top management with the industries in which the firm competed and with the factors that led to success and failure in those industries. Firms that followed a VIB diversification strategy may have realized economies of scale in management, control, scheduling, and inventories across their vertically integrated business.[10] If there were unexploited economies of scale in the industry, expansion by an SB firm through acquisition or by internal means would increase its efficiency and profits would increase unless this action lowered industry prices sufficiency to offset the efficiency gains. (This price effect would apply to the expansion of industry output resulting from any diversification strategy).

Regardless of the diversification strategy followed by a firm, it would have had to buy or develop its assets in the industries in which it operated at competitive market prices. These prices are determined by the supply of those assets on the market and the demand for them by other firms which are

[10] See Baumol [1977] for a theoretical (and empirical) analysis of the problem and possibilities of economies of scale and scope for diversified firms.

interested in acquiring them. For example, the price of a steel fabricating plant is determined by the demand for such a facility by steel producers (VIB), other metal fabricators (RD), firms in unrelated businesses (e.g., a firm in the beer industry), and firms already in the steel fabricating industry (SB). The profitability of acquiring this operation would depend on the difference between this market price and the discounted benefits realized by the firms which purchased it. Based on the preceding analysis, these benefits might be highest for SB firms (if there were unrealized economies of scale in the industry), followed by RB or VIB firms and then UB firms. This hypothesis is given some support by the average profitability of the four groups as reported in Table III.

This analysis can be taken a step further. The relatively high profitability of SB and RB strategies reported in the tables may be influenced by the average profitability of the industries in which the firms in the sample operated, as well as their diversification strategy. This effect can be taken into account by using the difference between the profitability of the firms in the sample and the weighted average profitability in the industries in which they operated. This tests the hypothesis that there may be intrinsic differences in the profitability of various strategies after controlling for the opportunities inherent in the firms' base industries—the industries into which they diversified. This hypothesis follows that of Rumelt and is contrary to that of Caves *et al.*

To test the relationship between profitability and diversification strategy, two equations were estimated by multiple regression analysis.

$$PDR_1 = a_0 + \sum_{i=1}^{8} a_i X_i$$

where:

PDR = the firm's return on equity plus retained earnings minus the weighted average return of the industries in which the firm operated divided by the firm's return on equity plus retained earnings. This variable essentially measures how well the firm performed relative to the industries in which it operated.

X_1 = a dummy variable equal to 1 *if* the firm followed a VIB strategy, 0 otherwise.

X_2 = a dummy variable equal to 1 *if* the firm followed an RB strategy, 0 otherwise.

X_3 = a dummy variable equal to 1 *if* it followed a UB strategy, 0 otherwise.

X_4 = the probability the firm was following the strategy it actually followed as given by the discriminant functions constructed from its base industry variables and its firm characteristics.

X_5 = the firm's weighted average market share in the industries in which it operated.

X_6 = the firm's growth rate relative to the weighted average of the growth rates of the industries in which it operated.
X_7 = the firm's debt to equity ratio.
$X_8 = X_7^2$.

The variables X_1, X_2 and X_3 are dummy variables for the three strategic groups. (The SB effect is impacted in the constant term). As the probability that the firm was following the strategy it actually did follow (X_4) increased, *PDR* should also increase since this probability was a measure of how appropriate the firm's strategy was, given its characteristics and those of its base industry. X_5, the firm's weighted average market share in the industries in which it operated, was included as a control variable since market share and profitability are often directly related (Buzzell [1981]). The relative growth rate of the firm's market share in the industries in which it operated (X_6) could have had two effects on its relative profitability. First, there may have been a trade-off between growth in market share and profitability if the firm were following a strategy of buying market share. In this case the coefficient of X_6 would be negative. Second, as suggested by Caves *et al.*, the relative growth in market share may reflect the possession by the firm of proprietary assets which were valued by the market and could not be duplicated by other firms. In this case, the coefficient of X_6 would be positive. X_7 and X_8 were included in the regression to test the hypothesis (as did Caves *et al.*) that the firm's financial structure did in fact influence its profitability, i.e., that there was an optimal capital structure.

The results of this regression are in Table VI. They support the hypotheses presented above: a firm's performance improved relative to that of the weighted average of the industries in which it operated if it followed a strategy of related diversification, if it followed a strategy that was appropriate to the characteristics of its base industry and the firm, and as its relative market share increased. The dummy variables for UB and VIB had the predicted sign but were not significant. There was weak evidence that there was optimal capital structure since the coefficient of X_7 was positive and X_8 was negative. Contrary to the results of Caves *et al.*, growth in market share was associated with lower relative profits, supporting the hypothesis that there was a trade-off between growth in market share and short run profitability.

The rather weak statistical support to the hypothesis that firm performance was influenced by strategic diversification choice given base industry structure may have been due to the specification on the equations. The dummy variables turned on and off depending on the strategy of the firm. This implies that, as a firm changed strategy, the effect on *PDR* was immediate and did not vary with the *extent* to which the firm followed this strategy. This may not be a reasonable assumption as can be illustrated by an example. As an SB firm began to diverisfy into an unrelated business, the bulk of its activities would still be in its base industry and hence any difference in return arising from its

TABLE VI
REGRESSION OF PDR ON STRATEGIC CHOICE AND INDUSTRY VARIABLES

Variables	*PDR* (*1*) ($\times 10^3$)	*PDR* (2) ($\times 10^3$)
Constant	+11.3	+13.2
Dummy VIB, X_1	0.75	—
	(1.34)	
Dummy RB, X_2	+10.1	—
	(1.98)	
Dummy UB, X_3	−8.5	—
	(1.67)	
Probability of Actual Strategy, X_4	+19.5	+17.4
	(2.53)	(3.14)
Weighted Average Market Share, X_5	+6.3	+7.2
	(2.35)	(2.73)
Weighted Growth Rate, X_6	−3.5	−4.3
	(2.17)	(2.56)
Debt to equity, X_7	+3.2	+4.1
	(1.42)	(1.69)
(Debt-equity)^2, X_8	−3.7	−2.7
	(1.52)	(1.66)
Percent Outside Base Industry VIB, X_9	—	+1.5
		(2.12)
Percent Outside Base Industry RB, X_{10}	—	+4.5
		(3.10)
Percent Outside Base Industry UB, X_{11}	—	−2.1
		(2.92)
$\bar{R}^2$	0.43	0.67
N	200	200

t statistics are in parenthesis

diversified activities (as measured by *PDR*) would be small, unless the additional assumption is made that is operations in the base industry also suffered a once and for all fall in profitability as management attention was diverted to operations in new industries. An alternative hypothesis would be that the extent of the benefits and costs of following a diversification strategy (as measured by *PDR*) would be related to the *extent* of the firm's activities its base industry contingent on the opportunity set of the base industry. This hypothesis could be tested by the regression equation:

$$PDR_2 = b_0 + \sum_{i=4}^{11} b_i X_i$$

where $X_4 \ldots X_8$ are as defined above and:

$X_9 =$ the percentage of a firm's operations outside its base industry *if* the firm were VIB

$X_{10} =$ the percentage of a firm's operations outside its base industry *if* the firm were RB

X_{11} = the percentage of a firm's operations outside its base industry *if* the firm were UB.

The variables X_1, X_2 and X_3 are dummy variables in the sense that they are 0 when the firm is not following a VIB, RB or VB strategy respectively. They are weighted by the percent of the firm's activities that were outside its base industry. This procedure allowed for the testing of the hypothesis that the strategy a firm followed directly affected its profitability relative to the profitability of the industries in which it operated *and* that this effect increased as activities outside its base industry increased, e.g., the more vertically integrated a firm became, the greater was the effect of this strategy on its relative profitability.

The results of this regression using samples of Canadian-owned and foreign-owned firms are reported in Table VI. In both equations $\bar{R}^2$ was higher and the strategic choice variables were significant. If a firm followed an RB or a VIB strategy it had significantly higher profits than the weighted average of the industries in which it operated and if it followed a UB strategy it earned lower than the weighted averaged profits. If a firm followed an appropriate strategy, its profits were also increased relative to the industries in which it operated. There was then a tradeoff for some firms between following a UB strategy if this strategy were indicated by the characteristics of the firm and its base industry since following the indicated strategy increased profits, but following a UB strategy decreased them.

As can be seen in Table VII, firms which were predicted to follow a UB strategy and actually followed that strategy diversified into industries whose profits were higher than profits in their base industries. The overall profitability of these firms was lower than the average profitability of the industries into which they had diversified, even though their overall profitability was higher than that of their base industries. Firms which were predicted to follow a UB strategy, but actually followed another strategy, diversified into industries with lower profitability than their base industries, earned higher

TABLE VII

	Predicted UB		*Predicted RB*	
	Actual UB	*Actual Other*	*Actual RB*	*Actual Other*
Profitability of industries into which firms diversified relative to base industry	+0.033[a]	−0.025[c]	−0.003	+0.011
Overall profitability relative to industries into which the firm diversified	−0.021[a]	+0.008	+0.035[a]	−0.028[a]
Overall firm profitability relative to base industry	+0.015[c]	−0.012[c]	+0.031[b]	−0.015[b]

a, b, c = significant at the 0.01, 0.05, and 0.10 levels respectively overall profits than the industries into which they had diversified, but lower overall profits than those in their base industries.

Firms whose base industry and firm characteristics indicated a UB strategy were in an unattractive situation. If they followed a UB strategy and diversified into higher profit industries, they earned low profits relative to other firms in those industries, yet their overall profits increased. If they did not follow the indicated UB strategy, the industries into which they could diversify via some other strategy were low profit industries and even though they performed relatively well, their overall profits were low. On average, however, firms which followed the predicted UB strategy earned higher profits than those that did not follow the predicted strategy. The optimal strategy for a firm whose base industry and firm characteristics indicated a UB strategy depended on the relative magnitudes of X_4 (probability of the firm following the strategy it actually followed) and the variables X_9, X_{10}, X_{11} (the percent of operations outside the base industry). If X_4 were low (i.e., a borderline UB firm) the negative impact of following a strategy other than the indicated UB strategy was low and was more than offset by the gain in following an RB or VIB strategy. Conversely, if X_4 was high (a strong correspondence between the firm's base industry characteristics and those indicating an UB strategy), then the penalty for following another strategy was high and outweighed the benefits of following an RB or VIB strategy.

The implications of these results are that, while firms that were predicted to follow a UB strategy and did follow that strategy have made the correct choice of *where* resources should go (i.e., into what industries), they made the incorrect decision of *how* the resources should be allocated, i.e., they allocated them within their firm rather than via the market through paid out dividends and reinvestment through the capital markets.

IV. SUMMARY

The analysis in this paper has found support for the following hypotheses based on a sample of the two hundred largest manufacturing firms in Canada:

1. For Canadian-owned firms, the characteristics of the base industry of a firm and the firm's characteristics influenced the diversification strategy it followed. For foreign-owned firms the diversification strategy was influenced both by the parent firm's strategy and by characteristics of the subsidiary and the base industry in which it operated.
2. There were often penalties for not following an appropriate diversification strategy, i.e., the strategy that reflected the influences of the characteristics of the firm and its base industry, for both Canadian and foreign-owned firms.
3. A firm's return on equity increased relative to the weighted average return on equity of the industries in which it operated to the extent it followed a

strategy of related diversification and vertical integration, if it followed an appropriate strategy, if its market share in the industries in which it operated was large, if it were growing more slowly than the industries in which it operated, and if it chose an optimal capital structure.

Donald J. Lecraw,
School of Business Administration,
The University of Western Ontario,
London, Canada, N6A 3K7

ACCEPTED SEPTEMBER 1983

REFERENCES

ALCHIAN, A. A. and DEMSETZ, H., 1972, 'Production, Information Costs, and Economic Organization', *American Economic Review*, Vol. 62, No. 5, pp. 777–95.

ANDREWS, K. R., 1971, *The Concept of Corporate Strategy*, (Dow Jones-Richard D. Irwin, Homewood, Ill.).

BAUMOL, W. J., 1977, 'Empirical Study of Scale Economics and Production Complementarity', *Journal of Political Economy*, Vol. 85, (October), pp. 1037–48.

BERRY, C. H., 1975, *Corporate Growth and Diversification*. (Princeton University Press, Princeton, N.J.).

BUZZELL, R. D., 1981, 'Are There "Natural" Market Structures?', *Journal of Marketing*, Vol. 45, (Winter), pp. 42–51.

CAVES, R. E., 1975, *Diversification, Foreign Investment and Scale in North American Manufacturing Industries* (Information Canada for the Economic Council of Canada, Ottawa).

CAVES, R. E., 1980, 'Industrial Organization, Corporate Strategy and Structure', *Journal of Economic Literature*, Vol. 18, (March), pp. 64–92.

CAVES, R. E., 1982, *Multinational Enterprise And Economic Analysis* (Cambridge Essays in Economics, Cambridge, England).

CAVES, R. E., PORTER, M. E., SPENCE, A. M. and SCOTT, J., 1980, *Competition in the Open Economy* (Harvard University Press, Cambridge, Mas.).

CHANDLER, A. D., JR., 1977, *The Visible Hand: The Managerial Revolution in American Business* (Harvard University Press, Cambridge, Mass.).

COASE, R. H., 1937, 'The Nature of the Firm', *Economica*, Volume IV, (November), pp. 386–405.

GLOBERMAN, S., 1977, *Mergers and Acquisitions in Canada* (Ministry of Supply and Services, Ottawa).

GORECKI, P., 1980, 'The Determinants of Foreign and Domestic Enterprise Diversification in Canada: A Note', *Canadian Journal of Economics*, Vol. 13, No.2, (May) pp. 329–39.

GORT, M., 1962, *Diversification and Integration in American Industry*, (National Bureau of Economic Research, General Series, No.77 Princeton University Press, Princeton, N.J.).

GREEN, P., 1978, *Analyzing Multivariate Data* (The Dryden Press, Hinadale, Illinois).

LAWRENCE, P. R. and LORSCH, J., 1967, *Organization and Environment: Managing Differentiation and Integration* (Division of Research, Graduate School of Business Administration, Harvard University Press, Boston).

LECRAW, D. and THOMPSON, D., 1978, *Conglomerate Mergers in Canada* (Minister of Supply and Services Canada, Ottawa).

MARFELS, C., 1976, *Concentration Levels and Trends in the Canadian Economy 1965–1973* (Ministry of Supply and Services, Ottawa).

PENROSE, E., 1959, *The Theory of the Growth of the Firm*, (Basil Blackwell, Oxford).
Royal Commission on Corporate Concentration, 1978, *Report*, (Ministry of Supply and Services Canda, Ottawa).
RUMELT, R. P., 1974, *Strategy, Structure, and Economic Performance*, (Division of Research, Graduate School of Business Administration, Harvard University, Boston, Mass.).
WILLIAMSON, O. E., 1975, *Markets and Hierarchies*, (Free Press, New York).
WRIGLEY, L., 1970, 'Divisional Autonomy and Diversification', unpublished DBA thesis (Graduate School of Business Administration, Harvard).

THE JOURNAL OF INDUSTRIAL ECONOMICS 0022-1821 $2.00
Volume XXXIII December 1984 No. 2

A "BRAND NAME FIRM" THEORY OF MEDICAL GROUP PRACTICE*

Thomas E. Getzen

Medical group practices are firms, voluntary contracts between two or more practitioners to jointly provide services, purchase inputs, and distribute income. It is hypothesized that one reason why such organizations are formed is to more efficiently convey information on quality of care to patients, and further, that the increased efficiency of doctor-patient exchange is usually more important than economies of scale in production. A "brand name firm" theory of medical group practice is presented and then tested by comparisons between medicine and dentistry, generalist and specialist practice, and by variations in mobility across patients and providers. Observed variation in the extent and contractual structure of group practice strongly supports the brand name firm hypothesis and is inconsistent with economies of scale explanations.

I. THE ECONOMIES OF SCALE HYPOTHESIS AND ITS DEFICIENCIES

In the first recorded discussion of group practice, Davis [1919] asserts that increasing medical specialization and capital intensity brought about by technological advances require a more organized type of practice for efficient operation. In simple terms, it was held that the gains from division of labor and the use of large expensive equipment created a lumpiness in inputs and, therefore, that average costs would decline with an increasing volume of service.[1]

The promised gains have proved elusive. Reinhardt's [1972] estimates of medical care production functions indicated that the use of large scale to overcome the lumpiness of specialized ancillary labor inputs (nurses, therapists, x-ray technicians, etc.) would be significant, yet studies by Bailey [1968] and Kimball and Lorant [1977] produced only equivocal results, Ernst and Schwartz [1974] found no effect, and Newhouse [1973] presented limited data which he argued demonstrated substantial diseconomies of scale. Bobula and Freshnock [1978] provide an excellent review of the literature. The consensus would appear to be that cost savings probably do exist, at least in

* Portions of this work were supported by grants from the W. K. Kellog foundation and the Pharmaceutical Manufacturers Association. Generous assistance and thoughful criticism were received from many persons, particularly Yoram Barzel, David Barton Smith and an anonymous referee. Of course, the opinions expressed herein and the remaining errors are solely my own responsibility.

[1] The dominant explanation for the slow growth of group practice has been the presumed willingness of physicians to forego profits in order to retain autonomy. This view is expressed most recently by Goodman and Wolinsky [1982].

some cases, although definitive evidence is still lacking, but they are small and hold only for modest sized (2–7 physician) groups.[2]

Ultimately an "economies of scale" hypothesis depends upon differences in transactions costs which make ownership less costly than other forms of contracting. Clearly some inputs would be easier to rent in partial units than others, and the greater part of capital and labor inputs in medical care are owned by hospitals, not physicians. Demonstrating a declining average cost function is appealingly direct, but ignores development of the hypothesis to make predictions regarding variations in group contracts or in the extent of group practice due to changes in prices, types of inputs, specialty, or conditions. Furthermore, exclusive focus on production and input transactions as explanations of economic organization seems somewhat inappropriate to medical care. Uncertainty and information asymmetry between doctors and patients are medicine's characteristic features (Arrow [1963] and Pauly [1978]) and would be expected to more significantly affect consumer transactions or "marketing".

II. A BRAND NAME FIRM HYPOTHESIS

Brand Name Transactions

When the quality of output is highly variable and the cost of quality information is much greater for consumers than producers, transactions are apt to be made in a relationship here termed a "brand name contract".[3] Consumer purchase decisions are made based on reputation, and producer lapses are punished by a loss of expected future business. A central feature of medical care, as noted by Arrow, is the asymmetry of information costs between providers and consumers. Treatment decisions can be made by the physician at lower cost so he acts as the patient's "agent".[4] The patient's information costs are also asymmetric over time. After treatment, outcome is (slowly) revealed to him by experiencing changes in his health status.[5] The accumulation of past experiences (his own or others) is the basis for the patient's trust in the physician. The identity of the physician is used in place of costly measurement at the time of transaction to determine quality. Patients depend upon

[2] Economies of scale increasing the efficiency or reducing the price of ancilliary inputs could actually increase the reported cost per unit if the elasticity of substitution with respect to physician time were sufficiently great.

[3] Throughout this paper there is a heavy dependence upon the work conducted by many economists over the last twenty years which has often been placed under the rubric of "transactions costs theory". Several of the most relevant articles are inluded in the references (Alchian and Demsetz [1972], Arrow [1963], Barzel [1982], Coase [1937], Klein and Leffler [1981] and Rothschild [1973]).

[4] Many authors use the term "agency" with regard to the doctor-patient relationship, most commonly citing as sources Bailey [1969] or Feldstein [1974].

[5] The patient must be able to determine outcome differences related to quality or he would have no way to enforce the agency relation. Indeed he would not need to, since, if forever unobservable, quality differences would not affect utility and would be irrelevant to him.

the reputation so formed and are willing to pay a premium for "brand name" quality services.[6]

Adam Smith [1976, p. 118] and John Stuart Mill [1909, p. 404] observed that "trusted" services were highly paid relative to apparent costs, but provided no adequate explanations. Klein and Leffler [1981] have described how such brand name premia act like guarantees, creating an incentive for a firm to fulfil the implicit contract by providing services of specified quality. Failure to do so results in a loss of income from expected future premia. In effect, the physician retains partial ownership of the product. As failure is revealed over time it causes a decline in the value of his "brand name" asset (in legal and accounting terminology, "goodwill").

The Brand Name Advantage of Group Practices

All medical care is transacted by brand name. The advantage of group practice firms over independent solo practitioners is that to some extent internal evaluation by physician colleagues can substitute for more costly patient search in monitoring quality. Patients and reputation can be transferred more efficiently and brand name is created at less cost.

The Mayo clinic, the first modern group practice, sprang from increased demand due to a reputation for quality, as documented in histories of this seminal group (Clapesattle [1941], Nagel [1966] and Rorem [1931]). No doubt the elder Dr. Mayo was efficient but, more importantly, he was perceived to be highly competent and was able to transfer his reputation and demand to his heirs and partners. The newly graduated doctor who joins the practice of established physicians benefits because reputation and patients are transferred early in his career rather than being laboriously built up over years. The established physicians are compensated for this brand name service by receiving a disproportionate share of joint income. Furthermore, sharing motivates them to bring in someone good and devote resources to monitoring so that the practice will remain growing and lucrative, thus patients obtain some guarantee that the quality of the new graduate will indeed meet expected standards. Similarly, the ability of groups to transfer patients for night coverage and vacations depends not on efficiency in production, but on the efficient formation of a contract which guarantees the patient he can obtain specified (quality) services and, not incidentally, guarantees the physician that he will not lose business to the competition.[7]

[6] Note that this implies that services of a particular brand should be homogeneous in quality, not necessarily of high quality. Sears and Neiman-Marcus are both brand name guarantors of quality for which consumers pay a premium, although the expected quality is very different in the two cases (Klein and Leffler [1981]).

[7] Informal agreements are used instead of contracts by solo physicians. That they are generally less satisfactory is apparent in survey responses that "adequate coverage for patients" and "less time on call" are major reasons for joining a group, and this is supported by the observation that group practitioners work for fewer nights than solo doctors (American Medical Association [1933] and Bailey [1968].

The partners are (to a degree) viewed by consumers as a single entity or "firm" producing a homogeneous service of equal quality regardless of the identity of the individual practitioner seen. In this regard the medical group is analogous to the licensed self-regulating profession at a micro level. The contract provides incentives for partners to act in concert by tying their income to that of the group—the behavior of all of them together. Any lapse of quality will result in a loss to all. The asymmetry of information cost is crucial in that it must be cheaper for the existing members to identify and enforce the quality of a potential partner than for consumers to do so for the group firm to achieve information cost savings.[8]

Formation of a group practice firm with perpetual identity independent of the individuals who comprise it ameliorates the "first period problem" (need to build a reputation) and "last period problem" (lack of incentive to maintain quality reputation as retirement nears) caused by the finite life of a solo practitioner. Having a single entity which spans several members who work together on one patient reduces the problem of "jointness", or confounding the estimate of the contribution of one physician by variability in the quality of the consulting specialist (or night replacement, anesthesiologist, assistant, etc). For a group including both, the distinction is irrelevant and all failures are clearly attributable to that single firm (Alchian and Demsetz [1972]). Purely static allocative efficiency is also increased. To the degree that information costs make the demand facing an individual producer inelastic (i.e., reduce cross-price elasticity), the price and marginal cost of services diverges, and consumer's business becomes a valuable commodity. It is precisely such a lack of cross-price elasticity we identify as "brand name loyalty". If the value of customers varies across producers who differ in reputation but are otherwise identical, there are gains from trade. The busy physician with a high cost of time can "sell" patients to his colleague if he can convince them that they are receiving the same quality. Forming a partnership firm makes the two physicians better substitutes (increases cross-price elasticity). Problems due to finite lives, jointness and allocation are alleviated by formation of a group practice. The firm constitutes a contract for the transaction of brand name so that it can be bought and sold somewhat like a capital asset. Incentives are thus provided to transfer patients and maintain quality so as to maximize its value.

In addition, "informational economies of scale" are obtained by partially substituting physicians monitoring of each other for costly evaluation by patients. With a group enforcing uniformity across members, the prospective patient can use information on any one of them to estimate the quality of

[8] The use of such cooperative linking of careers is not unique to doctors. Economists also bring on junior partners in research projects or consulting jobs, letting their reputation serve as a guarantee for the previously untested entrant. The standard incentive programs of corporations; promotions, raises and profit sharing, are movements toward a partnership solution. The greater extent of such a contractual form to the exclusion of others in medicine reflects the degree of asymmetry in information costs.

service he will receive. The body of experience or number of possible observations is larger, and search (predicting quality) is less costly.[9]

Different Quality Dimensions

Thus far it has been assumed that quality is a single dimension; probability of cure, increase in life expectancy, degree of functioning returned, etc. Multidimensionality in itself poses no particular problems so long as the asymmetry of information costs clearly favors physician colleagues relative to patients. Monitoring must occur along many margins and is thus more costly, but is also more costly to patients. Suppose, however, that one dimension of quality were in fact cheaper for patients to monitor than physicians—"bedside manner" for example.

The group not only has no advantage in monitoring bedside quality, but suffers from a free rider problem. The doctor who is surly, abrupt or inept bears only a part of the cost (loss of future business) because brand name is a shared asset. Hence groups should be less likely to form where quality is relatively more easily measured by patients (psychiatry, general practice) and, furthermore, groups will tend to specialize in the area where they have a comparative advantage relative to solo practitioners, in technical (physician evaluated) quality rather than bedside (patient evaluated) quality.

Exogenous Constraints

The value of brand name, and hence the advantage of group relative to solo practice, rises with increases in:[10]

(1) cost of search
(2) value of outcome differences
(3) variability of outcome
(4) infrequency and variability in disease occurrence
(5) jointness of production
(6) producer or consumer turnover (mobility)
(7) technical (as opposed to bedside) quality

[9] In this regard, a group practice is analogous to a department store whose reputation is used as an indicator of the quality of an appliance, or a clothier whose brand name is used to select a suit. Clearly the group will never become perfectly homogeneous, but informational economies of scale to patients will exist whenever the identity of the firm aids materially in evaluating the quality of the individual practitioner.

[10] The advantage of large relative to small groups similarly rises. A formal model and extended discussion of these constraints is provided in Getzen [1981]. Infrequency and variability of disease occurrence creates production economies of scale as well due to stochastic demand with discrete lumpiness in inputs. Asymmetry of information costs, on the other hand, is affected because consumers' stock of quality evaluation is used less often and must be acquired rapidly. From the patient perspective, the information problem is reduced if the disease is rare but chronic, or acute but signalled in advance, while the producer's problem remains unchanged.

III. THE CONTRACTUAL STRUCTURE OF MEDICAL GROUP PRACTICE: INCOME DISTRIBUTION

Variations in transaction costs determine not only the usefulness of a particular type of economic organization, but also the form of internal contract which governs it. The income distribution plan specifies what the individual physician owns, the incentive structure he faces. The variations are endless, but regardless of how complicated they may be in detail, virtually all group contracts distribute at least part and usually a majority of income either by equal shares, by productivity (i.e., proportional to individual service billings), by straight salary, or a combination of the three.

Under a pure productivity plan, the member retains ownership of his own earnings and hence faces incentives similar to those of a solo entrepeneur. *Ceteris paribus*, each physician will seek to maximize his individual revenues. If the number of group members is four, then a physician would divert effort from seeing patients to group management activities and monitoring partners only if the return is greater than 400%. Opportunistic quality reductions are rational since most of the current period gains accrue to him while the future costs (loss of business) are born mutually.

With equal sharing the individual's income depends solely on group income and *ceteris paribus* he will act to maximize the profits of the firm. The individual will optimally allocate his efforts between monitoring others, maintaining his own quality and transferring patients. The problem with equal sharing is that even though the incentive structure leads to an allocation of effort which maximizes profit, too little effort may be provided since at the margin the individual gains only a fraction (1 ÷ number of members) of the profits he generates for the firm.[11]

As management and technical quality become more important determinants of group earnings, the income distribution will shift toward sharing. If the quantity of individual physician effort is more important, productivity will be emphasized. The productivity plan also makes greater use of low cost patient information in controlling the "bedside" quality of practice by rewarding those doctors whom patients choose most frequently.

The group contract further refines the ownership structure through various practice restrictions. Part-time attending physicians may use the group's

[11] It might be suspected that under a sharing contract physicians would be prone to take extra time off, arrive late, etc. Repeated empirical studies however have demonstrated that group physicians work as many or more hours than solo physicians (Bobula and Freshnook [1978] and Held and Reinhardt [1979]). Upon reflection, this is not surprising since "hours" are very easy for the group to monitor and thus limit shirking behavior along this margin. It is rather the degree of effort and, in particular, the ability to provide "bedside" quality which is hard to determine. Intrinsic variation in earning power (due to education, manual dexterity or charisma) also occurs but is costly to negotiate (i.e., by providing unequal shares) and to renegotiate repeatedly as circumstances change. For these reasons combinations of productivity and sharing income distribution providing incentives for both individual and group effort, or the level and allocation of effort, are common. Examples of typical group contracts are provided in the references (American Association of Medical Clinics, [1974] and Medical Group Management Association [1978]).

brand name to build their own practice, and may see private patients during clinic hours. The part-timer also incurs a smaller loss from a decline in quality and his incentive to participate in group management is smaller. Allowing a member to keep "outside" earnings from honoraria, consultations and publications make it more difficult to monitor individual effort since they may be done using time "belonging" to the group; hence, it is frequently stipulated that all earnings related to medicine are to be treated as group income.

A hierarchical time structuring of membership progressing from salaried probation, to junior, and finally to full partner or shareholder, is used to bond the individual to the group. His rewards, obtained in the future, are tied to the satisfactory evaluation of his quality as it is revealed over time to the group. Even should other physicians be unable to detect his failures, such a time structuring prevents his "cheating" by providing quick and dirty services and then leaving for an equally attractive post elsewhere as the group's reputation starts to crumble.

A restrictive covenant is a contract clause which prohibits a physician who leave the group from practicing in the same market area or requires him to pay a cash indemnity for doing so (Gorlick [1978] and Medical Group Management Association [1976]). Not only could he cheat, as described above,but a member who set himself up in independent practice next door would expropriate a part of the group's brand name asset, its expected future business. The Oklahoma Supreme Court in "Herington vs. Heckler" explicitly recognized the restrictive covenant as a mechanism to preserve goodwill (brand name) (O'Hern [1968]).

All the practice restrictions discussed here serve to maintain group brand name. We predict that as the value of brand name rises, groups will be more likely to share income equally, prohibit part-time membership, own outside income, extend the membership hierarchy by increasing the compensation of a senior member relative to a new entrant, and stipulate restrictive covenants.

Costs of Group Organization

The cost disadvantages of group practice are due primarily to the problems of managing a larger and more complex organization. Under an equal shares income plan a physician may shirk or wastefully overuse ancillary inputs since he bears only part of the cost. Under a productivity plan there is insufficient incentive to devote time to group management activities or shared services. The inefficiencies arising from suboptimizing individualistic responses to uncontracted margins clearly increase with the size of the group under either alternative (Newhouse [1973] and Pauly [1970]).

The costs of initial contracting and search for compatible partners to form a group appear small and less important than the potential costs of dissolution. Approximately 25% of groups cease to exist within 10 years, with disagreements over income distribution being the main cause (Dickinson and Bradley

[1952] and Goodman and Freshnock [1978]). Protracted fights over accounts receivable, patient records and other assets are not uncommon. Acrimonious battles disrupt management and can lead to significant dissipation of brand name (Martin [1963] and Medical Group Management Association [1976]). The difficulty of maintaining harmony to avoid costly break ups would presumably rise with the number of members involved.

It is difficult to generalize regarding variations in organizational costs across practices (holding size constant) beyond the obvious statements that more standardized work (e.g., radiologists and pathologists) or less conflict (due for example to increasing rather than falling demand) reduce management problems. Across individual physicians, the choice of practice mode is probably largely determined by variations in management ability, or the ability to be "team" managed.

IV. EMPIRICAL EVIDENCE

Some Observations

The major hypothesis presented in this paper is that group practices increase "brand name" and thus more efficiently convey information on quality of care to patients. The demand for such economic organization increases as the ability of the patient to monitor quality declines relative to doctors, i.e., as the asymmetry of information costs increases. Furthermore, as the value of brand name rises, the internal contractual structure of the group shifts to facilitate quality control by increasing sharing and practice restrictions.

The Mayo Clinic, the Virginia Mason Clinic, the Ochsner Clinic and others clearly possess brand names that provide quality information to the consumer at low cost. The use of the partnership contract to transfer reputation and clientele from an established practitioner to a new entrant is also obvious. In one survey, 86% of all groups had grown from established solo practices that were more successful than most, as the Mayo Clinic did (Jordan [1958]). The common feature is the existence of a firm "identity" or name which is used by patients to evaluate quality and hence is a valuable asset. Assertions that patients come to the clinic rather than the individual doctor support the importance of the group identity as an advertising tool and are repeatedly made in the literature (American Foundation [1937], American Medical Association [1933], Jordan [1958], Medical Group Management Association [1976] and Rorem [1931]). A study at the Marshfield Clinic found that 43% of all patients considered the "clinic" rather than a particular doctor to be their regular provider of care (Mechanic [1980]). In this regard it is interesting to note that the use of a fictitious (corporate) name, even adding the word "clinic" after the practitioner's name, is unethical and (in some states) illegal for the solo physician but allowed to the group (American Medical Association [1971] and Stanford Law Review [1952]).

The existence of the group as an entity responsible for the quality of care is nowhere clearer than in the treatment of malpractice. All members are jointly held liable regardless of degree of involvement in the case or even presence in the country (Alsobrook [1977] and O'Hern [1970]). Similarly "fee splitting", payments from one doctor to another in return for referrals, are uniformly treated as fraudulent breaches of the agent-client contract when carried out between solo practitioners but are considered legal and ethical and commonly practiced within the firm (group) (American Medical Association [1971], Holman [1970], Medical Group Management Association [1976] and [1978]).[12] Integrating all care within the group reduces the need to distinguish the separate contributions of two independent providers. The enforcement of costly contractual practice restrictions is readily explainable in terms of transacting and maintaining brand name, but would appear useless if the sole function of the group were to reduce the costs of production.

Comparison of Medicine and Dentistry

For the majority of dental care the optimal outcome is "normal teeth"—a state that is relatively well defined, easily observed, and comparable across patients—and the worst outcome is the loss of all teeth, with some attendant pain, and loss of time and money. For medicine, the optimal outcome of treatment is more difficult to define and observe, and the worst outcome is death with a considerable outlay of time, pain and money. The cost and value of determining that a physician is among the top ten percent in quality is greater than for a dentist. Often the difference between high and low quality medical care hinges on small changes in probabilities of disastrous outcomes that occur long after treatment. Ascertaining that one physician is better than another in treating ulcers is tremendously difficult, and there are thousands of diagnoses. More observations are required and each is more costly for medicine because services are less comparable. Furthermore, the difference in the expected value of outcome of tenth percentile quality relative to fiftieth percentile quality is larger. The brand name of the medical doctor is worth more because the variability in the value of outcomes is greater and search costs are higher. Increased asymmetry of information costs make medical patients more likely to depend upon a professional evaluation of quality than dental patients. Therefore it is predicted that relatively more medical doctors will be organized into groups and that these groups will exhibit a greater degree of contract structuring to control quality.

[12] An interesting comparison is provided by the prohibition of pharmacy ownership by physicians on the (apparently well founded) grounds that they might raise prices and encourage extra purchases to increase profits. The attempt to discourage profiteering on drug sales by physicians can be traced as far back as the code of Hammurabi. The quality of drugs is fully controlled by the manufacturer and hence monitoring by the prescribing physician is of little value. The quality of service provided by referral practitioners is significantly variable, and net benefits can be obtained from the extra monitoring provided by a group.

The comparison between medicine and dentistry is particularly appropriate because a "production cost economies of scale" hypothesis leads to a contrary prediction. Dentists' expenses are higher than physicians' in both absolute terms, $56,300 vs. $42,000, and relative to gross, 56% vs. 43% (American Dental Association [1978] and American Medical Association [1978]). If group practice served primarily to reduce the ancillary input costs of production, then *ceteris paribus* groups would be more prevalent in dentistry because costs are greater.[13]

The extent of group practice depends upon how "group practice" is defined and measured, and the data for physicians and dentists are not perfectly comparable. Regardless of how group practice is measured though, the percentage of physicians organized into groups is clearly greater. Table I compares the size of the practice as determined by the AMA and ADA periodic surveys. With the strict AMA definition (3 or more with income distribution) Goodman, Bennett and Odem [1976] estimated that 23.5% of all physicians were in group practice. The comparable figure for dentists is less than 10%. The *Medical Economics* survey (Owens, [1980])estimated that over 50% of all physicians were in group practice, while in the similar *Dental Economics*' survey [1980] only 18% of all dentists identified themselves as being in a partnership, association or group.

TABLE I
GROUP MEMBERS AS A PERCENTAGE OF ALL PRACTITIONERS BY SIZE OF PRACTICE, 1976

Practice Size	*Physicians*	*Dentists*
Solo	56.5%	77.8%
2	10.6	13.6
3	8.3	4.4
4	5.5	2.2
5–25	14.6	2.0
26+	4.5	—

Sources: American Dental Association, *The 1977 Survey of Dental Practice*, Chicago, IL., American Dental Association, 1978; American Medical Association, *Profile of Medical Practice, 1978*, Chicago, IL., American Medical Association, 1978.

The types of income distribution plans are varied and hence more difficult to compare. In the 1975 AMA Survey (Goodman, Bennett and Odem [1976]), 30% of groups divided income primarily on the basis of equal shares, 9% on productivity, 20% on salary, and 41% on a combination or other

[13] Note that other contractual relations (such as renting space in a medical office building) exist which enable several dentists or doctors to share a receptionist or x-ray machine without forming a group.

formula. In the study of dental group practice conducted by Nash *et al.* [1979] 18% of group dentists were compensated on the basis of equal shares, 21% on the basis of productivity only, 17% on salary, and 44% on some combination or other formula. Despite the limited availability of data, one can conclude that dentists are less likely to divide income on the basis of equal shares, and more likely to use productivity measures.

Part-time practice appears to be much more common in dental groups. Nash *et al.* [1979] report that 20.3% of dentists in groups of 3 or more were part-time, while Goodman, Bennett and Odem [1976] estimate that only 8% of physicians in groups were part-time. Unfortunately, no data exist which would allow a comparison along other contract dimensions such as restrictive covenants or length of membership hierarchy.

The differences in the extent of group practice and contract structure between medicine and dentistry are consistent with the predictions of the brand name firm hypothesis. The cost of production "economies of scale" hypothesis leads to a prediction contrary to the findings presented above regarding the percentage of practitioners in groups, and gives rise to no predictions concerning the difference in income distribution plans and part-time membership.

Specialists vs. Generalist Practice

Search costs are greater for specialty care since fewer observations will provide relevant information. Furthermore, technical quality (best evaluated by physician colleagues) is relatively more important than bedside quality (best evaluated by patients) as care becomes more oriented to treatment and less personal.[14] Group practice is therefore predicted to be more prevalent among specialists.

The AMA survey reports that specialists are more likely to be in groups than are generalists (27% vs. 17%), more likely to share income equality (36% vs. 30%) and less likely to divide income on the basis of productivity (7% vs. 14%).[15] Findings of a higher percentage of group practice among specialists are consistently reported in other physician surveys (Owens

[14] The increases in specialization and technical capability to treat disease are probably responsible for much of the growth in group practice over time. It has been estimated that in 1900 a patient seeing a physician had only a 50–50 chance of being helped more than harmed. Quality was largely a matter of the personal relationship between patient and physician, cures were most commonly effected through the placebo effect, and technical quality which could be reliably assessed by colleagues of little import. Furthermore, specialization vastly increased jointness in production and the number of patient transfers.

[15] The source for all comparisons across specialties is Goodman, Bennett and Odem [1976] unless otherwise noted. Asymmetry of information costs is greater for technical services than for bedside care which can be personally evaluated. Hence one might predict, for example, that patients with functional (psychosomatic) illnesses requiring counselling rather than drugs or surgery would be more likely to patronize solo practitioners.

[1980]), among osteopaths (Cuzzolino [1979–80]), and among dentists (American Dental Association [1978]).

Expected differences between specialties are harder to sort out because separate dimensions may vary in opposite directions. Observations across specialties are generally consistent with a brand name firm explanation of group practice but cannot truly be said to provide a clean test of the hypothesis. For example, in pediatrics bedside quality is relatively more important than in other specialties and repeated use lowers the cost of search, yet because emergencies and night visits are common, patient transfers are more frequent. The predicted effects of these factors on group formation are opposed. In actuality, pediatricians are slightly more likely (30% vs. 27%) than other specialists to be in groups.

For some specialties the situation is more evident. Psychiatrists are high in bedside quality, rarely engage in joint production, and few (10%) practice in groups. At the other extreme radiologists virtually never come into contact with patients, quality is purely technical, and a large percentage (57%) are in groups. Orthopedic surgery is characterized by team production and many are in groups (38%). Opthamology is similar to dentistry, having lower information costs and less referral business, and group practice is less common (18%). The extent of group practice across specialties does not vary with expenses as a percentage of gross (American Dental Association [1978] and American Medical Association [1978]) and hence does not support a production cost economies of scale hypothesis.

Mobility

When a patient moves, his accumulated information is worth less in evaluating quality. Local friends and neighbors are harder to contact, and in an area of generally high mobility will have less useful information to impart. Mobility increases the cost of search and therefore is predicted to be positively associated with the extent of group practice.[16] Reported in Table II is the result of an OLS regression across 54 SMSA's for which data were available.[17]

The mobility coefficient is positive as predicted and significant at the 0.01

[16] For this reason one would predict that within any given area groups have a greater percentage of patients who are recent movers than solo practitioners and relatively fewer long term patients. No studies of patient tenure are available but Owens [1980] reports a *Medical Economics* survey indicating that group physicians attract more new patients per MD than solo practitioners.

[17] The unit of observation is the census bureau "Standard Metropolitan Statistical Area" (SMSA), which can reasonably be considered a local geographic market. The dependent variable is the percentage of physicians who reported themselves as being in groups, taken from unpublished data in the 1975 Physician Capacity Utilization Telephone Survey, Mathematica Policy Research, Princeton, New Jersey. "Mobility" is the percentage of households who had moved within the last twelve months as reported by U.S. Department of Commerce [1979]. Area total population in 1975, population growth 1970–75, and average per capita income are taken from the same publication. "MD's/population" is the number of MD's per 100,000 population reported by the AMA [1976]. None of the variables other than mobility obtains a conventional 0.05 level of significance.

Table II
Regression of Percentage of MD's in group Practice on Mobility and Area Characteristics, by 54 SMSA's, 1975.

%MD's in Groups	= 16.9	+ 1.49* mobility	+ 0.005 income	− 9.0 MD's/pop.	− 1.66 population	− 0.63 population growth
	(0.7)	(3.11)	(0.259)	(0.3)	(1.34)	(1.50)

$N = 54$ $R^2 = 0.24$ (t-values in parentheses) $* = p < 0.01$

Sources: Philip J. Held, Unpublished data from the 1975 Physician Capacity Utilization Telephone Survey, Mathematica Policy Research, Princeton, New Jersey; U.S. Department of Commerce, *Annual Housing Survey: 1976*, Washington, D.C., Bureau of the Census, Government Printing Office, 1979; American Medical Association, *Physician Distribution and Licensure in the U.S., 1975*, Chicago, IL, American Medical Association, 1976.

level.[18] None of the other variables obtains a conventional 0.05 level of significance. This study poses a clear test of the information cost hypothesis and provides strongly confirming evidence.

The cost of quality information is similarly increased for doctors who have newly entered the market. There is less experience (previous measurement) for patients to draw on and colleagues' brand name can be used to establish a reputation. Most of the literature, while not denying the importance of reputation, has given precedence to explanations based on capital market imperfection ("needs help getting started") even though the existence of personal debt has been shown not to influence the choice of group practice (Mahoney [1973]). A "brand name" theory stresses the fact that new entrants are more likely to have difficulty in attracting a sufficient number of patients rather than in obtaining capital equipment. New physicians (Freshnock and Goodman [1980]) and new dentists (*Dental Economics* [1980]) are both more likely to be in groups as predicted.

V. SUMMARY AND CONCLUSIONS

Medical group practices exist as economic organizations in part to perform a marketing role, acting as "brand name" firms to monitor quality and reduce the costs of information to consumers. Brand name exchange occurs when information costs are asymmetric, quality being measured at lower cost by providers before transaction and subsequently revealed at low cost to consumers over time by their own experience. The contract structure of the group, and equal sharing of income in particular, creates incentives for member physicians to use their low cost information on colleagues to maintain

[18] In a recent study of group practice conducted by Freshnock and Goodman [1980] a variable termed "migration" was associated with increased likelihood of group practice for 6 specialties and reduced likelihood for 3 specialties. Migration was measured by net population growth and actual mobility was omitted. It is interesting to note that while population growth has often been suggested as a proxy for mobility and the two are highly correlated ($R^2 = 0.51$), it enters here with a negative (although not significant) sign once mobility is controlled for (perhaps due to nonlinearities).

the quality of service. Failure to do so would depreciate the value of brand name through the loss of reputation and expected future patient business. Group practices have advantages as brand name firms because they allow patients to transact with a single entity incorporating several practitioners and also provide economies of scale in disseminating quality information. Gains become greater as the asymmetry of information increases due to increasing cost of search, value of outcomes, variance in quality, or jointness in production. The informational advantage of groups over solo practitioners in physician evaluated technical quality is reduced or reversed in "bedside" qualities readily evaluated by patients.

Medical groups, like other firms, exist for many reasons besides the monitoring of quality and dissemination of information. Excessive attention to "production economies of scale" explanations however has led researchers to ignore the demand side marketing role. Yet as emphasized by Arrow [1963], it is in consumer information rather than production that medicine is most different from other industries.

Efforts to demonstrate input cost savings empirically have met with very limited success, and there has been a failure to develop further testable implications. A brand name firm theory of medical group practice is richer in that it can elucidate and predict the structure of the contract (firm) as well as the conditions under which the formation of firms is more likely. Comparison of dentistry and medicine demonstrates the effects of a difference in technology which increases the value of brand name. The prediction of a higher proportion of groups in medicine is amply supported by the evidence and tends to contradict a "production cost economies of scale" explanation. Observed patterns of income distribution (more sharing) and membership (less part-time) are also implied by the theory. A similar technological shift is exhibited in the relation between generalists and specialists. New entrants furnish an example of higher information costs and greater propensity to join groups due to the characteristics of individual physicians. Finally, the regression across areas with different levels of mobility provides evidence that increasing consumer search costs are associated with more group practice.

The assertions that groups control quality and their reputation increases demand are hardly novel (American Foundation [1937], American Medical Association [1933] and Rorem [1931]). What has been done here is to more explicitly present a theory of firms as part of a brand name contract which increases the net gain from transactions. Disparate observations have been culled and drawn together so that it can be seen how they are explained by the role of medical group practice in information transfer.

ACCEPTED DECEMBER 1983

Thomas E. Getzen,
Temple University,
School of Business Administration,
Philadelphia, PA, 19122.

REFERENCES

ALCHIAN, ARMEN and DEMSETZ, HAROLD, 1972, 'Production, Information Costs and Economic Organization', *American Economic Review*, LXII (December), pp. 777–95.

ALSOBROOK, H., 1977, 'Legal Aspects of Group Practice', in F. F. Manning, ed., *Medical Group Practice Management* (Ballinger, Cambridge).

AMERICAN ASSOCIATION OF MEDICAL CLINICS, 1974, *Income Distribution: An Abstract and Analysis*, (American Association of Medical Clinics, Alexandria, VA).

AMERICAN DENTAL ASSOCIATION, 1978, *The 1977 Survey of Dental Practice* (American Dental Association, Chicago).

AMERICAN FOUNDATION, 1937, 'Group Practice', in *American Medicine: Testimony of Court*, Vol. 1 (The American Foundation, New York), pp. 567–678.

AMERICAN MEDICAL ASSOCIATION, 1933, 'Private Group Practice', *Journal of the American Medical Association*, **100** (May) pp. 1605–08, (June), pp. 1693–99, 1773–78.

———, 1971, *Opinions and Reports of the Judicial Council*, (American Medical Association, Chicago).

———, 1976, *Physician Distribution and Licensure in the U.S., 1975*, (American Medical Association, Chicago).

———, 1978, *Profile of Medical Practice, 1978*, (American Medical Association, Chicago).

ARROW, KENNETH, J., 1963, 'Uncertainty and the Welfare Economics of Medical Care', *American Economic Review*, LIII (December), pp. 943–73.

BAILEY, RICHARD M., 1968, 'Comparison of Internists in Solo and Fee-for-Service Groups', *Bulletin of the New York Academy of Medicine*, XLIV (November), pp. 1293–1303.

———, 1969, 'An Economist's View of the Health Services Industry', *Inquiry* VI (March), pp. 3–18.

BARZEL, YORAM, 1982, 'Measurement Cost and the Organization of Markets', *Journal of Law and Economics*, XXIV (April) pp. 27–48.

BOBULA, JOEL D. and FRESHNOOK, LARRY, J., 1978, 'The Supply of Medical Services and the Cost of Medical Care: A Review of the Literature', in *Report of the National Commission on the Cost of Medical Care 1976–1977*, Vol. 3 (American Medical Association, Chicago), pp. 95–108.

CLAPESATTLE, HELEN B., 1941, *The Doctors Mayo*, (University of Minnesota Press, Minneapolis).

COASE, RONALD H., 1937, 'The Nature of the Firm', IV *Economica*, (November) pp. 386–405.

CUZZOLINO, ROBERT, 1979–80, 'Alumni Survey: A Report', *The Digest of Philadelphia College of Osteopathic Medicine* XLII (Winter) p. 5.

DAVIS, MICHAEL M., 1919 'Group Medicine', *American Journal of Public Health* IX (May) pp. 358–63.

DENTAL ECONOMICS, 1980, 'Survey Results', *Dental Economics* LXIX (May) pp. 54–55.

DICKINSON, FRANK G. and BRADLEY, C. E., 1952, 'Discontinuance of Medical Groups 1940–1949', Bulletin #90, (Bureau of Medical Economics Research, American Medical Association, Chicago).

ERNST, RICHARD L. and SCHWARTZ, HERBERT J., 1974, 'Cost Functions for Physicians Practices: Evidence on Economies of Scale', in *An Original Comparative Economic Analysis of Group Practice and Solo Fee-for-Service Practice* (Final Report PB-241546, National Technical Information Service, Springfield, VA.).

FELDSTEIN, MARTIN, 1974, 'Econometric Studies of Health Economics', in M. Intrilligator and D. Kendrick, eds., *Frontiers of Quantitative Economics II* (North-Holland, Amsterdam).

Freshnock, Larry J. and Goodman, Louis J., 1980, 'The Organization of Physician Services in Solo and Group Medical Practice', *Medical Care*, XVIII (January) pp. 17–29.

Getzen, Thomas E., 1981, 'Quality, Reputation, and the Transaction of Patients: An Economic Analysis of Medical Group Practice', (unpublished Ph.D. dissertation, University of Washington, Seattle, WA.).

Goodman, Louis J., Bennett, Edward, and Odem, Richard, 1976, *Group Medical Practice in the U.S., 1975*. (American Medical Association, Chicago).

Goodman, Louis J. and Freshnock, Larry, 1978, 'Failure or Survival of Groups', *Medical Group Management*, XXV (November–December) pp. 10–14.

Goodman, Louis J. and Wolinsky, Frederic D., 1982, 'Conditional Logit analysis of Physicians' Practice Model Choices', *Inquiry* (Fall) pp. 262–70.

Gorlick, Sheldon H., 1978, 'Restrictive Covenants' *Medical Economics*, LV (September 18) pp. 250–56.

Held, Phillip J. and Reinhardt, Uwe, 1979, 'Analysis of Economic Performance in Medical Group Practices', (Mathematica Policy Research, Princeton).

Holman, E. J., 1970, 'Analysis of Fee Splitting Statutes', in *Best of Law and Medicine 68/70* (American Medical Association, Chicago) pp. 109–10.

Jordan, E. P., 1958, *The Physician and Group Practice* (Year Book Inc., Chicago).

Kimball, L. and Lorant, J., 1977, 'Physician Productivity and Returns to Scale', *Health Services Research* XII (Winter) pp. 367–79.

Klein, Benjamin and Leffler, Keith, 1981, 'The Role of Market Forces in Assuring Quality', *Journal of Political Economy* LXXXIX (August) pp. 615–41.

Mahoney, Anne R., 1973, 'Factors Affecting Physicians Choice of Group or Independent Practice', *Inquiry* (June) pp. 9–18.

Martin, William C., 1963, 'Death of a Group', *Medical Economics* XL (March 11), pp. 296–323.

Mechanic, David, Greenley, James R., Cleary, Paul D., Hoeper, Edwin, W. and Wenzel, Frederick, J., 1980, 'A Model of Rural Health Care: Consumer Response Among Users of the Marshfield Clinic', *Medical Care* XVIII, (June), pp. 597–608.

Medical Group Management Association, 1976, *The Organization and Development of a Medical Group Practice* (Ballinger, Cambridge).

———, 1978, *MGMA Digest of Medical Group Employment Contracts and Income Distribution Plans* (Medical Group Management Association, Denver).

Mill, John Stuart, 1909, *Principles of Political Economy*, ed. W. J. Ashley (Longmans, Green and Co., London).

Nagel, Gunther W., 1966, *The Mayo Legacy*, (C. C. Thomas, Springfield, Il.).

Nash, Kent D., Douglas, Chester W. and Wilson, Jock, 1979, 'Economies of Scale and Productivity in Dental Practices', (Division of Dentistry, Bureau of Health Manpower, Health Resources Administration, DHEW, (mimeo), Washington, D.C).

Newhouse, Joseph P., 1973, 'Economics of Group Practice', *Journal of Human Resources*, VIII (Winter), pp. 37–56.

O'Hern, V. M., 1968, 'Public Policy on Restrictive Covenants', in *Best of Law and Medicine 66/68* (American Medical Association, Chicago), pp. 129–30.

———, 1970, 'Physicians Employed by Physicians', in *Best of Law and Medicine 68/70* (American Medical Association, Chicago), pp. 49–50.

Owens, Arthur, 1980, 'Are You Getting Your Share of Referrals?' *Medical Economics* LVII (March 17), pp. 94–98.

———, 1980, 'Doctors' Earnings: A Brighter Picture This Time', *Medical Economics* LVII (September 15), pp. 118–31.

Pauly, Mark V., 1970, 'Efficiency, Incentives and Reimbursement for Health Care', *Inquiry* VII (March) pp. 114–31.

———, 1978, 'Is Medical Care Different?' in *Competition in the Health Care Sector*, Warren Greenberg, ed. (Federal Trade Commission, U.S. Govt. Printing Office, Washington, DC.).

Reinhardt, Uwe, 1972, 'A Production Function for Physicians' Services', *Review of Economics and Statistics* LIV (February), pp. 55–66.

Rorem, C. Rufus, 1931, *Private Group Clinics* (Publication No. 8, The Committee on the Costs of Medical Care, University of Chicago Press, Chicago).

Rothschild, Michael, 1973, 'Models of Market Organization With Imperfect Information: A Survey', *Journal of Political Economy* LXXXI (November–December), pp. 1283–1307.

Smith, Adam, 1976, *The Wealth of Nations*, Edward Cannon, ed. (University of Chicago Press, Chicago).

Stanford Law Review, 1952, 'Group Medical Practice and Clinics: Some Organizational Problems', *Stanford Law Review*, IV (April), pp. 401–14.

U.S. Department of Commerce, 1979, Bureau of the Census, *Summary of Housing Characteristics for Selected Metropolitan Areas*, (U.S. Government Printing Office, Washington, DC.).

THE JOURNAL OF INDUSTRIAL ECONOMICS 0022–1821 $2.00
Volume XXXIII December 1984 No. 2

SMALL FIRMS' SEEDBED ROLE AND THE CONCEPT OF TURBULENCE

M. E. Beesley and R. T. Hamilton

I. INTRODUCTION

An important role of independent small firms is often asserted to be to function as the 'seedbed' for new enterprises capable of challenging established businesses. The authors bring original data to bear on this, suggesting a workable definition of what constitutes a seedbed; measuring its industrial incidence; and defining the part played by independent firms in it. The study reveals substantial variation in the level of such activity among manufacturing industries. It is shown that seedbed activity is essentially innovative (the precursor of new industries) rather than a source of increased rivalry within existing industries. Conclusions are drawn about small firms policy, in particular that government aid for small business should be aimed more at reducing death rates among small firms.

II. THE SEEDBED FUNCTION

The notion of a seedbed process influencing industry population over time is implicit in Marshall's analogy with "... the young trees of the forest as they struggle upwards through the benumbing shade of their older rivals" [1920, Chapter 8, p. 263]. Marshall describes a continuous process of birth and death in the forest's undergrowth, with few undertakings reaching maturity and surviving, perhaps in perpetuity, as joint-stock companies. Since he was concerned at that point with aggregate industry structure, Marshall did not need to consider the variation of fertility and mortality across industries. The seedbed role was seized upon in 1971 by the Report of the Committee of Inquiry into Small Firms (the Bolton Report [1971]). This inquiry confined itself to small *independent* firms (i.e. those managed by the people who own them) and excluded from its scope the subsidiary units of large companies. To quote from the Report [1971, p. 85, para. 8.5]:

> "We believe that the health of the economy requires the birth of new enterprises in substantial number and the growth of some to a position from which they are able to challenge and supplant the existing leaders of industry. . . . This 'seedbed' function, therefore, appears to be a vital contribution of the small firm sector to the long-run health of the economy. We cannot assume that the ordinary working of market forces will necessarily preserve a small firm sector large enough to perform this function in the future."

The Committee thus expressed its major concern that, if left unattended, the fertile undergrowth may erode to such an extent as to jeopardize the continued propagation of the seedplants. In fact, in the event, the Committee went on to judge that erosion on such a scale was not then a serious prospect but that the situation be subject to "regular monitoring" [1971, p. 90, para. 8.16]. However, the seedbed process has proved more easily grasped as a concept than measured. No doubt due in large part to the lack of relevant data, the situation has not come under close monitoring. Given the public attention and resources now being devoted to the small business sector, it is important to gain some understanding on whether the benefits which it is thought society as a whole derives from the 'seedbed' are likely to exist.

The Bolton Committee perceived the challenge of independent small firms to be on two related fronts. The first emphasised the innovative role of new ventures and the threat to established industry leaders from the emergence of entirely new industries. Second, new firms expanding within established industries would erode the market power of the dominant suppliers, that is the incumbent firm's ability to deter actual entry. The major objectives of this paper are to establish the existence of a seedbed, and to clarify the extent to which the sector's contribution is either to establish new industries or to increase rivalry within well-defined industry orders.

The 'seedbed' can be viewed as the arena in which businesses are born and, judging by the body of evidence on the infant mortality of businesses (Boswell [1971]; Churchill [1955]; Gudgin [1978]; Marcus [1967]), where most will die. It follows that to show the extent and industrial composition of seedbed activity we need data on the birth and death rates of businesses by industry. Seedbed industries will be those with high birth and death rates. In other words, introducing a term which we develop below, the firm population of such industries will be subject to high levels of 'turbulence' because of the contemporaneous impact of these flows. By measuring births and deaths as distinct flows at the industry level we can identify the more active seedbed areas and begin to assess the extent to which this process is likely to lead either to more competitive industries or to more industries.

III. THE DATA

The work reported here is part of a wider study into the dynamics of industry structure. Data on births and deaths of establishments were extracted from the registers of HM Inspector of Factories (HMIF) for Scotland. Births are establishments observed to have opened in Scotland between 1 January 1976 and 31 March 1980. Deaths mean establishments which closed in Scotland between 1 January 1977 and 31 December 1979. A full account of the data collection and validation process is in Hamilton [1982]. The data's characteristic advantage was that they permitted the measurement of gross birth and death rates: almost all previous studies had had to be content with measuring the effect of differences between births or deaths over a period, i.e. the net increase or decrease in the total stock.

Unlike most official information sources, the HMIF registers extend to all sizes of establishment. This is most important in any study of new and small businesses since, at least in numerical terms, it is very small units which are likely to be predominant. However, for the purpose in hand, a measurement difficulty arises because the movement of an establishment to a new location will be recorded as both an opening and a closure. To minimize this distortion all businesses were traced which, in the relevant time period, moved location within Scotland. These businesses (82 in all) were excluded from the birth and death measures. Unfortunately it proved impossible to identify those businesses observed in the act of moving to or from Scotland. Thus, whilst the data are treated as births and deaths, 'births' include establishments which moved into Scotland and 'deaths' encompass units which transferred from the country. This renders the data somewhat imprecise but available statistics[1] do confirm business movement to and from Scotland to be much less frequent than internal movement. We are therefore confident that our measures closely approximate true births and deaths.

As seen earlier, we must distinguish between independent businesses and 'dependent' operations (i.e. subsidiary or associate companies; branch plants; and franchises). This is the dichotomy intended[2] in the Bolton Report. So in a 'birth' or 'death' the distinction must be maintained. Moreover, the processes leading up to the birth (or death) of a dependent unit are likely to be essentially different from those of an independent business. To achieve this distinction between dependence and independence, elements of the database were checked through trade directories and editions of *Who Owns Whom*. Each business was presumed to be independent in the absence of contrary evidence and so a number of dependent units—particularly the smallest—may have been misclassified as independent (rather than vice-versa).

The HMIF registers cover all of manufacturing and register entries (business premises) are classified to a Minimum List Heading (MLH) under the 1968 Standard Industrial Classification. At this stage the database was four absolute flows for each MLH industry: independent births (IB); dependent births (DB); independent deaths (ID); and dependent deaths (DD). The final step in the construction of the database involved transforming the individual flows into industry birth and death rates by dividing each flow by a count of the initial stock of establishments in that industry. The appropriate denominator for this calculation had to meet stringent requirements. Stock figures had to relate to Scotland at the MLH industry level. Enumeration must not have involved either sampling or the imposition of lower cut-off limits in terms of size (otherwise, this would have led to the exclusion of

[1] See *Regional Trends* 1981, Table 10.5, page 115.
[2] The Bolton Committee of Inquiry was not able to make this dichotomy in the quantitative sections of its report because official statistics are not compiled on this basis.

considerable numbers of small units). Finally, stock numbers were required to apply to a point in time before the start of the birth and death flows. These requirements were met by the data produced by the Annual Census of Employment (ACE) for June 1973, and this is the source of the denominators used to obtain industry birth and death rates. Table I aggregates the various flows to convey the size and structure of the database.

TABLE I
BIRTHS AND DEATHS IN MANUFACTURING INDUSTRY

	Births		*Deaths*	
	IB	*DB*	*ID*	*DD*
Employment:	*Period:*	*4½ years*	*Period:*	*3 years*
10 or less	719	163	890	175
11–49	259	88	341	102
50+	29	42	87	90
Unknown	287	104	121	50
TOTAL	1294	397	1439	417
Rates (based on June 1973 stock of 9606 units)				
Total/Stock %	13.5	4.1	15.0	4.3

Upon viewing Table I the reader is reminded that the birth and death flows relate to monitoring periods of different durations. This is a consequence of HMIF rules governing the retention period of register details on businesses which have closed. What information we have on the employment size of these establishments is sufficient to emphasize the extent to which we are indeed dealing with a host of small firms, independent and dependent. The birth and death rates calculated in Table I are global mean values for manufacturing in Scotland. Despite a shorter monitoring period,[3] deaths outnumber births—a result consistent with the general decline in Scottish manufacturing over the years to which our data relate.

IV. THE CONCEPT OF TURBULENCE

The term 'turbulence' is introduced to denote the flux created in an industry's total composition by flows of births and deaths. A few authors have come close to this concept but none appears to have carried through with the analysis. Caves and Porter [1976] suggest that:

> "Firms may go through life cycles, with lifespans varying from industry to industry. If some industries experience higher rates of generational turnover, perhaps due to greater frequency as amplitude of disturbances, they will show (*ceteris paribus*) more deaths and more births than other industries. . . . If industries vary in their rates of turnover, the occurrence

[3] To standardise for the different monitoring periods we presume the HMIF registers to operate with constant lags between birth or death and the monitoring thereof. Hence the annual rate of IB is (13.5 ÷ 4.5)% = 3.0%, cf. ID rate of 5.0% per annum. For DB and DD the annual rates are 0.9% and 1.4% respectively.

> of exit should be positively related to the occurrence of entry, with entry serving as a proxy for the unknown underlying forces that speed the generalizational turnover of settlers."

Caves and Porter go on to claim to have uncovered evidence of systematic differences in industries' rates of generational turnover. This evidence is in the form of a positive though weakly significant association between dummy variables which reflect the occurrence but not the extent of both entry and exit. Gudgin [1978, p. 193] broaches our concept of turbulence thus:

> "There are thus industries characterised by high turnover in firms and establishments and others with low turnover. This situation, which is also described by Wedervang for Norwegian industries, is only part of the story since some industries with high closure rates also have low entry rates."

Gudgin does not appear to have expanded on this casual observation. Our concept of turbulence reflects the same phenomenon which has attracted the attention of these authors. At this juncture it is useful to clarify terminology. A number of industrial economists have developed narrower measures of intra-industry mobility (or turnover). This also expresses the idea of challenge to established positions, in that it considers displacement of top ranking firms in industries by others. Such movements take place over many years. Thus particular studies (see Scherer [1980, pp. 54–56]) have been confined to analyses of changes over long periods of time in the size rankings of none but the largest corporations drawn from widely defined areas (e.g. the whole of manufacturing industry or the population of all non-financial corporations).

According to Boyle and Sorenson [1971] a general weakness of such studies has been their lack of industry specificity. Our turbulence analysis is conducted within narrowly defined (MLH) industries but the time-scale is short. We cannot identify the rank size order in each industry at any point in time. Hence our analysis is not of mobility (or turnover) as these terms have come to be used. Turbulence expresses a different source of challenge—by change in the identity of separate units in particular industries over a shorter period.[4]

V. EXTENT AND NATURE OF TURBULENCE

Drawing on the discussion of section III, our measure of industry turbulence is:

$$T = \frac{(\mathrm{IB} + \mathrm{ID}) + (\mathrm{DB} + \mathrm{DD})}{\mathrm{Stock}}$$

[4] In operating at industry level our measures also avoid a problem which arises with these studies' use of rank correlation coefficients as measures of mobility over time. These coefficients are sensitive to the ranks assigned to new entrants to, and exits from, the sector over the period. This measurement problem becomes more critical if rank correlation is used to reflect mobility within a larger number of more narrowly defined industries.

In the manufacturing industries as a whole, the global mean value of T is 0.37. In calculating T values for individual industries we must guard against the possibility of very small industries generating extreme values. Hence our detailed analysis of turbulence is confined to those MLH industries with a stock of at least 50 establishments. This serves to reduce our sample size to 57 MLH manufacturing industries (from 123).

In Figure 1 we have plotted birth rate against death rate for these 57 industries. The quadrants arise from imposing on to this scatter diagram the global mean rates for the whole of manufacturing (see Table I). The 10 industries in the upper right quadrant have above average rates of birth and death. The lower left quadrant contains the 26 industries with below average birth and death rates. Other quadrants contain industries with either an above average birth or death rate, but not both. The small group of high birth, high death rate industries are turbulent in the fullest sense with an average T value of 0.60. This compares with a mean of 0.21 for the low birth, low death grouping. (The difference between these means is highly significant on a Student's t test.) Remaining industries have an average T score of 0.39, close to the global mean (0.37) for all manufacturing.

Having revealed the extent to which turbulence varies across industries, let us now concentrate on the groups of high and low turbulence industries (upper right and lower left quadrants respectively of Figure 1). When the average turbulence values of these industries are decomposed into their independent and dependent components, the result is set out in Table II.

TABLE II
COMPONENTS OF TURBULENCE IN HIGH AND LOW TURBULENCE INDUSTRIES

Components of turbulence	*High T industries*	*Low T industries*	*All manufacturing*
IB + ID/Stock (mean)	0.49	0.15	0.28
DB + DD/Stock (mean)	0.11	0.06	0.09
Number of industries	10	26	123

It is readily apparent that turbulence is essentially a phenomenon involving independent businesses. In the group of high T industries, the contribution of the dependent component (mean 0.11) is not markedly different from its average over all manufacturing (0.09). It is the very large independent component which renders these industries highly turbulent. In the set of 26 low T industries, whilst both components are much lower, the bulk of the fall in total turbulence is due to the threefold reduction in the independent component. So it is correct to identify the seedbed as involving independent businesses primarily.

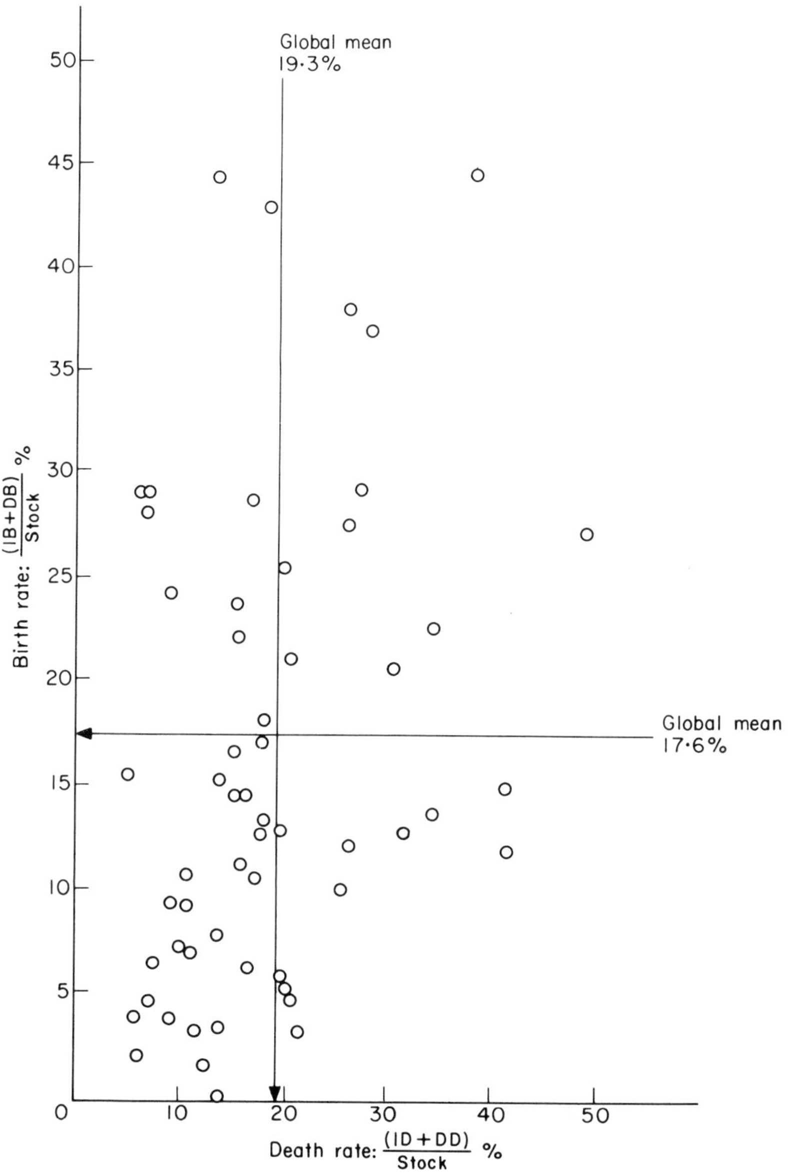

FIGURE 1
Plot of birth rate against death rate for 57 manufacturing industries

To take the analysis further, we note that the very highest levels of turbulence occur in the following industries:

MLH 349 Other mechanical engineering not elsewhere specified ($T = 0.65$)
MLH 399 Metal industries not elsewhere specified ($T = 0.66$)
MLH 479 Miscellaneous wood and cork manufacturers ($T = 0.76$)
MLH 496 Plastic products not elsewhere specified ($T = 0.83$)

These extremely turbulent industries have in common a lack of precise definition. Each is a residual category intended to capture those businesses whose products are such as to defy ready classification into more narrowly-defined MLH industries. It seemed very likely that these classifications are biased towards products which are either novel or unconventional (or both). Thus discussion of turbulence leads us to those ill-defined areas of the Standard Industrial Classification in which new industries are developed, later to become recognisable as independent industries. Turbulence indicates a process of commercial trial and error (birth and death), predominantly involving independent entrepreneurs. It is in this sense and to this extent that we might regard the 'seedbed' role of small firms as correlated with innovatory behaviour.

VI. INFLUENCES ON TURBULENCE

The foregoing analysis has been confined to the extremes of very high and very low turbulence. To generalise, we must extend our scope to include all 57 industries contained in Figure 1. So our concern in this section is to identify industry attributes (in addition to classification specificity) which seem to govern the variation in turbulence across industries.

We treat turbulence as the joint product of birth and death (or gross entry and exit) at the industry level. This enables us to draw on the separate birth and death (entry and exit) literature to generate hypotheses on what influences turbulence. We concentrate on five kinds of influence on births and deaths, viz. the capital cost of entry to an industry; the proportion of small units in it; industry profitability; industry growth; and concentration. Two of these are readily related to turbulence, but three are not and so we must make distinctions different from those of previous authors. This need arises because we deal with gross flows of births and deaths whereas previous studies have in the main been concerned with explaining the net effect of births and deaths, i.e. whether over a period the stock of businesses has risen or fallen. If a given influence is expected both to raise birth rates and raise death rates, there is a straightforward inference for effects on turbulence—it will be higher. The converse applies when the influence is likely to reduce both birth and death rates. But other cases are not clear. For example, if one anticipates a raised birth rate and a lower death rate, the effect on turbulence is unclear.

The higher the capital (and other) costs of entry, the more difficult it is thought to be to enter (Mansfield [1962]; Gorecki [1975]) and exit (Caves and Porter [1976]). Moreover, the greater the share of larger units (or conversely, the smaller the proportion of small units) the greater is inertia inherent in operations. Both these factors, obviously not unrelated themselves, would tend to be clearly related to turbulence—they would lower it. Higher profit is thought to encourage entry and lead to a net increase in units in an industry (Mansfield [1962]; Gorecki [1975]). But with respect to turbulence the effect is uncertain because circumstances favourably affecting profits would simultaneously increase births and decrease deaths (Marcus [1967]). So also for industry growth. Higher concentration would normally be expected to raise profit levels and so encourage entry (Duetsch [1975]). But rising concentration would also discourage births because of associations with entry barriers in general (Orr [1974]). We therefore expect the last three influences to be ambiguous for turbulence. To sum up: the level of industry turbulence (T) should be negatively related to the capital cost of entry to the industry; positively related to the proportion of very small units in the employment structure of the industry; but statistically independent of measures of industry profitability; growth; and concentration. In addition to these hypotheses, and drawing on the conclusion of the previous section, we also postulate a strong positive association between turbulence and the lack of specificity in an industry's classification. We now analyse these influences on turbulence. If and when the direction of the ambiguous effects is established, we can attempt further explanations.

Statistical analysis strongly confirms that two of the three ambiguous elements—profitability and concentration—are insignificant concomitants of total turbulence. The results of regression analysis involving the remaining explanatory variables[5] are presented in Table III. In equation (1) the small firm share (SHSM) coefficient is statistically insignificant. This can be attributed in part to the degree of correlation between entry cost (KINT) and SHSM (see correlation matrix). Omitting SHSM (equation (2)) has very little effect on the explanatory power of the regression. Introducing a dummy variable (DMY) reflecting the specificity of industry classification serves (equation (3)) to substantially increase the $\bar{R}^2$ value. In this final equation all the coefficients are highly significant (with no serious multicollinearity) and we explain 40% of the variation in industry levels of turbulence. The KINT and DMY coefficients have the expected signs and the size of the DMY coefficient confirms our earlier observation about the nature of the most turbulent industries. However, the significant positive relationship between turbulence and growth (GTH) is contrary to expectation. The most obvious explanation for this is that growth stimulates births but, even over the short

[5] The reader is referred to the Appendix for definitions and statistical sources of the explanatory variables used in this investigation.

TABLE III
MULTIPLE REGRESSION ANALYSIS OF TURBULENCE

Equation	*Y*	*Constant*	*KINT*	*SHSM*	*GTH*	*DMY*	*N*	$\bar{R}^2$	*F*
(1)	*T*	0.26 (2.07)	−0.004 (−1.75)	0.002 (1.19)	0.002 (2.77)		43	0.26	5.94 (3, 39)
(2)	*T*	0.40 (12.29)	−0.006 (−2.43)		0.003 (3.10)		43	0.25	8.12 (2, 40)
(3)	*T*	0.37 (11.60)	−0.005 (−2.41)		0.002 (2.87)	0.20 (3.30)	43	0.40	10.39 (3,39)

Notes: The figures in brackets are the *t*-values.
N represents the number of observations used.
Serial correlation absent in each estimated equation (Durbin-Watson test).

Correlation matrix

	KINT	*SHSM*	*GTH*	*DMY*
KINT	1.00	−0.40	−0.05	−0.10
SHSM		1.00	0.22	0.43
GTH			1.00	0.17
DMY				1.00

time span covered by this study, high birth rates themselves come to be associated with high death rates. (The simple correlation coefficient between the total birth and death rates plotted in Figure 1 is +0.31.) Death rates could thus be due to factors independent of industry types, but related to the fact that the population is young; seedlings are more vulnerable. To test this hypothesis would require data relating particular births to particular deaths.

VII. TURBULENCE AND INDUSTRY CONCENTRATION

The second aspect of small firms' seedbed challenge involves the erosion of the market power of dominant suppliers. We have just reported total turbulence (*T*) to be independent of the level of industry concentration. However, we can explore further the relationship between total turbulence and concentration by distinguishing the dependent and independent firm components.

The industry concentration ratios used are the percentage of 1973 industry employment in units each employing more than 500 people. Each of the 57 industries was allocated to one of three groups depending on the value of the concentration ratio. Within each grouping, we calculated the mean value of total turbulence (*T*) and the means of the independent and dependent components. This information is contained in Table IV.

The concentration ranges were chosen to ensure a reasonable spread of industry observations across the groups. Noting the mean concentration ratio for each group, we can reasonably regard the data as relating to low; medium; and high levels of concentration.

TABLE IV
TURBULENCE AND INDUSTRY CONCENTRATION

Concentration range	*0–15.9%*	*16.0–49.9%*	*50–100%*
Mean concentration	*4.5%*	*30.4%*	*65.9%*
T (mean)	0.34	0.34	0.37
IB + ID/Stock	0.28	0.26	0.24
BD + DD/Stock	0.06	0.08	0.13
Number of industries	22	20	15

The slight increase of turbulence (to 0.37) in the most concentrated industries is not statistically significant. The independent component of T falls slightly with increased concentration but this decline is more than offset by the large (and statistically significant) increase in the dependent component when we move into the highly concentrated industries. The immediate inference to be drawn is that, whilst dependent businesses are only involved to a minor degree in the overall turbulence of the less concentrated industries, such businesses do make a major contribution to turbulence in highly concentrated industries. We can in fact refine this conclusion because the simple correlation coefficient (r) between dependent birth and death rates is insignificant at +0.02 (between independent birth and death rates, $r = +0.44$). Thus, the high dependent component of turbulence in these industries is very much more likely to be the consequence of a high rate of birth or death, but not both. Table V sets out individual birth and death rates according to the level of industry concentration.

TABLE V
BIRTH AND DEATH RATES OF BUSINESSES AT DIFFERENT CONCENTRATION LEVELS

Concentration range	*0–49.9%*	*50–100%*
IB (%, mean)	11.5	13.0
DB	2.9	8.1
ID	15.8	10.4
DD	4.0	4.7

Of the increases and decreases reported in Table V, only the increase in dependent birth rate is statistically significant (Student's t test).

To refine our original inference, the increased contribution of dependent businesses to the turbulence of highly concentrated industries reflects their much higher birth rate in these industries. But why should dependent businesses gravitate so strongly into these areas? The most likely explanation, following Berry [1974], is that only large firms are able to encroach—via the setting up of dependent units—into areas already dominated by other large firms. Less likely, drawing on Brozen [1974], is that concentration is indeed a good proxy for profits and that, in this respect, established companies are more perspicacious than independent entrepreneurs. Thus, the overall level of seedbed activity is not influenced by concentration level but seedbed composition is markedly different in the most concentrated industries. Independent founders do not appear to be significantly repelled by increased concentration. However, the competitive challenge of dependent units is much more selective and directed at the areas of highest concentration. On these grounds we would argue that the more serious competitive threat to dominant suppliers is from the strategic entry moves of other large companies rather than the activities of the archetypal small entrepreneur.

VIII. CONCLUSIONS AND IMPLICATIONS FOR UK SMALL FIRMS POLICY

An essential function of the small business sector is alleged to be the seedbed of the new initiatives from which will emerge the successful businesses and industries of the future. This notion is intuitively plausible but we have so far lacked any measure of the extent or nature of seedbed activity. The concept of a seedbed cannot be disassociated from business trial and error (birth and death). Active seedbed industries will be in continuous flux due to contemporaneous birth and death flows. The usual measures of intra-industry mobility (or turnover) are inappropriate as indicators of this type of flux. We have developed the idea of turbulence into a direct measure of the flux created within individual industries due to the coincidence of birth and death flows.

The first point to emerge on the nature of seedbed activity is to confirm that it does involve independent much more than dependent units. The most turbulent MLH industries, we found, had the least specific definitions. It is to such open-ended industries that one would tend to classify those innovative ventures based on products sufficiently novel or unconventional as to prevent their being recorded in any narrowly-defined industry. Thus, seedbed activity is indeed associated with innovation. We intend to pursue the determinants of inter-industry variation in birth and death rates making up turbulence in subsequent work.

Further, we observed the nature of turbulence to be significantly influenced by industry concentration. Whilst independent founders do appear to be predominantly innovative, we see the major competitive challenge to dominant suppliers as coming from the diversification moves of other established companies.

From the early 1970s—provoked by the recommendations of the Bolton Committee—successive UK governments have contributed to the *ad hoc* development of a small firms policy. Towards the end of the decade the thrust of policy had become more selective in favour of new firms (rather than all small firms). Our evidence suggests that the benefits from such a policy will be in the form of innovation and new industries rather than the erosion of producer surplus in established industries. The more effective attack on this is likely to come from other established firms. In terms of the selectivity of policy instruments, we have traced high seedbed activity to a few ill-defined areas of industry. Our data reveal many independent entrepreneurs prepared to try something out of the ordinary—and that many fail in the attempt.

Initiatives intended to stimulate new business creation must anticipate turbulence and be able to tolerate high death rates. Their lack of industrial definition will make it difficult to channel specific support into such areas. To reduce the anticipated early failure rate of new businesses requires a method of choosing the 'best', *ex ante*, on the basis of formal plans and entrepreneurial skills. Apart from the question of the policy operators' ability to make the judgements, the method would require detailed analyses of 'industry' prospects and trends, when we have indicated that many entrepreneurs focus on ill-defined, and thus necessarily badly documented industries. Such individuals are likely to have extreme difficulty obtaining the data to support their claims. (They might have even greater difficulty accepting the need to reveal and justify their ideas on paper.)

These difficulties of running a policy based on *ex ante* encouragement are as desirable as they are inevitable. The willingness to act in the face of uncertainty is just what we require of entrepreneurs. Hence we are led to suggest that if aid to seedbed activity is to be given, it should be directed more at the problem of helping newly established firms recognise the symptoms of incipient failure in advance, i.e. of reducing the general tendency for young firms to be especially vulnerable. This, in turn, would redirect attention to increasing management skills, opportunities for finding consultancy advice, and like activities; that is, to a policy based on adding to the skills of entrepreneurs whilst engaged in running their business. This shift to a post-entry policy is supported by our finding less variance among death rates than among birth rates when industries are compared. But in general, the instinct to support small business, which has grown remarkably irrespective of government changes since the Bolton Committee reported, has been shown to have rather more solid support in fact than the Committee was itself able to demonstrate.

ACCEPTED NOVEMBER 1983

M. E. Beesley,
London Business School, Sussex Place,
Regent's Park, London NW1 4SA

R. T. Hamilton,
Department of Business Administration,
University of Canterbury, Christchurch 1, New Zealand

APPENDIX

DEFINITIONS AND STATISTICAL SOURCES OF THE EXPLANATORY VARIABLES

Variable	*Definition*	*Statistical sources*
Capital cost of entry (KINT) (£,000)	Net capital expenditure per employee (1975) *times* mid-point of modal employment size band (1975).	Scottish Abstract of Statistics (SAS) 1980, Table 12.7. Annual Census of Employment (ACE) 1975.
Share of small units (SHSM) (%)	Percentage number of units with less than 25 people in June 1974.	ACE 1974 (Scotland).
Industry profitability:		
* NQHD (£,000 per employee)	Net output per person employed (1975).	SAS 1980, Table 12.7.
* MARG (% profit margin)	Net output less wages and salaries, as % of industry sales.	Business Monitor PA1000, Census of Production 1976 (UK data).
Industry growth (GTH) (%)	Percentage change in industry employment between 1970 and 1977.	SAS 1974, Table 118. SAS 1981, Table 12.5.
* Concentration (CONC) (%)	Percentage of 1973 industry employment in units each employing more than 500 people.	ACE 1973 (Scotland).
Industry classification specificity (DMY) (dummy variable)	Value of 1 in following MLH industries: 229, 279, 349, 369, 399, 469, 479, 489, 496, 499.	Based on the 1968 Standard Industrial Classification.

* Statistically insignificant as determinants of the level of industry turbulence.

REFERENCES

BERRY, C. H., 1974, 'Corporate Diversification and Market Structure', *The Bell Journal of Economics*, Vol 5, No 1 (Spring), pp. 196–204.

BOLTON REPORT, 1971, Committee of Inquiry on Small Firms, Cmnd 4811, (HMSO, London).

BOSWELL, J., 1971, *The Rise and Decline of Small Firms*, (George Allen & Unwin, London).

BOYLE, S. E. and SORENSON, R. L. 1971, 'Concentration and Mobility: Alternative Measures of Industry Structure', *The Journal of Industrial Economics*, Vol 19, No 2 (April), pp. 118–32.

BROZEN, G., 1974, 'Concentration and Profits: Does Concentration Matter?', *Antitrust Bulletin*, Vol 19 (Summer), pp. 381–99.

CAVES, R. E. and PORTER, M. E., 1976, 'Barriers to Exit', Chapter 3 in *Essays on Industrial Organisation in Honor of Joe S. Bain*, edited by R. T. Masson and P. D. Qualls, (Ballinger Publishing, Cambridge, Mass.).

CHURCHILL, B. C., 1955, 'Age and Life Expectancy of Business Firms', *Survey of Current Business*, Vol 35, No 12 (December), pp. 15–19, 24.

DEUTSCH, L. L., 1975, 'Structure, Performance and the Net Rate of Entry into Manufacturing Industries', *The Southern Economic Journal*, Vol 41, No 3 (January), pp. 450–56.

GORECKI, P. K., 1975, 'The Determinants of Entry by New and Diversifying Enterprises in the UK Manufacturing Sector 1958–1963: Some Tentative Results', *Applied Economics*, Volume 7, No 2 (June), pp. 139–47.

GUDGIN, G., 1978, *Industrial Location Processes and Regional Employment Growth*, (Saxon House, Farnborough).

HAMILTON, R. T., 1982, *Measures and Determinants of Entry and Exit Rates of Businesses in Scotland*, Unpublished PhD thesis, University of London.

MANSFIELD, 1962, 'Entry, Gibrat's Law, Innovation and the Growth of Firms', *American Economic Review*, Vol 52, No 5 (December), pp. 1023–51.

MARCUS, M., 1967, 'Firms' Exit Rates and their Determinants', *The Journal of Industrial Economics*, Vol 16, No 1, (November), pp. 10–22.

MARSHALL, A., 1920, *Principles of Economics*, (8th edition), (Macmillan & Co Ltd, London).

ORR, D., 1974, 'The Determinants of Entry: A Study of Canadian Manufacturing Industries', *Review of Economics and Statistics*, Vol 56, No 1 (February), pp. 58–66.

SHERER, F. M., 1980, *Industrial Market Structure and Economic Performance* (2nd edition), (Rand McNally, Chicago).

THE JOURNAL OF INDUSTRIAL ECONOMICS 0022–1821 $2.00
Volume XXXIII December 1984 No. 2

EXCESS CAPACITY AND ENTRY: SOME EMPIRICAL EVIDENCE

JOHN C. HILKE*

I. INTRODUCTION

RECENT articles by Spence [1977], Dixit [1979], and Schmalensee [1981] have elaborated on Wenders' [1971] proposition that excess capacity can act as a barrier to entry. The intent of all of these treatments is to suggest that firms may rationally invest in excess capacity with the expectation that excess capacity will be seen by potential entrants either as a signal of aggressive intent[1] or as a credible threat.[2] When excess capacity does not lead to creation of a credible threat, it may still act as a barrier to entry by shifting the risk-return perceptions of potential entrants enough to divert the potential entrants' investments into other industries.[3] Alternatively, investment in excess capacity by incumbent firms may reduce the prospects of an active market for the used equipment of a defunct entrant and thereby help to convert fixed costs into sunk costs, consequently raising entry barriers.[4]

This paper represents an exploratory effort to investigate empirically the prevalence and efficiency of excess capacity in deterring entry. First, a simple and traditional model of entry is presented. This is followed by the description of the data used to explore the excess capacity-investment concept. A combined results and comments section follows the description of the data.

* I wish to thank Robert Smiley, William Burnett, Harold Saltzman, Ronald Bond, and Wendy Gramm for their comments at various stages in the preparation of this paper. Thanks also go to the editor and an anonymous referee for their assistance. The opinions, conclusions, and remaining errors are my own. This paper has not been reviewed by, nor does it necessarily reflect the views of the Federal Trade Commission or any of its members.

1 See Shelling [1960, especially ch. 8]. It may also be useful to think of excess capacity as capability of retaliating. In this sense, excess capacity raises the probability of effective retaliation even if the probability of retaliation were constant. A particular increase in output would be said to be a more effective instance of retaliation if it involved lower marginal costs than another instance.

2 Intent is distinguished from a credible threat in that a credible threat is self-enforcing. The firm finds that its shortrun best interest calls for carrying out the threat even if the other party has ignored the threat. An intention to retaliate, by contrast, may not involve actions in a firm's best short-term interest, once the firm being threatened has ignored the threat. See Salop [1979].

3 Under a capital asset pricing model of investment behavior, shifts in perception of the risk or return associated with a particular entry investment (that appeared on the initial investment-efficiency frontier) may shift the position of that investment away from the frontier into the interior. Since other investments will now provide greater utility, such a shift would effectively displace investment away from entry in that industry.

4 This follows from the discussion of Baumol and Willig [1981].

II. ENTRY MODEL

Assuming that entry decisions are not qualitatively different from other investment decisions, entry penetration (E) can be expected to depend on the return and risk perceptions that potential entrants hold about investment in an industry. Following traditional industrial organization research, anticipated high profit is the primary motivation and explanation for entry. Both past profits (PR) and growth (G) have been associated with entry as proxies for future profit opportunities. However, the potential entrants' profit expectations will systematically differ from profits currently realized by incumbent firms if there are significant cost differences between the established firms and potential entrants. These are usually termed barriers to entry (BE).

To this traditional formulation we now add excess capacity (EX). It can be viewed either as a measure of the risk of predation signaled by excess capacity or as a deflator that must be applied to preentry profit rates in estimating postentry profit rates because of incumbent firms' credible threats. Further, the signaling potency of excess capacity might be enhanced when there is evidence that previous entry met with a nonaccommodating response (EXNA).

Descriptions of the data used for these variables are contained in the next section.

If excess capacity has a widespread and consistent depressing effect on entry, the excess capacity measures should be negatively and significantly associated with entry in a regression model. If excess capacity only sporadically diminishes entry, then it will contribute to the explanation of entry in a few instances but will not have a significant effect throughout. If excess capacity is unrelated to entry in its entirety, no appreciable relationship will be observed.

The traditional entry model and the excess capacity extension sketched above are expressed in equation (1) below, where E is entry, PR is profit, BE is traditional barriers to entry, EX is excess capacity, and EXNA shows the record of nonaccommodating responses. The expected profit variables should be positively related to entry, while traditional barriers to entry and the excess-capacity variables should be negatively related to entry. The specifications for the regressions will then be as stated in equations (2) through (4).

$$\text{(1)} \qquad \mathrm{E} = f(\mathrm{PR}, \mathrm{G}, \mathrm{BE}, \mathrm{EX} \text{ or } \mathrm{EXNA})$$

$$\text{(2)} \qquad \mathrm{E} = \alpha + \beta_1\mathrm{PR} + \beta_2\mathrm{G} + \beta_3\mathrm{BE} + \varepsilon$$

$$\text{(3)} \qquad \mathrm{E} = \alpha + \beta_1\mathrm{PR} + \beta_2\mathrm{G} + \beta_3\mathrm{BE} + \beta_4\mathrm{EX} + \varepsilon$$

$$\text{(4)} \qquad \mathrm{E} = \alpha + \beta_1\mathrm{PR} + \beta_2\mathrm{G} + \beta_3\mathrm{BE} + \beta_5\mathrm{EXNA} + \varepsilon,$$

where β_1 and β_2 are expected to be positive and β_3, β_4, and β_5 are expected to be negative.

III. DATA

The dependent entry variable in this analysis is the sum of the market shares obtained by domestic entrants and gains (or losses) in the market share of imports between 1950 and 1966. The domestic-entry shares were estimated from financial press reports and from company publications.[5] Only new-capacity entries are included.[6] Entry by merger is not counted. Foreign market-share gains were derived from Government import publications. Observations are at the four- or five-digit level of industry classification.

Turning to the explanatory variables, profits in each industry are proxied by the average rate of profit on net worth of the leading firms.[7] This average is taken over the years *prior* to the last major new-capacity entry during the 1950–66 period.[8] Growth is represented by the average annual percentage increase in sales prior to the last major new-capacity entry.

Since the intent here is to study the possible strategic use of excess capacity to forestall entry, the industry sample is limited to manufacturing industries[9] with relatively attractive profit and growth rates. Industries were included only if their leading firms' preentry profits exceeded the manufacturing-average profit for that period. The sample is similarly limited to industries in which sales growth exceeded 1 percent annually. This exclusion is based on the expectation that in an industry with falling sales, excess capacity might be expected to arise for reasons wholly unrelated to strategic use of excess capacity.[10]

To maintain the maximum degrees of freedom, traditional barriers to entry are approximated by a trivariate dummy variable based on previous judgments of the overall level of barriers to entry.[11] Barriers were assessed as low, medium, or high.

In measuring excess capacity, the objective is to capture the industry leaders' general policy about the minimum level of excess capacity to hold. In periods of declining demand, actual excess capacity might be expected to exceed any strategically determined excess capacity for natural reasons. Downturns in the business cycle or recent entry episodes could therefore

[5] These data were obtained initially from Harris [1973] and subsequently modified by the author to reflect correspondence with individual firms to confirm entry activity.

[6] This specification does not provide a distinction between fringe entry and entry that directly threatens major firms. Consequently, relationships between mobility barriers and excess capacity cannot be addressed here.

[7] Use of the leading firms' profits can be considered as a proxy for industry profits or as the target variable of interest to potential entrants regardless of the profitability of secondary firms. The number of firms whose profits were included varied from two to four firms. Using firm data entails potential contamination problems when firms are engaged in more than one product line.

[8] Profit observations were truncated at the point of the last major entry to avoid simultaneity problems flowing from depression of profits due to the entry itself.

[9] The sample industries are involved in manufacturing. Service industries are not included in order to minimize the service competition aspects of excess capacity highlighted in De Vany [1976] and articles cited there. Service aspects of excess capacity cannot be ruled out as an alternative explanation. Case studies of excess capacity should, therefore, consider this factor.

[10] For a treatment including a less restricted sample, see Hilke [1978, ch. IV].

[11] See Mann [1966] and Shepherd [1970, pp. 274–84].

provide misleading indications of the industry's excess capacity policy. On the other hand, business cycle peaks make a reasonable period at which to assess the industry's posture because explicit capacity expansion decisions are required to maintain excess capacity in the face of peak demand. For this reason, excess capacity measured at the top of the business cycle from 1964 to 1966 is taken as the proxy for the industry's general stance on maintaining excess capacity.[12] Since readings of excess capacity at the top of the business cycle were unavailable for earlier peak periods, industries which faced entry primarily in the 1964–66 period were excluded from the sample since their excess capacity data could be biased, that is, it could reflect unanticipated reduced residual demand as a result of entry rather than any policy concerning the minimum acceptance level of excess capacity.[13]

The excess capacity data are available only at the three-digit level so observations at the four-digit level had to be assigned from the related three digit observation.[14]

The probability of a future nonaccommodating response to entry in an industry is proxied as the proportion of major new-capacity entries met by surges in advertising by leading incumbent firms[15] or by price declines that exceeded those implied by a Sylos-Labini hypothesis (incumbents hold their output constant).[16] The probability of a nonaccommodating price response is measured as the proportion of domestic entry instances after which the industry price index (U.S. Bureau of Labor Statistics, *Wholesale Prices and Price Indexes*) fell by more than would be expected if current producers had maintained rather than expanded their preentry output.

The Sylos-Labini price was calculated by adding a linear price trend from the three preceding years and the expected decline in price as a result of entry to the current price level. The expected decline in price is the result of multiplying the price elasticity of demand by the size of the entry relative to preentry capacity. The elasticity estimates are from Comanor and Wilson [1974, pp. 82–83] and Houthaker and Taylor [1970, pp. 55–159]. Entry size estimates are from Harris [1973]. If price declined by more than predicted by using the Sylos-Labini assumption, then production retaliation was assumed to have taken place. EXNA results from the multiplication of this non-accommodation probability by the excess capacity level.

The sample of industries consists of all of the industries for which both entry and excess capacity observations were available that also met the profit and sales growth criteria.[17] There are 16 four- and five-digit industries in the

[12] The McGraw-Hill capacity data were made available courtesy of H. Michael Mann.

[13] Tires and automobiles had to be eliminated for this reason.

[14] Excess capacity data for cigarettes are available at the four-digit level.

[15] Data from *National Advertising Investment*, 1950–67 were used to designate instances in which major new-capacity entry was met with advertising increases of more than 10 percent. For a discussion of the potential anticompetitive impact of advertising retaliation of new entry, see Hilke [1980].

[16] See Williamson [1977] for an elaboration of a legal rule following this definition.

[17] Profit must exceed the mean profit for the original Harris [1973] sample taken up to the date of the last major entry. Sales growth must exceed 1 percent per year on average.

sample. As previously noted, because excess capacity data are available only at the three digit level, four digit level excess capacity observations had to be assumed to be equal to the related three digit observation.[18]

Relatively low correlations between the independent variables (ranging from −0.14 for EXNA and G to 0.41 for PR and BE) suggest that multicolinearity should not be a major problem in interpreting the results.

IV. RESULTS AND COMMENT

Results from estimation of the model using OLS,[19] both with and without the excess capacity variables, are shown in Table I. In accordance with expectations, the sign of the growth coefficient is always positive. The growth coefficient is significant at the 10-percent level. The profit coefficient shows inconsistent signs and is not significant. This is consonant with the proposition that growth is perceived by entrants to be a better predictor of future profits than is a record of high profits.[20] The barriers coefficient is negative, as expected, and significant at considerably less than the 10-percent level. The

TABLE I
REGRESSION RESULTS
Dependent variable = E

Intercept	5.06	8.94	7.42
PR	0.04	0.68	−0.05
	(0.06)	(0.97)	(−0.08)
G	0.98	0.71	0.94
	(2.80)†	(1.96)*	(2.91)†
BE	−4.88	−6.80	−5.51
	(2.80)†	(−3.62)†	(−3.63)†
EX		−0.48	
		(−1.68)	
EXNA			−0.79
			(−1.77)
R^2	0.5652	0.6543	0.6613
F	5.20†	5.20†	5.37†

* Significant at the 10-percent level two-tailed or 5-percent one-tailed.
† Significant at the 5-percent level two-tailed or 2.5-percent one-tailed.

[18] In two instances, two four-digit industries are in the same three-digit category. Degrees of freedom are consequently treated as two less than they would otherwise be.

[19] Although none of the entry observations in this study had negative values, the variable is not theoretically constrained to positive values because decreases in imports would create a negative entry observation. For this reason, OLS is an acceptable regression technique.

[20] This result is also consistent with other hypotheses, ranging from sales maximization to differences between accounting profits for a firm and economic profits for a line of business. Similar results showing growth to be particularly conducive to entry have been reported previously in Harris [1976a and b] using the full version of the present entry data set. For additional citations see Scherer [1980, p. 249].

values of the significant coefficients are also fairly stable with respect to the introduction of the excess capacity variables.

Both the excess capacity and the excess capacity/nonaccommodation coefficients are negative as predicted. While EX and EXNA are not significant at the 10-percent level, they are nearly so. EX is significant at approximately the 14-percent level two-tailed and EXNA is significant at approximately the 12-percent level two-tailed. The corresponding incremental R^2 for the excess capacity variable is 8.9 percent and the incremental R^2 for the excess capacity/nonaccommodation variable is 9.6 percent. In parallel with the *t*-statistics above, the contributions to expanatory power are not significant at the 10 percent level two-tailed, but are nearly so.

These results indicate that excess capacity is likely to be related to entry in the predicted way but that the claim falls short of the usual standard of confidence for this limited sample size. One further bit of analysis seems worthwhile. Examination of the residuals and changes in residuals between the different versions of the model can provide some insight about the pattern of the changes in the error terms precipitated by the addition of the excess capacity variables. Table II displays the residuals for the three versions of the model and changes in residuals accompanying the addition of the excess capacity variables. Inspection of the last two columns shows that addition of

TABLE II
RESIDUALS AND CHANGES IN RESIDUALS

	0	*1*	*2*	*3*	*4*	*5*	*6*	*7*	*8*
Ind.	*E.*	*Predicted Entry (Exit) Using Variables PR, BR, GR*	*Resid.*	*1 With EX Added*	*Resid.*	*1 With EXNA Added*	*Resid.*	*Change in Resid. |4|−|2|*	*Change in Resid. |6|−|2|*
1	0.11	1.08	−0.97	−2.39	+2.50	−0.27	+0.38	+1.53	−0.59
2	1.50	7.99	−6.49	6.59	−5.09	5.30	−3.80	−1.40	−2.69
3	3.78	7.57	−3.79	7.63	−3.85	9.23	−5.45	+0.06	+1.66
4	2.60	4.27	−1.67	1.46	+1.14	−0.53	+3.13	−0.53	+1.46
5	0.16	−1.05	+1.21	2.33	−2.17	0.76	−0.60	+0.96	−0.25
6	1.00	2.34	−1.34	0.63	+0.37	1.36	−0.36	−0.97	−0.98
7	0.0	−0.27	+0.27	0.00	0.0	1.18	−1.18	+0.27	−0.91
8	0.83	2.31	−1.48	4.28	−3.45	2.57	−1.74	+1.97	+0.26
9	0.36	4.22	−3.86	4.05	−3.69	4.09	−3.73	−0.17	−0.13
10	9.48	4.53	+4.96	4.54	+4.94	4.68	+4.80	−0.02	−0.16
11	14.00	9.15	+4.85	10.38	+3.62	11.04	+2.96	−1.23	−0.19
12	10.32	1.28	+9.04	3.10	+7.22	2.94	+7.38	−1.82	−1.66
13	0.11	2.07	−1.96	1.22	+1.11	1.00	−0.89	−0.85	−1.07
14	18.40	14.92	+3.48	15.67	+2.73	15.24	+3.16	−0.75	−0.32
15	0.0	1.14	−1.14	1.45	−1.45	1.89	−1.89	+0.31	+0.75
16	10.00	11.08	−1.08	11.70	−1.70	12.16	−2.16	+0.68	+1.08

Legend: Industries in the sample are 1—cereals, 2—wet corn milling, 3—baking, 4—biscuits, 5—chewing gum, 6—soft drink bottling, 7—cigarettes, 8—drugs, 9—petroleum, 10—cement, 11—gypsum products, 12—steel, 13—elevators, 14—computers, 15—typewriters, and 16—radio and TV receivers.

the excess capacity variables increases or decreases residuals[21] considerably in a few instances but not by much in most cases.

Although this inconsistency of effect might make it difficult from a policy standpoint to reach any general recommendation, it may make it possible at least to make recommendations about industries which would make favorable candidates for additional research. The situation of most concern in this area occurs when excess capacity discourages entry from taking place. Translating this into the terms of the model, further research would be most interesting for those industries that exhibit positive residuals in column 2 in Table II and reductions in residuals as shown in the last two columns of Table II. Wet corn milling, soft drink bottling, petroleum, and elevators had these characteristics for both versions of excess capacity. Cereals and biscuits had reductions in residuals in one excess capacity version but not in the other. The largest impact of the excess capacity variables of this type occurs in wet corn milling.[22]

The co-occurrence of lower than expected entry and a reduction in residuals when excess capacity is introduced, does not, of course, prove that excess capacity strategies have caused a reduction in entry. However, these are the conditions in which further research would seem to have the best chance of finding successful excess capacity strategies at work during the period observed.

John C. Hilke,
Bureau of Economics,
Federal Trade Commission,
Washington, D.C., 20580.

ACCEPTED OCTOBER 1983

REFERENCES

BAUMOL, W. and WILLIG, R. 1981, 'Fixed Costs, Sunk Costs, Entry Barriers, and Sustainability of Monopoly', *Quarterly Journal of Economics*, XLVI, **3** (August), pp. 405–29.

COMANOR, W. and WILSON, T., 1974, *Advertising and Market Power* (Harvard University Press, Cambridge, Mass.).

[21] Inconsistency in an excess-capacity effect is not altogether surprising from the perspective of the excess-capacity and strategic-entry-deterrence literature; no one has claimed that excess capacity is a ubiquitously adopted strategy. Indeed, part of its appeal as a strategic device, aside from the precommitment aspects, may be that potential entrants may be unable to detect whether excess capacity represents an innocent capacity miscalculation, a strategic signal, or a credible threat through precommitment. An incumbent firm might welcome such uncertainty among potential entrants if potential entrants take excess capacity as a sign of a weak cartel organization that is likely to collapse if entry takes place. See Kirman and Masson [1980]. For a similar discussion with respect to predatory pricing, see Salop [1981, pp. 14–18].

[22] A number of investigations of wet corn milling have taken place, most prominently the 1950 Corn Products Refining Co. *et al.* decision of the F.T.C. (FTC Docket 5502) ordering the nine U.S. corn products producers to cease and desist from their cooperative pricing activities and arrangements. A related consent settlement also occurred in 1982. The investigations of corn milling firms have focused on cooperative behavior on pricing and not on entry deterrence, so cooperation or agreement on excess capacity remains an unknown aspect of the behavior of firms in this industry, despite antitrust scrutiny.

De Vany, A., 1976, 'Uncertainty, Waiting Time, and Capacity Utilization: A Stochastic Theory of Product Quality', *Journal of Political Economy*, LXXXIV, **3** (June), pp. 523–41.

Dixit, A., 1979, 'A Model of Duopoly Suggesting a Theory of Entry Barriers', *Bell Journal of Economics*, X, **1** (Spring), pp. 20–32.

Harris, M., 1973, "Entry, Barriers to Entry, and Limit Pricing', (Ph.D. dissertation, Columbia University, New York).

———, 1976a, 'Entry and Barriers to Entry', *Industrial Organization Review*, IV, **3**, pp. 169–74.

———, 1976b, 'Entry and Long-Term Trends in Industry Performance', *Antitrust Bulletin*, XXI, **2** (Summer), pp. 295–312.

Hilke, J., 1978, 'Determinants of Entry: Cost and Risk Barriers to Entry', (Ph.D. dissertation, Cornell University, Ithaca, N.Y.).

———, 1980, 'Advertising Prediction and the Areeda-Turner and Williamson Rules', *The Journal of Reprints for Antitrust Law and Economics*, X, **1**, pp. 367–97.

Houthaker, H., and Taylor, L., 1970, *Consumer Demand in the United States* (Harvard University Press, Cambridge, Mass.).

Kirman, W. and Masson, R., 1980, 'Excess Capacity and Credible Entry Deterrence', (unpublished, Cornell University, Ithaca, N.Y.).

Mann, H. M., 1966, 'Seller Concentration, Barriers to Entry and Rates of Return in Thirty Industries', *Review of Economics and Statistics*, XLIX, **3** (August), pp. 296–307.

Salop, S. 1979, 'Strategic Entry Deterrence', *American Economic Review*, LXIX, **2** (May), pp. 335–38.

———, 1981, 'Strategy, Predation, and Antitrust Analysis: An Introduction', in *Strategy, Predation, and Antitrust Analysis* (FTC, Washington, D.C.).

Schelling, T., 1960, *The Strategy of Conflict* (Harvard University Press, Cambridge, Mass.).

Scherer, F. M., 1980, *Industrial Market Structure and Economic Performance*, 2nd Edition (Rand McNally, Chicago, Illinois).

Schmalensee, R., 1981, 'Economies of Scale and Barriers to Entry', *Journal of Political Economy*, LXXXIX, **6** (December), pp. 1, 228–39.

Shephard, W., 1970, *Market Power and Economic Welfare* (Random House, New York).

Spence, A. M., 1977, 'Entry, Capacity Investment and Oligopolistic Pricing', *Bell Journal of Economics*, VIII, **2** (Autumn), pp. 534–44.

Wenders, J., 1971, 'Excess Capacity as a Barrier to Entry', *Journal of Industrial Economics*, XIV, **2** (November), pp. 14–19.

Williamson, O., 1977, 'Predatory Pricing: A Strategic and Welfare Analysis', *Yale Law Journal*, LXXXII, **2** (December), pp. 284–340.

THE JOURNAL OF INDUSTRIAL ECONOMICS 0022–1821 $2.00
Volume XXXIII December 1984 No. 2

STRUCTURE AND CONDUCT IN LOCAL ADVERTISING MARKETS: THE CASE OF IRISH PROVINCIAL NEWSPAPERS

R. S. Thompson*

INTRODUCTION

This note presents some results from an empirical investigation of the determinants of advertising rates for provincial newspapers in the Republic of Ireland. The county of origin of each newspaper is treated as its geographical market and the quoted rates for advertising space are related to firm and market characteristics. Finally, the price-concentration relationship is examined in more detail to determine whether a critical concentration threshold operated.

Provided that local markets can be determined satisfactorily, single product geographical analyses of structure-conduct-performance relationships appear valuable in so far as they avoid problems with the control variables necessary in inter-industry work.[1] The local newspaper industry has, moreover, a largely homogeneous product and possesses the advantage, important in the context of a small open economy such as Ireland, of being totally unaffected by foreign trade.

SAMPLE

Ireland, with its generally sparsely distributed population and correspondingly largely national T.V. and radio broadcasting system, possesses a substantial local weekly newspaper industry.[2] In common with those of other European countries, the Irish newspapers are heavily dependent on advertising revenue. The principal outside competition for this income appears to come from distribution papers ("freesheets") and a number of (until recently) semi-clandestine commercial radio stations. Both of these alternatives have been frequently short-lived and are typically restricted to major urban areas.

The basic sample used in this study consists of 50 weekly provincial newspapers drawn from 24 of the 26 administrative counties in the Republic of

* This note has benefited from the helpful suggestions of the editor of the *Journal*. The author would also like to thank Harry Anthony, Pat Lyons, Vivienne Murray, Michael O'Suilleabhain, Anne Thomspon and the author's 1982–83 Industrial Economics class for data and comments.

[1] United States commercial banking is most widely used in single industry work. Rhoades [1982] notes that 66 such studies were published between 1960 and 1982.

[2] In general, advertising may be relatively more expensive in smaller and more sparsely populated economies. For a comparison of the conditions in the U.S.A. and Canada, for example, see Caves *et al.* [1980, Chapter 6].

Ireland.[3] The papers published in the principal urban areas of Dublin (county and city) and Cork city have been omitted because they have a national circulation and have been the subject of detailed price control.

The criteria for inclusion were the availability of both advertising rates and circulation figures for 1982. Whilst the resulting sample is not exhaustive, it does appear to cover all but the very small local newspapers: only one member of the industry's trade association, for example, was omitted.[4]

DATA AND VARIABLES

The pricing of advertising space by local newspapers results in a wide variety of official and unofficial rates. Extensive price discrimination, by category of advertisement, is operated and a complex system of overt and covert discounts for bulk purchase may exist.[5] Two alternative rates were used as dependent variables in this study. These were: firstly, the price per standard column inch (SCI); and secondly, the price per page (PAG). In each case these were taken from published sources and rate cards and do not allow for any discounts. It is suggested that SCI is probably the more reliable measure: firstly, because these discounts are more likely to affect display advertising by the page; secondly, because it has not been possible to correct for differences in page size or position; and thirdly, chains of newspapers typically offer discounts for group-wide advertisements—these appear more likely at the page level.
The firm-specific explanatory variable was circulation (CIRC) which, of course, was expected to exert a positive impact on advertising rates.

The principal market concentration measure was the country Herfindahl (HERF) index:

$$\text{HERF} = \sum_{i=1}^{n} si^2$$

where si is the share of the ith newspaper-owning firm in the county market. The few newspapers which were identified but had to be excluded from the sample because of a lack of adequate data appeared typically to have very small circulations. Accordingly, the county Herfindahls have been adjusted, where necessary, on the assumption that these fringe firms' titles had a circulation of one half that of the smallest included paper in the country. Because of this assumption, the following alternative concentration measures were used: firstly, a monopoly binary variable (MON) equal to one if there was only a

[3] The other unrepresented county, Wicklow, was dominated by a newspaper chain whose individual circulations were unavailable.

[4] Some indication of the coverage of the sample is that its total weekly circulation (0.64m) implies about 1.18 copies per household over the areas represented.

[5] Discounting by U.S. T.V. companies is discussed by Peterman [1968]. Discussions with newspaper staff suggested that deals with regular and/or large advertisers could be complex. Favourable credit terms often figured in these: for example, auctioneers (estate agents) were offered preferential extended credit on the notional grounds that the item advertised took longer to sell than conventional goods.

single newspaper firm producing in the market, and zero otherwise; secondly, another dummy variable (COMP) set equal to one if there were three or more operating firms, if not COMP = zero; and finally, a general "extent of competition" variable (PEOP/N) was defined by dividing the county population by the number of operating firms.

Traditionally newspaper publishing, with its high fixed costs of production and the start-up costs of product differentiation and market entry, has been classified as a high barrier to entry industry.[6] However, technological change has almost certainly lowered the real cost of entry—particularly for those with access to already functioning production facilities and a co-operative labour force. In particular, modern print technology allows the separation of news gathering and printing functions. This has encouraged the growth of groups of papers with common production facilities.

The Irish provincial newspaper industry contains a number of recent additions which have emerged by one or more of several routes. Firstly, there is gradualist entry by production differentiation on the part of a neighbouring paper. This may take the form of extending the area of coverage; followed by the production of a separate edition; followed by the creation of a separate title and identity. Secondly, entry may be effected by a group producing a local version of a generally standardized paper. Thirdly, entry may result from the activities of a firm not previously engaged in the industry—often this involves a consortium of local business interests.

In an inter-market investigation, local variations in the cost of entry are the relevant consideration. It is expected that the specific attributes of both potential entrants and incumbent firms are relevant here insofar as they may indicate the anticipated degree of post-entry accommodation or competition. Unfortunately, the entry-detering characteristics of existing markets would appear to be very difficult to identify from the outside. It was postulated, however, that papers belonging to multiple groups might be seen as more capable of sustained price competition in the face of entry than individually-operated ones. Accordingly, a binary variable (MULT) was used to try to capture an entry-detering effect associated with groups. However, it must be accepted that the existence of possible group-wide discounts makes the interpretation of the coefficient on MULT more difficult, especially where PAG is the dependent variable.

It was expected that local newspaper markets would vary in attractiveness to national advertisers according to the income per head of the local reader-

[6] For a discussion of the scale economies see Pratten [1971, Chapter 26]. His discussion of the potential economies of joint production facilities assumed a degree of labour non-cooperation which is not typically present in the local press level—certainly in Ireland. The breakdown of costs for weekly newspapers given by the Royal Commission suggests a considerable scope of multiple paper operations. For example, 72% of weekly newspaper costs are accounted for by editorial (18%), production (35%) and administrative (19%) activities compared to a total of 53% for these activities for a popular daily paper. It is in these areas rather than in the direct costs (e.g. newsprint) that multiple product economies would appear important. See Royal Commission [1977, para, 5. 37, p. 42].

ship. Therefore county income per head (INCO) is included here as a market structural variable.[7]

It appeared plausible that significant cost differences existed across local markets. In particular, it was considered likely that both news gathering and newspaper distribution costs would be higher in sparsely populated areas. Accordingly, the county population density (POPD) is used to control for possible price differences resulting from cost variations.

To summarize, the basic model used in the regression analysis—with the predicted signs above the coefficients—was as follows:

$$\text{rate} = \alpha_0 + \overset{+}{\alpha_1}\text{CIRC} + \overset{+}{\alpha_2}\text{INCO} + \overset{-}{\alpha_3}\text{POPD} + \overset{+}{\alpha_4}\text{MULT} + \overset{+}{\alpha_5}\text{HERF} + \varepsilon \quad (1)$$

where: rate is alternatively taken as the 1982 price per standard column inch (SCI) or the cost per page (PAG), and the explanatory variables are as defined above.

RESULTS

Equation (1) was estimated by OLS using both SCI and PAG as dependent variables and each concentration measure in turn. The results, summarized in Table I, show substantial consistency whichever dependent variable is used.

In every specification tried CIRC emerged, as expected, with a highly significant positive coefficient—whose *t*-statistic did not fall below 5.85. At the same time the numerical value of the coefficient was surprisingly small. It implied that an increase of 1,000 in circulation added, on average, 14–16 pence to the rate per column inch. This appears small for a sample with a mean SCI of £4.73 and mean circulation of 16,000 copies.[8]

INCO attracted a positive coefficient which was significant at least at the 5% level for all specifications except those containing PEOP/N. The size of the coefficient in INCO is surprising. For example, taking the best fit with the SCI variable gives a coefficient on INCO of 0.008. This implies a *ceteris paribus* difference of £2 per standard column inch between the richest (Waterford) and poorest (Leitrim) counties in the sample, 42% of the actual mean value for SCI.

The population density variable (POPD) was universally insignificant. The newspaper chain dummy variable (MULT), by contrast, was invariably positive and consistently significant with PAG as dependent variable and insignifi-

[7] The source of these data was Ross and Jones [1977].

[8] Stigler [1964] reported a quadratic relationship for a regression of advertising rates on circulation for U.S. newspapers. However, including a squared CIRC term revealed no support for such a relationship here.

TABLE I
DETERMINANTS OF ADVERTISING RATES AMONG IRISH PROVINCIAL NEWSPAPERS: OLS ESTIMATES
(t-statistics in parentheses)

No.	Dependent Variable	Independent Variables: Constant	CIRC	INCO	POPD	MULT	HERF	MON	COMP	PEOP/N	R^2	R^{-2}	F
1.1	SCI, $n = 50$	−3.954**	0.145***	0.008***	−0.002	0.316	2.447***	–	–	–	0.62	0.58	14.65
		(−2.072)	(6.885)	(2.635)	(−0.599)	(0.985)	(4.067)						
1.2	SCI, $n = 50$	−1.734	0.145***	0.005**	0.000	0.378	–	1.641***	–	–	0.62	0.58	14.34
		(−0.978)	(6.863)	(1.921)	(0.066)	(1.169)		(3.968)					
1.3	SCI, $n = 50$	−3.027*	0.160***	0.009***	−0.004	0.331	–	–	−0.971***	–	0.55	0.50	10.82
		(−1.447)	(6.838)	(2.524)	(−0.986)	(0.945)			(−2.579)				
1.4	SCI, $n = 50$	−1.062	0.142***	0.004*	−0.000	0.173	–	–	–	0.001**	0.52	0.46	9.42
		(−0.535)	(5.857)	(1.347)	(−0.083)	(0.471)				(1.742)			
1.5	PAG, $n = 49$	1043***	32.74***	1.463**	−0.106	165.1**	403.5***	–	–	–	0.63	0.59	14.77
		(2.547)	(7.151)	(2.371)	(−0.162)	(2.389)	(3.126)						
1.6	PAG, $n = 49$	−667.1**	32.92***	1.091**	0.228	173.4***	–	247.8***	–	–	0.62	0.57	13.8
		(−1.723)	(7.042)	(1.787)	(0.346)	(2.449)		(2.755)					
1.7	PAG, $n = 49$	−1005**	35.69***	1.871***	−0.581	171.5***	–	–	−212.8***	–	0.62	0.57	13.96
		(−2.410)	(7.581)	(2.726)	(−0.813)	(2.434)			(−2.822)				
1.8	PAG, $n = 49$	−558.2*	32.93***	0.941*	0.182	147.3**	–	–	–	0.135	0.55	0.50	10.70
		(−1.345)	(6.445)	(1.433)	(0.256)	(1.916)				(0.761)			
1.9	PAG, $n = 49$	−1010***	32.79***	1.399***	–	163.4***	400.3***	–	–	–	0.63	0.60	18.87
		(−2.867)	(7.256)	(2.993)		(2.419)	(3.175)						

***, **, * Indicates significance (one-tail test) at the 1, 5 and 10% levels, respectively.

cant with SCI. The latter result does not indicate support for our hypothesised local entry barrier effect. However, it may be that the cost-reducing effects of multiple paper operation pull the rates in the opposite direction. Remembering that PAG is the page price for individual papers, it appears probable that the significant coefficient for MULT, with PAG as dependent variable, reflects a form of price discrimination against advertisers who do not avail themselves of groupwide space purchases.

Finally, the three principal concentration variables—HERF, MON and COMP—were invariably significant at the 1% level with the predicted signs. The consistency of these results appears to indicate strong support for the operation of the structure-conduct hypothesis within the industry. Furthermore, the size of the coefficients is remarkable. For example, the MON coefficient in equation (1.2) implies that *ceteris paribus* rates in monopolised markets are £1.64 per standard column inch higher than the average elsewhere.

The final concentration variable, PEOP/N, had the smallest impact. It was at most only weakly significant and its use invariably lowered the overall explanatory power of the regression. This is perhaps because it was the least valid measure of market concentration used here.

Ignoring those including PEOP/N, the adjusted R^2 for the regression equations varied between 0.5 and 0.6, according to the specification used. Given the simplified market definition and the inevitable unavailability of certain types of data—particularly relating to competing media and local entry (potential and realized) conditions—these fits appear satisfactory. They appear to compare reasonably well with those reported in other single industry studies.

A CRITICAL CONCENTRATION LEVEL?

An unresolved issue in the structure-performance literature concerns the existence of a crtitical threshold for concentration. Following Bain's [1951] initial finding of a critical level at a four-firm concentration ratio of 0.7, there has been a substantial but inconclusive empirical literature. Because of inter-industry differences in structural features, other than concentration, recent investigations of this phenomenon have tended to take the form of single industry studies using geographical markets. However, here again the results are mixed. For example, Marvel [1978] reported some evidence of a threshold effect in U.S. gasoline markets, but Geithman, Marvel and Weiss [1981] found no critical level for concentration in U.S. supermarket pricing, whilst Heggestad and Mingo [1972] found support for an *upper* threshold for the pricing of American banking services.

In view of the significant price-concentration relationship reported in the previous section of this paper, the data were examined for evidence of a critical concentration level. Piecewise linear regressions were run for alternative critical thresholds of HERF using an estimating equation of the form:

$$\text{rate} = \beta_0 + \beta_i X_i + \beta_j(\text{HERF} - \text{HERF}_j)D_j \qquad (2)$$

where the X_i are the explanatory variables (CIRC, INCO, POPD, MULT and HERF) as in equation (1); HERF_j is the critical threshold for HERF; and D_j is a binary variable equal to one where $\text{HERF} \geq \text{HERF}_j$.

Equation (2) was estimated over a range of alternative critical values of HERF from 0.3 to 0.6 and the $\hat{\beta}_j$ coefficients, their t-statistics and the adjusted R^2s are summarized in Table II. It can be seen that the slope dummy coefficients, whilst invariably positive, are insignificant and provide no clear evidence of a structural break in the price-concentration relationship.

TABLE II
PIECEWISE LINEAR REGRESSION TESTS FOR A STRUCTURAL BREAK IN THE PRICE–HERFINDAHL RELATIONSHIP
(t-statistics of the slope dummy in parentheses)

Critical Value of HERF	*DCI*	$\bar{R}^2$	*PAG*	$\bar{R}^2$
≥0.30	4.550 (0.822)	0.59	148.3 (1.264)	0.61
≥0.40	2.799 (0.946)	0.59	773.2 (1.238)	0.61
≥0.50	1.767 (0.779)	0.59	232.9 (0.772)	0.60
≥0.61	1.749 (0.781)	0.59	151.7 (0.317)	0.60

The lack of a critical concentration threshold was made further apparent when equation (1) was re-estimated after replacing HERF with binary variables for different concentration classes, as suggested by Geithman *et al.* [1981]. The results of this exercise are shown in Table III where the regression estimates from alternative classifications have been used to construct *ceteris paribus* price estimates for each concentration class. The estimated price is derived by multiplying the means of the variables by their coefficients and adding the constant term and the dummy variable coefficient for the appropriate size class. Each of the latter coefficients shows the price premium of the concentration class over the least concentrated group.

An inspection of Table III shows that for all but the third class there is a progressive increase in price with concentration category. This result appeared to be robust to alternative classifications and dependent variables employed. It does not indicate support for a critical level of concentration among newspaper markets.

TABLE III
ESTIMATED* ADVERTISING SPACE PRICES FOR ALTERNATIVE CONCENTRATION CLASSES BY HERFINDAHL, 1982

Concentration Class	*SCI*	*PAG*	*Concentration Class*	*SCI*	*PAG*
≤0.2	4.157 [4]	711.69 [4]	≤0.19	3.971 [4]	662.125 [4]
0.21–0.3	4.455 (0.45) [9]	724.828 (0.09) [9]	0.2–0.29	4.390 (0.62) [9]	705.131 (0.31) [9]
0.31–0.4 0.41–0.5	4.14 (−0.02) [15]	559.894 (−1.02) [14]	0.3–0.39 0.4–0.49	4.183 (0.31) [12]	561.272 (−0.71) [11]
0.51–0.6 0.61–0.7	4.886 (1.13) [14]	802.254 (0.67) [14]	0.5–0.59	4.692 (1.04) [13]	756.493 (0.67) [13]
0.71–0.8 0.81–0.9 ≤0.91	6.148 (2.86) [8]	955.759 (1.67) [8]	0.6–0.69 0.7–0.79 0.8–0.89 0.9–1.0	5.804 (2.65) [12]	923.473 (1.86) [12]

* Estimated prices are obtained by multiplying the mean values of variables by their regression coefficients and adding the constant term plus the appropriate binary variable coefficient. Numbers in parentheses are the *t*-values for the appropriate binary variable and those in square brackets are the number of observations in each size class.

CONCLUSION

This article has examined the determination of quoted advertising rates for a large sample of Irish provincial newspapers. It is recognized that there are a number of caveats to the reported results: firstly, the advertising rates could not be adjusted for discounts, credit term variation etc.; secondly, no data were available on the impact of free newspapers or the (then illegal) private local radio stations; thirdly, there are clearly limitations in defining local markets as co-terminous with administrative counties;[9] and finally, as with other structure-conduct studies, the results using data relating to a particular point in time do not necessarily indicate the price-concentration relationship in equilibrium. Despite these limitations, however, the consistency of the results reported in this paper does appear to provide strong support for the view that local market structure is important.

Concentration emerged as a consistently significant influence on price. Furthermore, there did not appear to be a critical concentration threshold

[9] In fact it is arguable that in Ireland the county possesses an identity which makes it more than a mere administrative unit: firstly, county boundaries have remained intact for over two centuries; secondly, the county is the basic unit for national sporting competition and Dail (parliamentary) elections; and finally it was noticeable that 25 (i.e. 50%) of the papers in our sample include the county name in their title.

evident across the sample. The size of the coefficients on the alternative concentration variables, however, indicated that competition in local markets is quantitatively important. This result supports the argument that local market conditions are a legitimate concern for antitrust policy where goods and services are locally provided. In the case of local advertising markets it appears that such a policy would need to have regard for the adverse consequence of newspaper mergers and policies restricting the entry of new media such as local commercial radio stations.

R. S. Thompson,
Department of Economics,
University College,
Cork, Ireland.

ACCEPTED JANUARY 1984

REFERENCES

BAIN, J., 1951, 'Relation of Profit Rate to Industrial Concentration: American Manufacturing, 1936–40', *Quarterly Journal of Economics*, **65** (August), pp. 293–324.

BOWLES, M., 1981, Word From Ireland *ADMAP*, (June) pp. 283–296.

CAVES, R., PORTER, M., SPENCE, A. M. and SCOTT, J., 1980, *Competition In the Open Economy: A Model Applied to Canada*, (Harvard University Press, Cambridge, Mass.).

GEITHMAN, F., MARVEL, H. and WEISS, L. W., 1981, 'Concentration, Price and Critical Concentration Ratios', *Review of Economics and Statistics*, **63** (August), pp. 246–53.

HEGGESTAD, A. R. and MINGO, J. J., 1972, 'The Competitive Condition of U.S. Banking Markets and the Impact of Structural Reform, *Journal of Finance*, **32** (June), pp. 649–61.

M.L.H. CONSULTANTS LTD., 1978, *A Study of the Evolution of Concentration in the Irish Publishing Industry*, (Commission of the European Communities, Brussels).

MARVEL, H., 1978, 'Competition and Price Levels in the Retail Gasoline Market, *Review of Economics and Statistics*, **60** (May), pp. 252–58.

PETERMAN, J. L., 1968, 'The Clorox Case and the Television Rate Structures', *Journal of Law and Economics*, **11** (October), pp. 321–422.

PRATTEN, C., 1971, *Economies of Scale in Manufacturing Industry*, University of Cambridge Department of Economics Occasional Paper. Number 28. (Cambridge).

RHOADES, S. A., 1982, *Structure-Performance Studies in Banking: An Updated Summary and Evaluation.* Federal Reserve Board Staff Studies 119.

ROSS, M. and JONES, R., 1977, *Personal Incomes by County in 1973*. National Economic and Social Council Report No. 50, (Dublin).

ROYAL COMMISSION ON THE PRESS, 1974–1977, (McGregor Commission), Final Report, 1977, Cmnd 6810 (HMSO, London).

STIGLER, G., 1964, A Theory of Oligopoly, *Journal of Political Economy*, **92** (February), pp. 44–61.

THE JOURNAL OF INDUSTRIAL ECONOMICS 0022–1821 $2.00
Volume XXXIII December 1984 No. 2

ON THE ABILITY OF SPATIAL COMPETITORS TO PRICE DISCRIMINATE

Bruce L. Benson

I. INTRODUCTION

Neil Dorward recently surveyed existing literature on spatial price discrimination in this journal and concluded that "where competitive firms are free of institutional constraints preventing any form of price discrimination, the pressures of profit maximization will force them to price discriminate spatially", [1982, p. 136]. Dorward's assessment of this literature is clearly accurate, *but* the literature itself generally has implicitly assumed away a large class of demand conditions which generate the potential for arbitrage among consumers.[1] Hoover [1937] demonstrated that certain demand conditions will lead a monopolist to desire a discriminatory pricing schedule which favors near buyers at the expense of distant buyers, but such discriminatory efforts cannot be maintained because of resale between buyers. Whether or not Hoover's spatial monopoly results extend to spatial competition and price discrimination has apparently not been adequately addressed. It shall become clear below, however, that a spatial competitor may not be able to price discriminatorily under certain demand conditions. Thus, the conclusions of the existing spatially competitive price discrimination literature should be modified to include an explicit recognition that they apply only under a "no arbitrage" condition.

II. SPATIAL MONOPOLY PRICING UNDER ALTERNATIVE DEMAND CONDITIONS

Assume, as in Greenhut [1975], and Benson [1980], that each individual consumer's demand is of the form

$$P = a - \frac{b}{x} Q^x, \tag{1}$$

where P is price, Q represents quantity demanded, and a, b, and x are parameters. The parameter x is central to the following analysis, since varying x allows equation (1) to represent a wide range of demand function shapes. For example, an $x > 1$ yields a curve which is convex upward, while $x = 1$ dictates

[1] Greenhut and Greenhut [1975] have explicitly recognized that discrimination does not apply to all the demand conditions.

a linear demand curve. Given $x < 1$, demand is concave upward, and an $x < 0$ implies an extremely concave curve (e.g. $x < 0$ in conjunction with $a = 0$ implies a constant elasticity function).

A spatial price discriminating monopolist sets a profit maximizing price for each consumer, assuming only one consumer is located at any site. For instance, if there are no transport costs (i.e. a consumer located at the monopolist's production site), price and quantity for that consumer are determined by equating marginal revenue and marginal cost:

$$P(1 - (1/e)) = MC, \tag{2}$$

where e is elasticity and MC is marginal cost (assumed to be constant). Since $dP/dQ = -bQ^{x-1}$ and $bQ^x = x(a - P)$, the own price elasticity of demand is

$$e = P/(x(a - P)). \tag{3}$$

Substituting (3) into (2) provides

$$P(1 + x) - xa = MC. \tag{4}$$

For consumers located at some distance from the firm,

$$P_D(1 + x) - xa = MC + D. \tag{5}$$

P_D denotes the delivered price to any point in space, while D is a variable representing transport costs from the seller's site to any consuming location. Transport costs are assumed to consist of a unitary transport rate times the units of distance, D. Solving equation (5) for P_D yields the monopolist's delivered price schedule:

$$P_D = (1/(1 + x))(xa + MC) + (1/(1 + x))D. \tag{6}$$

The first term on the right hand side of equation (6) is the price at the monopolist's production site (where $D = 0$). The slope of the delivered price schedule is given by $(1/(1 + x))$. The slope of an f.o.b. delivered price schedule would be one since the transport rate is assumed to be constant and unitary. Thus, a slope less than one implies discrimination in favor of distant buyers and against near buyers, while a slope greater than one indicates discrimination in favor of near buyers and against distant buyers. The monopolist ships out to the point where P_D equals the demand intercept (a when $x > 0$ and infinity when $x < 0$).

The relevant points of Hoover's monopoly analysis can now be summarized. The slope of the discriminatory schedule obviously depends upon the value of x, or the convexity of consumer demand. If $x > 0$ the slope is less than one and discrimination in favor of distant buyers occurs. Note that profitable consumer resale or arbitrage is not possible under such circumstances since the firm is absorbing freight. Resale requires buyers to reship the product so the delivered resale price including full transport costs would have to be greater than the monopolist's delivered price.

When $x < 0$, the slope of the delivered price schedule exceeds one.[2] Consequently arbitrage is possible. Favored buyers can resell the product at a lower delivered price than the monopolist sets for more distant buyers, while still charging the full freight cost and some additional profit mark-up. This is the essence of Hoover's analysis. Therefore, it deserves further emphasis and discussion. The point is that demand conditions exist in theory under which a spatial monopolist will be unable to maintain a profitable price discriminating system. Thus, f.o.b. pricing may be the most profitable pricing strategy the monopolist is *able* to employ.

The reason that the value of x plays the role it does in determining the slope of the discriminating delivered price schedule is straightforward. When transport costs are netted from a positive exponential demand the elasticity of demand rises at every price. This can be seen by noting that the effect of subtracting transport costs from demand is to lower a in equation (3). Thus, distant buyers have relatively elastic demand. The discriminatory firm sets increasingly lower prices net of transport costs for increasingly distant consumers as a consequence. When transport costs are added to the discriminatory prices to obtain the delivered price schedule the slope is less than one, as freight to distant buyers is absorbed due to the lower and lower prices net of transport costs.

On the other hand, when $x < 0$ and transport costs are netted, the elasticity of demand falls at each price.[3] Distant buyers, as a consequence, have relatively inelastic demand. A discriminator would want to set increasingly higher prices net of transport costs for increasingly distant buyers. Thus, when delivery costs are added to the discriminatory prices net of such costs, the impact is that delivered prices rise by more than just transport costs—phantom freight if you will. Profitable discrimination is likely to be prevented by arbitrage in this case. Furthermore, given elasticities of demand, profits would be lower under a pricing policy which discriminates against near buyers than they are under f.o.b. pricing, so f.o.b. pricing is the most profitable of the available pricing strategies.

One might ask if it is reasonable to assume a negative exponential demand rather than a positive exponential. Of course, the opposite question is just as plausible! Certainly once one leaves the spatial literature negative exponential (i.e. constant elasticity) demands are often employed. Such demands are

[2] An $x = 0$ leads a monopolist to choose f.o.b. pricing. Of course, this is unlikely since $x = 0$ implies a perfectly elastic *individual* consumer demand.

[3] Note that when $x < 0$, a is the asymptote of the curve as Q approaches infinity. Thus, $P > a$.

easily derivable from reasonable appearing utility functions (something that some would claim cannot be said about the linear function employed in many spatial models), so it seems both reasonable and necessary to consider the implications of both $x > 0$ and $x < 0$ before drawing any general conclusions for spatial models.

III. SPATIALLY COMPETITIVE PRICING UNDER ALTERNATIVE DEMAND CONDITIONS

In order to see that the potential for arbitrage can arise in a spatially competitive model as well as under spatial monopoly, consider Löschian competition. The Löschian behavioral assumption is that each spatial entrepreneur expects his market area to be fixed and prices as a spatial monopolist in that area. The difference between a Löschian competitor and a spatial monopolist is that the competitive firm's market is constrained by the proximity of a distant competitor rather than by the demand intercept. Thus, the Löschian entrepreneur should set discriminatory prices if he can. Since a monopoly (or Löschian) price discriminator sets a profit maximizing price at each consumer location, the loss of some buyer sites due to distant competition will have no impact on the prices set for remaining customers (assuming constant marginal cost). Price at each location is still given by equation (4) and the delivered price schedule is given by (6). Furthermore, successful price discrimination yields greater profits than f.o.b. pricing. Thus, *given positive exponential demands* and free entry to zero profits, Löschian competitors may practise price discrimination. However, negative exponential demand and the resulting profitability of discrimination in favor of near buyers obviously will have the same impact on Löschian competitors as it does on a spatial monopolist. Arbitrage should prevent such disrimination so the best this Löschian competitor can do is set an f.o.b. price.[4]

More is needed for effective price discrimination than differences in elasticities of demand. Hoover, in his analysis of spatial monopoly pricing, stressed that in addition "the more-favored buyers must somehow be prevented from selling to the ones discriminated against" [1937, p. 183]. This point also applies to spatial competition.

Bruce L. Benson,
Department of Agricultural Economics and Economics,
Montana State University,
Bozeman, Montana, 59717.

ACCEPTED OCTOBER 1983

[4] The same is true of the Cournot and Greenhut-Ohta models of spatial competition mentioned in Dorward's survey, but space constraints prevent the detailed development needed to demonstrate this. Interested readers can contact the author to obtain a demonstration.

REFERENCES

Benson, B. L., 1980, 'Löschian Competition Under Alternative Demand Conditions'. *American Economic Review*, **70**, 5 (December), pp. 1098–105.

Dorward, N., 1982, 'Recent Developments in the Analysis of Spatial Competition and Their Implications for Industrial Economics', *Journal of Industrial Economics*, **31**, 1/2 (September/December), pp. 133–51.

Greenhut, J. and Greenhut, M. L., 1975, 'Spatial Price Discrimination, Competition and Location Effects', *Economica*, **42**, 168 (November), pp. 401–19.

Hoover, E., 1937, 'Spatial Price Discrimination', *Review of Economic Studies*, **4**, 3 (June), pp. 182–91.

ANNOUNCEMENT

The Third Annual Meeting of the Association of Managerial Economists (AME) will be held in New York, December 28–30, 1985.

Three sessions of competitively selected papers will be featured in conjunction with the ASSA meetings. Theoretical, empirical and policy analyses across a broad spectrum of topics will be featured. Especially encouraged are papers integrating the theory of accounting, finance and industrial organizations in topic areas such as: the market for corporate control (buyouts, mergers, share repurchases, spinoffs), managerial labor market, measuring monopoly profits, and the information content of accounting data.

Both members and nonmembers are invited to submit papers and/or make program suggestions to Professor Mark Hirschey (AME Program Chair), Graduate School of Business Administration, 1100 14th Street, University of Colorado, Denver, CO 80204 (303/623-4436).

Submission deadline. June 15, 1985.

THE JOURNAL OF INDUSTRIAL ECONOMICS

Published first in October 1952, the Journal has a very wide international circulation, and has established itself as the leading journal in the field of industrial economics. It was founded to promote the analysis of modern industry, particularly the behaviour of firms, and the functioning of markets. More specifically it seeks to bring the tools of modern economic analysis of real problems of industrial economies.

Contributions are welcomed covering all the major areas of industrial economics. One such area is the relationship between market structure and market behaviour in the areas of pricing, product differentiation, advertising and the dissemination of information and R and D. Another area focuses more directly on the firm, its objectives, finance, investment and growth. A third area comprises the background environment within which industrial firms operate: the changing structure of industry, public policy on monopoly and restrictive trade practices, regulation, fiscal and monetary policy as they affect firms, and underlying changes in productivity and international competitiveness.

The Journal has a tradition of publishing a blend of theory and evidence. Theoretical discussion is welcomed provided that the more abstract theory includes sufficient introduction and other explanation to convey the significance of the material to the general reader who wants to decide whether to follow the analysis through. Empirical analysis, and especially econometric analysis, should include an explanation of the data sources used, of the methods applied and of the underlying theoretical basis of the study. The Journal has a particular tradition of case studies of firms and industries, which the Editors would wish to continue. However contributors of such studies are asked to remember that a study will be of interest to the international readership of the Journal only if it makes a particular contribution to the methodology of such studies, or if the empirical results are exceptionally interesting.

Alongside articles of more normal length, the Editors are ready to publish shorter notes, especially where these give interim results of important research studies, or where they report significant new empirical results. Books are not reviewed, although books received will be listed, sometimes with a short note: but substantial review articles will be considered.

Information for contributors

Typescripts from North America should be sent to Professor H. Michael Mann, Department of Economics, Boston College, Chestnut Hill, Massachusetts, 02167, U.S.A. Typescripts from *all* other countries should be sent to the General Editor, Journal of Industrial Economics, Institute of Economics and Statistics, The University of Oxford, St. Cross Building, Manor Road, Oxford, OX1 3UL, U.K. Detailed Information for Contributors is available from the General Editor. Contributors are asked to send an Abstract, not exceeding 100 words, with their article. No payment is made for articles accepted, but authors are provided with 25 free offprints.

Information for subscribers

The journal is published four times a year, in September, December, March and June, by Basil Blackwell Publisher Ltd., 108 Cowley Road, Oxford OX4 1JF, England. Prices are as follows:

	UK	Overseas	USA	Canada
Institutions	£26.50	£33.50	$65.75	$80.50
Individuals	£16.25	£20.35	$35.00	$47.00
Single issue prices for				
Institutions	£7.20	£8.80	$17.70	$21.50
Individuals	£5.20	£6.40	$12.00	$14.70

CONTRIBUTORS TO THIS NUMBER

PANKAJ GHEMAWAT: Assistant Professor of General Management at the Graduate School of Business Administration, Harvard University.

DAVID M. BARTON: Staff Economist, Bureau of Economics, U.S. Federal Trade Commission, Washington D.C.

ROGER SHERMAN: Professor of Economics, University of Virginia, Charlottesville.

DONALD J. LECRAW: Associate Professor, School of Business Administration, The University of Western Ontario, London, Ontario.

THOMAS E. GETZEN: Assistant Professor of Health Economics, School of Business Administration, Temple University, Philadelphia.

M. E. BEESLEY: Professor of Economics, London Business School.

R. T. HAMILTON: Senior Lecturer in Business Administration, University of Canterbury, Christchurch, New Zealand.

JOHN C. HILKE: Staff Economist, Federal Trade Commission, Bureau of Economics, Washington D.C.

R. S. THOMPSON: Lecturer in Economics, University College, Cork.

BRUCE L. BENSON: Associate Professor of Economics, Department of Agricultural Economics and Economics, Montana State University, Bozeman.

US Mailing: Second class postage paid at New York. Postmaster: Send address corrections to: Journal of Industrial Economics, c/o Expediters of the Printed Word Ltd., 515 Madison Avenue, New York, NY 10022 (US Mailing Agent).

Reprints of Back Volumes: Volumes 1–28 of the journal are available (in complete volumes only) from the Kraus Reprint Corporation, Route 100, Millwood, New York 10546, USA. More recent back issues are available from the publisher at the current single issue price.

Microfilm: An agreement for the supply of microfilm copies from Volume 1 onwards has been made with University Microfilms International, Department PR, 30–32 Mortimer Street, London W1N 7RA, England, or 300 North Zeeb Road, Ann Arbor, Michigan 48106, USA.

Set by Santype International Ltd., Salisbury, Wilts.
Printed and bound by Whitstable Litho Ltd., Whitstable, Kent.

THE JOURNAL OF INDUSTRIAL ECONOMICS

Volume XXXIII MARCH 1985 No. 3

ROBERT A. TAGGART, Jr.,
Effects of Regulation on Utility Financing: Theory and Evidence 257

JAMES A. BRANDER and BARBARA J. SPENCER
Tacit Collusion, Free Entry and Welfare 277

DOUGLAS TODD
Productive Performance in West German Manufacturing Industry 1970–80: A Farrell Frontier Characterisation 295

DAMIEN NEVEN
Two Stage (Perfect) Equilibrium in Hotelling's Model 317

M. S. KUMAR
Growth, Acquisition Activity and Firm Size: Evidence from the United Kingdom 327

Short Articles and Notes

GEIR GRIPSRUD and KJELL GRØNHAUG
Structure and Strategy in Grocery Retailing: a Sociometric Approach 339

M. S. SILVER
On the Measurement of Changes in Aggregate Concentration, Market Concentration and Diversification 349

ALAN J. DASKIN
Dynamics of Canadian Deposit-Taking Institutions: Comment 353

ARUN K. MUKHOPADHYAY
Returns to Scale in R&D and the Schumpeterian Hypothesis: a Comment 359

MEIR KOHN and JOHN T. SCOTT
Scale Economies in Research and Development: a Reply 363

ISSN 0022-1821
BASIL BLACKWELL OXFORD ENGLAND

THE JOURNAL OF INDUSTRIAL ECONOMICS 0022-1821 $2.00
Volume XXXIII March 1985 No. 3

EFFECTS OF REGULATION ON UTILITY FINANCING: THEORY AND EVIDENCE*

ROBERT A. TAGGART, JR.

THE determinants of cross-sectional variations in corporate capital structure have yet to be convincingly identified. There is a prevailing notion that industry characteristics are somehow related to differences in firms' debt ratios, but while this notion enjoys some empirical support, it is difficult to pinpoint the industry factors responsible for such differences.[1] A deeper understanding of these cross-sectional variations might be afforded by the detailed examination of specific industry characteristics and their relationship to firms' financing patterns.

The present study offers a methodology for approaching this issue. The first step is to assemble joint theories of industry and financial structure in order to identify the ways in which changing industry conditions might be associated with changes in financing. Evidence on such simultaneous changes can then be examined in an attempt to identify the most plausible joint theory.

The methodology is used to investigate the effects of state commission regulation on the financing of electric utilities. This is a natural candidate for study since regulation is such a salient feature of the industry. In addition, the regulatory system imparts some interesting special features to the very nature of utility capital structures. Inherent in all capital structures, for example, are opportunities for shifting wealth between bondholders and shareholders, but under regulation these wealth-shifting opportunities are expanded to encompass consumers as well. Finally, the study of regulation has resulted in several relatively well-specified theories of why regulation is imposed and what its observable effects should be.

In Section I, the different theories of capital structure and regulation are discussed and their joint implications are derived. The capital structure theories include the 'perfect capital market' theory, the 'debt capacity' theory and the 'financing hierarchy' theory. The regulatory theories include the 'public interest' or 'market failure' theory, the 'political economy' theory and the 'imperfect monitoring' theory. In Section II, financing data from the early days of state commission utility regulation are used to try to distinguish

* I am grateful to Leslie Edison and Suk Heun Yoon for able research assistance and to Paul Asquith, James Bicksler, Gregory Connor, Patrick Hess, Robert McDonald, Ingo Vogelsang and a referee for helpful comments on earlier drafts. Support from the National Science Foundation under Grant No. SOC 77-07251 is also gratefully acknowledged.

[1] For evidence in support of industry effects on capital structure, see Schwartz and Aronson [1967], Scott [1972], Scott and Martin [1975] and (to a limited extent at least) Ferri and Jones [1979]. Of special relevance to this study, Flath and Knoeber [1980] reported a capital structure effect associated with regulated industries.

among the theories, and conclusions are offered in Section III. For the period studied the most plausible interpretation of the evidence appears to be that state regulation made the business environment safer for utilities, thereby encouraging greater use of debt financing. This is consistent with the political economy theory of regulation in conjunction with the debt capacity theory of capital structure. However, the evidence does not eliminate all ambiguity. The possibility cannot be ruled out that some utilities, as suggested by the imperfect monitoring theory of regulation, may have adopted higher debt proportions in an attempt to win price concessions from regulators. In addition, the financing hierarchy theory of capital structure is consistent with some, but not all, of the results.

I. THEORIES OF CAPITAL STRUCTURE AND REGULATION

A. *Capital Structure Theories*

Although there are many different models of the capital structure decision, they are grouped for purposes of this study in three categories. The first of these is labeled the 'perfect capital market' category and includes the models of Modigliani and Miller [1958] and Miller [1977]. The distinguishing feature of these models is that perfect competition in the capital market drives out any advantages to financial structure. In equilibrium, firms are willing to substitute debt for equity indefinitely at a constant exchange rate. Likewise, in the Modigliani-Miller version at least, equity funds raised either externally or internally are perfect substitutes for one another. Because of these properties, no one firm can increase its total market value by changing its capital structure, and financing changes that do take place would be expected to occur randomly.

The second, or 'debt capacity' category includes the tax-saving-bankruptcy costs model,[2] the agency model[3] and the signalling model.[4] In each version, there is some initial advantage to corporate debt financing, but the marginal net benefit diminishes as the firm encounters increased costs that are related in a variety of ways to the threat of bankruptcy. Each firm thus has an optimal debt level, or debt capacity, that depends on such factors as its business risk, the potential severity of shareholder-bondholder conflicts and the proportion of its assets suitable for use as collateral.

The third category comprises different versions of the 'financing hierarchy' theory. Under this notion, internal funds are preferred by firms and used first.

[2] See Robichek and Myers [1966], Kraus and Litzenberger [1973] and Kim [1976]. The DeAngelo and Masulis [1980] model could also be included under this heading in the following sense: Since interest deductions are a substitute for other tax shelters, too much debt entails the cost of losing the benefits of other tax shelters in low-income states of nature.

[3] See Jensen and Meckling [1976], Myers [1977] and Smith and Warner [1979].

[4] See Ross [1977]. In this model the firm's shareholders do not directly bear any costs of substituting debt for equity, but its managers are confronted with a kind of bankruptcy cost through the incentive compensation schedule.

If needed, debt financing is used after internal funds have been exhausted, while external equity is issued only as a last resort. This view has long held sway among observers of business practice (see Donaldson [1961]) but has only recently found its way into formal finance theory. In the most recent versions of this theory, the factors underlying firms' reluctance to issue stock include personal taxation (Stiglitz [1973]) and the adverse selection problem associated with stock issues (Myers and Majluf [1983].[5] In its extreme form, in which no corporate stock is issued at all, this theory suggests that each firm's debt issuance in a given period will be determined by the relative magnitudes of its investment opportunities and internal funds.

B. *Theories of Regulation*

The theory of regulation that is perhaps most frequently invoked (sometimes as a straw man) in the electric utility context is the 'public interest' or 'market failure' theory.[6] According to this theory, regulation is introduced to enhance efficiency in those markets where the competitive system fails. Natural monopoly is the category of market failure usually ascribed to the electric utility industry, and regulation of prices is thus aimed at expanding the monopolist's inefficiently restricted output. Much of this theory's attention is devoted to the regulatory price-setting process, and it is implicit that the regulator need not concern himself with other aspects of utility operations.

The "political economy" theory takes the position that market forces, working through the political system, shape the formation and ongoing activities of the regulatory process itself.[7] Regulation is recognized as an instrument not so much for achieving economic efficiency as for shifting wealth, and both firms and consumer groups are seen as competing in the political marketplace, using votes and resources in an attempt to win favorable outcomes. The distinguishing feature of this model is fully rational behavior on the part of all participants: consumers, producers and regulators (legislators) alike maximize well-defined objective functions subject to well-defined constraints. Although the regulatory process may sometimes favor consumers and sometimes producers, depending on the relative strengths of their desires and their relative capacities to marshal resources, its outcomes are never unintended. Of particular interest to this study, Peltzman [1976, p. 227] infers one such set of fluctuating, but nevertheless intended, outcomes from his model: "Regulation will tend to be more heavily weighted toward producer protection in depressions and toward consumer protection in expansions." This implies that regulation should reduce the systematic risk of utilities' operating cash flows.

The third theory of regulation is the "imperfect monitoring" theory, which

[5] If managers have better information than investors about their firms' prospects, they will be tempted to issue stock when they feel it is overvalued in the market. Since investors are aware of this incentive, however, they will bid down the price of a firm that issues stock.

[6] It is difficult to find a pure statement of the public interest theory. Discussions can be found in Posner [1974], Jarrell [1980] and Kahn [1970]

[7] See Stigler [1971], Posner [1974] and Peltzman [1976] for different versions of this theory.

emphasizes informational asymmetries between parties to the process, the importance of procedural rules and the regulator's pursuit of a quiet life.[8] As in the political economy theory, firms and consumers compete for economic benefits through the regulatory process and, in a broad sense, this results in intended outcomes. In the Owen and Braeutigam [1978] version, participants are ultimately seeking a level of "fairness" that does not exist in unregulated markets, and this is accomplished through well-established procedural rules that all parties can understand and rely upon. Unlike the political economy theory, however, the mechanical nature of such rules, or differences in information, or even mistaken perceptions[9] on the part of one or more groups create opportunities for strategic behavior. In the short run, one group might be able to capture benefits by means that its adversaries did not anticipate.[10] In the long run, however, such opportunities should tend to disappear, or at least change in nature, as the different parties learn from experience and procedural rules are updated.

C. *Joint Theories of Capital Structure and Regulation*

Combining the theories from Sections I.A and I.B results in nine possible joint theories. Distinctions among them can be made by contrasting their predictions of what happens when an unregulated utility is suddently subjected to regulation. The primary focus of this study is predictions about capital structure changes that result from the move to a regulated environment. Nevertheless, more complete discrimination is facilitated if the predictions are specified in greater detail. Where possible, therefore, predictions about electricity prices and utility profits and about the sequence of the various changes are also derived.

The capital structure effects of regulation under the different theories can be derived with the aid of a simple model: Consider a utility operating over a single period. At the beginning of this period, it chooses a capital stock, K, which it finances with some combination of either debt, D, or equity, E. For a given capital stock, then, the financing decision is fully specified once D has been chosen. If the utility is an unregulated monopolist, it also chooses an output price, p. On the other hand, if competition is the initial condition, this price is determined in the market, while under regulation it is set by a commission. Given the capital stock, financing mix and output price, the utility then employs variable inputs (fuel and labor, say) in the amount necessary to satisfy end-of-period demand.[11]

[8] Examples from this category include Joskow [1974] and Owen and Braeutigam [1978].

[9] In Joskow [1974], for example, consumers suffer from money illusion and become exercised only about increases in nominal prices.

[10] Owen and Braeatigam [1978] give numerous examples of strategies that regulated firms might find profitable.

[11] Uncertainty could enter the model in a variety of ways. Demand may be uncertain as of the beginning of the period, in which case the firm must choose K without knowing how much of the variable input it will need to employ. Alternatively, end-of-period fuel costs or wage rates may be uncertain. The exact source of the uncertainty is not crucial to the analysis.

The utility's cash flow in any given state of nature is thus a function of three variables, K, D and p. When filtered through investors' expectations, this state contingent cash flow in turn determines the utility's beginning of period market value, V:

$$(1)\qquad V = V(K, D, p).$$

The unregulated monopolist simply chooses K, D and p to maximize V. The regulated utility is not allowed to choose p, but its choices of K and D could in principle influence the regulator's choice of p. If we hold K constant, so as to focus on the financing mix,[12] the optimal debt level for the regulated utility is given by

$$(2)\qquad \frac{dV}{dD} = \frac{\partial V}{\partial D} + \frac{\partial V}{\partial p}\frac{dp}{dD} = 0.$$

The first term in (2) reflects those channels through which financial policy would affect market value even in the absence of regulation. We will refer to this term as the pure capital structure effect. The onset of regulation could, of course, alter the magnitude of this effect. The second term in (2) is unique to the regulated case, as it reflects the influence of the utility's capital structure on the output price chosen by the regulator. It will be called the price-influence effect.

Capital structure effects of regulation can now be traced through both terms in (2) for each of the nine theories. In conjunction with price and profit predictions, this yields the set of implications summarized in Table I.

Working through the table by rows, suppose first that regulation is imposed on a monopolist. The public interest theory predicts that electricity prices and profits will fall.[13] In addition, there is no price-influence effect on capital structure under public interest regulation. The regulator chooses the price that maximizes a well-defined weighted sum of producer and consumer surplus, and this price is independent of the utility's actual financing choice. Any influence of financing under public interest regulation, therefore, must stem from the pure capital structure effect.

This effect is identically zero under the perfect capital market theory, so the upper left-hand cell of Table I shows no effect on financing. Under a debt capacity model, the financing effect of public interest regulation depends on its impact on the costs associated with debt. If these costs vary directly with utility profits (as is likely, though not necessary, depending on relative risks of the regulated and unregulated profit streams) public interest regulation will

[12] Regulation's effect on the capital stock choice is already the subject of an extensive literature. The seminal paper is Averch and Johnson [1962]. Bailey [1973] provides a survey.

[13] It should be noted for completeness that public interest regulation might also be imposed in a situation where inefficiently small firms are competing with one another. We would also expect prices to fall here as the industry is consolidated and economies of scale are realized. Replacement of competing smaller firms by a regulated monopolist would not necessarily reduce industry profits, however.

TABLE I
EFFECTS OF IMPOSING REGULATION UNDER NINE JOINT THEORIES OF REGULATION AND CAPITAL STRUCTURE

Capital Structure Theory: / *Theory of Regulation:*	*Perfect Capital Market*	*Debt Capacity*	*Financing Hierarchy*
Public interest	Prices, profits decrease; no effect on debt financing	Prices, profits decrease; debt financing decreases if debt capacity varies directly with profitability	Prices, profits decrease; debt financing increases in response to reduced profits
Political economy	Prices, profits increase if producers are favored; no effect on debt financing	Prices, profits increase if producers are favored; debt financing increases	Prices, profits increase if producers are favored; debt financing decreases in response to increased profits
Imperfect monitoring	Prices, profits increase in response to increase or decrease in debt financing	Prices, profits increase in response to increase or decrease in debt financing	Prices, profits increase in response to increase or decrease in debt financing; debt financing may subsequently decrease in response to increased profits

reduce debt capacity. Finally, under the financing hierarchy theory, public interest regulation reduces profits and hence internal funds, so for a given investment plan debt financing is increased.

In the second row of the table, the political economy theory of regulation predicts that prices and profits rise if producers are favored and fall if consumers are favored. Once again, there is no price-influence effect on utility capital structure. The regulator sets price so as to benefit producers or consumers, with the allocation of benefits determined by the relative votes and resources that each side can muster. Given the outcome of their political competition, the regulator does not allow extraneous factors, such as the utility's actual financing choice, to influence his pricing decision. Regulation under the political economy theory, then, likewise affects utility financing only through the pure capital structure effect.

In a perfect capital market regime, this effect remains identically zero. In a debt capacity regime, however, regulation's effect on risk is important. As predicted by Peltzman [1976], counter-cyclical swings in the allocation of regulatory benefits reduce the utility's operating risk and hence its probability of bankruptcy for a given debt level. Regulation's tendency to soften extreme outcomes may also reduce the actual cost of bankruptcy. For example, regulators would probably prevent a bankrupt utility from shutting off service to consumers. As Titman [1984] has argued, the costs imposed on consumers in such events are indirectly borne by the firm and hence are relevant to its capital structure choice. Taken together, then, regulation's tendency to reduce both the probability and cost of bankruptcy will increase utility debt proportions.[14] Finally, under the financing hierarchy theory, the capital structure effect depends on utility profits. If regulation favors producers, increased profits mean that new investment will be more heavily financed with internal funds and utility debt proportions will decrease. If regulation favors consumers the converse will be true.

Under the imperfect monitoring theory, firms manipulate the regulatory process to win benefits for themselves. Thus regulation results in higher prices and profits, similar to pro-producer regulation under the political economy theory. The pure capital structure effect is also similar. Like Peltzman, Owen and Braeutigam [1978] suggest that regulation tends to mitigate extreme outcomes for both producers and consumers, and in a debt capacity regime the resulting decrease in operating risk will induce utilities to increase their debt proportions. In a financing hierarchy regime, by contrast, higher profits result in less use of debt financing.

The imperfect monitoring theory is really distinguished from its competitors, though, by its allowance for price-influence effects. Regulator's

[14] A remark by Jensen and Meckling [1976, p. 335] is also worth noting in this context. They argue that ". . . in industries where the freedom of management to take riskier projects is severely constrained (for example, regulated industries such as public utilities), we should find more intensive use of debt financing". This suggests that certain regulatory activities supplement the monitoring of the firm undertaken by bondholders.

simple and clearly-defined pricing rules are seen under this theory as particularly susceptible to exploitation by firms. In particular, to the extent that these pricing rules depend on their actual financing proportions, utilities may manipulate their capital structures in an attempt to win higher prices.

Such manipulation may take on a variety of guises, depending on the regulator's specific pricing rule.[15] For example, it has been argued (see Sherman [1977]) that some regulators set the allowed return to equity independently of the firm's financing proportions. Since the cost of equity declines as financial risk is reduced, a utility operating in such an environment would want to substitute equity for debt in order to maximize the differential between the allowed return on equity and its cost. An alternative price-influence opportunity presents itself if regulators react strongly to any hint of financial distress. If output price is set so as to allow maintenance of a target fixed charge coverage ratio, the utility could expand its debt proportion now, thereby increasing both the probability that this target ratio will be breached and the chance that regulators will allow higher prices in some future states of nature.

In summary, the price-influence effect could tend toward either more debt or less, depending on the regulator's pricing rule and it could be operative under any of the three capital structure regimes.[16] In part, the three regimes could be distinguished by the magnitude of the overall financing effect. For example, any tendency toward increased debt stemming from the price-influence effect would be amplified by the capital structure effect in a debt capacity regime.

Empirical evidence can be gathered in an attempt to discriminate among these nine joint theories of capital structure and regulation. One relevant piece of information is whether utility debt proportions increase, decrease or remain the same in response to a change in regulatory status. However, it is clear from Table I that other information is also needed. Knowledge of concomitant changes in prices and profits is clearly useful, and the sequence of these changes also contains some discriminatory power. Under the financing hierarchy theory, for example, changes in debt proportions should follow any changes in profits, since debt issuance is driven by the availability of internal funds. Under the imperfect monitoring theory of regulation, on the other hand, financing changes should come first, since they are aimed at influencing prices and profits. Suppose it is found, then, that the imposition of regulation

[15] The small literature on capital structure decisions of regulated utilities is primarily concerned with the direction and magnitude of price-influence effects. See, for example, Gordon [1961], Elton and Gruber [1971], Sherman [1977] and Taggart [1981]. Implicitly, then, this literature comes under the imperfect monitoring theory of regulation. Although Litzenberger and Sosin [1979] discuss capital structure decisions in a more normative vein, they do suggest that regulators sometimes force utilities to adopt more debt in an inefficient attempt to pass on tax benefits to consumers. Because of these inefficiencies, that paper could also be classified under the imperfect monitoring theory of regulation.

[16] Strictly speaking, imperfect monitoring and a perfect capital market environment are unlikely to coincide. The same kinds of frictions that lead to imperfect monitoring in the regulatory process are likely to impose costs on debt and/or equity financing as well.

is associated with increased prices and profits and decreased debt. Such a finding would be consistent with either the political economy theory of regulation in conjunction with the financing hierarchy theory or the imperfect monitoring theory of regulation in conjunction with any of the three capital structure theories. However, if it could be shown that debt issuance decreased only after the increase in prices and profits, this would tend to favor the political economy plus financing hierarchy interpretation.

II. EMPIRICAL TESTING

A. *Choosing an Experimental Setting*

The ideal setting for empirical tests would be a period during which regulation was imposed on some of the firms in a sample, while the others remained unregulated throughout. Any changes in prices, profits and financing could then be observed for the firms that came under regulation and compared with analogous changes during the period for firms that did not. It would also be desirable to have evidence on business conditions and on the determinants of political coalitions for the various jurisdictions in which the sample firms operated. It might thus be possible to establish a direct link between political characteristics (and hence the regulatory environment) of a jurisdiction and the financing behavior of its utilities. Alternatively, it might be possible to show that regulation affects utility financing primarily through its effect on business conditions.

For electric utilities in the U.S., two candidates for an experimental setting are the current period and the early years of the twentieth century, during which many state regulatory commissions were established. Both periods have certain advantages, but neither conforms exactly to the ideal specifications. For example, extensive data are available on both individual firms and states in the current period. However, each state now has some kind of regulatory commission and it is thus impossible to observe the capital structure decisions of unregulated utilities. In principle it should be possible to make inferences about the different regulatory environments on the basis of political and business conditions and to test for systematic differences in financing across regulatory environments. While some attempts (e.g. Hagerman and Ratchford [1978]) have been made, though, to link pricing decisions to characteristics of the regulatory environment, neither the theories of regulation nor of capital structure seem sufficiently well developed to draw the needed inferences very precisely. In view of this difficulty, the earlier period was chosen as the setting for the empirical tests. This earlier period offers one disadvantage but two major advantages.

The disadvantage is the lack of data. Financial data for electric utilities are available in the *Census of Electrical Industries*, but these are reported only on a statewide, not an individual firm basis, and they are available only for the years 1912, 1917 and 1922. Market values of utility securities are not available on a comparable basis to these book value data. Moreover, the small number of years of available data makes it difficult to assess differences in operating risk across states, a variable that would be crucial to the financing decision under the debt capacity model of capital structure.

One offsetting advantage is that the earlier period offers an identifiable and significant change in the regulatory environment. The earliest electric utility companies in the U.S. were granted special franchises by municipalities to use the public streets.[17] These franchise agreements often specified maximum prices and other conditions of service so, strictly speaking, there is no period in which utilities were entirely free of regulation. Nevertheless, significant changes occurred as regulation shifted to the state level.

Although Massachusetts began regulating gas utilities in 1885, the era of state regulation is generally acknowledged to have begun in 1907 with the establishment of commissions in New York and Wisconsin. Many other states immediately followed suit, with twenty-seven such commissions established between QOPU and 1914, and the movement continued, though at a slower pace, after 1914. There were two common elements to state regulation: first, utility franchises granted by states were exclusive and of indefinite term. This marked a departure from municipal regulation, under which duplicate franchises were frequently awarded and competitors could vie for a utility's franchise upon expiration. Second, regulation of output prices was continuous under state commissions. When it existed, municipal price regulation took the form of specifying maximum prices over the franchise period. Whereas utilities faced potential, if not actual, competition under municipal regulation, they became regulated monopolists, subject to formal price-setting procedures, when state commissions were established.

A second advantage to studying the earlier period is the availability of Jarrell's [1978; 1980] extensive evidence on utility prices and profits. Jarrell found that the establishment of state commissions resulted in significant increases in the prices and profits of utilities in those states. However, state-regulated utilities did not move to higher levels of prices and profits than those subject to municipal regulation. Rather, state regulation tended to be imposed first in those states where prices and profits were low under municipal regulation. After state commissions were established, utility prices and profits then moved up to levels that were more commensurate with those experienced in other states.

Jarrell interpreted these results as favoring the political economy theory of regulation over the public interest theory. He argued that utilities' demand for state regulation was heaviest in those states where they faced the stiffest competitive pressure under municipal regulation. This competitive pressure

[17] A capsule review of the early history of electric utility regulation can be found in Jarrell [1978]. See also Behling [1938], Glaeser [1927] and Troxel [1947] for further details on the transition from municipal to state regulation.

manifested itself in the initially lower price and profit levels. Then, as pro-producer state regulation was established, prices and profits rose to the levels prevailing in other states.

If Jarrell's evidence on prices and profits is accepted, the task of discriminating among the nine joint theories of capital structure and regulation is made easier, since the three entries in the top row of Table I can be eliminated. His evidence does not discriminate between the political economy and imperfect monitoring theories of regulation, however, since both are consistent with an increase in utility prices and profits. In addition, it remains to be seen whether the establishment of state regulation was associated with any significant changes in utility financing.

B. *State Regulation and Utility Financing, 1912–22*

The first step is to specify an equation describing utility financing decisions in the absence of state regulation. This can then be used to test for significant changes when state regulation is imposed.

A simple working hypothesis is that these decisions are governed primarily by a target ratio of long-term debt to total assets. This would be consistent with a debt capacity model where the target reflects a firm's optimal debt ratio. It would also be consistent with a financing hierarchy model, where the target would be related to a firm's return on assets and hence its need for external funds. In a perfect capital market model, on the other hand, cross sectional differences in financing would be random, and we would not expect an equation based on this hypothesis to fit the data very well.

Ideally, the target ratio would itself be specified as a function of explanatory variables, particularly if one believes in the debt capacity model. Under that model, the target is determined by the costs and benefits of debt, but unfortunately these are difficult to measure for the period under study. Tax variables are of little use, since corporate tax rates were so low at this time (see Taggart [1984]) that the tax benefits of debt were negligible. Other possible advantages to debt are its ability to convey information (Ross [1977]) or to mitigate the agency costs of outside equity (Jensen and Meckling [1976]), but these are difficult to measure for any period. On the cost side, a prime explanatory variable would be operating risk, which in turn reflects the severity of bankruptcy and other agency costs. As has been pointed out above, though, the paucity of time series and market value data make this variable impossible to measure.

In view of these problems, the change in long-term debt for a state's utilities over a five-year period is simply hypothesized to be proportional to the change in total assets over that period.[18] That is,

$$(3) \qquad \Delta D_{it} = \alpha_0 \Delta A_{it} + \varepsilon_{it},$$

[18] Empirical studies of corporate financing behavior (surveyed by Marsh [1982]) have typically specified a pattern of partial short run adjustment to target debt ratios. It is assumed here that the five-year periods covered by the data are of sufficient length that complete adjustment occurs.

where ΔD_{it} and ΔA_{it} are changes in long-term debt and total assets for utilities in state i between times $t-1$ and t, and ε_{it} is a random error term.[19] This specification implicitly assumes that cross-sectional differences in α_0 are random and impounded in the error term.

Formation of state regulatory commissions, however, may lead to systematic differences in α_0. If state regulation makes the operating environment safer, then under a debt capacity model, α_0 should increase. By contrast, in a financing hierarchy model any tendency of state regulation to increase utility profits should reduce α_0. Such changes in the financing targets can be estimated using dummy variables, R_{ij}, that take on a value of unity if state i formed a regulatory commission in period j and zero otherwise. Given the available data, three such dummy variables were defined: R_{i1} takes on a value of unity if state i had formed a commission by 1912, R_{i2} takes on a value of unity if a state commission was formed between 1912 and 1917, and R_{i3} takes on a value of unity if a state commission was formed between 1918 and 1922.[20] In all remaining states, regulation was not instituted until after 1922, and thus the dummy variables partition the states into four mutually exclusive sets. Adding these dummy variables to equation (3) gives

$$(4) \qquad \Delta D_{it} = \left(\alpha_0 + \sum_{j=1}^{3} \alpha_j R_{ij} \right) \Delta A_{it} + \varepsilon_{it}.$$

The available data permit estimation of (4) over the cross section of states for the periods 1912–17 and 1917–22. At first glance, it would appear that analyzing the significance of the coefficient estimates $\hat{\alpha}_j$ provides a good test for regulatory effects. Unfortunately, however, several econometric problems threaten to vitiate the results of such a test unless further adjustments are made.

The first of these difficulties is that the regulatory dummy variables may serve as a proxy for some other factor affecting utility capital structures. The nature of a state's business environment, for instance, could be systematically related to the adoption of regulation in that state, and thus the dummy variables may not reflect regulatory effects alone. This would be suspected particularly if any of the dummy variables had a significant coefficient during a period when regulation was not yet in effect ($\hat{\alpha}_3$ in the period 1912–17, for example).

One way to correct for this problem is to look for significant *changes* in the dummy variable coefficients between periods. Examining these differences

[19] Preferred stock has been added to long-term debt in the estimation for two reasons. First, tax factors that give rise to distinctions between the two instruments were negligible during this period. Second, if price-influence effects exist, they would apply to preferred stock as well as debt. If a utility is attempting to build up a high level of fixed charges in order to win price concessions from regulators, preferred stock should serve this purpose as well as debt.

[20] Following the convention of Stigler and Friedland [1962], it is assumed that effective commission regulation began three years after the law was passed establishing a commission in that state. Dates on which the various state commissions were established are available in Stigler and Friedland.

increases the chance that spuriously correlated factors will cancel, leaving only the regulatory effect.[21] A convenient way to test the significance of such changes is to estimate (4) for the two periods combined, with slope dummies included to allow for changes in the coefficients between periods. That is, the equation to be estimated may be expressed as

$$\Delta D_{it} = [\alpha_0 + \alpha'_0(DUM_t) + \sum_{j=1}^{3} \alpha_j R_{ij} + \sum_{j=1}^{3} \alpha'_j R_{ij}(DUM_t)]\Delta A_{it} + \varepsilon_{it} \tag{5}$$

where $DUM_t = 1$ if $t = 1922$ and zero otherwise. In this formulation, α_0 and the α_j represent the coefficients of the model for the period 1912–1917, while $(\alpha_0 + \alpha'_0)$ and the $(\alpha_j + \alpha'_j)$ are coefficients for 1917–1922. When the equation is estimated in this form, the t-statistics for the α'_j are in precisely the form needed to test for the significance of changes in the regulatory dummy variable coefficients between the two periods.

Econometric difficulties also surround the implicitly assumed error structure in equations (4) or (5). In particular, wide differences in the scale of utility operations might cause heteroscedasticity as well as contemporaneous correlations among the errors of firms (states) in different size classes. Although one can never be completely confident that such problems have been eliminated, more efficient estimates might be achievable if the data are deflated by a variable that may be related to the error terms in (5). A likely candidate would seem to be A_{it-1}, the beginning-of-period asset level for utilities in state i.

A given utility will try to maintain its target debt ratio in each period subject to scale economies in the transaction costs associated with security issues. If a very small debt or equity issue is needed to maintain the target ratio, the utility may prefer to let the actual ratio deviate from target this period and make the adjustment all at once with a larger issue next period. Similarly, it would be inefficient from a transaction cost standpoint to pay a large dividend this period and raise external funds next period. If internal funds are temporarily large relative to financing needs, it would make sense to let the debt ratio fall below target for now and adjust with a large debt issue later.

Such departures of this period's debt financing from the target proportion of total current financing needs are likely to have greater standard deviations

[21] An attempt was also made to identify these factors. This was done through analyses of variance for a number of state characteristics across the four state categories defined by the dummy variables. The factors examined included the number and total revenues of state and municipal electric stations operating in the state prior to state regulation, total utility employment, the number of utility customers, absolute and percentage growth in utility output and the degree of urbanization in 1910. Most of these factors exhibited little difference in mean values across state categories. Urbanization (defined by the Census Bureau as percentage of the state's population living in incorporated areas of 2500 or more inhabitants), however, was significantly higher on average for those states regulated by 1912 and for those that adopted regulation during 1912–17. This may reflect Peltzman's [1976] contention that regulation occurs where the costs of organizing for political action are lowest. The most urbanized states were probably also those in which competition among utilities was the heaviest prior to regulation.

precisely when beginning-of-period assets are large relative to this period's financing needs. In that event, the percentage change in assets is small and the proportion financed with debt can deviate further from target without throwing the overall balance sheet too far out of line. Internal funds availability might likewise be large relative to current financing needs in these circumstances, reinforcing the tendency to let debt issues deviate from target and perhaps leading to positive correlations among the error terms for different asset sizes.[22] If we attempt to correct for these problems by deflating the variables in (5) by A_{it-1}, the equation to be estimated becomes

$$(6) \qquad \frac{\Delta D_{it}}{A_{it-1}} = \alpha_0 \frac{\Delta A_{it}}{A_{it-1}} + \alpha_0' \frac{\Delta A_{it}}{A_{it-1}} (DUM_t) + \sum_{j=1}^{3} \alpha_j R_{ij} \frac{\Delta A_{it}}{A_{it-1}} + \sum_{j=1}^{3} \alpha_j' R_{ij} \frac{\Delta A_{it}}{A_{it-1}} (DUM_t) + u_{it},$$

where u_{it} is the adjusted error term.

Estimates of (6), with a constant term included, are present in Table II.[23] The estimated equation fits the data well, and this evidence of a regular pattern in utility financing might be interpreted as weighing against the perfect capital market theory. Primary interest, however, centers on the coefficients of the regulatory dummy variables. All of these are negative (although the coefficient of R_1 is not significantly negative) for the period 1912–17, indicating that utilities in those states regulated earliest employed lower debt proportions prior to or even coincident with the establishment of regulation. In the subsequent period, the coefficients of the slope dummies for the regulatory variables are all positive. In particular, the changes between the two periods in the coefficients R_2 and R_3 are significantly positive, suggesting that the establishment of regulation in these states was associated with an increase in debt proportions.

One possible interpretation of these results is that they are in line with Jarrell's [1978] findings. If, as Jarrell argues, the states that moved to state regulation earliest were those in which the utility industry was most competitive this may explain the initially lower debt proportions in these states. To the extent that a competitive environment adversely affects the level and stability of utility cash flows, a debt capacity model would predict that it is less conducive to debt financing. If state regulation then imposed a more stable environment, we would expect to see a subsequent increase in utility debt

[22] An ancillary point is that holding company activity might have been more likely in a given state during this period the larger were beginning-of-period assets. To the extent that utilities in holding companies followed similar financing patterns, this would also lead to contemporaneous correlation in the error terms.

[23] While the potential for econometric difficulties still suggests caution in interpreting the results, an examination of the residuals from (6), plotted against asset size and regulatory status, revealed no obvious tendencies toward heteroscedasticity or contemporaneous error correlation.

TABLE II
ESTIMATES OF EQUATION (6) FOR THE PERIODS 1912–17 AND 1917–22 COMBINED

Independent Variable	*Estimated Coefficient*	*Standard Error*	*t-Statistic*
Constant	−0.031	0.027	−1.17
Constant (DUM_t)	0.007	0.039	0.19
$\frac{\Delta A_t}{A_{t-1}}$	0.672	0.038	17.51
$\frac{\Delta A_t}{A_{t-1}}(DUM_t)$	−0.127	0.066	−1.92
$\frac{R_1 \Delta A_t}{A_{t-1}}$	−0.089	0.085	−1.05
$\frac{R_1 \Delta A_t}{A_{t-1}}(DUM_t)$	0.190	0.124	1.53
$\frac{R_2 \Delta A_t}{A_{t-1}}$	−0.126	0.046	−2.74
$\frac{R_2 \Delta A_t}{A_{t-1}}(DUM_t)$	0.158	0.072	2.18
$\frac{R_3 \Delta A_t}{A_{t-1}}$	−0.100	0.040	−2.50
$\frac{R_3 \Delta A_t}{A_{t-1}}(DUM_t)$	0.326	0.140	2.33

$DUM_t = 1$ for $t = 1922$, 0 otherwise
$R^2 = 0.944$
S.E. = 0.124
Number of Observations = 92
$R_1 = 1$ if regulatory commission formed by 1912, 0 otherwise
$R_2 = 1$ if regulatory commission formed during 1912–17, 0 otherwise
$R_3 = 1$ if regulatory commission formed during 1917–22, 0 otherwise

financing.[24] This interpretation of the evidence is consistent with the political economy theory of regulation in conjunction with the debt capacity model of capital structure.

There are alternative interpretations that cannot be categorically rejected for a subset of the regulated states, but they seem less plausible in terms of the evidence as a whole. Consider, for example, the political economy theory of regulation in conjunction with the financing hierarchy theory of capital struc-

[24] A bit of rough evidence supporting the contention that regulation generally was associated with greater industry stability is Peltzman's [1976] finding that the systematic risk of the utility industry as a whole declined somewhat after 1907. Using correlations between utility stock price indexes and industrial stock price indexes as his measure of systematic risk, Peltzman estimated a correlation of 0.67 for the period 1871–1906 and 0.60 for the period 1907–42.

ture. This joint theory predicts that pro-producer regulation should increase utility profits and that, as a result, the use of debt financing should decrease. In fact, the evidence for those states that established regulation between 1912 and 1917 is consistent with that prediction. Jarrell found that utility profits rose in those states during the 1912–17 period but subsequently fell again during 1917–22.[25] Simultaneously, as indicated in Table II, the use of debt financing was low in these states relative to others in the 1912–17 period, but increased during 1917–22. It is possible, then, that financing behavior in these states was driven by the rise and fall of profits.

However, the financing hierarchy theory is not at all consistent with the financing pattern of those states that formed commissions in the 1917–22 period. There, the increase in debt financing coincided with the increase in utility prices, contrary to what the theory would predict.[26] Moreover, the extreme version of the financing hierarchy theory, whereby firms issue no stock, can be rejected simply on the grounds that utilities were issuing substantial amounts of stock during this period.[27] To the extent that financing hierarchy considerations were at work, they must have been operating in conjunction with some notion of debt capacity.

Consider also the imperfect monitoring theory of regulation, under which firms may have arranged their financing with an eye toward influencing regulated prices. If utilities in those states that adopted regulation between 1912 and 1917 were following this strategy, they must have been purposely increasing the proportion of equity financing. The increase in debt financing occurred only later, after prices had already risen. But if equity were increased in the 1912–17 period in an attempt to increase prices, it is not at all clear why this pattern would have been reversed during 1917–22. It is also possible that utilities in states that adopted regulation in the 1917–22 period were trying to influence prices with their financing choices, but in this case the strategy must have been to increase debt financing. If price-influence effects existed, therefore, they were not consistent across states.

One final bit of evidence on the imperfect monitoring theory comes from the evolution of state regulatory statutes. This evidence suggests that, while price-influence financing strategies may have been followed initially in some jurisdictions, regulators rather quickly became aware of them and took steps to combat them. This would be expected in a political economy model, in which unintended wealth transfers would be suppressed.

Statutory powers of the state regulatory commissions were often limited at first to such matters as prices, entry and conditions of service. Although some

[25] In his other paper, Jarrell [1980] found that the downward movement in prices in 1917–22 was temporary. Utility prices in these states rose again in 1927, 1932 and 1937.

[26] Unfortunately, Jarrell [1978] estimated only the effect on prices and not on profits for utilities in these states during 1917–22.

[27] Although stock issues are not reported in the data, increases in the par value of common stock give a rough indication of stock issue activity. These increases amounted to 26 percent of the increase in total utility assets during 1912–17 and 17 percent during 1917–22.

states gave their commissions approval power over utility securities issues, many initially did not.[28] Even in those states where commissions initially had some power over utility financing, the feeling became widespread that these powers were not used effectively and that at least some utilities were tailoring their financing proportions to exploit this situation.[29] A trend gradually developed, therefore, toward increasing the state commissions' powers to regulate utility financing. In Wisconsin, for example, a special act was passed in 1911, four years after establishment of the state commission, granting the commission wider financial regulatory powers. Among these, the commission was charged with making sure that the amount of bonds bore "a reasonable proportion to the amount of stock."[30] An additional measure in 1931 granted still further powers, among which was the authority to halt the payment of common stock dividends if these would impair the utility's financial integrity.[31] In several other states, commissions eventually gained authority to "control the issuance of additional bonds under each mortgage, require sinking funds for most bond issues, specify provisions for depreciation and maintenance costs and limit the payment of common stock dividends."[32] A few states even passed statutory limitations on utility debt ratios.[33]

The similarity between these measures and the restrictive covenants ordinarily written into bond indentures is striking.[34] To some extent, the enforcement of such measures could subsidize the monitoring costs usually borne by the utility's securityholders, but it is not clear why that should have been their primary intent. A more plausible interpretation is that legislators came to realize the wealth-shifting implications of utility capital structures and these measures were adopted, not to protect bondholders, but to reduce unintended wealth transfers from consumers to utility shareholders.[35]

In summary, then, the full range of evidence seems most consistent with the political economy theory of regulation together with the debt capacity theory of capital structure. Financing behavior in the states that established regulation during 1912–17 is not inconsistent with the financing hierarchy theory,

[28] Jones and Bigham [1931, p. 495] complain, for example, that of the states that had established regulation by 1926, eighteen had given their commissions no power over securities issues.

[29] Jones and Bigham [1931, p. 505] conclude that "overcapitalization, whatever its form, but particularly overcapitalization in the form of excessive issues of bonds and preferred stock, does affect the rate of return regarded by commissions and courts as fair". See also Glaeser [1957, Chapter 7] for further assertions that utility commissions initially lacked either the power or the perspicacity to halt such price-influence financing strategies.

[30] Jones and Bigham [1931, p. 185].

[31] See Glaeser [1957, Chapter 7].

[32] Troxel [1947, p. 160]. The Securities and Exchange Commission also began exercising similar controls over utility holding companies under the Public Utility Holding Company Act of 1935.

[33] Jones and Bigham [1931, p. 543].

[34] See Smith and Warner [1979] for an extensive description and analysis of these covenants.

[35] Vigilance against such transfers has continued to the present. In a 1977 rate case, consumer intervenors accused the New England Power Company of employing "an ingenious scheme . . . to qualify for excessive rates of return based on thin common equity ratios." See *Public Utilities Reports* [1977, p. 456].

which implies that debt usage varies inversely with the availability of internal funds. However, the states regulated during 1917–22 do not fit this pattern. In addition, the fact that it took some time for utilities in the states regulated during 1912–17 to increase their use of debt financing does not run counter to the debt capacity theory. Utilities may have needed this time to convince themselves that their environment had in fact become more stable. The presence of price-influence financing strategies is also not ruled out, but if they were used they do not leave a very clear track in the data. Moreover, steps were taken to combat them, so any success they had may have been fleeting.

III. CONCLUSION

This study has investigated one possible source of industry influences on capital structure: the effect of regulation on utility financing. Evidence from the early days of electric utility regulation by state commissions supports several conclusions about this effect. First, the effect exists: the establishment of regulation is associated with a discernible increase in utility debt proportions. Second, this effect appears to result primarily from regulation's tendency to reduce business risk. The evidence is consistent with the idea that regulation was imposed first where municipalities had fostered the most competitive environments. Subsequent increases in utility debt financing in these states can be plausibly attributed to the more stable environment brought on by state regulation. However, the third conclusion is that price-influence effects cannot be rejected entirely. The delayed adoption of legislative measures to combat these effects suggests that they may have enjoyed temporary success in at least some jurisdictions.

It is not surprising that the evidence fails to eliminate all ambiguity. The effect of regulation on utility financing depends crucially on the behavior of individual state commissions and thus the effect may not be uniform. A prerequisite for tracing this effect in recent times, in fact, is the development of more precise measures of how regulatory behavior differs across states.

Robert A. Taggart, Jr.,
Boston University,
School of Management,
704 Commonwealth Avenue,
Boston, MA 02215, *U.S.A.*

ACCEPTED MAY 1984

REFERENCES

Averch, H., and Johnson, L. L., 1962, "Behavior of the Firm Under Regulatory Constraint," *American Economic Review*, 52, 5 (December), pp. 1052–69.

Bailey, E. E., 1973, *Economic Theory of Regulatory Constraint* (Lexington Books, Lexington, MA).

Behling, B., 1938, *Competition and Monopoly in Public Utility Industries* (University of Illinois Press, Urbana, IL).

DeAngelo, H., and Masulis, R. W., 1980, "Optimal Capital Structure Under Corporate and Personal Taxation," *Journal of Financial Economics*, 8, 1 (March), pp. 3–29.

Donaldson, G., 1961, *Corporate Debt Capacity* (Harvard Business School, Division of Research, Boston).

Elton, E. J., and Gruber, M., 1971, "Valuation and the Cost of Capital for Regulated Industries," *Journal of Finance*, 26, 3 (June), pp. 661–70.

Ferri, M. G., and Jones, W. H., 1979, "Determinants of Financial Structure: A New Methodological Approach," *Journal of Finance*, 34, 3 (June), pp. 631–44.

Flath, D., and Knoeber, C. R., 1980, "Taxes, Failure Costs and Optimal Industry Capital Structure: An Empirical Test," *Journal of Finance*, 35, 1 (March) pp. 99–127.

Glaeser, M. G., 1927, *Outlines of Public Utility Economics* (Macmillan, New York).

———, 1957, *Public Utilities in American Capitalism* (Macmillan, New York).

Gordon, M. J., 1961, "Some Estimates of the Cost of Capital to the Electric Utility Industry, 1954–57: A Comment," *American Economic Review*, 57, 5 (December), pp. 1267–77.

Hagerman, R. L., and Ratchford, B. T., 1978, "Some Determinants of Allowed Rates of Return on Equity to Electric Utilities," *Bell Journal of Economics* 9, 1 (Spring), pp. 46–55.

Jarrell, G. A., 1978, "The Demand for State Regulation of the Electric Utility Industry," *Journal of Law and Economics*, 21, 2 (October), pp. 269–95.

———, 1980 "Regulation of the Electric Utility Industry: A Historical Perspective and Empirical Study," Conference Paper No. 67, National Bureau of Economic Research, Cambridge, MA (October).

Jensen, M. C. and Meckling, W. H., 1976, "Theory of the Firm: Managerial Behavior, Agency Costs and Ownership Structure," *Journal of Financial Economics*, 3, 4 (October), pp. 305–60.

Jones, E., and Bigham, T. C., 1931, *Principles of Public Utilities*, (Macmillan, New York).

Joskow, P. L., 1974, "Inflation and Environmental Concern: Structural Change in the Process of Public Utility Price Regulation," *Journal of Law and Economics*, 17, 2 (October) pp. 291–327.

Kahn, A. E., 1970, *The Economics of Regulation*, 2 Vols (John Wiley, New York).

Kim, E. H., 1976, "A Mean-Variance Theory of Optimal Capital Structure and Corporate Debt Capacity," *Journal of Finance*, 33, 1 (March), pp. 45–63.

Kraus, A. and Litzenberger, R. H., 1973, "A State-Preference Model of Optimal Financial Leverage," *Journal of Finance*, 28, 4 (September), pp. 911–22.

Litzenberger, R. H., and Sosin, H. B., 1979, "A Comparison of Capital Structure Decisions of Regulated and Non-Regulated Firms," *Financial Management*, 8, 3 (Autumn), pp. 17–21.

Marsh, P., 1982, "The Choice Between Equity and Debt: An Empirical Study," *Journal of Finance*, 37, 1 (March), pp. 121–44.

Miller, M. H., 1977, "Debt and Taxes," *Journal of Finance*, 32, 2 (May), pp. 261–75.

Modigliani, F., and Miller, M. H., 1958; "The Cost of Capital, Corporation Finance and the Theory of Investment," *American Economic Review*, 48, 3 (June), pp. 261–97.

Myers, S. C., 1977, "Determinants of Corporate Borrowing," *Journal of Financial Economics*, 5, 2 (November), pp. 147–75.

——— and Majluf, N. S., 1983, "Corporate Financing and Investment Decisions

When Firms Have Information That Investors Do Not Have," Sloan School of Management Working Paper, M. I. T. (March).

OWEN, B. M., and BRAEUTIGAM, R., 1978, *The Regulation Game: Strategic Use of the Administrative Process*, (Ballinger, Cambridge, MA).

PELTZMAN, S., 1976, "Toward a More General Theory of Regulation," *Journal of Law and Economics*, 19, 2 (August), pp. 211–40.

POSNER, R. A., 1974, "Theories of Economic Regulation," *Bell Journal of Economics*, 5, 2 (Autumn), pp. 335–58.

Public Utilities Reports, 1977, 4th Series, Vol. 20, (Public Utilities Reports, Inc., Washington, D. C.).

ROBICHEK, A. A., and MYERS, S. C., 1966, "Problems in the Theory of Optimal Capital Structure," *Journal of Financial and Quantitative Analysis*, 1, 1 (June), pp. 1–35.

ROSS, S. A., 1977, "The Determination of Financial Structure: The Incentive-Signalling Approach," *Bell Journal of Economics*, 8, 1 (Spring), pp. 23–40.

SCHWARTZ, E. and ARONSON, J. R., 1957, "Some Surrogate Evidence in Support of the Concept of Optimal Capital Structure," *Journal of Finance*, 22, 1 (March), pp. 10–18.

SCOTT, D. F., 1972, "Evidence on the Importance of Financial Structure," *Financial Management*, 1, 1 (Summer), pp. 45–50.

——— and MARTIN, J. D., 1975, "Industry Influence on Financial Structure," *Financial Management*, 4, 1 (Spring), pp. 67–73.

SHERMAN, R., 1977, "Financial Aspects of Rate-of-Return Regulation," *Southern Economic Journal*, 44, 2 (October), pp. 240–48.

SMITH, C. W., and WARNER, J. B., 1979, "On Financial Contracting: An Analysis of Bond Covenants," *Journal of Financial Economics*, 7, 2 (June), pp. 117–61.

STIGLER, G. J., 1971, "The Theory of Economic Regulation," *Bell Journal of Economics*, 2, 1 (Spring), pp. 3–21.

——— and FRIEDLAND, C., 1962, "What Can Regulators Regulate? The Case of Electricity," *Journal of Law and Economics*, 5, 1 (October), pp. 1–16.

STIGLITZ, J., 1973, "Taxation, Corporate Financial Policy and the Cost of Capital." *Journal of Public Economics*, 2, 1 (February), pp. 1–34.

TAGGART, R. A., 1981, "Rate-of-Return Regulation and Utility Capital Structure Decisions," *Journal of Finance*, 36, 2 (May), pp. 383–93.

———, 1984, "Secular Patterns in the Financing of U.S. Corporations." in B. M. Friedman, ed. *Corporate Capital Structures in the United States*, (University of Chicago Press, Chicago).

TITMAN, S., 1984, "The Effect of Capital Structure on a Firm's Liquidation Decision," *Journal of Financial Economics*, 13, 1 (March), pp. 137–51.

TROXEL, E., 1947, *Economics of Public Utilities* (Rinehart, New York).

U.S. Bureau of the Census, 1912, 1917, 1922 *Census of Electrical Industries, Central Electric Light and Power Stations* (U.S. Government Printing Office, Washington, D.C.).

THE JOURNAL OF INDUSTRIAL ECONOMICS 0022–1821 $2.00
Volume XXXIII March 1985 No. 3

TACIT COLLUSION, FREE ENTRY AND WELFARE

JAMES A. BRANDER AND BARBARA J. SPENCER*

I. INTRODUCTION

THE effect of collusion under free entry has a long history of analysis in economics, yet many of the central issues remain unresolved. Of particular interest is the interaction between the number of firms in the industry and the degree of collusion in the industry. There are two relationships that might reasonably exist between the number of firms and collusion. On one hand, collusion is made easier if the number of firms is small, but on the other hand, an industry that successfully colludes will earn short run above normal profits and attract new entry until profits are driven to zero.

In this paper we model the interaction between these two forces and present, in a simple diagram, an illustration of the determination of equilibrium entry and collusion. We are also concerned with the implications of such a structure for public policy. In particular, direct anti-collusive policies and entry fees are examined.

One preliminary point to address is why collusion should occur at all if profits are going to be driven to zero in any case.[1] First of all, it is only marginal firms that must earn zero profits, so if there are asymmetries between firms, inframarginal firms might hope to gain from collusion even in the long run. Our analysis, however, focusses on the case of symmetric firms: all firms earn zero profits in the long run. Even in this case the profit that can be earned in the short run implies that the present discounted value of an increase in the degree of collusion is positive. Furthermore, once a collusive zero profit equilibrium is reached, industry participants will want to maintain collusion so as to avoid the short run losses that would result from a breakdown in collusive arrangements. (This is similar to the "transitional gains trap" described in Tullock [1975]).

Certainly a fairly large class of industries seem to be characterized by partial collusion and free entry. Providers of professional services are an important example. There is a wide variation in the ability and income of different providers of the same professional services; nevertheless, in most professions there are individuals at the margin earning zero economic profit. Moreover in many countries professionals such as lawyers and dentists are

* We would like to thank two anonymous referees for their very helpful comments, which led to improvements in the paper, and for correcting a number of small errors in the paper.

[1] For example, Dewey [1982] asserts that, although collusion has been observed in such low profit industries as barber shops or hot dog stands in midtown Manhattan, it cannot be aimed at increasing monopoly rents because free entry keeps monopoly profits equal to zero.

strongly discouraged or even prevented by their professional organizations from advertising prices. Partly because of this, prices set by different suppliers tend to be similar, particularly when the association provides "guidelines". That such prices are not competitive is apparent if some suppliers are underemployed in the sense that they would like to work more at the going price, as often seems to be the case with lawyers, for example.

The subtle and complex bargaining that underlies tacit collusion in professional service organizations and other collusive structures is a difficult process to model accurately. We use the conjectural variation model as a relatively simple representation of the possible outcomes of such collusive interaction. If one is to focus on the relation between free entry and collusion some simplification of (or abstraction from) the actual collusive process is necessary.

The principal feature of the conjectural variation (or "generalized Cournot") model is that each firm forms an expectation concerning how the rest of the industry would vary its output in response to a change in own output. This expectation is the "conjectural variation." In principle, the conjectural variation would vary as output levels vary (see, for example, Boyer and Moreaux [1983]) and could be different for different firms, but a normal simplification is to assume that the conjectural variation, λ, is fixed and the same for all firms. We adopt this simplification. In this case the conjectural variation is, for any fixed number of firms, a single structural parameter reflecting the degree of output restriction in the industry.

There are at least two interpretations of the link between behaviour and the conjectural variation parameter. One interpretation is that the conjectures about other firms' behaviour are not taken literally.[2] Instead, the value of the conjectural variation, which is associated with a particular price and industry output given the number of firms, is interpreted as a proxy for or a representation of the level of tacit (or explicit) collusion in the industry.[3] Alternatively, even with tacit collusion, the conjectural variation, λ, may be the literal expectation held by firms. If λ exceeds 1, each firm expects to be punished if it raises output, in the sense that the rest of the industry will also raise output. Tacit partial collusion can be maintained if such expectations are held. The use of the conjectural variation parameter to reflect collusion is a useful but not uncontroversial simplification.

A second simplification to which attention should be drawn is that the conjectural variation model is a static representation of the actual complicated dynamic model that would be needed to capture the real time action

[2] In a fully non-cooperative setting where the conjectural variation parameter is taken as a firm's "best guess" concerning the expected behaviour of other firms, it has been argued that firms would revise their conjectures until they coincided with the actual responses that would occur in the event of a change in own output. This is the "consistent conjectures" approach. See Bresnahan [1981], Perry [1982], Kamien and Schwartz [1983].

[3] See Seade [1980]. See also Thompson and Faith [1981] on the selection of optimal behavioural rules with tacit collusion.

and reaction structure of imperfectly competitive firms. A recent paper by Kalai and Stanford [1983] explicitly analyzes conjectural variations in a repeated game framework, showing that various different conjectural variations can be maintained as "credible" equilibria.[4]

In any case, the important point is that a particular value of λ is associated with a particular price and industry output given the number of firms. A conjectural variation of zero is associated with pure competition, while a conjectural variation equal to the number of firms gives rise to the fully collusive level of output. As shown in the paper, for any given number of firms, higher levels of λ induce higher prices and lower levels of industry output. Use of the conjectural variation model makes it possible to examine the interaction between the number of firms and the level of collusion.[5]

In section II we set out the conjectural variation model and briefly derive results concerning the effects on industry and firm output of changes in the conjectural variation parameter and of entry or exit. In section III the combinations of numbers of firms and levels of collusion that allow zero profit are characterized. Each such point is a possible long run equilibrium. The actual equilibrium is then determined by introducing a schedule reflecting how the ease of collusion depends on the number of firms. The equilibrium is illustrated in a simple diagram.

Section IV is devoted to output, price, and welfare effects of government policies which reduce tacit collusion, and section V develops the second best contour, which shows how the optimal number (and scale) of firms varies with the degree of tacit collusion.

One important aspect of some industries characterized by free entry is that existing firms manage to impose entry costs on new entrants. (Consider, for example, professional service organizations in which large initial costs in the form of high opportunity costs incurred in qualifying for "certification" have a major impact on the entry decision.) Entry is still free in the sense that no arbitrary limit is set on the number of firms, and entry will take place until the profit of new entrants is driven to zero. In section VI we examine such entry costs, and also consider government imposed license fees. Section VII contains concluding remarks.

[4] There is an extensive recent literature on modelling oligopolies as repeated games in an attempt to capture the dynamic structure. Shubik [1982] is a good pedagogical source. Kalai and Stanford [1983] is the only paper (apart from a related paper by the same authors) that explicitly deals with trying to reconcile the conjectural variation and repeated game approaches. Their work is, however, confined to the 2 firm case. Incorporating free entry would be a major undertaking. Porter [1983] has a repeated game structure with uncertainty in which collusive outcomes are supported by credible finite punishment strategies, and has the attractive feature, in contrast to most of the repeated game literature, that output during cooperative phases is increasing in the number of firms. This result is broadly consistent with the model presented in this paper.

[5] The possibility of partial collusion is important. It has been argued (see Dewey [1982] and Patinkin [1947]) that such a situation would not be a true equilibrium; the collusive firms would form a profit maximizing cartel which would operate plants so as to minimize unit costs of production and use side payments to share profits. It seems to us that with large numbers of firms the organization of such a cartel would be extremely difficult.

II. THE MODEL

There are n identical firms, each with profit π, output y, variable cost function $c(y)$ and fixed cost F. Each firm maximizes expected profit π subject to its conjecture $dY/dy = \lambda$, where Y is industry output.

$$\pi = yp(Y) - c(y) - F \tag{1}$$

The first and second order conditions for maximization of π are respectively,

$$\pi_y = p - c' + yp'\lambda = 0 \tag{2}$$

$$\pi_{yy} = 2p'\lambda - c'' + yp''\lambda^2 < 0 \tag{3}$$

where primes or subscripts denote derivatives. From (2) it is immediate that $\lambda = 1$ yields the Cournot model and $\lambda = 0$ yields pure competition. The following conditions are necessary and sufficient for local stability with identical firms. (See Seade [1980, p. 483].)

$$p'\lambda - c'' < 0 \tag{4}$$

$$\alpha \equiv p'\lambda - c'' + n(p' + yp''\lambda) < 0 \tag{5}$$

First we examine the effect of changes in n and λ on the output of the industry and on the profit of an individual firm.[6] Because firms are identical actual equilibrium changes have the property that $dY/dy = n$ in contrast to the belief held by firms that $dY/dy = \lambda$. Consequently comparative static results are related to α rather than to second order condition (3).

Totally differentiating (2) with respect to y and n yields

$$\alpha\, dy + (\partial\pi_y/\partial n)\, dn = 0 \tag{6}$$

Since $\partial\pi_y/\partial n = p'y + y\lambda p''y$ it follows that

$$y_n \equiv dy/dn = -y(p' + \lambda yp'')/\alpha \tag{7}$$

and

$$Y_n \equiv dY/dn = y + ny_n = y(1 - n(p' + \lambda yp'')/\alpha) \tag{8}$$
$$= y(\lambda p' - c'')/\alpha > 0$$

From (8) industry output must expand with entry if stability conditions (4) and (5) hold. The effect of entry on profit is obtained by differentiating (1):

$$\pi_n = yp'Y_n + (p - c')y_n \tag{9}$$

$$= -(p - c')(Y_n - \lambda y_n)/\lambda \tag{10}$$

using $yp'\lambda = -(p - c')$ from (2).

[6] We treat the integer variable n as though it were continuous in taking derivatives and for the comparative statics. This approximation is, of course, a problem only if n is very small.

From (7), (8) and (3), we have $Y_n - \lambda y_n = y\pi_{yy}/\alpha$. Therefore

$$\pi_n = -(p - c')y\pi_{yy}/a\lambda < 0 \tag{11}$$

From (11), the second order and stability conditions, each firm's profit at the Nash equilibrium declines with entry. The effect of λ on Y and π is obtained using a similar methodology. From (2)

$$\alpha\, dy + (\partial\pi_y/\partial\lambda)\, d\lambda = 0 \qquad \text{where } \partial\pi_y/\partial\lambda = p'y \tag{12}$$

so

$$y_\lambda = -p'y/\alpha < 0 \tag{13}$$

and

$$Y_\lambda = -np'y/\alpha < 0 \tag{14}$$

Higher values of λ are associated with less output and a higher price, other things equal. As for profit, from (1)

$$\pi_\lambda = yp'Y_\lambda + (p - c')y_\lambda \tag{15}$$

$$= -(p - c')(n - \lambda)y_\lambda/\lambda \text{ using (2) and } Y_\lambda = ny_\lambda \tag{16}$$

π_λ is positive provided n exceeds λ and price exceeds marginal cost. The joint profit maximum ($\pi_\lambda = 0$) is achieved when $\lambda = n$.

Summarizing the results yields the following proposition.

Proposition 1: (i) Given the level of collusion, entry causes industry output to rise and the profit of each firm to fall. (ii) Given the number of firms, an increase in the level of collusion causes industry output and output per firm to fall and profit to rise.

The effects of entry in this model are available in Seade [1980] and Perry [1984], and Seade has some brief comments about the effect of changes in λ on profit and output. Our derivation of these results is slightly different from and more streamlined than earlier work. The results are required for the analysis of industry equilibrium and welfare effects.

III. ZERO PROFIT EQUILIBRIUM

Because changes in n and λ (the "collusion parameter") affect profit independently, there is a locus of n, λ combinations which allow zero profit for each firm. Thus $\pi(n, \lambda) = 0$ implicitly defines $\lambda = f(n)$: the zero profit locus. We assume that only points on this locus are candidates for long run equilibrium under free entry.

There are several concerns one might have about this assumption, most of which are related to the perceptions of potential entrants. In particular, if there are only a few firms in the industry, a potential entrant might reasonably expect to have a large negative impact on profit per firm, should it enter.

Thus existing profits might be positive because profits with further entry are expected to be negative. Secondly, there is the awkward issue of whether potential entrants should have the same sort of expectations as firms already in the industry, or whether they should have perfect foresight concerning the effects of entry, or some other kind of expectations. Other possibilities include Bertrand expectations, as in the contestable markets approach (see Baumol, Panzar and Willig [1982]), or Cournot expectations.

Our specification is as follows. We assume that there is a large number of firms in the industry so that the entry of any one firm has a negligible impact on profit per firm. The exact perception held by firms is then not particularly important, since the most plausible candidates approximate each other. One perception that is in the spirit of the paper is that entrants understand that if they enter they will join an implicitly collusive process governed by conjectural variation $\lambda(n)$; that is, an entrant correctly foresees that its entry will lower industry profit, but only by a negligible amount since n is large. The zero profit equilibrium then becomes a convenient approximation.[7]

In any case, differentiating $\pi(n, \lambda) = 0$ yields,

$$\pi_n \, dn + \pi_\lambda \, d\lambda = 0 \tag{17}$$

Substituting for π_n and π_λ from (10) and (16) gives

$$f'(n) = d\lambda/dn \Big|_{\pi=0} = -(Y_n - \lambda y_n)/(n - \lambda)y_\lambda \tag{18}$$

Provided $n > \lambda$, $d\lambda/dn$ must be positive since $y_\lambda < 0$ and $Y_n - \lambda y_n = y\pi_{yy}/\alpha > 0$. Greater tacit collusion is required to absorb more firms earning zero profit (provided price is below the joint profit maximizing level.) For example, in the case of linear demand, $p = a - bY$, and constant marginal cost, the equation for the zero profit locus[8] is

$$n = -\lambda + (a - c')\sqrt{\lambda/Fb} \tag{19}$$

From expression (19) it follows that, for the case of linear demand and constant marginal cost, the competitive outcome, $\lambda = 0$, is consistent only with $n = 0$. This is a manifestation of the familiar observation that, if marginal cost is below average cost, the competitive pricing rule, price = marginal cost, implies negative profits if $n > 0$. Therefore the trivial ($n = 0$) equilibrium is the only competitive zero-profit equilibrium: a non-trivial zero-profit equilibrium must be imperfectly competitive.

[7] The problems of small numbers and possible asymmetric expectations between entrants and incumbents is not, of course, unique to our model and has been much discussed, particularly in connection with the contestable markets hypothesis, but also whenever the Chamberlinian zero profit equilibrium is formalized.

[8] With linear demand, profit maximization implies $y = (a - c')/b(n + \lambda)$. The relationship between n and λ at zero profit, $n = -\lambda + (a - c')\sqrt{\lambda/Fb}$ is obtained by substituting this value of y into $\pi = 0$ and assuming c' constant.

With "U-shaped" average cost curves, on the other hand, there is some positive value of n at which $\lambda = 0$ along $\lambda = f(n)$. The number of firms at this "purely competitive" zero profit point depends on the technology and the size of the market and is not necessarily large. In general, for the zero profit equilibrium to exist with $\lambda > 0$ average cost must be downward sloping at the solution because average cost must be tangent to perceived demand, which slopes downward.

As illustrated in Figure 1, the 45° line is the locus of joint profit maximizing points ($n = \lambda$). From (18), the zero profit locus is vertical at the point $n = \lambda$. Line OA passing through the origin represents the linear example. The shape of the contour reflects the fact that in this case $f''(n)$ is strictly positive if $n > \lambda$. For completeness we continue the contour to the left of the 45° line ($n < \lambda$), but it should be noted that this region is not economically relevant. Line NB illustrates a zero profit contour for the case of "U-shaped" average cost curves. N is the number of firms at the competitive outcome.

We examine the fully symmetric case. Clearly providers of professional services do not all have the same costs and differences in ability and training lead to some differentiation in the product. Fortunately, generalization to asymmetric firms does not affect the nature of the problem, but it does substantially complicate the analysis. In the case of cost asymmetry and asymmetric product differentiation the zero profit contour is defined with reference to the marginal firm. The convenient assumptions of continuity and differentiability are harder to justify. With asymmetric conjectures and product differentiation, there is a conjecture λ_{ij} associated with each pair of firms i and j and the analysis of output and price affects would have to be carried out using some average or index of firm perceptions.

In this paper, equilibrium with free entry is defined as a situation in which the (symmetric) firms earn zero profit in the long run, given their conjectures, λ. New firms, once they enter, will have the same expectations as established firms. For example, with tacit collusion via a professional organization, new

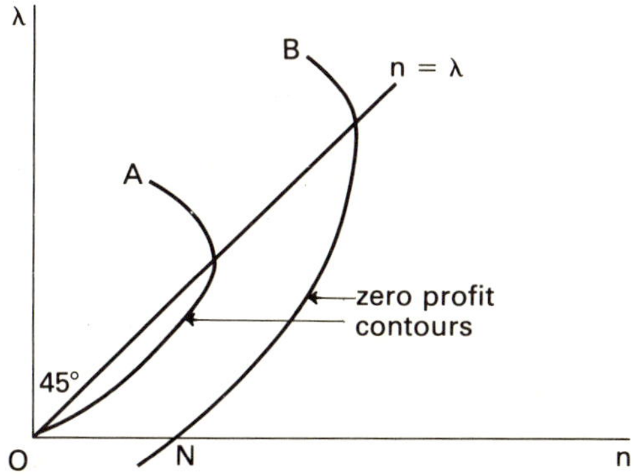

FIGURE 1

professionals joining the system follow the same pricing behaviour as will existing professionals after entry. Nevertheless, the maintenance of the tacit agreement becomes more difficult as entry occurs, which is reflected by a decrease in the value of λ.

To determine which point on the zero profit locus is the industry equilibrium with free entry, consider the way the collusion parameter, λ, is likely to vary with entry. This relationship is denoted $\lambda = g(n)$. More precisely, $g(n)$ shows the λ that would emerge if the number of firms were fixed at n while λ adjusted. In the case of monopoly, since firm output is industry output, $\lambda = 1$. In general, profit-maximizing collusion is achieved if $\lambda = n$ as entry occurs. Since a greater number of firms makes collusion more difficult, we assume that $\lambda = g(n)$ falls below the 45° line after some n ($g(n)$ may be coincident with the 45° line for some n) and eventually decreases in n, until the axis (competitive expectations) is reached. This is illustrated by $g(n)$ in Figure 2. For low values of n, $g(n)$ is in a region of positive profits to the left of the zero profit contour $\lambda = f(n)$. Industry equilibrium with free entry (if it exists) is given by the intersection of f and g. Two possible positions of the zero profit contour, f_1 and f_2, are illustrated. f_1 intersects g at A so that at the free entry equilibrium there are more firms and price is higher than at the competitive point N_1. If the zero profit contour is f_2, $g(n)$ meets the n axis ($\lambda = 0$) with firms earning positive profits. Additional entry then moves the industry from short run purely competitive equilibrium to the zero profit long run equilibrium at N_2.

The function $\lambda = g(n)$, expressing the conjectural variation as a function of the number of firms, is simply imposed exogenously. One would prefer to derive $g(n)$ from the underlying technological and strategic structure. This is, however, a substantial problem and is beyond the scope of the present paper. One could, however, look to the repeated game literature for some sort of justification. Porter [1983] develops a repeated game structure in which the

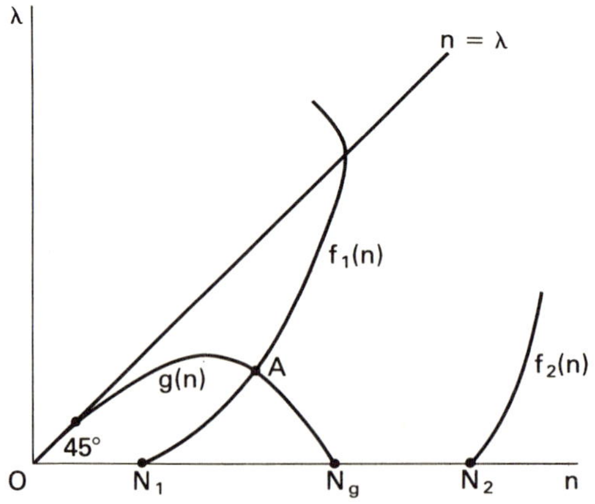

FIGURE 2

level of collusion that firms are able to maintain, as reflected by the output level, falls as the number of firms in the industry rises. This is broadly consistent with our assumption concerning $g(n)$. Our assumption is also consistent with the "free rider" problem discussed by Stigler [1974] and Kalai and Stanford [1983]. Specifically, in any implicitly collusive arrangement each firm bears some costs should it be called upon to punish deviant behaviour. With many firms, output restriction by any firm is attributable mainly to the enforcement effort of others: each firm has a tendency to free ride. This effect is stronger as the number of firms rises, making the achievable strength of collusion fall as n rises.

It could be argued that the "free rider" problem might lead to other formulations. For example, a referee suggested that, with large numbers of firms, collusion would be organized by trade associations, who in turn were financed by firms in the industry. Through this avenue the cost of collusion might show up as a part of fixed costs for each firm, hence λ would be an increasing function of F. This strikes us as a potentially fruitful modelling approach, although quite different from our model. In any case, neither Porter's argument nor the free-rider issue is formally connected to our model, so we would not wish to overstate the case. Nevertheless, we feel that these arguments do lend rough support to the assumed nature of the "ease of collusion" function.

IV. WELFARE AND THE ZERO PROFIT LOCUS

Now consider the effect of government policy on the placement of the $\lambda = g(n)$ schedule. If policy acts to make tacit collusion more difficult for any given number of firms and there is free entry, the industry moves down the zero profit locus, reducing the equilibrium number of firms. For example, one such policy might be for the government to ensure that members of professional associations such as lawyers and dentists can advertise the price of their services. This reduces the power of the association to maintain prices. This section is concerned with the welfare implications of such policies.

Assuming that partial equilibrium analysis is appropriate, consumer utility can be approximated by the form $U = u(Y) + m$ where m is expenditure on a numeraire commodity. Let $S(n, \lambda)$ be the sum of consumer surplus plus profit given n and λ. Since the marginal utility of income is constant and equal to one,

$$S(n, \lambda) = u(Y) - n(c(y) + F) \tag{20}$$

Using $p = du/dY$, $ny_n = Y_n - y$ and $Y_\lambda = ny_\lambda$, we have

$$S_n(n, \lambda) = (p(Y) - c'(y))Y_n - (c(y) + F - c'(y)y) \tag{21}$$

$$S_\lambda(n, \lambda) = (p(Y) - c'(y))ny_\lambda \tag{22}$$

where S_n and S_λ are partial derivatives.

Zero profit means price equals average cost, $p = (c(y) + F)/y$, and (21) becomes

$$(23) \qquad S_n(n, \lambda) = (p - c')(Y_n - y) = (p - c')(ny_n)$$

Along the zero profit locus $\lambda = f(n)$. Therefore, using (22) and (23), we have

$$(24) \qquad dS/dn\Big|_{f(n)} = S_n + S_\lambda f'(n) = n(p - c')(dy/dn)\Big|_{f(n)}$$

where

$$dy/dn\Big|_{f(n)} = y_n + y_\lambda f'(n)$$

The effect on welfare of an increase in the number of firms along the zero profit locus depends on the sign of $(dy/dn)|_{f(n)}$, that is, on whether the output of a typical firm rises or falls along the contour. Substituting (18) for $f'(n)$ and some rearrangement using $Y_n = ny_n + y$ yields

$$(25) \qquad dy/dn\Big|_{f(n)} = -y/(n - \lambda)$$

which is negative, since $n > \lambda$. Since in this case (from (18)), $f'(n) > 0$, additional firms earning zero profit can only be accommodated with a higher value of λ (greater tacit collusion) and a lower level of output for each firm.[9] Therefore, from (24), welfare falls along the zero profit locus as n increases with λ. Greater numbers of firms do not offset the anti-competitive effect of increased collusion along $f(n)$. The industry performs better at low levels of n and λ and welfare is maximized at $\lambda = 0$. Government policies which reduce collusion in equilibrium necessarily increase welfare.

Since profit is zero along the contour the changes in welfare are just changes in consumer welfare and therefore can be related to price changes. The Nash equilibrium levels of Y and p along the zero profit contour can be represented by $Y = Y(n, f(n))$ and $p = p(Y(n, f(n)))$. The effect on price of an increase in the number of firms along $\lambda = f(n)$ is

$$(26) \qquad dp/dn\Big|_{f(n)} = p'(dY/dn)\Big|_{\pi = 0}$$

Since $dY/dn|_{f(n)} = n(dy/dn)|_{f(n)} + y$, using (25) yields

$$(27) \qquad dY/dn\Big|_{f(n)} = -\lambda y/(n - \lambda)$$

If $n > \lambda > 0$, from (27) and (26), industry output falls and price rises along the zero profit contour. These results are summarized in Proposition 2.

[9] This model captures the argument made by Machlup [1952] that collusion with free entry causes firms to move up their average cost curves, increasing the average cost of production.

Proposition 2: Provided $n > \lambda > 0$, both the output of each firm and total industry output are decreasing and price is increasing as both n and λ increase along the zero profit contour. Industry output and welfare are maximized at $\lambda = 0$.

To see the welfare change directly as a function of the price change, first substitute (27) into (26) and use first order condition (2) to obtain

$$(28) \qquad dp/dn\Big|_{f(n)} = (p - c')/(n - \lambda)$$

Then substituting (25) into (24) and using (28), we obtain

$$(29) \qquad dS/dn\Big|_{f(n)} = -Y(p - c')/(n - \lambda) = -Y\, dp/dn\Big|_{\pi = 0}$$

The change in welfare along the zero profit contour is just the marginal loss in consumer surplus from the rise in the price of Y.

V. THE SECOND BEST CONTOUR

In markets with economies of scale it has long been recognized that entry of firms into the industry may reduce welfare. (See von Weizsäcker [1980] for an analysis of the Cournot case.) An additional firm normally increases industry output, but it may also cause production to occur at a higher average cost. Perry [1984] has illustrated this in the context of the conjectural variation model. He shows that if entry reduces the output of each firm, $y_n < 0$, then welfare would be increased by reducing the number of firms below the level at the free entry equilibrium. This can be seen from our equation (24). As in Perry [1984], given the behaviour of the firms (characterized by the value of λ), the (second best) optimal number of firms, n^*, is defined by $S_n(n^*, \lambda) = 0$, where S_n is given by (21).

For the purpose of illustrating this effect in our diagram and for the welfare results in section VI, we extend this analysis to show how the second best optimal number of firms varies with the degree of tacit collusion. We refer to the schedule $n^* = n^*(\lambda)$, defined implicitly by $S_n(n^*, \lambda) = 0$, as the second best contour. It relates the (second best) optimal value of n to λ. From total differentiation of $S_n(n, \lambda) = 0$ with respect to n and λ the slope of this contour is

$$(30) \qquad dn^*/d\lambda = -S_{n\lambda}/S_{nn}$$

Under most demand and cost conditions one would expect the second best optimal number of firms to increase with λ. With greater tacit collusion, the output increasing effect of a larger number of firms becomes more important. This is indeed the case if economies of scale are caused by a fixed cost, F, (with constant marginal cost) and if demand is linear. The equation for the second best welfare contour[10] with $p = a - bY$ is then

$$n^* = -\lambda + (\lambda^2(a - c')^2/Fb)^{1/3} \tag{31}$$

with slope $dn^*/d\lambda = (2n^* - \lambda)/3\lambda$. Since with linear demand, $y_n < 0$, from (7), the second best welfare contour lies to the left of the zero profit locus and is illustrated in figure 3.

If demand is sufficiently convex ($p'' > p'/\lambda y > 0$) from (7), y_n may be positive and the second best contour may lie to the right of the zero profit contour. However, we take $y_n < 0$ as the normal case, leading to a second best contour along which firms' profits would be positive, unless lump sum entry or license fees are imposed.

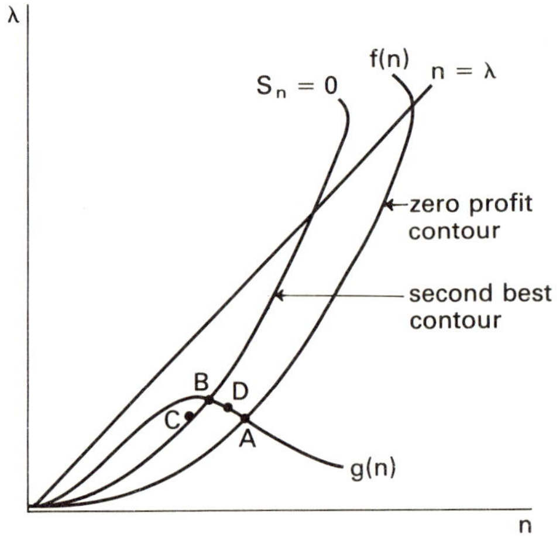

FIGURE 3

[10] With linear demand, $p = a - bY$, and constant marginal cost, from (21), the second best contour becomes,

$$S_n(n^*, \lambda) = (a - c' - bn^*y)Y_n - F = 0$$

The first order condition (2) for profit maximization implies $y = (a - c')/b(n + \lambda)$. Also from (5) $\alpha = p'(\lambda + n)$ so that from (8), $Y_n = \lambda y/(\lambda + n)$. Substituting y and Y_n into $S_n = 0$, we obtain

$$(\lambda + n^*)^3 = \lambda^2(a - c')^2/Fb$$

which implies $n^* = -\lambda + (\lambda^2(a - c')^2/Fb)^{1/3}$

$$\begin{aligned} dn^*/d\lambda &= -1 + (1/3)(\lambda^2(a - c')^2/Fb)^{-2/3}(2\lambda(a - c')^2/Fb) \\ &= -1 + 2(\lambda + n^*)^{-2}(\lambda + n^*)^3/3\lambda \\ &= (2n^* - \lambda)/3\lambda \end{aligned}$$

VI. WELFARE IMPLICATIONS OF ENTRY COSTS AND LICENSE FEES OR SUBSIDIES

It is sometimes suggested that professional associations set conditions so that it is more difficult and expensive for a professional to obtain a license than is strictly necessary based on professional standards. Long periods of study or apprenticeship before certification are particularly common entry barriers. The natural reaction of economists is that such impediments to entry are welfare reducing. However, as pointed out by von Weizsäcker [1980], in connection with a free entry Cournot model, it is conceivable that restricting entry could improve welfare. In this section such a possibility is examined using our model. We find that entry barriers imposed by the industry, and which consume real resources, definitely lower welfare, but government license fees will improve welfare if output per firm is increased.

So far we have treated F as a fixed cost: a cost which must be borne if any output at all is to be produced, but which is implicitly avoidable if no output is produced. Some license fees are well-modelled as increases in F: for example a license fee may be charged every year. True entry fees, on the other hand, such as the costs of law school for a lawyer, are more like sunk costs inasmuch as they are irreversible whether or not output is produced. However, if one is careful about the conceptual experiment being considered, these sunk costs can also be modelled as increases in F. First of all, the model is a static one period model, so the minor complication that a sunk cost must be amortized over the life of the industry rather than applied to a single period is avoided. (This is easy to deal with in any case.) The slightly more subtle point is that we do not consider the conceptual experiment of raising F for potential entrants while allowing incumbents to remain in the industry. Instead we compare two different equilibrium configurations, one in which there is a low fixed cost F for all participants and one in which there is a high F, including the entry cost or license fee, for all participants.

Since the entry cost, F, is a fixed cost from the viewpoint of an individual firm, its only direct positive effect is to reduce the equilibrium number of firms. To determine this effect it is useful to first consider the implications of a change in F for the zero profit locus implicitly defined by $\pi(n, \lambda; F) = 0$ (given by (1)). Differentiating $\pi = 0$ with respect to n and F holding λ fixed, and using $\pi_F = -1$ and $\pi_n < 0$ (from (11)) we obtain

$$(32) \qquad \partial n/\partial F\bigg|_{\tau=0} = 1/\pi_n < 0$$

The higher cost of entry shifts the zero profit locus to the left reducing n for a given value of λ. The equilibrium number of firms is determined by the intersection of this (shifted) locus with $\lambda = g(n)$. If $g'(n) < 0$, a reduction in the number of firms increases the level of the tacit collusion in equilibrium. From total differentiation of $\pi(n, g(n); F) = 0$ we obtain the effect of F on the equilibrium number of firms allowing λ to vary. If $g'(n) \leq 0$, then

$$(33) \qquad dn/dF\Big|_{\pi=0} = 1/(\pi_n + \pi_\lambda g'(n)) < 0$$

If $g'(n) < 0$, then an increase in F reduces the equilibrium number of firms, but by less than would occur if $g'(n) = 0$.

The decrease in the number of firms due to a higher entry cost may increase the equilibrium level of output per firm. This is easily shown by recognizing that in zero profit equilibrium $y = y(n, \lambda; F)$ where $\lambda = g(n)$. Therefore

$$(34) \qquad dy/dF\Big|_{\pi=0} = (y_n + y_\lambda g'(n))(dn/dF)\Big|_{\pi=0}$$

which from (33) is positive if $g'(n) = 0$ and $y_n < 0$. If $g'(n) < 0$, output per firm may still rise if $y_\lambda g'(n)$ is small.

Despite this, if $g'(n) \leq 0$ industry output always falls and price rises with an increase in F. Since in equilibrium $Y = Y(n, \lambda : F)$, from (8), (14) and (33),

$$(35) \qquad dY/dF\Big|_{\pi=0} = (Y_n + Y_\lambda g'(n))(dn/dF)\Big|_{\pi=0} < 0$$

$$(36) \qquad dp/dF\Big|_{\pi=0} = p' \, dY/dF\Big|_{\pi=0} > 0$$

Now suppose that F is a real resource cost imposed by the industry. Since profit is zero, the change in welfare is then due only to changes in consumer surplus. Since price rises, consumer surplus and welfare must fall with an increase in F.[11] These results are summarized in Proposition 3.

Proposition 3: Provided $g'(n) \leq 0$, an increase in the real cost of entry, F, increases price and reduces industry output and welfare at the zero profit equilibrium.

In addition, the second best contour $n = n^*(\lambda; F)$ implicitly defined by $S_n(n^*, \lambda; F) = 0$ is dependent on a real entry cost F as in (21). Since $S_{nF} = -1$ (from (21)) and $S_{nn} < 0$ from the second order condition for a welfare optimum, for any given value of λ, n^* is decreasing in F.

$$(37) \qquad dn^*/dF = 1/S_{nn} < 0$$

This implies that the second best contour (as well as the zero profit contour) is shifted to the left by an industry policy to increase the real cost F. In the context of figure 3, although an increase in the real entry cost reduces the equilibrium number of firms, it may not bring the equilibrium closer to the second best contour.

[11] This can be shown directly using the welfare function $S(n, \lambda; F)$ as given by (20).

On the other hand, the second best contour would be unaffected if, rather than a real cost F, the government imposed a license fee, T. The license fee reduces the profit of a typical firm, but this is just offset by the additional revenue collected by the government, which is included in total welfare.

(38) $$S(n, \lambda; F, T) = u(Y) - nc(y) - n(F + T) + nT$$

The welfare function therefore reduces to the same form as before (see (20)).

However, a license fee does affect welfare through its influence on the number of firms in equilibrium. A license fee has the same effect on profit and the equilibrium number of firms as the real entry cost F.

Therefore, expressions (33) and (34) describe the marginal effects of T on n and y, respectively, along the zero profit contour, just replacing F by T. Now consider the optimal value of T, which is characterized by setting the derivative of $S(n, \lambda; F, T)$ to zero, recognizing that $\lambda = g(n)$ in equilibrium.

(39) $$dS/dT\Big|_{\pi=0} = (S_n + S_\lambda g'(n))\ dn/dT\Big|_{\pi=0} = 0$$

Noting that $c(y) + F = py - T$ and using (21), we obtain

(40) $$S_n(n, \lambda)\Big|_{\pi=0} = (p - c')ny_n + T$$

Then, from (40) and (22), (39) becomes

(41) $$dS/dT\Big|_{\pi=0} = (n(p - c')(y_n + y_\lambda g'(n)) + T)(dn/dT)\Big|_{\pi=0} = 0$$

The optimal license fee is then (using (34) with T instead of F):

(42) $$T = -n(p - c')[(dy/dT)/(dn/dT)]\Big|_{\pi=0}$$

Since $dn/dT < 0$ from (33), Proposition 4 follows.

Proposition 4: At the zero profit equilibrium, the optimal license fee, T, is positive if and only if an increase in the license fee increases the equilibrium level of output of each firm.

If there is no change in λ with entry ($g'(n) = 0$), then from (34) and (42) the optimal license fee is $T = -n(p - c')y_n$, which is positive in the normal case of $y_n < 0$. With this value of T, S_n is zero from (40). This means that if tacit collusion is unaffected by the number of firms and $y_n < 0$ then the second best optimal license fee shifts the zero profit locus to the left so that it cuts the second best contour at the constant value of λ. Assuming $g(n)$ is horizontal this is illustrated in figure 3 by the move from point A to point C. In the unusual case in which $y_n > 0$, the optimal value of T is then a subsidy. If $g'(n) = 0$, it will also bring the industry to the second best contour, which in this case lies to the right of the zero profit locus.

On the other hand, if $g'(n) < 0$, from (41) the optimal license fee is lower but still positive (by Proposition 4) if it increases firm output in equilibrium. In this case from (40), the value of S_n at zero profit is negative indicating that the optimal license fee leaves the industry to the right of the second best contour (at a point such as D in figure 3). The policy takes account of the fact that a further cutback in the number of firms (as in the move from D to B in figure 3) will increase tacit collusion sufficiently to reduce welfare. The improvement in welfare from the increase in output per firm is more than offset by the loss from the increase in tacit collusion.

These results are summarized in Proposition 5.

Proposition 5: If $g'(n) = 0$, the optimal license fee, T, ensures that the zero profit equilibrium lies on the second best contour. If $g'(n) < 0$ and $T > 0$, then at the optimal fee, the number of firms exceeds the number on the second best contour, given λ.

One qualification to Propositions 4 and 5 raised by a referee is that license fees or certification costs might be used to exclude inefficient producers or low quality producers, leading to rather different and perhaps significant welfare affects. These possibilities are excluded by our model due to the assumption that firms are symmetric.

VII. CONCLUDING REMARKS

Freedom of entry is regarded as an important source of economic efficiency in market economies. In combination with purely competitive behaviour by firms, it leads to pareto-efficient outcomes. However, even industries with large numbers of sellers seem to appreciate the value of achieving some degree of collusion, despite free entry. As mentioned in the paper, this is perfectly rational behaviour consistent with pursuit of short run excess profits and avoidance of short run losses. Therefore it seems important to understand the positive and normative implications of the relationship between free entry and partial collusion.

The nature of this relationship can conveniently be understood within the context of the general conjectural variation model. We show that greater tacit collusion is required to absorb more firms earning zero profit, as reflected in a zero profit locus of combinations of the number of firms, n, and conjectural variation, λ. The idea that ease of collusion falls as entry occurs yields a second (n, λ) locus. Industry equilibrium occurs when both relations are satisfied. We are also able to characterize the second best optimum number of firms given the level of tacit collusion in the industry. There is a trade-off in that more firms lead to more competitiveness, but normally reduce output per firm so that firms move up their average cost curves.

The welfare analysis of impediments to entry yields some interesting results. First, not surprisingly, policies which render tacit collusion more difficult are in the public interest. Also attempts by the industry to increase the real cost of entry are welfare reducing. However, a positive government license fee, which simply taxes entrants rather than forcing them unnecessarily to use up real resources in entering, is normally welfare improving. The number of firms falls, reducing competitiveness, but output per firm rises, lowering average cost. The license fee is just a transfer and overall welfare rises.

James A. Brander,
Faculty of Commerce and Business Administration,
University of British Columbia,
Vancouver, B.C. V6T 1Y8, Canada.

ACCEPTED MARCH 1984

Barbara Spencer,
Department of Economics,
Boston College,
Chestnut Hill,
Massachusetts, 02167, U.S.A.

REFERENCES

BAUMOL, W., PANZAR, J. and WILLIG, R., 1982, *Contestable Markets and the Theory of Industry Structure* (Harcourt, Brace, Jovanovich, New York).

BOYER, M. and MOREAUX, M., 1983, "Consistent Versus Non-Consistent Conjectures in Duopoly Theory: Some Examples," *Journal of Industrial Economics* 32 (September), pp. 97–110.

BRESNAHAN, T. F., 1981, "Duopoly Models with Consistent Conjectures," *American Economic Review* 71 (December), pp. 934–45.

DEWEY, D., 1982, "Welfare and Collusion: Reply," *American Economic Review* 72 (March), pp. 276–81.

KALAI, E. and STANFORD, W., 1983, "Conjectural Variations Strategies in Dynamic Cournot Games with Fast Reactions," Northwestern University, Center for Mathematical Studies in Economics and Management Science, Discussion Paper No. 575 (September).

KAMIEN, M. and SCHWARTZ, N., 1983, "Conjectural Variations," *Canadian Journal of Economics* 16 (May), pp. 191–211.

MACHLUP, F., 1952, *The Economics of Seller's Competition: Model Analysis of Sellers' Conduct*, (John Hopkins Press, Baltimore).

PATINKIN, D., 1947, "Multiplant Firms, Cartels and Imperfect Competition," *Quarterly Journal of Economics* 61 (October), pp. 173–80.

PERRY, M. K., 1982, "Oligopoly and Consistent Conjectural Variations," *Bell Journal of Economics* 13 (Spring), pp. 197–205.

PERRY, M. K., 1984, "Scale Economies, Imperfect Competition and Public Policy," *Journal of Industrial Economics* 32 (March), pp. 313–33.

PORTER, R. H., 1983, "Optimal Cartel Trigger Price Strategies," *Journal of Economic Theory* 29 (April), pp. 313–38.

SEADE, J., 1980, "On the Effects of Entry," *Econometrica* 48 (March), pp. 479–89.

SHUBIK, M., 1982, *Game Theory in the Social Sciences: Concepts and Solutions* (The MIT Press, Cambridge, Massachusetts).

STIGLER, G. J., 1974, "Free Riders and Collective Action: An Appendix to Theories of Economic Regulation," *Bell Journal of Economics and Management Science* 5 (Autumn), pp. 359–65.

TULLOCK, G., 1975, "The Transitional Gains Trap," *Bell Journal of Economics* 6 (Autumn), pp. 671–78.

THOMPSON, E. A., and FAITH, R. L., 1981, "A Pure Theory of Strategic Behaviour and Social Institutions," *American Economic Review* 71 (June), pp. 366–80.

VON WEIZÄCKER, C. C., 1980, "A Welfare Analysis of Barriers to Entry," *Bell Journal of Economics* 11 (Autumn), pp. 399–420.

THE JOURNAL OF INDUSTRIAL ECONOMICS 0022-1821 $2.00
Volme XXXIII March 1985 No. 3

PRODUCTIVE PERFORMANCE IN WEST GERMAN MANUFACTURING INDUSTRY 1970–80: A FARRELL FRONTIER CHARACTERISATION

DOUGLAS TODD*

I. INTRODUCTION

Some measure of the success with which economic resources are utilised lies at the heart of any meaningful indicator of economic performance. A traditional and obvious point of departure is to say that for a given state of technical knowledge and initial endowments of factor inputs, resource allocation depends on the degree of ability to transform inputs into outputs and the relative returns which these resources can earn.

In this paper, the more recent productive performance of the West German manufacturing sector is appraised from one particular viewpoint whilst remaining firmly within what might be called the conventional framework of relating outputs to the factor inputs labour and capital[1]. Section II provides an initial brief overview of the West German manufacturing sector over the period 1970–80, in which some of the more interesting trends are noted for a more detailed analysis in later sections. Section III sets out the approach used. Again, this is not very extensive given the relatively well documented nature of the methodology. Section IV takes the form of some notes on the data used with a more substantial Section V containing the major analysis. Some more general observations and concluding comments are brought together in a final Section VI.

II. THE WEST GERMAN MANUFACTURING SECTOR: AN OVERVIEW

In many respects, the post-war productive performance of the West German economy overall can be regarded as a remarkable success story. In the thirty years 1950 to 1980, GDP grew at an annual rate of over 5 per cent. This figure does however mask a considerable slowing down in the trend increase as the following Table illustrates clearly.

* The author is a Senior Economic Adviser in H.M. Treasury, London, and on leave as Economic Adviser in the Directorate General for Economic and Financial Affairs, European Commission, Brussels. This is a revised version of a paper given at an SSRC Panel Conference on Capital Productivity, London, November 1983. Whilst the usual disclaimer applies, the author is nevertheless grateful for having received helpful comments from an anonymous referee.

[1] This study is the first part of a larger comparative exercise concerned with both static productive efficiency and total factor productivity growth in the larger EEC countries.

GDP growth (%)[2]	
1950–80	5.2
1950–60	8.0
1960–70	4.7
1970–80	2.8
1973–80	2.3

Thus the most rapid expansion occurred during the reconstruction period, a standard which makes performance over the last decade appear rather modest. It was during these last ten years that the economy was subjected to the two oil shocks and it is of interest to see what changes have taken place. Breaking this period down a little more reveals the following picture:

Annual Average Growth Rates[3]

	GDP	*Manufacturing Output*
1960–73	4.5	5.2
1970–80	2.8	2.1
1970–73	3.8	3.4
1973–80	2.3	1.6
1975–80	3.5	3.3
1976–80	3.2	2.6

The West German economy proved to be quite resilient to the wave of oil price increases. External competitiveness was maintained and a relatively strong exchange rate helped to reduce inflationary pressure. Both GDP and manufacturing output recovered to something closer to the performance achieved prior to 1973. Here it is worth noting the contrast with the United Kingdom where in the face of such price increases, the existence of substantial oil reserves brought about a rise in the real exchange rate. This tended to depress output and reduce the share of manufacturing.[4] The German manufacturing sector in effect has had little choice but to try to absorb the oil price increases and attempt to maintain competitiveness in its tradeable goods sector. Nevertheless, capacity utilisation in the German manufacturing sector has declined from 96.2 per cent in 1970 to a low of 82.9 per cent in the greatly depressed year of 1975. Thereafter, it has recovered to remain at around 90 per cent over of the last four years of the decade.

From 1970, there has been an almost unbroken decline in numbers employed totalling nearly 1.16 millions, that is a fall of 1.45 per cent per annum. The volume of capital measured by the stock of gross fixed assets, on the other hand, has exhibited a steady rise at an annual average rate of 3.06 per cent. The ratio of capital to labour therefore rose at a rapid rate (4.6 per annum) over the ten years, whereas capital productivity fell at a rate of 1 per cent per annum.

Labour productivity growth measured in terms of numbers employed rose at 3.6 per cent per annum. Measured in terms of output per man hour

[2] Source: OECD National Accounts.
[3] Source: Jahresgutachten 1981/82, November 1981.
[4] See Byatt *et al.* [1982].

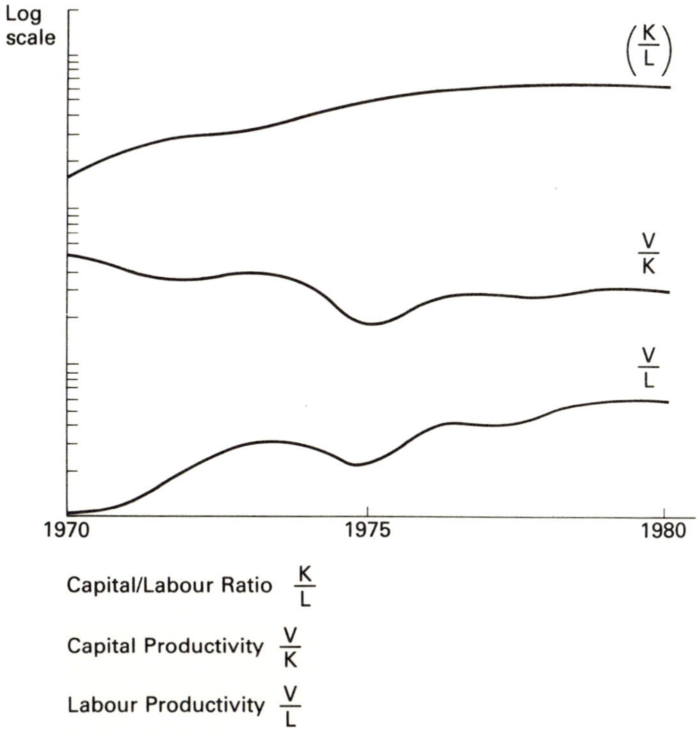

CHART I
WEST GERMAN MANUFACTURING INDUSTRY 1970–80

worked, the figure is 4.8 per cent. Unit labour costs given here by the ratio of wages and salaries to volume of net output increased at an annual average rate of 5.1 per cent. Hence, on average, unit cost increases were not very much out of line with increases in labour productivity, taking the period as a whole. There were, however, periods when significant departures occurred; 1970 to 1974 for example, when the growth of unit wage costs exceeded output per man hour by 2 per cent per annum and output per employee by 2.8 per cent per annum.

There has been also a strongly inverse relationship between labour productivity on the one hand and capital productivity on the other. Chart I illustrates the main trends in productivity growth over this period.

This view is, however, somewhat superficial; when the contributions of both labour and capital are taken into account the picture becomes somewhat more complex. Further, the kind of interpretation which is placed on these factors depends to some extent on the techniques used and this is the area to which we now turn.

III. THE PRODUCTIVE EFFICIENCY APPROACH

The relevant literature provides an enormous number of examples of comparative performance measures which are based on one or more partial indicators. Easily the most popular are the rate of return on capital and output per unit of labour, with the relevant variables being defined in a variety of ways. However, if social efficiency or some notation of national resource allocation is the object of interest, it makes no real sense to assume that maximising say the return to labour alone is necessarily preferable to any other measure of performance. In economic terms, a low figure for say labour productivity can be generated just as 'efficiently' as a much higher figure. In the production process, all factors are relevant and a meaningful performance measure or assessment of performance should attempt to take these into account.

Economists traditionally have attempted to cope with the multi-factor case by specifying and estimating explicit forms of production function in order to identify contributions separately. In the time series case it is usual to make some assumptions about the embodiment or otherwise of technical progress. Alternatively, one might specify one or more total factor productivity measures taking account of technical progress as a residual element.

In this exercise, observations on sectors of manufacturing industry cover ten years only which effectively rules out a fully fledged econometric time series study. However, one candidate for consideration is set in static productive performance terms being an application of the technique suggested first by M. J. Farrell in his seminal article [1957]. We start with a description of the motives underlying this methodology leading to a discussion of strengths and weaknesses.

III(i). TECHNICAL EFFICIENCY

In economic terms, as we have mentioned, a fundamental approach to the productive efficiency problem is to use the notion of a production function which relates flows of factor services to a given output. In its more general form, the production function being essentially a micro concept defines either a maximum output yielded by given inputs, or alternatively the minimum inputs required to achieve a given output. Figure 1 illustrates these two versions for the single output single input case.

If output V is held constant, one measure of relative productive efficiency is given in Figure 1 by

$$\frac{X1}{V1}\Big/\frac{X2}{V1} = \frac{X1}{X2}\bigg|_{V\ \mathrm{const.}} \tag{1}$$

Alternatively, for constant input we have:

$$\frac{X2}{V2}\Big/\frac{X2}{V1} = \frac{V1}{V2}\bigg|_{X\ \mathrm{const.}} \tag{2}$$

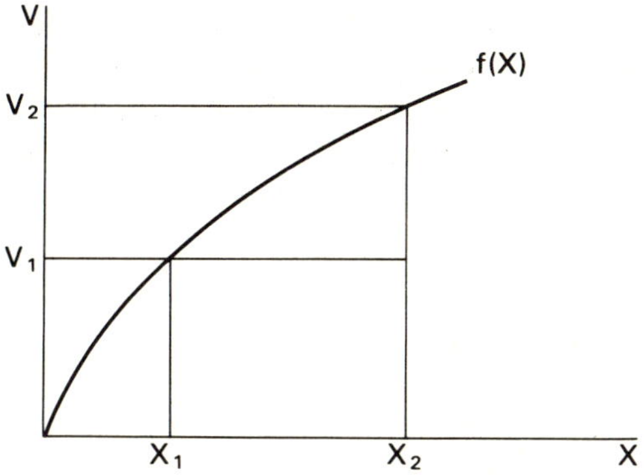

FIGURE 1

We have therefore a production boundary conditional on a given state of technical knowledge and set of production techniques. An agent cannot do better in a purely technical sense than produce on the boundary or frontier as defined by the function $f(X)$. It should be noted however that the above two measures are not necessarily the same and we will return to this point again later in the discussion.

One well known interpretation is to say that prior to an investment taking place, the production function takes an *ex-ante* form. The set of latest or best practice techniques yields a frontier or isoquant which is convex from below. Once the investment decision is taken however, the production function is in effect frozen and assumes an *ex-post* character embodying the more recent techniques and remaining unchanged. The boundary now is defined by the maximum utilisation of the chosen capital stock and labour supply. Over time, the *ex-ante* frontier will tend to move as improvements in the state of technical knowledge take place. In addition to this, as relative factor prices change, the convolution of price changes, of both labour skills and capital goods of the latest vintage makes such *ex-ante* relationships very difficult if not impossible to identify.

From the viewpoint of an individual firm, the best that can be achieved is to be on the boundary or frontier of the best practice technique at the correct set of relative factor prices. The position of other firms can then be compared with such a point on the best practice boundary and this provides one standard against which efficiency differences can be compared. Excluding price or allocative efficiency effects, simply being on the frontier is the relevant criterion for maximum success in technical terms.

This basic idea was first given empirical significance by Farrell in his paper cited above. The approach is to construct an innermost or 'technically efficient' frontier from a set of observations on factor inputs per unit of output defined for a given set of firms or industries. The frontier thus generated is best practice, only but nonetheless importantly, in the sense that those observations which define it *reveal* that they are capable of producing a unit of net output whilst utilising smaller factor input proportions than are other firms.

Figures 2 and 3 below illustrate the Farrell approach in two factor input space.

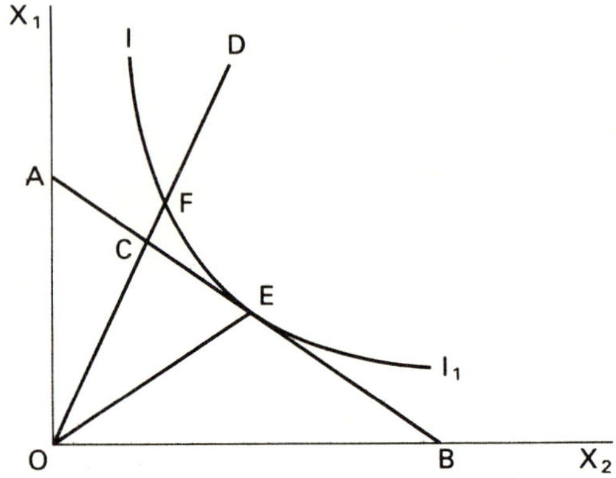

FIGURE 2

Figure 2 is the usual isoquant diagram where the preferred point of production is E; here the production unit is producing maximum output at the correct relative price given by the tangency of AB to the frontier $I - I_1$. Production unit D however is inefficient on two criteria. Firstly, it is operating away from the production frontier and the ratio OF/OD is Farrell's indicator of this technical inefficiency. Secondly, the ray OD cuts the frontier at an implied relative price ratio which is different from that at E. That is to say, input X_2 is relatively more expensive than would be the case at E. Such price

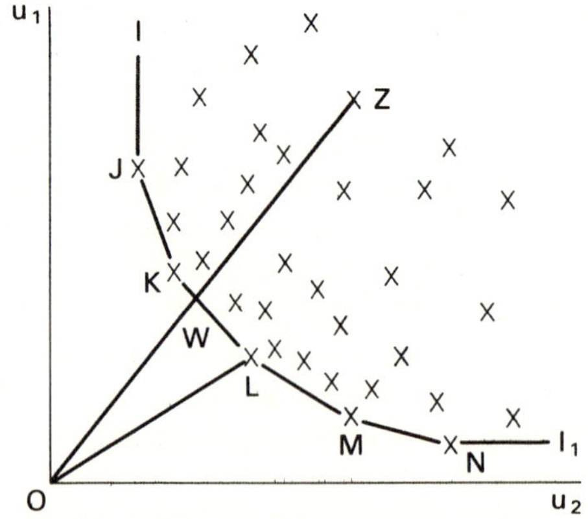

FIGURE 3

or allocative inefficiency, Farrell denoted by OC/OF. Overall efficiency is thus OF/OD. $OC/OF = OC/OD$.[5]

Concentrating on technical or productive performance, the empirical analogue of the above is represented in Figure 3.

Each point represents the observed unit factor requirements of a firm or industry. Observation Z has technical efficiency OW/OZ relative to the convex frontier $I - I_1$ constructed from the inner-most set of observations. All points such as J, K etc have maximum revealed efficiency of unity, e.g., $OL/OL = 1$. Observation Z is thus assessed relative to a *hypothetical* observation W along the ray OZ and which is assumed to lie in the efficient production set as defined by $I - I_1$. Hence comparisons are set in terms of maintained factor proportions such that if say industry Z could produce using input ratio $u1/u2$ at lower cost, it would move inwards along the factor ray OZ.

Whilst the ideas which lie behind the above are extremely simple and certainly appealing, the implied assumptions necessary to generate meaningful results can be demanding.

First of all, one can see intuitively that efficiency comparisons made on the above basis assume first degree homogeneity in the underlying production technology. In the absence of such a restriction, standardising along the unit input ray such as OZ in Figure 3 would not be possible in these same terms.

Taking this a little further, if the production function is

$$V = f(x_1, x_2, x_3 \cdots x_n),$$

following Frisch [1965, Chapter 5] we can write

$$(3) \qquad f(\lambda x_1, \lambda x_2, \ldots, \lambda x_n) = f \qquad (\lambda X) = f(X)\lambda^e$$

where Frisch defines e as the average size of the elasticity of scale or passus coefficient over the interval $(\lambda : 1)$. Interest in this particular formulation arises from the fact that as demonstrated by Forsund and Hjalmarsson [1974], the two measures of productive or technical efficiency illustrated in Figure 1 and relationships (1) and (2) can be related in a simple way.

Given (3), any actual input X_i can be defined in terms of the technical frontier as λX_i. Hence, comparisons can be made by means of the scaling factor λ. From Figure 1 and expression (1) we can then write

$$E_1 = \frac{\lambda X}{X} = \lambda$$

and

$$E_2 = \frac{f(\lambda X)}{f(X)}$$

[5] The Farrell construction bears some close similarity to the welfare 'distance' measure used in Section 9 of the early paper by Debreu [1951].

from (3)

$$\lambda e = \frac{f(\lambda X)}{f(X)}$$

or

$$e = \log\{f(\lambda X)/f(X)\}/\log \lambda$$

so that

$$e = \frac{\log E_2}{\log E_1}$$

We now see that if and only if the elasticity of scale is equal to unity, will the two alternative measures of technical efficiency be identical, i.e., $E_1 = E_2$. In other words, since from (3), the elasticity of scale is the degree of homogeneity, it is only production technologies of degree one homogeneity which have this property.

It is now clear that the convex hull approach suggested and as employed by Farrell imposes this particular restriction and the fact must be borne in mind in application.[6]

III(ii). FURTHER LIMITATIONS

Extensive discussions on the characteristics and limitations of the Farrell frontier method are available in the references cited already. However, it is helpful to mention briefly some of the more important elements since these bear heavily upon the interpretation of any empirical results derived from use of this particular methodology.

Unlike the more conventional production function approach, the Farrell technique applied strictly is a non-parametric technique. It is therefore difficult, if not impossible, to apply the usual classical methods of statistical inference. Secondly, the constructed convex hull is a support set generated from marginal data only. It is the innermost 'outliers' which define the frontier rather than the whole sample and in the classical inferential context, the technique makes inefficient use of all information. Finally, there is always the problem of different qualities of factor inputs employed. A production unit could be judged efficient in a purely static technical sense and yet be operating with older machines and a labour force which lacks more up to date training skills. These are points which are all taken up again at various stages of the analysis.

[6] The literature in this area has grown enormously in the last eight years or so. Many approaches and analyses of efficiency measures for both homogeneous and inhomogeneous functions have been suggested and developed; see for example Färe and Lovell [1978], Kopp [1981], the excellent article by Forsund and Hjalmarsson [1974] and Forsund *et al.* [1980].

Despite these restrictions, the Farrell approach remains a very simple technique in that set of more recent approaches to frontier function estimation[7]. In this respect, one is closer to the textbook concept as opposed to the average function which is used more often in econometric work.

IV. THE DATA

The analysis is based on observations on net output volume, capacity net output, numbers employed, average hours worked, wages and salaries per employee and the volume of fixed assets for 32 sectors of West German manufacturing industry over the period 1970–80.[8] The observations on output and capital are expressed in terms of base year 1970.

Whilst 32 industry groups are worthy of investigation in their own right, for the purposes of the analysis here this does nevertheless represent a high degree of aggregation. The basic theoretical underpinnings as we know, are expressed quite explicitly in terms of single production units with homogeneous product markets. Faced with this, it is tempting to argue that comparisons are likely to be meaningless, or at best somewhat misleading. There are two replies to this, which although not entirely satisfactory, suggest nevertheless that the investigation is worth continuing.

The first quite simply is that questions are and indeed can be expected on such matters as whether manufacturing as a whole is performing well; whether say the chemicals sector is better or worse than engineering or whatever. In an everyday situation it is not sufficient to argue that before any inferences can be made, one needs to disaggregate and yet disaggregate further. Answers are needed at different levels, e.g., plants within firms, firms within product groups, industries within the economy and so on.

A second and more formal reply is to regard an industry's ratios of labour and capital per unit of net output as weighted averages of those ratios of its constituent firms. Denoting an input ratio for a given firm by u, e.g. $(K/V)_i = u_i$, then for the whole industry we can write

$$\sum_i K \Big/ \sum_i V_i = \sum_i u_i V_i \Big/ \sum V_i$$

This obscures, of course, any variations within broad industry groups and thus focuses attention on variations between such groups. If the former is known or thought to be the more important, then if possible this will demand further disaggregation.

[7] See for example Meller [1976] and Todd [1971], [1977].

[8] The Data source is DIW *Produktionsvolumen* etc—Rolf Krengel *et al.*, Berlin, October 1981. The OECD *Historical Statistics 1960–1981–1983*, suggest that industrial production in 1970 was slightly more above trend than was the year 1980. Thus whilst neither end year can be described as 'normal', the discrepancy is not great.

Whereas the DIW published series provides for each industry a single estimated figure for fixed assets employed[9], there are several alternative definitions for the labour input. Numbers employed is probably the most widely recognised definition of labour input, and figures for output per employee are quoted extensively in most countries. Although output per head is of interest in its own right there are other possibilities. Hours worked per employee is somewhat closer to a flow of services concept and which seems more appropriate in a production function context. This however does not take into account differences in quality or work intensity. Here it is possible that real earnings per employee has some attractions insofar as payments to labour are expected to reflect, in part, different skills and perhaps, differences between male and female work intensity.

Because there is no unique preference for one specification over another in the results which are quoted, some examples from all three are sometimes given. In fact, however, the average hours and real earnings variants turned out to be very close indeed in the vast majority of cases.

On the question of which deflator for earnings per employee, again the choice is not entirely obvious. From the viewpoint of the employee, the purchasing power of his money reward is what matters and hence a general consumer price index is appropriate. The firm or industry however may view things differently and assess factor returns in terms of its own product price. That is to say the 'own product' real wage is the relevant specification. Fortunately, this problem is easily resolved because for the West German economy over the period 1970–80, the consumer price and ex-works manufacturing output price indices tracked each other closely so that choice of deflator is not a serious problem.

In presenting and discussing results in experiments of this sort, inevitably one runs into a problem of selection. It is clear that one cannot set out everything and this makes the issue of exactly what to concentrate on something of a problem.

The decade 1970–80 as we know is an awkward one for economic analysis. The first oil shock of 1973 led to a sharp recession in the manufacturing sector in 1975. The year 1976 was one of very rapid recovery followed by an easing down in the next two years. 1979, however, was another year of relative boom in output which preceded the second oil price hike. Hence, there is something in the notion that almost every year is a special event. Simple averaging obscures significant changes, whereas too much concern with individual years diverts attention from the trend. Further, given the sharp divergences it is almost impossible to choose a suitable base year for all purposes.

The simplest but by no means wholly satisfactory approach adopted here is to focus attention on the two end years 1970 and 1980. (See footnote 8). At various points however, explicit reference is made to an individual intermediate year where this is thought to illuminate the discussion.

[9] Smith [1961] seems to favour a stock concept.

V. PRODUCTIVE EFFICIENCY

The discussion here describes the set of experiments using the Farrell frontier methodology. The approach initially is to estimate a set of two-factor Farrell frontiers for each of the years in the sample. Detailed figures for the two end years only are given in the Annex Table.

Charts II and III provide an illustration of the estimated technical frontiers for actual output and also for the comparison between actual and capacity output—1970 and 1980; where the labour input is expressed in terms of numbers employed and hours per man respectively.

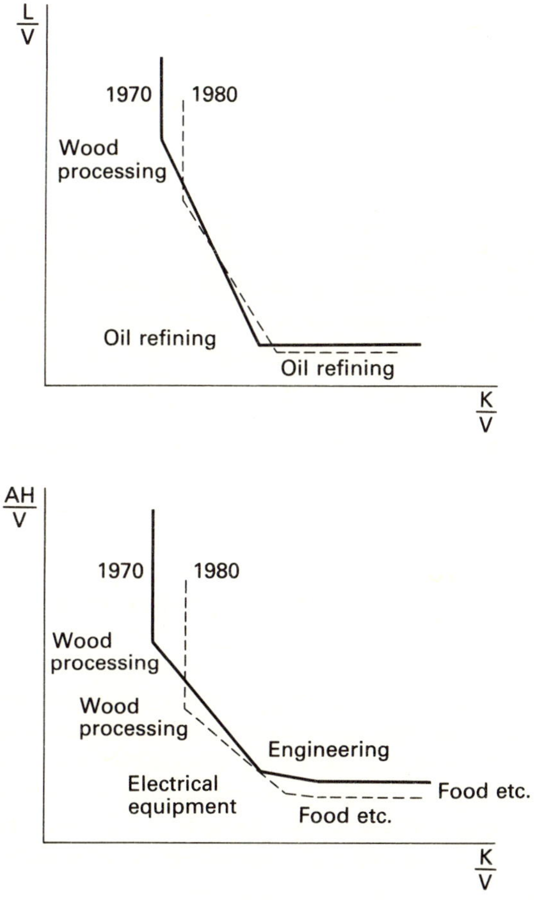

CHART II
WEST GERMAN MANUFACTURING

Farrell Frontiers

The first point to note in Chart II is that there is not a great deal of difference between the two sets of points. There is some suggestion that the technical frontier has shifted inwards slightly towards the origin over the decade. The frontier for 1975, the most depressed year in the sample and omitted in order to avoid overcomplicating the graphs, lies well outside the two boundaries given here. The second point is that almost identical industries lie on the frontiers. Indeed for each individual year, what might be called the technical leaders in these static terms change hardly at all. These are Oil Refining, Wood Processing, Food, Drink and Tobacco, Engineering, Electrical Equipment, where each of these, of course, has a revealed efficiency index of unity. Thus oil refining because it has a relatively high capital/labour ratio is in these terms no more or less efficient than wood processing which is relatively labour intensive. This is the simple essence of the multi-factor approach. A labour productivity comparison taken in isolation would, of course, produce a different ranking, and more is said about this later. One further point of interest is that over time, the technical frontier tends to shift downwards and to the right which is an indication of increasing capital intensity. The mean value of the capital/labour ratio in 1970 was 3.91, by 1980 it had risen to 6.12.

Chart III is a simple representation of how the gap between actual and capacity output compared at best efficiency as revealed, has opened up over the period. The two frontiers for the most depressed year 1975 (again not shown), produce a much wider divergence as one might expect.

Because each industry is assessed relative to the frontier generated in any given year, individual comparisons of industries across years are neither obvious nor easy to make. What is of some interest, however, is the distribution of industries by technical efficiency relative to any given frontier and how this might have moved through time. Chart IV shows that the cumulative frequency distribution of industries by efficiency index moved relatively little when the two end years are compared. In other words, relative to own frontier there is little other than a slight suggestion that the movement is north easterly, the final point of which is where all industries would lie on the technical frontier.

The question arises as to how one might interpret such information. In static snapshots such as those given here, one view is that it is desirable that industries and firms be close to the frontier. If this is so, one may feel that the resource allocation system is operating reasonably well. A relatively small dispersion would then be judged more satisfactory than one which is larger. On the other hand, the market economy is a witness of constant change. Capital equipment is replaced and labour skills adapt. Both the economy and individual industry frontiers are shifting. This vintage factor input interpretation suggests, therefore, a rather different picture. If firms are following something close to an optimal replacement policy, those best practice firms which adapt quickly to increases in market demand will push the productive frontier

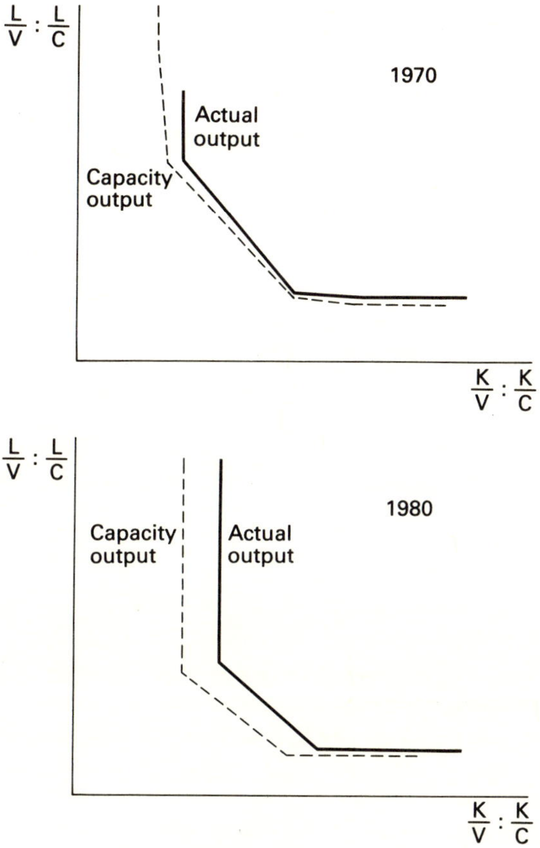

CHART III
WEST GERMAN MANUFACTURING

Actual and Capacity
Output Farrell Frontiers

inwards. Firms and industries in weaker and technically less progressive sectors will not be able to respond in the same fashion. This will, if anything, increase the dispersion from the revealed efficiency boundary[10].

The technique as used here can therefore lead to an apparently pessimistic view of the allocative process. A wide dispersion of a skew distribution when viewed as a cross-section of information need not be an indication that industrial structure is 'inefficient'. Hjalmarrson [1973] has suggested that the real problem is one of knowing how to optimise the process of structural *change*. In

[10] On the other hand, if the earnings measure of the labour input is used, it could be argued that in the weaker sectors, competitive forces will tend to drive real wages down relative to those in stronger markets. This will help to maintain efficiency and thus act in the opposite way.

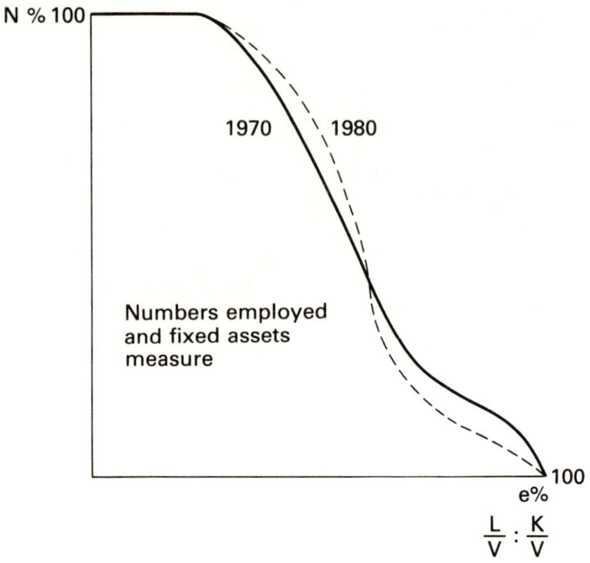

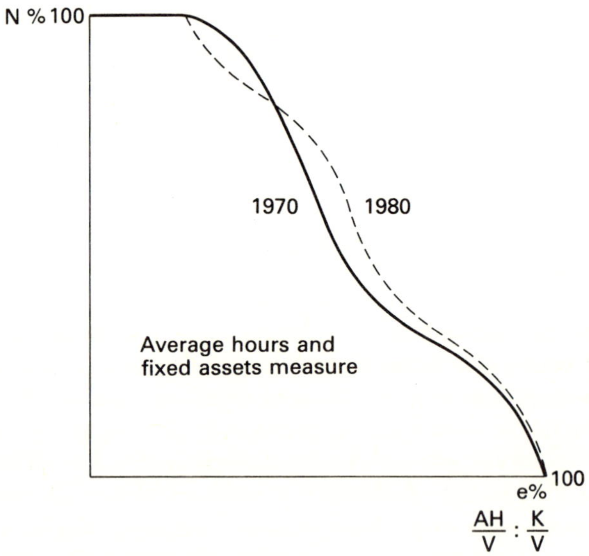

CHART IV
CUMULATIVE DISTRIBUTION OF PRODUCTIVE EFFICIENCY 1970 AND 1980

(Numbers employed and Average Hours worked)

the absence of knowledge on plant vintages, replacement policies and labour skills, it is impossible to be more precise about the issues involved.

Looking at the frontiers individually, all variants on the labour input indicate a declining variance of the efficiency indices around the mean over the sample period. Table I gives the profile for a few of the years in question. One interpretation of this trend might be that gradual slowing down in the growth performance overall in the West German Manufacturing Sector is consistent with a narrowing of differences in productive efficiency between individual industries. 'Best practice' technologies have not been introduced and grown fast enough to maintain the impetus so characteristic of the earlier post-war decades. Again, the static comparisons show little change in either the positioning or the constituent members of the convex frontiers 1970 to 1980.

TABLE I
STANDARD DEVIATION—FARRELL TECHNICAL EFFICIENCY %

	Nos. Employed	*Average Hours*	*Real Average Compensation*
1970	19.56	24.04	23.68
1973	18.82	24.10	22.49
1976	18.19	22.66	21.10
1978	17.0	22.24	21.03
1980	17.2	22.10	20.08

Further light on this observation is provided by a series of rank correlations of indices for the 32 sectors between individual years. First of all, the Spearman coefficient of rank correlation for the three variants was computed for the end year 1980. These are

$$r(e_L\, e_H) = 0.814, \quad r(e_L\, e_W) = 0.868 \quad \text{and} \quad r(e_H\, e_W) = 0.988.$$

where e_L, e_H and e_W refer to the index based on numbers employed, hours and earnings variants. As one might expect intuitively, the correspondence by rank is greatest between the two flow specifications of the labour input.

Next, year by year rankings were computed using the average hours variant. Surprisingly we find that on the basis of the Farrell approach the industry rankings change very little indeed through the sample period. Some examples are

$$r\left(\frac{1980}{1970}\right) = 0.951, \quad r\left(\frac{1975}{1970}\right) = 0.946 \quad \text{and} \quad r\left(\frac{1976}{1970}\right) = 0.953.$$

Where the rank order coefficient compares ranks in 1980 with those in 1970 and so on.

We noted earlier that the best performers in static terms remain virtually unchanged and now we see that this applies to virtually the whole sample. Thus those improvements which have occurred would seem to be through a movement in the sector overall, with rather less emphasis on relative movements within the sector. The weakest sectors, for example, namely Shipbuilding, Iron and Steel Foundries, Non-Ferrous Metals and Cellulose, Paper and Board, maintain their positions in the rankings also.

V(i). EXTENSIONS OF THE STATIC INTERPRETATION

A number of the more important weaknesses of the Farrell characterisation of productive efficiency have been mentioned already. The non-parametric nature of the technique is a particular limitation.

One way of accommodating this is to specify say a Cobb-Douglas technology

$$V = F(x)e^{-u}$$

where $\log F(\cdot) = \sum \alpha_i \log x_i$; the error term u_j has the property which implies $V \leq F(X)$. This conforms with the basic requirements of a deterministic production frontier in that all deviations fall on one side of the convex hull. (In this formulation one need not of course constrain the $\sum \alpha_i = 1$, the linear homogeneity assumption.) A very simple intuitive procedure therefore is to estimate a functional form

$$\log V = \log \alpha + \sum \beta_i \log X + \varepsilon$$

with the intercept term $\log \alpha$ scaled so that all but one of the ε_j lie beneath the regression plane. The one supporting point will therefore be maximally 'efficient'. This procedure has been shown to provide a consistent estimate of the intercept α. (See Green [1980]).

Simple Cobb–Douglas type equations were fitted to data for the two end years 1970 and 1980; the parameter estimates are given in Table II[11].

Shifting the intercept upwards as described enables one to calculate indices of divergence from the regression surface in much the same way as is done in the Farrell method. This was done in each case and rank orders were compared with the Farrell results for each year. The resulting Spearman coefficients are given in Table III using 1980 as an example.

Thus in no case was the rank correlation coefficient below 92 per cent (the same pattern emerged in the 1970 comparisons with the lowest coefficient being 0.926).

For the numbers employed relationships, the two unadjusted intercepts turned out to be negative and of doubtful significance. (In all other cases the constant terms were insignificant also). For 1970 and 1980 we have a natural

[11] Some experiments using Kmenta's Taylor's series expansion of the standard CES form which leads to a trans-log formulation suggested again that an elasticity of substitution of around unity is what the data yields. (See Kmenta [1967]). One remains uneasy however given the persistently odd discrepancy between time-series and cross-section estimates. Frequently in applied work the former yields elasticities of substitution which are well below and significantly different from unity. The cross-section evidence tends to support the Cobb-Douglas technology hypothesis.

TABLE II

	Capital	Nos. Employed	Deflated Employee Compensation	Hours Worked
1970	0.6003	0.3978		
	(6.397)	(3.801)		
	0.5333		0.4623	
	(4.789)		(3.684)	
	0.5853			0.4102
	(5.954)			(3.742)
1980	0.7367	0.2951		
	(7.473)	(2.800)		
	0.6364		0.3981	
	(5.658)		(3.319)	
	0.7253			0.3074
	(7.141)			(2.816)

Figures in brackets are the usual 't' statistics.

TABLE III
RANK CORRELATION COEFFICIENTS

Farrell (e_F)	Nos. Employed	Deflated Employee Compensation	Hours Worked
Cobb-Douglas (e_{CD})			
Nos. Employed	0.920		
Deflated Employee Compensation		0.967	
Hours Worked			0.961

logarithm -1.3375 and -1.3073 respectively, which implies an annual average rate of growth of productive efficiency of around 0.3 per cent. Given the obvious degree of uncertainty surrounding these estimates one might not wish to attach much importance to them. On the other hand, the Farrell frontiers given in the Charts were seen to have moved very little over the period and the rankings obtained from the elementary Cobb–Douglas forms were very close indeed to those obtained via the non-parametric approach.

V(ii). SOME COMPARISONS

It is useful to compare the static productive efficiency measures here with the more popular single factor productivity indicators; output per head and output per unit of capital, for example.

Coefficients of rank correlation relating to the end year 1980 are given in Table IV for Farrell frontier indices in association with the various definitions of the labour input.

TABLE IV

e_F		e_F		e_F	
L/V	K/V	$\bar{H}/V$	K/V	$\bar{W}/V$	K/V
0.355	0.930	0.678	0.794	0.669	0.868

In every instance there is a closer association between overall productive efficiency and capital per unit of output than with labour per unit of output. The same procedure followed with respect to the adjusted Cobb-Douglas implied indices yielded an essentially similar picture. The Spearman coefficients being 0.38 with respect to labour per unit of output and 0.88 with respect to the normalised capital variable. Given this, the suggestion is that the observations in the normalised input space are grouped in a form broadly similar to that in the illustration provided by Figure 4.

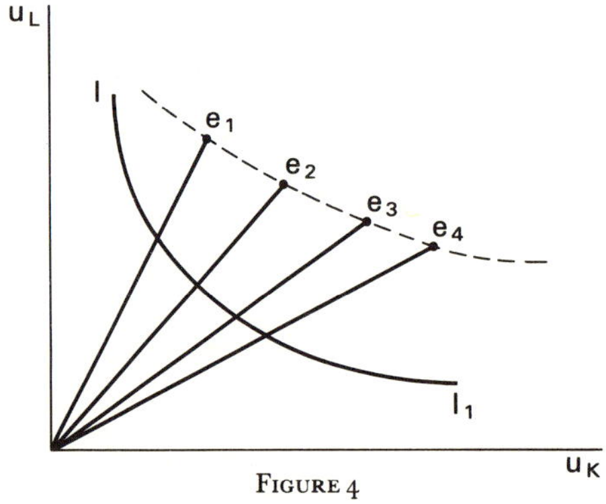

FIGURE 4

In this extreme case, observations with low capital per unit of output would have high efficiency and here the ranking would be exactly the opposite with $e4$, the least efficient being ranked the highest in terms of labour productivity.

An alternative way of looking at this feature is to say that proportionately the biggest gains to productive efficiency are likely to be achieved via increases in capital productivity. Simple log linear multiple regression relationships for the two years 1970 and 1980 yielded the results in Table V[12].

Once again, whilst one would not wish to place too much weight to the precise figures here, the coefficient on u_k is a good deal larger than that on u_L and has risen somewhat over the decade. This is a reflection of the fact that the capital/labour ratio has risen as we have seen. The 1980 Cobb-Douglas based productive efficiency estimates for example, suggest that at constant efficiency, a unit percentage change in capital requires a reduction in labour of 2.49 per cent; this elasticity is the ratio of the coefficient (elasticity) on capital to that on labour in Table II[13]. For 1970 the figure is 1.51.

[12] Strictly speaking, the linear regression model is inappropriate given that the dependent variable cannot exceed unity in value. Thus a 'Tobit' model is more appropriate.
[13] This aspect is analysed in greater detail in Todd [1984].

TABLE V
INDEPENDENT VARIABLE*

Dependent Variable		log u_L	log u_k	$\bar{R}^2$
log e_F	1970	−0.198	−0.764	0.982
log e_F	1980	−0.174	−0.804	0.975
log e_{CD}	1970	−0.323	−0.687	0.844
log e_{CD}	1980	−0.259	−0.811	0.954

* All coefficients were significant at the one per cent level.

Referring back to Table II we see again that the coefficients on capital are much larger than those on labour and the 1980 figure has increased. This all suggests therefore that technical progress in West German Manufacturing over this period and on average is more likely to have been non-neutral and capital augmenting. The underlying production function has shifted in a more capital intensive manner.

If the market is operating reasonably well as an allocator of resources available, it would be comforting to know that those industries which improve or maintain productive performance see this reflected in their position in the market. In order to look at this, changes in market share between 1970 and 1980 were compared with changes in static productive efficiency assessed relative to the revealed 'best practice' frontiers.

Out of the 32 sectors examined, 15 increased or had unchanged marked share over the period. Of these, 12 showed an increase in productive performance, one of which remained on the frontier in both years. Thirteen industries experienced both a decline in market share and productive performance which leaves a remaining seven sectors where the direction of change differs.

The picture overall is summarised below[14].

Industries showing increases in or maintained market share and productive performance	*Industries showing both a decline in market share and in productive performance*	*Industries which do not conform*		
			Change in Market share	*Change in efficiency*
4	2	1	−	0
8	3	6	+	−
9	5	7	−	+
10	11	15	+	−
18	12	17	+	−
21	13	20	−	+
24	14	30	−	+
25	16			
26	19			
27	22			
28	23			
32	29			
	31			

[14] The numerical key is that used in the Annex where the complete set of industries is listed.

In fairly general terms and referring back to the earlier observations made in Section V, the consistently declining sectors include more basic sectors of the iron and steel industries together with Shipbuilding. Included also are the two engineering sectors which appear to be weakening in terms of comparative advantage. Both of these, whilst having increases in output per employee of 1.86% in each case, experienced also a reduction in output per unit of capital of 2.6% for engineering and 3.34% for precision engineering.

Of the so-called 'non-conforming' sectors, textiles, oil refining, metal products and steel drawing have declined, but in a manner which is consistent with efficient use of inputs. The case of textiles is especially interesting insofar as gradual withdrawal of government support and encouragement of rationalisation, including scrapping of older vintage capital seems to have produced a desired result. Clearly industries can decline but remain successful in resource use. Subsidised sectors such as Aircraft and Aerospace exhibit the opposite tendency.

VI. CONCLUDING COMMENTS

The approach used in the major part of this exercise has a number of limitations. Being non-parametric it lies outside what might be called the more conventional statistical framework. It should be regarded as the title of this paper suggests, as one possible *characterisation* of productive performance; there are others.

Looking at the disaggregated picture, the results seem to be broadly consistent with the macro observation that manufacturing growth has slowed down[15]. The leading and declining sectors in Farrell efficiency terms have changed little over the past decade. The general impression therefore is one of a relatively slight movement only between the various sectors, with improvements in output per head being offset to some extent by declining capital productivity. The productive efficiency frontier moves inwards somewhat and drifts in a more capital intensive direction.

The set of comparative indices of productive efficiency for any year display considerable variability as the tables indicate. The static dispersions suggest substantial differences, being a reflection also of big differences between inputs per unit of output across the industry set. In a number of respects one would not wish to become over-committed to cardinal differences of this scale. The simple intercept adjusted Cobb-Douglas derived indices rank very closely with the Farrell set, hence an ordinal view of comparative performance seems to be a safer interpretation.

The comparisons are based on snapshots or static views of the industry set which obscures a more dynamic analysis. It is hoped that the latter will emerge from work which is continuing in this area.

Douglas Todd,
Brussels.

ACCEPTED MAY 1984

[15] See, for example, Klaus Hennings' Chapter 16 in Boltho [1982].

ANNEX

INDICES OF TECHNICAL EFFICIENCY AND FACTOR INPUT RATIOS 1970 AND 1980.

	1970			*1980*		
	L/V	K/V	e_F	L/V	K/V	e_F
1. Oil Refineries	3.1	0.86	1.00	2.50	0.90	1.00
2. Stone, Clay, Sand etc.	20.93	1.33	0.52	14.51	1.54	0.51
3. Iron and Steel Industries	24.71	2.14	0.35	19.42	2.49	0.33
4. Non Ferrous Metals	18.76	2.26	0.36	29.78	2.16	0.33
5. Iron and Steel Foundries	28.74	1.89	0.37	37.71	1.41	0.38
6. Non-Ferrous Metals Foundries	32.44	1.79	0.37	37.71	1.65	0.38
7. Steel Drawing and Cold Rolling Mills	16.80	0.95	0.71	12.47	1.03	0.72
8. Chemical Industry	18.26	1.83	0.42	12.37	1.74	0.47
9. Sawmills and Timber	27.96	1.30	0.49	18.08	1.41	0.52
10. Cellulose, Paper & Board	26.33	2.21	0.33	13.29	1.96	0.42
11. Rubber and Asbestos	32.75	1.07	0.53	23.27	1.32	0.51
12. Steel Forging	27.14	1.01	0.59	21.63	1.20	0.56
13. Steel Construction	37.61	0.83	0.63	32.84	1.11	0.56
14. Engineering	30.92	0.86	0.62	25.69	1.11	0.56
15. Vehicle Building & Repairs	22.68	1.11	0.58	19.47	1.26	0.56
16. Shipbuilding	35.45	1.46	0.42	26.25	1.87	0.38
17. Aircraft and Aerospace	21.81	0.65	0.95	34.37	0.54	0.98
18. Electrical Equipment	21.51	0.93	0.67	34.63	0.86	0.62
19. Precision Engineering	27.34	0.84	0.74	32.89	0.60	0.87
20. Metal Products	28.47	0.81	0.65	19.97	0.98	0.66
21. Office & Data Processing Machinery	31.49	1.00	0.56	14.19	1.10	0.67
22. Musical Instruments, Toys, Games	31.60	0.65	0.82	28.19	1.07	0.58
23. Fine Ceramics	45.56	1.29	0.41	38.47	1.58	0.39
24. Glass Industries	28.01	1.12	0.54	14.29	1.11	0.66
25. Wood Processing	14.16	0.62	1.00	19.13	0.53	1.00
26. Paper and Board	31.61	1.04	0.55	20.74	1.24	0.55
27. Printing	23.32	0.81	0.71	16.20	0.93	0.73
28. Plastics Manufacturing	29.04	0.93	0.60	19.02	1.03	0.65
29. Leather & Leather Products	36.30	0.89	0.59	32.84	1.25	0.49
30. Textiles	38.57	1.59	0.39	22.04	1.51	0.47
31. Clothing Industry	47.58	0.57	0.93	37.35	0.79	0.78
32. Food, Drink and Tobacco	14.06	1.03	0.70	9.04	1.03	0.77

REFERENCES

BOLTHO, A., 1982, *The European Economy* (Oxford).

BYATT, IAN, *et al.* 1982, 'North Sea Oil and Structural Adjustment', *Government Economic Service Working Paper*, No. 54, March.

DEBREU, G., 1951, 'The Coefficient of Resource Utilisation, *Econometrica*, 19, pp. 273–92.

FÄRE, R. and LOVELL, C. K., 1978, 'Measuring the Technical Efficiency of Production', *Journal of Economic Theory*, 19, pp. 150–62.

FARRELL, M. L., 1957, 'The Measurement of Productive Efficiency', *Journal of the Royal Statistics Society*, Series A, 120 (Part III), pp. 253–66.

FORSUND, F., and HJALMARSSON, L., 1974, 'On the Measurement of Productive Efficiency', *Swedish Journal of Economics*, 76 (No. 2), pp. 141–54.

Forsund, F., Lovell, C. K., and Schmidt, P., 1980, 'A Survey of Frontier Production Functions etc.', *Journal of Econometrics*, 13 (No. 1), pp. 5–25.

Frisch, R., 1965, '*The Theory of Production*' (Dordrecht: D. Reidel Publishing Co.).

Green, W. H., 1980, 'Maximum Likelihood Estimation of Econometric Frontier Functions', *Journal of Econometrics*, 13 (No. 1), pp. 27–56.

Hjalmarsson, L., 1973, 'Optimal Structural Change and Related Concepts', *Swedish Journal of Economics*, 75 (No. 2), pp. 176–92.

Kmenta, J., 1967, 'On Estimation of the CES Production Function', *International Economic Review*, 8, pp. 180–89, June.

Kopp, R. J., 1981, 'The Measurement of Productive Efficiency: A Reconsideration', *Quarterly Journal of Economics*, pp. 477–503, August.

Meller, P., 1976, 'Efficiency Frontiers for Industrial Establishments of Different Sizes', *Explorations in Economic Research*, Occasional Papers of National Bureau of Economic Research, 3, pp. 379–407.

Smith, V. L., 1961, '*Investment and Production*' (Cambridge, Mass.).

Todd, D., 1971, 'The Relative Efficiency of Small and Large Firms', *Research Report No. 18* of Committee of Inquiry on Small Firms, HMSO London.

Todd, D., 1977, 'Efficiency and Size', *Economic and Social Review*, 8 (No. 4), pp. 305–12.

Todd, D., 1984, 'Total Factor Productivity Growth and The Productivity Slowdown in the West German Industrial Sector, 1970–1981', *Economic Papers*, No. 32, Commission of the European Communities, Directorate-General for Economic and Financial Affairs, February.

THE JOURNAL OF INDUSTRIAL ECONOMICS 0022–1821 $2.00
Volume XXXIII March 1985 No. 3

TWO STAGE (PERFECT) EQUILIBRIUM IN HOTELLING'S MODEL

Damien Neven*

I. INTRODUCTION

Hotelling [1929] suggests that his spatial competition model can be used to describe a wide range of differentiation problems. He points to the selection of product variety within an industry as a potential application. Most of the subsequent work in his tradition has taken the equivalence of the two problems for granted. In this note, we look more closely at this equivalence. We distinguish between two types of differentiated products according to the variety of preferences assumed with respect to those products. Building on this distinction, we recognize that the demand faced by a firm locating on Hotelling's line is analogous to the demand faced by a firm selecting a horizontally differentiated product. It should be emphasized, thus, that the equivalence between the geographical and the product selection problem is by no means general and relies on specific assumptions about consumers' preferences.

Next, we formulate a small model, close to Hotelling's one in which firms select a horizontally differentiated product. Within this model, it will be shown that a pure strategy price equilibrium exists for every pair of products. This statement is to be contrasted with the results of d'Aspremont *et al.* [1979], who have shown that in the original Hotelling's setting an equilibrium fails to exist when firms are too close together.[1]

In addition, we will examine the product selection problem faced by firms in a two-stage game: in the first stage, each firm selects a product; in the second stage, the firm defines a price for its product.

We will seek the existence of a perfect equilibrium in this game. A perfect equilibrium in this context can be viewed as a Nash equilibrium in a game in which firms select a product, aware of the non-cooperative price equilibrium that will occur for each of their choices. It will be shown that contrary to Hotelling's principle, the two firms will maximise their differentiation (i.e. firms will locate at opposite ends of the market).

* I am grateful to D. Hay, L. Phlips and J. F. Thisse for helpful comments and to J. Kremers for many discussions. This paper builds upon part of my M.Phil. thesis at the University of Louvain. I wish to thank J.-F. Thisse and J. Jaskold Gabszewicz, whose supervision of this project was most stimulating.

[1] Several attempts have been made to overcome this difficulty. Usually, it is assumed that firms locate on a circle (see Salop [1979], Novshek [1980]), and/or alternative equilibrium concepts are used (Novshek [1980] and Novshek and Kohlberg [1982]).

II. TWO TYPES OF DIFFERENTIATION

In this journal, Phlips and Thisse [1982] emphasized the distinction between horizontal and vertical differentiation.[2] They assume that differentiated products can be viewed as bundles of characteristics and their exposition reads as follows: "the degree of differentiation can be expressed in two different ways. (i) Differentiation is said to be horizontal when the commodity comprises products that are differentiated in space or quality in the following manner: between two products, the level of some characteristics is augmented while it is lowered for some others, as in the case of different versions—called varieties—of a car" and "(ii) Differentiation is called vertical when the commodity refers to products that are differentiated in time or quality in the following manner: between two products the level of all characteristics is augmented or lowered, as in the case of cars of different series . . . there is unanimity to rank the products according to a certain order".

We shall take up their distinction and apply it in two ways. Firstly, we shall propose to draw this distinction without reference to a characteristics framework. Secondly, we shall extend the definition to sets of products.

Two products will be vertically differentiated if all consumers prefer a unit quantity of one of them to a unit quantity of the other. More generally, a set of products will be vertically differentiated if all consumers unanimously rank unit quantities of them. A set of vertically differentiated products can be thought of as a commodity sold in several qualities.[3] This type of differentiation has been extensively treated in a series of papers by Gabszewicz and Thisse [1979], [1980], [1982], Gabszewicz, Shaked, Sutton and Thisse [1982] and Shaked and Sutton [1981], [1982].

Two products will be horizontally differentiated if there is no consensus among consumers to prefer a unit quantity of one of them to a unit quantity of the other. Similarly, a set of products will be horizontally differentiated if there is no pair of products among them, such that a unit quantity of one of these two products is unanimously preferred by the consumers to a unit quantity of the other. A set of horizontally differentiated products can be thought of as a commodity sold in several varieties.[4]

Next, let us look at the analogy with Hotelling's spatial model. In this model, instead of having different preferences, consumers are located at different places. More specifically, it is assumed that they are evenly spread over a bounded interval of the real line. Each consumer purchases the same commodity and supports a transportation cost if this commodity is not available at its own location. (Hotelling assumes transportation costs linear in the

[2] The terminology already appears in Lancaster [1979], within a rather specific model, though. Much earlier, Chamberlin [1933], already formulated the idea behind the distinction drawn here (p. 173).

[3] "Quality" is sometimes used in the literature in a sense which does not imply a common ranking, e.g. Leland [1977] uses quality for what we call here "variety".

[4] Instead of variety, Lancaster [1979] uses "specification".

distance). A consumer is, therefore, not indifferent between a commodity available at its own location and a commodity available somewhere else, at the same price. Hence, two commodities available, for the same price, at different locations can be thought of as two differentiated products. Next, let us recognise that there is no pair of locations in Hotelling's model such that a commodity available at one of these two locations is unanimously preferred to a commodity available at the other, for the same price. This is straightforward as for any pair of locations (a, b), there is, under Hotelling's assumptions, at least one consumer located at a and one consumer located at b. These two consumers will certainly disagree on deciding whether a commodity available at a is better than a commodity available at b. No consensus can be reached and a set of commodities available at different locations in Hotelling's model is, therefore, analogous to a set of horizontally differentiated products.

It should be emphasized, thus, that Hotelling's location model cannot be used to describe the choice of product qualities. The analogy between his analysis and a product choice is limited to the problem of selecting product varieties.

III. THE MODEL

Let us assume that all the possible varieties of a product can be represented by a continuous variable x. Moreover, we assume that x belongs to the unit interval, which can be thought of as the "product line".

Consumers have different preferences with respect to the varieties. Still, we assume that each consumer will never purchase several units of a variety. The other goods available in the economy will be represented by a composite commodity (q). We assume that the preferences of all consumers with respect to this commodity are identical and strongly separable with respect to the differentiated product. Under these assumptions, the utility function of a consumer (i), can be written:

$$U_i = U(V_i, q) \tag{1}$$

We must specify the subutility function V_i, in such a way that the products will, indeed, be horizontally differentiated. The following set of conditions will be sufficient for this purpose:

(i) V_i is continuous and has a unique maximum.

(ii) $\forall x \in [0, 1]$, there is one and only one function V_i such that $V_i(x) = \max_x V_i(x)$.

Each consumer (i) will, thus, have a "most preferred" variety which we shall denote x^*. In turn, every variety is "most preferred" by a consumer. Each consumer can, therefore, be indexed by his most preferred variety and (1) can be written:

$$U_{x^*}(x, q) = U(V_{x^*}(x), q) \tag{2}$$

In addition, we shall assume that the subutility functions $V_{x^*}(x)$ have the same functional form, for every x^*. Each consumer will maximise (2) under the following budget constraint: $P_x + q = Y$, in which Y stands for income (same for all consumers), P_x for the price of the variety x and in which it is assumed that the price of the composite good is one. We assume that the marginal utility of income is also unity, so that (2) is written:

$$U_{x^*}(x, q) = V_{x^*}(x) + q.$$

As the utility function is strongly separable, this maximisation problem can be split into two stages. In the first stage, each consumer decides on the allocation of this income between the composite good and the differentiated product. The decision taken at this first stage can be illustrated by a conditional indirect utility function:

$$L_{x^*}(x) = V_{x^*}(x) + (Y - P_x)$$

Each consumer will buy a differentiated product if he can find a variety x such that $L_{x^*}(x)$ is higher than Y (i.e. $(V_{x^*}(x) - P_x)$ is positive). In order to be as close as possible to Hotelling, we will assume that it is, indeed, the case. In other words, each consumer will always purchase a differentiated product; the outcome of the first stage maximisation is the same for all consumers. In the second stage, each consumer (x^*) selects a variety by maximising $L_{x^*}(x)$. Finally, we specify $V(x)$ and re-write $L_{x^*}(x)$ accordingly:

$$L_{x^*}(x) = [a - b(x - x^*)^2] + [Y - P_x]$$

This function specifies the "utility cost" suffered by a consumer purchasing a variety x at price P_x, different from his most preferred one. The parameter a gives the utility level achieved by a consumer purchasing his most preferred variety at zero price and b can be thought of as the "utility cost" of moving in the product space apart from his most preferred variety. This function is, then, the equivalent of a transportation cost function in a geographical space. Contrary to Hotelling who assumes a linear cost function, we use a quadratic form. The shape of the cost function is crucial to establish the existence of a price equilibrium. The quadratic form, however, seems more natural than the linear one when consumers "move" in a product space. At least, it seems reasonable to assume that the marginal disutility of "moving" on the product line is increasing.

Finally, we assume a uniform distribution of tastes; consumers, uniquely characterised by their most preferred variety, are supposed to be evenly distributed over the interval [0, 1].

On the supply side, we maintain the usual assumptions of two firms and constant marginal cost of production (zero without loss of generality), and like Hotelling, we will stick to the case in which each firm markets a single product.

IV. STATEMENT OF RESULTS

We will first look at a price equilibrium, holding product varieties fixed, i.e. we will compute a Nash equilibrium in price for every pair of products chosen by the firms. Let x_1, x_2 be the products chosen by firm 1 and 2 respectively; x_1, $x_2 \in [0, 1]$, $x_1 < x_2$.

In order to define the market shares of the two firms, we compute the "marginal consumer", i.e. the consumer just indifferent between purchasing product 1 and 2, for given pairs of prices and products. This marginal consumer x' is such that $L_{x'}(x_1) = L_{x'}(x_2)$.

An easy computation leads:

$$x' = \frac{(1/b)(P_2 - P_1) - (x_1^2 - x_2^2)}{2(x_2 - x_1)}$$

It can be easily checked that x' remains well defined even if it is greater than x_2 or less than x_1. We can, therefore, write the profit functions in the following way:

$$R_1 = P_1 x' M \tag{3}$$

$$R_2 = P_2(1 - x')M \tag{4}$$

Where M is the density of consumers (uniform), R_1 is the profit function of firm 1 and R_2 the profit function of firm 2.[5]

The first proposition can be stated as follows:

Proposition 1: for any given value of x_1 and x_2, there is a unique Nash equilibrium (P_1', P_2') in the two person game with players 1 and 2, strategies $P_1 \in S_1 = [0, \infty)$ and $P_2 \in S_2 = S_1$, and payoff functions given by (3)–(4).

Proof: the payoff functions (3)–(4) are continuous and twice differentiable everywhere. (Contrary to Hotelling's piecewise functions). The first order conditions for this problem can then be written:

$$\frac{M[P_2/b - 2P_1/b - (x_1^2 - x_2^2)]}{2(x_2 - x_1)} = 0 \tag{5}$$

$$M\left(1 + \frac{[P_1/b - 2P_2/b + (x_1^2 - x_2^2)]}{2(x_2 - x_1)}\right) = 0 \tag{6}$$

An equilibrium in this game is a pair of prices (P_1', P_2') satisfying the simultaneous equations (5)–(6). We first solve (6) for P_2 as a function of P_1: $P_2(P_1)$. We substitute this function in (5). Reducing it in P_1, we get P_1', the optimal

[5] Writing these profit functions, we effectively restrict x' to the interval $[0, 1]$. We, therefore, narrow the strategy set of each firm to prices implying that x' belongs to $[0, 1]$. Still, the stragegies excluded could never be optimal as they are dominated by the strategies implying $x' = 0$ or $x' = 1$.

strategy for 1. Finally, $P_2(P'_1)$ gives the optimal strategy for 2. This equilibrium pair of prices is given by:

$$P'_1 = (x_2 - x_1)2b/3 + (x_2^2 - x_1^2)b/3 \quad (7)$$

$$P'_2 = (x_2 - x_1)4b/3 - (x_2^2 - x_1^2)b/3 \quad (8)$$

It is easy to check that the second derivatives of the profit functions are both negative. Consequently, the second order conditions are satisfied. Moreover, for any given x_1 and x_2, (P'_1, P'_2) is the unique vector of prices satisfying (5) and (6) simultaneously. The equilibrium is therefore unique. It is also apparent from these equations that, when firms choose the same product, the Bertrand solution occurs. Both firms charge zero price at the equilibrium and no profit is earned.

We will now consider a two-stage game in which each firm selects a product in the first stage and defines a price for this product in the second stage. We will look for a perfect equilibrium in this sequential game. The strategy set of player 1 and 2 in this game will be denoted as S_1 and S_2: S_1 and S_2 are redefined as:

$$S_1 = \mathop{\times}_{i=1}^{2} S_{1i}$$

$$S_2 = \mathop{\times}_{i=1}^{2} S_{2i}$$

S_{ij} being the strategy set of player i in stage j.

and $S_{11} = \{x_1/x_1 \in [0, 1]\}$

$S_{21} = \{x_2/x_2 \in [0, 1]\}$

$S_{12} = S_{22} = [0, \infty]$ as before.

A sequence of strategies for player i will be denoted by $f_i = (x_i, P_i)$. Accordingly, $f = (f_1, f_2)$ will be a strategy combination. The second proposition can now be stated as follows:

Proposition 2: in the two person, two stage game, in which the sequence of strategies of player 1, $f_1 \in S_1$ and the sequence of strategies of player 2, $f_2 \in S_2$, and the payoff functions are given by (3)–(4), the unique perfect equilibrium is the strategy combination $f = [(0, b), (1, b)]$.

Proof: A strategy combination, f, is in perfect equilibrium if its restriction to any subgame is in Nash equilibrium (see Selten, [1956]). According to this definition, (x'_1, P'_1, x'_2, P'_2) will be a perfect equilibrium if $(x'_1(P'_1, P'_2), x'_2(P'_1, P'_2))$ is a Nash equilibrium in the first stage where (P'_1, P'_2) is the equilibrium vector of prices in the second stage. The payoff functions of this subgame are given by:

$$R_1' = Mb[(x_2 - x_1)2/9 + (x_2^2 - x_1^2)(2/9 + 1/18(x_1 + x_2))] \tag{9}$$

$$R_2' = Mb[(x_2 - x_1)8/9 - (x_2^2 - x_1^2)(4/9 - 1/18(x_1 + x_2))] \tag{10}$$

where we have substituted the price equilibrium equations (7)–(8) into the payoff functions (3)–(4).

The first-order conditions for this problem are given by the usual $K - T$ conditions of firm 1 maximising (9) subject to $x_1 \in [0, 1]$ and firm 2 maximising (10) subject to $x_2 \in [0, 1]$. These conditions can be written as:

$$A = Mb/9[2 + 4x_1 - 1/2(x_2^2 - x_1^2) + (x_1 + x_2)x_1] + u_1 > 0$$

$$x_1 A = 0$$

$$x_1, u_1 > 0, \quad u_1(x_1 - 1) = 0$$

$$B = Mb/9[-8 + 8x_2 - (x_1 + x_2)x_2 - 1/2(x_2^2 + x_1^2)] + u_2 > 0$$

$$x_2 B = 0$$

$$x_2, u_2 > 0, \quad u_2(x_2 - 1) = 0$$

It can be easily checked that $x_1 = 0$, $x_2 = 1$, $u_1 = 0$, $u_2 = Mb3/18$ are the only values satisfying these conditions. Moreover, it is easy to verify that (9) is concave in x_1 and (10) is concave in x_2. Consequently, the maximum characterised by these values is global.

$x_1' = 0$, $x_2' = 1$ is therefore a Nash equilibrium in the subgame defined above and the prices corresponding to this pair of products are given by $P_1' = P_2' = b$ (substitute $x_1 = 0$, $x_2 = 1$ in (7)–(8)).

Consequently, the strategy combination $f = [(0, b), (1, b)]$ is a perfect equilibrium, i.e. the two firms locate at opposite ends of the market and charge the same price. Moreover, the equilibrium strategies are uniquely defined in each stage. This guarantees the uniqueness of the equilibrium.[6]

V. CONCLUSIONS

A first conclusion emerging from this note is that the non-existence-result due to d'Aspremont *et al.* [1979] in Hotelling's model can be naturally avoided when firms locate in product space instead of geographical space.

The existence of a price equilibrium enables us to examine the location tendencies of the firms in a sequential game. In the recent literature, the

[6] Uniqueness follows, partly, from the assumption that $x_1 < x_2$ (this assumption is embodied in the profit functions (3)–(4)). Without this restriction, there will be two similar equilibria with the two firms located at the extremities of the market. This is simply a question of labelling the firms and the equilibrium configuration would still be unique.

location problem has been tackled mainly through a simultaneous price-location game (see Novshek [1980], Kohlberg and Novshek [1982], Lancaster [1979]). Still, the behavioural assumption behind this price-location game seems rather myopic. In this specification, the firms do not take full account of the interdependence between their price and location strategies. On the contrary, the perfect equilibrium in a sequential game can be viewed as an equilibrium in a location game in which the firms are perfectly aware of the price equilibrium that will occur for each of their strategies. To the extent that behavioural interpretations of equilibrium points are meaningful, this solution can be considered as a kind of rational expectations equilibrium.

The conclusion reached in this sequential game can be stated as a "maximum differentiation" behaviour. Firms tend to relax price competition through product differentiation. This result appears to be consistent with Hotelling's basic observation that firms effectively avoid the zero profit Bertrand solution through some kind of differentiation. Moreover, Shaked and Sutton (1981) reach a similar conclusion in a context of vertical product differentiation. Consequently, it seems to us that this differentiation behaviour could be fairly general.

Damien Neven,
Nuffield College,
Oxford, OX1 1NJ

ACCEPTED JANUARY 1984

REFERENCES

D'ASPREMONT C., JASKOLD-GABSZEWICZ, J. and THISSE, J.-F., 1979, 'On Hotelling's Stability in Competition', *Econometrica*, 47, pp. 1145–50.

CHAMBERLIN, EDWARD, 1933, *The Theory of Monopolistic Competition*, (Harvard University Press, Cambridge).

HOTELLING, H., 1929, 'Stability in Competition', *Economical Journal*, 39, pp. 41–57.

JASKOLD GABSZEWICZ, J. and THISSE, J.-F., 1979, 'Price Competition, Quality and Income Disparities', *Journal of Economic Theory*, 20, pp. 340–59.

JASKOLD GABSZEWICZ, J. and THISSE, J.-F., 1980, 'Entry (and Exit) in a Differentiated Industry', *Journal of Economic Theory*, 22, pp. 327–38.

JASKOLD GABSZEWICZ, J. and THISSE, J.-F., 1982, 'Product Differentiation with Income Disparities: An Illustrative Model', *Journal of Industrial Economics*, 31, pp. 115–29.

JASKOLD GABSZEWICZ, J., SHAKED, A., SUTTON, J. and THISSE, J.-F., 1982, Segmenting the Market: The Monopolist's Optimal Product Mix, CORE discussion paper 8242.

KOHLBERG, E. and NOVSHEK, W., 1982, 'Equilibrium in a Simple Price-Location Model', *Economics Letters*, 9, pp. 7–15.

LANCASTER, K., 1979, *Variety, Equity and Efficiency*, (B. Blackwell, Oxford).

LELAND H., 1977, 'Quality Choice and Competition', *American Economic Review*, 67, pp. 127–35.

NOVSHEK, W., 1980, 'Equilibrium in Simple Spatial (or Differentiated Product) Models', *Journal of Economic Theory*, 22, pp. 313–26.

Philips, L. and Thisse, J.-F., 1982, 'Spatial Competition and the Theory of Differentiated Products: An Introduction', *The Journal of Industrial Economics*, 31, pp. 1–11.

Salop, S., 1979, 'Monopolistic Competition With Outside Goods', *Bell Journal of Economics*, 10, pp. 141–56.

Selten, R., 1956, Spieltheoretische Behandlung eines oligopomodels mit Nachtfragetragheit, *Zeitschrift fur die Gesamte Staatswissenschaft*, Bd 121, 301–24 and 667–89.

Shaked, A. and Sutton, J., 1981, Natural Oligopolies, ICERD Discussion paper 35, London School of Economics.

———, 1982, 'Anti-Hotelling: Relaxing Price Competition Through Product Differentiation', *Review of Economic Studies*, 44, pp. 3–13.

THE JOURNAL OF INDUSTRIAL ECONOMICS 0022–1821 $2.00
Volume XXXIII March 1985 No. 3

GROWTH, ACQUISITION ACTIVITY AND FIRM SIZE: EVIDENCE FROM THE UNITED KINGDOM*

M. S. KUMAR

INTRODUCTION

THIS PAPER provides new empirical evidence on the relationship between size, growth and acquisition activity of quoted companies in the United Kingdom. The evidence is based on some two thousand companies and covers the period 1960–76. There has been no detailed systematic study for this period. The results suggest some revisions to generally accepted views in the area and they have certain implications for industrial and competition policy pursued in the U.K. and the factors affecting aggregate concentration. The paper is arranged as follows: Section I considers the broader economic context for the study whilst Section II notes some *a priori* expectations regarding the relationship between size and growth, and size and acquisition activity. Sections III–V present empirical evidence and the last section provides a summary and policy implications of the results.

I. THE ECONOMIC CONTEXT

Examining the rise in Industrial Concentration in the Post War period, Prais in a major study concluded the following:

> "The observed rise of 19 percentage points in the share of the hundred largest firms in the period 1949–70 (from 22 to 41 percent) may be divided into a portion to be expected from the general diffusion process and amounting to some 10 percentage points or half of the total rise, and the remaining half to be attributed to the systematic factors which have particularly favoured the growth of large concerns in this period." (Prais [1976, p. 37]).

Hannah and Kay [1977], and the authors of the Review of Monopolies and Mergers Policy [1978], seem to accept this position. Whilst there is some evidence of a positive size-growth relationship for the 1950s, there is no conclusive evidence for the period since 1960. There are two studies which suggest a positive relationship: (i) Utton [1972] for 1954–65 and (ii) Samuels and Chesher [1972] for 1960–69. Equally, however, three other studies (i) Aaronovitch and Sawyer [1975] for 1958–67 (ii) Smyth *et al.* [1975] for 1971–73

* I am grateful to Ajit Singh, Alan Hughes, Bruce Lyons, Geoffrey Meeks, the Editor of the Journal and an anonymous referee, for helpful comments and suggestions. The usual caveat applies.

and Meeks and Whittington [1976] for 1964–69 indicate a negative relationship. All these studies, however, cover limited samples of firms, are based on rather limited time periods, or generally consider growth measured by one or two variables only. The first main objective of this paper is to provide comprehensive evidence for the size-growth relationship for a large population of UK quoted firms for the period 1960–76, using a range of variables.

With regard to the relationship between size and growth by acquisition, there is again no conclusive evidence for the recent period. For example, Aaronovitch and Sawyer [1975] find no significant relationship between the two variables for their sample of large firms for the period 1958–67, but find a positive relationship for the sub-period 1963–67 [p. 141]. The Monopolies Commission Survey [1970] suggests a positive relationship for 1958–68, but its methodology suffers from the 'regression' bias. Utton [1972, p. 193] using similar data but a more appropriate methodology finds an inverse relationship. In view of the diversity of findings, the second objective of this paper is to investigate the relationship between size and growth by acquisition. In addition, evidence is presented on serial correlation in growth rate.

II.1. SIZE AND GROWTH OF FIRMS

There are a number of analytical frameworks within which one can examine the relationship between the size and growth of firms. (See for example, Singh and Whittington [1975]). One main framework which has been used extensively in the literature, and which provides an explicit link between the size and growth of firms and concentration in the economy is the Stochastic Framework (see Hay and Morris [1979, pp. 501–508]). This postulates that the growth of firms is a random process; whilst there may be a large number of systematic factors affecting growth, collectively they exercise only a limited influence on firms' proportionate growth. (For further discussion see Hart [1962]).

There are a number of models which have been fitted into this general framework. Of these, the simplest is the Law of Proportionate Effect (LPE). It has three main propositions: (i) that firms of different size classes have the same average proportionate growth; (ii) that the dispersion of growth rates about the common mean is the same for all size classes; and (iii) that there is no serial correlation in growth rates.

Our main purpose is to test the extent to which the first proposition is valid (although evidence is provided on the second and the third propositions as well). In the past, it has often been empirically tested by estimating the following model:

$$(1) \qquad \log S_{t+1} = \alpha + \beta \log S_t + U_t$$

where S_t is a measure of firm size at time t, and U_t is a homoscedastic error term. If $\beta = 1$, this means that the proposition can be sustained. If $\beta > 1$, this means that systematic factors favour large firms and that they grow faster than small firms; $\beta < 1$ implies the opposite, that is, small firms grow faster than large ones. However, as Chesher [1979] has argued, proposition (iii) is unlikely to hold in practice, and tests using equation (1) may yield inconsistent estimates of β (see Section 4 for further discussion).

Concerning the change in aggregate concentration, and the size—growth relationship, it is worth noting that from (1) we can obtain the following:

$$\text{Var}(\log S_{t+1}) = \beta^2 \text{Var}(\log S_t) + \text{Var}(U_t) \tag{2}$$

According to one measure, concentration increases between period t and $t+1$, if the following holds:

$$\frac{\text{Var}(\log S_{t+1})}{\text{Var}(\log S_t)} > 1 \tag{3}$$

From (2) this yields the following condition:

$$\text{Var}(U_t) > (1 - \beta^2)\,\text{Var}(\log S_t) \tag{4}$$

since Var $(U_t) > 0$, (Var $(U_t) = 0$ if there is no variability in growth rates across firms), if the first proposition of LPE holds (i.e. $\beta = 1$), concentration will increase over time. *A fortiori* concentration will also increase if $\beta > 1$. More interestingly, even if $\beta < 1$, concentration may still increase, if Var (U_t) is sufficiently large relative to Var (S_t), so that (4) continues to hold. (See Kalecki [1945 pp. 161–62]).

II.2. SIZE AND ACQUISITION ACTIVITY

The overall growth of firms consists of internal growth (due to new investment) and acquisition growth. That overall growth may satisfy the propositions of LPE does not necessarily mean that acquisition growth, and internal growth each satisfy LPE individually, since deviations from the LPE may cancel each other to satisfy the LPE (see Ijiri and Simon, [1977, p. 193]).

Whilst there has been a considerable analysis of the determinants of acquisition growth, its relationship with firm size has received much less attention. There are some factors which suggest a positive relationship, whilst others suggest a negative one. The former is suggested by the following types of factors: There may be high fixed costs involved in searching for suitable acquisitions, in obtaining the technical, marketing and other relevant information concerning them, and in actually making the purchase. Large firms may be better placed to bear these costs (Lynch [1971]). Opportunities for acquisitions may also be greater for larger firms, for example, because of their ability to undertake acquisitions overseas. They are also much more likely to have the 'Multi-Divisional' ('M') form structure and it would be easier to incorporate the operations of the acquired firm into the existing operations, than in the 'Unitary' ('U') form structure of the majority of small and medium sized firms (see Scherer [1980]). This is because within the 'M' form it need not be necessary to assimilate the operations of the taken-over firm—the latter could operate as a subsidiary with considerable autonomy. Lastly, to the extent that larger firms are more active in diversification, acquisitions would offer a convenient method of doing so (see Kumar [1984]).

A number of other factors suggest large firms may not necessarily exhibit greater acquisition activity than smaller firms. The most important of these is when inducement to grow arises from new products or new technology. Due to indivisibilities, large firms are considered to be more likely to undertake their own research and development, and to develop new processes and products. These may generally be exploited best if the firm itself undertakes investment embodying the new techniques, or manufactures and markets the products itself. But this will only decrease the desire or ability of large firms to grow by acquisition if there is a limited capacity to manage overall growth. (See Meeks [1977] and Kumar [1981]). Finally, it is worth noting that if, as is sometimes suggested, smaller firms are more 'dynamic', they may grow faster than other firms by both acquisitions and by new investment (*cf.* Newbould and Luffmann [1978]).

In view of these factors, on *a priori* grounds, it is difficult to predict whether in general one set of factors would predominate. However, in terms of the importance of the first set of factors, and the general impression provided by the existing literature, it would not be unwarranted to expect a positive relationship between size and growth by acquisition.

III.1. DATA

The data used in the empirical analysis are obtained from the Company Accounts Data-bank in Cambridge.[1] These data are very carefully prepared and provide one of the best sources of information available on quoted UK companies. The companies were engaged in manufacturing industry, or a limited range of services including wholesale, retail and transport, within the UK. Our objective was to study the seventeen year period 1960–76 inclusive (1976 was the last year for which records were available). However, due to the vast merger wave in the 1960s and early 1970s, the number of firms surviving this period was a small proportion of the firms continuing for any given, shorter, sub-period.[2] Accordingly, the period was divided into three sub-periods, and three populations of firms surviving over these periods were studied: population 1 consisted of 1747 firms which survived with records in the data-bank from 1960–65, population 2 was the 1021 companies which survived from 1966–71 and population 3 was the 824 companies which sur-

[1] I am grateful to Dr G. Meeks and Esmee Fairbairn Charitable Trust for allowing me access to this Data-bank. For details of the Data-bank, see Meeks [1977].

[2] In addition there is a size criterion which excluded the smallest firms, in 1969 and 1974.

vived from 1972–76. In addition two populations surviving over longer periods were studied, viz 1960–71 and 1966–76 (denoted by 1′ and 2′ respectively): (see Appendix).[3] Studying the sub-periods separately gives a considerably greater number of firms than if we consider the period as a whole. The benefit of this is that it provides a good cross section of firms; if we consider only the population of firms surviving the seventeen year period, it will be biased towards larger firms. (Typically, in the merger wave a very large number of small and medium sized firms were taken over).

III.2. VARIABLES

The variables used for each company were as follows:

a. Size Measures[4]

1. Net Assets: Total assets less current liabilities (as measured in the balance sheet).
2. Physical Assets: This includes tangible fixed assets (net of depreciation) and stocks and work in progress.
3. Equity Assets: Total issued capital (ordinary), plus capital and revenue reserves plus future tax reserves.
4. Employees.
5. Sales.

b. Growth Measure

1. Total growth: This is calculated as size in period $t + 1$ as a proportion of size in period t.
2. Growth by acquisition: This is calculated as expenditure on acquisitions of new subsidiaries as a proportion of opening size (measured by net assets).

IV. SIZE AND GROWTH: EMPIRICAL EVIDENCE

There are a number of ways of estimating the systematic relationship between firm size and growth. In the past it has been estimated by applying OLS to equation (1). As noted above, Chesher [1979] has shown that this may lead to inconsistent estimates of the parameter β. It is important to note, however, that the inconsistency arises from serial correlation in the error term in (1).

[3] The population of firms, surviving over the entire period 1960–76, was also examined. Some results using this are noted below.

[4] For the first two size measures, revaluations of assets were excluded from 1968 onwards (when data on revaluations became available). Since companies were not required to publish figures on sales or employees before the 1967 Companies Act, size measures 4 and 5 are only available for population 3 (covering the period 1972–76). The acquisition growth rates were calculated on an annual basis and the arithmetic average of the annual values was then calculated over the relevant period. For the appropriateness of this variable, see Meeks and Whittington [1975].

The shorter the time period over which growth is examined, *ceteris paribus*, the higher the persistency of growth rates, and so the greater the probability of inconsistency. Conversely the *longer* the unit of time, the smaller the serial correlation in growth, and the less unreliable the estimates obtained by using this equation.[5] Since in our case, estimates are obtained for an average of at least five years, inconsistency using equation (1) is unlikely to be of import.[6]

Nevertheless, for the main results, past growth, to account for serial correlation, was incorporated and the following equation was estimated using OLS:

$$\text{(4)} \qquad \log\,(Si,_{t}/Si,_{t-1}) = \alpha + \beta \log Si,_{t-1} + \gamma \log\,(Si,_{t-2}) + \varepsilon_{it}$$

where S is a measure of firm size and, t, $t-1$ and $t-2$ refer to 1976, 1971 and 1966 (or 1971, 1966 and 1960) respectively. This equation postulates that proportionate growth (approximately) over the period $t-1$ to t is a function of size at time $t-1$ and proportionate growth in the period $t-2$ to $t-1$.[7]

TABLE I
REGRESSION RESULTS
Equation: $\log\,(Si,_{t}/Si,_{t-1}) = \alpha + \beta \log Si,_{t-1} + \gamma \log\,(Si,_{t-1}/Si,_{t-2}) + \varepsilon_{it}$

Time period	*Size measure*	$\hat{\alpha}$	$\hat{\beta}$	$S\varepsilon(\hat{\beta})$	$\hat{\gamma}$	$S\varepsilon(\hat{\gamma})$	$\bar{R}^2$
1960–71							
	Net assets	0.08	−0.003	0.002	0.11*	0.03	0.02
	Physical assets	0.82	−0.04*	0.01	0.07*	0.03	0.02
	Equity assets	0.54	−0.02	0.01	0.08*	0.03	0.01
1966–76							
	Net assets	1.12	−0.05*	0.01	0.12*	0.03	0.04
	Physical assets	1.13	−0.04*	0.01	0.07*	0.03	0.02
	Equity assets	1.20	−0.05*	0.01	0.09*	0.03	0.03

Notes: For 1960–71, $Si,_{t}$, $Si,_{t-1}$ and $Si,_{t-2}$ denote size in 1971, 1966 and 1960 respectively. For 1966–76 $Si,_{t}$, $Si,_{t-1}$ and $Si,_{t-2}$ denote size in 1976, 1971 and 1966 respectively.
The sample included 832 and 694 firms for 1960–71 and 1966–76 respectively.
* indicates significantly different from zero at the 5% level.

The results of fitting this equation to the two populations of firms, 1′ and 2′, surviving over 1960–71, and 1966–76, respectively are given in Table I. For both time periods, and for the three size measures, the coefficient on opening size is negative. For the more recent period, it is significantly different from 0 on all three size measures. These results are contrary to the belief that during the intense acquisition activity of the 1960s, large firms grew faster than small ones, mainly due to their reliance on acquisition.[8] They also contrast with the results obtained by Singh and Whittington [1975] for an earlier period. Using

[5] This can be seen from Table I in Chesher [1979, p. 406].
[6] This was confirmed in a private correspondence with Andrew Chesher.
[7] The equation was first estimated by Singh and Whittington [1975] for analysis of firm growth in the 1950s.
[8] There was found to be negligible heteroscedasticity, using the Spearman's Rank Correlation test, and the Glejser test. (Detailed results are available from the author).

Table II
Regression Results
Equation: $\log Si,_t = \alpha + \beta \log Si,_{t-1} + \varepsilon i,_t$

		All industries			
		Coefficients		*s. error*	
Size measure	*Population*	$\hat{\alpha}$	$\hat{\beta}$	$\hat{\beta}$	$\bar{R}^2$
Net assets	1	0.77	0.96*	0.01	0.88
	2	0.70	0.96	0.02	0.79
	3	0.29	0.93*	0.01	0.85
Physical assets	3	1.24	0.95*	0.01	0.91
Equity assets	3	1.71	0.90*	0.02	0.78
Employees	3	0.32	0.96	0.02	0.79
Sales	3	0.96	0.99	0.01	0.92

Notes: $\hat{\beta}$ in this Table is equivalent to $(1 + \hat{\beta})$ in Table I.
* indicates significantly different from unity at the 5% level.

net assets as a measure of size they found a weak positive relationship between firm size and growth over the period 1948–60.

A sharper contrast between the 1950s, and the more recent period, is in the serial correlation of growth rates. Singh and Whittington obtained an estimate of around 0.30, compared to our estimate of 0.12. This difference may be due to two factors: (i) With the increasing international integration of UK's industries, domestic environment has become less certain. This may make planning by firms to maintain some stable growth path more difficult, and so lead to a lower inter-temporal persistency in growth rates. (ii) There has been a sharp increase in growth by acquisition in firms' overall growth in the period since 1960. It may be argued that acquisition growth by its very nature, is unlikely to be as persistent as internal growth (*cf.* Ijiri and Simon [1977]). If the two forms of growth are not substitutes, this would lower persistency in overall growth.

Finally, results of fitting equation (1) to populations (1) to (3) are given in Table II.[9] In general they show that $\hat{\beta}$ was significantly less than unity for the different populations of firms.[10] There are two additional interesting features: (i) There is no evidence that the capital/labour ratio of larger firms has been increasing over time. For population (3), employment grew faster for smaller firms, but the growth in their capital employed (measured by net assets or physical assets) was greater still. (ii) As might be expected, in relation to capital employed, large firms did show a relatively faster growth in sales.

[9] It was not possible to fit the preferred equation (4) to these populations, because of data constraints. Note that in view of the low serial correlation found in Table I, the estimates are likely to be quite reliable.

[10] There was evidence of mild heteroscedasticity in this equation, but correcting for it did not alter the significance of the results. (Results available from the author). This equation was also fitted to the population of firms surviving over the entire period 1960–76; OLS estimate of $\hat{\beta}$, using net assets as a measure of size, was 0.84 with standard error of 0.02; it was significantly less than unity.

V. SIZE AND ACQUISITION GROWTH

The main equation used to examine the effect of size on growth by acquisition also incorporated serial correlation in acquisition growth. It had the following form:

$$(5) \qquad g^A_{i,t} = \alpha + \beta \log S_{i,t} + \gamma g^A_{i,t-1} + \varepsilon i_t$$

where $g^A_{i,t}$ and $g^A_{i,t-1}$ refer to acquisition growth over the period 1966–71 and 1960–65 respectively (or 1972–76 and 1966–71) and $S_{i,t}$ refers to firm size in 1966 (or 1972). The null hypothesis would be that $\beta = 0$, and the alternate hypothesis is that $\beta > 0$. The data used were for populations 1′ and 2′, and the results are given in Table III. They show that for firms in all industries, with serial correlation taken into account, there is a slight positive relationship between size and acquisition for the period 1960–71, but a negative one for the period 1966–76 ($\hat{\beta}$ equals 0.08 and -0.31 for the two periods respectively).

There is a noticeable difference in the firms in manufacturing industries, and those in non-manufacturing. (This includes non-financial service industries). For both periods there is a negative size-acquisition relationship in manufacturing which is statistically significant at the 5 percent level in the second period. However, there was evidence of heteroscedasticity in the second period; correcting for it made the result barely significant at the 10 percent level.

As for the size-growth relationship, an analysis was also undertaken of the size-acquistion relationship for each of the three populations 1–3, over shorter time periods. The equation fitted was of the following form:[11]

$$(6) \qquad g^A_{i,t} = \alpha + \beta \log S_{i,t} + \varepsilon_{it}$$

where $g^A_{i,t}$ = average growth by acquisition over the periods 1960–65, 1966–71 or 1972–76; and S_{it} = firm size in 1960, 1966 or 1972 (ε_{it}, as before, is the error term). The results showed that for non-manufacturing, there was now a negative relationship for the first two periods and a mild positive one for the third. For firms in manufacturing, and for 'all firms', there was a weak negative relationship, which was significant at the 5 percent level for the sample of all firms during 1960–65, and for firms in manufacturing during 1971–76. To the extent than any generalisation about the results is possible, it has to be a negative one: In the period under consideration, there was no tendency for large firms to grow faster by acquisition than small ones.

Table III also provides estimates of serial correlation in acquisition growth ($\hat{\gamma}$); it is significant for 'all firms' in both periods. Interestingly, its magnitude for firms in manufacturing in the first period is considerable, and it is greater than that for total growth (see Table I). This supports the view that a substantial number of firms do adopt acquisitions as a regular strategy, and attain

[11] As in the earlier case, it was not possible to fit the preferred equation (5) to these populations, because of data constraints.

TABLE III
GROWTH BY ACQUISITION AND FIRM SIZE
$g^A_{i,t} = \alpha + \beta \log Si,_t + \gamma g^A_{i,t-1} + \varepsilon it$

Time period	n	Section	$\hat{\alpha}$	$\hat{\beta}$	$SE(\hat{\beta})$	γ	$SE(\hat{\gamma})$	$\bar{R}^2$
1960–71	635	Manufacturing	3.46	−0.09	0.39	0.32*	0.03	0.04
	197	Non-Manufacturing	0.25	0.38	0.43	0.01	0.04	0.004
	832	All Industries	2.58	0.08	0.32	0.17*	0.04	0.02
1966–76	510	Manufacturing	7.56	−0.49*	0.25	0.03	0.02	0.01
	184	Non-Manufacturing	−0.91	9.52	0.55	0.10*	0.04	0.04
	694	All Industries	0.10	−0.31	0.23	0.05*	0.02	0.01

Notes: For 1960–71 $g^A_{i,t}$ and $g^A_{i,t-1}$ denote growth by acquision over 1966–71 and 1060–65 respectively, and $S_{i,t+1}$ denotes size in 1966. For 1966–76 $g^A_{i,t}$ and $g^A_{i,t-1}$ denote growth by acquision over 1972–76 and 1966–71 respectively, and $S_{i,t-1}$ denotes size in 1972. n denotes number of firms.

above average growth by this method over a number of time periods (*cf.* Newbould and Luffman [1978]). But the value for manufacturing for 1966–76, is very low. One explanation for this could be that in the merger boom of late 1960s, many more firms were drawn into the activity than would have been the case under 'normal' conditions. (*cf.* Meeks and Whittington [1975]). These firms would be unlikely to continue sustained growth by acquisition.

Finally, an analysis was undertaken of the relationship between variation in acquisition growth and firm size. It is generally accepted that large firms tend to have more uniform overall growth rates than small firms, but there is no recent evidence available for variability of acquisition growth. The above OLS estimation suggested the presence of some heteroscedasticity. This was further examined by computing standard deviations of acquisition growth for firms arranged in six discrete size classes with assets in 1960 of less than the following: £1m, £2m, £4m, £8m, £16m and assets greater than £16m. It was found that for 1966–71, and 1972–76, the standard deviation of acquisition growth declined systematically with size; using the 'F' test the hypothesis of homogeneity in the dispersion of growth rates of firms in the 1st, 3rd and the largest size classes was rejected as the 1 percent level for both time periods.

VI. SUMMARY AND ECONOMIC IMPLICATIONS

The following main results have emerged from the investigation of the records of over 2000 quoted companies for the UK over the period 1960–76.

(1) There was a mild tendency for firm growth to be negatively related to size. This was found to persist over various sub-periods and for the period as a whole. This result held for both manufacturing and non-manufacturing industries and for alternate measures of size.

(2) There was some persistency in firm growth over time, but it was considerably weaker than that found for earlier periods.

(3) There was in general a weak negative relationship between size and growth by acquisition for firms in manufacturing, which was again found to persist over time.

(4) For all firms, there was no systematic relationship between size and acquisition growth. The persistency in growth by acquisition was much less stable over time than the persistency in total growth.

(5) There was a significant decline in the dispersion of growth by acquisition with an increase in firm size.

An overall important conclusion is that the choice of population (and *a fortiori* that of a sample) can exercise a significant influence on the results. Given this, it does appear that for the period 1970–76, results (1) and (2) do run counter to the propositions of the LPE noted in Section I. Further, as the analysis of heteroscedasticity showed, larger firms have lower dispersion in growth rates than smaller ones. It is worth noting, however, that as far as the stochastic framework itself is concerned, it is possible to incorporate serial correlation in growth rates and still have some sort of stochastic model. Similarly by adopting the assumption that the aggregate of firms in a particular size stratum has an expected percentage change which is independent of size, the decrease in variance of firm growth rates with size can be accommodated. (*cf.* Ijiri and Simon [1976]).

The results are in keeping with the evidence obtained by a number of other researchers, for the period since 1960. For example, as noted in Section I, Aaronovitch and Sawyer [1975] found a weak negative relationship between firm size and growth for the large, mainly quoted, companies for the period 1958–67. Meeks and Whittington [1976] found that for the period 1964–71, the smallest third of the population of UK quoted firms had average annual growth of 14.7%; the middle third had growth of 9.0% and the top third had 10.9%. There is also some complementarity between (1) and the evidence on profitability and size of UK companies. Whittington [1980, p. 350] found that the average profitability of quoted companies was largely independent of firm size 'but such relationship as there is tends to be negative'. In view of the strong positive relationship between firm profitability and growth, this finding gives some support to our study.

The results do, however, differ from the period in the 1950s when there was found to be a weak positive relationship between size and growth (see Singh and Whittington [1975]). They also seem somewhat surprising in view of recent arguments which might prompt the opposite expectation.

With regard to the result (3), it is interesting to note that in manufacturing during the period 1966–71, when there was considerable state encouragement for acquisitions (by the Industrial Reorganization Corporation), there is an insignificant relationship between size and growth, whilst during the more recent period 1972–76, there is a significantly negative relationship.

With regard to the implications of the results for concentration, it is worth emphasizing that concentration can still be increasing, as it was in the period under consideration, even if large firms grow less fast than smaller ones. Further, since large firms have not relied proportionately more on growth by acquisition, it cannot, of course, be concluded that restricting this form of growth would have little or no impact on concentration change. This is so since one of the main causes of increasing concentration has been the disappearance of companies through acquisitions (see Hannah and Kay [1981]). Nevertheless, as Prais [1981] has noted, it is unlikely that 'restraining all mergers and takeovers would make more than a partial contribution towards inhibiting the general growth of concentration'. If continuing high concentration is regarded undesirable, clearly further research is needed to discover specific policy measures to restrain or reverse it.

M. S. Kumar,
Department of Applied Economics,
Sidgwick Avenue,
Cambridge, CB3 9DE

ACCEPTED APRIL 1984

APPENDIX

The 'populations' of firms:

The 'populations' studied in the text included the following set of firms:

Population	*Firms 'surviving' over at least this period*	*Number of firms*
1	1960–65	1747
2	1966–71	1021
3	1972–76	824
1′	1960–71	832
2′	1966–76	694

REFERENCES

AARONOVITCH, S. and SAWYER, M. C., 1975, 'Mergers, Growth and Concentration', *Oxford Economic Papers*, 27, 1 (March), pp. 136–55.

CHESHER, A., 1979, 'Testing the Law of Proportionate Effect', *Journal of Industrial Economics*, XXVII, 4 (June), pp. 403–11.

GLEJSER, H., 1969, 'A New Test for Heteroscedasticity', *Journal of the American Statistical Association*, 64 (March) pp. 316–23.

HANNAH, L. and KAY, J. A., 1977, *Concentration in Modern Industry* (Macmillan, London).

HANNAH, L. and KAY, J. A., 1981, 'The Contribution of Mergers to Concentration Growth: A Reply to Professor Hart', *Journal of Industrial Economics*, XXIX, 3 (March) pp. 305–13.

HART, P. E. and PRAIS, S. J., 1956, 'The Analysis of Business Concentration: A Statistical Approach', *Journal of the Royal Statistical Society*, Series A, 119, (Part II) pp. 150–91.

HART, P. E., 1962, 'The Size of Growth of Firms', *Economica*, 29 (February), pp. 29–39.

HAY, D. and MORRIS, D., 1979, *Industrial Economics: Theory and Evidence.* (Oxford University Press, London).

IJIRI, Y. and SIMON, H. A., 1977, *Skew Distribution and the Size of Business Firms* (North-Holland, Amsterdam).

KALECKI, M., 1945, 'On the Gibrat Distribution', *Econometrica*, 13 (January), pp. 161–70.

KUMAR, M. S., 1981, 'Do Mergers Reduce Corporate Investment?' *Cambridge Journal of Economics*, 5, 2 (June), pp. 101–18.

KUMAR, M. S., 1984, *Growth, Acquisition and Investment* (Cambridge University Press, Cambridge).

LYNCH, H., 1971, *Financial Performance of Conglomorates* (Harvard University Press, Boston).

MARRIS, R., 1964, *The Economic Theory of Managerial Capitalism* (Macmillan, London).

MARRIS, R., 1979; *The Theory and Future of the Corporate Economy and Society.* (North-Holland, Amsterdam).

MARRIS, R. and WOOD, A., 1971, *The Corporate Economy* (Macmillan, London).

MEEKS, G. and WHITTINGTON, G., 1975, 'Giant Companies in the United Kingdom', *Economic Journal*, 85, 340 (December), pp. 824–43.

MEEKS, G. and WHITTINGTON, G., 1976, *The Financing of Quoted Companies in the UK.* (Background Paper No. 1. Royal Commission on the Distribution of Income and Wealth. HMSO, London).

MEEKS, G., 1977, *Disappointing Marriage: A Study of Gains From Merger* (Cambridge University Press, Cambridge).

The Monopolies Commission, 1970, *A Survey of Mergers* 1958–1969 (HMSO, London).

MUELLER, D. C. ed., 1980, *The Determinants and Effects of Mergers* (Oelgeschlages, Gunne and Hain, London).

NEWBOULD, G. and LUFFMAN, G., 1978, *Successful Business Policies* (Gower, London).

PENROSE, E. T., (1959), *The Theory of the Growth of the Firm* (Blackwell, Oxford).

PRAIS, S. J., 1976, *The Evolution of Giant Firms in Britain* (Cambridge University Press, Cambridge).

PRAIS, S. J., 1981, 'The Contribution of Mergers to Industrial Concentration: What do we know?' *Journal of Industrial Economics*, XXIX, 3 (March), pp. 321–29.

H.M.S.O., 1978, *A Review of Monopolies and Mergers Policy* (HMSO, London).

SAMUELS, J. M. and CHESHER, A. D., 1972, 'Growth, Survival and Size of Companies 1960–69', in Cowling, K. ed. *Market Structure and Corporate Behaviour* (Gray-Mills, London).

SCHERER, F. M., 1980, *Industrial Market Structure and Economic Performance*, (2nd edition), (Rand McNally, Chicago).

SINGH, A. and WHITTINGTON G., 1968, *Growth, Profitability and Valuation* (Cambridge University Press, Cambridge).

SINGH, A. and WHITTINGTON, G., 1975, 'The Size and Growth of Firms', *Review of Economic Studies*, XLII, 1, (January) pp. 15–26.

SMYTH, D., BOYES, W. and PESEAU, D., 1975, *Size, Growth, Profits and Executive Compensation in large Corporations* (Gower, London).

UTTON, M., (1972), 'Mergers and the Growth of Large Firms', *Bulletin of Oxford University Institute of Economics and Statistics*, 34, 2 (May), pp. 189–97.

WHITTINGTON, A., 1980, 'The Profitability and Size of United Kingdom Companies, 1960–74', *Journal of Industrial Economics*, XXVIII, 4 (June), pp. 335–52.

THE JOURNAL OF INDUSTRIAL ECONOMICS 0022–1821 $2.00
Volume XXXIII March 1985 No. 3

STRUCTURE AND STRATEGY IN GROCERY RETAILING: A SOCIOMETRIC APPROACH*

GEIR GRIPSRUD AND KJELL GRØNHAUG

I. INTRODUCTION

THE purpose of the present paper is to contrast the "objective" market structure of a conventionally defined geographical market area with the relevant structure as perceived by individual retailers and to examine the impact of perceived competitive structure on the retailers' choice of strategy. Special attention will be given to the question of interdependence in the strategy formulation of close competitors.

II. HYPOTHESES

The marketplace is the arena for competition. Typically, rival sellers seek to attract and serve the same potential customers and are—to some extent at least—aware of this fact. It is usually assumed that structural dimensions of the market will influence the strategies chosen by sellers. In industrial organization studies all retailers within a conventionally defined market area tend to be regarded as potential competitors. The extent of the market area is determined by available statistical data[1] and empirical tests of the structure-strategy relationships are based on "objective" measures of market structure, such as number and concentration of firms.

This way of defining the market fails, however, to consider two important points. First, the relevant "objective" market may not coincide with the conventional statistical classifications. Second, the behavior of individual sellers is motivated by their perceptions of the relevant market, which—for bounded rationality reasons (Williamson [1975])—may differ from the relevant "objective" market.

A number of authors have emphasized the local nature of retail markets.[2] This means that the relevant competitive environment of a store located in an urban area may consist of only a small subset of the total number of stores in the area, usually the stores located in the immediate neighbourhood. Thus,

* The authors are grateful to the editor and an unknown referee for their constructive comments on an earlier version of this article.

[1] In the U.S. Standard Metropolitan Statistical Areas are typically used in defining market areas, *cf.* Marion *et al.* [1979] and McFall Lamm [1981].

[2] This includes Chamberlin [1933] with his reference to the "chain" linking of retail markets, and Holdren [1960] who concludes that "the brunt of any competitive move is usually borne by the geographically closest rival" [1960, p. 181].

the structure of a retail market as a determinant of retail conduct is probably not adequately assessed by the number and size distribution of all stores in the area. Furthermore, it is the *perceived competitive structure* that is instrumental in determining the *strategy* chosen by individual retailers.

The idea that only a fraction of all the retailers in an area is considered to be potential competitors coincides with the notion of an "evoked set", i.e. the subset of all alternatives considered. The term "evoked set" is primarily thought of as the alternatives considered by a buyer (Howard and Sheth [1969]). Simon and March [1958], however, apply the term "evoked alternatives" at a more general level which subsumes the present use of the concept. Studies on "evoked sets" have demonstrated that the number of alternatives considered in most cases is modest, partly due to limited cognitive capacity. Hence, our first hypothesis is:

> H1: Retailers will only perceive a modest fraction of all the stores in a conventionally defined market area as competitors.

It is possible to identify salient store dimensions which determine whether a store is likely to be perceived as a competitor or not by individual retailers. If attention is focused on the most important competitor reported by individual retailers, the average *size* of such stores will probably be larger than the average size of all retailers in the area. That is, a large store will—other things equal—be perceived as a larger threat than a small one. Furthermore, a large store may be selected as the most important competitor by *many* retailers. Hence, there will be a discrepancy between the size distribution of all stores in the conventionally defined market area and the size distribution of stores perceived to be the most important competitor.

> H2: (a) The mean size of stores perceived to be the most important competitor will be larger and (b) the number of such stores will be lower than in the total population of stores in a conventionally defined market area.

In addition to size the *spatial distance* is crucial in determining the content of the "evoked set" of competitors. A short distance between stores makes it easy for consumers to compare and choose between them. Among equal alternatives, the *nearest* one is the most easy to observe, which also coincides with the observation that search for alternatives starts in the immediate surroundings (Cyert and March [1963]). It seems reasonable to assume that this argument also should apply to the retailer's perception of competitors. Thus, disregarding size differences, the nearest store will tend to be perceived as the most important competitor.[3]

[3] Stern and El-Ansary [1982] contend that "the bulk of any establishment's sales may be traced to persons in the immediately surrounding area" [1982, p. 56], which also indicate that the closest stores are the most important competitors.

Firms may, however, vary in sales, reputation and profile, and thus appeal to different consumer segments.[4] The more homogeneous the stores are in terms of sales and profile the more likely it is that a retailer perceives the nearest store to be the most important competitor. The degree of homogeneity of stores does in general differ between retail trades. In some trades spatial distance as opposed to other store characteristics is relatively more important to consumers. This is the case in trades where the shopping frequency is high and the extent of product differentiation is relatively low as in the grocery trade.

In a recent study White [1981] observed that in industrial markets consisting of few firms, these were continuously watching each other and mutually adapting their strategic behavior. In retail markets a similar interdependence in strategy formulation and behavior is probably taking place within subsets of retailers. Thus, the perceived competitive environment or "evoked set" will influence the choice of strategy by individual retailers.[5] When the *nearest* store is perceived as the most important competitor the store has *no* differential advantage with regard to location. Hence, to create a differential advantage in such a situation the retailer is apt to differentiate his store from the competitor in other ways. When the nearest store is *not* perceived as the most important competitor, the firm will still perceive the situation as a competition for the same consumer segment(s). In this case the store has a differential advantage in its location, and has not the same need to differentiate its strategy from the competitor's. Thus, the following hypothesis:

H3: (a) When the nearest store is perceived to be the most important competitor, the retailer will differentiate his strategy from his most important competitor's. (b) When the most important competitor is not the nearest store, the retailer will be less inclined to differentiate his strategy from his most important competitor's.

III. FINDINGS

The present study is restricted to grocery stores as defined at the four digit level by SIC-data in one convential market area. The market area chosen is a small Norwegian town, which encompassed 51 grocery stores.[6] The data were

[4] If the retailers in an area can be segmented into subsets of retailers competing for different groups of customers with different strategic approaches, "strategic groups" are present (Porter [1980]).

[5] In his well known article Hotelling [1929] argues that two retailers watching each other will tend to imitate each other to attract demand from the competitor. The analysis conducted by Graitson [1982] does, however, indicate that this is not a general phenomenon. Empirical research in the area is scarce. In a study of retail pricing in an oligopolistic context, Baumol *et al.* [1964] found no firm evidence of either differentiation or imitation.

[6] In Norway published statistics offer two definitions of the local retail market, the municipality and the trade district. The latter encompasses two or more municipalities. In the present study the municipality level was chosen as the most appropriate starting point.

collected by means of personal interviews with store managers.[7] A complete *sociometric* mapping was undertaken, i.e. all the retailers in the market area were asked about their most important competitor in addition to own size and strategy. See appendix A for further description of the research methodology applied. The average store was small (mean sales 1.8 mill. N. kr or $300,000; mean sales area 183.7 square meters). All the competitors mentioned belonged to the total set of stores included in the study, indicating that an adequate mapping of the total market as perceived by the retailers involved had been done.

Hypothesis 1 stated that retailers will only perceive a modest fraction of all the stores in the total market as competitors. The empirical results are reported in Table I. The reported number of observations (43) is lower than the total number of stores in the market area due to lack of information about competitors. Respondents not submitting this information are excluded in Table I.

From Table I it is seen that the average number of competitors is 3.2. This is slightly over 6 percent of the total number of potential competitors in the area and must be termed a modest fraction. By inspecting the frequency distribution it is furthermore observed that a small fraction (2.3%) is perceiving no competitors at all. Seven is the highest number of reported competitors. Thus, Table I strongly supports H1.

Hypothesis 2 claimed that there is a discrepancy between the "objective" size distribution of sellers in the market and the size distribution of stores

TABLE I
NUMBER OF PERCEIVED COMPETITORS

Number of competitors	
0	2.3%
1	16.3
2	20.9
3	16.9
4	20.9
5	14.0
6	7.0
7	2.3
$\sum$	100.0
$n =$	(43)
$\bar{x} =$	3.2

[7] In Norway, most grocery stores are owned and operated by the same person who seldom operates more than one store. The only multi-store chain located in the area is the Consumer Cooperatives. However, most strategic decisions, such as price and assortment decisions are made at the store level. The competition among grocery stores in this specific market area can primarily be classified as "intratype" competition.

TABLE II
SIZE DISTRIBUTIONS

Sales area m^2	All firms	Perceived most important competitors
< 100	39.2%	13.0%
100–299	39.2	43.5
≥ 300	21.2	43.5
	$\sum =$ 100.0	100.0
	$n =$ (51)	(23)*
	$\bar{x} =$ 183.7	280.7
	SD = (24.6)	(44.8)
Sales mill. N. kr		
<2	76.3%	55.6%
2–5	15.8	27.7
>5	7.9	16.7
	$\sum =$ 100.0	100.0
	$n =$ (38)	(23)
	$\bar{x} =$ 1.811	2.832
	SD = (314.3)	(568.5)

* Number of perceived competitors was 24, but one of these did not submit information about sales and sales area.

reported to be the most important competitor. The size distributions found for all stores and for the stores claimed to be the most important competitor, respectively are reported in Table II. Of the 51 stores 24 were regarded as the most important competitor one or more times. Furthermore, it is evident from Table II that the average size of the stores being considered as the most important competitor is much larger than the population average ($p < 0.5$).[8] Thus, the first part of our second hypothesis is strongly supported by the data. The results do also indicate that the perceived relevant market is more concentrated than is the market measured by conventional "objective" measures. Most of the stores (54.9%) in the area are not reported to be the most important competitor by any retailer (*cf.* H2 b). 33.3% are mentioned once, while the remaining 11.8% are reported twice or more. One particular store is claimed to be the most important competitor by 11 of the retailers in the market. This store has the largest sales in the area.

When relating store size to number of choices received for the whole population very high correlation coefficients were observed, i.e. $r = 0.79$ ($p < 0.001$) for sales and $r = 0.46$ ($p < 0.01$) for sales area. This supports the idea that store size is one dimension that is instrumental in determining the "evoked set" of competitors. Our discussion above also indicated that the nearest store is likely to be regarded as the most important competitor in many cases when the profiles of the stores are fairly equal. In this specific grocery retail market it turns out that 26 stores (51%) claimed that the nearest store was the most important competitor.

[8] *t*-test, two-sided.

Aspects of the perceived competitor structure were assumed to influence the strategy chosen by the retailer. By relating relative choice of strategy to whether or not the most important competitor was the nearest one, the following was found:

TABLE III
STRATEGY BY DISTANCE

		Strategy:		
		Same	*Differential*	Σ
Most important competitor	No	11	5	16
Nearest store	Yes	4	19	23
	Σ	15	24	39

Due to lacking information submitted with regard to competitors and own strategy and thus information needed to construct our measure of relative strategy (*cf* variable 6 (b) in appendix A), the number of observations ($n = 39$) is lower than the total number of stores in the market area. Missing data were observed somewhat more frequently among firms not perceiving the most important firm to be the nearest store. Our test of H3 is, however, still valid. The lacking information does mainly influence the distributions of events, and only indirectly due to reduced number of observations the test of the hypothesis.

Differential strategy is applied in 24 and equal strategy in 15 of the cases. From Table III it may be observed that the same strategy is applied most often when the most important competitor is not the nearest store (11 of 16), while a differential strategy is used in most of the cases when the nearest store is perceived as the most important competitor (in 19 of 23 cases). H3 states that competitors located close to each other will tend to differentiate their strategies, while this will not be the case to the same extent when the most important competitor is located more distantly. The findings presented in Table III suport this hypothesis.

The data also allowed us to consider the case when the most important competitor was a mutual choice, i.e. store 1 perceives store 2 to be the most important competitor, and store 2 perceives store 1 to be the most important competitor. Ten retailers reported such mutual choices and they all referred to the nearest store. All the ten applied differential strategies. By using the information from Table III, the probability of applying such a strategy may be estimated as 24/39. The probability that all the ten firms will apply this strategy is $P(b = 10) < 0.001$ (for $n = 10$, and $p = 24/39$). Thus, this is even a stronger support for the assumption that competitors watching each other with no differential advantage in location will try to differentiate their strategies. One might ask whether the tendency to differentiate the strategy rela-

TABLE IV
STRATEGY BY SIZE AND DISTANCE

		Size						
		L		*M*		*H*		
		Distance		*Distance*		*Distance*		
		0	1	0	1	0	1	Σ
Differential strategy:	No	7	1	3	3	1	—	15
	Yes	3	3	1	7	1	9	24
	Σ	10	4	4	10	2	9	39

tive to the strategy of the most important competitor is uniform across store size. In order to answer this Table IV has been computed. The table is to be read in the following way. The firms have been grouped into three size categories, L(ow < 100 sq meters), M(edium = 100–199), and H(igh ≥ 200 sq meters). The perceived competitor can be the nearest store (1) or not the nearest store (0). Inspecting the ratios between equal and differentiated strategies, when the most important competitor is not the nearest store, reveals the following pattern: $\frac{7}{3}\,\frac{3}{1}\,\frac{1}{1}$, i.e. a curvilinear, but downward sloping relationship. The same curvilinear, downward sloping relationship occurs when inspecting the various size groups for the "nearest store" ($\frac{1}{3}\,\frac{3}{7}\,\frac{0}{9}$). This indicates that store size may have some impact on choice of relative strategy in addition to the distance-variable. The latter is, however, by far the most important of the two variables in explaining relative choice of strategy.

The empirical results reported in this study indicate that the question of imitation or differentiation by close competitors is related to whether intervening competitors of less importance exist or not. Furthermore, the findings suggest that an adequate assessment of retail structure as a determinant of retail strategy and performance is difficult to make from 'objective' market structure data alone.

ACCEPTED MARCH 1984

Geir Gripsrud,
The Norwegian Fund for Market and Distribution Research,
Fredensborg v.24,
Oslo, 2
Norway.

Kjell Grønhaug,
The Norwegian School of Economics and Business Administration,
Breiviken 2,
N-5035 Bergen,
Sandviken,
Norway.

APPENDIX A. METHODOLOGY

Below are reported the variables used and their operational definitions.

Variables:	*Operational Definitions**
1. Number of retailers ("objective")	Based on counting of the retailers (1, 2, . . .).
2. Number of competitors ("perceived")	Based on counting the retailers who were chosen as *perceived* competitor (1, 2, . . .).
3. Most important competitor	"Please submit the names of your competitors. Start with your most important competitor."
4. Distance from most important competitor	"Is your most important competitor the store located nearest to you?" (1 = yes, 0 = no).
5. Size	(a) Sales measured in N. kr based on the annual report for last year (1, 2, . . .).
6a. Strategy	(a) A list of the following strategies: low general price level, width of assortment, quality products, price deals, service, depth of assortment (specialities) was presented, and the following question was asked: "Which strategy is most important to you"?
6b. Relative strategy	(b) Based on contrasting the most important strategy chosen by the firm and the strategy of its most important competitor (1 = different, 0 = equal).

* Most variables and operational definitions shown above are straightforward. However, a few clarifying comments may be necessary. As noted previously, interviews were made with all the retailers in the area. Each retailer was asked to indicate his most important strategy from six alternatives presented to him (*cf.* variable 6(a)) and to name his most important competitor (*cf.* variable 5). Thus, it was possible to trace the principal strategy chosen by the competitor. The strategy chosen by the respondent and the strategy chosen by the retailer perceived to be his most important competitor could then be compared. The dependent variable, i.e. relative strategy choice, defined as differentiation or no differentiation, could then be determined (*cf.* variable 6(b)).

REFERENCES

BAUMOL, W. J., QUANDT, R. E. and H. T. SHAPIRO, 1964, "Oligopoly Theory and Retail Food Prices," *Journal of Business*, 37, pp. 346–63.

CHAMBERLIN, E. H., 1933, *The Theory of Monopolistic Competition*, (Cambridge, Mass., Harvard University Press).

CYERT, R. M. and J. G. MARCH, 1963, *A Behavioral Theory of the Firm*, (New Jersey, Prentice-Hall).

GRAITSON, D., 1982, "Spatial Competition à la Hotelling: A Selective Survey," *Journal of Industrial Economics*, Vol. XXXI, (Sept./Dec.), pp. 13–25.

HOLDREN, B. R., 1960, *The Structure of a Retail Market and the Behavior of Retail Units*, (Prentice-Hall, Englewood Cliffs, N.J.).

HOTELLING, H., 1929, "Stability in Competition," *Economic Journal*, 39, pp. 41–57.

HOWARD, J. A. and J. N. SHETH, 1969, *The Theory of Buyer Behavior*, (New York, John Wiley & Sons).

MARION, B., MUELLER, W., COTTERILL, R., GEITMAN, F. and J. SCHMIELZER, 1979, *The Food Retailing Industry*, (New York, Praeger Publis).

MCFALL LAMM, R., 1981, "Prices and Concentration in the Food Retailing Industry," *Journal of Industrial Economics*, XXX, (September), pp. 67–78.

PORTER, M. E., 1980, *Competitive Strategy*, (New York, The Free Press).

SIMON, H. and J. G. MARCH, 1958, *Organizations*, (New York, John Wiley).

STERN, L. W. and A. I. EL-ANSARY, 1982, *Marketing Channels*, (New Jersey, Prentice-Hall).

WHITE, H. C., 1981, "Where Do Markets Come From?", *American Journal of Sociology*, 83, pp. 517–47.

WILLIAMSON, O., 1975, *Markets and Hierarchies*, (New York, Free Press).

THE JOURNAL OF INDUSTRIAL ECONOMICS 0022–1821 $2.00
Volume XXXIII March 1985 No. 3

ON THE MEASUREMENT OF CHANGES IN AGGREGATE CONCENTRATION, MARKET CONCENTRATION AND DIVERSIFICATION

M. S. Silver*

In a recent article Clarke and Davies [1983]—henceforth C & D—developed a framework for the analysis of concentration and diversification based on the Herfindahl index of concentration. They demonstrated how aggregate concentration could be decomposed into the product of two components, one associated with diversification between, and the other with concentration within, industries at a lower level of aggregation. Their key finding is given by:

$$(1) \qquad H_A = (1 - D)^{-1} \sum^{K} w_j H_j$$

where H_A is the Herfindahl index of aggregate concentration $= \sum_{i=1}^{N} S_i^2/S^2$ for $i = 1, \ldots, N$ independent firms with S_i as an indicator of size of firm (employment) and $S = \sum S_i$; D is an aggregate (weighted) index of diversification $= \sum_{i=1}^{N} w_i D_i$ and $\sum_{j=1}^{K} w_j H_j$ for $j = 1, \ldots, K$ industries, a weighted average of market concentration Herfindahl indexes. The weights for the diversification and market concentration indexes are given by $w_i = S_i^2/\sum^N S_i^2$ and $w_j = S_j^2/S^2$ respectively.

This framework was applied to consider changes in diversification and concentration in UK manufacturing between 1963 and 1968 and between 1971and 1977 at a number of different levels. The decomposition of *changes* in concentration was derived, between period 0 and 1, using:

$$(2) \qquad \frac{H_{A1}}{H_{A0}} = \left[\frac{(1 - D_0)}{(1 - D_1)}\right] \left(\frac{\sum_{j=1}^{K} w_{j1} H_{j1}}{\sum_{j=1}^{K} w_{j0} H_{j1}}\right) \left(\frac{\sum_{j=1}^{K} w_{j0} H_{j1}}{\sum_{j=1}^{K} w_{j0} H_{j0}}\right)$$

"Thus, the overall change in concentration depends on (a) the change in aggregate diversification; (b) the change in the shares of individual industries (note that this involves weighting by end period H_j); (c) the change in industry concentration (where each industry is weighted by its base year share." (C & D, [1983, p. 186]).

The concern of this paper is with the correct specification of the measurement of changes in aggregate concentration and its constituent elements given the importance of this major contribution by C & D. The numerator and denominator of equation (2) are both derived from equation (1) for periods 1

* The author wishes to thank Roger Clarke, University of Sheffield, for helpful comments.

and o respectively, each being multiplied by $\sum_{j=1}^{K} w_{j0}H_{j1}$ to give the changes in weights a separable identity. C. & D might as well have used $\sum_{j=1}^{K} w_{j1}H_{j0}$ to give:

$$\text{(3)} \qquad \frac{H_{A1}}{H_{A0}} = \left[\frac{(1-D_0)}{(1-D_1)}\right]\left(\frac{\sum_{j=1}^{K} w_{j1}H_{j1}}{\sum_{j=1}^{K} w_{j1}H_{j0}}\right)\left(\frac{\sum_{j=1}^{K} w_{j1}H_{j0}}{\sum_{j=1}^{K} w_{j0}H_{j0}}\right)$$

Equation (3) provides a (Paasche) current period weighted index of market concentration and a (Laspeyres) base period weighted index of weight changes in contrast to C & D's equation (2) which reverses the index number formulae used. Neither equation can be justified from the framework used nor are such equations exclusive[1] and, furthermore, need not yield identical results for the constituent elements. An alternative formulation derives from the Divisia [1925 and 1926] approach.[2]

From the definition of equation (1):

$$\text{(4)} \qquad H_A = (1-D)^{-1}\sum_j w_j H_j = \left(1-\sum_i w_i D_i\right)^{-1}\sum_j w_j H_j$$

Let w_i, D_i, w_j, H_j and H_A be functions of time. Differentiate (4) with respect to time and divide by H_A to derive proportionate changes given by (with subscripts omitted):

$$\text{(5)} \qquad \frac{dH_A}{H_A} = \frac{\sum_j wdH}{\sum_j wH} + \frac{\sum_j Hdw}{\sum_j Hw} + \frac{\sum_i wdD}{\left(1-\sum_i wD\right)} + \frac{\sum_i Ddw}{\left(1-\sum_i wD\right)}$$

Changes in equation (4) can be identified as being made up of aggregate changes in the separate components of equation (5), i.e., concentration, weight change (concentration), diversification and weight change (diversification) indexes. Each component can be defined as Divisia line integrals following the usual derivation (see, for example, Forsyth and Fowler, [1981]). Thus the concentration component in period t would be defined as:

$$\text{(6)} \qquad H_j(t) = H_j(0)\exp\int_0^t \frac{\sum_j wdH}{\sum_j wH}$$

[1] As long as the two (not necessarily different) formulae satisfy Fisher's 'factor reversal test' the comparison in terms of C & D's framework will hold—see Fisher [1922] for details of such formulae.

[2] See Forsyth and Fowler [1981] for an application in a different context.

Corresponding results can be obtained for other components. The Divisia index, in adjusting its weights over infinitesimal periods, cannot of course be applied in practice. However, the approach gives support to the process of chaining as the natural discrete approximation. Chaining involves the combination of binary comparisons of consecutive periods (or links) through successive multiplication, thus updating the weights over discrete periods as opposed to using (as with C & D's study) a fixed set of weights for all comparisons. Whilst the Divisia approach gives no indication as to which formula to use for the links, it is apparent that as the duration of each link becomes shorter, the choice of formula becomes less important all formulae being equal, for infinitesimal links, to the Divisia index. The use of Laspeyres and Paasche is, however, to be avoided if market concentration (diversification) is associated with the size of the industry (firm). As a 'compromise solution' a formula based on some form of average of the base and current period weights in any link may be advocated, the Tornqvist or Fisher's 'ideal' index being suitable. For alternative grounds for support see Diewert [1976] and Trivedi [1981]. The use of the chained Tornqvist or Fisher's 'ideal' index have been proposed for the measurement of changes in the elements of aggregate concentration. These formulae will be applied to study changes in weighted sector concentration over the period 1971 to 1977 for UK manufacturing. The results will be compared with those derived by C & D using fixed period weights as given by equation (2).

Table I shows the percentage changes in indices of aggregate sector concentration and the related weights for the period 1971 to 1977. Changes in concentration are given by the base period weighted Laspeyres formula (as proposed by C & D)[3], the chained Laspeyres and chained Fisher's 'ideal' formulae. Changes in weights are given by the current period weighted Paasche formula (as proposed by C & D)[3], the chained Paasche and chained Fisher's 'ideal' formulae. All formulae show little change in concentration and weights over this particular period. This is not to say that the choice between these formula is unimportant. C & D have estimated that overall concentration fell by 6% over this period and, as such, the magnitude of the figures presented may be expected to be small. Yet the *relative* differences between the results, especially regarding the decision to chain, can be identified as being

[3] Figures presented using C & D's method differ from those given in the original paper. This revision arises from their use of employment in *private* manufacturing enterprises for calculating S^2 and *all* manufacturing enterprises for $\sum S_j^2$ when calculating the weights $w_j = \sum S_j^2/S^2$. Data for all manufacturing enterprises are used for S^2 in the revised figures for all columns of Table I. The revision has little effect on the measurement of *relative* changes in sector concentration though pinpoints a measurement problem. Data relating to the analysis of size of all manufacturing industries relates to private enterprises whilst similar data at the industry level relates to private and public enterprises (*Business Monitor*, PA1002, tables 12 and 13 respectively.) Adjustments need to be made to Table 12 in applying C & D's framework. The residuals reported in C & D's tables should be noted to also incorporate the effects of public enterprises on overall concentration.

TABLE I
PERCENTAGE CHANGES IN AGGREGATE SECTOR CONCENTRATION AND WEIGHTS RELATIVE TO 1971 FOR UK MANUFACTURING

	Percentage change in sector concentration relative to 1971			*Percentage change in weights for sector concentration relative to 1971*		
	Base period weights (revised C & D)	*Chained base period weights*	*Chained Fishers' 'ideal'*	*Current period weights (revised C & D)*	*Chained current period weights*	*Chained Fishers' 'ideal'*
1972	0.54	0.54	0.50	0.19	0.19	0.23
1973	−1.63	−1.52	−1.57	1.99	1.87	1.92
1974	−3.72	−4.27	−4.38	0.14	0.72	0.84
1975	0.79	0.36	0.22	0.64	1.07	1.22
1976	−2.18	−2.65	−2.75	−1.47	−1.00	−0.89
1977	−1.91	−1.76	−1.79	0.75	0.59	0.62

quite large. Given changes in these aggregates may also be large in absolute terms (for example, C & D estimated a 50% change in sector concentration for 1963–68) the relative differences isolated here argue for the use of the proposed formulae under C & D's most useful framework.

M. S. Silver,
School of Management,
University of Bath,
Claverton Down,
Bath BA2 7AY

ACCEPTED MARCH 1984

REFERENCES

CLARKE, R. and DAVIES, S. W., 1983, 'Aggregate Concentration, Market Concentration and Diversification', *Economic Journal*, Vol 93, No. 369, pp. 182–92.

DIEWERT, W. E., 1976, 'Exact and Superlative Index Numbers', *Journal of Econometrics*, No. 4, pp. 115–45.

DIVISIA, F., 1925 and 1926, 'L'indice monetaire et la theorie de la monnaie, *Revue Economique Politique*, Societie Anonyme de Recueil Sirey, Paris.

FISHER, I., 1922, *The Making of Index Numbers*, (Boston: Houghton Mifflin).

FORSYTH, F. G. and FOWLER, R. F., 1981, 'The Theory and Practice of Chain Price Index Numbers', *Journal of the Royal Statistical Society*, Series A, Vol. 144, Part 2, pp. 224–47.

TRIVEDI, P. K., 1981, 'Some Discrete Approximations to Divisia Integral Indices, *International Economic Review*, Vol. 22, No. 1, pp. 71–77.

THE JOURNAL OF INDUSTRIAL ECONOMICS 0022-1821 $2.00
Volume XXXIII March 1985 No. 3

DYNAMICS OF CANADIAN DEPOSIT-TAKING INSTITUTIONS: COMMENT

ALAN J. DASKIN*

IN a recent article in this journal, Raj, Kirkham, and Clarke [1979] (henceforth RKC) conclude that "the ten-year period between the Bank Act revisions does not appear to be sufficiently long to allow the Canadian deposit-taking institutions fully to adjust to legislative changes" [p. 187]. That conclusion, however, stems from an inappropriate application of the theory of Markov processes. Specifically, in investigating the evolution of their Markov process over time, they implicitly start the process at an unrealistic starting point. In fact, for the period they consider, ten years is adequate to allow the institutions to adjust to legislative changes, and their model suggests a rather rapid convergence of deposit shares towards their predicted long-run equilibrium values.

The first section of this note reviews RKC's Markovian approach and defines the required notation. The second section analyzes their discussion of the system's adjustment towards equilibrium.

I. RAJ, KIRKHAM, AND CLARKE'S MARKOVIAN MODEL

Let $y(t)$ be the 4-component vector whose values give the shares of deposits held by commercial banks (CBs), trust companies (TCs), mortgage loan companies (MLs), and credit unions (CUs), respectively, in quarter t. The transition probabilities are given by a 4×4 matrix $P = [p_{ij}]$, where "p_{ij} is . . . the probability that a customer (or a group of customers), will be a depositor in institution [of type] j after having been a depositor in institution [of type] i in the previous period" (see RKC, [1979, p. 181]). If the distribution of deposits follows a Markov process, the predicted values of liability shares in the $(t + 1)^{st}$ quarter, given the vector of shares in quarter t, is given by $y(t + 1) = y(t)P$. In such a process, as t goes to infinity, deposit shares will approach long-run equilibrium values given by a vector $\mathbf{a}$ where $\mathbf{ap} = \mathbf{a}$.

RKC report three estimates of P based on data from 1962Q2–1974Q1 and from two subperiods, 1962Q2–1967Q4 and 1968Q1–1974Q1 (see Tables III, IV, and VI in RKC, [1979]). In their Table V, reproduced here as Table I, they report three corresponding estimates of $\mathbf{a}$, the vector of long-run equilibrium shares.

* The views expressed are those of the author and do not necessarily reflect those of the Board of Governors of the Federal Reserve System or its staff. I would like to thank Mark S. Daskin and John D. Wolken for helpful discussion, Elizabeth Gordon and Ronnie McWilliams for capable research assistance, and an anonymous referee for helpful comments and suggestions on an earlier draft. I, of course, retain full responsibility for any errors.

TABLE I
RAJ, KIRKHAM, AND CLARKE'S LONG-RUN EQUILIBRIUM MARKET SHARES

Period Used to Estimate P	CBs(%)	TCs(%)	CUs(%)	MLs(%)
1962–67	69.9	12.5	9.5	8.1
1968–74	65.6	13.5	13.5	7.4
1962–74	65.0	14.0	13.9	7.1

In anticipation of results to be discussed below, I have recomputed estimates of these long-run equilibrium market shares using the transition matrices reported in RKC. Those shares can be found by solving the system of simultaneous equations $\mathbf{a}P = \mathbf{a}$ for $\mathbf{a}$.

TABLE II
LONG-RUN EQUILIBRIUM MARKET SHARES CALCULATED FROM TRANSITION MATRICES REPORTED BY RKC

Period Used to Estimate P	CBs(%)	TCs(%)	CUs(%)	MLs(%)
1962–67	70.49	12.22	9.46	7.83
1968–74	64.92	13.61	14.23	7.24
1962–74	67.36	13.90	11.25	7.48

Note that the first two rows of Table II are close to the corresponding rows in Table I. The third rows in the two tables differ somewhat, however, particularly for the long-run shares of CBs and CUs.[1]

II. ADJUSTMENT TO EQUILIBRIUM

In the second part of their paper, RKC try to determine whether 10 years is long enough to allow depository institutions to adjust to changes in the Bank Act, particularly the 1967 revisions. To do so, they note first that $\lim_{t\to\infty} (P^t) = A$, where A is a 4×4 matrix, *each* of whose rows is equal to the vector $\mathbf{a}$. To examine the time path of adjustment, therefore, they raise P to successive powers and compare the rows of the resulting matrix to the equilibrium shares, given by $\mathbf{a}$. Specifically, in their Table VIII, they record the first row of P^t (for $t = 5, 10, 20, 30, 40$), where P is estimated using the entire 1962–74 period, and compare those rows (especially the first row of P^{40}) to the

[1] There are at least two ways to find $\mathbf{a}$. One way, as indicated in the text, is to solve the simultaneous equation system $\mathbf{a}P = \mathbf{a}$ for $\mathbf{a}$. The second method exploits the fact that $\lim_{t\to\infty} (P^t) = A$, where A is a 4×4 matrix, *each* of whose rows is $\mathbf{a}$ (see section II of the text above). Thus one could estimate $\mathbf{a}$ by raising P to successively higher powers until the rows of P^t were identical. Both techniques yield the values in Table II above. It is not clear which technique RKC [1979] used. On p. 182, they suggest that they used the second technique. On p. 184, they suggest that they used a technique in Padberg [1962] that is formally identically to the first technique mentioned above.

equilibrium vector **a** in the last row of Table I above. "A comparison of the results in Table VIII and the third row of Table V [Table I above]," they conclude on page 187, "indicates that from a pragmatic point of view a ten-year period does not appear sufficiently long to allow the Canadian deposit market to respond to legislative changes". They note in a footnote that other rows of P^{40}, in addition to the first row, lead to similar conclusions.

Although their procedure is mathematically valid in some sense—each row of P^t will converge to **a** as $t \rightarrow \infty$—it is not appropriate to compare any particular row of P^{40} to **a** when trying to determine if the system is relatively close to equilibrium after 10 years (40 quarters). The reason is quite simple: The ith row ($i = 1, 2, 3, 4$) of P^{40} gives the predicted shares of the four types of deposit-taking institutions after 10 years, *assuming* that institutions of type i held *all* deposits at the beginning of the 10-year period. To see why, let e_i be a 1×4 vector with a 1 in the ith position and zeros elsewhere, and assume that e_i represents the initial distribution of shares. We could then generate the predicted vector of shares 40 quarters later by multiplying e_i by P^{40}. By the definition of e_i, though, $e_i P^{40}$ also picks out the ith row of P^{40}. Q.E.D.

The first row of P^{40}, given in RKC's Table VIII, therefore, gives predicted liability shares 10 years after an initial period in which CBs held 100% of deposits. That hypothetical initial distribution, however, bears little resemblance to the actual distribution of shares in 1968Q1, immediately after the Bank Act revisions. RKC's Table II indicates that CBs held 69.6% of deposits in 1968Q1; TCs, 12.7%; CUs, 9.8%; and MLs, 7.9%. In assessing the difference between predicted shares 10 years after the revisions and long-run equilibrium shares, the first row of P^{40}—or any other row of P^{40}—is irrelevant.[2]

The appropriate vector to compare to **a** is $y(68Q1)P^{40}$, where $y(68Q1)$ is a 1×4 vector giving the actual shares in the first quarter of 1968. Table III gives two values of $y(68Q1)P^{40}$, one using RKC's estimate of P based on 1968–74 data (after the 1967 revisions) and the other using their estimate of P based on 1962–74 data.

The first and second lines of Table III can then be compared with the second and third lines, respectively, of Tables I or II above.

TABLE III
VALUES OF THE VECTOR $y(68Q1)P^{40}$

Period Used to Estimate P	*CBs*(%)	*TCs*(%)	*CUs*(%)	*MLs*(%)
1968–74	66.63	13.64	12.38	7.35
1962–74	68.16	13.77	10.47	7.60

[2] If the initial distribution of shares *were* given by $e_i = [1\ 0\ 0\ 0]$, the first row of P^{40} in RKC's Table VIII would suggest a rather *speedy*, if incomplete adjustment toward equilibrium. In 10 years, for example, commercial banks' share of deposits would fall from 100% to 72.57%; trust companies' share would rise from 0% to 12.8%, etc. (See RKC's Table VIII.)

The shares on the first line of Table III are quite close to the equilibrium shares given on the second line of Table I, and not very different from those on the second line of Table II. The rest of the adjustment to equilibrium will involve primarily the transfer of 1 to 2 percentage points from CBs to CUs.

The second line of Table III is reasonably close to the third line of Table I: TCs' and MLs' shares in Table III are quite close to their equilibrium values; the rest of the adjustment will involve primarily the transfer of roughly three percentage points from CBs to CUs. The second line of Table III is remarkably similar to the third line of Table II: Shares for TCs and MLs are essentially identical in the two tables, and shares reported in Table III for CBs and CUs are within 0.8 percentage points of their equilibrium shares in Table II.[3]

In short, RKC's estimated transition matrices predict that deposit-taking institutions' shares 10 years after the Bank Act revisions of 1967 *will* be close to their long-run equilibrium values, contrary to the conclusion of RKC. That conclusion is relatively insensitive to the choice between Tables I and II for long-run equilibrium shares or the choice of period used to estimate *P*. Thus, for the period RKC consider, ten years is adequate to allow the institutions to approach equilibrium.

An anonymous referee has correctly pointed out that the similarity between Table III and Tables I and II may indicate that the process is converging rapidly, or it may simply reflect the fact that the system started near equilibrium in 1968. Note, however, that for some policy questions, that distinction may not be critical. Legislators who are deciding whether or not to amend the Bank Act, for example, might ask about the consequences of not revising the Act. In such circumstances, the similarity between equilibrium shares and predicted shares 10 years after the last revision (as in the tables above) effectively answers their question: If the two share distributions are particularly close, deposit-taking institutions' shares are not likely to change much after 10 years. In that case, it hardly matters for policy purposes whether the very small remaining adjustment to equilibrium occurs rapidly or not.

Nonetheless, for some purposes, it may be interesting to see if the predicted convergence to equilibrium in the 10 years after 1968 is rapid or not. To address that question, I have computed for each type of deposit-taking institution the percentage of the adjustment from its actual share in 1968Q1 to its equilibrium share that will be made in 40 quarters, given the estimated transition matrices.[4] Tables IV and V report those percentages. Table IV is based on the equilibrium shares in Table I; Table V, on the equilibrium shares in Table II. For both tables, actual shares in 1968Q1 are taken from RKC's

[3] It is also interesting to note that the *actual* distribution in 1974Q1, only *six* years after the Bank Act revisions, was for all intents and purposes identical to the equilibrium distribution in row 3 of Table II in the text above. According to RKC's Table II, the actual shares in 1974Q1 were 67.5% for CBs, 13.8% for TCs, 11.3% for CUs, and 7.4% for MLs.

[4] I am indebted to an anonymous referee for suggesting this measure.

TABLE IV
PERCENTAGE OF ADJUSTMENT TO EQUILIBRIUM AFTER 40 QUARTERS
(Equilibrium shares as given in Table I)

Period Used to Estimate P	*CBs*	*TCs*	*CUs*	*MLs*
1968–74	74%	118%	70%	110%
1962–74	31%	82%	16%	38%

TABLE V
PERCENTAGE OF ADJUSTMENT TO EQUILIBRIUM AFTER 40 QUARTERS
(Equilibrium shares as given in Table II)

Period Used to Estimate P	*CBs*	*TCs*	*CUs*	*MLs*
1968–74	63%	103%	58%	83%
1962–74	64%	89%	46%	71%

Table II (see also the text above, where I have reproduced those numbers), and predicted shares 10 years later are taken from Table III above.

The entries in Table V suggest a reasonably rapid convergence toward equilibrium in 10 years, as do the entries on the first line of Table IV. The second line of Table IV suggests somewhat slower convergence than the second line of Table V, reflecting the differences between the third lines of Tables I and II. Table V, however, is a more appropriate indicator of the speed of convergence than Table IV, since Tables II and III, which were used to construct Table V, are both based on RKC's published transition matrices. Table IV, on the other hand, uses equilibrium shares from Table I, which are not consistent with RKC's reported transition matrices, especially the matrix estimated over the 1962–74 period.

III. CONCLUSION

RKC's conclusion that the ten-year period between Bank Act revisions does not provide enough time for institutions to adjust to legislative changes is unwarranted, at least for the 1967 revisions on which they focus their attention. In fact, the predicted shares of various deposit-taking institutions 40 quarters after the revisions are quite close to the long-run equilibrium shares for the Markov process they model. The similarity between those two share distributions reflects two factors: (i) The 1968Q1 distribution was already close to the equilibrium distribution; and (ii) the Markov process does converge rather quickly towards equilibrium from the 1968 distribution.[5]

[5] For an example of a similar Markovian approach where the initial distribution is *not* close to equilibrium and does not approach it quickly, see Adelman's model of the U.S. steel industry [1958, especially p. 901].

These conclusions, although contrary to those of RKC, actually lend some analytical support to their Markovian approach and their interest in the equilibrium distribution of shares. If the initial distribution is not near equilibrium and does not converge quickly, it seems likely that the transition matrix *P* will change long before the process approaches equilibrium. If *P* does change, so will the equilibrium distribution. Under such circumstances, any "equilibrium" distribution based on a particular current estimate of the matrix *P* becomes virtually irrelevant, since the system might *never* approach that distribution.

Alan J. Daskin,
Department of Finance and Economics,
School of Management,
Boston University,
704 Commonwealth Avenue,
Boston, Massachusetts 02215,
U.S.A.

ACCEPTED DECEMBER 1983

REFERENCES

ADELMAN, IRMA G., 1958, 'A Stochastic Analysis of the Size Distribution of Firms', *Journal of the American Statistical Association*, **53**, **284** (December), pp. 893–904.

PADBERG, D. I., 1962, 'The Use of Markov Processes in Measuring Change in Market Structure', *Journal of Farm Economics*, XLIV, **1** (February), pp. 189–99.

RAJ, BALDEV, KIRKHAM, PETER G. and CLARKE, EDWARD W., 1979, 'Dynamics of Canadian Deposit-Taking Institutions: A Markovian Approach', *Journal of Industrial Economics*, XXVIII, **2** (December), pp. 177–88.

THE JOURNAL OF INDUSTRIAL ECONOMICS 0022–1821 $2.00
Volume XXXIII March 1985 No. 3

RETURNS TO SCALE IN R&D AND THE SCHUMPETERIAN HYPOTHESIS: A COMMENT

ARUN K. MUKHOPADHYAY

IN the literature on research and development (R&D) behavior of firms, many empirical studies have investigated the Schumpeterian hypothesis that larger firms are more efficient in conducting R&D.[1] These studies have regressed R&D intensity (either output or input of R&D, deflated by firm size) on firm size to see if the coefficient of size is significantly positive. Fisher and Temin (henceforth, F–T), [1973; 1979] have criticized the empirical tests by showing that greater efficiency in research does not necessarily imply that research intensity will also be higher, and that the empirical tests therefore do not verify the Schumpeterian hypothesis. Later, Kohn and Scott (henceforth, K–S), [1982] using a modified formulation of the F–T model, have claimed that "An empirical test of the Schumpeterian Hypothesis is a legitimate test of Schumpeter's own hypothesis," [1976, p. 248]. The purpose of this paper is to show that this conclusion is inappropriate.

To examine the K–S conclusion, we start with a list of different statements which have been or can be termed the "Schumpeterian hypothesis" (SH).

(SH1): Larger firms are more research-efficient, that is, they are more productive in their research efforts.

Two special forms of (SH1) are:

(SH1a): In the F–T model, "if both R and N increase in the same proportion, so that both research and production divisions of the firm grow at the same rate, then average returns per research worker go up"[2] [1979, p. 387].

(SH1b): In the K–S version, there are increasing returns to scale in the production of R&D, and a given level of R&D produces a greater value added in a larger firm.

(SH2): R&D output increases more than proportionately with firm size. Note that this is equivalent to the proposition that research output intensity (research output as a fraction of firm size) is higher for a bigger firm.

Of the above-listed forms of (SH), K–S have termed (SH1b) as the "Schumpeterian postulate" and (SH2) as "Schumpeter's own hypothesis".

[1] For reviews of this literature, see Kamien & Schwartz [1982, pp. 75–84] and Scherer [1980, pp. 418–22). For Schumpeter's own version of the hypothesis, see Schumpeter [1976, Ch. 8].

[2] This formulation is a revised version of their original formulation which had a problem as pointed out by Rodriguez [1979].

F–T call (SH1a) "The Schumpeterian hypothesis", and (SH2) "Schumpeter's own conclusion".[3]

There are two types of empirical tests (ET) which are relevant to our discussion:

(ET1): R&D input increases more than proportionately with firm size. Note that this is equivalent to the proposition that research input intensity (research input as a fraction of firm size) is higher for a bigger firm.

(ET2): The same proposition as (SH2). Neither F–T nor K–S have mentioned this proposition as one that has been tested directly in empirical tests.[4]

Now, F–T have shown as a result of their model that (SH1a) does not imply either (ET1) or (ET2), and therefore, the empirical tests are not meaningful tests of the Schumpeterian hypothesis (SH1a). The same result comes out of the K–S model as well: (SH1b) does not imply either (ET1) or (ET2). Yet, K–S claim that their results show that the empirical tests of (ET1) are meaningful. This is because, in their model, (ET1) implies (ET2). Since (ET2) is the same as (SH2), and is called "Schumpeter's own hypothesis" by K–S, they conclude that a test of (ET1) is a valid test of Schumpeter's own hypothesis. This conclusion is unwarranted for the following reason.

In the K–S model, (SH2) can be true whether or not (ET1) is true. Therefore, a rejection of (ET1) on the basis of empirical tests would not allow us to reject (SH2). As a result, (SH2) becomes a non-refutable hypothesis, if the hypothesis is sought to be verified through (ET1). In that case, there is no point in testing the hypothesis.[5] Moverover, the K–S result that (ET1) implies (ET2) is derived by assuming that (SH1b) is true. The validity of (SH1b), however, cannot be taken for granted. Indeed, this hypothesis of increasing returns to scale in R&D could itself be made a candidate for empirical tests under the name of a test of "the Schumpeterian hypothesis".

Arun K. Mukhopadhyay,
Department of Economics,
Saint Mary's University,
Halifax, Nova Scotia, B3H 3C3

ACCEPTED OCTOBER 1983

[3] F–T state (SH2) as a formalization of yet another proposition that "more innovations will be forthcoming if small firms are combined into big ones" [1973, p. 57]. However, this proposition is not really equivalent to (SH2). Even if the combined firm produces more research output, this increase may be proportionately less than an increase in firm size at the new equilibrium over the sum of the pre-merger sizes of the small ones.

[4] Kamien & Schwartz [1982, pp. 82–84] and Scherer [1980, p. 420] give reviews of these tests, where the usual measure of R&D output is the number of patents.

[5] Lunn [1982] has made a similar point by concluding that "the empirical tests are incapable of discriminating between various models of the relationship between innovative inputs and output" [1982, p. 216]. The issue here is different from Lunn's in that we are concerned here with the non-refutability of (SH2) within the context of K–S's own model, and not through the comparison of different models.

REFERENCES

FISHER, FRANKLIN M. and PETER TEMIN, 1973, "Returns to Scale in Research and Development: What Does the Schumpeterian Hypothesis Imply?" *Journal of Political Economy* 81, No. 1 (January–February), pp. 56–80.

———, 1979, "The Schumpeterian Hypothesis: Reply", *Journal of Political Economy* 87, No. 2 (April), pp. 386–89.

KAMIEN, MORTON I. and NANCY L. SCHWARTZ, 1982, *Market Structure and Innovation* (Cambridge, Cambridge University Press).

KOHN, MEIR and JOHN T. SCOTT, 1982, "Scale Economics in Research and Development: The Schumpeterian Hypothesis", *Journal of Industrial Economics* 30, No. 3 (March), pp. 239–49.

LUNN, JOHN, 1982, "Research and Development and the Schumpeterian Hypothesis: Alternate Approach", *Southern Economic Journal* 49, No. 1 (July), pp. 209–17.

RODRIQUEZ, CARLOS ALFREDO, 1979, "A Comment on Fisher and Temin on the Schumpeterian Hypothesis", *Journal of Political Economy* 98, No. 2 (April), pp. 282–85.

SCHERER, F. M., 1980, *Industrial Market Structure and Economic Performance*, Second Edition (Chicago, Rank McNally).

SCHUMPETER, J. A., 1976, *Capitalism, Socialism and Democracy* (London: George Allen & Unwin).

THE JOURNAL OF INDUSTRIAL ECONOMICS 0022–1821 $2.00
Volume XXXIII March 1985 No. 3

SCALE ECONOMIES IN RESEARCH AND DEVELOPMENT: A REPLY

MEIR KOHN AND JOHN T. SCOTT

MUKHOPADHYAY objects to our use of the term "empirical test" [1982, p. 248] and to the fact that one aspect of our conclusions follows from our assumptions (A1) and (A2) which characterize [1982, pp. 242–43] increasing returns to scale in the product of R&D and characterize the value added of R&D. What we intended is clear in our paper.

First, Corollary 3 [1982, p. 244] clearly states that the relation that Mukhopadhyay addresses holds under (A1) and (A2). Second, the complaint that our "test" does not allow refutation of the theory misinterprets our use of the idea of an empirical test.

Fisher and Temin set out to ask what if anything could be inferred about the relation between R&D output and firm size via observation of input-size relations. That is not an uninteresting question because it is easier to measure inputs than to measure outputs. Patents, for example, are an imperfect indicator of R&D outputs. Our notion of an empirical test is based on the need to learn from observation about whether a phenomenon does occur even though we cannot observe it directly. Can we learn about the unobservable via what we can observe? Fisher and Temin reach nihilistic conclusions on that score in the present context. We do not.

Suppose we could observe only inputs accurately, can we infer anything about outputs? Although we cannot observe output directly, we can observe something else which, if we find it to be true, is consistent with the Schumpeterian story. If A1 and A2, then the observation $eR/eS > 1$ is equivalent to the observation $eQ/eS > 1$. It is in this sense that estimating the input-size relation is a test of the output-size relation. Of course, empirical workers have looked at both output-size and input-size relations. But we have set out to answer the Fisher and Temin question. Because output is more difficult to measure and compare across observations than is input, the question we answer is an important one.

Meir Kohn and John T. Scott,
Department of Economics,
Dartmouth College,
Hanover, New Hampshire, 03755

ACCEPTED OCTOBER 1983

REFERENCE

KOHN, MEIR and JOHN T. SCOTT, 1982, "Scale Economies in Research and Development", *The Journal of Industrial Economics*, **30**, 3 (March), pp. 239–49.

THE JOURNAL OF INDUSTRIAL ECONOMICS
Volume XXXIII March 1985 No. 3

PUBLICATIONS RECEIVED

Agenda for the Study of Macroeconomic Policy, by Herbert Stein. Published by American Enterprise Institute, 1983.

American Banks in the International Interbank Market, in the Monograph Series in Finance and Economics, by Stephen V. O. Clarke. Published by Soloman Brothers Center for the Study of Financial Institutions.

Authority and Participation in Industry, by Peter Brannen. Published by Batsford Academic and Educational Ltd., 1983, £6.95.

Biotechnology, Chemical Feedstocks and Energy Utilization, by D. F. Gibbs and M. E. Greenhalgh. Published by Frances Pinter (Publishers) Limited, 1983, £16.50.

Britain and the EEC, edited by Roy Jenkins. Published by Macmillan Press, 1983, £20.00 (hardback), £7.95 (paperback).

Britain with the European Community: The Way Forward, edited by A. M. El-Agraa. Published by Macmillan Press, 1983, £25.00 (hardback), £8.95 (paperback).

Capital Budgeting Techniques, 2nd edition, by F. M. Wilkes. Published by J. Wiley and Sons Ltd., 1983, £16.60.

Case in Hand—Cases in Industrial Relations, by Alun Phillips and Geoffrey Stuttard. Published by Cambridge University Press, 1983, £2.95.

Commerce, Industry and Transport: Studies in Economic Change on Merseyside, edited by B. L. Anderson and P. J. M. Storey. Published by Liverpool University Press, 1983, £14.50.

The Competitive Strength of the Information and Communication Industry in Europe, edited by H. van Houten. Published by Martinus Nijoff Publishers BV, 1983, $32.50, Dfl. 75.00.

The Corporate Imagination, by Peter Earl. Published by Wheatsheaf Books Ltd, 1984, £18.95 (cloth), £7.95 (paper).

Corporate Structure and Performance, by M. Lawriwsky. Published by Croom Helm Ltd., 1984, £19.95.

Craft Enterprises in Britain and Germany: a Sectoral Study, by Alun Doran, Economists Advisory Group. Published by Anglo-German Foundation, 1984, £9.50.

Developing Electric Power: Thirty Years of World Bank Experience, by Hugh Collier. Published by The Johns Hopkins University Press, 1984, $22.50.

The Economic Analysis of Capital Investments for Managers and Engineers, by G. T. Stevens Jr. Published by Prentice/Hall International, 1983, £26.95.

Economic Analysis of Technical Change, by Paul Stoneman. Published by Oxford University Press, 1983, £19.50 (hardback), £8.95 (paperback).

Economic Growth in a Nordic Perspective, edited by Gunnar Eliasson. Published by the Industrial Institute for Economic and Social Research, 1984, SEK 223.

The Economics of Distribution, Proceedings of the 2nd International Conference on the Economics of Distribution held in Venice, April 28–29, 1983. Published by CESCOM—Centro di Studi Sul Commercio, 1983.

Effective Management Skills: Managing People, by John Scott and Arthur Rochester. Published by Sphere Books Ltd., 1984, £2.95.

The Effectiveness of Antitrust Policy towards Horizontal Mergers, by David B. Audretsch. Published by UMI Research Press, 1983.

Energy and Economic Adjustment, edited by Bengt-Christer Ysander. Published by the Industrial Institute for Economic and Social Research, 1983, SEK 200:

Energy in Swedish Manufacturing, edited by Bengt-Christer Ysander. Published by the Industrial Institute for Economic and Social Research, 1983, SEK 200:

Essays in Contemporary Economic Problems, project directed by William Fellner. Published by the American Enterprise Institute, $19.95 (cloth), $10.95 (paper).

Exchange-Rate Regime Selection in Theory and Practice, in the Monograph Series in Finance and Economics, by Gordon Weil. Published by New York University.

The Financial Impacts of Social Security, in the Monograph Series in Finance and Economics, by R. Glenn Hubbard. Published by New York University, 1983.

The Food Industry—Economics and Politics, edited by Jim Burns, John McInerner and Alan Swinbank. Published by Heinemann Ltd., 1983, £10.95.

Fugitive Industry: The Economics and Politics of Deindustrialisation, by Richard B. McKenzie. Published by Pacific Institute for Public Policy Research, 1984, $29.95 (hardcover), $11.95 (softcover).

Future for Automotive Technology, by Ulrich Seiffert and Peter Walzer. Published by Frances Pinter (Publishers) Ltd., 1984, £15.00.

The Future of Industrial Societies, by C. Kerr. Published by Harvard University Press, 1984, £14.00.

Governments and Multinationals: Policies in the Developed Countries, by A. E. Safarian. Published by the British-North American Committee, £4.00.

Growth in the American South, by Robert J. Newman. Published by New York University Press, 1984, $39.00.

Humanism and Capitalism: A Survey of Thought on Morality and the Economic Order, by Bernard Murchland. Published by American Enterprise for Public Policy Research, 1984, $3.95.

Industrial Economics: Australian Studies, by L. R. Webb and R. H. Allan. Published by George Allen and Unwin, 1983, £18.00.

Interindustry Differences in Productivity Growth, by John W. Kendrick. Published by American Enterprise Institute, 1983.

International Business and Global Technology, by J. Davidson Frame. Published by Lexington Books, 1983, £21.00.

The International Ceramic Tableware Industry, by R. L. S. Smyth and R. S. Weightman. Published by Croom Helm Ltd., 1984, £25.00.

Intra-industry Trade, edited by P. K. M. Tharakan. Published by North-Holland Publishing Company, 1983, $40.50, Dfl. 105.00.

IUI Yearbook 1982–1983, Microeconometrics, edited by G. Eliasson and H. Fries. Published by the Industrial Institute for Economic and Social Research, 1983.

Investment in Technology, by Barry Bozeman and Albert N. Link. Published by Praeger, 1983, $21.95.

Inward Investment: Policy Options for the United Kingdom, by Michael Brech and Margaret Sharp. Published by the Royal Institute of International Affairs, 1984, £4.95.

Japan's Reluctant Multinationals—Japanese Management at Home and Abroad, by Malcolm Trevor. Published by Frances Pinter (Publishers) Limited, 1983, £16.50.

Macro-electronics, Robotics and Jobs, YICCP, OECD, 1982, £12.50.

Making Economic Policy in Congress, edited by Allen Schick. Published by American Enterprise Institute for Public Policy Research, 1984, $19.95 (cloth), $10.95 (paper).

Managing Corporate Pension Plans: The Impacts of Inflation, by Dennis E. Logue and Richard J. Rogalski. Published by the American Enterprise Institute for Public Policy Research, 1984, $5.95.

Managing Work, by John Scott and Arthur Rochester. Published by Sphere Books Ltd., 1984, £12.50.

Manpower Planning—Strategy and Techniques in an Organizational Context, by John Edwards, Chris Leek, Ray Loveridge, Roger Lumley, John Mangan and Mick Silver. Published by John Wiley and Sons Ltd., 1983, £6.75.

Market, Firm and Economics Performance, from the Monograph Series in Finance and Economics, by Stephen Martin. Published by New York University, 1983.

Market Integration in the European Community—Studies in Industrial Organization, Vol. 5, by Jacques Pelkmans. Published by Martinus Nijhoff Publishers BV, 1984, £29.25, $46.50, Dfl. 115.00 (cloth); £15.25, $24.90, Dfl. 60.00 (paper).

Marketing Theory and Practice, 2nd edition, by M. Baker. Published by Macmillan Press, 1983, £8.95.

The Military Origins of Industrialisation and International Trade Rivalry, by Gautam Sen. Published by Frances Pinter (Publishers) Ltd., 1984, £16.00.

Modern Industrial Economy: Its Working under Different Economic Systems, by Mohammad Shabbir Khan. Published by L. N. Mishra Institute of Economic Development and Social Change, 1983.

A Muslim's Reflections of Democratic Capitalism, by Muhammad Abdul-Rauf. Published by American Enterprise Institute for Public Policy Research.

Natural Gas Markets after Deregulation, Methods of Analysis and Research Needs, by H. G. Broadman, W. D. Montgomery, with assistance of M. B. Zimmerman. Published by Johns Hopkins University Press, 1983, $18.00.

Policy and Trade Issues of the Japanese Economy, edited by Kozo Yamamura. Published by University of Washington Press, 1983, £18.75.

Policy Making in a Disorderly World Economy, edited by Gunnar Eliasson, Marc Sharefkin, and Bengt-Christer Ysander. Published by the Industrial Institute for Economic and Social Research, 1983, SEK 180:

Productivity and Prices: The Consequences of Industrial Concentration, by Steven Lustgarten. Published by American Enterprise Institute for Public Policy Research, 1984, $4.95.

Proposals for Line-Item Veto Authority. Published by the American Enterprise Institute, 1984.

Proposals to Establish a Department of Trade. Published by American Enterprise Institute, 1984.

Public Sector Accounting and Financial Control, by Sir Douglas Henley, Andrew Likierman, Clive Holtham and John Perrin. Published by Van Nostrand Reinhold (U.K.) Co. Ltd., 1983, £8.50.

Renewal of the Generalized System of Preference. Published by American Enterprise Institute, 1984.

Rights and Regulations: Ethical, Political, and Economic Issues, edited by Tibor R. Machan and M. Bruce Johnson. Published by Pacific Institute for Public Policy Research, 1983, $35.00 (cloth), $11.95 (paper).

Sogo Sosha, The Vanguard of the Japanese Economy, by Yoshihara. Published by Oxford University Press, 1983, £7.95.

Strategies for Vertical Integration, by Kathryn Rudie Harrigan. Published by Lexington Books, 1983, £25.00.

Strikes in Europe and the United States, by Kenneth Walsh. Published by Frances Pinter (Publishers) Limited, 1983, £15.75.

Structural Changes in the World Economy, by Béla Kádár. Published by Frances Pinter (Publishers) Limited, 1984, £12.50.

Taxing the Family, edited by Rudolf G. Penner. Published by American Enterprise Institute for Public Policy Research, 1983.

The United Brotherhood of Carpenters, by Walter Gallensen. Published by Harvard University Press, 1984, £21.25.

United States Oil Pipeline Markets: Structure, Pricing and Public Policy, by John A. Hansen. Published by MIT Press, 1983, £20.25.

Vertical Integration and Joint Ventures in the Aluminium Industry, by J. A. Stuckey. Published by Harvard University Press, 1983, £24.00.

Water Rights: Scarce Resource Allocation, Bureaucracy and the Environment, edited by Terry L. Anderson. Published by Pacific Institute for Public Policy Research, 1983, $11.95 (softcover), $35.00 (hardcover).

The Way People Work: Job Satisfaction and the Challenge of Change, by Christine Howarth. Published by Oxford University Press, 1984, £12.50 (hardback), £3.95 (paperback).

What is a Manager? by John Scott and Arthur Rochester. Published by Sphere Books Ltd., 1984, £2.95.

Women and Employment: A Lifetime Perspective, by Jean Martin and Ceridwen Roberts, HMSO, £9.50.

Workers Participation and Self-management in Turkey, from the Research Report Series No. 13, by Mehmet Nezir Uca. Published by Institute of Social Studies, 1983, 11 guilders.

Journal of Business Finance & Accounting

Editors: Richard Briston & John Perrin

Spring 1985 Vol.12 No.1

Contents

A Post Keynesian View of Modern Financial Economics: In Search of Alternative Paradigms
M. C. FINDLAY and E. E. WILLIAMS

Assessing the Vulnerability to Failure of American Industrial Firms: A Logistic Analysis
CHRISTINE V. ZAVGREN

Dividend Yield, Regulation, and the Return on U.S. Public Utility Stocks
MICHAEL A. GOLDBERG and ASHOK VORA

Inflation, Taxes and Bank's Market Values
JEAN DERMINE

UK Building Societies – A Study of the Gains from Merger
PAUL BARNES

Studies of the Information Content of Qualified Audit Reports
A. T. CRASWELL

A Note to Barlev-Levy Theory of the Information Content of Accounting Data and the Management of Security Portfolios Which Include the Least Correlated Stocks: An Empirical Analysis
AVI RUSHINEK and SARA RUSHINEK

Safety Margin Allocation and Risk Assessment Under the NPV Method
SANG-HOON KIM and HUSSEIN H. ELSAID

On Unanimity and Monopoly Power
VAROUJ A. AIVAZIAN and JEFFREY L. CALLEN

The Efficiency of the Finnish Market for Rights Issues: An Application of the Black-Scholes Model
TOM BERGLUND and BJORN WAHLROOS

The Role of the Payback Period in the Theory and Application of Duration to Capital Budgeting: A Comment
LUTZ KRUSCHWITZ

The Role of the Payback Period in the Theory and Application of Duration to Capital Budgeting: A Reply
CALVIN M. BOARDMAN

1985 subscription £40 in UK and £50 elsewhere (or US $99; Can $121.50) to library and business subscribers; £21.25 in UK and £26.75 elsewhere (or US $52.50; Can $65) to individual teachers and students. Order from Journals Dept., Basil Blackwell Publishers, 108 Cowley Road, Oxford, OX4 1JF, UK. Editorial communications to JBFA/CRIBA, University of Warwick, Coventry CV4 7AL, UK. Students and teachers in the UK and members of the E.A.A. and E.F.A. may qualify for a specially reduced subscription price; details may be obtained on request from the editors.

ANNOUNCEMENTS

The Third Annual Meeting of the Association of Managerial Economists (AME) will be held in New York, December 28–30, 1985.

Three sessions of competitively selected papers will be featured in conjunction with the ASSA meetings. Theoretical, empirical and policy analyses across a broad spectrum of topics will be featured. Especially encouraged are papers integrating the theory of accounting, finance and industrial organization in topic areas such as: the market for corporate control (buyouts, mergers, share repurchases, spinoffs), managerial labor market, measuring monopoly profits, and the information content of accounting data.

Both members and nonmembers are invited to submit papers and/or make program suggestions to Professor Mark Hirschey (AME Program Chair), Graduate School of Business Administration, 1100 14th Street, University of Colorado, Denver, CO 80204, U.S.A.

Submission deadline: June 15, 1985.

The Twelfth Annual Conference of EARIE, the European Association for Research in Industrial Economics, will be held on 11–13 September, 1985, at the Department of Applied Economics, University of Cambridge, Cambridge, England.

Sessions include the economics of industry and firm organization, industrial and competition policy, industrial organization and international trade, industry studies, regulation of industries and firms, industrial organization theory, technological and organizational change and industry structure, public enterprise economics, as well as other areas of current research interests in industrial economics.

Those interested in presenting a paper should send three copies of the paper, not later than 1 April, 1985, to the Chairman of the Programme Committee: Dr. A. Singh, Department of Applied Economics, Sidgwick Avenue, Cambridge CB3 9DE, England.

P. W. S. ANDREWS MEMORIAL ESSAY PRIZE – £300

The PWSA Memorial Prize of £300 is awarded annually. Competitors for the prize are asked to submit an essay on a subject of their own choice within the general field of Industrial Economics and Theory of the Firm, broadly interpreted. Entry to the competition is open to anyone under 30 years of age (or over 30, if not more than eight years have elapsed since taking a first degree). The essay, written in English, and not exceeding 10,000 words in length, should be a work of original research by the candidate only, not previously published and not previously awarded any other prize.

The winning essay may, at the discretion of the Editors, be published in *The Journal of Industrial Economics*.

The closing date for entries is 31st December.

Further details are available from:

Miss B. Cox,
University House,
The University of Lancaster,
Bailrigg, Lancaster, LA1 4YX, England.

The General Editor,
Journal of Industrial Economics,
The Institute of Economics and Statistics,
The University of Oxford,
St Cross Building, Manor Road,
Oxford, OX1 3UL, England.

The North American Editor,
Journal of Industrial Economics,
Graduate School of Business Administration,
New York University, 90 Trinity Place,
New York 10006, U.S.A.

THE JOURNAL OF INDUSTRIAL ECONOMICS

Published first in October 1952, the Journal has a very wide international circulation, and has established itself as the leading journal in the field of industrial economics. It was founded to promote the analysis of modern industry, particularly the behaviour of firms, and the functioning of markets. More specifically it seeks to bring the tools of modern economic analysis to bear on the analysis of real problems of industrial economies.

Contributions are welcomed covering all the major areas of industrial economics. One such area is the relationship between market structure and market behaviour in the areas of pricing, product differentiation, advertising and the dissemination of information and R & D. Another area focuses more directly on the firm, its objectives, finance, investment and growth. A third area comprises the background environment within which industrial firms operate: the changing structure of industry, public policy on monopoly and restrictive trade practices, regulation, fiscal and monetary policy as they affect firms, and underlying changes in productivity and international competitiveness.

The Journal has a tradition of publishing a blend of theory and evidence. Theoretical discussion is welcomed provided that the more abstract theory includes sufficient introduction and other explanation to convey the significance of the material to the general reader who wants to decide whether to follow the analysis through. Empirical analysis, and especially econometric analysis, should include an explanation of the data sources used, of the methods applied and of the underlying theoretical basis of the study. The Journal has a particular tradition of case studies of firms and industries, which the Editors would wish to continue. However contributors of such studies are asked to remember that a study will be of interest to the international readership of the Journal only if it makes a particular contribution to the methodology of such studies, or if the empirical results are exceptionally interesting.

Alongside articles of more normal length, the Editors are ready to publish shorter notes, especially where these give interim results of important research studies, or where they report significant new empirical results. Books are not reviewed, although books received will be listed, sometimes with a short note: but substantial review articles will be considered.

Information for Contributors

Submissions (*three* copies are required) should be in typescript, double-spaced, and conform to the style of the Journal. Detailed Information for Contributors is available from the General Editor. The submission should include an Abstract, not exceeding 100 words.

Typescripts from North America should be sent to the North American Editor, Journal of Industrial Economics, Graduate School of Economics and Business Administration, New York University, 100 Trinity Place, New York, NY 10006, U.S.A.

Typescripts from *all* other countries should be sent to the General Editor, Journal of Industrial Economics, Institute of Economics and Statistics, University of Oxford, St Cross Building, Manor Road, Oxford OX1 3UL, U.K.

Information for Subscribers

The Journal is published four times a year, in September, December, March and June, by Basil Blackwell Publisher Ltd., 108 Cowley Road, Oxford OX4 1JF, U.K. Prices are as follows:

	UK	Overseas	USA	Canada
Institutions	£26.50	£33.50	$65.75	$80.50
Individuals	£16.25	£20.35	$35.00	$43.25
Single issue prices for:				
Institutions	£7.20	£8.80	$17.70	$21.50
Individuals	£5.20	£6.40	$12.00	$14.70

CONTRIBUTORS TO THIS NUMBER

ROBERT A. TAGGART, Jr: Professor of Finance, Boston University.

JAMES A. BRANDER: Associate Professor, Faculty of Commerce and Business Administration, University of British Columbia.

BARBARA J. SPENCER: Associate Professor, Department of Economics, Boston College.

DOUGLAS TODD: Senior Economic Adviser in H.M. Treasury, London, on leave as Economic Adviser in the Directorate General for Economic and Financial Affairs, European Commission, Brussels.

DAMIEN NEVEN: Graduate Student, Nuffield College, University of Oxford.

M. S. KUMAR: Fellow of Sidney Sussex College, University of Cambridge, and Research Officer, Department of Applied Economics, University of Cambridge.

GEIR GRIPSRUD: Research Director at the Norwegian Fund for Market and Distribution Research, Oslo.

KJELL GRØNHAUG: Professor at the Norwegian School of Economics and Business Administration, Bergen.

M. S. SILVER: Lecturer in Industrial Economics and Statistics, School of Management, University of Bath.

ALAN J. DASKIN: Department of Finance and Economics, School of Management, University of Boston.

ARUN K. MUKHOPADHYAY: Associate Professor, Department of Economics, St Mary's University, Canada.

MEIR KOHN: Associate Professor, Department of Economics, Dartmouth College, New Hampshire.

JOHN T. SCOTT: Associate Professor, Department of Economics, Dartmouth College, New Hampshire.

US Mailing: Second class postage paid at New York. Postmaster: Send address corrections to: Journal of Industrial Economics, c/o Expediters of the Printed Word Ltd., 515 Madison Avenue, New York, NY 10022 (US Mailing Agent).

Reprints of Back Volumes: Volumes 1–28 of the Journal are available (in complete volumes only) from the Kraus Reprint Corporation, Route 100, Millwood, New York 10546, USA. More recent back issues are available from the publisher at the current single issue price.

Microfilm: An agreement for the supply of microfilm copies from Volume 1 onwards has been made with University Microfilms International, Department PR, 30–32 Mortimer Street, London W1N 7RA, England, or 300 North Zeeb Road, Ann Arbor, Michigan 48106, USA.

Printed and Bound in Great Britain by T. J. Press (Padstow) Ltd, Padstow, Cornwall

THE JOURNAL OF INDUSTRIAL ECONOMICS

A SYMPOSIUM ON OLIGOPOLY, COMPETITION AND WELFARE

Edited by P. A. GEROSKI
L. PHLIPS and A. ULPH

ISSN 0022-1821
BASIL BLACKWELL OXFORD ENGLAND

CONTENTS

Volume XXXIII JUNE 1985 No. 4

P. A. GEROSKI, L. PHLIPS and A. ULPH
Oligopoly, Competition and Welfare: Some Recent Developments 369
RAY REES
Cheating in a Duopoly Supergame 387
KEVIN ROBERTS
Cartel Behaviour and Adverse Selection 401
ROBERT H. PORTER
On the Incidence and Duration of Price Wars 415
JONATHAN B. BAKER and TIMOTHY F. BRESNAHAN
The Gains from Merger or Collusion in Product-Differentiated Industries 427
DAVID EASLEY, ROBERT T. MASSON and ROBERT J. REYNOLDS
Preying for Time 445
CHRISTOPHER HARRIS and JOHN VICKERS
Patent Races and the Persistence of Monopoly 461
HUW DIXON
Strategic Investment in an Industry with a Competitive Product Market 483
NORMAN J. IRELAND
Product Diversity and Monopolistic Competition under Uncertainty 501
G. K. YARROW
Welfare Losses in Oligopoly and Monopolistic Competition 515
THOMAS von UNGERN-STERNBERG and CARL CHRISTIAN von WEIZSÄCKER
The Supply of Quality on a Market for "Experience Goods" 531

Bibliography 541

THE JOURNAL OF INDUSTRIAL ECONOMICS 0022-1821 $2.00
Volume XXXIII June 1985 No. 4

OLIGOPOLY, COMPETITION AND WELFARE: SOME RECENT DEVELOPMENTS*

P. A. GEROSKI, L. PHLIPS AND A. ULPH

I. INTRODUCTION

IN THIS essay, we wish to highlight three particular areas in the enormous literature on oligopoly where, we believe, recent work has proved particularly productive and illuminating. One recent development of interest has been the application of game theory to the well known "interdependence of expectations" problem. While interesting in its own right, it has also had a major impact in clarifying thinking about rational strategic choice, and the role of information in affecting outcomes. Our view is that the information structure of the oligopoly problem plays a crucial role in conditioning the nature of its solution, and this is the first topic that we propose to discuss. These developments in theory have occurred in tandem with and, indeed, have stimulated empirical work. One important empirical problem is that of identifying the exercise of monopoly power in practice, and recent work has focussed on the problem of inferring conduct from observed price-output configurations. This obviously has a high order of policy importance, and it constitutes the second topic in our discussion. Rational strategic choice involves, *inter alia*, the use of various types of competitive weapons, and such modes of rivalry produce outcomes which differ substantially from competition in simple homogeneous goods markets. We wish to briefly highlight these, and then turn to one of the more interesting features of such competitive processes. When firms can strategically invest and pre-commit themselves to markets, the timing of competitive movements becomes important. A recent body of work has focussed on pre-emption, and the likelihood that monopoly positions—however created—can persist for long periods of time. This material is of major importance for those concerned with market dynamics, and we shall close this essay by highlighting some of the recent work on this topic.

II. OLIGOPOLY AND IMPERFECT INFORMATION

A number of interesting new developments on the oligopoly front can be traced back to Stigler [1964] who examined the relationship between collusion and the information structure of an oligopolistic market. He argued that the basic problem in colluding to maximize joint profits is that of policing the agreement (rather than joint profit maximization as such; see Roberts [1985] on this

* We are obliged to Beth Allen, Tim Bresnahan, Jean Jaskold Gabszewicz, and Bentley MacLeod for comments on various portions of early drafts. The usual disclaimer applies.

second issue). This is a problem in the theory of information, since secret price cutting must be detectable for retaliation to be possible, or for a threat of retaliation to be credible. Given this framework, subsequent research has tried to clarify a number of questions, three of which we shall consider in some detail.[1]

First, how much information (among rivals) is needed for collusion to be possible?

Second, does less information (among rivals) promote "active competition" or more frequent "price wars"? Interpreting "active competition" as a move from the profit frontier to a non-cooperative Nash equilibrium, this question can be reformulated as: does a non-cooperative Nash equilibrium require perfect information? If not, related questions are: (a) do duopolists, taken individually, wish to acquire more information in a non-cooperative equilibrium?; (b) do they wish to share information in such an equilibrium?

Third, can price wars or "active competition" be shown to result from (intertemporally) rational behaviour, rather than the result of a myopic pursuit of self interest? That is, can one define a non-cooperative equilibrium that includes both episodic price wars, as well as periods of effective collusion?

(i) *The Prisoners' Dilemma and Imperfect Information*

Credit should be given to Osborne [1976] for unveiling the information structure that is required for a group of oligopolists to come to a workable collusive agreement which maximizes joint profits on the one hand, and which deters cheating on the other. The basic dilemma is that whatever the point chosen on the profit frontier (see Figure 1), each member finds it profitable to produce more than the quota allotted to him and so has an incentive to cheat whether the other members cheat or not. The situation is that of the familiar prisoners' dilemma[2] in which each player has two strategies (observe the agreement or cheat) and the profits are such that for each player, cheating is a dominant strategy—i.e. the best strategy no matter what strategy the other player chooses. However, the strategy pair (cheat, cheat) is off the profit frontier (since profits to both firms could be increased by both observing the agreement), and so is "Pareto dominated" (it could be a Cournot–Nash equilibrium; see section (ii)). The other three strategy pairs are on the profit frontier (or "Pareto optimal"), since one firm's profit cannot be increased without decreasing others'

[1] We do not discuss oligopoly with asymmetric market information, such as badly informed buyers (see Nermuth [1979], Stahl [1982] and von Ungern-Sternberg [1984a, Chapter 5]) or badly informed sellers (see de Palma *et al.* [1983]). We will also not discuss the question of how firms may systematically mislead their less well informed rivals. Such signalling models have recently featured in discussions of entry; see, for example, Milgrom and Roberts [1982a] and [1982b], Kreps and Wilson [1982b] and Easley *et al.* [1985].

[2] Shubik [1982, p. 254] formulates the usual verbal scenario as follows: "Two prisoners who are suspected of having committed a crime are interrogated separately by the police. If both maintain silence, at most they can be booked on a minor charge. Each is encouraged to incriminate the other with a promise of leniency if he is not himself incriminated. If they double-cross each other, they are both in trouble."

profits. Explicit pooling of revenue agreements has long been thought to be the only way out of this problem, so that tacit collusion and explicit collusion without pooling seemed doomed to failure (see Patinkin [1947]). Osborne showed that the dilemma can be solved without explicit pooling if each firm is assigned an operating rule incorporating a deterrent to cheating. This "best reply" rule to cheating involves loyal firms increasing their output in the same proportion as the cheaters increase theirs.[3]

However, it should be realized that everything hinges on the information that is available to the players. To begin with, to locate their Pareto optimal strategy pairs, the members of an agreement should know the production of non-members. In addition, they should have adequate and compatible information on the payoff matrix itself, which implies compatible forecasts about future developments in the market and compatible time horizons. In short, they should be well informed about the rules of the game itself; i.e. their information should be "complete" (in the terminology of Selten [1982]). Clearly, this difficulty can be overcome, but it is likely to become more severe as the number of players increases. The detection of cheating also raises problems of "imperfect" information. For example, to deter cheating with quotas, information on the actual output of the players is essential. In order to be able to use Osborne's operating rule, either the output of each player or the total output of all players should be known. (In the latter case, the rule could be modified by supposing that the cheater has an average quota, but this would not deter small cheaters.)

At this point, an important caveat is in order. Osborne's rule is *not* a theoretical solution to the prisoners' dilemma as defined above: that dilemma occurs in a one-period game and remains without solution, while Osborne's rule implies the passage of time, with some cheaters increasing their output first and other firms reacting to this subsequently. Osborne's rule thus refers to a game in which history matters, and a satisfactory theoretical treatment should consider it as a strategy in a supergame (see section (iii)).

(ii) *Cournot–Nash Equilibrium and Imperfect Information*

Suppose information is incomplete and sufficiently imperfect for the players to be off the profit frontier. Is even a non-collusive equilibrium possible under these conditions? The answer is: yes. A non-cooperative game with "incomplete" information can be redefined as a game with complete information in extensive form, i.e. with all possible decisions, and the sequence of these decisions fully described.[4] The possibility of writing a game in extensive form

[3] Holahan [1978] has shown that this rule may leave loyal members worse off if sufficiently large differences exist between the profit functions of loyalists and cheaters. Rothschild [1981] identifies conditions under which loyal firms are worse off than they would have been if they had stood pat, even when all firms have identical profit functions.

[4] The classic reference is Harsanyi [1967–8]; Selten [1982] explains (in a not too technical way) how this can be done using fully worked out examples.

solves the problem of imperfect information analytically through the use of "information sets" which describe the lack of information at each stage of the game for each player.

A series of experiments have suggested much the same answer.[5] Experimental games conducted by Hoggatt ([1959], [1967]), Fouraker and Siegel [1963], Friedman ([1963], [1969], [1970]), Dolbear *et al.* [1968] and Sauermann and Selten [1967] show that when information about competitors is limited, and in the absence of communication between players, (posted) prices actually tend to a competitive equilibrium when Bertrand price strategies are played, even with very few players. With quantity decisions, the outcome is most often a non-cooperative Cournot–Nash equilibrium.[6] The accuracy of the joint maximization model was found to decrease with a reduction of information about other agents' actions, but joint profit maximization was the outcome under perfect information with experienced players (Stoecker [1980] and Friedman and Hoggatt [1980]). These results suggest that under imperfect information

> "the number of sellers becomes a very important treatment variable in that an increase in the number destroys the accuracy of the joint maximum model. In duopoly markets, significant (but less than perfect) cooperation occurs but, with an increase in the number of firms, it vanishes almost completely and the Cournot model is very accurate by comparison." (Plott [1982], p. 1516–1517).

These experimental results are compatible with the theoretical and econometric findings of Spence [1978] on tacit coordination and imperfect information. Spence introduces both *event uncertainty* (for example unforeseen changes in demand) and *imperfect information* (firms do not observe their competitors' behaviour directly but receive market signals, such as changes in total industry output or market shares), so that the reaction functions have market signals as arguments. These signals are, in turn, functions of the competitors' outputs and of the states of nature. Spence defines signalling equilibria (in terms of these reaction functions) such that no firm has an incentive to cheat when it takes the probability of being detected (and punished) into account, and the Cournot–Nash equilibrium turns out to be such an equilibrium; i.e. it has the property that the expected profit if one does not cheat is always larger than the expected profit if one cheats. To these equilibria correspond a region of payoffs (represented by a circle in Figure 1) around the Cournot–Nash equilibrium payoffs inside the profit frontier (Π_1 and Π_2 are their respective profits. m_1 and m_2 are the profits after penalties are inflicted on player 1 or 2 when a deviation from the equilibrium is detected).

[5] Excellent reviews of experiments in this field can be found in Selten [1979] and Plott [1982].

[6] The distinction between Bertrand price strategies and Cournot quantity strategies appears as less fundamental once it is realized that the Cournot outcome is also a perfect equilibrium in a two stage game in which the players choose their capacity in the first stage and compete in prices in the second stage, as shown by Kreps and Scheinkman [1983]. See also MacLeod [1984], and Dixon [1985].

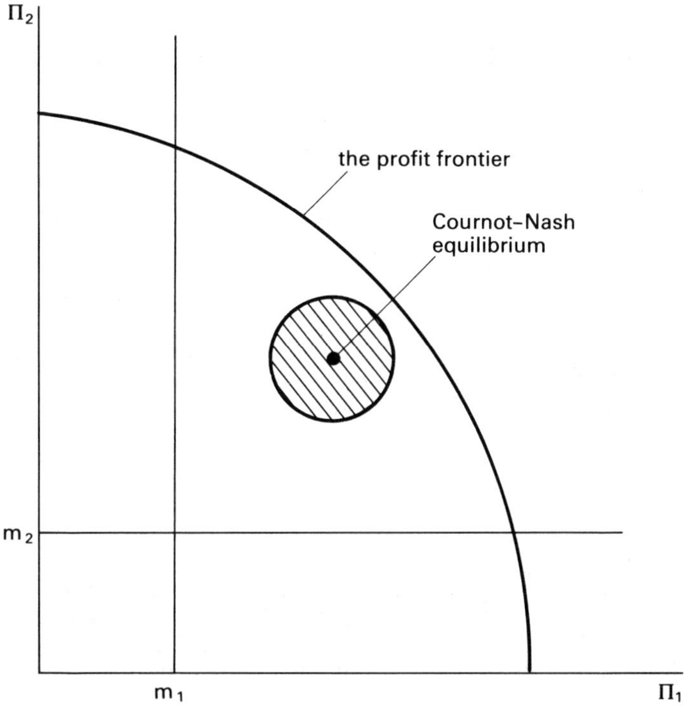

FIGURE 1

Thus, perfect information seems not to be a necessary ingredient of Cournot–Nash equilibria. This leaves open the question of whether non-cooperating oligopolists care about acquiring more private market information, and whether they are indifferent to sharing it. Novshek and Sonnenschein [1982] argue that they do want more information but are indifferent about sharing it if they have access to the same information set. Clarke ([1983a], [1983b]) shows that, if a crucial assumption made by Novshek and Sonnenschein is dropped, they do not wish to share information. The assumption is one of "fulfilled expectations". Expectations are "fulfilled", when, given the equilibrium, the expected joint evolution (the joint distribution) of a signal and the random variable on which it provides information is correct. The signal provides information about the value of the (random) intercept of the (linear) market demand equation, and each signal is defined as the simple average of observations on the intercept drawn from a sample owned by an independent information agency. Each firm's profit is defined in terms of these observations. It turns out that the profit of a firm increases with the information acquired by itself (or by a competitor if the latter pools some of it), but is the same whether all information is kept private or pooled. In a signalling Cournot–Nash equilibrium, players are thus indifferent with respect to information pooling.

However, total welfare (consumer surplus plus producer surplus) increases with the amount of information acquisition *and* with the amount of information release. Clarke ([1983a], [1983b]) replaces this *ex post* fulfilled expectations assumption by a "Bayes–Cournot" assumption, that firms make their quantity decisions based on their best Bayes estimates of their opponents' information. Using results obtained by Basar and Ho [1974], Clarke finds that in all cases where expectations are not actually fulfilled, firms would prefer not to share information[7] (even if they have less accurate information than their rivals) unless they will cooperate once the information has been shared.[8]

> "This situation is unfortunate as society's welfare is maximized only when firms share information, but act competitively. Thus society faces a dilemma. Information pooling is good if firms behave competitively, but shared information makes anticompetitive agreements easier to construct." (Clarke [1983b, p. 383]).

The policy implication is clear:

> "If all industry firms are observed to pool information without paying each other compensation, they must be setting quantities cooperatively on the basis of the homogenized information. Hence information-pooling mechanisms like trade associations can be considered *prima facie* evidence that firms are illegally cooperating to restrict output. This result strengthens Posner's [1976] informal analysis of the desirability of information-sharing agreements. On the other hand, lack of information-pooling mechanisms can be taken as fairly good evidence that cooperative behaviour is impeded." (Clarke [1983b, p. 392]).

(iii) *Tacit Collusion, Price Wars and Imperfect Information*

Having discussed the informational requirements of a collusive equilibrium and of a non-cooperative Cournot–Nash equilibrium, it seems natural to ask whether the two could not constitute the components of a non-cooperative Nash equilibrium in a "supergame". Not surprisingly, time now explicitly enters the picture: players are now viewed as playing (stationary) repeated game (also called "supergame") with an infinite horizon. The strategic variables are either quantities or prices and Osborne's instantaneous operating rule is replaced by the following intertemporal strategy. In the first period of the game, all players choose the collusive Pareto optimal quantities q_1^* (or prices). In any subsequent period, they continue to do so if, in all past periods, all players were loyal. If, however, this is not the case, then all players shift to the Cournot–Nash

[7] See also Crawford and Sobel [1982] and Palfrey [1982]. Empirical evidence on the exchange of information and collusion can be found in Eisenberg [1980].

[8] Gal–Or [1982] and Vives [1983] find this result to hold only if the goods produced are substitutes, and to be reversed for the case of Bertrand price competition (with substitutes).

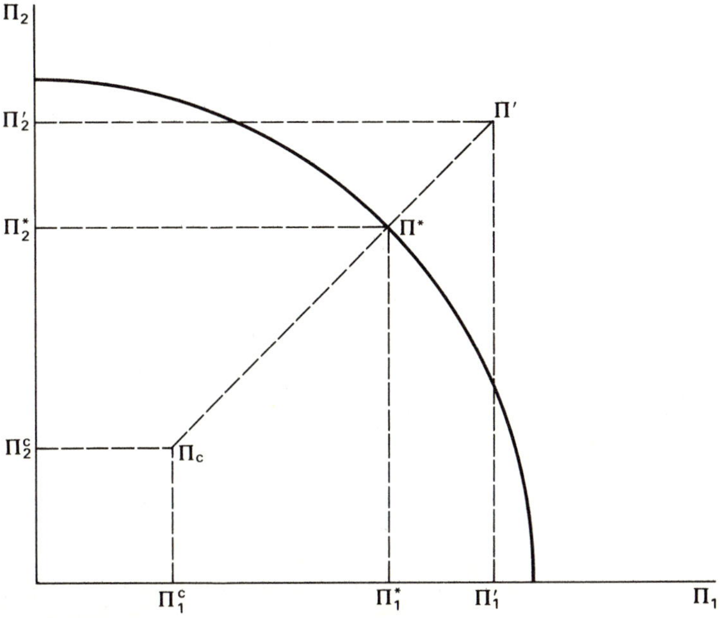

FIGURE 2

quantities q_i^c. The profit possibilities for a single period are represented in Figure 2.[9] Π^* represents the collusive profits and Π^c represents the profits when all firms have shifted to the Cournot–Nash equilibrium. It turns out that the collusive payoff Π^* can be obtained without an explicit agreement; "tacit collusion" can thus be defined in game-theoretic terms as the non-cooperative achievement of the collusive outcome.

To understand this, suppose the intertemporal strategy defined above is not played by a firm j in period t. Then its immediate profit is Π'_j. However, in period $t+1$ all rivals will switch to q_i^c, so the cheater's profit will be reduced to the level associated with the Cournot–Nash equilibrium. A tacitly collusive outcome occurs if the discounted flow of j's profits when j cheats is smaller than the discounted flow of profits when nobody cheats. This inequality will be satisfied if the discount factor $(1/(1+r))$, is close to one, i.e. if the rate of interest is sufficiently small. The discount factor plays such a crucial role because the important comparison for form j is between the immediate additional profit due to cheating $(\Pi'_j - \Pi^*_j)$ and the present value of subsequent per period losses of $(\Pi'_j - \Pi^c_j)$. This supergame approach gives a precise meaning to the concept of "tacit collusion" but solves the prisoners' dilemma too well: no firm ever has an

[9] These arguments were first presented by Friedman [1971] following an idea by Aumann [1960], and then included in his 1977 textbook (chapter 8); see also Friedman and Hoggatt [1980, chapter 1], Friedman [1972], Rees [1985], and, for a survey, Fudenberg and Tirole [1984].

incentive to cheat in this equilibrium![10] Porter ([1983a], [1983b]) and Green and Porter [1984] introduce imperfect information into the supergame, allowing for random shocks in demand so that firms are imperfectly informed on their rivals' output. An observed price decrease may then be blamed on the demand shock rather than on cheating, and this may give rise to some cheating. An intertemporal strategy that combats this problem is to switch to the Nash equilibrium as soon as the observed price is less than some "trigger price" which depends, *inter alia*, on the extent of uncertainty. The collusive quantities pertaining to this strategy are above their joint-profit-maximizing levels, but tend towards this level as the variance of the unobserved disturbance term (of demand) goes to zero. Interestingly, price wars now occur with positive probability; however, their occurrence is not the result of cheating, but of unusual demand shocks to which firms must respond in order to maintain the credibility of the punishment strategy.

III. THE EMPIRICAL ANALYSIS OF PRICING BEHAVIOUR

After several decades and countless inter-industry regressions, empirical work has begun to turn from examining simple correlations between industry concentration and average industry profitability towards looking more closely at the pricing behaviour underlying them. This recent work seeks to make inferences about existence of monopoly power from observed data on costs, demand, and equilibrium prices and quantities, and we wish to highlight some of its features here.[11]

(i) *Testing Price-Taking Behaviour*

Easily the simplest exercise one can perform is to attempt to test whether firms appear to be price takers. In general, however, an integral feature of the problem is the need to simultaneously estimate a marginal cost function and detect significant differences between it and prices at observed outputs.[12] With data on inputs and input costs, one can do this in a straightforward fashion by jointly estimating the parameters of a production function and the marginal revenue curve, and testing to see whether the latter is horizontal (one may date

[10] Price wars can occur only when the inequality just defined is reversed, and thus only a change in the interest rate could take an industry back into a non-cooperative equilibrium. Furthermore, with a sufficiently small interest rate, tacit collusion is likely to occur only in certain types of markets, such as geographically segmented markets (of the Loschian type—see MacLeod *et al.* [1984]) or markets with no rapid growth or slow technical progress, in which Friedman's inequality is relatively easy to compute in practice.

[11] The precise relationship between the work to be reviewed below and these earlier studies becomes evident when the profits-concentration link is written out in precise form; e.g. see Cowling and Waterson [1976]. For further remarks on this relationship, see Geroski [1982a].

[12] This is the natural way of dealing with the well known ambiguity of interpreting profit-concentration correlations as indicators of monopoly power or of superior efficiency (e.g. Demsetz [1974]). For other empirical work on this problem, see (*inter alia*) Caves and Pugel [1980], Mueller [1981] and Clarke *et al.* [1984], and the discussion in Scherer [1980].

this approach at least as early as Rosse [1970]; Appelbaum [1979] is a good recent example). However, testing for price-taking behaviour becomes considerably more complex when industry outputs cannot be reasonably taken as homogeneous. In this case, one must carefully specify and estimate the parameters of the demand functions for the products produced before one can examine whether the associated marginal revenue functions are horizontal.

Bresnahan [1981] attempted such an exercise for the U.S. Automobile industry in a cross-section study for 1977 and 1978. The basic simplification he used was to take products as being vertically differentiated. Consumers were modelled as differing in their valuation of product quality, and the demand for each product was built up from the demands of those consumers in its "quality segment" of the market. The cost side of the model was characterized by multiproduct production, and equilibrium was assumed (but not tested) to be Nash in prices. Using the first order conditions for equilibrium prices and quantities together with observed data on prices, quantities, and so on, enables one to infer the parameters of the unobserved cost and demand functions. Departures of prices from marginal costs can then be gauged by inspection (the statistical testing of this difference seems all but impossible given the complexity of the model). Bresnahan observed markups of the order of 10% over marginal cost, with higher markups observed for higher quality models, perhaps due to higher product bunching and more extensive foreign competition at the lower quality end of the product range.[13]

Since these exercises are rather data expensive, it is worth remarking that one can dispense with *precise* characterizations of equilibrium and the associated high demand for data. By inspecting these first order conditions, it is clear that the change in equilibrium prices and quantities induced by a perturbation of any of the exogenous variables will differ depending on pricing conduct (or, solution concept). It ought to be possible, then, to make some inferences about solution concepts by observing the responses of firms to outside shocks. Sumner [1981] (see also the comments of Bulow and Pfeiderer [1983]) and Just and Chern [1980] report interesting exercises of this variety, looking at the effects of taxes and technical changes respectively. However, it does seem to be exceedingly difficult to do more than observationally distinguish the responses of price takers from those of non-price takers without being very precise about characterizing equilibria, and this would seem to limit the appeal of this approach. Baker and Bresnahan [1985] have, however, developed a technique for assessing the change in market power (say, due to a merger) from pre-change data alone, without looking at post-change pricing conduct explicitly, and this

[13] This varying distortion of prices from marginal costs leads to some distortion of consumer purchases away from preferred models, and Bresnahan's estimates of this source of welfare loss suggests that it dominates conventional dead-weight loss, both of which sum to an aggregate loss of about 8% of industry revenues. It should be added that there are some doubts about the statistical significance of his loss estimates (deriving at least in part from the unsatisfactory estimates of the product quality scalar).

may turn out to be a data cheap way of predicting potential changes in monopoly power.

The importance of the work discussed thus far lies not so much in what it yields by way of conclusions on pricing conduct, but in the light it sheds on other, familiar empirical exercises. It is standard practice to use observed prices and quantities to make inferences about the parameters of costs (or production functions) and demand, and there seem to be no good grounds for believing that estimating these cost and demand parameters conditional on the assumption of price taking behaviour will yield unbiased estimates.

(ii) *Estimating Conjectural Variations*

In order to make progress and to develop a more detailed analysis of industry conduct, it is necessary to specify marginal revenue functions in a precise way. A natural way to parameterize various oligopoly solution concepts is by using conjectural variations—the expected change in rival's (or total industry) output consequent upon a change in the output of firm i.[14] Including these amongst the parameters to be estimated opens up the possibility of estimating and evaluating more precisely the departure of price from marginal cost (see Bresnahan [1982] on identifying conjectures). This is the focus of Iwata's paper [1974]. He generated extraneous estimates of cost and demand functions for the Japanese Flat Glass industry and then, using the first order conditions describing output choice together with observed prices and outputs, solved directly for the implied values of the conjectural variations. The sources of statistical uncertainty in the demand and cost functions were then used to develop confidence intervals around these calculated conjectural variations under various null hypotheses about their values. A very similar approach was taken by Cubbin [1975] in an examination of the U.K. Car industry, who used the equilibrium relation between price-cost margins and the elasticity of demand to make some inferences about changes in conduct over the period 1956–69 by (in effect) solving for the implied values of conjectural variations.[15]

The most elaborate exercise of this type is the study done by Gollop and Roberts [1979] on firms in the U.S. Coffee Roasting industry. They attempted to estimate a *pattern* of conjectural variations (together with production function parameters[16]) across rival firms i rather than either a single conjectural vari-

[14] It is often argued that conjectural variations are hard to interpret in the one shot games characteristic of static oligopoly theory, since the action-reaction sequence posited by such conjectures has no meaning (e.g. see Friedman [1983]). This is not a very compelling criticism of the work we are discussing here. Our lack of knowledge of solution concepts can, as a matter of econometric convenience, be parameterized as a lack of knowledge about conjectures. It is then natural to think of such conjectural variations parameters as *describing* the different equilibrium positions which may have generated the data, but not necessarily as *explaining* them in a theoretically satisfying manner.

[15] An alternative way to reach much the same goal is to try to estimate a "conjectural variation elasticity" (e.g. Dickson [1982], Geroski [1983], and Applebaum [1982]).

[16] Gollop and Roberts used an extraneous estimate of the elasticity of demand which is extraordinarily low and, in particular, rules out the possibility that pricing behaviour could be cooperative. It appears (footnote 15, p. 322) that their estimates of the values of the conjectural

ation parameter for firm i *vis-à-vis* all rivals, or a single summary number aggregated across all firms i. Since there are $N(N-1)$ such cross conjectural variations between i and j in an N firm industry, they imposed an *a priori* structure expressing the conjectures of all firms in terms of those of certain "benchmark firms", thus dramatically shrinking the set of parameters to be estimated. This procedure naturally enables one to consider asymmetric models of oligopoly, and Gollop and Roberts were able to reject Cournot and price-taking behaviour in favour of something reminiscent of Dominant Firm or Stackelberg models.[17]

The main difficulty with all of these studies is that the results are, in a sense, difficult to interpret, for the numbers estimated differ from those corresponding to the familiar solution concepts of oligopoly theory (e.g. zero conjectural variations correspond to Cournot and conjectural variations equal to minus unity correspond to price-taking behaviour). Clearly, it would be useful to estimate conjectures subject to the constraint that the estimates are interpretable in the light of familiar oligopoly models. The important point to grasp is the fact that different solution concepts place precise restrictions on the values of conjectural variations.[18] Thus, for each solution concept taken in turn, conjectural variations are not an unknown parameter to be estimated; rather, they can be expressed as a number or in terms of the fundamental underlying parameters of costs and demand, depending on the details of the particular oligopoly model under consideration.

A start has been made on this problem by Geroski [1982b] and M. Roberts [1983], using the Gollop and Roberts [1979] database. Both authors examine several solution concepts (including Price-Taking, Cournot, Stackelberg, Collusion, Dominant Firm, and Consistent Conjectures Models) and conclude that the Dominant Firm model best describes the data. There is some disagreement about the size of the Dominant Firm group in the two papers (the leading five or two firms respectively), and a puzzle about precisely how to explain the very high levels of concentration in this industry,[19] but there is no doubt that there

---

variations (though perhaps not their pattern) are rather sensitive to the precise value of the demand elasticity used.

[17] Slade [1984] and Anderson [1984] both push this type of exercise one step further, and try to explain the variations in conjectures across firms they observe by a variety of firm specific factors. Spiller and Favaro [1984] look at the effects of entry regulation on pricing conduct, in the process comparing a Stackelberg model to others somewhat in the manner of the studies discussed immediately below.

[18] This is easiest to see in the case of Cournot and price-taking behaviour where the conjectural variations are just numbers. In the case of the Stackelberg model, the followers are Cournot while the conjectural variations of the leader are equal to the slope of the follower's reaction function. Much the same is true in the Dominant Firm model, where the followers in this case are Price-Takers. Consistent Conjectures, to take a final example, are defined at an equilibrium where each firm correctly conjectures the slope of its rival's reaction functions.

[19] A basic problem applying to almost all the work discussed thus far is to explain the degree of concentration in the industries studied. The usual practice of assuming that all firms in the industry operate on a common production frontier implicitly assumes (in a homogeneous goods industry) that variations in factor prices and/or asymmetry in conjectures adequately explain the observed distribution of output across industry members.

are fairly strong grounds for believing that this oligopoly model is a superior description of the U.S. Coffee Roasting industry to most of the well known alternatives.

(iii) *Varying Conduct Models*

The studies that we have examined are useful for the positive and precise information that they yield about industry conduct. However, their value is clearly dependent on the stability of conduct patterns. To the extent that conduct is stable over time in industries, then the knowledge of conduct in some year t can be used to predict and evaluate industry performance in the future.[20] This observation, in turn, suggests that it is important to develop models which allow for systematic conduct change over time. The gain here comes not only from testing the proposition that conduct is stable, but also from developing models capable of explaining price wars, cartel formation, pricing behaviour over the business cycle, and so on.

Porter [1983b] provides one example of this type of work (see also the extension in Lee and Porter [1984], and Porter [1985]; Bresnahan [1981] is also interesting in this regard).[21] His model posits discrete shifts in industry conduct between cooperative and non-cooperative pricing regimes, the trigger shifting the industry into a "price war" being an unexpected drop in demand (see section II above). Applying his model to the Joint Executive Committee, a cartel controlling freight shipments from the East Coast of the U.S. at the end of the last century, he estimated demand and cost functions with a varying parameter indicating whether an industry wide conjectural variations term varied from price-taking values to something less than full collusive values.[22] He observed that cooperative periods were, in fact, characterized by Cournot prices (giving the cartel added 11% higher revenue in cooperative periods), that non-cooperative periods lasted about 10 weeks on average, and that two of the three "price wars" observed occurred following significant entry. Whether it was, in fact, demand which triggered the price wars (which were identified by using trade reports of the time which identified whether a war was occurring) is a little unclear since they did not appear to occur in periods of low demand. In any case, it does seem clear from his results that significant shifts in conduct occurred.

[20] Perhaps through the use of "industry-performance gradients" (e.g. Dansby and Willig [1979]; see the computations of M. Roberts [1983] for the U.S. Coffee Roasting industry), or the construction of "appropriate" indices of concentration (see Geroski [1983] for the U.S. Cigarette industry).

[21] By contrast, Geroski and Ulph [1984] parameterized the conduct of the oil producing nations in terms of "co-efficients of cooperation" (see Cyert and DeGroot [1973]) rather than conjectural variations. These were taken to shift in a continuous fashion depending on an assortment of factors, including past conduct, financial needs and capacity. Their model easily outperformed a "constant conduct" version in accounting for the 1973 and 1978 price "shocks".

[22] His model suggests that, because of uncertainty, cooperative prices will be below full joint profit maximizing levels, and he regards the evaluation of just how high they are to be part of the goals of estimation.

IV. NON-PRICE STRATEGIC COMPETITION

Textbook models of non-cooperative behaviour with homogeneous products give rise to a presumption of competitive outcomes when markets are "large enough" and economies of scale become negligible (Novshek and Sonnenschein [1980] and others) or when conduct is Nash in prices. However, this presumption does not survive the introduction of non-price competition (see Marris and Mueller [1980] who develop this theme). Non-price strategies weaken the impact of price competition by partially isolating any one firm's product from the effects of a price cut by other producers, and by providing a richer set of strategies for firms to consider. Further, in these more complex competitive processes, one is led to focus on issues and types of analyses rather different from those used in homogeneous goods industries.

(i) *Product Differentiation and the Localization of Competition*

From the viewpoint of oligopoly theory, the introduction of non-price competition (especially product or locational differentiation) substantially complicates the expectations that firms must form. In a homogeneous goods industry, it is only the *aggregate* response of rivals' outputs that matters to any particular firm; with differentiated goods, the firm not only has to weigh the likely price or output response of *individual* rivals, but also must consider how a change in the equilibrium set of prices or outputs will in turn affect the choice of advertising, production, location and so on. Indeed, non-price competition may so successfully blunt the impact of price competition that, at the level of price/output choice, firms can quite legitimately ignore the effect they have on other firms.[23] These effects, however, are somewhat mitigated if firms are only concerned with a relatively small number of (possibly "local") rivals.

Here one can usefully distinguish two approaches in the literature to modelling product differentiation. The first approach is that of *horizontally differentiated* goods. This arises when all goods offered at the same price are ranked differently by different consumers because they value the characteristics in these goods differently. An important further distinction here is between *symmetric* and *asymmetric preferences*. With asymmetric preferences (e.g. Phlips and Thisse [1982], Lancaster [1979], and others), there is an ordering of goods such that if a consumer has a strong preference for good i he will also have strong preference for goods close to i; with symmetric preferences (see Dixit and Stiglitz [1977], Perloff and Salop [1983], Sattinger [1983], and Hart [1983], amongst others), a consumer's preference for good i tells one nothing about his preference for goods $i+1$. All spatial models generate asymmetric preferences and, by analogy, one conjectures that as long as the number of characteristics is small relative to the number of goods, one is likely to have asymmetric preferences.

[23] This latter insight may be useful in rationalizing certain solution concepts such as Nash or Bertrand (Hart [1983]).

However, if one believes that the number of characteristics is very large compared to the number of goods, then symmetric preferences may be more plausible (Hart [1983]). With symmetric preferences, as the number of firms grows, the influence of any one firm on others diminishes and the appropriate equilibrium notion is monopolistic competition.[24] This corresponds roughly to the kind of presumption found in textbook stories. With asymmetric preferences, however, even if the number of firms becomes very large, each firm has a small number of close neighbours who are affected by the price it sets (Salop [1979b], Lancaster [1979], Stern [1972], Schmalensee [1978]). Competition is thus localized within the industry, and individual firms still face a downward sloping demand curve.

The second approach to modelling product differentiation can be found in the work of Shaked and Sutton on natural oligopolies ([1982], [1983a], [1983b]). Here the framework is that of *vertical product differentiation*: if all goods were offered at the same price, consumers would unanimously select only the "highest quality" good. In this case, all the characteristics of the different goods can be aggregated into a single "quality" index. Shaked and Sutton show that if the *variable* costs of production rise only slowly with quality then there is a limit on the number of firms that can exist irrespective of how product quality is chosen. Once this number of firms is reached, then no further reduction in fixed costs or expansion of the market could increase the number of firms in equilibrium, and hence these markets will remain "naturally oligopolistic". As with the asymmetric preferences case, the usual limiting arguments about competition will fail to apply. This, of course, eliminates the presumption that markets will reach a perfectly competitive equilibrium outcome.

(ii) *Sequential Competition, Pre-emption and First Mover Advantage*

Non-price competition not only blunts the effects of price-competition, but, also widens the set of weapons available to firms. At the very least, this means that decisions on price and non-price variables need to be taken simultaneously, recognizing the interaction they have on each other and recognizing the variety of responses rivals may make to price changes (Lambin *et al.* [1975]). But, there is a more important point. The weapons of non-price competition (choice of product, advertising, R&D level, capacity investment) often have the characteristic of involving sunk and irreversible investment, and this gives these weapons a powerful additional role to play as commitments that make threats against rivals credible (see Salop [1979a]; Dixit [1982] and Encaoua *et al.* [1984]). The area in which this effect has played a most prominent role is that of entry, where the weapons of non-price competition can be used as pre-emptive investments by incumbents to bias post-entry outcomes against en-

[24] Indeed, not only do cross price effects become negligible, but own price effects may become so large that equilibrium tends towards perfect competition; see Perloff and Salop [1983].

trants, and so enable incumbent monopolists to persist (Geroski and Jacquemin [1984]).

The simplest context in which to analyse the role of non-price competition in creating credible commitments is that of capacity (Spence [1977], Dixit [1980] and the extension by Ware [1984], Spence [1979], Eaton and Lipsey [1980] and [1981], and Salop [1979a]). A threat by incumbents to maintain high output in the face of entry (i.e. the "Sylos" postulate) is not a credible one, for output decisions are easily reversed. After entry occurs, it is generally more profitable for the incumbent to cut output and share the market than to maintain output at pre-entry levels, the potential entrant can calculate this, and so will not be rationally deterred by such empty threats. Such threatened actions by the incumbent to make entry unprofitable for the entrant often damage the incumbent as well and, to make it credible that the incumbent will carry out such actions post-entry, the incumbent will have to alter the nature of the post-entry game in a way that makes it profitable to carry out his threat (the classic reference on "self-crippling" strategies is Schelling [1960]). Such actions taken pre-entry to alter the payoffs in the post-entry game are called pre-commitments, and by the argument just advanced, they must be irreversible to be credible. The use of *capacity* as a threat is promising because once the incumbent has sunk his capital costs,[25] it is only the *variable* costs of production that are relevant to the incumbent. The entrant must incur both fixed and variable costs, and so suffers a disadvantage. Similar analyses can be carried out in which the variable chosen at the first stage is not capacity, but product specification. Assuming that there are *sunk* costs of product choice, then a strategy of carefully scattering products throughout the product space will leave no gaps for subsequent entrants to profitably exploit (Eaton and Lipsey [1978], Schmalensee [1978], Hay [1976], Prescott and Visscher [1977], Lane [1980]). One interesting consequence of this is that the clustering result of the original Hotelling [1929] spatial model does not appear in general (Eaton and Lipsey [1975] and [1976] and Shaked and Sutton [1982]).

A rather different type of first mover advantage emerges in the discussion of pre-emptive patenting as an entry barrier (Gilbert and Newbery [1982], [1984a] and [1984b], Reinganum [1981], [1983] and [1984], Lee and Wilde [1980], Loury [1979], Dasgupta and Stiglitz [1980] and, for a survey, Dasgupta [1984]). Here the notion is that an incumbent seeks to protect an existing monopolized market from the development of a close substitute product by a potential entrant. If the incumbent patents the substitute first, he will be able to maximize profit across both markets, whereas if the entrant develops it, the resulting equilibrium will be a duopoly. Since total profit across both products will be lower under duopoly than monopoly, the patent is worth more to the

[25] Much of the analysis assumes infinitely lived capital (see Eaton and Lipsey [1980] and [1981]). When investments are not sunk, markets may become contestable (see Baumol *et al.* [1982]), in which case monopolists can be completely disciplined by entry threats.

monopolist than the entrant, and so the incumbent will "outbid" the entrant, and pre-empt.[26] One rather special patent race occurs where firms seek a new process to produce an already existing product at the same cost. In this case, the incumbent has no interest in the patent *per se*, but he still wants to prevent the potential entrant winning the patent because that will erode his monopoly position. Obviously, the patent will be left "sleeping" by the incumbent if he develops it first. This case is discussed by Gilbert and Newbery [1982] and emphasized by Harris and Vickers [1985]. Harris and Vickers also introduce the notion that R&D may involve many stages of expenditure. If this is the case, then, in a perfect equilibrium, the incumbent may be able to gain a winning advantage very early in the race and force the entrant to retire. Note that, in the R&D context, one does not necessarily have to impose some first mover advantage on the game to observe pre-emption; the asymmetry that produces the result arises solely from the fact that a monopoly already exists and so the monopolist has more to lose if he does not gain the patent than just the cost of the R&D.

Two final points should be mentioned. Much of the discussion so far has been focussed on the context of the entry problem, in which some asymmetry between incumbent and entrant was assumed. Some work has been done on multi-stage strategic games without asymmetries—e.g. models of capacity choice by Kreps and Scheinkman [1983] and Dixon [1984]. They show that if all firms choose capacity at the first stage and in the second stage prices are set either in a competitive market (Dixon) or as a Bertrand equilibrium modified to take account of capacity restrictions (Kreps and Scheinkman), then the final outcome is identical to a one-stage Cournot equilibrium. This is a move towards trying the solution concept employed in the price setting game more closely to the outcome of the strategic competition. Work on symmetric models of strategic competition is more prevalent in the R&D literature (see Dasgupta [1982] for a survey). There the link between the market structure that prevails in the output stage of the model and the level of strategic competition is addressed directly (although no notion of causality is implied). Second, the notion of credibility employed in the above literature effectively assumes that there is perfect information—the entrant needs to know the characteristics of the incumbent so that it can compute rational behaviour by the incumbent in the post-entry game, while the incumbent needs to know the characteristics of the entrant to choose the level of entry-deterring precommitment. In the context of entry, the assumption of perfect information seems especially in-

[26] Reinganum [1983] shows that this asymmetry in favour of the incumbent can be eroded if there is some uncertainty in the R&D process. If there is some uncertainty about the date at which a given investment of R&D resources will yield results, then, by bidding a bit less, the incumbent only marginally reduces his chance of winning the patent, but extends the likely time before the product is patented, and hence lengthens the period over which his existing market earns monopoly profits. There is a rather confused debate about whether the original Gilbert–Newbery result also depended on first move advantage, but the fact that the problem can be viewed as a bidding game suggests that move order is not crucial (Reinganum [1984], Gilbert and Newbery [1984]).

appropriate,[27] but the problem is more pervasive than that, and requires some fairly extensive modifications along the lines mentioned in section II above.

(iii) *Welfare Implications*

As is well known, with horizontally differentiated products, one has to consider not only the familiar welfare losses arising from suboptimal levels of production by oligopolistic firms, but also the question of whether the range of products provided is socially optimal. One of the important developments in the recent literature has been a careful treatment of the problem of optimal product variety, for which Spence [1976], Dixit and Stiglitz [1977], Lancaster [1975] and Meade [1974] are the seminal sources. What gives the issue bite is increasing returns to scale. If there were non-increasing returns, the first best solution would be to price each variety at marginal cost and produce every variety for which there was a positive demand at marginal cost. With increasing returns, it will pay to reduce the range of products offered in order to reap economies of scale on those that are produced. The first best can be achieved by price discrimination (Spence [1976], Phlips [1983]), since this will achieve both the right quantity setting rule (marginal price equals marginal cost) and the right product choice rule (produce all products with non-negative profits). This option is attractive if there are 100% profit taxes and lump sum handouts to deal with the surpluses. An alternative is to have marginal cost pricing (which achieves the right output rule), and some calculating by the government of consumer surpluses to decide which products to produce and hence subsidize. However, the design of lump sum taxes to finance these subsidies is a delicate matter (Brown and Heal [1979]). Obviously first best policies are not of much interest for the usual reasons, but only rather limited forms of constrained (or second best) analyses are available (for example, Dixit and Stiglitz [1977] examine optimal product variety under the constraint of average cost pricing). Usually authors compare the product variety selected by the market with that in a first best (or very simple second best) equilibrium. The interesting result is that there is no general conclusion about whether markets achieve too little or too much product variety. Again, textbook presumptions about the beneficial workings of free markets fail to carry through.

When goods are vertically differentiated, a rather different set of welfare issues arises, for there is now no intrinsic consumer benefit from variety (*ceteris paribus* all consumers would prefer to have the highest quality product).[28] If

[27] A discussion of what form credibility constraint should take in the absence of perfect information (together with an analysis of the resulting equilibria) can be found in Geroski, Ingham and Ulph [1984].

[28] One topic of some importance is the analysis (positive and normative) or markets where consumers are unsure of product quality (e.g. von Ungern-Sternberg and von Weizsäcker [1985], Grossman and Shapiro [1984], Ireland [1985], and Wolinsky [1983] [1984]). Once again, this calls for further development of models involving information acquisition and evaluation along the lines discussed above.

there are identical constant costs of producing each quality, only the best quality would be produced (compared with horizontal differentiation where *every* variety would be produced), and economies of scale only add to the argument for concentrating on one product. What gives rise to the need to produce different qualities is inequalities in the distribution of income and this introduces a wider set of welfare concerns.[29]

Finally, let us turn briefly to the welfare aspects of strategic competition. The issues are not unrelated to those just discussed in the debate on optimal product variety, and once again we would expect the results to be ambiguous. Two broad forces are at work. Unless perfect price discrimination is practised, the private gains from strategic investment will be below social gains and this will be a factor leading to too little investment. For example, if R&D can be easily imitated despite patents, then there will be no private incentives to innovate, though social gains may be large (e.g. Kamien and Schwartz [1982]). On the other hand, the value of strategic investment as a precommitment suggests that there will be overinvestment and a "dissipation of rents". In the R&D context, having more than one firm do R&D may create waste (Dasgupta [1984]). Waste can occur if one firm pre-empts but leaves the resulting patent "sleeping", and there may still be overinvestment in that all the profits of the potential entrant are eliminated in R&D expenditure. How these factors balance out in practice will be a matter of empirical investigation; Yarrow [1985] provides some orders of magnitude to suggest that conventional measures of welfare loss may be substantial underestimates.

ACCEPTED NOVEMBER 1984

P. A. GEROSKI AND A. ULPH,
Department of Economics,
The University,
Southampton SO9 5NH,
U.K.

and

L. PHLIPS,
CORE,
Université Catholique de Louvain,
34 Voie du Roman Pays,
1348 Louvain-la-Neuve,
Belgium.

[29] At first sight, it might appear that moves to equalize income distribution would work in the *same* direction as cost minimization by justifying only producing one quality of good. However, Beath and Ulph [1984] argue that if the cost of producing higher quality products rises quite slowly with quality (precisely the condition needed to generate natural oligopolies), then the indirect utility of income may not be concave (essentially because this may cause a sharp increase in the quality people choose as income rises). Then, even if one has a welfare function which has inequality aversion (except only extreme Rawlsian inequality aversion), it may be desirable to have an unequal distribution of income with low income households consuming low quality goods and high income families consuming high quality goods.

THE JOURNAL OF INDUSTRIAL ECONOMICS 0022-1821 $2.00
Volume XXXIII June 1985 No. 4

CHEATING IN A DUOPOLY SUPERGAME[1]

RAY REES

I. INTRODUCTION

THIS PAPER examines an approach to oligopoly theory, first proposed in a relatively neglected paper by George J. Stigler [1964]. Suppose that the firms in an oligopoly have achieved, tacitly or explicitly, a collusive agreement, and that open defection, in a sense to be made more precise below, does not pay. Given that the other firms observe the agreement, it pays any one of them to cheat, that is, to make secret price cuts to selected buyers in order to secure sales it may not otherwise have made. Stigler then sets out to define the likely extent of the gain a cheat can make without detection and to relate this to observable market parameters. This would allow prediction of the probable incidence of cheating in a market and hence of the effectiveness of the collusive agreement.

Stigler first argues that in a purely deterministic world, there could be no scope for cheating. Each firm's sales could be fully anticipated and any deviation from the expected level would be immediate evidence of cheating, which becomes, in effect, open defection. Implicit in this, of course, is the assumption that firms can observe each others' outputs at negligible cost—a reasonable assumption which will be maintained throughout the rest of this paper. If the world is not in fact deterministic, then scope for cheating may arise. Suppose that in each period any one buyer buys from any one seller with a probability between zero and one. Then, each seller's sales in each period are a random variable and it is possible that a seller may attribute to chance a well above average sales level which in fact was due to cheating. In deciding whether to accept this, the other sellers are involved in hypothesis testing and the critical level of this test will determine how far a cheat dare go.

Stigler's development of this idea in a formal model is open to a number of specific criticisms. McKinnon [1966] criticized the excessively simplistic decision-theoretic basis of Stigler's model. In deciding whether a rival has gained above average sales by cheating or simply by chance, a firm is assumed to use a standard significance test with conventional critical levels, the choice of which is entirely unexplained in the model. There is also an unnecessary separation of tests according to the precise source of the buyers won by cheating—previous customers of the cheat, other firms' customers or newly-

[1] Earlier versions of this paper have been presented at seminars at Exeter, Hull and Southampton Universities in the U.K., and at the Center for Mathematical Studies in Economics and Management Science, Northwestern University, Evanston, Illinois. I am grateful to participants in those seminars for many helpful comments, and in particular to Ray Deneckere, Peter Dolton, Paul Geroski, and Alistair Ulph. A referee made some especially helpful comments. I am also very grateful to Neil Manning for help in carrying out the simulations reported in section III of the paper.

entered buyers. To these criticisms, I would add the observation that Stigler's model is internally inconsistent. In calculating the gains from cheating, Stigler appears to assume that the cheat is able to control precisely the total number of buyers he receives so as to remain below the critical level at which the hypothesis of no cheating would be rejected. This explains the implication of Stigler's model that cheating is always profitable, and also the absence in the model of any specific analysis of retaliation to detected cheating, or of an enforcement mechanism. Consider, however, the following description of the market. At the collusive price, there is a given population of buyers with given probabilities of buying from each seller. A seller cheats by approaching some subset of these buyers and offering each of them, secretly and individually, a price cut if they will buy from him for sure. However, the cheating firm will also still receive, at random, some of the buyers to whom it does *not* offer secret price cuts and there is no guarantee that, given the level of cheating, the sum of the cheating sales and the sales made by chance will not exceed the critical level. Thus, a cheat can never be sure that he will get away with cheating, and the question of detection, retaliation and enforcement becomes a relevant one.[2]

Perhaps the main criticism of Stigler's model is, however, that it does not specify the equilibrium outcome in the market. Stigler is content to tabulate the gains from cheating as a function of market parameters with resulting behavior left implicit. But, what precisely will be the market outcome when each firm knows that there are gains to cheating, and knows the others know, etc? Does Stigler's basic insight, that randomness permits cheating, have interesting and well-defined implications for market equilibrium? This paper sets up a simple formal model to explore these questions, using the concept of a "supergame".

A supergame consists of an infinitely repeated "constituent game". In the following section, a constituent game is constructed which embodies Stigler's main ideas. It is shown that viewed in isolation, or in single-play terms, this game is uninteresting. It yields the conclusion that whenever cheating is profitable, the collusive agreement will collapse. This can be viewed as simply an illustration of the difficulty of rationalizing collusive behavior in a single-period oligopoly model—adherence to a collusive agreement which maximizes joint profits is not a best response for one firm to the strategy of adherence by the others. In the supergame, on the other hand, adherence to the collusive agreement can become an individually rational strategy and we find that Stigler's ideas (which clearly were formulated for a world of successive market periods) have some interesting implications.

[2] One could, of course, assume that the cheat could turn away random buyers if he is in danger of exceeding the critical level of sales (though actually it would be more profitable to turn away buyers to whom he has offered a secret price cut). In that case, the model analysed in this paper would not apply in its entirety—some other mechanism would have to be found for detecting cheating. However, if, as we assume, such rejection of would-be buyers can always be observed by the other firms, or is technically not possible, then our objection continues to hold. Moreover, it seems to be consistent with Stigler's approach to assume that the number of buyers each seller gets cannot be perfectly controlled, since, if it could, the collusive agreement could specify individual firms' outputs and no possibilities of cheating would then arise.

Specifically, we consider a model of a duopoly market in which the individual firms' demands, at the collusive price, are random variables. We suppose that one firm wishes to enforce the collusive agreement on the other by choosing a critical level of the other's sales which, if exceeded, will be taken as evidence of cheating and so will induce retaliatory price competition, so as to punish the "cheat". We find that where the number of buyers is reasonably large—at least 70—and for a reasonable range of per-period interest rates, an "enforcement equilibrium" exists in which the threat of retaliatory action is enough to induce the other firm never to cheat.

It is, of course, a rather one-sided approach to cast one firm in the role of the enforcer and the other in the role of the cheat. However, *given* that enforcement is effective and no cheating takes place, the analysis is symmetrical: each firm can be thought of, in turn, as the enforcer and the potential cheat. The analysis of the paper then defines a Nash equilibrium: one firm's best reply to choice of a particular critical level and the decision not to cheat by the other, is itself not to cheat and to adopt its own optimal critical level. Moreover, the expected cost to each firm—in terms of the expected value of the loss of profit from adopting the retaliatory pricing strategy—is very small. Thus, the enforcement equilibrium, implying a stable collusive agreement, seems to be a plausible market outcome. This is in contrast to Stigler's analysis, which seemed to suggest that cheating would be widespread.

II. THE CONSTITUENT GAME

Let $t = 0, 1, \ldots$ denote the time period, and at each t, the same game will be played. There are two firms, indexed $i, j = 1, 2, i \neq j$, with homogeneous outputs and equal, constant unit costs c. The market demand function $x(p)$, with $p = \min(p_1, p_2)$, is assumed to be both certain and constant over time. Each firm chooses a price. If $p_i = p_j$, then $q_i = 1/2$ is the probability that each buyer in the market at that price will buy from i, expressing the idea that buyers are indifferent between sellers. $p_i < p_j \Rightarrow q_i = 1$, so the firm with a lower price would capture the entire market. If x_{it} is firm i's sales at t, then when $p_i = p_j = p$ at t, x_{it} is a binomial variable, that is, $x_{it} \sim B(q_i x(p), q_i q_j x(p))$, although in this paper it will be assumed that market demand x is sufficiently large that x_{it} can be regarded as a normally distributed real variable on $[0, x]$. Let $f_i(x_{it}, x)$ denote the probability density function for x_{it}, when x is the total demand which will be allocated between the firms randomly.

Given this simple model, it is straightforward to define a number of equilibrium concepts for the constituent game. Since the model is essentially one of homogeneous, symmetric price-setting duopoly, it is well known that the Nash or non-competitive equilibrium in this model implies $p_i = p_j = p^c = c$, the marginal-cost pricing or perfectly competitive outcome. If, therefore, the game was played non-competitively, at any t expected profit of firm i is $\bar{\pi}_i^c \equiv (p^c - c) q_i x(p^c) = 0$. Note that this solution is the only equilibrium having the best-reply property in a single-play of the constituent game: given any $p_j \neq c$, the p_i which maximizes i's profit $\neq p_j$, but $p_i = c$ maximizes i's profit when $p_j = c$, $i, j = 1, 2$, $i \neq j$.

The *collusive equilibrium*, of course, looks much better for the firms. Since market demand is certain and constant, at each t, the joint-profit maximizing price p^* is the same. Then, when $p_i = p^*$, expected profits in each period are $\bar{\pi}_i^* \equiv (p^* - c)q_i x^* > 0$, $i = 1, 2$ with $x^* = x(p^*)$.

Open defection occurs when at some t, firm i chooses a price $p_i^D = p^* - \varepsilon$, $\varepsilon > 0$. Since, by assumption, j has set $p_j = p^*$ at this t, i will make "defection profits" of $\pi_i^D = (p_i^D - c)x(p^D) > \bar{\pi}_i^*$, with j's resulting profit $\pi_j^D = 0$. We have $\pi_i^D > \bar{\pi}_i^*$ because, since outputs are homogeneous, ε can be arbitrarily small, and the entire market output at $p^* - \varepsilon$ must yield more profit[3] than the expected output $q_i x^*$ at p^*.

We can now introduce the concept of a *balanced temptation equilibrium* (bte).[4] Suppose i were to defect openly at some t, and j retaliated by moving to the Cournot equilibrium $p_j = p^c$ from $t+1$ onward. Such open defection would not be worthwhile to i if, given the per period interest rate r, we have:

$$(1) \qquad \pi_i^D - \bar{\pi}_i^* \leqslant \frac{\bar{\pi}_i^*}{r}$$

since this implies that the single period profit gain from open defection, $\pi_i^D - \bar{\pi}_i^*$, is at least offset by the value at t of the loss of profit in each future period resulting from j's retaliation, $(\bar{\pi}_i^* - \bar{\pi}_i^c)/r = \bar{\pi}_i^*/r$. Then, define:

$$(2) \qquad r_i^0 \equiv \frac{\bar{\pi}_i^*}{\pi_i^D - \bar{\pi}_i^*}, \qquad i = 1, 2$$

and the set

$$(3) \qquad \mathcal{R} = \{r \in \mathbb{R}_+ \mid r \leqslant \min(r_1^0, r_2^0)\}$$

Assuming both firms face the same interest rate, a bte is said to exist when this interest rate $r \in \mathcal{R}$. Although each firm might be tempted to defect openly, it pays neither to do so. Of course, in any given market, the interest rate may be too high for a bte to exist—future losses are discounted sufficiently heavily that they do not offset the immediate gain from open defection. However, we can interpret Stigler's assumption that open defection is ruled out as implying that the market is in a bte.[5]

[3] More precisely, given continuity of the demand function, it is always possible to find small enough ε to make this statement true for $q_i = 1/2$.

[4] The concept was introduced by Friedman [1977], though the underlying idea can be found in Luce and Raiffa [1966].

[5] In fact, this assumption is not a terribly strong one in the present model. Since ε can be very small, we can take

$$r_i^0 = \frac{\bar{\pi}_i^*}{\bar{\pi}_i^D - \bar{\pi}_i^*} \approx \frac{(p^* - c)q_i x^*}{(p^* - c)x^* - (p^* - c)q_i x^*} = \frac{q_i}{1 - q_i} = 1$$

Finally, then, we come to the *cheating constituent game*. We consider first i's choice of a cheating strategy *given that* j adheres to the agreement and that no detection-retaliation mechanism is in force. Let $s_{it} \in [0, x^*]$ denote the amount of sales i acquires at time t by making secret offers of price cuts to selected buyers. Then, his expected payoff at time t is:

$$(4) \qquad \bar{P}_{it}(s_{it}) = (p_i^D - c)s_{it} + (p^* - c)\int_0^{x^* - s_{it}} x_{it} f_{it}(x_{it}, x^* - s_{it})\, dx_{it}$$

$$= \bar{\pi}_i^* + \{(p_i^D - c) - q_i(p^* - c)\}s_{it}$$

Thus, i's expected payoff consists of the sure profit on cheating sales *plus* the expected profit on the remaining sales he will get by chance, $x_{it} \in [0, x^* - s_{it}]$. This exceeds $\bar{\pi}_i^*$ for $s_{it} > 0$ iff

$$(5) \qquad \frac{p_i^D - c}{p^* - c} > q_i = 1/2$$

In fact, $\bar{P}_{it}$ is linear and increasing in s_{it} if condition (5) is satisfied. This condition has a nice intuitive meaning. To cheat is essentially to convert a possible sale with *expected* profit $q_i(p^* - c)$ into a sure sale with profit $(p_i^D - c)$, and this is profitable as long as the latter exceeds the former—not too large a discount must be given. Since in this model p_i^D can be arbitrarily close to p^*, we assume condition (5) is always satisfied.

It then follows that i's best reply to the choice $p_j = p^*$ in any t is to set $s_{it} = x^*$, since this maximizes i's expected payoff. Now of course, we must accept that each firm realizes this, and so would *not* regard itself as having the payoff function (4) in the cheating game, since this assumes the other is not cheating. But, in this case, we are back with the conclusion that the equilibrium of this single-play game is the Nash equilibrium in prices, $p_i = p_j = c$. To see this, suppose at any t, i expects j to set $s_j^0 \in [0, x^*]$ and to offer a price $p_{jt}^D = p^* - \varepsilon^0$, $\varepsilon^0 \geqslant 0$ on these sales. But then, i's best response is to set $s_{it} = x^*$ at a price $p_{it}^D = p^* - \varepsilon^1$ where $\varepsilon^1 > \varepsilon^0$. But then, j's best response is to set $s_{jt} = x^*$ and price $p_{jt}^D = p^* - \varepsilon^2$ where $\varepsilon^2 > \varepsilon^1$, and so on. Essentially, even though firms are cheating, we have a non-cooperative game with prices as the strategy variables, and so we must revert to the unique Nash price equilibrium of the constituent game. The difference is that output is $x^* < x^c$, but firms still earn zero profit. In the sense, therefore, that price and profits are the same with and without cheating, the analysis of cheating in the one-shot game is essentially uninteresting.[6] Its main purpose is to allow definition of the expected payoff function in (4), and to suggest the need for some kind of enforcement mechanism. But, since such a

[6] The only difference is that price competition, if "secret", does not expand the market beyond x^* and so, unlike the "open" game in prices, market output does not change throughout the process of adjustment to the Nash equilibrium. There is, however, something artificial in this. Since equilibrium profits in each case are the same, it is hard to see why *open* price competition would not break out, so that we are essentially back with the open constituent game, and cheating is neither here nor there.

mechanism is necessarily intertemporal, we need to consider it in the context of the supergame, to which we now turn.

III. CHEATING IN THE SUPERGAME

Given that the constituent game is to be repeated at each t, a strategy for player i in the supergame is now a set of functions $\{\sigma_{it}(H_t^i)\}$, where $\sigma_{it}(H_t^i)$ specifies a particular choice of action for i at time t, as a function of H_t^i, the information i possesses about the entire previous history of the game. In the present case, we would have for firm i

$$H_t^i \equiv [\{(x_{10}, x_{20}), \ldots, (x_{1t-1}, x_{2t-1})\}, \{(p_{10}, p_{20}), \ldots, (p_{1t-1}, p_{2t-1})\}, \{s_{i0}, \ldots, s_{it-1}\}] \quad (6)$$

that is, i knows the past sequence of outputs, open price choices, and his own level of cheating in each period. He would then choose p_{it} and s_{it} in the light of H_t^i.

It would be interesting to pursue the general analysis of these supergame strategies, but in the present paper, in line with Stigler's analysis, we adopt a simpler approach. We consider the situation from the point of view of one firm, say j, which wants to *enforce* the collusive equilibrium on the other. It does this by choosing a critical level of i's sales which, if exceeded, and given that it itself does not cheat, will trigger a retaliatory strategy which takes the form of setting price at the competitive level forever. More formally, firm j is considering an enforcement strategy of the form:

$$s_{jt} = 0, \qquad t = 0, 1, \ldots$$

$$p_{jt-1} = p^* \text{ and } x_{it-1} \leq \hat{x}_{it-1} \Rightarrow p_{jt} = p^*, \qquad t = 1, \ldots$$

$$p_{jt-1} = p^* \text{ and } x_{it-1} > \hat{x}_{it-1} \Rightarrow p_{jt} = p^c, \qquad t = 1, \ldots$$

$$p_{jt-1} = p^c \Rightarrow p_{jt} = p^c, \qquad t = 2, \ldots$$

Since $p_j = p_i = p^c$ is the Nash equilibrium of the constituent game, the kind of retaliatory strategy envisaged here is very similar to that underlying Friedman's balanced temptation equilibrium. The difference, apart from the fact that firms choose prices and not outputs, is that "defection" cannot now be observed with certainty, but must be inferred from the observed output of the "defector". Each firm is thought of as casting itself in the role of j as well as i. There is a possible inconsistency here, in that when j views himself as the "enforcer", he sets $s_{jt} = 0$, $\forall t$, and so the equilibrium choice of sequence of critical levels is based on the assumption that only i cheats. But then, if each firm's choice of critical levels implies that the other firm would find cheating profitable, these critical levels could not constitute an equilibrium—each "enforcer" is also a "cheat" and so could not rationally calculate its critical levels on the assumption that it does not cheat. However, in the model of this paper, we find that the simplification involved in the assumption that the enforcer does not cheat can be sustained: we find that when j chooses his optimal critical level, i sets $s_{it} = 0$, $i, j = 1, 2, i \neq j$. Thus, when each firm adopts its optimal critical level, neither firm would cheat, and each is justified in adopting a critical level which assumes it itself does not cheat. In other words, the critical levels we derive constitute a Nash equilibrium.

Figure 1 shows the structure of the supergame. We suppose firm i faces a given sequence of critical levels $\{\hat{x}_{i0}, \hat{x}_{i1}, \ldots\} \equiv \{\hat{x}_{it}\}_0^\infty$, with $p_{j0} = p^*$. At $t = 0$, firm i may choose $s_{i0} = 0$ or $s_{i0} > 0$—the precise positive value of s_{i0} does not matter at the moment. Following a move along an initial branch, chance "makes a move" at the nodes marked C_0 and C_0^1. Let

$$F_i(\hat{x}_{it}, s_{it}) \equiv \int_0^{\hat{x}_{it} - s_{it}} f_i(x_{it}, x^* - s_{it})\, dx_{it}, \qquad t = 0, 1, \ldots, s_{it} \geqslant 0,$$

denote the probability that the sales i obtains at random at t do not exceed the level $\hat{x}_{it} - s_{it}$. This is also the probability that i's *total* sales at t do not exceed the critical level $\hat{x}_{it}$. Then, if $s_{i0} = 0$, chance's move at C_0 is to send i along the upper branch with probability $F_i(\hat{x}_{i0}, 0)$, and along the lower branch (dashed line) with probability $1 - F_i(\hat{x}_{i0}, 0)$. Alternatively, if $s_{i0} > 0$, at C_0^1 chance sends i along the upper branch (dashed line) with probability $F_i(\hat{x}_{i0}, s_{i0})$, and along the lower with probability $1 - F_i(\hat{x}_{i0}, s_{i0})$. Whatever the route by which i returns to the node marked $t = 1$, the future game looks exactly the same and, moreover, is identical to that which faced i at $t = 0$. This recursive form of the supergame will be exploited in what follows. If, at C_0 or C_0^1 chance sends i to N_0, the game is, in a sense, over. At $t = 1$ and forever after, expected profits will be zero because the game enters the "retaliation phase", the Cournot–Nash equilibrium in prices. Essentially then, i's choice of s_{i0} determines the probability with which he will be faced with the same game at $t = 1$, or, more generally, choice of s_{it} determines the probability of repeating the game at $t+1$.

We can use Figure 1 to define the value of the game to i at $t = 0, 1, \ldots$ as a function of any sequence $\{s_{i\tau}\}_t^\infty$, given some sequence $\{\hat{x}_{i\tau}\}_t^\infty$. Denote this value by $\bar{V}_{it}$. Then

$$(7) \qquad \bar{V}_{it} = \bar{P}_i(s_{it}) + F_i(\hat{x}_{it}, s_{it}) V_{it+1}(1+r)^{-1}, \qquad t = 0, 1, \ldots, \quad s_{it} \in [0, x^*]$$

where $\bar{P}_i(s_{it})$ is defined as in (4). By successive substitution, we have:

$$(8) \qquad \bar{V}_{it} = \bar{P}_i(s_{it}) + \sum_{k=t+1}^{\infty} \frac{\bar{P}_i(s_{ik})}{(1+r)^{k-t}} \prod_{\tau=t}^{k-1} F_i(\hat{x}_{i\tau}, s_{i\tau}), \qquad t = 0, 1, \ldots, \quad s_{it} \in [0, x^*]$$

We shall refer to (7) as the *recursive form* and to (8) as the *expanded form* of $\bar{V}_{it}$. Each $\bar{V}_{it}$ is bounded above since $r > 0$, $F_i(\hat{x}_{it}, s_{it}) \leqslant 1$, $\forall t$, and

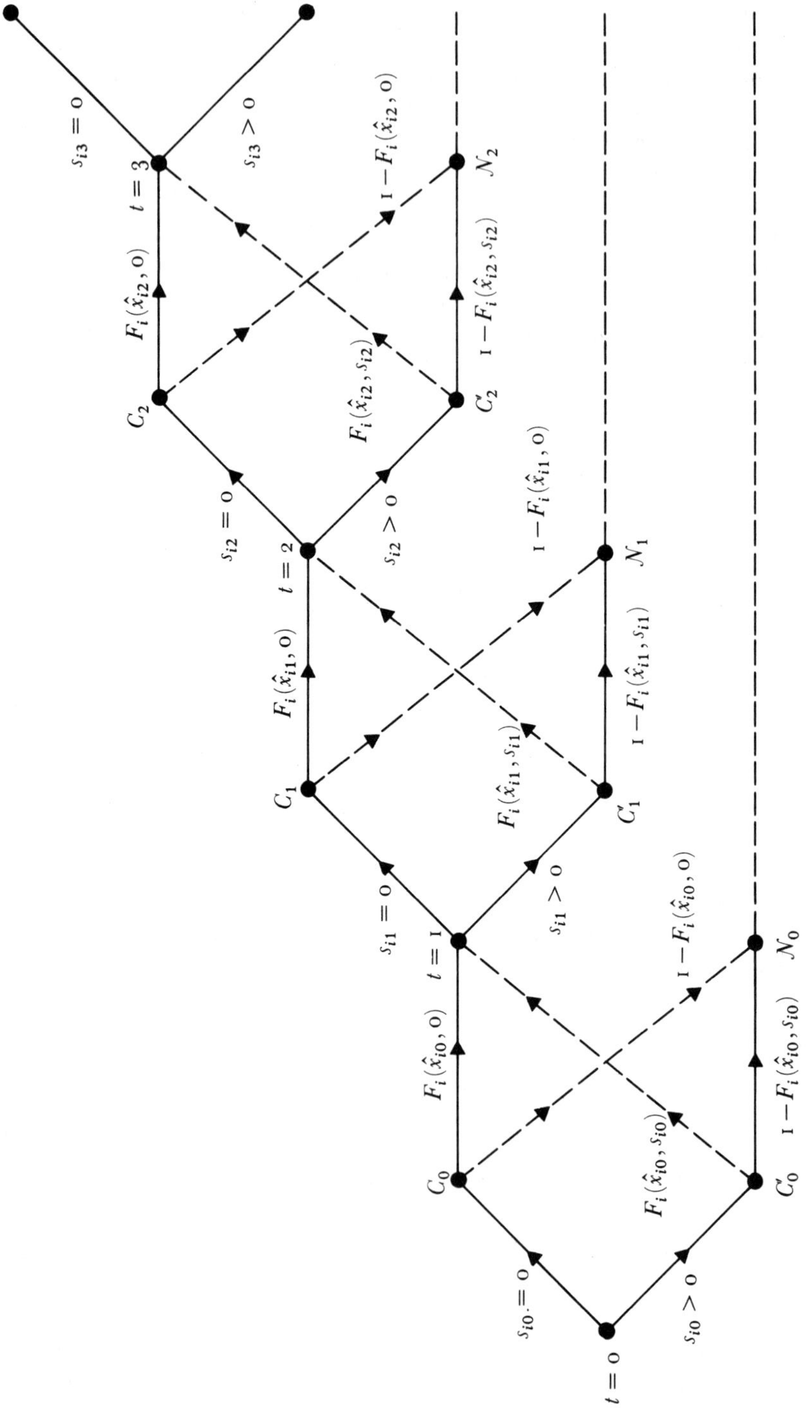

FIGURE 1
Game Tree for Cheating Supergame

$\bar{P}_{it}(s_{it}) \leqslant \bar{\pi}_i^* + \alpha_i x^*$, where $\alpha_i \equiv (p_i^D - c) - q_i(p^* - c)$. Each $\bar{V}_{it}$ is also bounded below since $\bar{P}_i(s_{it}) \geqslant \bar{\pi}_i^*$ and $F_i(\hat{x}_{it}, s_{it}) \geqslant 0$.

It seems reasonable to assume that for any sequence $\{\hat{x}_{it}\}_0^\infty$, i will choose $\{s_{it}\}_0^\infty$ in such a way as to maximize $\bar{V}_{i0}$. It can be shown by straightforward differentiation that over the relevant range, $\bar{V}_{i0}$ is strictly concave in each s_{it}, and so there is a unique sequence $\{s_{it}\}_0^\infty$ for each $\{\hat{x}_{it}\}_0^\infty$. Thus, denote

$$\text{(9)} \qquad \bar{V}_{i0}^* = \max_{\{s_{it}\}_0^\infty} \bar{V}_{i0} = \bar{V}_{i0}(\{s_{it}^*\}_0^\infty; \{\hat{x}_{it}\}_0^\infty)$$

It follows from the fact that j knows the function $\bar{V}_{i0}$ that he can find $\{s_{it}^*\}_0^\infty$ for any $\{\hat{x}_{it}\}_0^\infty$, that is, he can predict exactly i's response to his own choice of sequence of critical levels. Thus, j's problem is not really one of "detecting" cheating, but rather of setting up an optimal incentive mechanism given the rule embodied in (9), which can be thought of as a form of *incentive constraint.*[7] The mechanism which is optimal for j is that which maximizes the value of the game to himself, subject to the incentive constraint. We can define this value at each t in recursive form as

$$\text{(10)} \qquad \bar{V}_{jt} = \bar{P}_j(s_{it}) + F_i(\hat{x}_{it}, s_{it})\bar{V}_{jt+1}, \qquad t = 0, 1, \ldots, \qquad s_{it} \in [0, x^*]$$

where $\bar{P}_j(s_{it}) = \bar{\pi}_j^* - q_j(p^* - c)s_{it}$ is j's expected payoff at t when i cheats by $s_{it} \geqslant 0$, since $q_j(p^* - c)$ is j's expected profit on each unit i secured by cheating. The idea here is exactly that used in defining $\bar{V}_{it}$: choice by j of $\hat{x}_{it}$ and by i of s_{it} at any t determines the probability of facing exactly the same game at $t+1$, or of earning zero forever—essentially the end of the game. In expanded form, we have:

$$\text{(11)} \qquad \bar{V}_{jt} = \bar{P}_j(s_{it}) + \sum_{k=t+1}^{\infty} \frac{\bar{P}_j(s_{ik})}{(1+r)^k} \prod_{\tau=t}^{k-1} F_i(\hat{x}_{i\tau}, s_{i\tau}), \qquad t = 0, 1, \ldots, \qquad s_{it} \in [0, x^*]$$

The problem for j is then that of maximizing $\bar{V}_{j0}$ subject to the constraint that i will choose $\{s_{it}\}_0^\infty$ to maximize $\bar{V}_{i0}$ given any choice of $\{\hat{x}_{it}\}_0^\infty$ by j.

To simplify the analysis, we can make use of the recursive nature of the supergame. Let $\{\hat{x}_{it}^*\}_0^\infty$, $\{s_{it}^*\}_0^\infty$ denote the optimal solution sequences for j's problem. Then, the optimality principle of dynamic programming says that $\{\hat{x}_{i\tau}^*\}_t^\infty$, $\{s_{i\tau}^*\}_t^\infty$ must be optimal sequences for the supergame beginning at $t = 0, 1, \ldots$. Furthermore, if $\bar{V}_{it+1}^*$, $\bar{V}_{jt+1}^*$ denote these optimal values for the supergame beginning at $t+1$, then j's choice of $\hat{x}_{it}$ and (*implied*) s_{it} must solve the problem:

$$\text{(12)} \qquad \max_{\hat{x}_{it}, s_{it}} \bar{P}_j(s_{it}) + F_i(\hat{x}_{it}, s_{it})\bar{V}_{jt+1}^*(1+r)^{-1} \text{ subject to}$$

$$\frac{\partial \bar{V}_{it}}{\partial s_{it}} = \alpha_i + \frac{\partial F_i}{\partial s_{it}} \bar{V}_{i1}^*(1+r)^{-1} \leqslant 0, \qquad s_{it}^* \geqslant 0, \qquad s_{it}^* \frac{\partial \bar{V}_{it}}{\partial s_{it}} = 0, \qquad t = 0, 1, \ldots$$

[7] The problem is obviously very similar in structure to that studied in the literature on principal-agent problems. See, for example, Rees [1984].

where the constraint expresses the condition that s_{it} must maximize $\bar{V}_{it}$ for given $\hat{x}_{it}$.

We then immediately have the first proposition: sequences which are optimal solutions to (12) are in fact *constant* sequences $\{\hat{x}_i^*, \ldots\}$, $\{s_i^*, \ldots\}$. The reason is that since the supergames beginning at each t are all identical, they have the same optimal values $\bar{V}_{jt}^*$, $\bar{V}_{it}^*$. But that implies that the problem in (12) has exactly the same parameters at each t, and so must have the same solution at each t. Hence, the optimal solutions form constant sequences.

With the help of this proposition, the problem of characterizing the optimal solution to j's problem then becomes very straightforward. Since we know that the solutions are constant sequences, we can state the problem as that of finding values $\hat{x}_i$, s_i which solve the problem, expressed in the expanded form

$$(13) \qquad \max_{\hat{x}_i, s_i} \bar{V}_{j0} = \bar{P}_j(s_i)\left[1 + \sum_{t=1}^{\infty}\left\{\frac{F_i(\hat{x}_i, s_i)}{1+r}\right\}^t\right] \text{subject to}$$

$$s_i = \operatorname{argmax} \bar{V}_{i0} = P_i(s_i)\left[1 + \sum_{t=1}^{\infty}\left\{\frac{F_i(\hat{x}_i, s_i)}{1+r}\right\}^t\right], \qquad s_i \in [0, x^*]$$

Since $[F_i(\hat{x}_i, s_i)]/(1+r) < 1$, the sums to infinity in (13) certainly converge and the terms in square brackets can be replaced by the term

$$(14) \qquad \phi(\hat{x}_i, s_i) \equiv \left[1 - \frac{F_i(\hat{x}_i, s_i)}{1+r}\right]^{-1}$$

where ϕ can be thought of as a "risk-adjusted annuity factor". Hence, the optimal critical level $\hat{x}_i^*$ and associated cheating level s_i^* must maximize the Lagrangean function $L_j(\hat{x}_i, s_i, \lambda) = \bar{V}_{j0} - \lambda(\partial \bar{V}_{i0}/\partial s_i)$ subject to $s_i \geqslant 0$. These optimal values are therefore characterized by the conditions:

$$(15) \qquad \frac{\partial L}{\partial s_i} = -q_i(p^* - c)\phi + \bar{P}_j\frac{\partial \phi}{\partial s_i} - \lambda^*\left\{2\alpha_i\frac{\partial \phi}{\partial s_i} + \bar{P}_i\frac{\partial^2 \phi_i}{\partial s_i^2}\right\} \leqslant 0, \qquad s_i^* \geqslant 0$$

$$s_i^*\frac{\partial L}{\partial s_i} = 0$$

$$(16) \qquad \frac{\partial L}{\partial \hat{x}_i} = \bar{P}_j\frac{\partial \phi}{\partial \hat{x}_i} - \lambda^*\left\{\alpha_i\frac{\partial \phi_i}{\partial \hat{x}_i} + P_i\frac{\partial^2 \phi_i}{\partial \hat{x}_i \partial s_i}\right\} = 0$$

$$(17) \qquad \frac{\partial L}{\partial \lambda} = -\frac{\partial \bar{V}_{i0}}{\partial s_i} \geqslant 0, \qquad \lambda^* \geqslant 0, \qquad \lambda^*\frac{\partial \bar{V}_{i_0}}{\partial s_i} = 0$$

The main interest in examining these conditions is to ascertain whether $s_i^* > 0$, so that there would be positive cheating at the equilibrium. If this were the case, then the simplistic approach adopted so far is inadequate to analyse the equilibrium of the market, since firm $j = 1, 2$ could not determine its enforcement strategy on the assumption that $s_j = 0$ if it is in fact profitable for it to set $s_j > 0$, given firm i's optimal critical level. The conditions themselves, however, do not give a clear answer. It is straightforward, if tedious, to show that $\partial F_i/\partial s_i < 0$, and $\partial^2 F_i/\partial s_i^2 < 0$, from which we have that in (15), $\partial\phi_i/\partial s_i < 0$, and $\partial^2\phi_i/\partial s_i^2 < 0$. Thus, we cannot conclude that in (15), $\partial L/\partial s_i < 0$ unambiguously—it will all depend on the relative magnitudes of all the terms in conditions (15) and (16). It does not appear possible to obtain clearcut conclusions analytically.

However, it is relatively straightforward to carry out simulations of the model, particularly given the assumption that $x^* > 70$, so the normal distribution can be used. The basic parameters of the model are x^*, the total market size, and r, the per-period interest rate. Since p_i^D can be arbitrarily close to p^*, we set $p_i^D = p^*$, the most favorable case to cheating. Combinations of cases were taken for the following parameter ranges:

$$x^* = 70, 100, 500, 1000$$

$$r = 0.05, 0.1, 0.2, 0.5$$

The range of interest rates in particular seems to encompass all reasonable possibilities, since the time-period considered in the model is unlikely to be longer than a year and could be as short as one week. The main results of the simulations[8] were then as follows:

(i) In *all* cases, $s_i^* = 0$, that is, the optimum for j involves choice of a critical level which makes no cheating optimal for i.

(ii) The critical level $\hat{x}_i^*$ lay between 2 and 3 standard deviations above $1/2x^*$, i's mean sales, with lower values for high r and low x^*.

(iii) In general, because the probability with which j would have to retaliate in any one period was very low, the expected cost of the enforcement mechanism—the difference between $\bar{V}_0^* \equiv \pi_j^* \, (1 + 1/r)$ and $\bar{V}_{j0}^*$, the expected present values of profits with and without the enforcement mechanism, with $s_i = s_j = 0$ in either case, was very small.

Figure 2 illustrates the typical results for a case which would tend to favor cheating, with high r and low x^* (resp. 0.5 and 70). In each part of the figure, the vertical axis shows the value of the game to one firm as a proportion of the value the game would have if there were no cheating *and* no enforcement. The upper figure shows that for given $\hat{x}_i$, $\bar{V}_{i0}$ is strictly concave in s_i. As $\hat{x}_i$ increases, the curve shifts down. The lower figure shows that the critical level is optimally set at about 2.2 standard deviations above the mean. The large majority of the other simulations had even higher critical values and higher value ratios. Thus, we conclude that in the model examined in this paper, deterrence of cheating is both cheap and fully effective, over a wide range of plausible parameter values.

Intuitively, the reason for the "no-cheating" result is that the normal distribution with $q_1 = 1/2$ has very nice properties: it is possible for the

[8] Copies of the Appendix setting out the simulation method and numerical results are available from the author.

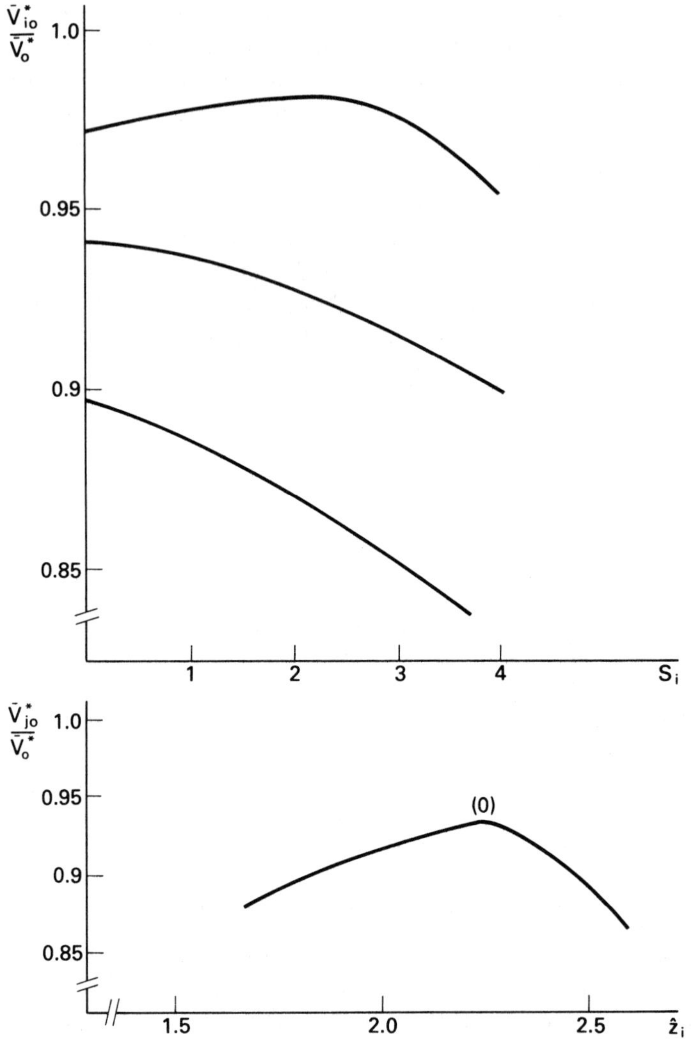

FIGURE 2
Gain from Cheating and Cost of Deterrence

enforcing firm to choose a critical level far out in the upper tail of the distribution, thus ensuring a very low probability that it will have to retaliate, but at the same time, just a little cheating so increases the probability that this retaliation will take place that the potential cheat finds it not worthwhile. Thus, the conclusion may fail to hold if the assumptions about the random process which generates firms' demands yielded a less nice distribution.

The picture of market equilibrium which emerges from this analysis is then the following: each firm adopts its optimal critical level $\hat{x}_i^*$, $i = 1, 2$, neither cheats and market price continues at p^* as long as one of the two mutually exclusive events $x_{it} > \hat{x}_i^*$, $i = 1, 2$, does *not* occur. The question then arises of the rationality, in a game-theoretic sense, of this "enforcement equilibrium". First, we have to assume that each firm communicates its choice of critical level to the other because if they had to learn these by experience, it would be too late. Then, each firm's choice of $s_i = 0$ is a best reply to the other's choice of critical level. Moreover, neither firm has an incentive to change its critical level in equilibrium because, given that the other firm would know of such a change, this would either induce cheating (if the critical level were raised) or deter cheating at higher expected cost (if the level were lowered). In either case, this reduces the value of the supergame to that firm, and so cannot be optimal. Thus, the enforcement equilibrium has the self-reinforcing "best-reply" property of a Nash equilibrium, provided communication of critical levels is permitted.

A less attractive aspect of the equilibrium is the very "grim" nature of the punishment strategy—moving to the competitive equilibrium forever. The choice of the competitive equilibrium is perfectly acceptable once we allow firms to choose prices, since this is the noncompetitive equilibrium of the constituent game. What seems objectionable is that punishment goes on forever. In fact, along the lines of a recent paper by Green and Porter [1984],[9] it would be possible to define retaliation in terms of a move to the competitive equilibrium for some finite time period. In the present model, this would reduce critical levels[10] and so increase the probability of observing competitive episodes in the market. Some preliminary simulations done for this case suggest that the basic conclusion of no cheating at the equilibrium, for the parameter values considered in this paper, continues to hold, with the duration of punishment as well as the critical level at which punishment is applied being jointly determined.[11]

IV. CONCLUSIONS

This paper takes a market in which there is symmetric, homogeneous price-setting duopoly with constant costs. The firms have reached an agreement to set

[9] The subject of Green and Porter's paper is closely related to this one, and, in a sense, that paper and this are dual to each other. Green and Porter consider two firms which choose outputs—unobservably to the other—the sum of which then determines market price *via* a stochastic market demand function. Retaliation to an observed market price below some critical level takes the form of a move to the Cournot output-equilibrium for some finite time-period. Though clearly inspired by Stigler's original paper, Green and Porter's analysis does not attempt to develop Stigler's analysis as closely as that of this paper.

[10] Note that compensation for a reduced-punishment period could not be provided by cutting price below the competitive level, thus inflicting negative rather than zero profits on the cheat, because zero production is always possible: the lowest profit either firm can inflict on the other is zero.

[11] On the other hand, some simulations with unequal probabilities q_i show that the no-cheating result ceases to hold when q_i is very small—around 0.1 and x^* is close to its lower limit of 60. There is an asymmetry, with firm j "allowing" i to cheat at the equilibrium, but i not allowing j to do so. Intuitively, this is because i is so small relative to j that it has a lot to gain from cheating and little to lose by retaliating, whereas for j, the converse applies. It is hoped to pursue the case of unequal probabilities in a further paper.

the joint-profit maximizing price and there is no incentive for open defection on the agreement. We then explore the implications of Stigler's original idea that randomness in individual firms' demands permits cheating, in the form of secret price cuts to selected buyers. To have any interest at all, the situation must be modelled as a supergame, in which each firm chooses a critical level of the other's sales, such that if this is exceeded at any time, the firm retaliates by setting price at the competitive level forever. It also chooses a level of cheating for itself in the light of the other's choice of critical level. In this model, detection of cheating as such is not a problem. Since each firm knows the other's profit function, it can predict what the other's profit-maximizing cheating level is in response to its own choice of critical level. The problem is to find the critical level which maximizes each firm's profit, given the level of cheating by the other firm induced by the critical level, that is, it is a problem in incentive design. The particular features of the supergame model are used to solve this problem in quite a simple way. The general analytical form of the solution does not appear to offer any clearcut conclusions. However, simulations over a very wide and reasonable set of parameter values show that, at the optimum, neither firm cheats, the critical levels adopted are far out on the upper tails of the respective output distributions, and the expected cost of enforcing the collusive agreement is very small. This simultaneous choice of critical level and zero cheating constitutes a Nash equilibrium in the supergame.

The results of this paper then suggest that, at least for the case where the number of buyers is large enough for each firm's sales to be normally distributed and each buyer is indifferent to which seller it buys from (that is, $q_i = 1/2$), a collusive agreement is easily enforced, with no cheating. This contrasts with the results of Stigler's original paper. On the other hand, although at any one time the probability of reversion to the competitive equilibrium is very small, in the long-run, as $t \rightarrow \infty$, it becomes virtually certain that this will take place. In this respect, it would be attractive to assume a *finite* period of retaliation, as in Green and Porter [1984], so that the market would be subject only to competitive episodes. But this, along with relaxation of some other assumptions in this paper, will have to be pursued elsewhere.

RAY REES,
Department of Economics,
University College,
P.O. Box 78,
Cardiff CF1 1XL,
U.K.

ACCEPTED NOVEMBER 1984

THE JOURNAL OF INDUSTRIAL ECONOMICS 0022-1821 $2.00
Volume XXXIII June 1985 No. 4

CARTEL BEHAVIOUR AND ADVERSE SELECTION

KEVIN ROBERTS

I. INTRODUCTION

CARTELS ARE central to any general theory of market structure. For, given the prevailing notion of rationality based upon self-interest, the rational behaviour of a group of firms should be to form together into a cartel and maximize joint profits or, more generally, act in a manner efficient to the group. If other forms of conduct, or market structures compatible with such conduct, are to be rationalizable then an exploration of why firms fail to act in this way is central.

Some constraints on firms can be imposed by a society's legal structure, broadly defined. If, as is common, collusive action by firms is deemed to be illegal, collusion may still occur but be hampered; for instance, side-payments made between firms to encourage members of a cartel to act in the group interest may be hard to disguise and in consequence may be ruled out. As well as these, what may be termed, external constraints, there are internal constraints which are part and parcel of a society's economic system. Here, one naturally thinks of the costs of communication which are often used as an argument against collusion. However, a more basic constraint is the informational structure of an economic system—in loose terms, what information about the economic system is known or can be found out by agents within the system. Assume that transfers of goods or income cannot take place between firms; then in a world of full information—all tastes, technologies and behaviour known to all—there is no need for direct communication between firms. Each firm can calculate what would be the result under costless communication and act accordingly; there is an incentive to do so because, as behaviour can be observed, firms can respond to any erring firm in exactly the same way as if there was direct communication. It is the lack of full information which makes communication between firms necessary or useful.

A lack of full information can take different forms and have different implications. For present purposes, it is desirable to distinguish between *moral hazard* and *adverse selection*. Moral hazard exists when the behaviour of other agents is less than perfectly observable whereas adverse selection arises when it is the preferences of other agents which are unobservable. Following the seminal work by Stigler [1964], the extensive literature on the problems of implementing rules for cartels has tended to equate lack of full information with moral hazard.[1] The classic example of moral hazard occurs when the demand for a firm's product is stochastic and other firms can observe only the level of demand

[1] See, for instance, McKinnon [1966], Osborne [1976], Scherer [1980, ch. 6], Porter [1983a] and Green and Porter [1984].

but not the price being charged. If there is a high demand for the firm's product then the other firms do not know whether the high demand is a stochastic "fluke" or the result of "secret" price-cutting. For this case, interest centres on the policing of cartel rules, i.e. to provide a disincentive to price-cutting, action must be taken against firms with high demand but, at the same time, it must be recognized that this will sometimes involve action when a firm is not erring. However, notice that as the preferences of firms are known under pure moral hazard, it is clear to all firms how much "cheating" will occur under any particular cartel rule and policing policy.

Unlike moral hazard, adverse selection has not been the subject of careful investigation in the cartel literature.[2] Both demand and cost considerations will affect a firm's preferences and a firm's information about its own demand and cost position is likely to be better, or at least different, to information possessed by other firms.[3] Thus, the reasonableness of assuming that adverse selection problems exist seems clear. However, it is the *implications* of assuming the existence of adverse selection that are relevant for judging whether it is an important feature of cartel problems. Its most basic implication can be uncovered by considering a situation without an adverse selection problem but, perhaps, where moral hazard exists. As all preferences are known to all, there is no need for direct communication for a cartel rule to be implemented—there is the initial problem of deciding what rule is to be followed but, even here, it is not completely untenable that firms can work out, in isolation, the rule that would be agreed upon if they were to meet together. This point was clearly made by Chamberlin [1929], now more than half a century ago. The implication of this is that with only moral hazard present, what can be achieved under explicit collusion by firms can also be achieved under "tacit" collusion with each firm acting in isolation and following some decentralized rule. In consequence, there has been little underpinning to arguments which suggest that tacit and explicit collusion will differ. The existence of moral hazard restricts the possibilities of what rules can be implemented but it is adverse selection which draws tacit and explicit collusion apart.

With moral hazard, the natural focus of attention is the incentive for a firm to "cheat" in the hope that its action will go undetected and, together with this, the form of cartel rules with respect to the detection and punishment of cheating, e.g. trigger strategies (see, for instance, Green and Porter [1984]). With adverse selection and no moral hazard, behaviour is observed without error so cheating, as such, has no role.[4] Instead, attention must focus on the

[2] Adverse selection problems are considered in Roberts [1983] and, though not labelled as such, in Simpson and Waterson [1984].

[3] The following example is considered in Roberts [1983]: By looking at a firm's published accounts, its level of costs may be observable to other firms. However, it may be impossible to disentangle marginal costs—the crucial parameter necessary to determine efficient behaviour—from this observation. The net result of this is that cartel rules tie the behaviour of firms to their level of total costs—under some conditions, mark-up pricing becomes the optimal response to the posited informational parsimony.

[4] Under pure adverse selection, there is still the problem that a firm may wish to break the cartel

fact that if the implementation of a cartel rule depends upon the use of information private to one firm, that firm must be given an incentive to correctly reveal the information.

To simplify the problems to be investigated, the consequences of adverse selection when moral hazard is *not* present will be examined. Roberts [1983] considered rules of tacit collusion under adverse selection, but explicit collusion gives a greater degree of freedom for the form of cartel rules. In particular, under explicit collusion, the cartel rule for one firm can be made sensitive to information provided by another firm. More generally, explicit collusion permits the transmission of information between firms and a lessening of the problems created by adverse selection.

The next two sections examine the implications of mutually determined behaviour and explicit information transmission. In both sections, side-payments are assumed to be ruled out by some external constraint but their potential role is considered in section 4.

II. INTERDEPENDENT BEHAVIOUR

Throughout, the problem of entry into an industry is avoided: it is assumed that there are a fixed number of firms producing goods which are substitutes for each other. For convenience, attention will concentrate on the two-firm case. Firm i is assumed to possess a profit function of the form

$$(1) \qquad \Pi_i = \Pi_i(q_1, q_2, \alpha_i)$$

where q_1, q_2 are the outputs of firms 1 and 2 and α_i is a parameter known only to firm i—the other firm knows the functional form of the profit function and that α_i is drawn from some support A_i. However, the other firm has a Bayesian belief about α_i which is captured by a probability density function $f_i(\alpha_i)$ (with support A_i). The parameter α can affect the profit function in any way but two extreme cases of interest are

$$(2) \qquad \text{I:} \quad \Pi_{q_j\alpha_i} \text{ is negligible if } i \neq j, \text{ non-negligible if } i = j$$

$$(3) \qquad \text{II:} \quad \Pi_{q_j\alpha_i} \text{ is non-negligible if } i \neq j, \text{ negligible if } i = j$$

In case I, the unknown parameter relates solely to firm i's preferences with regard to its own output; for instance, this will be the case when α relates to the firm's cost structure. Case II is less plausible but captures the idea that only firm i knows how interdependent it is with the other firm. The example developed in section 3 is compatible with such an information structure.

The purpose of this section is to consider the usefulness of mutually

rule when, through the operation of the rule, it finds out information (about other firms) that it did not know when the rule was determined. To simplify the problems to be studied, it will be taken for granted that there exist credible punishment strategies which deter rule-breaking. Because there is no randomness, these strategies are never employed.

determined behaviour for a cartel. For this, asymmetric information of the type embodied in case I will be considered. It will also be assumed that α can take on only two values and that the profit function is of the form (where $Qd(Q)$ is assumed to be strictly concave in Q):

$$(4)\qquad \begin{aligned} \Pi_1(q_1,q_2,\alpha) &= q_1(d(q_1+q_2)+\alpha) \\ \Pi_2(q_1,q_2,\alpha) &= q_2(d(q_1+q_2)+\alpha) \end{aligned}$$

This corresponds to the classic Cournot case of a homogeneous good being produced under conditions of constant marginal cost, the marginal cost of a firm being in direct negative relation to α.

If interdependence is not admitted then a cartel rule for the two firms would take the form of specifying output as a function of own α. If interdependence is admitted, then a firm's output will be dependent on the α values of each firm. The simplest way of achieving this is to adopt a rule which specifies one firm's output as a function of own α and the other firm's output $(q_1(\alpha_1, q_2), q_2(\alpha_2, q_1))$. More generally, each firm can report a signal to a coordinating agency, the signal being dependent upon one's own α value, and the agency can then specify the output of each firm as a function of signals received. As specified, one can do no better than have the firms signal their α type so that it is rules of this form that will be investigated.[5] Notice, however, that recontracting is not permitted, i.e. a firm cannot change the α value reported on finding out what the other firm reported. This is closer in spirit to the situation considered in the next section.

There are two issues that need looking at. First, the above story of information transmission does not include a specification of incentives—as the α value of a firm is known only to that firm, it must have the incentive to reveal it truthfully. Second, there is the problem of objective for the cartel. With no asymmetric information problem, the two firms would face a standard co-operative bargaining problem which would be expected to entail a resolution that embodied efficiency and symmetry, e.g. the Nash bargaining solution which involves the maximization of the product of the gains of the agents as compared to some *status quo* position. What happens under asymmetric information?[6] To simplify the problem, assume that α can take on only two values, 0 or β, $\beta > 0$. Furthermore, if p_i is the prior probability, held by the other firm, that i is of type 0, then assume that $p_i = p_j = p$—the two firms are in a symmetric position. By bargaining and attempting to secure particular outcomes, the firms may reveal more information about themselves. Transmission of information will be considered in the next section—for present purposes, assume that the stage has been reached where firms do not wish or have no credible way of transmitting more information.[7] Under symmetry, the cartel

[5] This is the so-called revelation principle.

[6] For an axiomatic extension of the Nash bargaining solution to asymmetric information situations, see Myerson [1984].

[7] The point here is that no more information is being transferred *before* the cartel rule is to be

rule decided upon by the two firms will be symmetric between the two firms and will specify four output levels—$q_{00}, q_{0\beta}, q_{\beta 0}, q_{\beta\beta}$—where the subscript denotes one's own type and the type of the other firm. Efficiency will have the implication that the bargaining resolution will occur at a position where the weighted sum of the expected profits for firms of each type, E_0 and E_β, is at a maximum. Thus, the rule will maximize (for some $y > 0$)

$$E = \gamma p E_0 + (1-p) E_\beta \tag{5}$$

where

$$E_0 = p q_{00} d(2q_{00}) + (1-p) q_{0\beta} d(q_{0\beta} + q_{\beta 0}) \tag{6}$$

$$E_\beta = p q_{\beta 0}[d(q_{0\beta} + q_{\beta 0}) + \beta] + (1-p) q_{\beta\beta}[d(2q_{\beta\beta}) + \beta] \tag{7}$$

For the correct incentives to exist, a firm of each type cannot expect to gain by reporting itself to be a firm of the other type, this revelation occurring after the rule is determined. As the output of a firm produces an external diseconomy on the other firm, the rule used is likely to involve output being restricted, the level of restriction being higher for an 0-type. Thus, the relevant incentive constraint will take the form that an 0-type must not prefer to misreport itself as a β-type (it will be shown below that a β-type will never wish to misreport itself). This constraint is given by

$$p q_{00} d(2q_{00}) + (1-p) q_{0\beta} d(q_{0\beta} + q_{\beta 0}) \geqslant p q_{\beta 0} d(q_{0\beta} + q_{\beta 0}) + (1-p) q_{\beta\beta} d(2q_{\beta\beta}) \tag{8}$$

The chosen rule will maximize (5) subject to (8). With a multiplier $\lambda \geqslant 0$ for the constraint, first-order conditions are given by

$$q_{00} \geqslant 0; \quad d(2q_{00}) + 2q_{00} d'(2q_{00}) \leqslant 0 \qquad \text{(c.s.)} \tag{9}$$

$$q_{0\beta} \geqslant 0; \quad (1-p)(\gamma p + \lambda)[d(q_{0\beta} + q_{\beta 0}) + (q_{0\beta} + q_{\beta 0}) d'(q_{0\beta} + q_{\beta 0})] - [\lambda + (\gamma - 1) p (1-p)] q_{\beta 0} d'(q_{0\beta} + q_{\beta 0}) \leqslant 0 \qquad \text{(c.s.)} \tag{10}$$

$$q_{\beta 0} \geqslant 0; \quad (1-p-\lambda) p [d(q_{0\beta} + q_{\beta 0}) + (q_{0\beta} + q_{\beta 0}) d'(q_{0\beta} + q_{\beta 0})] + p(1-p)\beta + [\lambda + (\gamma - 1) p (1-p)] q_{0\beta} d'(q_{0\beta} + q_{\beta 0}) \leqslant 0 \qquad \text{(c.s.)} \tag{11}$$

$$q_{\beta\beta} \geqslant 0; \quad (1-p-\lambda)[d(2q_{\beta\beta}) + 2q_{\beta\beta} d'(2q_{\beta\beta})] + (1-p)\beta \leqslant 0 \qquad \text{(c.s.)} \tag{12}$$

where (c.s.) denotes a complementary slackness relationship.

Unsurprisingly, the rule depends upon the weight in the maximand γ. If γ is very different from unity then the rule is biased in favour of one particular type of firm and it is unlikely that firms reaching such a bargaining outcome would not convey more information to the other firm about their type. Consider, first, the case where the incentive constraint fails to bite ($\lambda = 0$). Equations (9)–(12)

---

determined. After the cartel rule is determined, the incentives for revelation change and revelation will be a feature of the operation of the rule.

then solve to give

$$(13)\quad \begin{cases} q_{00} = \dfrac{q_0^m}{2}, \qquad q_{\beta\beta} = \dfrac{q_\beta^m}{2} \\ \gamma < 1 + \dfrac{\beta}{d(q_\beta^m)} \rightarrow q_{0\beta} = 0 \quad \text{and} \quad q_{\beta 0} = q_\beta^m \end{cases}$$

where q^m is the monopolistic output that would be produced by a firm if it had sole control of the market (notice that the complementary slackness relationships in (10) and (11) are important for deriving (13)).[8] (13) shows very clearly the desirability of coordination of firms. If the objective is not biased too much in favour of o-type firms, it is desirable for production to take place by the most efficient firm so that a signal of high efficiency leads to permission to produce a higher output with the output of the other firm being cut back.

In a second-best situation where the incentive constraint bites, the solution is not so simple. Manipulation of (9)–(12) gives

$$(14a)\quad q_{00} = \frac{q_0^m}{2}$$

$$(14b)\quad q_0^m \leqslant q_{0\beta} + q_{\beta 0} \leqslant 2q_{\beta\beta}$$

$$(14c)\quad q_{\beta\beta} \geqslant \frac{q_\beta^m}{2}$$

and using this information in (8) for the case where the constraint bites gives

$$(14d)\quad q_{0\beta} \leqslant q_{\beta 0}$$

Before going further, it can now be seen why the incentive constraint that a β-type firm must have no incentive to say that it is an o-type firm can be ignored in the optimization exercise. When $\lambda = 0$ and (13) holds, this incentive constraint is obviously satisfied and when λ is positive and (8) bites, $q_{\beta 0} \geqslant q_{00}$, $q_{\beta\beta} \geqslant q_{0\beta}$ and equality in (8) again ensures satisfaction of the constraint. Thus it can be ignored.

Turning to the second-best solution (14), (14a) is a standard feature of incentive problems—if both firms are willing to say that they have the low productivity then the first-best solution is implemented. Given the form of the incentive constraint, (14b) and (14c) are natural responses though it is somewhat surprising that such clear-cut results are possible. The second-best solution preserves the feature that if a firm chooses to say it is efficient (a β-type rather than an o-type) then it is permitted to produce a higher output. However, to induce the correct incentives, it is necessary to counteract the effect in the first-best outcome which leads to a reduction in the other firm's output if efficiency is reported. The second-best solution will usually involve a strictly

[8] If γ exceeds $1 + \beta/d(q_\beta^m)$ then the rule is sufficiently biased in favour of o-type firms for $q_{0\beta}$ to be positive and, for γ large enough, $q_{0\beta}$ will equal q_0^m and $q_{\beta 0}$ will be zero.

positive $q_{0\beta}$ and a $q_{\beta 0}$ which is reduced relative to $q_{\beta\beta}$ as compared with the first-best. Thus there are two, partially offsetting, arguments for why a central coordinating agency is useful: (1) efficiency considerations suggest the desirability of a coordinated policy with the output of the other firm dropping when it is desirable to produce a higher output; (2) coordination itself acts as an incentive device and a firm can be discouraged from misreporting by ensuring that the output of the other firm rises if the firm makes a report which allows it to produce a higher output.

Finally, it is worth considering when the first-best solution is achievable. Putting (13) into (8), gives

$$(15) \qquad \left(\frac{p}{p+1}\right) q_0^m d(q_0^m) \geqslant q_\beta^m d(q_\beta^m)$$

so that, as q_0^m maximizes $qd(q)$, (15) is satisfied when β exceeds a critical β^* (q_m^β is an increasing function of β). Thus, the incentive constraint fails to bite when the two types are sufficiently different and q_β^m is "too high" an output for a type-0 firm to wish to produce.

III. EXPLICIT INFORMATION TRANSMISSION

In the last section it was mentioned that in a cooperative bargaining set-up, the cartel rule that a group of firms would decide upon could change as a result of information about others being gleaned from the operation of the cartel rule. Knowing that this will happen affects the incentive to report or misreport information.

With evolution, one is interested in the final rule that will be implemented and this will depend upon the reporting behaviour of firms. In the last section, the form of the final rule was examined, taking for granted the uncertainty that firms possessed about each other. Here, attention will be directed to the process of movement towards a final rule. Given that the final rule to be used is not decided upon at the outset, firms now have an incentive to pretend that they are of a type with strong bargaining power. When recontracting takes place concerning the rule to be used, firms can hope that a rule will be chosen which is biased in their favour.

The bargaining power of a firm will depend upon the effect that the firm can have on other firms and the effect that other firms can have on it. In terms of private information, it is the effect that other firms can have on a particular firm which is likely to be private to that firm. This corresponds to the case II which was considered at the beginning of the last section.

As in the last section, assume that there are only two firms and that a firm can be of only two types—a dependent type (d) or an independent type (i). The profit function of an i-type is independent of the other firm's output and q^i is the profit-maximizing output for such a firm. For convenience, assume that only one other output, q^d, can be produced. A d-type firm has a profit function which depends upon both firms' outputs. Let Π_{di} be profit if it produces q^d and the other firm produces q^i. Let Π_{dd}, Π_{id}, and Π_{ii} be defined in a similar way. These profits are assumed to be of the form so that two d-type firms are in the classic "prisoners' dilemma" position:

$$\Pi_{id} > \Pi_{dd} > \Pi_{ii} > \Pi_{di} \tag{16}$$

As a repeated situation will be looked at, it is also convenient to assume that

$$\Pi_{id} + \Pi_{di} \leqslant 2\Pi_{dd} \tag{17}$$

This ensures that a cooperative correlated policy which moves between *id* and *di* does not dominate *dd*.

Given the output of the other firm, a dependent firm would prefer to produce q^i—the output chosen by an independent firm. However, with two dependent firms, a situation where both firms produce q^d is superior to one where they both produce q^i.

Each firm has to choose what output to produce in each period. This will convey information to the other firm about the likely type of the firm in question. An i-type firm will profit maximize by always producing q^i so this can be assumed to be its strategy. A d-type firm would like to produce q^i but, if it thinks that its opponent is a d-type, it may wish to encourage a situation which allows the cooperative solution to arise where both firms produce q^d.

At date t, let P_t^1 (P_t^2) be the prior probability held by firm 2 (1) that firm 1 (2) is of type i. A firm of type d must choose a probability p_t with which to produce output q^i. Given that this probability can be inferred by the other firm, its prior can be updated:

$$P_{t+1}^1 = \begin{cases} 0 & \text{if } q^d \text{ produced at } t \\ \dfrac{P_t^1}{P_t^1 + p_t^1(1-P_t^1)} & \text{otherwise} \end{cases} \tag{18}$$

What strategy should a d-type firm follow? If it has revealed itself to be of a d-type by choosing q^d then it does not wish to allow a situation where it produces q^d and the other firm produces q^i to continue. The most appealing strategy for a d-type takes the form:

(i) if q^i chosen in the past and other firm has always chosen q^i, choose q^i with probability p_t;
(ii) if q^i chosen in the past and other firm has just chosen q^d, choose q^i with probability 0;
(iii) if q^d chosen at $r < t-1$ and other firm has chosen q^i after r, choose q^i with probability 1;
(iv) if q^d chosen at r and other firm has chosen q^d at every date after r, choose q^i with probability 0.

Thus, if a firm has not revealed itself to be a d-type, it follows some mixed strategy; if it has revealed itself then it gives the other firm one chance to allow itself to be a d-type before it reverts to q^i forever. This strategy for each firm will be a perfect equilibrium if a d-type firm finds it optimal to respond to the other firm announcing that it is a d-type by declaring itself to be a d-type.[9] Thus, if δ is the firm's discount factor, equilibrium requires

$$\Pi_{dd} + \frac{\delta}{1-\delta}\Pi_{dd} \geqslant \Pi_{id} + \frac{\delta}{1-\delta}\Pi_{ii} \tag{19}$$

which is the standard condition for the cooperative solution to be achievable in an infinitely repeated prisoners' dilemma problem. If both firms are of type d then, once one firm has revealed itself, the strategy produces an efficient outcome from then on for the two firms.

The probability p_t has still to be determined. The expected discounted profit for firm 1 of type d at time t, given that both firms have yet to reveal themselves, is given by

$$\begin{aligned} {}^iV_t^1 = (1-P_t^2)(1-p_t^2)\left[\Pi_{id} + \frac{\delta}{(1-\delta)}\Pi_{dd}\right] \\ + (1-(1-P_t^2)(1-p_t^2))\,[\Pi_{ii} + \delta V_{t+1}^1] \end{aligned} \tag{20}$$

if q^i is chosen and

$$\begin{aligned} {}^dV_t^1 = (1-P_t^2)p_t^2\left[\Pi_{di} + \frac{\delta}{(1-\delta)}\Pi_{dd}\right] + (1-P_t^2)(1-p_t^2) \\ \times\left[\Pi_{dd} + \frac{\delta}{(1-\delta)}\Pi_{dd}\right] + P_t^2\left[\Pi_{di} + \delta\Pi_{di} + \frac{\delta^2}{(1-\delta)}\Pi_{ii}\right] \end{aligned} \tag{21}$$

if q^d is chosen. V_{t+1}^1 is the expected discounted profit at $t+1$, given that an optimal policy is followed from then on. Thus

$$V_t^1 = p_t^1\,{}^iV_t^1 + (1-p_t^1)\,{}^dV_t^1 \tag{22}$$

and optimizing behaviour implies that

$$\begin{cases} {}^iV_t^1 > {}^dV_t^1 \Rightarrow p_t^1 = 1 \\ {}^dV_t^1 > {}^iV_t^1 \Rightarrow p_t^1 = 0 \end{cases} \tag{23}$$

In the non-degenerate case where p lies between zero and unity for both firms, p_t^1 and p_t^2 can be derived from the two equations

$$\begin{cases} {}^iV_t^1 = {}^dV_t^1 \\ {}^iV_t^2 = {}^dV_t^2 \end{cases} \tag{24}$$

As (20) is a difference equation, the solution to (24) will be a difference equation.

[9] As is common in infinitely repeated games, there are many perfect equilibria of which this is only one. Kreps *et al.* [1982] examine a perfect equilibrium in a repeated prisoners' dilemma game with a different type of incomplete information; there, agents with non "prisoners' dilemma" preferences have preferences biased in favour of cooperation.

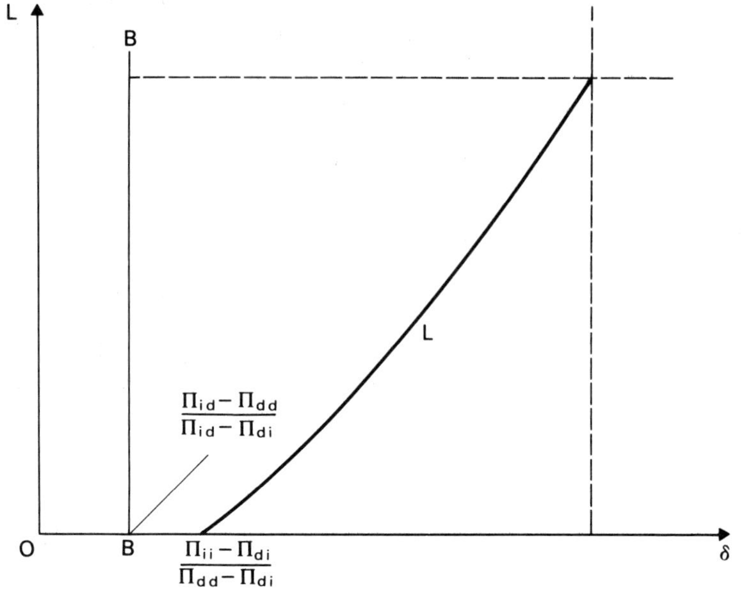

FIGURE 1

The information transfer will be complete if a firm's type is eventually known with probability one. This will be the case if P_t rises to unity so that a firm who never reveals itself is, in probabilistic terms, certain to be an *i*-type. The question to ask is what states of the system (P_1, P_2) have the feature that $p_1 = p_2 = 1$ so that (P_1, P_2) is not updated and no further information is transferred? If this steady state is reached, $V_{t+1} = {}^iV_t$, and (20), (21), (23) imply

$$(25) \qquad P \geqslant \frac{\dfrac{\delta}{1-\delta}[\Pi_{dd}-\Pi_{ii}]-[\Pi_{ii}-\Pi_{di}]}{\dfrac{\delta^2}{1-\delta}[\Pi_{dd}-\Pi_{di}]+\delta[\Pi_{ii}-\Pi_{di}]} = L$$

where each term in square brackets is positive (from (16)). With $\delta < 1$, (25) can be satisfied with $P < 1$ so that information is not always transferred in the limit. Figure 1 shows L as a function of δ. If the discount factor δ lies below $\Pi_{ii} - \Pi_{di}/\Pi_{dd} - \Pi_{di}$ then whatever the level of initial beliefs held by the two firms, neither will ever reveal itself to be a *d*-type firm. The line B is defined by (19) so that collusion cannot be sustained at lower values of δ. As shown, it is possible for δ to be high enough for collusion to be sustained but too low for information transfer, which would engender profitable collusion, to take place. Whatever the value of δ below unity, if both firms have the belief that it is very likely that the other firm is of type i then, again, no information transfer will take place.

In this model, the cost to a firm of revealing itself to be a *d*-type is a loss of profit for two periods. However, if a *d*-type is in a poor bargaining position because of its dependence on the other firm, the model could be easily amended to allow for the fact that a firm may suffer permanently from revelation. If a *d*-type firm gains from being thought an *i*-type after the other firm has revealed itself, revelation only occurs in the model because both firms can gain if they both reveal themselves to be *d*-types at the same time. The strategy probabilities p for both firms will either be low or unity—after some time, the probabilities "jump" to unity and no revelation can occur thereafter.[10]

What is interesting about this story is that though it is useful to have information transfer when asymmetric information is present, the incentive structure may be such that full revelation never occurs. What is suggested is that firms have an incentive to present themselves in a way so that they appear to have a strong bargaining position and as one of the most obvious ways of being in a strong bargaining position is to be unaffected by other firms' actions, collusive equilibria will, in probabilistic terms, be shifted towards what would happen under limited interdependence in a world of full information. These inefficient equilibria are cooperative equilibria but have features of non-cooperative equilibria; for instance, if other firms can observe the local behaviour of the own demand curve that a firm faces—other firms' outputs being held constant—then to convince these other firms of its independence from them, a Cournot strategy becomes optimal.[11] Thus, non-cooperative equilibria can be viewed as "poor" cooperative equilibria that arise when information fails to be transferred between firms.

IV. SIDE-PAYMENTS

Thus far, it has been assumed that side-payments between firms cannot be made. The most obvious role that they have is to increase the set of opportunities available to a group of firms. The sharing out of benefits can be divorced from production decisions so that, in a world of full information, an efficient co-operative bargaining solution will always involve the maximization of joint profits together with a sharing rule dependent upon the exact form of the bargaining solution. But in a world of asymmetric information, side-payments also have the role of an incentive device—if the share out depends upon what a firm reports then incentives for misrepresentation are affected by the share out.

To see how side-payments can be used as an incentive device, consider again the model of section 2. Side payments which do not favour one of the firms in an arbitrary way will affect the objective only through the effect on incentives. In the model assume that the coordinating agency tries to implement the

[10] Other equilibria are also possible. For instance, revelation may only occur at odd dates but not at even dates.

[11] The form that the equilibrium takes depends on what other firms observe. If other firms observe the slope of the demand curve with other prices constant then independence is exhibited by adopting Bertrand strategies.

first-best rule given by (13) and specifies a transfer t to be paid by a firm announcing itself to be a β-type if the other firm announces itself to be an o-type. Putting down the appropriate incentive constraints, a firm will always wish to reveal itself correctly (whatever the other firm announces)[12] if

$$(26)\quad \begin{cases} \dfrac{q_0^m}{2} d(q_0^m) \geqslant q_\beta^m d(q_\beta^m) - t \\ t \geqslant \dfrac{q_\beta^m}{2} d(q_\beta^m) \\ q_\beta^m d(q_\beta^m) + \beta q_\beta^m - t \geqslant \dfrac{q_0^m}{2} d(q_0^m) + \beta \dfrac{q_0^m}{2} \\ \dfrac{q_\beta^m}{2} d(q_\beta^m) + \dfrac{\beta q_\beta^m}{2} \geqslant t \end{cases}$$

As q_0^m and q_β^m are the profit-maximizing outputs for monopolistic firms of types o and β respectively, it is clear that (26) is satisfied by

$$(27)\qquad t = \frac{q_\beta^m}{2} d(q_\beta^m)$$

The present problem is very similar to an auction scheme. Attainment of the first-best requires that production should be undertaken by the most efficient firm and this can be ensured by allowing the firms to bid for the right to produce. (27) is the amount an o-type firm would be willing to bid to be allowed to produce when the other firm is of type β. Thus with such a transfer, the coordinating agency is similar in operation to a second price auction where the highest bidder wins but only pays the second highest price. As is well known (Vickrey [1961]), this auction mechanism has the property that truthful revelation is the dominant strategy so it is unsurprising that (27) ensures satisfaction of (26).

When a firm is called upon to report its type before it can observe what the other firm reports, and no recontracting is possible—the set-up of section 2—it is clear that by making side-payments sensitive to what a firm reports, one could hope to be able to provide appropriate incentives without requiring the cartel rule implemented by the coordinating agency to be used as an incentive device.[13] But when bargaining can take place after a firm has obtained information about another firm, the usefulness of side-payments is less certain. The problem here is that side-payments are within the domain of what is bargained over and can no longer be specifically formulated to cope with the problem of incentives. To take the example of the last section, in the steady state

[12] Truth will be, in this case, a dominant strategy.

[13] For a general analysis of the implementation of rules when agents have beliefs about the preferences of other agents and side-payments are possible, see d'Aspremont and Gerard-Varet [1979].

with no further revelation of information, side-payments will be determined through a bargaining process that takes place between firms uncertain of the type to which the other firm belongs. The side-payment will depend upon the state of the system (P^1, P^2) and though the firms may decide upon a particular side-payment to induce more information transmission, they may not be able to commit themselves to a particular side-payment structure in the future as this will be the outcome of the negotiation process at that time—side-payments can be used to enlarge the set of opportunities available under the bargaining process but there may be little role for side-payments as an incentive device.

KEVIN ROBERTS
Department of Economics,
University of Warwick,
Coventry CV4 7AL,
U.K.

ACCEPTED NOVEMBER 1984

THE JOURNAL OF INDUSTRIAL ECONOMICS 0022-1821 $2.00
Volume XXXIII June 1985 No. 4

ON THE INCIDENCE AND DURATION OF PRICE WARS*

ROBERT H. PORTER

I. INTRODUCTION

THE PURPOSE of this paper is to test some theoretical predictions about the incidence and duration of price wars, when these price wars are viewed as an enforcement device to maintain a cooperative or tacitly collusive agreement in an uncertain environment. The theoretical model of Green and Porter [1984] and Porter [1983a] predicts that price wars should be triggered by unanticipated demand fluctuations, and that they will be more frequent the greater the number of firms in the industry, or the greater the degree of market concentration. Correspondingly, the optimal duration of price wars is also affected by the number of firms.

The tests employ weekly time series data on the Joint Executive Committee railroad cartel (henceforth referred to as the JEC) from 1880 to 1886. Porter [1983b] and Lee and Porter [1984] previously used this data in order to identify periods in which price wars occurred, and to test whether pricing behavior in co-operative periods was consistent with predictions of the theoretical model. The present paper will look more closely at the price wars themselves, in order to test another set of predictions about their incidence and duration.

Section 2 summarizes the theoretical model in more detail, with emphasis on markets with price-setting firms. The models in Green and Porter [1984] and Porter [1983a] consider quantity-setting firms, but the railroads in the JEC chose prices, not quantities. The distinction has some bearing on the econometric work, but the basic ideas from the theory still apply.

There is a brief description of the JEC and the data set in section 3. Empirical results are covered in section 4, and section 5 contains some concluding comments.

II. NONCOOPERATIVE COLLUSION UNDER UNCERTAINTY

Consider an industry analogous to that originally studied by Stigler [1964]. A number of price-setting firms produce a good of relatively homogeneous quality in a market that is immune from entry. Individual firms cannot monitor the prices chosen by their competitors, so that any tacitly collusive scheme must face the problem of detecting and deterring deviations from the agreement.

* I have benefited from the research assistance of Cristina Mazon and the financial support of a Sloan Foundation Grant to the University of Minnesota Economics Department. I am also indebted to Tom Ulen, who made this data set available to me, and to Paul Geroski for helpful comments.

The static noncooperative outcome is that associated with Bertrand, with firms pricing at marginal cost. Any scheme by the firms to jointly raise their prices would benefit them all, assuming that their cost and demand functions are well behaved (for example, marginal costs not declining too rapidly). However, any single firm would profit from a unilateral price cut which attracted enough customers away from its competitors. Thus the collusive price vector is not an equilibrium point in a one-shot market game. It pays to defect. (For more detail, see Friedman [1983].)

Suppose, however, that the firms operate in this market in perpetuity and that there is no exogenous source of uncertainty. As Friedman [1983] and Telser [1972] show, it is then possible to support the collusive price vector as a noncooperative equilibrium of this repeated game by "trigger strategies", as long as future profits are not discounted too heavily. Absent uncertainty, detection of cheating is straightforward. Firms know what market shares they should get if they all adhere to the agreed-upon price vector, and any discrepancy between actual and anticipated shares (in particular, any shortfall) occurs only when some rival has surreptitiously lowered its price.

In this context, trigger strategies are quite simple. Firms choose prices according to the following rules:

(1) As long as no firm has ever defected from the agreement, firms continue to price at collusive levels.
(2) If at any point someone cheats on the agreement, firms permanently revert to noncooperative price levels, i.e., price at marginal cost.

Any firm contemplating a secret price cut would face a tradeoff. It could increase its short-run profits by earning more than it would at the agreed-upon prices, but it would then permanently sacrifice the present discounted value of the difference between collusive and competitive profits, beginning with the next period. Here periods are determined by the length of time it takes rivals to learn of the decrease in their market share and the additional time it takes them to cut their prices in response. Spence [1978] refers to these as the observation and response lags, respectively, and their sum as the reaction lag. As long as the firm does not discount its future profit stream too heavily, the threatened future retaliation will be sufficient to dissuade it from deviating.

The rate at which firms discount profits will depend on a number of factors, as enumerated by Telser [1972]. The longer the reaction lag, the longer the relevant time period, and so the more future profits are discounted. In addition, the firms will discount both according to their subjective rate of time preference (perhaps the market rate of interest), and according to their beliefs about the expected duration of the market. The expected length of the market game could be finite, perhaps because either government regulation or nationalization is possible, and yet the game can appropriately be modelled as one of infinite duration whenever there is some chance of its not ending. Suppose, for example, that the probability of the game ending in any period is described by a geometric distribution. That is, there is a constant probability p that the game will end in any period, given that it has lasted that long. Then, if r is the subjective rate of time preference, firms will use a discount factor of $\beta = (1-p)/(1+r)$. A dollar next period is worth β dollars today, where $0 < \beta < 1$.

As long as β is large enough, the agreement will be noncooperatively viable, since it does not pay to defect when every other firm cooperates. Thus we require that both p and r be relatively small. Note that the threatened punishment is a credible threat, because firms revert to static noncooperative prices. By definition, if every other firm reverts to that level, any single firm maximizes its profits by doing so as well. Note also that the critical level of the discount factor depends on the cooperative price vector chosen. If β is smaller than the level necessary to support prices which maximize joint profits (perfectly collusive prices) as a noncooperative equilibrium with simple trigger strategies, it may still be possible to support prices greater than competitive prices but less than perfectly collusive prices by a simple trigger mechanism. It is easy to show that the closer prices are to perfectly collusive levels, the greater the critical level of β, as the short run gains from cheating increase with prices more rapidly than does the difference between cooperative and competitive profits. The closer cooperative prices are to competitive levels, the smaller the critical value of β.

Now suppose that there is an exogenous source of demand uncertainty, so that market shares are a random function of prices. Firms are then faced with an inference problem. For any firm, a smaller market share than had been anticipated could be the result of cheating by a competitor, or an adverse demand shock. If competitors' prices are not directly observable, uncertainty about the source of market share movements cannot be resolved. Nevertheless, it is still possible for firms to tacitly raise prices above marginal cost and create incentives to adhere to the collusive prices, provided that there is not too much exogenous demand variability, and if future profits are not discounted too heavily.

Consider the following amendment of simple trigger strategies. Rather than having price wars triggered by any deviation from anticipated market shares, let the required deviation be some percentage of the total industry output. For example, sum the absolute value (or the square) of the individual discrepancies, and if this sum exceeds a given fraction of total demand (or demand squared), start a price war. Alternatively, suppose that some firm acts as a price leader. Then reversions to competitive prices would be triggered if the market share of the price leader falls enough below its allotted share. In both of these cases, price wars are triggered by large deviations of actual from allocated market shares, an event caused either by actual cheating or by an atypical interfirm demand pattern. Actual cheating by some firm would increase the likelihood of these deviations being large, and so be more likely to trigger a price war. According to Ulen [1983], the JEC monitored these deviations in order to detect cheating. In addition, rather than have a permanent reversion to competitive prices, suppose that the price war is of finite length. This is a more "forgiving" punishment, which takes into account the fact that price wars could be triggered by random events, and not by actual cheating.

Whether this scheme will be stable, i.e. whether it pays to defect, depends on a number of factors. Any firm considering a secret price cut again faces a tradeoff. As before, there are short run profits to be had. However, by cutting price, the firm increases the probability that a price war will occur, and so decreases the expected discounted value of future profits. If the cartel is to be stable, the costs of cheating—the increased probability of foregone future earnings—must exceed the short run benefits for any price cut. Thus we again require that firms' discount factors be sufficiently close to one.

Now suppose that prices in cooperative periods, the trigger mechanism, and the price war length are chosen optimally, that is to maximize total industry expected discounted profits subject to the constraint that no firm benefits by deviating from cooperative prices. (This is the problem studied by Porter [1983a] for quantity-setting firms.) This could be accomplished either by an explicit mutual agreement, or by firms following the strategy of an industry leader. In either case, firms are pursuing their own interests in charging cooperative prices and so have no incentive to secretly cut prices.

One conclusion which emerges is that, when there is uncertainty, the prices charged in cooperative periods will not be as high as those which would maximize joint profits in a single period. In equilibrium, the marginal gains from cheating in cooperative periods must be exactly offset by the marginal losses implicit in the increased probability of a reversion to competitive behavior. The gains from cheating increase as prices in cooperative periods increase towards perfectly collusive levels, so expected losses must be increased by decreasing the market share deviations necessary to trigger a price war, or by increasing the length of reversionary episodes. Expected discounted industry profits will be maximized at price levels between competitive and perfectly collusive levels. Furthermore, the greater the number of symmetric firms or the greater the degree of demand uncertainty, the closer the cooperative price is to competitive levels. If there are too many firms, or if demand uncertainty is too large, the only equilibrium is that of competitive prices.

It is important to note that in equilibrium, the incentive structure is designed to guarantee that firms do not deviate from agreed-upon-prices in cooperative periods, but that price wars will still occur as random demand shocks will occasionally induce large discrepancies between allotted and actual market shares. Rational firms will realize that, in equilibrium, this occurs only when demand shocks are unusually asymmetric, and never because of individual firm deviations. Nevertheless, rational firms will revert to competitive prices for the prescribed number of periods, precisely because the enforcement mechanism must be employed on these occasions if firms are to have the correct incentives in cooperative periods. If they do not believe that the enforcement mechanism will be employed, they will then have an incentive to cheat on the agreement. Thus observed price wars will always be preceded by a period with an unexpectedly large deviation of actual from allotted market shares.

It is difficult to predict how the frequency and duration of competitive reversions will be affected by changes in market structure without specifying how the joint distribution of market share shocks is affected. However, Stigler's [1964] intuition that collusion is more difficult the greater the number of firms seems reasonable, so that the frequency of reversions might be expected to increase with the number of firms. This intuition is borne out in the simple environment studied by Porter [1983a]. However, no simple comparative statics result is available for the duration of price wars. When duration is selected optimally, there are several conflicting considerations. As the number of firms increases, so does the incentive to free ride on the gains from cooperation, and so the penalty to cheating must increase. For essentially this reason, the expected frequency of reversions will increase. However, the cartel may want to employ shorter, and so more forgiving, punishments when reversions occur, in order to partially offset the increased fraction of time spent at competitive prices. In the case of the JEC, this second effect appears to have predominated.

In the following sections we examine the JEC to see whether these theoretical predictions are correct.

III. THE JOINT EXECUTIVE COMMITTEE

This section contains a brief description of the JEC, with emphasis on the period to 1880 to 1886. A more complete account is contained in Ulen [1983], and the references cited there.

The JEC was a cartel formed by the railroads which controlled eastbound freight shipments from Chicago to the Atlantic seaboard in the 1880s. The agreement was publicly acknowledged, as it preceded the passage of the Sherman Act (1890) and the formation of the Interstate Commerce Commission (1887).

The assumption that a homogeneous good was sold seems to have been approximately satisfied. Through shipments of grain accounted for 73% of all dead freight tonnage handled by the JEC. The railroads also carried flour and provisions, but the prices charged for transporting these commodities were tied to the grain rate. While different railroads shipped grain to different port cities, most of the wheat handled by the cartel was subsequently exported overseas, and the rates charged by different firms adjusted to compensate for differences in ocean shipping rates.

The JEC cartel agreement took the form of market share allotments rather than absolute amounts of quantity shipped. Firms set their rates individually, and the JEC office took weekly accounts so that each railroad could see the total amount transported. Total demand was quite variable, and the actual market share of any particular firm depended on both the prices charged by all the firms and unpredictable stochastic forces. Thus, the problem faced by the members of the JEC seems to be comparable to that posed in the preceding section.

In their model, Green and Porter [1984] explicitly rule out the possibility of entry into the market. In the case of the JEC, entry occurred twice between 1880 and 1886. It appears that the cartel passively accepted the entrants, allocated them market shares, and thereby allowed the collusive agreement to continue. The reason for this is undoubtedly that when a firm entered the rail freight industry in this period, it faced a "no-exit" constraint. To put it briefly, bankrupt railroads were relieved by the courts of most of their fixed costs and instructed to cut prices to increase business. Therefore, it would not be rational for a railroad cartel to engage in predatory pricing practices in response to entry. Of course, entry may have increased the frequency of future price wars as the collusive agreement became more difficult to maintain.

Lake steamers and sailships were the principal source of competition for the railroads, and at no point did they enter into an agreement with the JEC. The opening and closing of the Great Lakes to navigation therefore resulted in semi-annual fluctuations in demand for the JEC. These predictable fluctuations should not have disrupted industry conduct, according to the theory.

A principal function of the JEC was weekly information gathering and dissemination to member firms. This can be viewed as an effort to reduce the observation lag mentioned in the previous section. As a result, the following data is available from week 1 in 1880 to week 16 in 1886:

Q, total quantity of grain shipped; in tons (times 10^{-5})
L, dummy variable; 1 if Great Lakes were open to navigation, 0 otherwise
W, regime classification indicator; 1 if colluding reported by *Railway Review*, 0 otherwise
I, estimated regime classification indicator; 1 if colluding predicted by Lee and Porter [1984], 0 otherwise
H, Herfindahl index of allotted market shares
SSD, sum of squared deviations of actual from allotted market shares.

The data set employed is weekly time series, a frequency which is probably close to the actual reaction lag of the firms in the JEC, so that temporal aggregation bias is not likely to be a problem here.

A price variable is also available, but it is somewhat suspect. The JEC polled member firms and provided an index of prices charged. This index may not reflect secret price cuts, since there is a moral hazard problem in reporting actual prices. Therefore, any price war that was precipitated by secret price cuts may have been recorded with a lag. In this case, *I*, the estimated dummy variable which indicates when the cartel was successfully maintaining high prices, may also record cartel breakdowns with a lag. For each week t, I_t is the maximum likelihood estimator of whether a price war was occurring, given the observed price, quantity and the exogenous variables listed above. It is also assumed that the reported adherence series, W, is correct some fraction of the time, and so its value is accounted for. The calculation of I is done according to Bayes' rule. Typically, I_t predicts that price wars occurred in period t when prices are unaccountably low, and so is inaccurate if the price series is subject to measurement error. As a result, both I and W, the incidence of competitive episodes reported by the trade press at the time, will be employed as indicators of cartel adherence. Whether I or W is more accurate will depend on the relative accuracy of the price series and the reports of cartel success. Note also that, while the price series is suspect, the existence of this sort of imperfect information structure is necessary if an enforcement mechanism involving reversions to competitive behavior, or price wars, is to be witnessed. It is of crucial importance that firms monitor some variable (in this case their own market share) which only imperfectly reflects the actions of other firms. Here firms knew the prices they charged their own customers, but the reported price index would not be of much use in determining whether other firms were secretly cutting prices.

The Herfindahl index, H, is computed using the allotted market shares of JEC firms. These varied following entry, and because allocations were revised periodically to satisfy internal conflicts. I use H rather than the number of firms as an explanatory variable in order to see whether these reallocations reflected changes in the degree of competition. Of course, the reallocations subsequent to entry had a more dramatic effect on the Herfindahl index.

The L variable documents when the JEC faced its main source of competition. It would be preferable if the prices charged by lake steamers, or some other index of whether lake steamers were successfully colluding, had been used in the econometric work, but such data are not available.

There are five distinct periods in the sample, separated by either entry, additions to existing networks, or the temporary departure of the Chicago and Atlantic from the JEC (due to a dispute with a non-JEC railroad (the Erie) which provided it with access to the eastern seaboard). From week 1 through week 28 in 1880, three firms were members. The Grand Trunk then entered. In week 10 of 1883, the New York Central added another line to its network. In week 26 in 1883, the Chicago and Atlantic entered, and then in week 12 of 1886, through the end of the sample (week 16 of 1886), it departed due to its dispute with the Erie. The second and fourth of these episodes encompass the greater portion of the sample (281 of 328 sample points), and all reversionary periods occurred during these intervals, according to I. A very brief reversion began in week 17 of 1883, according to W. I therefore will run my regressions for both the full sample and these two subsamples separately to test for evidence of structural change.

I now turn to the econometric results, as well as a heuristic description of the pattern of price wars in this sample.

IV. EMPIRICAL RESULTS

Before discussing the econometric results, we examine the pattern of cooperation in the JEC in the 1880–86 sample, employing both W, the series reported at the time by trade publications and newspapers, and I, the series estimated by maximum likelihood methods from price movements by Lee and Porter [1984]. I consider two subsets of the sample. During period 1, from week 28 in 1880 to week 10 in 1883, there were four active firms in the market. In period 2, from week 26 in 1883 to week 11 in 1886, there were five firms. The former period lasted 139 weeks and the latter 142 weeks.

According to the contemporaneous press reports, as captured by W, there were three price wars in period 1 and seven in period 2. In period 1, their average duration was 14 weeks. As a result, 30.2% of the weeks in the period involved relatively competitive behavior by the firms. The probability of a price war beginning in any particular week, given that the preceding week was cooperative, was 0.0395. When the number of firms increased in period 2, the seven price wars had an average duration of 11.6 weeks. The increase in the frequency of competitive reversions was greater than the fall in their duration, and so 57% of the weeks in this period witnessed competitive behavior. The probability of a price war beginning increased to 0.1167.

The estimated adherence series, I, reflects a similar pattern, although fewer weeks are labelled as reversionary and their pattern differs somewhat. According to I, there was one 37 week long price war in period 1, and seven reversions

TABLE I
DETERMINANTS OF W_t (GIVEN $W_{t-1} = 1$)*

Independent Variable	1. *Full Sample*	2. *Period 1*	3. *Period 2*
Constant	−2.25 (1.67)	15.89 (16.58)	−6.12 (15.35)
L_{t-1}	0.331 (0.349)	0.767 (0.636)	0.387 (0.477)
Q_{t-1}	1.38 (1.86)	2.91 (4.17)	2.43 (2.56)
H_{t-1}	9.79 (4.52)	−42.38 (47.31)	22.01 (52.00)
SSD_{t-1}	3.26 (6.22)	7.73 (11.62)	0.81 (9.37)
N	201	94	62
$-2 \log L$	7.30	2.05	1.69

* Estimated standard errors are in parentheses. N is the number of observations. The statistic $-2 \log L$ is twice the difference between the log likelihood function and that when all parameters but the constant are set equal to zero. Under the null hypothesis of no explanatory power, it has a chi-squared distribution with 4 degrees of freedom.

TABLE II
DETERMINANTS OF I_t (GIVEN $I_{t-1} = 1$)*

Independent Variable	1. *Full Sample*	2. *Period 2*
Constant	−1.72	−0.62
	(2.12)	(9.32)
L_{t-1}	−0.286	0.093
	(0.386)	(0.442)
Q_{t-1}	−3.55	0.25
	(1.84)	(2.43)
H_{t-1}	15.13	7.56
	(6.82)	(31.36)
SSD_{t-1}	−6.77	−9.52
	(6.19)	(7.40)
N	232	85
$-2 \log L$	12.86	1.99

* Estimated standard errors are in parentheses. The statistic $-2 \log L$ is calculated as in Table I, with the same distribution under the null hypothesis.

in period 2, which were on average 8.1 weeks long. The percentage of weeks involving competitive behavior was 26.6 % in period 1 and 40.1 % in the second period. The probability of a price war being triggered increased from 0.0099 to 0.0833 when the additional firm entered.

Both I and W indicate that, as the number of firms increased, the frequency of price wars increased as their duration fell. The net effect was a less stable cartel, as a greater percentage of weeks were accounted for by periods of reversionary conduct. In addition, the estimates of Porter [1983b] and Lee and Porter [1984] indicate that, *ceteris paribus*, prices were 9–10% lower in the second period. One goal of the econometric work of this section is to determine whether the JEC was less successful in maintaining cooperative prices in the second period because of the entry of an additional firm, as the theoretical model would predict, or because of some other developments. The lower prices in the second period are consistent with the theory of noncooperative collusion under uncertainty.

The econometric work estimates the determinants of both the frequency and the duration of price wars, for the full sample and for periods 1 and 2 separately. (The Herfindahl index of allotted shares varied within the two subsamples because of occasional renegotiations, as mentioned in the previous section, and so can be employed as an additional explanatory variable.) Tables I and II display the results of a probit regression of whether or not a price war begins, conditional on the preceding period witnessing cooperative behavior, for each of the three possible samples. (Tables I and II employ W and I as the dependent variable, respectively. In the latter case, there was only one price war in period 1, so that a separate regression cannot be run.) Thus the periods selected are those in which the previous period was cooperative. The regression is designed to determine which variables cause price wars to begin. (See Ulen [1983] for a similar logit regression of cooperation versus noncooperation in which all the sample points are used.)

The results reported in Table I are discouraging. The regressions for the cartel adherence series reported by the press do indicate that the frequency of reversion increased when the number of firms increased. (H has a positive and significant coefficient for the full sample.) No other variable has significant explanatory power, however. In the case of L, this conforms with the theory, since predictable demand disturbances should not influence cartel stability. The statistic $-2 \log L$, which is a likelihood ratio test statistic for the hypothesis that the independent variables do not explain variations in W (see Maddala [1983]), lead one to accept the hypothesis of no explanatory power, except for the full sample, where changes in H affected price war incidence. Within periods 1 and 2, changes in H associated with changes in allotted market shares had no effect. Here H may simply be a proxy for some unspecified difference between the two periods. Total eastbound grain shipments were similar in these two periods (see Porter [1983b, Table 6]), however, and so the effect of entry is the most likely difference.

The results in Table II conform more closely with the theory of section 2. Again H has a significant coefficient for the full sample, although not for period 2, and L is not significant. At a 90% confidence level, SSD is now significant and has the right sign in both samples. In addition, Q is significant for the full sample. Curiously, its coefficient indicates that price wars were more likely to begin the larger the quantity sold in the previous period. Perhaps large values of Q were associated with greater incentives to cheat. In any event, the regressions show that the incidence of price wars increased as the number of firms increased, and as the sum of squared deviations of actual from allotted market shares increased, consistent with the theory.

Tables III and IV show the results of regressions with the duration of price wars as the dependent variable, for the full sample and for period 2. (There were not enough price wars in period 1 to do a separate regression for it.) The duration variables of Tables III and IV are obtained from W and I, respectively. $\hat{W}$ and $\hat{I}$ are predicted values of W and I in the first period of the price war, given by the appropriate probit equation in Table I or II. The other explanatory variables are also computed using their values at these dates.

In the models of Green and Porter [1984] and Porter [1983a], it was assumed that the price war length was fixed, although the optimal duration could vary with the number of active firms. This restriction was imposed for reasons of computational tractability. More generally, one might expect that the length of the price war could depend on the factors which triggered it. Therefore, both $\hat{W}$ (or $\hat{I}$) and SSD were employed as regressors, in order to

TABLE III
DETERMINANTS OF PRICE WAR LENGTH*

Independent Variable	1. *Full Sample*	2. *Period 2*
Constant	3.32 (6.96)	−191.3 (115.2)
$\hat{W}$	—	249.5 (137.8)
L	—	−30.11 (12.25)
SSD	277.6 (203.0)	—
R^2	0.172	0.603
N	11	7
F	1.87	3.04

* *W* is used to calculate price war length. Estimated standard errors are in parentheses.

TABLE IV
DETERMINANTS OF PRICE WAR LENGTH*

Independent Variable	1. *Full Sample*	2. *Period 2*
Constant	−121.7 (23.8)	12.33 (3.00)
L	−7.71 (3.89)	−7.33 (3.96)
H	455.6 (80.4)	—
R^2	0.865	0.406
N	8	7
F	19.28	3.42

* *I* is used to calculate price war length. Estimated standard errors are in parentheses.

determine whether the duration of price wars was positively correlated with the predicted probability of its occurring or the size of the discrepancy between actual and allotted market shares, respectively. If this was the case, then a firm contemplating defection would risk losing future profits, both because of an increase in the probability of a price war, and because of an increase in expected duration should one occur. Once a price war has begun, it is assumed that its length is determined solely by the factors which triggered it, and not by firms' behavior during the price war. If other firms behave competitively, each has no incentive to alter its behavior, and so to affect the duration of the reversion.

The results reported in Tables III and IV represent the best fits available in each case. Since degrees of freedom are limited, insignificant variables have been dropped. Both tables indicate that price wars were longer when the lakes were closed. While this predictable shift in demand does not appear to have influenced the likelihood of reversions to competitive behavior, their expected duration increased 6 to 8 weeks, according to the equations in Table IV. For the reported cartel adherence series W, reported in Table III, the length of a price war is positively correlated with the predicted probability of its occurring, $\hat{W}$, or with SSD, the sum of squared deviations of actual from allotted market shares. In the case of I, the estimated adherence series, price wars were significantly shorter when the number of firms increased (and so H fell). Thus the conjectures of the preceding paragraph, and those of section 2, are substantiated by the empirical results, at least to some extent. Note, however, that only the full sample results of Table IV can be viewed with confidence, according to the F-statistics. Also, because degrees of freedom are limited, these results are merely suggestive.

V. SUMMARY

The operation of the JEC appears to conform with the theoretical model of Stigler [1964], Green and Porter [1984] and Porter [1983a]. As the number of active firms increased from four to five, collusion became more difficult to enforce. As estimated by Porter [1983b], prices in cooperative periods were approximately 10% lower when there were five firms, *ceteris paribus*, presumably to reduce the short run gains from cheating. Furthermore, as documented in the previous section, the percentage of time spent in reversions to relatively competitive pricing behavior increased from 26.6% to 40.1%, according to the estimated incidence series of Lee and Porter [1984], or from 30.2% to 57% according to contemporaneous press reports. While the average duration of price wars decreased, there was a dramatic increase in the frequency of their incidence.

ROBERT H. PORTER,
Department of Economics,
State University of New York at Stony Brook,
Stony Brook, NY 11794,
U.S.A.

ACCEPTED NOVEMBER 1984

THE JOURNAL OF INDUSTRIAL ECONOMICS 0022-1821 $2.00
Volume XXXIII June 1985 No. 4

THE GAINS FROM MERGER OR COLLUSION IN PRODUCT-DIFFERENTIATED INDUSTRIES*

JONATHAN B. BAKER AND TIMOTHY F. BRESNAHAN

I. INTRODUCTION

A MERGER in an industry with differentiated products increases the market power of the merging firms to the extent that their products are close substitutes and that other firms produce only more distant substitutes.[1] Such a merger makes the residual demand curve of each partner steeper, by shifting each in the direction of the industry demand curve.[2] The extent of this increase in market power depends upon the own-elasticity of demand for each merging firm's product, as well as the cross-elasticity of demand for each with all other firms' products. As a result, evaluating the effect of a merger between two firms with $n-2$ other competitors would seem to require the estimation of at least n^2 parameters (all of the price elasticities of demand), a formidable task.

That extremely difficult estimation task is unnecessary, however. The necessary information is contained in the slopes of the two single-firm (residual) demand curves before the merger, and the extent to which the merged firm will face a steeper demand curve. For example, suppose a merger between two U.S. brewing firms, say Pabst and Anheuser–Busch, were proposed. It is not particularly important to determine whether it is competition from Miller or competition from Stroh (or from Heileman, or . . .) which puts the most effective brake on Anheuser–Busch's pricing. Only the total effect of these other firms and the particular effect of competition from Pabst are of interest.

This paper proposes econometric procedures for estimating the demand system that merger partners will face, based only on pre-merger data. The key to the procedures is that the effects of all other firms in the industry are summed together. Formally, we start with a model of an n-firm product-differentiated industry. Manipulation of the model removes the prices and quantities of all but two firms. This reduces the dimensionality of the problem to manageable size; rather than an n-firm demand system, we estimate a two-firm residual demand system. In this way the technique extends our econometric method for

* We would like to thank Paul Geroski and an anonymous referee for comments on an earlier draft. Acknowledged is grant support from the Sloan Foundation to the Department of Economics at Stanford University.

[1] This definition of the increase in market power from a merger ignores possible changes in industry conduct resulting from the change in industry structure. If the merger raises the likelihood of collusion (Stigler [1964]), the definition underestimates the change in market power. If the merger induces entry by new firms or competitive product introductions by existing firms, the definition overestimates the change in market power.

[2] Our definition of the residual demand curve is distinct from, but closely related to, Chamberlin's [1933] *dd'*. We make the distinction precise in Note 6 below.

evaluating single-firm demand elasticities in product-differentiated industries (Baker and Bresnahan [1984]).

Throughout, we do not distinguish a merger between two firms from a bilateral collusive arrangement between them. We use the language "the increase in market power from a merger" but could equally well use the phrase "the gains from a bilateral collusive arrangement between these two firms".

We apply our technique to three U.S. brewing firms: Anheuser–Busch (A–B), Pabst and Coors. Since U.S. brewing is quite concentrated, and since all of these firms are large,[3] a merger between any two of the three would likely be challenged under current U.S. antitrust guidelines. The question of bilateral collusion is therefore more interesting. Our estimates show that neither of the two smaller firms, Pabst and Coors, would have a significant increase in market power from bilateral collusion, although A–B would gain substantially from colluding with either of the other two.

II. TWO FIRMS IN A PRODUCT-DIFFERENTIATED INDUSTRY

This section derives the residual demand curve facing two firms in a product-differentiated industry. The residual demand curve is the relationship between those two firms' prices and quantities, taking the reactions of all other firms into account. This is a natural generalization of the residual demand curve facing a single firm: the relationship between its price and quantity, taking other firms' reactions into account. In product-differentiated industries, it is natural to suppose that there will be a (private) gain to merger, because the merged firm will face a steeper residual demand curve.[4]

A simple location model of product differentiation can illustrate these ideas. Suppose stores are distributed along a road as in Figure 1 (a). The road goes on forever, but we show only the four firms at locations ℓ_1, ℓ_2, ℓ_3 and ℓ_4. Each initially charges the price P_0. Customers need to travel to the stores; their costs per mile are given by the slopes of the delivered-price lines. Customer c_{12} is just indifferent between going to store 1 or 2, but everyone located to the right of c_{12} would rather buy at store 2 than store 1. Suppose that competition in the industry takes the Bertrand (price) form, and that the stores are spaced such that the reaction functions have slope $+\frac{1}{3}$. That is, every store would respond to a price increase by either of its neighbors with a price increase $\frac{1}{3}$ as large.

To define the residual demand curve facing firm 2, suppose that firm 2's costs increased, leading it to increase its price to P_1. After all other stores have reached equilibrium, both of firm 2's neighbors will have increased their prices by slightly over $\frac{1}{3}$ as much.[5] Figure 1 (b) shows that firm 2 will lose customers to both stores 1 and 3. The slope of firm 2's residual demand curve can be

[3] In 1983, Anheuser–Busch had a 32.9 percent national market share (in unit sales), Coors 7.5 percent, and Pabst 7.0 percent.

[4] This presumption is typically false in homogeneous-product industries. See Salant *et al.* [1983].

[5] It is slightly over $\frac{1}{3}$ because store 3's increase leads to an increase by 4, which feeds back to 3, and so on.

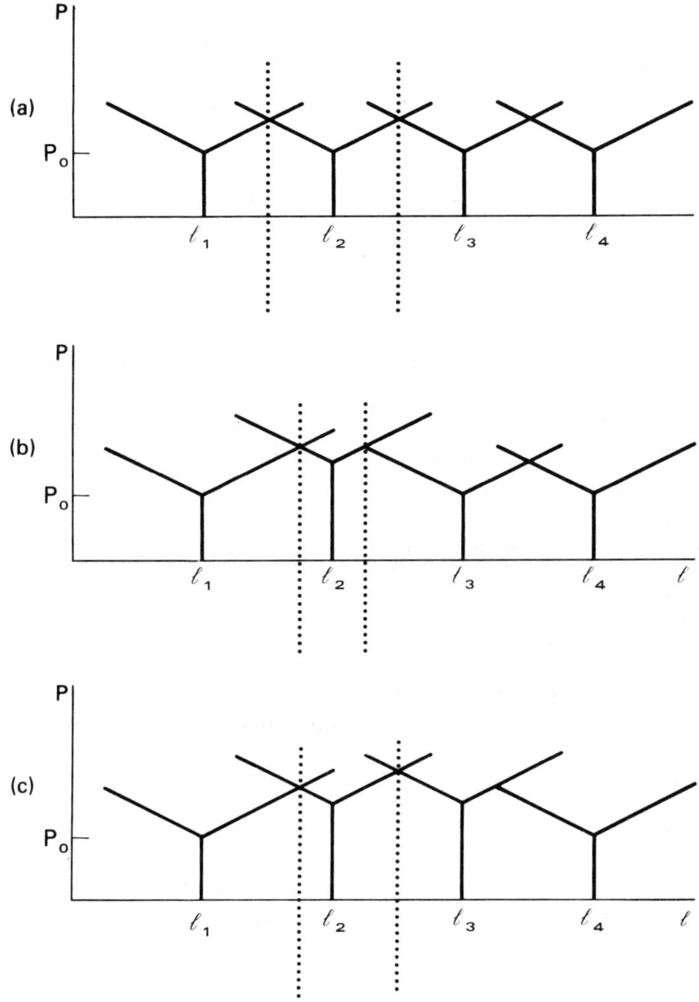

FIGURE 1
Spatial Example

calculated by the amount of sales it loses for a given price increase.[6] As the figure is drawn, the slope of residual demand for firm 3 is identical to that for firm 2, since the firms are symmetric to one another.

Alternatively, stores 2 and 3 might be merged into a single firm. Since its two stores are identical, this firm would set a single price. Figure 1 (c) shows what

[6] The slope of the residual demand curve is different from the slope of Chamberlin's *dd'*. The latter would be defined in our spatial-Bertrand context keeping other firms' prices constant. The residual demand curve lets other firms adjust. It is possible to estimate the slope of *dd'* as well as a residual demand: see, for example, Bresnahan [1981].

would happen if the merged firm raised price. Now, customers switch from store 2 to store 1 *but not to store* 3. Similarly, store 3 loses customers to store 4 but not to store 2. As a result, each store loses only half as many customers as it would have acting independently. The residual demand elasticity for the merged firm is only half that of the pre-merged firms, a considerable increase in market power.

Any real-world product-differentiated industry is likely to be much more complicated than this example. If there are n firms with different products in the industry, one might expect a price increase by any one firm to lead some customers to switch to most or all of the other $n-1$ firms. The situation is unlikely to be symmetric; some particular firms' products will have greater cross-elasticities of demand than others. Further, the assumption of price (Bertrand) competition in our example might be incorrect; firms might exhibit Cournot or other forms of behavior. It therefore seems that calculating the increase in market power due to a real-world merger involves an extremely difficult econometric task. All of the own- and cross-elasticities of demand must be estimated and the nature of competitive interaction must be determined.

Let firms 1 and 2 propose a merger in an industry with $n-2$ other firms. The inverse demand curves for the merger partners may be written

$$P_1 = h_1(Q_1, Q_2, \underset{\sim}{Q}, Y; \eta_1) \tag{1}$$

$$P_2 = h_2(Q_1, Q_2, \underset{\sim}{Q}, Y; \eta_2) \tag{2}$$

Here $\underset{\sim}{Q}$ is an $(n-2)$ vector of quantities produced by all other firms, Y denotes a vector of exogenous variables which shift demand, and η_i is a parameter vector. The remaining $(n-2)$ demand curves in this industry may be written compactly as follows:

$$\underset{\sim}{P} = \underset{\sim}{h}(Q_1, Q_2, \underset{\sim}{Q}, Y; \underset{\sim}{\eta}) \tag{3}$$

Note that estimation of (1), (2) and (3) can be very difficult. Denoting the elasticity of h_i with respect to Q_j as η_{ij}, (1), (2) and (3) might be approximated as

$$p_1 = \eta_{10} + \eta_{11}q_1 + \eta_{21}q_2 + \sum_{j=3}^{n} \eta_{j1}q_j + \langle \eta_{1Y}, Y \rangle, \tag{1'}$$

$$p_2 = \eta_{20} + \eta_{12}q_1 + \eta_{22}q_2 + \sum_{j=3}^{n} \eta_{j2}q_j + \langle \eta_{2Y}, Y \rangle, \tag{2'}$$

$$p_i = \eta_{i0} + \eta_{1i}q_1 + \eta_{2i}q_2 + \sum_{j=3}^{n} \eta_{ji}q_j + \langle \eta_{iY}, Y \rangle, \qquad i = 3, \ldots, n \tag{3'}$$

where $q_i = \log(Q_i)$, $p_i = \log(P_i)$ and $\langle \cdot, \cdot \rangle$ is the inner product of two vectors. There are n^2 elasticities of demand η_{ij}, even before considering the exogenous-variable elasticities, η_{iY}. Unless some further structure can be put on (1′), (2′)

and (3′), for example, by grouping firms into market segments, direct estimation will be very difficult if not impossible.[7]

Next we specify the behavior of the $(n-2)$ non-merging firms. It can be cooperative or non-cooperative, and if non-cooperative it can be Cournot, Bertrand, or some other oligopoly equilibrium. Each firm will satisfy a first-order condition equating marginal cost with *perceived* marginal revenue. For the non-merging firms, perceived marginal revenue, which differs across oligopoly solution concepts, is written as follows:

$$(4) \qquad \tilde{MR} = \tilde{P} + \tilde{g}(Q_1, Q_2, \tilde{Q}, Y; \tilde{\eta})\tilde{Q}$$

In equation (4), $\tilde{g}$ is a vector of slopes of the demand curves $\tilde{h}$ perceived by each of the $(n-2)$ non-merging firms.

Although (4) is written as if quantity were the choice variable of the oligopolists, appropriate choice of $g(\cdot)$ can make (4) correspond to any behavioral rule, including equilibria in which firms choose prices.

The vector of marginal costs for the $(n-2)$ non-merging firms depends on output $\tilde{Q}$, factor prices W, and parameters $\tilde{\beta}$.

$$(5) \qquad \tilde{MC} = \tilde{MC}(\tilde{Q}, W, \tilde{\beta})$$

Thus the first-order conditions describing the behavior of the non-merging firms take the following form[8]

$$(6) \qquad \tilde{MC}(\tilde{Q}, W; \tilde{\beta}) = \tilde{P} + \tilde{g}(Q_1, Q_2, \tilde{Q}, Y; \tilde{\eta})\tilde{Q}$$

Solving the $2(n-2)$ equations in the vector relations (6) and (3) for the vector $\tilde{Q}$, we derive

$$(7) \qquad \tilde{Q} = \tilde{E}(Q_1, Q_2, Y, W; \tilde{\eta}, \tilde{\beta})$$

A different equation $\tilde{E}_j$ corresponds to each of the $(n-2)$ outputs of non-merging firms. We denote the elasticities of $\tilde{E}_j$ with respect to Q_i $(i = 1, 2)$ as ε_{ji}; this is the elasticity of firm j's reaction function (to firm i).

Equation (7) defines a partial reduced form for the $(n-2)$ non-merging firm outputs; it defines equilibrium $\tilde{Q}$, given Q_1 and Q_2. Substituting equation (7) into demand curves (1) and (2) for the merger partners, we derive *partial residual demand curves* for those two firms:

$$(8) \qquad P_1 = h_1(Q_1, Q_2, \tilde{E}(Q_1, Q_2, Y, W; \tilde{\eta}, \tilde{\beta}); Y; \eta_1)$$
$$= r_1(Q_1, Q_2, Y, W; \eta_1, \tilde{\eta}, \tilde{\beta})$$

$$(9) \qquad P_2 = r_2(Q_1, Q_2, Y, W; \eta_2, \tilde{\eta}, \tilde{\beta})$$

[7] For methods which use such further structure, see Bresnahan [1980], Cowling and Cubbin [1972], and Joskow [1983], all applied to the Automobile industry.

[8] Note that (6) are supply relations, functions of both $\tilde{P}$ and $\tilde{Q}$. They are the analog of the supply function $P = MC(Q)$ in the theory of perfect competition.

We estimate equations (8) and (9), the partial residual demand system applicable to firms 1 and 2. They are *residual* demand curves because the actions of firms 3 to n have been taken into account. They are *partial* residual demand curves because, for each firm, the potential merger partner's action remains to be specified. Note that this approach includes as a special case the possibility of perfect competition. If P_1 and P_2 are completely explained by Y and W, so that Q_1 and Q_2 have coefficients of zero in (8) and (9), then firms 1 and 2 have no power over price, even acting jointly.

In our empirical work, we approximate (8) and (9) with log–log functional forms

$$p_1 = \eta_{10} + \eta_{11}^{PR} q_1 + \eta_{21}^{PR} q_2 + \Gamma_1 y + \Delta_1 w + v_1 \tag{10}$$

$$p_2 = \eta_{20} + \eta_{12}^{PR} q_1 + \eta_{22}^{PR} q_2 + \Gamma_2 y + \Delta_2 w + v_2 \tag{11}$$

The interpretation of the parameters η^{PR} may be obtained by logarithmically differentiating (8) and (9). This yields

$$\eta_{11}^{PR} = \eta_{11} + \sum_{j=3} \eta_{j1} \varepsilon_{j1} \tag{12}$$

$$\eta_{21}^{PR} = \eta_{21} + \sum_{j=3} \eta_{j2} \varepsilon_{j2} \tag{13}$$

$$\eta_{12}^{PR} = \eta_{12} + \sum_{j=3} \eta_{j1} \varepsilon_{j1} \tag{14}$$

$$\eta_{22}^{PR} = \eta_{22} + \sum_{j=3} \eta_{j2} \varepsilon_{j2} \tag{15}$$

Thus the partial residual demand elasticities η_{ij}^{PR} depend both on the structural demand elasticities η_{ij} and on the reaction function elasticities ε_{ij}. By estimating only the parameters η_{ij}^{PR}, we obtain only a subset of the information about the industry. For example in (12), we cannot separate the effects of firms 3 through n; only the total effect enters the equation.

Calculation of post-merger market power from the partial residual demand curve is straightforward. Suppose that the merged firm will decrease Q_1 and Q_2 in the same proportion to exploit its increased market power.[9] Then a decrease of both Q_1 and Q_2 of one percent will raise P_1 by $\eta_{11}^{PR} + \eta_{21}^{PR}$ and will raise P_2 by $\eta_{22}^{PR} + \eta_{12}^{PR}$.

Pre-merger (current) market power depends on the residual demand curve facing each of firms 1 and 2 acting alone. Since the formal derivation closely follows that of the partial residual demand curve, we present it in Appendix I and just give the main ideas here. The residual demand curve facing firm 1 will take the form

$$P_1 = R_1(Q_1, Y, W, \underset{\sim}{\eta}_1, \underset{\sim}{\eta}, \underset{\sim}{\beta}) \tag{16}$$

[9] The merged firm may not find it optimal to decrease Q_1 and Q_2 in the same proportion to exploit its market power. See Orr and MacAvoy [1964] for analysis of when proportional-quantity rules are jointly profit maximizing for two firms.

This is exactly the same as (8), except firm 2 has been "equilibrated out" along with firms 3 to n. The elasticity of P_1 with respect to Q_1 defined by (16) is η_1^R, the residual demand elasticity for firm 1.

Suppose instead of solving the $2(n-2)$ equations (3) and (4) for $Q_3, \ldots, Q_n$, we expanded them by one demand curve (2) and a first-order condition for firm 2. Then we would have $2(n-1)$ equations for $Q_2, \ldots, Q_n$. We solve for the $(n-1)$ outputs as functions of Q_1:

$$\begin{pmatrix} Q_2 \\ \vdots \\ Q_n \end{pmatrix} = \hat{E}(Q_1, Y, W; \underset{\sim}{\eta}, \underset{\sim}{\beta}) \tag{17}$$

where (17) differs from (7) because Q_2 is on the left, not right. Let the elasticity of Q_i with respect to Q_1 in (16) be ξ_{i1}. Note that there is no obvious relationship between the *partial* residual demand elasticity η_{11}^{PR} and the residual demand elasticity η_1^R, since they are defined by different conceptual experiments. In the partial residual demand system, firm 2's output is held fixed along with firm 1's. In the residual demand curve, firm 2's output is solved out along with all of the other $n-2$ firms.

$\hat{E}(\cdot)$ is the vector of outputs of all firms except firm 1. The elasticity of firm 1's residual demand curve is

$$\eta_1^R = \eta_{11} + \eta_{21}\xi_{21} + \sum_{j=3} \eta_{j1}\xi_{j1} \tag{18}$$

We could similarly define a residual demand curve for firm 2. It would have elasticity

$$\eta_2^R = \eta_{22} + \eta_{12}\xi_{12} + \sum_{j=3} \eta_{j2}\xi_{j2} \tag{19}$$

To summarize, the difference between the residual demand curve facing a single firm and the partial residual demand curve facing two firms is this: the price discipline that each of the two firms exerts on the other is isolated. When we estimate the residual demand curve for firm 1, the slope depends (in part) on how firm 1's customers defect to firm 2. When we estimate the partial residual demand curve, we can perform the conceptual experiment of raising both firms' prices together.[10]

Calculation of the exact, quantitative increase in market power as a result of the merger rests on the assumption that the elasticity of demand does not change along the demand curve. Estimates based on pre-merger historical data cannot reveal the elasticity of demand at the hypothetical post-merger point. What they can do is measure the extent to which the merger will change

[10] In a product differentiated industry, residual demand elasticities correspond directly to a firm's markup of price over marginal cost. For an explanation, and a discussion of other circumstances in which the markup is related to residual demand elasticities, see Baker and Bresnahan [1984, section B].

1

price-quantity incentives. If the demand curve grows steeper as a result of the merger, we can be sure that the merged firm will have an incentive to raise price from the pre-merger level. But we cannot be sure how far; if for some (unlikely) reason the demand curve rapidly flattens at quantities slightly below those observed in the market, the merger will have little effect.

III. THREE BREWERS

In this section, we empirically investigate the extent to which existing competition from other firms' products limits market power in the U.S. brewing industry. Three hypothetical mergers are considered: between Anheuser–Busch (A–B), the largest firm in the national market, and Pabst, another important producer of "premium" beer; between A–B and Coors, the largest firm in the Western states; and between Pabst and Coors.[11] After a discussion of the structure of the industry,[12] we estimate residual demand curves for each of the three firms, and partial residual demand curves for each of the three pairs of firms.

The brewing industry is highly concentrated. In 1983, the last year of our sample, the two-firm (A–B and Miller) concentration ratio was over 50 percent. Four more firms (Pabst, Coors, Heileman and Schlitz) had market shares between seven and thirteen percent. There is also considerable evidence of product differentiation. An FTC study[13] shows substantial long-term trends in the relative prices of different kinds of beer ("popular", "premium", etc.) indicating they must be imperfect substitutes in demand. Similarly, the correlations over time among the prices charged by our three firms suggest they are selling distinct products. Table I reports correlation coefficients for the log of the real price of each firm's primary brand in mid-summer in Northern California, over the period 1962–83.

Data limitations prevent straightforward extension of our techniques to Miller, Heileman or Stroh–Schlitz. Each of these firms has acquired a rival or been acquired. Miller and Heileman have both been closely held within our sample period. Thus firm-specific data on these firms cannot be assembled from published sources.

Given the concentration and the product differentiation present in the industry, it is natural to ask whether there are gains to collusion or merger. If we find that coordinated pricing between two firms would substantially increase their market power, we can draw two conclusions. First, a merger between them would worsen industry conduct, and would therefore worsen performance if it did not yield cost savings. Second, the firms are not now

[11] None of these hypothetical mergers is likely to occur without antitrust challenge. For a history of brewing mergers and their antitrust treatment, see Ornstein [1981].

[12] Elzinga [1982] presents a detailed review of brewing industry history. The demand for beer has been discussed by Greer ([1971], [1981]), Hogarty and Elzinga [1972], Kelton and Kelton [1982], and McConnel [1968]. Product differentiation issues are discussed in Greer [1981].

[13] Keithahn [1978].

TABLE I
CORRELATIONS AMONG PRICES[a]

	$P_{\text{A-B}}$	P_{Coors}	
$P_{\text{A-B}}$	1.0	0.83	0.93
P_{Coors}		1.0	0.61
P_{Pabst}			1.0

[a] Log of real prices. See Appendix II for description of price data.

pursuing completely colluding pricing policies, which follows directly from the nature of our estimates. If a coordinated pricing policy *would* yield a steeper demand curve than the firm *does* face, we can conclude that a completely coordinated pricing policy is not now being used.

Several long-term trends in the brewing industry's environment and structure affect the specification of residual demand curves for our 1962–83 sample period. First is the question of what variables to include in the equation. The derivation of (8) and (9) shows that variables shifting the cost curves of other firms in the industry must be included, as must variables that shift the demand curve for any brand. The second issue is whether the residual demand system is stable over time.

Regarding the question of cost-side variables, w, we first include two indexes of factor prices. One is short-run average variable cost (SRAVC) for the industry, defined to include labor, agricultural inputs, and energy inputs.[14] The other is a price of capital series (PK). A third variable is suggested by the increasing exploitation of scale economies over time (Elzinga [1982]). If marginal costs are falling because of exploitation of scale economies, then it is important to capture this effect econometrically. Our variable is the average plant size (APS) in the industry, defined to be industry-wide capacity divided by the number of operating plants. The fourth variable is suggested not by long-term trends but by the cyclicality of the demand for beer. If firms $3, \ldots, n$ have excess capacity, then their marginal costs are likely to be lower. We capture this with the variable EKTI, defined as $\text{EKTI} = \Sigma_{j=3}^{n} (K_j - Q_j)$, excess capacity of the other $n-2$ firms.

On the demand side, economic and marketing studies suggest the inclusion of several economic demographic variables.[15] We include *per capita* disposable income (PCDI), firm advertising expenditures, the percentage of the drinking-age population under 45 years old, and the percentage of drinking-age women who ever drink beer. Of these, only PCDI ever approaches significance in our regressions. It is therefore the only demand variable reported below. We suspect the insignificance arises because most demographic variables move very slowly.

On the question of structural stability, there are two important considerations. One is the increasing concentration of the industry over our sample

[14] See Appendix II for precise definitions of all variables.
[15] Hatten and Schendal [1977]; Ellison and Uhl [1964].

period. Two-thirds of the firms in the industry in 1962 exited before 1983; over the same period, the five firm concentration ratio rose from 35 percent to 84 percent. Thus we allow for the possibility that residual demand curves are getting steeper over time by interacting both their slopes and intercepts with a variable which increases by one each year, TIME. The second issue of structural change is the introduction of the heavily advertised "LITE" brand beer by Miller.[16] Other firms responded with the introduction of their own "light" beers. We take account of the effect of this structural change on residual demand by introducing a dummy variable LITE that takes in the value of 1 beginning in 1975. This dummy variable is allowed to shift both the residual demand elasticity and the intercept of the residual demand curve.

Our procedure for estimating these residual demand elasticities regresses both P_1 and P_2 on the two quantities Q_1 and Q_2, demand shift variables Y, and industry-wide cost variables W. In double-log form, we estimate:

$$p_1 = \eta_{10} + \eta_{11}^{PR} q_1 + \eta_{21}^{PR} q_2 + \Gamma_1 y + \Delta_1 w + v_1 \tag{20}$$

$$p_2 = \eta_{20} + \eta_{12}^{PR} q_1 + \eta_{22}^{PR} q_2 + \Gamma_2 y + \Delta_2 w + v_2 \tag{21}$$

The primary econometric problem that must be solved to estimate (20) and (21) is the simultaneity of these equations with as yet unspecified supply relations for the two merging firms. The solution to this problem will also prove that equations (20) and (21) are econometrically identified. The supply relations are derived from equating marginal revenue with marginal cost:

$$MC_1(Q_1, W, W_1; \beta_1) = P_1 + Q_1 t_1(Q_1, Q_2, Y, W; \eta_1, \underset{\sim}{\eta}, \underset{\sim}{\beta}) \tag{22}$$

$$MC_2(Q_2, W, W_1; \beta_2) = P_2 + Q_2 t_2(Q_1, Q_2, Y, W; \eta_2, \underset{\sim}{\eta}, \underset{\sim}{\beta}) \tag{23}$$

Equilibrium in the industry at issue is defined by the simultaneous determination of the two partial residual demand curves (8) and (9) with the two supply relations (22) and (23). As is evident, identification of the parameters of the residual demand curve requires the presence of the firm-individuated cost variables W_1 and W_2. We therefore estimate (20) and (21) by employing firm-specific cost variables as instruments for quantities q_1 and q_2.[17] In addition, to conserve degrees of freedom, we impose a cross-equation restriction that the different industry-wide prices W enter proportionately for both firms. Finally we estimate partial residual demand curves jointly for the two merging

[16] Miller acquired the rights to Meister Brau Lite beer in 1972, which had been unsuccessfully marketed as a diet beer for women by a small Chicago brewery. Miller's innovation was in the nationwide marketing of light beer. Light beers, now made by many firms, are lower in alcohol and calories than premium beers. In estimating demand curves from time series data, we implicitly assume that no unobserved changes in product quality or reputation occur. The one exception to this is the obvious change in the relative attractiveness of different brands after the invention of light beer, which we treat by introducing a dummy variable in the residual demand curve of each firm.

[17] In our earlier paper, we showed that even if we lack such instruments, the estimation of single firm residual demand elasticities will be biased in the conservative direction of disproving market power. Baker and Bresnahan [1984].

TABLE II
PARTIAL RESIDUAL DEMAND CURVES FOR A–B AND COORS

Dependent:	P_{ab}	P_{cs}
Independent		
Constant	1.97	3.67
	(1.71)	(0.92)
q_{ab}	−0.466	0.036
	(−1.94)	(5.35)
q_{cs}	0.093	−0.661
	(5.6)	(−1.76)
SRAVC	0.148	0.699
	(0.75)	(1.17)
APS	−0.009	−0.452
	(−1.10)	—
PK	0.057	0.272
	(2.93)	—
EKTI	0.00019	0.00094
	(2.2)	—
LITE	0.610	
	(2.18)	
q_{ab}*LITE	−0.219	
	(−2.88)	
q_{cs}*LITE	0.043	
	—	
TIME		0.0849
		(1.57)
PCDI	0.404	−0.012
	(0.824)	(−0.007)

partners by three-stage least-squares, a procedure which takes advantages of information available from the correlation of errors in those equations.[18]

Substantial experimentation with the specification produced some simplifications. First, advertising and the demographics were never significant. Thus "Y" in (20) and (21) consists only of PCDL. Second, only the slope and intercept of A–B's residual demand equation are changed by the LITE dummy; this change in industry structure appears to have had little effect on the other two firms. Finally, the TIME coefficient appears to enter the intercept of each of the Pabst and Coors equations, but not to affect the slope of any residual demand curve. The following tables report only the estimates for specifications after these simplifications have been imposed.[19]

[18] If we begin with all of the structured equations of the model (1′), (2′), (3′) and (4) linear in the logs with additive error, then (10) and (11) will have additive error, but v_1 and v_2 will be correlated. Thus three-stage least-squares will increase the power of our estimators.

[19] Baker and Bresnahan [1984] reports on the specification tests in considerably greater detail.

Table II reports the partial residual demand curve for A–B and Coors. Most of the coefficients have the expected signs: a decrease in either firm's quantity would raise its own price and lower that of the other firm. If factor prices were higher (SRAVC or PK), the residual (inverse) demand curve would shift up, as one expects. Similarly an increase in APS (and the resulting lowering of industry-wide costs) shifts the residual demand curve down. The coefficient of excess capacity is of the incorrect sign but small. The demand elasticities appear to be substantial: a one-percent quantity decrease by A–B would lower its price by 0.466 percent, and raise Coors price by 0.093 percent—these price effects take into account the reactions of all firms but Coors. A–B's partial residual demand curve is somewhat flatter when the LITE dummy is turned on. Taking into account the competitive responses of all other firms, A–B plus Coors would have only about half as much control over P_{ab} when LITE = 1.

The results for the partial residual demand curve for A–B and Pabst (Table III) are similar in some respects. The coefficients again have mostly the ex-

TABLE III
PARTIAL RESIDUAL DEMAND CURVES FOR A–B AND PABST

Dependent:	P_{ab}	P_{pb}
Independent		
Constant	1.50	3.92
	(8.42)	(1.57)
q_{ab}	−0.523	−0.011
	(−3.27)	(0.58)
q_{pb}	0.185	−0.035
	(1.82)	(0.077)
SRAVC	0.133	0.096
	(1.22)	(2.44)
APS	−0.193	−0.139
	(−1.6)	—
PK	0.072	0.028
	(2.40)	—
EKTI	0.0015	0.0012
	(2.68)	—
LITE	0.805	
	(0.81)	
q_{ab}*LITE	−0.67	
	(−4.1)	
q_{pb}*LITE	0.016	
	—	
TIME		−0.01
		(−1.7)
PCDI	0.249	−0.11
	(4.33)	(−0.13)

TABLE IV
PARTIAL RESIDUAL DEMAND CURVES FOR PABST AND COORS

Dependent:	P_{pb}	P_{cs}
Independent		
Constant	3.96	3.34
	(12.6)	(2.20)
q_{cs}	0.16	−0.648
	(0.312)	(−2.61)
q_{pb}	−0.006	−0.028
	(−0.16)	(−1.18)
SRAVC	0.105	0.225
	(1.71)	(1.44)
APS	−0.197	−0.422
	(−1.39)	—
PK	0.042	0.090
	(1.66)	—
EKTI	0.00033	0.00071
	(0.503)	—
TIME	−0.011	0.041
	(−1.42)	(1.39)
PCDI	−0.218	0.991
	(−1.76)	(1.37)

pected sign. A–B's demand curve is again downward-sloping in own-quantity and increasing in Pabst's quantity. The LITE effect is again to substantially flatten A–B's demand curve. The Pabst equation, however, shows very little market power for the firm.

The results for Pabst and Coors (Table IV) are consistent with what one would expect from the first two tables. Pabst has no market power, even with the cooperation of Coors. The Coors partial residual demand curve is again quite steep.

To use the information in Tables II–IV to evaluate mergers or collusion, we need to estimate the residual demand curves for each of the three firms. This is reported in Table V. The estimates show that Coors, acting alone, has a steep demand curve. Pabst, acting alone, has very little power over price. A–B's market power appears to vary over time, because of the effects of LITE.

Table VI summarizes the coefficients needed to evaluate the gains from a merger or collusion. The first section reports η_{11}^{R} for each firm, the inverse demand elasticity when all other firms act independently. The second section reports $\eta_{11}^{PR}+\eta_{12}^{PR}$, the inverse demand elasticity if two firms moved their quantities proportionately. Looking first at the A–B/Coors merger, we observe that the A–B demand curve would be steeper after a merger with Coors. In the 1967–74 period the A–B demand elasticity grows slightly as a result of the merger (−0.373 *vs.* −0.313), while it grows substantially after the "LITE"

TABLE V
RESIDUAL DEMAND CURVES FOR ALL THREE BREWERS

Dependent:	P_{ab}	P_{cs}	P_{pb}
Independent			
Constant	2.625 (7.77)	2.85 (3.73)	3.53 (12.00)
q_{ab}	−0.313 (−5.99)		
q_{cs}		−0.633 (1.82)	
q_{pb}			−0.028 (−0.961)
SRAVC	0.094 (1.811)	0.326 (2.33)	0.086 (1.81)
APS	−0.079 (−1.15)	−0.277 —	−0.073 —
PK	0.025 (1.31)	0.082 —	0.024 —
EKTI	0.0023 (0.54)	0.008 —	0.0023 —
LITE	0.629 (0.918)		
q_{ab} *LITE	−0.311 (9.07)		
TIME		0.042 (2.91)	−0.011 (−2.57)
PCDI	0.115 (0.775)	0.537 (1.50)	−0.026 (−0.19)

TABLE VI
GAINS TO MERGER OR COLLUSION

I. RESIDUAL DEMAND ELASTICITIES: η_{11}^{R}		
Coors:	−0.633	(−10.07)
Pabst:	−0.028	(−0.961)
A–B, 1962–74:	−0.313	(−5.99)
A–B, 1975–83:	−0.002	(−0.014)
II. POST-MERGER DEMAND ELASTICITIES: $\eta_{11}^{PR}+\eta_{12}^{PR}$		
Merger of A–B and Coors:		
Coors:	−0.625	(−7.81)
A–B, 1962–74:	−0.373	(−3.45)
A–B, 1975–83:	−0.176	(−2.57)
Merger of A–B and Pabst:		
Pabst:	+0.024	(+0.14)
A–B, 1962–74:	−0.338	(−6.28)
A–B, 1975–83:	−0.151	(−2.14)
Merger of Pabst and Coors:		
Coors:	−0.676	(1.97)
Pabst:	+0.01	(0.103)

dummy is turned on (-0.176 *vs.* -0.002). Hence, as expected, a merger with Coors would substantially increase A–B's market power. The Coors demand curve, by contrast, grows slightly less steep as a result of the merger. We conclude from this insignificant change that Coors' market power would be unaffected by merger with A–B.

The merger of A–B and Pabst would be similar. The Pabst demand curve moves from being small, negative, and insignificantly-sloped, to being small, positive, and insignificantly-sloped. Just as Pabst is a price-taker now, so would the merged A–B/Pabst firm be a price-taker in its Pabst product line. The A–B demand curve, however, again grows steeper by a small amount before the introduction of "LITE" and by a large amount after it.[20] The Pabst/Coors merger does not substantially enhance the market power of either product; though the Coors elasticity grows slightly; this occurs because Pabst and Coors appear to be *complements* in demand.

All three sets of estimates show an increase in the slope of the demand curve only for A–B. We can determine the importance of this increase by a simple calculation. Suppose a merger increased the inverse demand elasticity for Budweiser, A–B's flagship product, by 0.05. This is conservative: except for the merger with Pabst in the pre-1975 period, all of our estimates show a larger increase. An increase of 0.05 means that the price–cost margin for Budweiser would increase by five percent of cost. A conservative estimate A–B marginal cost is $50/barrel. In 1983, A–B sold 42 million barrels of this brand. Thus collusion or a merger with a smaller firm would yield additional monopoly profits of at least $105 million per year.

IV. CONCLUSION

Our estimates show that collusion or a merger between A–B and either Pabst or Coors would lead to a substantial increase in market power for A–B. No merger among any two of the three firms yields any increase in market power for the other two brands.[21] We draw a strong and a weak conclusion about the nature of competition in brewing.

Our strong conclusion is that these three brewers are not colluding in price, even though there is substantial market power in the industry. The evidence for the absence of complete collusion is compelling; a change from the pricing rules firms now use to coordinated pricing would yield very large increases in profits. Market power such as we measure can exist even without collusion in a product-differentiated industry.

[20] The Pabst/A–B merger suggests that our convention of assuming proportional decreases in post-merger quantities may be too conservative. Since the post-merger Pabst demand curve remains flat, but decreases in Pabst sales shift the A–B demand curve out, the merged firm would find it profit-maximizing to decrease Pabst quantity much more sharply than A–B.

[21] This statement presumes that the merger will not increase the probability of collusion on an industry-wide basis. In general, we would expect mergers between larger firms to have a greater effect on the probability of collusion. Thus we think our assessment of A–B's gains to merger is conservative.

Our weak conclusion concerns the competitive role of the producers, such as Coors and Pabst, with market shares in the 5–15 percent range. These firms seem to provide an important brake on the pricing power of the market leader, A–B. This conclusion is weak because data limitations prevent extension of the analysis to other firms. First, we do not know whether our results about Coors and Pabst also apply to the other "second tier" firms; Schlitz, Stroh, and Heileman. We conjecture that we would also find substantial anti-competitive effects of bilateral collusion (or merger) between any of these and A–B. Second, the conclusion is weak because we can say nothing about the role of Miller, the second-largest producer.

JONATHAN B. BAKER AND TIMOTHY F. BRESNAHAN,
Department of Economics,
Encina Hall,
Stanford University,
Stanford,
California,
U.S.A.

ACCEPTED NOVEMBER 1984

APPENDIX I*

The (inverse) demand function for firm 1, the firm of interest, is

$$P_1 = P^1(Q_1, \hat{Q}, \tilde{Y}, \eta^1) \tag{A.1}$$

Here P_1 and Q_1 are price and quantity for firm 1's product, $\hat{Q}$ is a vector of quantities for other firm's products, $\tilde{Y}$ are exogenous variables entering the demand system, and η^1 are parameters. Q_i is a typical element of $\hat{Q}$. $\hat{Q}$ includes Q_2, as well as $Q_3, \ldots, Q_n$.

The model also includes (inverse) demand equations for $\hat{Q}$, the vector of quantities of all other relevant products, including 2.

$$P_i = P^i(\hat{Q}, Q_1, Y, \tilde{\eta}^i), \qquad i = 2, \ldots, n \tag{A.2}$$

$\tilde{P}$ is a vector composed of the P_i.

The third element of the model is the supply behavior of all the firms i. Their supply relations are written in the form marginal cost equals marginal revenue:

$$MC^i(Q_i, W, \beta^i) = MR^i(\hat{Q}, Q_1, Y, \eta^i), \qquad i = 2, \ldots, n \tag{A.3}$$

The first step in deriving the single-firm residual demand is to solve the equations (2) and (3) simultaneously for the vectors $\hat{Q}$ and $\hat{P}$.

$$\hat{Q} = \tilde{E}(Q_1, Y, W; \eta, \beta) \tag{A.4}$$

The elasticity of Q_i with respect to Q_1 in this partial-reduced form is denoted ξ_{i1}:

$$\xi_{i1} = \frac{\partial \ell n E^i}{\partial \ell n Q_1}$$

* A complete development of this appendix can be found in Baker and Bresnahan [1984].

The residual demand curve facing firm 1 is derived by substituting $\underset{\wedge}{E}(\cdot)$ into (A.1):

$$P_1 = P^1(Q_1, \underset{\wedge}{E}(Q_1, Y, W, \eta, \beta), Y, \eta^1) \tag{A.5}$$

Substituting out the redundancies, we have:

$$P_1 = R(Q_1, Y, W, \eta, \beta) \tag{A.6}$$

where the notation $R(\cdot)$ means (inverse) residual demand. The arguments of the residual demand curve are threefold; own quantity, structural demand variables, and other firm's cost variables.

Note that the elasticity of residual demand depends on all the ordinary demand elasticities and on the elasticities of other firms' reactions, ξ_{i1}:

$$\eta_1^R = \eta_{11} + \sum_i \eta_{i1}\xi_{i1} \tag{A.7}$$

where η_1^R is (inverse) residual demand elasticity, and η_{i1} is the own- or cross- (inverse) demand elasticity in the usual sense.

APPENDIX II

This appendix describes the sources for the variables employed in our study.

Price and Quantity

Nationwide production figures are available from trade publications, such as the yearly *Modern Brewery Age Blue Book* and *Brewers Almanac*. Q in our regressions is annual production of the flagship brand. *Per capita* adjustments were made using the U.S. population over age 18. Prices were transformed into real terms by dividing by GNP deflator. Flagship brand prices are reported in issues of the *Beverage Industry News of Northern California* until 1978. After 1978, newspaper advertisements are used.

Factor Prices (Cost Variables)

Time series on four factors of production were assumed to apply industry-wide: labor, materials, variable capital, and advertising. The price of labor is the average hourly wage of brewing production workers collected by the Bureau of Labor Statistics, reprinted annually in *Brewers Almanac*. The price of variable capital is the user-cost measure from Hazilla and Kopp [1983] for food and beverage industries, and updated by us through the end of the sample period.

Two variants of the materials price series were used. The first uses data on the prices and quantities of a list of specific inputs: malt, corn, rice, hops, cans, bottles, and power. The second divides cost of materials for brewers, as reported in *Brewers Almanac*, by quantity of beer manufactured in barrels. The quantities consumed of all specific inputs are found in *Brewers Almanac*, except power. *MBA Blue Book* reports expenditures on power. The price series for the specific inputs are from *Producer Prices and Prices Indexes*. In real terms, the two materials price series are correlated at 0.99. The advertising price series is computed as an index of media prices; brewing industry weights are from *Leading National Advertisers*.

Demand Variables

Population and income variables are taken from Census and other Commerce Department Sources.

Instruments

Brewer capacity, by plant, is reported in *Beer Marketer's Insights*. This is the basis of both K and APS. The Colorado manufacturing wage rate series is from the *Statistical Abstract of the United States*.

Other Variables

Advertising variables, include each firm's expenditures on advertising, as reported in *Brewers Almanac*. These variables are normalized either by sales, or by the industry price of advertising as described above and a population index.

THE JOURNAL OF INDUSTRIAL ECONOMICS 0022-1821 $2.00
Volume XXXIII June 1985 No. 4

PREYING FOR TIME

David Easley, Robert T. Masson and Robert J. Reynolds*

I. INTRODUCTION

The recent antitrust policy literature which seeks to define predatory pricing contains a flood of proposals which have "pervasively transformed an entire body of law".[1] One theme of this literature is that a readily anticipatable standard should be established, so that firms will not fear being sued for normal competitive responses; another is that, since predation is presumed to be rare, the standard should be lax so as to minimize the possibility of stifling competition in the overwhelming majority of more competitive markets.

Perhaps the most striking feature of these arguments is the omission of any analysis of predatory behavior when business firms are sophisticated and "rational". McGee [1980, pp. 295–6], for example, points out that predation only pays if the present discounted value of future high prices exceeds the costs of suffering today's low prices. But if this is so for the monopolist, then why not for the competitor?

> "It only *seems* paradoxical, therefore, that if a victim were sure this is a predatory campaign, rather than normal competition . . . , he would *surely* want to stick it out."

The argument that predation generally costs a predator more than it costs the prey (and other arguments) led McGee to conclude that predation is nonexistent or rare, and that the best standard against predation would be no standard at all [p. 317].

To resolve whether some antitrust rule would work as desired requires analysis of an equilibrium with predation assuming that businessmen are reasonably intelligent. McGee points the way in qualifying his statements. His businessman is said to be "sure" the low price is not due to normal competition. This requires certainty: i.e., the businessman always knows exactly when a price is "predatory" versus when it is simply "competitive". If the process were so simple that businessmen could always be "sure", the difference between predation and competition should also be readily demonstrable to courts. But

* We are grateful to numerous individuals—Lucinda Lewis and Paul Geroski, in particular. We owe a special debt to the late Richard B. Heflebower. His interpretations of some chain store behavior sowed the seeds that led to this paper. The initial work was funded in part by the United States Department of Justice and later work by the National Science Foundation (grant numbers SES-8111237 and ISI-8120315). The views presented are those of the authors.

[1] Brodley and Hay [1981, p. 740]. Brodley and Hay review much of this literature as does McGee [1980]. Some other contributors are Areeda and Turner [1975], [1976], Baumol [1979], Greer [1979], Joskow and Klevorick [1979], Ordover and Willig [1981], Posner [1976], Schmalensee [1979], and Scherer [1976a], [1976b].

if businesses cannot always distinguish the precise point at which prices cease being "normally competitive", then predation may be both profitable and hard to detect by businessmen, courts or academic economists.

This paper develops a model of predatory pricing using the tools of incomplete information games. When the problem is seen as one of incomplete information, the standard reasons for saying predation is rare are not compelling. Further the lack of proof of predation is an unreliable empirical indicator of its prevalence. The model is designed to facilitate analysis of the efficiency of the various proposed antitrust rules when predation is rational. The result is that most of the rules may not prevent all instances of predation. For example the precise standard "Price must not fall below average variable costs" (Areeda and Turner [1975], [1976]), may in some cases serve as an instruction manual on how to avoid liability when preying.

II. AN INCOMPLETE INFORMATION GAME

II.1 *Entry with Imperfect Information*

The model is developed to analyse entry dynamics when the incumbent firm is a multimarket monopolist. An entrant who experiences a negative entry value in one market will analyse its cause prior to entry into another of the monopolist's markets. For example, if the entrant decides that the incumbent's production was more efficient than it had anticipated, it should consider whether the monopolist's other markets use the same or similar production processes and revise future anticipations accordingly. If negative entry value in one market slows or deters entry to other markets, the multimarket monopolist has an incentive to assure that an entrant is met with a negative entry value. This is true even if the Nash response of the monopolist, if it were only a single market monopolist, would yield positive entry value. Thus, if the cost of driving the entrant's value negative in one or a few markets is exceeded by the margin protected by forestalling entry into other markets, the multimarket monopolist has an incentive to "prey"—as long as this behavior actually inhibits entry.

From the monopolist's point of view, the success of this strategy depends upon keeping its identity hidden from potential entrants. If it were generally known that the single market Nash response would yield a positive entry value, entrants would rapidly enter the markets, predation would then be unprofitable, so a threat to prey would not be carried out. The dynamics of entrants' expectations and the monopolist's responses is critical. If an entrant knows, or believes, that predatory responses will never occur, it will conclude that a negative entry value resulted from inaccurate estimation of real competitive factors and will halt entry after a single episode: the expectation that predation will never occur makes it quite profitable. On the other hand, if entrants expected that all markets would be profitable absent predation they would be undeterred by initially negative entry values: the unprofitability of predation in that case would mean it would never occur. Where there is imperfect information, entrants are not able to definitively attribute negative entry values to either misestimation or predation, and so some predation is liable to occur.

Two other models also analyse predation using incomplete information games. These models (Milgrom and Roberts [1982a] and Kreps and Wilson [1982b]) significantly restrict the strategies available to the players. In each period a new market appears. They require that predation, once it has begun *in any market* must continue in that market, so formally they have a series of one shot games. Since giving up is not permitted, predation, once started, is automatically credible for any market. The classical question (cf. Telser [1966], McGee [1980]), "How long can it pay to prey?" is swept aside.[2] This paper presents a model in which all prices are endogenous in all periods so that a richer strategy space appears: (a) entrants may now enter new markets to force a rise in profits in previously entered markets; (b) some monopolists may decide to prey only to gain extra time, with full knowledge that the predation will not preclude eventual entry of all of their markets. This adds three elements to the analysis: (1) the duration of predation in each market is endogenous; (2) entrants' abilities to cause predation to cease are modeled; (3) the anti-competitive potential of a type of predation which is ineffective in the longrun is also demonstrated. Each of these elements is important for antitrust analysis.

II.2 *The Model*

The model will be developed as a dynamic game with "imperfect but complete information". In each period several potential entrants consider entry into the markets of an incumbent monopolist. The monopolist in turn selects market parameters (e.g., prices, rebates, advertising...) for each market at each time. Information is "imperfect" in the sense that the potential entrants do not know all the competitive aspects of the monopolist's markets. Despite the fact that entrants do not have a perfect description of the monopolist they face, they have "complete information" about the types of monopolists they may be facing.[3] More specifically, they know that the monopolist is one of H possible monopolists and they know the probability that it is any individual type of monopolist. The formal game theoretic model structure and proofs are detailed in the Appendix.

(i) *Predatory Acts*

A definition of predatory behavior is a prerequisite to further analysis. For the purposes of this paper, predation will be defined as:

> The selection of strategy in any *entered market* which does not maximize present value in that market when it is considered in isolation, but which

[2] In terms of Figure 1 their firms only play on the diagonal of each matrix. Once a monopolist reveals it will not prey, additional markets can only be entered at a rate of one per period. Further, unlike strategy (b), any predator which does not prey in an additional entered market has "failed".

[3] If predation is rational with complete information, it may be rational with incomplete information. See, for example, Rosenthal [1981].

is selected for the purpose of *slowing or stopping* future entry of *equally efficient* firms.

It is at times convenient to think of this "strategy" as a low price. Unlike "limit pricing", predatory pricing is only used *in response* to entry. These acts serve to slow or stop entry and need not require elimination of an entrant. They are knowingly selected in a fashion that does not maximize the monopolist's present value in each market separately. They occur where the Nash equilibrium for each market in isolation would lead to a positive entry value and involve the monopolist sacrificing profits in order to create a negative entry value. Further, the potential for a positive entry value demonstrates that the result does not simply reflect competitive overcrowding. The equal efficiency assumption (which is not essential) assures that the results do not simply reflect superior efficiency on the part of the incumbent firm.[4]

(ii) *Basic Structure of the Model*

There are J potential entrants indexed by $j = 1, \ldots, J$. They observe a monopolist which is operating in m identical markets indexed by $i = 1, \ldots, m$. From their knowledge about technology, demand, prices, and other observable characteristics the potential entrants know that the monopolist must be one of only H possible monopolists, indexed by $h = 1, \ldots, H$. They further know that of these H possible types, only for a "type 1" monopolist would these markets be "inherently competitive" (markets for which the form of the non-predatory post-entry Nash equilibrium for a single market monopolist would yield a negative present value to any of the potential entrants). They know that the other possible types of monopolists, $h = 2, \ldots, H$, all operate in "beneficial markets" (ones for which single market Nash reactions would lead to positive entry values for any entrant).

The monopolist's type is indistinguishable pre-entry. Even the post-entry results do not necessarily reveal the monopolist's type. If entry leads to profits which indicate that the entry has a positive present value, then the monopolist will have revealed itself to be a beneficial type, i.e., not of type 1. But the converse is not true. If entry leads to the level of profits which would be expected from entering a market of a type 1 monopolist, this is not a reliable indicator that the monopolist is actually a type 1 monopolist. It could instead be a beneficial monopolist feigning the reactions of a type 1 monopolist. If this occurs, a type $h > 1$ monopolist may be said to "play as a type $h = 1$ monopolist" or more simply, this may be called a "predatory response" (if the entrant is as efficient as the monopolist). Type $h > 1$ has an incentive to play as a type 1 only if, by doing so, it can slow or stop entry.

The problem of not knowing whether a non-remunerative entry episode

[4] As Brodley and Hay [1981] point out, successful entry of somewhat less efficient firms may raise welfare. Our standard is intended to be a non-controversial sufficient condition for predation. It allows the incumbents' fixed sunk entry costs, valued at either original cost or replacement value, to be as high as, or higher than, those of entrants.

occurs from a type 1 playing as a type 1 (competition) or a type $h > 1$ playing as a type 1 (predation) demonstrates how imperfect information creates the potential for strategic behavior. It is assumed that entrants have complete information about the distribution of possible monopolist types in two respects. Prior to any entry all potential entrants know exactly the probability that the monopolist is of each type. After entry, by observing monopolist behavior, entrants accurately revise their prior probabilities.

A simple numerical example can illustrate model dynamics. For notational ease the markets are modeled as having static demand. As a consequence, the flow profits for any market, divided by the interest rate, r, are the present value of flow profits for that market unless competitive conditions change. The monopolists' flow profits are assumed to be ΠM in any unentered market. Predation by any $h > 1$ yields monopolist flow profits of ΠP. To simplify notation, without altering qualitative results, heterogeneity is introduced in only one parameter. This parameter is Πh, the flow profits monopolist h would receive were it to react to entry by playing its Nash present value maximizing strategy for the market. It follows that $\Pi h < \Pi M$, and for $h > 1$, $\Pi h > \Pi P$.

There is little cost in the richness of qualitative results from introducing heterogeneity for the J potential entrants through only one parameter—fixed sunk entry costs. The entry costs of entrant j are f_j. Again for notational ease there are only two entrant types, entrant 1 and all others, defined by $f_1 < f_2 = f_3 = \ldots = f_J$. If an entrant enters a market of a type 1 monopolist it receives "competitive" flow profits of πC. These do not induce exit, $\pi C \geqslant 0$, but are non-remunerative in the present value sense that $\pi C/r - f_j < 0$ for all of the J potential entrants. Similarly, if an entrant meets a predatory response it receives flow profits of πC because a predatory monopolist must act so as to be indistinguishable from a type 1 monopolist. If the monopolist is of type $h > 1$ and "plays as itself" (e.g., plays to receive Πh), then entrant flow profits are πB. These are "beneficial" in the present value sense: $\pi B/r - f_j > 0$ for all of the J potential entrants.

For predation to be optimal J must be greater than 1, but the simplest case mathematically, $J > m$, is selected. Also the presence of entrant adjustment costs leads to the most interesting equilibria. This is incorporated using a simple adjustment cost rule: each entrant can enter only one market in any period.[5] Finally, no market can profitably absorb infinite entry. The simplest convention is to assume that no market can accommodate more than one entrant. Then to avoid the complications of modeling mistaken multiple entry, the extensive form of the game in each time period permits potential entrant J to go first, $J-1$ goes second, and so on until entrant 1 chooses whether to enter. After all entry decisions are made, the monopolist responds for that time period.

[5] With no adjustment costs the game collapses. For an airline to be certain not to face predation it must enter every city pair of every competitor in each entered market simultaneously. This might require entering on a single day virtually all U.S., European, Pacific, etc., city pairs. Leaving aside evidence of adjustment costs one should note that most entry is sequential. This fact should be instructive in terms of interpreting litigated predation cases as well.

(iii) *A Simple Example*

Suppose there are only three markets ($m = 3$),[6] that there are only three monopolist types ($H = 3$), and that the monopolist is drawn from a sample composed of 49 type 1 monopolists, 50 type 2 monopolists, and a single type 3 monopolist. Direct solutions for equilibria are difficult, even for simple examples, but some equilibria can be constructed by working backwards. First, assume a behavior rule for each monopolist type and then derive optimal entrant reactions, "best replies". Second, assume an entry behavior rule and derive the best reply for each monopolist type. If the model parameters are selected such that: (a) the entrants' best replies are identical to the behavior rule assumed in solving for the monopolists' best replies; and (b) the monopolists' best replies are the behavior rules assumed in solving for the entrants' best replies, then a full game Nash equilibrium has been derived.

The first step is to analyse optimal entry. Suppose any of the 50 type 2 monopolists would always prey if only one market were entered, but would always play as type 2 if two or more markets were entered. Suppose that the type 3 monopolist's rule is to prey if one or two markets are entered but not if all three are entered. What is the optimal entrant response? One potential solution involves entrant J entering market 1 in period 1. Since $(J-1)$ is identical to J, then $(J-1)$ would enter market 2 in period 1, and similarly $(J-2)$ would enter market 3. The outcome of the first stage of the game would entail steady state flow profits of $(\Pi 1, \pi C)$ with probability 0.49; $(\Pi 2, \pi B)$ with probability 0.50; and $(\Pi 3, \pi B)$ with probability 0.01. Thus if J would enter there would be a flood of entry in stage 1. Neither predation nor sequential entry would be observed. Alternatively, if not even entrant 1 is willing to enter in period 1, no entry ever occurs. Again neither predation nor sequential entry would be observed.

One interesting case for predation occurs if there are entrant parameters which yield the following entry sequence:

Time 1:	Entrant 1 enters market 1.
Time 2:	Entrant 1 enters market 2.
Time 3:	If πB has occurred in markets 1 and 2 then entrant J enters market 3, and if πC has occurred in markets 1 and 2 there is no further entry.
Time 4–anon:	No entry, the profit steady state is that of period 3.

Such parameters exist. The extremely low probability of type 3 monopoly relative to type 2 monopoly makes this intuitively clear. All that is needed is:

[6] Predation is more likely to occur as m is increased, but it can occur with only three markets. Easley, Masson and Reynolds [1981] demonstrate this result in a decision theoretic version of this model. As m increases, the monopolist's value of markets protected goes up for any level of entry. But the entrant's breakeven point, assuming πB would be revealed upon its last entry, is unaltered.

(1) entrants $2, \ldots, J$ do not find roughly even odds of πB to be attractive; (2) entrant 1 finds even odds to be attractive if it requires entering two markets sequentially; but (3) having entered 2 markets without observing πB, entrant 1 would not find entry of a third market to be attractive if the probability of πB were only 0.02 ($=0.01/(0.49+0.01)$), the conditional probability that the monopolist is of type 3 if it has not played to yield πB in markets 1 and 2.

The technical statements of conditions (1)–(3) above are:

(1) $$[0.49\pi C/r + 0.51\pi B/r] - f_j < 0, \quad j > 1;$$

(2) $$\{\pi C - f_1\} + \{[2(0.5\pi C/r + 0.5\pi B/r) - f_1]/(1+r)\} > 0;$$

(3) $$\{3(0.98\pi C/r + 0.02\pi B/r) - f_1\} - \{2\pi C/r\} < 0.$$

Conditions (1)–(3) are readily seen to be compatible (e.g., if $\pi C = 0$; $\pi B = 0.1$; $r = 0.1$; $J \geqslant 4$; $0.06 < f_1 < 0.3$; and $1 > f_2 = f_3 = f_4 > 0.51$, these conditions are met). This leads the entrants' best replies to be the behavior pattern described above in the sequence from time 1 to 4–anon.

There are parameters for a type 2 monopolist such that its reaction to the above entry behavior rule would be to prey in response to a period 1 entry, but to not prey in response to the second entry. There are also parameters such that a type 3 monopolist would prey in response to entry in both periods if it knew that by so doing its third market would not be entered. To demonstrate this it is useful to give the sequencing a visual representation in matrix form. The monopolist's flow profits can be represented for each of its three markets by the rows of the matrix; the columns represent time 1, time 2, etc. Since the profit steady state is reached after the last play in time 3, the additional infinite sequence of columns which replicate the time 3 profit outcomes can be suppressed. Using the entry rule above and recalling that if any monopolist $h > 1$ selects a response with profits of Πh, then any remaining unentered markets will be entered, matrices (a) and (b) in Figure 1 show the profit sequences underlying a necessary condition for a type 2 monopolist to prey in the first time period. The only difference between matrices (a) and (b) are the "starred" profit levels in (b), elements (1, 1) and (3, 2). By foregoing period 1 profits in market 1, monopolist 2 gains by retarding entry into market 3 by one period. This condition is that profits from preying only one time exceed those from no predation.

(4) $$(\Pi 2 - \Pi P) < (\Pi M - \Pi 2)/(1+r)$$

Further, monopolist 2 must not find it profitable to prey in period 2. A sufficient condition for this is that predation in the second period would not be remunerative even if it would stop all entry. This condition can be visualized by contrasting matrix (b) with (c): The difference is in those elements which are "starred" in matrix (c) (and for the continuing values of the third column elements in periods 4–anon). The condition for ceasing predation is found by the difference in present values between matrix (c) and (b). This difference is

Matrix (a)
No Predation

market \ time	1	2	3
1	Π2	Π2	Π2
2	ΠM	Π2	Π2
3	ΠM	Π2	Π2

Matrix (b)
Preying Only Once

market \ time	1	2	3
1	ΠP*	Π2	Π2
2	ΠM	Π2	Π2
3	ΠM	ΠM*	Π2

Matrix (c)
Preying Twice—
Stopping All Entry

market \ time	1	2	3
1	ΠP	ΠP*	ΠP*
2	ΠM	ΠP*	ΠP*
3	ΠM	ΠM	ΠM*

FIGURE 1

composed of ΠP rather than $\Pi 2$ in two markets in perpetuity, and then starting one period later, ΠM rather than $\Pi 2$ in a third market in perpetuity. Rearranging terms this is:

$$(5) \qquad 2(\Pi 2 - \Pi P)/r > (\Pi M - \Pi 2)/r(1+r)$$

Conditions (4) and (5) are consistent. By multiplying by r, the type 2 monopolist follows the conjectured strategy if

$$2(\Pi 2 - \Pi P) > (\Pi M - \Pi 2)/(1+r) > (\Pi 2 - \Pi P)$$

In order for a type 3 monopolist to behave as posited it must satisfy a condition similar to condition (4):

$$(6) \qquad (\Pi 3 - \Pi P) < (\Pi M - \Pi 3)/(1+r)$$

Furthermore, it is necessary that it satisfy a condition which is the inverse of condition (5):

$$(7) \qquad 2(\Pi 3 - \Pi P)/r < (\Pi M - \Pi 3)/r(1+r)$$

These conditions can be obtained by substituting $\Pi 3$ for $\Pi 2$ in matrices (a), (b) and (c). These are met for any parameters for which

$$(\Pi M - \Pi 3)/(1+r) > 2(\Pi 3 - \Pi P)$$

The type 3 monopolist has more to lose from a duopoly game ($\Pi 3 < \Pi 2$) than does the type 2. Generally, the more competitive is the non-predatory outcome, the greater the incentive to prey.

These conditions are sufficient for demonstrating the existence of an equilibrium with predation in the example. No monopolist can improve its profits given the entry decision rules and no entrant can improve its expected value given the monopolists' decision rules. In many discussions of predatory pricing the assumption is made that a predator's goal is either to eliminate a firm or attain submission (agreement or merger). Although the model can be used to illustrate these types of predation, the examples above demonstrate the existence of two other predatory strategies.[7]

The first strategy, used by monopolist 3, looks like classical "deep-pockets" predation, but it is not. The monopolist preys in some markets in perpetuity to protect others in perpetuity. In "deep-pockets" predation firms are alleged to use earnings from profitable markets to finance predation in others. That is certainly not the causality underlying this example. In fact the predatory markets may yield non-negative cash flows ($\Pi P \geqslant 0$). Thus, a "long purse" (see [Telser 1966]) is not required for predation to have anticompetitive effects in some markets in perpetuity.

The second strategy, used by the type 2 monopolist, involves the use of predation only to slow entry; it recognizes that it will subsequently cease its predation and face complete entry of its markets. Despite this fact, it can attain a greater present value by preying and retarding the rate of growth of competition. The fact that eventual entry is not stopped does not mean that predatory behavior has not occurred or that it has been unsuccessful. Profits can be made from slowing the inevitable.

Both of these strategies work despite the fact that potential entrants know these strategies and do their best to counteract them. For example, suppose that entrant one uses sequential entry to call the bluff. It continues to enter until it knows that accommodation is sufficiently unlikely that it is no longer profitable to enter. When it ceases to enter it knows that if it faces a predator it could force accommodation by yet further entry, and it knows it may be facing a predator. Despite this sophisticated entrant behavior, the model demonstrates that successful predation may stifle competition without either eliminating competitors or even stopping (some) competitors from entering!

[7] Another interesting equilibrium pattern is not demonstrated. Suppose that if there had been only monopolists $1, \ldots, (H-1)$ that no entrant would have entered, but since type H was possible, entrant 1 did enter. It is possible that once behavior reveals that the opponent is not of type H, the entrant will continue to enter. This is because it has already invested the sunk costs in some markets and it may pay at the margin to try to force the monopolist to yield πB in these, and new, markets.

(iv) *Equilibria*

For any parameters the model generates a steady state within a finite horizon (see the Appendix).[8] It is useful to note that entrants, $j > 1$, will enter at only one stage of any game. This will be either the first period or after a monopolist $h > 1$ plays as an $h > 1$ (see the Appendix).

It follows that there are equilibria of three generic types:

(1) *Instantaneous Entry:* The probability of a type 1 monopolist is so low that all markets are entered in the first period.

(2) *Zero Entry:* This has two subcases: (a) *Benign:* The probability of a type 1 monopolist is so great that even a type 1 entrant who expects no predation would not enter; (b) *Latent Deterrence:* Only a type 1 entrant would enter if all $h > 1$ monopolists would play their true types; it does not enter, however, in light of probabilities that type $h > 1$ monopolists would prey and it would be excessively costly to enter sufficient markets to force some of them to cease to prey.

(3) *Sequential Entry:* This may involve pure or mixed strategy equilibria. There are three subcases: (a) *Competition:* The monopolist is of type 1. The type 1 entrant enters some markets and then ceases entry; (b) *Predation in Perpetuity:* The type 1 entrant enters only some markets, the monopolist is of type $h > 1$, but plays as type 1. The monopolist gains by initially slowing entry to only one market per period and then by halting all entry after that; (c) *Predation to Slow Competition:* The monopolist is of type $h > 1$, but plays as type 1 for some time. It later responds to entry by playing its own type and having all of its remaining unentered markets entered in the next period. Slowing competitive entry benefits the monopolist despite the fact that it knows it may not ("will not" in pure strategies) deter eventual entry to all of its markets.

One characteristic of sequential entry equilibria is worth stressing. Given the model structure, observed sequential entry of two or more markets can mean only one thing: there is a positive probability that the monopolist is a predator. The only possibilities are that πB is observed initially and a flood of entry precludes sequential entry or that πC is observed. Continued entry to the latter set of markets is only optimal if there is some chance that πC will be revised to πB. If πC may be revised to πB then this means that one possible reason πC is being observed is that the incumbent firm is a predator.

III. POLICY ISSUES

Since 1975 there has been "...a virtual explosion in the legal and economic literature dealing with predatory pricing [which] has rapidly and pervasively

[8] A monopolist may be willing to prey longer if this would stop all future entry, than if it could only slow entry. When such a gap occurs the equilibrium may involve mixed strategies (within this gap). These equilibria are discussed more fully in Easley, Masson and Reynolds [1984] and a pure strategy decision theoretic solution is presented in Easley, Masson and Reynolds [1981].

transformed an entire body of [U.S. Antitrust] law, and within the briefest period of time" (Brodley and Hay [1981, p. 740]). The economic literature underlying this revolution has generally attempted to define predation without formally analysing its rationality. However, knowing when predation might work—the credibility issue—is an important step in knowing how and when to expect it. This issue is discussed in the policy literature, but its importance is not fully recognized. A closer examination of the role of imperfect/incomplete information in predatory pricing reveals fundamental infirmities in the current policy debate.

III.1. *Criteria for Policy Analysis*

The various proposals for predatory pricing rules have, either implicitly or explicitly generally contained the following points. First, some economic definition of predation is formulated. These vary by author depending upon numerous factors such as whether "fairness" is considered to be relevant. Next, a judicial definition is offered: How should courts define predation given the imperfect information that will be faced by courts? The policy goal can be seen as a rule which weighs the costs against the benefits from deterring or stopping predators. The costs are: (1) Enforcement costs; (2) Costs of type 1 errors (punishing the innocent); (3) Costs of type 2 errors (acquitting or not even detecting the guilty); (4) Costs from firms using alternative strategies to achieve the same ends; (5) Costs due to non-predatory firms acting to avoid being mistaken for predators. The potential for both benefits and costs from any rule against predation is highly dependent upon the incidence of predation. If predation is extremely rare, then costs (2) and (5) may easily outweigh the benefits. If it is very common (3) and (4) may be the primary costs, and the relative benefits from deterrence may be great.

III.2. *The Incidence of Predation*

Economists who opine that predation is rare have little evidence to go on.[9] Predators are unlikely to admit to predation lest they lose their bluff or get prosecuted. Only if it does not expect to be detected will a monopolist prey.

[9] If economists could definitively detect predation then; (1) it might not pay to prey if potential entrants could hire economists, and (2) predators could be easily brought to justice.

Koller [1971] examines the results of 123 cases since 1890. Only 26 out of 95 convictions have complete records. To be categorized as predatory by Koller an episode must pass three tests. The third test is that a competitor must be eliminated or merged or that there be "improved market discipline". The predators demonstrated in this model would never violate this criterion. Koller finds 5 total cases of predation by his standards.

It is noteworthy that many filed Sherman Act cases involve a multi-geographic market firm allegedly preying in a subset of markets, and many of the remaining cases involve a firm with several related products allegedly preying for only some of these products. Defendants and others argue that many allegedly threatening statements are the rhetoric of tough competition, but if threat-like statements come from type 1's they should also come from type $h > 1$. Finally, as noted above, markets more predisposed to competitive results are, *ceteris paribus*, more predisposed to predation.

Furthermore, predators will not wish to maintain evidence (e.g., incriminating memos) where it can be discovered. Although unambiguously incriminating evidence sometimes emerges, these firms have every incentive to settle the case out of court, leaving only the atypically ambiguous cases to go to court and become publicly reported. These cases are the bulk of the available evidence on the incidence of predation.[10] It would thus seem risky to assume that predation is rare, and hence that costs (3) and (4) may be high.

III.3. *The Model and Proposed Antitrust Rules*

At the risk of oversimplifying numerous and varied analyses in the policy literature, the literature can be viewed as based upon the case of a single market industry with high entry barriers and long entry lags. Therefore, if an entrant can be swiftly eliminated, a monopolist may enjoy a long period of elevated profits. The role of conjectures in these discussions is generally implicit or simplistic. Multimarket considerations are then tacked on as an after-thought (cf. Brodley and Hay [1981, pp. 789–790] or McGee [1980, p. 326]).

Although the model presented here has no pretense of encompassing all possible types of predation, it demonstrates that previous analyses leave out many potentially important aspects of the problem. In contrast to one common view, predation need not imply economic murder (the elimination of an entrant) or coercion (to force conspiracy or merger upon an entrant). By simply making life tough for entrants the monopolist may intimidate future entry. By the same token, large entry barriers need not be present for predation to be an optimal strategy.[11] Indeed relatively low entry barriers and the threat of rapid mass entry may motivate a monopolist to artificially manufacture an additional entry deterrent through predation.

The new proposed "economic rules" against predation have had a profound effect upon legal decisions in the last decade. It is accordingly useful to see how these rules stack up against this model in which predation is in fact a rational strategy with sophisticated players. Several of the new rules propose "bright-line" standards, which describe precisely what is predatory and, by exclusion,

[10] Of course additional circularity is added because if a particular predatory price does not fit the current legal precedent the case will probably not be filed. Conversely, the Robinson–Patman Act requires only the showing of injury, not predation, so there is a danger that loose use of judicial language could misbrand other cases.

[11] What courts have traditionally called monopoly is not needed either. Suppose every city has the same non-conspiring 4 grocery stores (A–D) located in a ring around the central city. An entrant entering near A (e.g., between A and B) might experience predation for precisely the reasons incorporated above, or because A (and/or B) attempt to induce it to try entering near C in the next city. If the entrant suspects all monopolists (A–D) are of the same type it may continue to enter A's markets to attempt to force a shift to πB. If A may differ from B–D (e.g., product differentiation may lead to differences in perceived or actual cross elasticities of demand, or firm cost structures may differ) it may shift to entering near C. For this type of spatial oligopoly neither entry barriers nor large city market shares are required for predation to be effective. Finally, as discussed above, markets more prone to competitive results will, *ceteris paribus*, be more prone to predation.

what is not. Stripped to their essentials, the existing proposals can be summarized as follows.[12] "The courts should find it illegal for a dominant firm to..." (1) "Set price below average variable costs"; or (2) "Set price below marginal costs"; or (3) "Eliminate a competitor by ..."; or (4) "Increase price following exit"; or (5) "Set price below average costs with intent to ..." or (6) "Increase output when experiencing entry".

One advantage of the "bright-line" approaches is that they let firms know exactly what they are not permitted to do, so that the fear of violating the law "by mistake" does not have a chilling effect on all activity. By the same token, a list of interdicted activities tells firms exactly what competition-stifling tactics they are permitted to employ. The parameters of the model in section II above were selected to demonstrate this. None of the predators described there could be held in violation of standards (1)–(4). Prices are not below AVC or MC and exit is not induced.[13] Nor need they necessarily violate (5) using accounting costs. Measuring costs correctly (e.g., replacement value, learning effects) reduces the rule's precision (see Brodley and Hay [1981]). Also, depending upon technological and demand factors (some of which may be manipulated prior to entry) there is no logical necessity for the modeled firms to violate standard (6). Ironically, for the modeled firms, some bright-lines may constitute the instruction manual on how to prey with impunity.

Scherer [1976a], [1976b], Brodley and Hay [1981], and Schmalensee [1979] suggest using a Rule of Reason approach. Litigation may be more costly with this approach, but the unseen portion of the evidentiary iceberg, documents or admissions of intent,[14] often come from the wider scope of inquiry. Many of the cases brought under the Sherman Act involve slashing prices by large margins (not infrequently by 50%). It seems doubtful that many firms are inhibited from socially desirable competitive price cuts due to fear of Sherman Act litigation.[15] The burden of proof is high, the number of cases filed as a proportion of price cuts is no doubt minuscule. But, to the extent that there is a small chilling effect, the by-product is that even non-predatory firms may be forced to keep pre-entry prices more closely aligned with costs in order to avoid the appearance of predation if there is entry.[16] Thus if fear of litigation

[12] These standards are for predatory pricing. It is notable that most cases involve allegations of complementary coercion as well (e.g., bribing suppliers, threatening buyers). Standards (1)–(6) are simplified from their originals. They are respectively from: (1) Areeda and Turner [1975]; (2) Posner [1976]; (3) Ordover and Willig [1981]; (4) Baumol [1979]; (5) Greer [1979]; (6) Williamson [1977]. Joskow and Klevorick [1979] use a combination of (1), (4) and (5).

[13] If (4) did not require an exit, the rule would lower an entrant's incentive to enter a potential predator's markets because it could not achieve πB in its infra-marginal markets for a quasi-permanent time period.

[14] Good documentary evidence is seldom made public because when it is available the case is typically settled before trial.

[15] The Robinson–Patman Act does not require a showing of predation. Any effect it has on pricing should not be attributed to a predation standard.

[16] Contestable market theory depends upon an incumbent not being able to respond to match the entry price for a finite period of time. If sunk costs are non-zero this time period expands. Although this limits the applicability of contestability to a general curiosum (cf. Schwartz and Reynolds [1983]), its basic elements might come into play if firms feared litigation if they cut prices in response to entry.

has any effect at all upon non-predators, whether this leads to on average higher or lower prices, is itself an open question.

DAVID EASLEY,
ROBERT T. MASSON,
Department of Economics,
Uris Hall,
Cornell University,
Ithaca,
New York 14853,
U.S.A.

ROBERT J. REYNOLDS,
ICF, Inc.,
1850K St., N.W.,
Washington D.C. 20006,
U.S.A.

ACCEPTED NOVEMBER 1984

APPENDIX: STRATEGIC PLAY AND EQUILIBRIUM

The model has a "sequential equilibrium" as defined by Kreps and Wilson [1982b]. All players know that the monopolist's markets are ordered in an entry sequence of 1, 2, ... m. At stage "0" of the game, nature selects the monopolist. The probability of type h is p_h, where $\Sigma_{h=1}^{H} p_h = 1$. These and all other parameters are in the entrants' stage 1 information set. At stage 1, entrant J has the first move, an entry decision (on market 1). Then entrant $J-1$ moves. It can infer J's move from the model structure. If it infers that J entered 1, it decides whether to enter 2; if it infers J did not enter, its decision is on market 1. This sequence of, in effect, simultaneous moves continues until 1 has moved. Then the monopolist selects its move given the information set derived from knowing its type and knowing all entry moves. (A type $h > 1$ will clearly play only 1 or its own type in equilibrium.) The stage 2 entrant information set includes all parameters and the revealed knowledge of all moves in stage 1. The game is then infinitely repeated.

Sequential equilibria exist for finite games. The game can be made finite by imposing a finite duration on the markets. Alternatively, suppose that once entry ceases there will be no future entry (certainly no new information would be generated if the monopolist changes its play only in response to entry). In this case the model has at most m stages before reaching a steady state which defines terminus values, for a finite game.

The information of entrant j is represented as a partition, Γ^j, of the nodes of the game tree at which j must move. At time t the possible nodes are denoted S_t^j and the partition is Γ_t^j with its elements the information sets I_t^j. These indicate which monopolist(s) entrant j may be playing at time t. A monopolist's information set at any time is the individual node associated with its identity. The set of possible nodes for a monopolist at t is denoted S_t^m, and this is partitioned into individual nodes, s_t, the information sets for the monopolist at time t.

A strategy for entrant j is a sequence of functions $g^j = \{g_t^j\}_{t=1}^{m}$, where the function $g_t^j : \Gamma_t^j \rightarrow \{x \in R_+^m : \Sigma_{i=1}^{m} x_i \leqslant 1\}$ assigns a probability to entering each market as a function of entrant j's information at stage t. A strategy for monopolist h is also a sequence of functions $G^h = \{G_t^h\}_{t=1}^{m}$. The monopolist's possible information sets are S_t^h, so $G_t^h : S_t^h \rightarrow \{x \in R_+^H : \Sigma_{h=1}^{H} x_h = 1\}$ assigns the probabilities the monopolist will play as any type h in $\{1, \ldots, H\}$ in any entered market. (A type 1 must play as type 1, so $G_t^1(s_t) = (1, 0, \ldots, 0)$ for all t.) A monopolist of type $h > 1$ may assign positive probabilities to any play, but optimal behavior leads to zero probabilities always being assigned to all but the first and h^{th} element of the vector.

Let $g \equiv \{g^1, \ldots, g^J; G^1, \ldots, G^H\}$ describe the vector of entrants' and monopolists' strategies. Nature selects the monopolist's type using probabilities $(p_1, p_2, \ldots, p_H)$. This probability vector and any strategy vector g induces a probability p^g on the nodes of the game. The probability of reaching any node s is denoted $p^g(s)$ and the probability of reaching any set of nodes, for example I^j, is denoted $p^g(I^j)$.

Define $\mu^j(s)$ as the probability j assigns to being at node $s \in I^j$ if it arrives at information set $I^j \in \Gamma^j$. (Note $\mu^j(s)$ is implicitly conditioned upon I^j.) For any strategy vector, g, and expectation, μ^j, entrant j can assign probabilities to the terminal nodes, conditional upon any information set during the play of the game. Define $\rho^{\mu^j,g}(s \mid I^j)$ as the conditional probability entrant j assigns to terminal node s given the information set I^j. Then expected payouts are $E^{\mu^j,g}[\cdot \mid I^j]$. (For the monopolist, expected payouts are $E[\cdot \mid s]$ for any node.) Let $\mu = (\mu^I, \ldots, \mu^J)$ be the vector of entrants' expectations.

Then (μ^*, g^*) is a *Sequential Equilibrium* if three conditions are met.

(i) For all $j \in \{1, \ldots, J\}$ and $I^j \in \Gamma^j$,

$$E^{\mu^{*j},g^*}[\pi^j(s) \mid I^j] \geqslant E^{\mu^{*j},g}[\pi^j(s) \mid I^j] \text{ where}$$

$$g \equiv (g^{*1}, \ldots, g^j, \ldots, g^{*J}; G^{*1}, \ldots, G^{*H}), \text{ for all strategies } g^j.$$

(ii) For all $\bar{s} \in S^h$ and all $h \in \{1, \ldots, H\}$

$$E^{g^*}[\Pi^h(s) \mid \bar{s}] \geqslant E^g[\Pi^h(s) \mid \bar{s}] \text{ where}$$

$$g \equiv (g^{*1}, \ldots, g^{*J}; G^{*1}, \ldots, G^h, \ldots, G^{*H}), \text{ for all strategies } G^h.$$

(iii) There exists a sequence (μ_n, g_n) with $\lim_{n\to\infty} (\mu_n, g_n) = (\mu^*, g^*)$ such that for each n:

(a) $1 \gg g_n^j(I^j) \gg 0$ for all $I^j \in \Gamma^j$,
(b) $G_n^h(s) \gg 0$ for all s for each $h \in \{2, \ldots, H\}$ and
(c) $\mu_n^j(s) = p^{g_n}(s)/p^{g_n}(I^j)$ for any $s \in I^j$, for all $I^j \in \Gamma^j$, and all j.

Conditions (i) and (ii) are simply that all entrants and the monopolist maximize expected profits given the equilibrium strategies of all other players. Condition (iii) is the "consistency condition". One heuristic interpretation is that (a) and (b) force positive probabilities on all possible outcomes. Condition (c) requires that expectations be derived from Bayes rule where applicable. The positive probabilities in (a) and (b) allow for expectations to be defined when attaining information sets which are logically possible, but off any equilibrium path. The limit assures that this assignment rule accurately presents expectations along any equilibrium path.

With these definitions, Proposition 1 follows directly from Kreps and Wilson's Proposition 1:

Proposition 1. The extensive form game of section II and this Appendix has at least one sequential equilibrium.

The model generates at most two truly strategic players, entrant 1 and the monopolist, if the monopolist is of type $h > 1$. This vastly simplifies constructing examples like those in the text.

The intuition is simple, if any $j > 1$ is willing to enter at stage 1, then all are willing at stage 1, so the game ends. Further, unless πB is observed in some later stage, entrants $j > 1$ have only "bad news", so they will not enter. Hence types $j > 1$ can be treated as "exogenous", entering all unentered markets only at stage 1 or at the stage after observing πB. Proposition 2 demonstrates these two entry equilibria for $j > 1$ in sections (i) and (ii) respectively.

Define: p_1 as the initial probability of a type 1 monopolist; $h(I_t^j)$ as the monopolist type played in stage $t-1$ (which entrant j observes at stage t); $n(I_t^j)$ as the number of markets entered at information set I_t^j; and $\|g_t^j\|$ as the norm of g_t^j. (Note that $\|g_t^j\| = 1$

only if j chooses to enter some market with probability one and $\|g_t^j\| = 0$ if j chooses not to enter.)

Proposition 2. There exists an equilibrium where:

(i) *If* $(p_1\pi C + (1-p_1)\pi B)/r \geqslant f_2$ *then:*

$$\|g_1^j\| = \{1, \text{ if } j \in \{J, \ldots, J-m\};\ 0, \text{ otherwise}\} \text{ and}$$

$$\|g_t^j\| = 0 \text{ for all } t > 1, \text{ for all } j.$$

(ii) *If* $(p_1\pi C + (1-p_1)\pi B)/r < f_2$ *then for all* $j > 1$ *and all* t:

$$\|g_t^j\| = \{1, \text{ if } h(I_t^j) > 1 \text{ and } j > J-(m-n(I_t^j));\ 0 \text{ otherwise}\}.$$

Proof

(i) If $(p_1\pi C + (1-p_1)\pi B)/r \geqslant f_j$ for all j then entry is profitable if there will be no predation (if $h > 1$ yields πB). From Proposition 1, condition (ii), if all m markets are entered h will play its true type. Entrants $J, \ldots, J-m$ will enter sequentially, as for any $j' > J-m$ to delay for one period would lead to pre-emption by the entry of $J-m-1$.

(ii) If $(p_1\pi C + (1-p_1)\pi B)/r < f_j$ for $j > 1$ then the optimal stage 1 strategy for $j > 1$ is $\|g_1^j\| = 0$. This results because j's payoff from entry, even with the most favorable strategies for its opponents, is negative. Thus no entrant $j > 1$ will enter in stage 1.

At any information set I_t^j, j will enter ($\|g_t^j\| = 1$) if there is an unentered market, that is, $j > J-(m-n(I_t^j))$ and if $\mu(s) = 1$ for any node $s \in I_t^j$ on a branch of the tree following a selection by nature of $h > 1$ (that is, if Πh is played and πB received). This strategy is optimal for the same reason as in (i) above.

At any information set I_t^j, $j > 1$ will not enter ($\|g_t^j\| = 0$) if $h(I_t^j) = 1$ because $\Sigma\,\mu(s) \leqslant (1-p_1)$ for $I_t^j \subset I = \{s : s$ is on a branch following selection by nature of $h > 1\}$.

THE JOURNAL OF INDUSTRIAL ECONOMICS 0022-1821 $2.00
Volume XXXIII June 1985 No. 4

PATENT RACES AND THE PERSISTENCE OF MONOPOLY*

Christopher Harris and John Vickers

I. INTRODUCTION

Patent races are important determinants of market structure. For a new firm, a patent can be an entry ticket into the market. For an incumbent firm already in the market, patents for related technologies can ensure that no new firm enters. In this spirit recent work has explored the implications of patenting for the persistence of monopoly (see, for example, Dasgupta [1982], Gilbert [1981], Gilbert and Newbery [1982]). Much attention has been given to "pre-emptive patenting"—the strategic acquisition of patents by an incumbent firm solely to prevent potential rivals from entering the market.

In this context it is important to distinguish between two kinds of patent race. A *standard race* is a competition in which a prize is awarded to the first player to reach the finishing line. An *asymmetrical race* is a competition in which one player loses something of value if one of his rivals reaches the finishing line (he is content if nobody wins), but a prize is won by the first of the other players to reach the finishing line, if any of them does so. A patent race in which an incumbent firm's sole concern is to prevent potential rivals from entering his market is an asymmetrical race and not a standard race.

The distinction between the two kinds of race can be captured only in models with a sufficiently rich dynamic structure. This, and other, advantages of a properly dynamic model are explained in section II. A model of an asymmetrical race with two firms is presented in section III. In this model the "challenger" wins a prize, and the "incumbent" loses a prize, if the challenger is first to reach the finishing line. It is shown that the challenger is often automatically deterred from making any effort to win the race, because the strategic interactions between the players are such that the incumbent would outdo any reasonable effort made by the challenger in order to stop the challenger being first to reach the finishing line. Then the incumbent has no need to make any effort in the race in order to maintain his existing monopoly. The reason is that the incumbent—unlike the challenger—does not need to go all the way to the finishing line to achieve his objective. On the other hand, it may be true—depending on the parameters describing the firms—that the challenger wins the patent, proceeding to the finishing line just as if he were the only contender for the patent. Of particular interest is the case in which the firms are identical

* We are very grateful to Jim Mirrlees, John Sutton and an anonymous referee for their helpful comments and suggestions.

except for the incumbent/challenger asymmetry. It turns out that the incumbent generally has strategic supremacy here: the challenger is automatically deterred from actively pursuing the patent.

In section IV we briefly set out a variant upon our (1985) model of a standard race, which we compare with the model of an asymmetrical race of section III. The comparison illustrates generally the strategic advantages of wanting one's rival *not* to win, rather than wanting to win oneself.

In section V we solve an explicit example to obtain a clear picture of the solutions to the standard and asymmetrical races—and the differences between them. In order to do this neatly, we look at the models in the limit as the intervals between the rivals' actions and reactions become shorter. This limiting case may also be of independent interest.

The concluding section discusses the implications of our results for the theory of the persistence of monopoly.

II. THE ECONOMICS OF PATENT RACES

Patent Races as Bidding Games

It has been suggested that the essence of a patent race among fully informed competitors can be distilled by analysing bidding games: see Dasgupta [1982, p. 30] and Gilbert and Newbery [1982, p. 517]. In their simple models, each of two players makes an irrecoverable bid (his R & D expenditure) for an indivisible prize (the patent), which the players may value differently. This highest bidder wins the prize. It turns out that the prize is won by the player most keen to win it, since he is prepared to pay the most for it.

It is often supposed that one player is an incumbent monopolist, currently supplying a product with which the future invention would compete. If his rival does not win the patent, then his monopoly persists. But if the challenger does win the new patent, he will enter the market and compete with the current incumbent. It is reasonable to assume that the firms' joint profits in this latter case are lower than the incumbent's profits if he retains his monopoly position. Hence it is argued that the incumbent has more incentive than the challenger to win the patent, and so will "pre-empt" the patent.[1]

Our criticism of the structure of this simple model is that it neglects important features of strategic interaction between players during the course of the race. In the simple model each player has just one bid, which would be appropriate only if the competitors made unconditional, once-and-for-all commitments of effort at the outset of the race. In fact there is action and reaction between the rivals as the race progresses. A competitor makes a series of decisions during the race, each one in the light of the moves made by his

[1] For a critical discussion of Gilbert and Newbery [1982] see Reinganum [1983] and the debate between Reinganum, Salant and Gilbert and Newbery in the *American Economic Review*, March 1984, Vol. 74, pp. 238–53.

rivals and with a view to influencing the moves that they make in their turn.[2]

In an attempt to capture these considerations we develop the structure of the simple model. In our framework, each player makes a series of bids, each one of which is made in the light of the bids made previously. The players take turns to bid: thus there are opportunities for action and reaction. The richer structure enables one to analyse questions that could not previously be handled. For example, we can make precise the idea that a player would give up in the race once his rival was far enough ahead; we can see why this might be so; and we can see what exactly it is to be "far enough ahead" in this sense. Moreover, the richer structure permits one to distinguish between a standard race and an asymmetrical race.

Two Kinds of Patent Race

We discuss the distinction between the two kinds of race in terms of a two-firm example which is related to the models in the following sections. In a standard race it is true of each firm that its profits increase if it obtains the patent, but that if it loses the race it forgoes only its R & D expenditures. An asymmetrical race is different. Let A be the name of a challenger to an incumbent firm B. A's payoff is as in the standard race above. But B's profits fall if A wins the patent. So if B loses the race to A, he loses not only his R & D expenditures, but also suffers a fall in profits. If A does not win the race, B avoids this latter loss, irrespective of whether he actually wins the patent himself.

To summarise: (i) in a standard race, both A and B want to win the prize; but (ii) in an asymmetrical race, A (the challenger) wants to win the prize, but B's (the incumbent's) concern is that his rival should not win the prize.

There are cases intermediate between these two types of race. For example, B might strictly prefer to have the patent than not have it, although he would rather that no one have it than his rival have it. In this paper we shall not discuss such hybrid cases. Our main concern is with "pure" asymmetrical races, in which the incumbent's sole motive is to prevent his rival from winning. Because we are concerned with the question of the persistence of monopoly, this is the natural focus of attention.

III. A MODEL OF AN ASYMMETRICAL RACE

Two players, A and B, compete for a single indivisible prize. Initially A and B are at distances x_0 and y_0 from a "finishing line". Progress by A towards the finishing line depends on his irrecoverable R & D efforts, called "bids". Thus a bid of z moves him a distance $w_A(z)$ closer to the finishing line. We assume

[2] In independent work, Fudenberg *et al.* [1983, section 4] have also presented a model that attempts to capture these features of strategic interaction through time. For a discussion of the relationship between that paper and our work, see Harris and Vickers [1985].

that w_A is continuous, increasing and that it exhibits increasing returns to scale for low effort levels. We assume also that $w_A(0) = 0$.[3]

We make exactly the same assumptions about B and his "progress" function w_B. It is not assumed that the w functions are necessarily identical, since we wish to allow for the possibility that the players are not equally efficient at R & D. Players bid alternately: first A, then B, then A again, and so on. We denote the sequence of bids by: $a_1, b_1, a_2, b_2, \ldots$. The prize is awarded to the first player to reach the finishing line.

If player A wins the prize his payoff is $V_A - \Sigma a_i$. If he does not win the prize his payoff is $-\Sigma a_i$. Player B's payoffs are as follows. If A wins the prize, B's payoff is $-V_B - \Sigma b_i$. If A does not win the prize, B's payoff is $-\Sigma b_i$, whether or not B wins the prize himself. Thus we think of A as a challenger to an incumbent monopolist B.

For simplicity of exposition we adopt the convention that, if player A is indifferent between winning the prize with a net payoff of zero and not winning the prize, he will choose to win the prize. And if B is indifferent between thwarting A's victory and not doing so, then he will do so. It will be clear that these conventions do not significantly affect the analysis.

Players are perfectly informed of one another's bids, and condition their choices on this information. Thus a player's strategy specifies what bid he would make contingent upon any possible history of bids. Since we want to rule out the making of threats that are not credible, Selten's [1965] notion of perfect equilibrium is the natural solution concept. While the arguments that follow are intuitive, the underlying solution concept is perfect equilibrium.

The game is most conveniently analysed by partitioning the space of pairs of distances from the finishing line in terms of two sequences of critical distances: $\{C_n\}$ for A and $\{E_n\}$ for B. (See Figure 1.)

The sequence $\{C_n\}$ is defined purely in relation to A. First, $C_0 = 0$. Then if C_{n-1} has been defined for some $n \geqslant 1$, C_n is the maximum distance from the finishing line that A can profitably cover if he is subject to moving to within C_{n-1} of the finishing line with his first bid. More formally:

Definition 1. $C_0 = 0$. For $n \geqslant 1$, C_n is the maximum x such that there exists a sequence $a_1, a_2, \ldots, a_r$ of non-negative bids such that

$$\sum_{i=1}^{r} w_A(a_i) \geqslant x$$

$$w_A(a_1) \geqslant x - C_{n-1}$$

$$V_A \geqslant \sum_{i=1}^{r} a_i$$

To gain another perspective on $\{C_n\}$, let us define $\Omega_A(x)$ as the value to A of

[3] These assumptions on w_A are similar to those models about the hazard function in the literature on R&D under uncertainty: see for example Kamien and Schwartz [1982, p. 181].

a "free run" from distance x.[4] That is to say, $\Omega_A(x)$ is the payoff that A would get if he started a distance x from the finishing line and faced no rivalry from B. Then he would face the one-player decision problem of finding the optimal path to the line. Now, if $C_{n+1} > C_n$, we have

$$(1) \qquad C_n - C_{n-1} = w_A(\Omega_A(C_{n-1}))$$

The RHS of (1) is the distance that A would travel if he bid the full value to him of a "free run" from C_{n-1}. It is simple to show that Ω_A is strictly decreasing if it is strictly positive. Hence $C_{n+1} - C_n < C_n - C_{n-1}$ so long as $\Omega_A(C_{n-1}) > 0$.

The sequence $\{E_n\}$ is defined purely in relation to B.

Definition 2. $E_n = nw_B(V_B)$.

Thus $E_n - E_{n-1} = w_B(V_B)$. That is, increments in the $\{E_n\}$ sequence are all equal to $w_B(V_B)$, which is the distance that B would travel if he bid the maximum amount he would pay to prevent A from winning. Note that while $E_n - E_{n-1}$ is exactly equal to $w_B(V_B)$, $C_n - C_{n-1}$ is strictly less than $w_A(V_A)$ for all $n > 1$. This is because $C_n - C_{n-1}$ also reflects the cost of getting from C_{n-1} to the finishing line. If the firms are identical except for the incumbent/challenger asymmetry, that is $V_A = V_B$ and $w_A = w_B$, then $E_n > C_n$ for $n > 1$. Moreover, the ratio E_n/C_n increases with n.

Figure 1 shows the partition of the space of pairs of distances from the finishing line.

If A is within C_n of the finishing line for some n, but B is more than E_n away from it, then we say that (x,y) lies in A's *safety zone*. If B is within E_n of the line, but A is more than C_n from it, then (x,y) lies in B's safety zone. If $C_{n-1} < x \leqslant C_n$ and $E_{n-1} < y \leqslant E_n$ for some n, then we say that (x,y) lies in a *trigger zone*. The final, uninteresting, possibility is that $x > C_n$ for all n, in which case A could not profitably reach the line, even without rivalry from B.

The following proposition states what happens in the race.

Proposition 1. Suppose that the players' strategies are in equilibrium:

(i) *If (x,y) lies in player A's safety zone then A wins the prize. His bids are those he would make in the absence of rivalry from B. B always bids zero.*
(ii) *If (x,y) lies in B's safety zone both players always bid zero and no one wins the prize.*
(iii) *If (x,y) lies in a trigger zone and it is A's move then A wins the prize. His bids are those he would make if, in isolation, he were subject only to reaching his safety zone with his first bid. B always bids zero.*
(iv) *If (x,y) lies in a trigger zone and it is B's move then no one wins the prize. B moves immediately to the boundary of his safety zone and both players bid zero thereafter.*

[4] Appendix A contains a more formal discussion of $\Omega_A(x)$, including a proof that equation (1) holds.

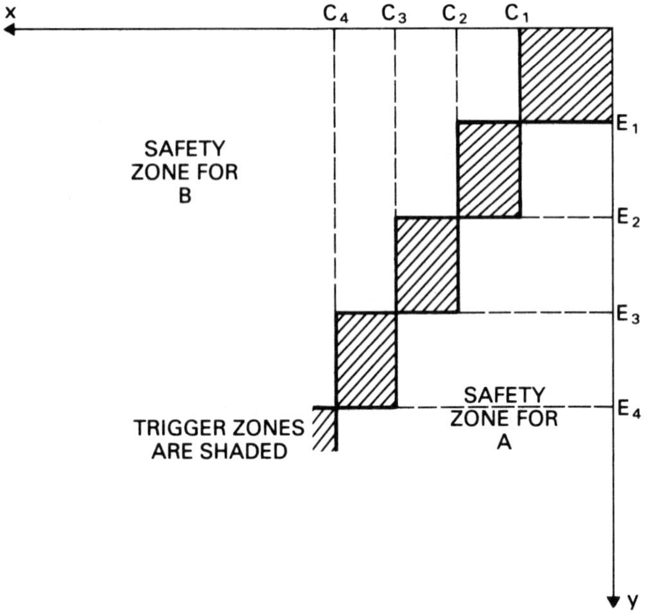

FIGURE I
The Partition of the Space of Distances from the Finishing Line in the Asymmetrical Race

Proof. The proof is by induction. In Figure 2, consider the first trigger zone, T_1, and the first parts of A's and B's safety zones, denoted by A_1 and B_1.

If it is A's turn to bid in $T_1 = \{(x,y) \mid 0 < x \leqslant C_1 \text{ and } 0 < y \leqslant E_1\}$ then A wins the prize. Otherwise his payoff is at best zero, whereas he obtains a positive payoff by moving directly to the finishing line. Moreover, A moves immediately to the line. For otherwise it would become B's turn to move in T_1, in which case A would not win since B would do better to move to the line himself and prevent A's victory than to allow it. Finally, if it is B's turn to move in T_1 he moves immediately to the line. If he did not, it would become A's turn to move in T_1 in which case A would win: then B would get at most $-V_B$ which is worse than moving immediately to the line himself. Thus we have shown that whoever's turn it is to move in T_1 moves immediately to the line.

Next we show that A is safe in $A_1 = \{(x,y) \mid 0 < x \leqslant C_1 \text{ and } y > E_1\}$. It can never be optimal for B to finish in one move from any point in A_1. For to do so would cost him more than V_B, whereas $-V_B$ is the worst payoff that B can get if he does nothing. Nor can it be optimal for B to move into T_1 from A_1. For if he did so, A would finish immediately, and B's payoff would be $-V_B$ less the cost of his move. This is again worse than bidding zero always. Since B never moves out of A_1, A's behaviour is unaffected by B, and his bids are those he would make if he acted in isolation. Since B cannot affect A's behaviour he always bids zero.

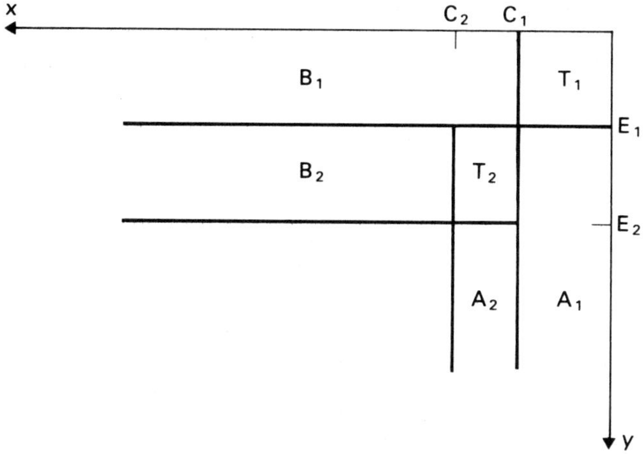

FIGURE 2

Furthermore B is safe in $B_1 = \{(x,y) \mid x > C_1 \text{ and } 0 < y \leqslant E_1\}$. For it is not optimal for A to finish in one move from any point in B_1, or for him to move from B_1 into T_1. In either case his payoff would be negative, whereas complete inaction yields a payoff of zero. Hence A never moves out of B_1. Indeed, he never moves at all, and B faces no effective rivalry. B therefore bids zero, and achieves a payoff of zero, the best payoff he can possibly obtain.

If it is A's turn to bid in $T_2 = \{(x,y) \mid C_1 < x \leqslant C_2 \text{ and } E_1 < y \leqslant E_2\}$ then A wins. If he did not win, his payoff would be at most zero, whereas he can obtain a positive payoff by moving directly to A_1. Moreover, A moves out of T_2 immediately. For if he did not, B would be motivated to pre-empt A by moving directly to B_1 where B is safe. By pre-empting A in this way, B's payoff would exceed $-V_B$, since he can reach B_1 at a cost less than V_B. This would be better for B than allowing A to win. Moreover, if it is B's turn to bid in T_2, he moves immediately to B_1. For otherwise A would win, by the previous argument. Thus we have shown that whoever is to move from T_2 moves immediately to his safety zone, A_1 or B_1 as the case may be.

Next we show that A is safe in $A_2 = \{(x,y) \mid C_1 < x \leqslant C_2 \text{ and } y > E_2\}$. It cannot be optimal for B to move from A_2 to B_1, since this would cost more than V_B. Nor can it be optimal for B to move from A_2 to T_2, since A would then win, which is worse for B than doing nothing. Therefore A faces no effective rivalry and proceeds as if in isolation. B always bids zero.

Finally we show that B is safe in $B_2 = \{(x,y) \mid x > C_2 \text{ and } E_1 < y \leqslant E_2\}$. It is not optimal for A to move from B_2 to A_1, since this would cost more than V_B. Nor is it optimal for A to move from B_2 to T_2 since B would then move to his safety zone B_1. Therefore A bids zero, since he cannot win the prize. And B secures his maximum possible payoff by bidding zero himself.

These arguments can be iterated. Thus the proof is complete.

Q.E.D.

Several remarks are in order. In the incumbent's (that is B's) safety zone the "race" is at a standstill. Even if the challenger (A) could profitably reach the finishing line if he were alone, he makes no attempt to do so since B credibly threatens to outdo any such attempt and beat A to the line. Of course B need never carry out this threat, and he makes no effort at all, since A is completely stymied. If the race begins with B to move from within a trigger zone, he makes an immediate dash to safety after which no player makes any further effort. In A's safety zone, A proceeds at his own pace to the finishing line, because if B attempted to thwart A's victory then A would foil B's attempt by increasing his efforts.

Note that the location of the trigger and safety zones depends upon the players' valuations of the prize (i.e. the V's) and upon their efficiency at R & D (i.e. the w functions). Not surprisingly, C_n increases the more that A wants to win the prize and the more efficient he is at R & D. Likewise E_n increases the more that B wants to avoid A winning, and the more efficient he is.

The size of the incumbent's safety zone is striking. Increments in the $\{C_n\}$ sequence (that is $C_n - C_{n-1}$) decrease and ultimately vanish, and the $\{C_n\}$ sequence is bounded above. The increments of the $\{E_n\}$ sequence, however, are constant.

It follows from this that A might be deterred from challenging the incumbent even though the incumbent was further from the line, less efficient at R & D, and less concerned to stop A's victory than A was to achieve it. This result stands in contrast to the theme of much of the literature on pre-emptive patenting and the persistence of monopoly.

The intuition behind our result is that the incumbent does not need to go all the way to the finishing line to prevent the rival from winning the prize. Once the incumbent has reached his safety zone, he has achieved his objective and makes no further effort. The rival, however, has to proceed all the way to the finishing line to attain his objective of winning the prize. The effect of this is that the incumbent's safety zone is relatively large. This point is illustrated by an example at the end of section V.

IV. A MODEL OF A STANDARD RACE

We now describe a model of standard race, which we will compare, in the following section, with that of the asymmetrical race. The model is adapted from that in Harris and Vickers [1985], to which it is closely related. In that paper we assumed that players discounted the future, whereas here we assume that they do not. This change is necessary in order to obtain direct comparability with the asymmetrical race of section III.

We have assumed that players do not discount the future in the asymmetrical race in order to render its analysis tractable. With discounting, the effort that the incumbent is prepared to make to stop his rival depends in part upon when the rival would win. This complexity is avoided if discounting is not introduced. However, in order to guarantee the existence of the C_n, and so the existence of equilibrium, in the absence of discounting, the additional assumption that the w functions exhibit increasing returns to scale for low effort levels is needed.

Our description of the standard race will be brief. A more detailed and rigorous analysis is available in our earlier paper.

The Model

The only differences between the model in this section and that in the previous section is the specification of B's payoffs. In the asymmetrical race, B lost V_B if A won the prize. Here, in the standard race, B gains V_B if he wins the prize. Thus B's payoff is now $V_B - \Sigma b_i$ if he wins the prize, and $-\Sigma b_i$ if he does not win the prize. Otherwise the model remains the same: the w functions and the structure of moves are as explained at the beginning of the previous section.

Once again, the key to analysing the game is to partition the space of pairs of distances from the finishing line in terms of two sequences of critical distances: $\{C_n\}$ for A and $\{D_n\}$ for B. The $\{C_n\}$ sequence is given by Definition 1 above. The $\{D_n\}$ sequence is defined exactly as the $\{C_n\}$ sequence:

Definition 3. $D_0 = 0$. For $n \geqslant 1$, D_n is the maximum y such that there exists a sequence $b_1, b_2, \ldots, b_r$ of non-negative bids such that

$$\sum_{i=1}^{r} w_B(b_i) \geqslant y$$

$$w_B(b_1) \geqslant y - D_{n-1}$$

$$V_B \geqslant \sum_{i=1}^{r} b_i$$

Using the sequences $\{C_n\}$ and $\{D_n\}$ we can characterise the outcome of the standard race in a fashion similar to that used to analyse the asymmetrical race in the previous section.

Figure 3 shows the partition of the space of distances from the finishing line. Once again we employ the terminology of safety zones and trigger zones. The following proposition states what happens in the race.

Proposition 2. Suppose that players' strategies are in equilibrium.

(i) *If (x,y) lies in player A's (B's) safety zone then A (B) wins the prize. His bids are those he would make in the absence of rivalry from B (A). B (A) always bids zero.*

(ii) *If (x,y) lies in a trigger zone, and it is A's (B's) move, then A (B) wins the prize. His bids are those he would make if, in isolation, he were subject only to reaching his safety zone with his first bid. B (A) always bids zero.*

(iii) *If, for all n, $x > C_n$ and $y > D_n$ then both players always bid zero.*

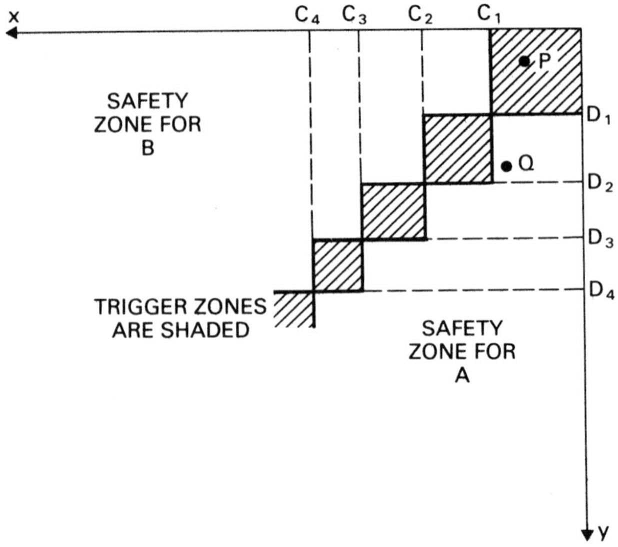

FIGURE 3
The Partition of the Space of Distances from the Finishing Line in the Standard Race

This result can be seen as follows. If (x,y) lies in the first trigger zone, such as point P in Figure 3, and if it is A to move, then A must win. For he can profitably pre-empt any attempt by B to win, simply by winning in one move. Moreover, A must win immediately, in one move. For if he did not, it would become B's move from within the first trigger zone, in which case B would win, by the previous argument. This contradiction shows that whoever's turn it is to move from within the first trigger zone must win the prize immediately.

Next consider a point such as Q, where $x \leqslant C_1$, but $y > D_1$. From here, B cannot win. For if he did so his path to the finishing line would involve him either (i) jumping over the first trigger zone; or (ii) passing through it. By the definition of D_1, (i) is unprofitable, and we have already established that A would win if B moved into the first trigger zone. So B cannot win in either case, and therefore he bids zero always. Thus A faces no effective rivalry from B, and his bids are those he would make if he were in isolation. That is, A is "safe". Similarly, B is safe if $y \leqslant D_1$ and $x > C_1$.

The second trigger zone, and the parts of the safety zone adjacent to it, can be analysed in much the same way as the first; and so on, inductively. Thus equilibrium takes the form described in the Proposition and illustrated in Figure 3.

V. AN EXAMPLE

In this section we present an explicit example of our models of standard and asymmetrical races. To do this neatly, we examine the models in the previous two sections as the intervals between bids become short.

In respect of each type of race (i.e. standard and asymmetrical) we consider a sequence of races defined as follows. In race 1 in the sequence, each player makes a bid each unit of time; we have already analysed this case. In race k in the sequence each player bids each kth of a unit of time. We preserve the alternating move structure throughout. Thus, as k becomes large, the process of action and reaction between rivals becomes more rapid. We are interested in what happens in the limit as k goes to infinity. This limiting case is of interest for several reasons. First, under suitable assumptions, the trigger zones collapse to form a curve, which can be characterised. Secondly, explicit examples can conveniently be solved in the limiting case; these may be illuminating. In particular, examples reveal clearly how different are standard and asymmetrical races. Thirdly, and rather speculatively, the limiting case can perhaps be regarded as the appropriate solution to the model in continuous time.

The present section contains an informal derivation of the limit of the equilibrium as k tends to infinity. A full statement of the technical conditions required to justify our analysis is given in Appendix B. One more substantive assumption should however be noted. We assume that $w_i(z)/z \to 0$ as $z \to \infty$. This means that it is impossible to move a strictly positive distance in zero time with a fixed budget.

Now let us consider race k in the sequence (the following applies equally to standard and asymmetrical races). A bid of an *amount* z implies expenditure at a rate kz, since the effort is applied for $1/k$ units of time. Expenditure at rate kz implies progress at rate $w_i(kz)$. Therefore, in race k, a bid of z moves player i a distance $w_i(kz)/k$ towards the finishing line.

Using this fact, we can define the $\{C_n^k\}$ sequence for race k in the natural way. Rather than state a formal definition, let us extend equation (1) to characterise the sequence $\{C_n^k\}$. If $C_{n+1}^k > C_n^k$ then

$$C_n^k = C_{n-1}^k + w_A(k\Omega_A^k(C_{n-1}^k))/k, \tag{2}$$

where $\Omega_A^k(x)$ is the value to A of a free run from x in race k.

Similarly, the $\{E_n^k\}$ sequence for race k is given by

$$E_n^k = nw_B(kV_B)/k \tag{3}$$

(cf. Definition 2 in section III).

Inspection of (2) and (3) reveals that our assumption that $w_i(z)/z \to 0$ as $z \to \infty$ implies that the trigger zones vanish, both in the standard and asymmetrical races. Consider first equation (2). The width of the nth trigger zone in race k is $C_n^k - C_{n-1}^k = w_A(k\Omega_A^k(C_{n-1}))/k$. Clearly $\Omega_A^k(\cdot) < V_A$, and therefore the RHS $\to 0$ as $k \to \infty$. The same is true for B's sequence $\{D_n^k\}$ in the kth standard race. Therefore the trigger zones vanish in the standard race as $k \to \infty$.

To show that the same is true for the asymmetrical race, consider equation (3). The height of the nth trigger zone in the kth asymmetrical race is $E_n^k - E_{n-1}^k = w_B(kV_B)/k$. Clearly the RHS $\to 0$ as $k \to \infty$, by our assumption. This completes the argument that the trigger zones vanish.

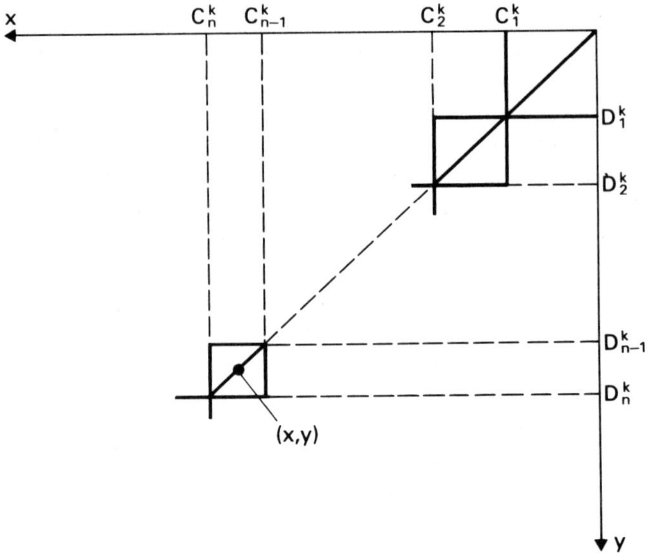

FIGURE 4
The Diagonals of Trigger Zones in Race k

Naturally the next step is to characterise the curve to which the trigger zones collapse. First we sketch how this is done for the standard race. Suppose that (x,y) lies on the diagonal of the nth trigger zone in race k: see Figure 4. Then the slope of the diagonal at (x,y) is given by

$$\text{(4)} \qquad \frac{dy}{dx} = \frac{D_n^k - D_{n-1}^k}{C_n^k - C_{n-1}^k} = \frac{w_B(k\Omega_B^k(D_{n-1}^k))}{w_A(k\Omega_A^k(C_{n-1}^k))}$$

from equation (2). If (x,y) lies on the limiting curve formed by the collapsed trigger zones, then the slope of this curve at (x,y) is given by

$$\frac{dy}{dx} = \lim_{k\to\infty}\left(\frac{w_B(k\Omega_B^k(D_{n-1}^k))}{w_A(k\Omega_A^k(C_{n-1}^k))}\right)$$

or

$$\text{(5)} \qquad \frac{dy}{dx} = \lim_{k\to\infty}\left(\frac{w_B(k\Omega_B(y))}{w_A(k\Omega_A(x))}\right)$$

where $\Omega_i(x)$ is the value to i of a free run from x in the limit as $k \to \infty$. That is, the slope of the limiting curve is the limit of the slopes of the diagonals that converge to it. The limiting curve is then characterised by equation (5).

It must be noted that informal arguments such as the present one can easily be mistaken: the slope of a limiting curve need not in general be the limit of the slopes of the curves that converge to it. However, we have derived an independent, rigorous, justification of that conclusion in the context of the

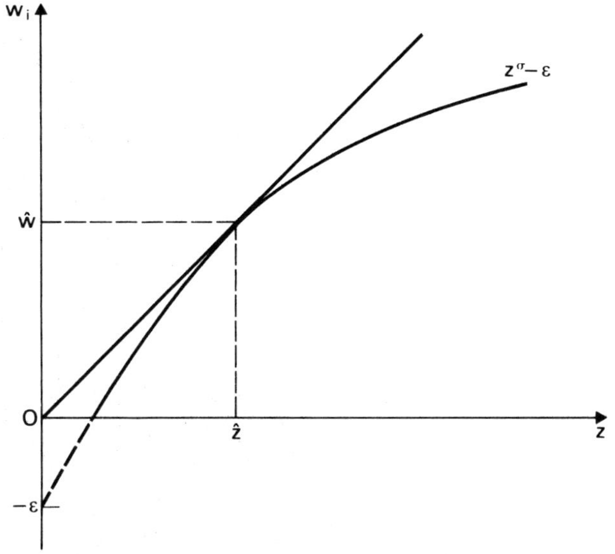

FIGURE 5
The Progress Function in the Example

present model. This rigorous argument is outlined in Appendix B.

The analysis for the asymmetrical race is much the same. The only difference is that V_B replaces $\Omega_B(y)$ in equation (5), due to the way that the $\{E_n^k\}$ sequence is defined.

The Example

Suppose that w_i has the form

(6) $$w_i(z) = \max\{0, z^{\sigma} - \varepsilon\}$$

for $i = A, B$, where $\varepsilon > 0$ and $0 < \sigma < 1$.

The most efficient rate of effort is $\hat{z} = (\varepsilon/(1-\sigma))^{1/\sigma}$. The value to A of a free run from x as $k \to \infty$ is therefore

(7) $$\Omega_A(x) = V_A - \frac{x\hat{z}}{\hat{w}} = V_A - \gamma x, \quad \text{say.}$$

The Standard Race

Using (5), (6), and (7) we find that the equation of the limiting curve for the standard race is

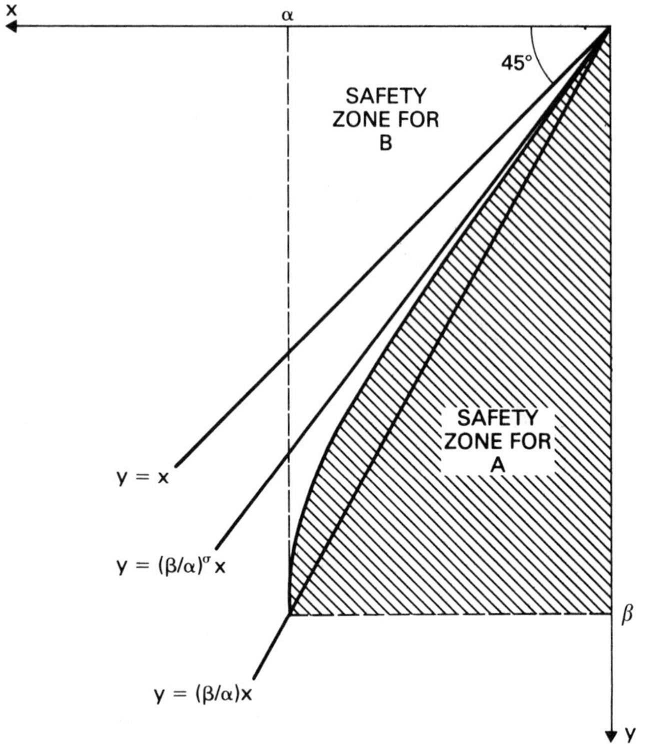

FIGURE 6
The Limiting Curve in the Standard Race

$$\frac{dy}{dx} = \lim_{k\to\infty}\left(\frac{k^\sigma (V_B - \gamma y)^\sigma - \varepsilon}{k^\sigma (V_A - \gamma x)^\sigma - \varepsilon}\right) = \left(\frac{\beta - y}{\alpha - x}\right)^\sigma \tag{8}$$

where $\alpha = V_A/\gamma$ and $\beta = V_B/\gamma$. The solution to the differential equation (8) is

$$y = \beta - ((\alpha - x)^{1-\sigma} - \alpha^{1-\sigma} + \beta^{1-\sigma})^{1/(1-\sigma)} \tag{9}$$

Assuming for instance that $\beta > \alpha$, the slope dy/dx increases with x and approaches infinity as $x \to \alpha$. At the origin the slope is $(\beta/\alpha)^\sigma$. The curve thus lies entirely to one side of the 45° line, reflecting the assumption that $\beta > \alpha$. Figure 6 sketches the curve.

The Asymmetrical Race

In this case the equation of the limiting curve is

$$\frac{dy}{dx} = \lim_{k\to\infty}\left(\frac{k^\sigma V_B^\sigma - \varepsilon}{k^\sigma (V_A - \gamma x)^\sigma - \varepsilon}\right)$$

$$= \left(\frac{\beta}{\alpha - x}\right)^\sigma \tag{10}$$

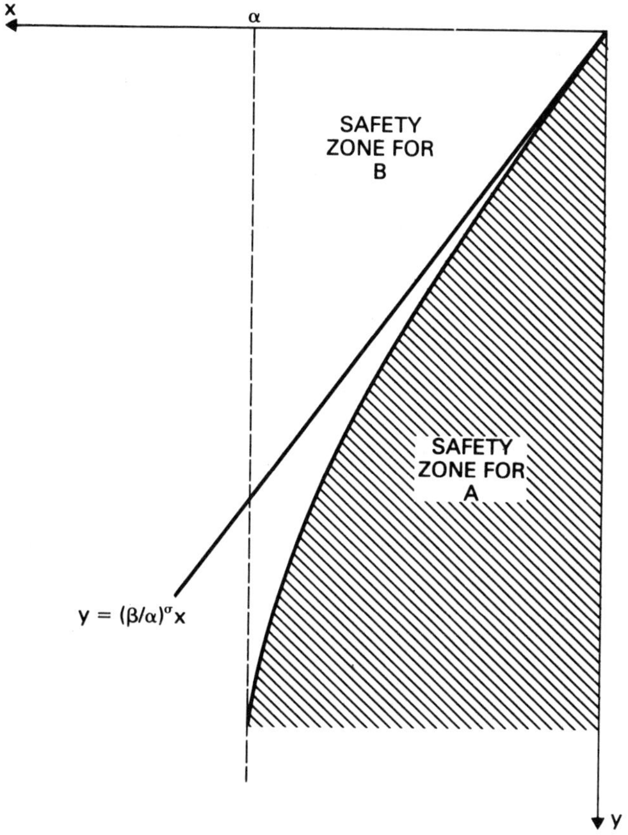

FIGURE 7
The Limiting Curve in the Asymmetrical Race

The solution to this differential equation is

$$y = \frac{\beta^{\sigma}}{1-\sigma}\left(\alpha^{1-\sigma} - (\alpha - x)^{1-\sigma}\right) \tag{11}$$

The slope of this curve is $(\beta/\alpha)^{\sigma}$ at the origin, is increasing in x, and goes to infinity as x goes to α. The curve is sketched in Figure 7.

The slope dy/dx for the asymmetrical race is everywhere steeper than it is for the standard race. The value of y at which $x = \alpha$ is therefore greater, and B's safety zone is larger. In Figure 8 we plot both curves for the case in which $V_A = V_B$ (that is $\alpha = \beta$).

VI. CONCLUSION

In a patent race between a firm already in a market and a firm attempting to enter it, there are several reasons why the incumbent and potential entrant

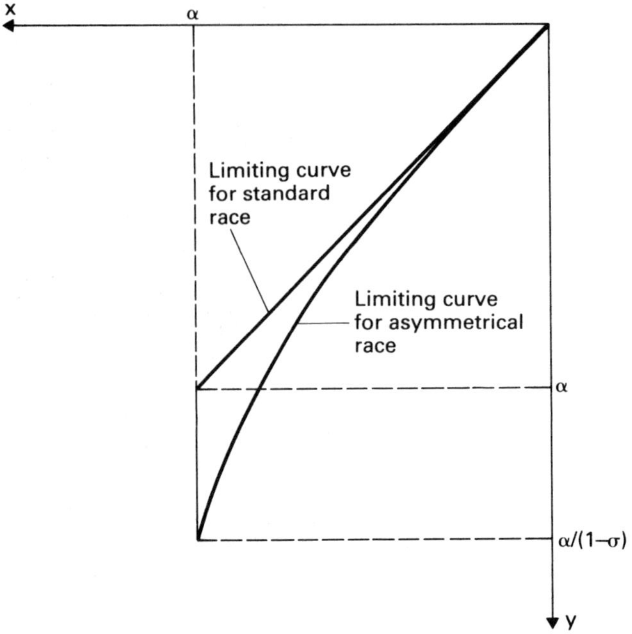

FIGURE 8
Comparison between the Two Limiting Curves

might be in an asymmetrical position. First, the two firms might value the patent differently. In particular, it is probable that the incumbent values the patent more highly than his rival, since monopoly persists if he wins the patent whereas there is competition if the rival is successful. Secondly, the firms might begin the race at different distances from the finishing line. For example, due to his past experience, the incumbent might have more knowledge than his rival at the outset of the race. Thirdly, the firms might differ in terms of R & D efficiency—that is, in terms of their ability to transform R & D effort into R & D output.

As well as these factors, there is another important asymmetry, which this paper has sought to explore. It is that the incumbent's aim is to *prevent* his rival from winning the patent, and not necessarily to win the patent himself. The rival, on the other hand, is out to *win* the patent. The analysis of our model reveals that this last asymmetry can be rather important. Indeed, it can happen that the rival is deterred from actively competing in the patent race even though he has the advantage over the incumbent in terms of all the three asymmetries described in the previous paragraph.

In this paper we have concentrated on the "pure" case, in which the incumbent's only concern is to prevent his rival from winning the patent. This is appropriate if, for example, the patent is for a technology no better than already possessed by the incumbent. If, however, the new technology is for a superior patent, then the incumbent has an incentive to win the patent in addition to his desire to stop the rival winning. The presence of this extra incentive in the "hybrid" case strengthens our conclusions regarding the pure case.

In summary, there are several sources of strategic advantage that an incumbent firm might enjoy in a patent race against a potential entrant into his market. An important one of these is that the incumbent is concerned to prevent the rival from winning, and not necessarily to obtain the patent for himself. This asymmetry appears to favour the incumbent considerably—especially if the players begin far from the finishing line. We suggest it as a possible ingredient for a theory of the persistence of monopoly.

CHRISTOPHER HARRIS AND JOHN VICKERS,
Nuffield College,
Oxford,
U.K.

ACCEPTED NOVEMBER 1984

APPENDIX A

In this appendix we prove that the sequences $\{C_n\}$ and $\{D_n\}$ exist. Since the analysis for $\{D_n\}$ is identical to that for $\{C_n\}$ we treat only $\{C_n\}$ explicitly. We also explore the properties of $\{C_n\}$ briefly. We drop the subscripts on w_A, V_A, and Ω_A since there is no risk of confusion.

Let us assume that w is increasing and continuous, that $w(0) = 0$, and that w exhibits increasing returns to scale for low effort levels, in the sense that there exists $\alpha > 0$ such that w is convex on the interval $[0, \alpha]$. Our first step is to show that $\Omega(x)$, the value of a free run from x, is well defined and continuous for all x.

Let $\omega_r(x)$ be the value of a run with r bids from x. A might choose to move to the finishing line with these r bids, or he might remain stationary. In particular, some of the bids may be zero. $\omega_r(x)$ is the solution to the problem

$$\text{(A1)} \qquad \underset{a_1, a_2, \ldots, a_r}{\text{maximise}} \; V - \sum_{i=1}^{r} a_i$$

$$\text{subject to } a_i \geqslant 0 \qquad \text{all } i$$

$$V - \sum_{i=1}^{r} a_i \geqslant 0$$

$$\sum_{i=1}^{r} w(a_i) \geqslant x$$

when this problem is feasible, otherwise $\omega_r(x) = 0$. Standard arguments show that ω_r is well defined and continuous everywhere. Notice that $\omega_{r+1} \geqslant \omega_r$ for all r. Also, if there is a solution to the problem with $r+1$ bids in which one bid is zero then no loss of generality results from considering only the problem with r bids.

If either of the expressions $\Omega(x)$ and $\max\{\omega_r(x) \mid r \geqslant 1\}$ is well defined, then both expressions are well defined and each is equal to the other. Our strategy of proof is to show that there exists an N such that if $r > N$ then there is a solution to the problem with r bids in which at least $r - N$ of the bids are zero. It will follow that $\sup\{\omega_r \mid r \geqslant 1\} = \max\{\omega_r \mid 1 \leqslant r \leqslant N\} = \omega_N$, and so that $\Omega = \omega_N$. In particular, Ω is well defined and continuous.

Let β be a value which yields a solution to the problem

$$\text{(A2)} \qquad \underset{a}{\text{maximise}} \ \frac{1}{a} w(a)$$

$$\text{subject to } 0 < a \leqslant V$$

β is well defined because w is convex in a neighbourhood of the origin. β is one of the most efficient effort rates. We assume that $w(\beta) > 0$ in order to avoid trivialities. We also assume w.l.o.g. that $\beta > \alpha$, reducing α slightly if necessary. Further, let $\bar{x} = Vw(\beta)/\beta$. This is the distance that could be covered profitably if it were possible to proceed at the most efficient rate. If it is profitable to finish from x, then $\bar{x} \geqslant x$.

Fix r and consider the problem (A1). If it is infeasible then the number of non-zero bids that A will make in a run of length r from x is zero. We now show that if (A1) is feasible then there is an upper bound to the number of non-zero bids that A will make in such a run. The cases $w(\alpha) = 0$ and $w(\alpha) > 0$ must be considered separately.

Suppose that $w(\alpha) > 0$. Let the number of non-zero bids be m. Because w is convex in $[0, \alpha]$ we may assume w.l.o.g. that at most one of these bids is less than α. Moreover the total distance moved will be exactly x. Hence

$$x \geqslant (m-1)w(\alpha)$$

But (A1) is feasible, and so $x \leqslant \bar{x}$. We conclude that $m \leqslant (\bar{x}/w(\alpha)) + 1$.

Suppose instead that $w(\alpha) = 0$. Let K be the smallest integer such that $K\alpha \geqslant \beta$. Next, $w(a)/a$ is continuous for $a \in [\alpha, \beta]$, strictly positive for $a = \beta$, and zero for $a = \alpha$. Hence there exists γ, $\alpha < \gamma < \beta$, such that $w(\gamma) > 0$ and such that the efficiency $w(a)/a$ of any bid a in the range $\alpha \leqslant a \leqslant \gamma$ is at most $1/K$ of the efficiency of β. Now the number of non-zero bids not exceeding γ must be less than K. For suppose by way of example that to the contrary $\alpha \leqslant a_i \leqslant \gamma$ for $1 \leqslant i \leqslant K$. Then

$$\begin{aligned} \sum_{i=1}^{K} w(a_i) \leqslant Kw(\gamma) &= K\gamma \frac{1}{\gamma} w(\gamma) \\ &\leqslant K\gamma \frac{1}{K}\left(\frac{1}{\beta} w(\beta)\right) \\ &< w(\beta) \\ &\leqslant w(K\gamma) \end{aligned}$$

A could therefore strictly increase his payoff by amalgamating the a_i, $1 \leqslant a_i \leqslant K$, into a single bid. This is a contradiction. Hence the number of non-zero bids not exceeding γ must indeed be less than K. Suppose that the number of non-zero bids is m. We have

$$x \geqslant (m-K)w(\gamma),$$

and, since $\bar{x} \geqslant x$, $m \leqslant K + \bar{x}/w(\gamma)$.

We have thus shown that, whether or not $w(\alpha) = 0$, there exists an upper bound N to the number of non-zero bids in a run of length r from x. In calculating $\Omega(x)$, then, we can restrict our attention to $\{\omega_r \mid 1 \leqslant r \leqslant N\}$ w.l.o.g., and $\Omega = \omega_N$ is well defined and continuous.

It is now straightforward to show that $\{C_n\}$ is well defined. For suppose that C_{n-1}

is well defined. Then C_n is the solution to the problem

$$\begin{aligned}&\underset{a,\,c}{\text{maximise}}\ c\\&\text{subject to } a \geqslant 0\\&\qquad c-w(a) \leqslant C_{n-1}\\&\qquad a \leqslant \Omega(c-w(a)),\end{aligned}$$

and consequently well defined.

We conclude this appendix with a few observations about $\{C_n\}$. Notice first that it is possible to finish profitably from x iff (A1) is feasible for $r = N$. Hence there exists $C_\infty < \infty$ such that it is possible to finish profitably from x iff $x \leqslant C_\infty$. Since $\{C_n\}$ is increasing and $C_n \leqslant C_\infty$ for all n, $C_n - C_{n-1} \to 0$ as $n \to \infty$.

Next, the increments $C_n - C_{n-1}$ are decreasing in n, and strictly decreasing where they are strictly positive. In order to see this, suppose for a contradiction that $C_n - C_{n-1} > 0$ and that $C_{n+1} - C_n \geqslant C_n - C_{n-1}$. Any solution to the problem of finishing from C_{n+1} subject to moving to within C_n of the finishing line with the first bid is feasible in the analogous problem for C_n and C_{n-1}. However, in this latter problem it involves moving strictly beyond the finishing line, contradicting the construction of C_n, which is by definition the furthest distance from which it is profitable to finish subject to moving at least to within C_{n-1} of the finishing line with the first bid.

Thirdly, $C_n \to C_\infty$ as $n \to \infty$. The proof of this is almost identical to that of Property 3 in Harris and Vickers [1985] (set $\rho = 1$ in the proof in the Appendix of that paper).

Fourthly, $C_n \to C_\infty$ finitely as $n \to \infty$. For let $a_1, a_2, \ldots, a_r$ be a solution to the problem of finishing profitably from C_∞, and suppose w.l.o.g. that $a_i > 0$ for all i. There exists n_0 such that $C_\infty - C_n < w(a_1)$ for all $n \geqslant n_0$. Now, if $C_{n_0} = C_\infty$ there is nothing left to prove. Suppose therefore that $C_\infty - C_{n_0} > 0$. Then, since $a_1, a_2, \ldots, a_r$, which is the solution to the problem of finishing from C_∞ profitably, remains feasible when the additional constraint that $w(a_1) \geqslant C_\infty - C_{n_0}$ is introduced, we have that $C_{n_0+1} = C_\infty$. Hence $C_n \to C_\infty$ finitely as claimed.

Finally we prove the result, used in the text and in the following appendix, that if $C_{n+1} > C_n$ then $C_n = C_{n-1} + w(\Omega(C_{n-1}))$. For consider the problem of covering C_n subject to moving at least to within C_{n-1} of the finishing line with the first bid. If the constraint on the first bid binds then certainly $C_n = C_{n-1} + w(\Omega(C_{n-1}))$. If it does not, then, as in the previous paragraph, $C_{n+1} = C_n$. Thus the result claimed holds.

APPENDIX B

Let w_i^δ be player i's progress function when δ is the duration of a bid. In this appendix we show how a meaningful calibration for the w_i^δ can be derived from consideration of the continuous time case. We then examine the behaviour of the solution of the δth game as $\delta \to 0$.

If, in the continuous time case, player A's bid rate at time t is $a(t)$ then his total progress over the interval $[0, T]$ is

$$\int_0^T w_A(a(t))\,dt$$

and the cumulative cost to him over the same interval is

$$\int_0^T a(t)\,dt.$$

B's cumulative cost and progress are defined analogously in terms of his bid rate $b(t)$.

Naturally a player is awarded the prize only if he reaches the finishing line in finite time. With this understanding we define $\Omega_i(v)$ as the value to player i of a free run from v.

Consider the δth game. If we think of player i as choosing a bid rate z which, once chosen, must remain constant over an interval of length δ, then i's progress over that interval will be $\int_0^\delta w_i(z)\,dt$, or $\delta w_i(z)$. Thus we define

$$w_i^\delta(z) = \delta w_i(z)$$

The cost of this bid is $\int_0^\delta z\,dt$, or δz.

We impose the following conditions on w_A and w_B in addition to those already imposed in Appendix A.

(i) For each i, $\delta w_i(1/\delta) \to 0$ as $\delta \to 0$.

(ii) There exist $h: (0, \infty) \to (0, \infty)$ and functions $\bar{w}_A$ and $\bar{w}_B$ continuous on $(0, \infty)$ such that $\bar{w}_i(z) > 0$ for each i and all $z > 0$, and such that

$$h(\delta)\delta w_i\left(\frac{z}{\delta}\right) \to \bar{w}_i(z) \qquad \text{as} \qquad \delta \to 0$$

for each i and all $z \geqslant 0$.

The earlier assumptions guarantee the existence of Ω_i^δ and sequences $\{C_n^\delta\}$ and $\{D_n^\delta\}$ for the δth game. Condition (i) states that it is not possible to move a finite distance in zero time with a fixed budget. It guarantees that the trigger zones collapse. In conjunction with the earlier assumption that w_i is convex in a neighbourhood of the origin, condition (i) also guarantees the existence of Ω_i. Condition (ii) is purely technical, and is needed in order to give a rigorous derivation of the limiting "trigger line". h is independent of i, and in effect normalises $\delta w_i((1/\delta)z)$.

The Standard Race

Let $C_\infty^\delta = \max\{C_n^\delta \mid n \geqslant 0\}$ and let C_∞ be the maximum distance from which A can finish in the continuous time case. (In the notation of Appendix A, this distance is $\bar{x}$.) C_∞ is finite, $C_\infty^\delta \leqslant C_\infty$, and $C_\infty^\delta \to C_\infty$ as $\delta \to 0$. Then D_∞^δ and D_∞ can be defined analogously for B, and similar remarks apply. Also, $0 \leqslant \Omega_i^\delta \leqslant \Omega_i$ and $\Omega_i^\delta \to \Omega$ pointwise on $[0, \infty)$ for each i. In what follows we show how the limiting behaviour of the trigger zones can be characterised in the rectangle $[0, C_\infty) \times [0, D_\infty)$.

Observe first that the widths and heights of the trigger zones are dominated by

$$\delta w_A\left(\frac{1}{\delta} V_A\right) \qquad \text{and} \qquad \delta w_B\left(\frac{1}{\delta} V_B\right)$$

respectively, and so converge to zero uniformly with δ. It follows, first, that we can restrict our attention to the line traced out by the diagonals of the trigger zones, and secondly that we can ignore the possibility that

$$C_n^\delta - C_{n-1}^\delta \neq \delta w_A\left(\frac{1}{\delta}\Omega_A^\delta(C_{n-1}^\delta)\right)$$

for the last strictly positive increment $C_n^\delta - C_{n-1}^\delta$.

The line traced out by the diagonals of the trigger zones of the δth model, parameterised by s, can be described by the following pair of differential equations:

$$X_\delta'(s) = h(\delta)(C_n^\delta - C_{n-1}^\delta) \qquad \text{if} \qquad C_{n-1}^\delta \leqslant X_\delta(s) < C_n^\delta$$
$$Y_\delta'(s) = h(\delta)(D_n^\delta - D_{n-1}^\delta) \qquad \text{if} \qquad D_{n-1}^\delta \leqslant Y_\delta(s) < D_n^\delta$$

X_δ and Y_δ are strictly increasing as long as $X_\delta(s) < C_\infty^\delta$ and $Y_\delta(s) < D_\infty^\delta$. We can therefore invert them to obtain $Q_\delta : [0, C^\delta_\infty) \to [0, \infty)$ and $R_\delta : [0, D^\delta_\infty) \to [0, \infty)$ respectively. We analyse only Q_δ explicitly.

Let $N(x, \delta)$ denote the maximum n such that $C^\delta_{n-1} \leqslant x < C^\delta_n$. Then Q_δ satisfies the differential equation

$$Q'_\delta(x) = \frac{1}{h(\delta)\,(C^\delta_{N(x,\delta)} - C^\delta_{N(x,\delta)-1})} \qquad \text{for} \qquad 0 \leqslant x < C^\delta_\infty$$

Let

$$q(x, \delta) = h(\delta)\delta w_A\left(\frac{1}{\delta}\Omega_A(C^\delta_{N(x,\delta)-1})\right)$$

Then

$$Q_\delta(x) = \int_0^x \frac{1}{q(\xi, \delta)}\, d\xi$$

for $0 \leqslant x < C^\delta_\infty$. It can be shown that $q(\xi, \delta) \to \bar{w}_A(\boldsymbol{\Omega}_A(\xi))$ uniformly in ξ over compact sub-intervals of $[0, C_\infty)$. Thus, if

$$Q(x) = \int_0^x \frac{1}{\bar{w}_A(\boldsymbol{\Omega}_A(\xi))}\, d\xi,$$

we have that $Q_\delta \to Q$ pointwise on $[0, C_\infty)$.

Now Q_δ and Q are strictly increasing, Q is continuous, and $Q_\delta \to Q$ pointwise on $[0, C_\infty)$. It follows that $Q_\delta^{-1} \to Q^{-1}$ pointwise on $[0, \bar{s})$, where $\bar{s} = \sup\{Q(x) \mid x < C_\infty\}$. Let $X = Q^{-1}$. Then we have shown that $X_\delta \to X$ pointwise on $[0, \bar{s})$. In exactly the same way one can show that $R_\delta \to R$, where

$$R(y) = \int_0^y \frac{1}{\bar{w}_B(\boldsymbol{\Omega}_B(\xi))}\, d\xi,$$

and that $Y_\delta \to Y$, where $Y = R^{-1}$ too is defined on $[0, \bar{s})$.

We have therefore shown that the line traced by the diagonals of the trigger zones of the δth model converges to the line $\{(X(s), Y(s)) \mid 0 \leqslant s < \bar{s}\}$. Then X and Y can be found directly from the differential equations

$$X'(s) = \bar{w}_A(\boldsymbol{\Omega}_A(X(s)))$$
$$Y'(s) = \bar{w}_B(\boldsymbol{\Omega}_B(Y(s)))$$

($s \in [0, \bar{s})$). This result underlies the discussion of section V.

The Asymmetric Race

In the asymmetric case the line traced by the diagonals of the trigger zones of the δth model converges to the line $\{(X(s), Y(s)) \mid 0 \leqslant s < \bar{s}\}$, where

$$X'(s) = \bar{w}_A(\boldsymbol{\Omega}_A(X(s)))$$
$$Y'(s) = \bar{w}_B(V_B)$$

($s \in [0, \bar{s})$). Here X and $\bar{s}$ are exactly as before, and the argument which establishes the form of X is unchanged. The argument which establishes the form of Y is similar but rather simpler.

THE JOURNAL OF INDUSTRIAL ECONOMICS 0022-1821 $2.00
Volume XXXIII June 1985 No. 4

STRATEGIC INVESTMENT IN AN INDUSTRY WITH A COMPETITIVE PRODUCT MARKET*

HUW DIXON

I. INTRODUCTION

THIS PAPER explores the scope for, and effect of, strategic behaviour by firms in an industry where the product market is "competitive" in the usual sense that firms are effectively price-takers. Traditionally the literature on imperfect competition has concentrated on the product market, employing the notions of the Cournot equilibrium or monopolistic competition. The model presented shows that even if firms are unable to obtain any such market power in the product market, they can still influence the market outcome through investment behaviour which determines their actual cost structure. The ability of firms to thus influence the market outcome is directly related to their market share. This is a result which is not only of theoretical interest. It is sometimes argued that for some industries concentration does not lead to welfare loss because the market may be competitive even with only a few producers (see Fisher *et al.* [1983, pp. 24–25] for the U.S. computer industry and I.B.M.). The message of this paper is that even in such competitive industries concentration still matters since firms can still behave strategically with factors such as investment and R&D.

This paper considers a model of strategic investment in the context of a two stage dynamic equilibrium with two factors of production, capital and labour. In the first "strategic" stage, firms choose their capital stocks. In the second "market" stage the capital stocks are fixed, and a competitive equilibrium occurs. The two stages of the model can be seen as capturing the distinction between the long run and the short run. The equilibrium rests on the reasonable assumption that the capital decisions of firms are irreversible in the market stage. We are thus implicitly assuming that there is no rental market for capital. In the competitive market stage the price equates supply with demand. In essence, the choice of the capital stock in the strategic stage determines the supply function that the firm has in the market stage. Thus firms are able to influence the market equilibrium to their favour through their choice of capital stock. The resultant equilibrium can be interpreted as a Nash equilibrium in supply functions (see for example Grossman [1981], Dixon [1984a]).

In evaluating the welfare consequences of the model, it is necessary to realise that the cost structure of the firm is endogenous. The choice of capital

* This is part of my D.Phil thesis. I would especially like to thank my supervisor Jim Mirrlees for his guidance, and George Yarrow for useful comments and encouragement. Paul Geroski and an anonymous referee were also extremely helpful. The financial assistance of the ESRC is acknowledged.

determines the firms "short-run" cost function. If we were only to consider the *actual* cost structure of firms, then, since price equals marginal cost in the competitive market stage, the standard welfare analysis would tell us that there was no restriction of output, and no loss of consumer surplus. However, since investment alters the firm's actual cost structure, welfare considerations need to concentrate on possible rather than actual costs. In equilibrium we find that firms are able to restrict investment and output so that the price exceeds least cost, and there is a loss of consumer surplus relative to the socially optimal outcome. This is not the only source of welfare loss.

Because capital is used strategically in this model, there is an asymmetry between capital and labour. In equilibrium the strategic use of investment leads to a bias away from capital, so that there is undercapitalisation and an excessive labour-capital ratio. This results in inefficient production, in the sense that the actual costs of producing the firm's output are in excess of the minimum technically required.

The result of undercapitalisation provides an interesting contrast with existing models of the strategic use of investment. The model which most closely resembles ours is Brander and Spencer's model of R&D expenditure [1983]. The crucial difference between the models is the assumption made about the market stage: they assume that it is Cournot. Under this assumption, they show that there is the opposite factor bias, with overcapitalisation in equilibrium. Furthermore, whereas strategic behaviour improves social welfare in the Brander and Spencer [1983] model as compared with the non-strategic case, in the model presented it leads to a loss in social welfare. Overcapitalisation can also occur in Dixit's model of strategic entry deterrence [1980, pp. 103–4].

The assumption of a competitive market stage, coupled with constant returns to scale gives the model a particularly tractable and intuitive form. In section I of the paper the basic framework is presented. In section II we explore the general properties of the equilibrium. We show that the profit to sales ratio that is, the price-cost margin) is inversely related to the elasticities of demand and supply. In section III two specifications of the general model are presented. First we derive an explicit solution to the model in the case of identical firms with Cobb–Douglas technology and constant elasticity industry demand. This example enables us to relate the strategic investment model with the standard (one stage or non-strategic) Cournot equilibrium. Furthermore, depending on the technical parameter, the strategic investment equilibrium has Cournot and Bertrand outcomes as limiting cases. We also provide a linearised model in section III, which is particularly useful for explicitly analysing the welfare properties of the model. We are able to show, in this case at least, that the welfare loss due to strategic inefficiency may be large relative to the standard welfare "triangle".

The main body of this paper treats the number of firms as given: there is a given set of active incumbents. However, the impact of entry on the model is briefly discussed. Entry adds an additional welfare loss to the model, since sunk set-up costs will in general lead to more firms than are socially optimal in the industry.

I. A MODEL OF STRATEGIC INVESTMENT

We present the general model in this section, and will consider more specific cases in section III. All functions are assumed to be differentiable when required.

Firms have a standard two-input constant-returns production function:

A1: Each firm's production function $f_i : R^2_+ \to R_+$ is homogeneous to degree one and strictly concave in each input:

$$x_i = f_i(k_i, L_i) \qquad f_k, f_L > 0 > f_{LL}, f_{kk}$$

where k_i and L_i are capital and labour inputs of the ith firm.

This assumption is stronger than required, but it simplifies the analysis. We can then define the firm's cost function in the standard manner taking the factor prices w and r as parameters.

(a) *Long-Run Cost function*: $a \cdot x$

$$a(x) = \min_{L,k \in R_+} (w \cdot L + r \cdot k) \qquad \text{subject to} \qquad f(k,L) - x \geqslant 0$$

$$= a \cdot x$$

where a is (constant) least average cost.

(b) *Short-Run Cost Function*: $k \cdot c(x/k)$

$$C(K,x) = \min_{L \in R_+} (w \cdot L + r \cdot k) \qquad \text{subject to} \qquad f(k,L) - x \geqslant 0$$

Under constant-returns we can define $k \cdot c(x/k) = k \cdot C(1, x/k)$.

Concavity of f in L implies that c is convex in output-per-unit-capital x/k. Given the technology, we can then define the "short-run" supply function, again taking advantage of constant returns.

(c) *Supply Function*: $k \cdot s(p)$

$S(k,p)$ is the output which solves:

$$\max_{x,L \in R^2_+} [p \cdot x - w \cdot L - r \cdot k] \qquad \text{subject to} \qquad f(k,L) - x \geqslant 0$$

Under A1 this can be written as $k \cdot s(p)$.

Thus $s(p)$ is the profit-maximising output-per-unit-capital. Obviously, the strict convexity and differentiability of $c(x/k)$ imply that s is strictly increasing in p, and its second derivative s'' will be positive or negative depending on c'''. In effect, through its choice of k_i, the ith firm chooses the supply function it will have in the market-stage.

We consider a two stage model. In the first "strategic" stage, firms precommit their capital stock. In the second "market stage", firms' capital stocks are fixed, and a competitive equilibrium occurs. In order to define the competitive price we need to state our assumptions about the industry demand function.

A2: Industry demand $F: R_+ \to R_+$ is bounded, continuous, and strictly decreasing when positive.

The competitive price θ which occurs in the market stage is defined implicitly by the relation:

$$(1.1) \qquad F(\theta) - \sum_{i=1}^{n} k_i \cdot s_i(\theta) = 0$$

We can thus define the implicit function which gives the competitive price θ ruling in the market stage to the n-vectors of capital stocks $\underline{k}$ chosen in the strategic move, $\theta : R^n_+ \to R_+$

$$(1.2) \qquad \theta = \theta(\underline{k})$$

Total differentiation of (1.1) yields:

$$(1.3) \qquad \frac{\partial \theta}{\partial k_i} = \frac{s_i(\theta)}{F' - \sum_{j=1}^{n} k_j \cdot s_j'} < 0$$

where primes denote derivatives with respect to price, which are evaluated at $\theta(\underline{k})$. The numerator s_i will vary between firms, whilst the denominator is common to all firms, and reflects the fact that as the price falls, firms' outputs will fall. If firms are identical then (1.1) and (1.3) simplify, since θ will depend only on the total capital stock Σk_j, as will $\partial\theta/\partial k_i$.

We are now in a position to define the firm's payoff function U_i, giving the profit earned as a function of the capital stocks chosen in the strategic move. First, however, we define the firm's profit-per-unit-capital conditional upon $\theta, \pi : R_+ \to R$

$$(1.4) \qquad \pi(\theta) = \theta \cdot s(\theta) - c(s(\theta))$$

Thus π is the nett or supernormal rate of profit on capital, once the cost-per-unit-capital r has been covered (since r is included in $c(\cdot)$, from definition (*b*)). We now have the firm's profit-function $U_i : R^n_+ \to R$.

(d) *Profit Function*: $U_i(\underline{k}) = k_i \cdot \pi(\theta(\underline{k}))$.

Having defined firms' payoffs in terms of their choices of k_i in the strategic move, we can define the equilibrium in the two stage model as a Nash equllibrium $\{\underline{k}^*, \theta^*\}$ in the game $[R_+, U_i : i = 1 \ldots n]$. The Nash equilibrium assumption seems perfectly natural here, since the capital decision is irreversible, so that firms are unable to react to each other. Whilst the model is formally defined as a Nash equilibrium in capital stocks, it is really a Nash equilibrium in supply functions. We will have more to say about this subsequently.

II. THE PROPERTIES OF THE EQUILIBRIUM

Supposing an equilibrium $\underline{k}^*$ to exist, what does it look like? We will restrict ourselves to those equilibria where all firms are producing, that is, $\underline{k}^* \gg 0$, and we shall denote the equilibrium market price $\theta^* = \theta(\underline{k}^*)$. Then $\underline{k}^*$ will be a Nash equilibrium if for all firms $i = 1 \ldots n$:

$$(2.1) \qquad U_{ki}|_{k^*} = \pi_i(\theta^*) + k_i^* \cdot \frac{d\pi}{d\theta} \cdot \frac{\partial \theta}{\partial k_i} = 0$$

where U_{ki} is the partial derivative of U_i with respect to k_i (since we shall never need cross-partials, this notation should be unambiguous). We can define the elasticity of θ with respect to k_i as:

$$(2.2) \qquad \varepsilon_i =_{\text{def}} -\frac{k_i}{\theta} \cdot \frac{\partial \theta}{\partial k_i}$$

substituting (2.2) into (2.1), and noting that by Hotelling's Lemma $d\pi/d\theta = s(\theta)$, at $\underline{k}^*$:

$$(2.3) \qquad \frac{\pi(\theta)}{\theta^* \cdot s_i(\theta^*)} = \varepsilon_i$$

Note that the LHS of (2.3) is the ith firm's profit to sales ratio. Hence in equilibrium, each firm's profit to sales ratio will be equal to the elasticity of the market price with respect to its own capital. Clearly, the profit to sales ratio must equal the price-average-cost-margin, and when we expand the LHS of (2.3) we obtain:

$$(2.4) \qquad \frac{\theta^* - \dfrac{c(s(\theta^*))}{s(\theta^*)}}{\theta^*} = \varepsilon_i$$

where $c(s(\theta))/s(\theta)$ is average cost. It should be noted that we have made no assumption of average-cost being equal to marginal cost to derive (2.4): the LHS is in principle a directly observable variable (if we leave aside problems of measuring profits, of course).

It is easily shown that the equilibrium price θ^* in the market stage will be greater than the long-run (least) average cost a_i for all firms that produce in equilibrium. If $\theta^* < a_i$, then the ith firm will make a loss if it produces anything at all, and if $\theta^* = a_i$ it will earn nothing. Since we restrict ourselves to $\underline{k}^* \gg 0$, the price must be greater than or equal to a_i. But if $\theta^* = a_i$, then the firm could reduce k_i slightly, thus increasing θ and hence earn positive profits.

In the case of identical firms (2.3) simplifies further. Since $\partial\theta/\partial k_i$ is then a function of total capital only, and so is identical across firms:

$$\frac{\partial\theta}{\partial k_i} = \frac{s(\theta)}{F' - s' \cdot \Sigma k_j} \qquad j = 1 \ldots n \tag{2.5}$$

so that from (2.2) and (2.5) we have:

$$\varepsilon_i = \frac{k_i}{\Sigma k} \cdot \frac{1}{\varepsilon_s - \varepsilon_d} \tag{2.6}$$

where ε_s and ε_d are the familiar price elasticities of supply and demand, $\varepsilon_s = (\theta/s) \cdot s'$, $\varepsilon_d = (\theta/F) \cdot F'$. Hence if all firms have an identical technology, then (2.3) becomes:

$$\frac{\pi(\theta^*)}{\theta^* \cdot s(\theta^*)} = \frac{1}{n(\varepsilon_s - \varepsilon_d)} \tag{2.7}$$

Thus the profit to sales ratio equals the reciprocal of the sum of demand and supply elasticities (evaluated at θ^*), divided by the number of firms. In an industry with $\varepsilon_s = -\varepsilon_d = 1$, and fifteen firms, the profit to sales ratio would be $1/30^{\text{th}}$.

Equation (2.7) is clearly similar to the equilibrium condition in the Cournot–Nash model. As we argue in Dixon [1984a], perhaps the most natural and convincing interpretation of the standard Cournot model is that firms pre-commit both factors of production, so that in the strategic move firms choose a capacity, and in the market stage a competitive equilibrium (occurs that is, the price clears the market). Hence the symmetric Cournot equilibrium is given by:

$$\frac{\theta^c - a}{\theta^c} = \frac{-1}{n \cdot \varepsilon_d} \tag{2.8}$$

Comparing (2.8) with the equilibrium condition for the strategic investment case, we can see that they differ in two important respects. First, on the LHS of (2.8) the price cost margin is given as a mark-up on a. Second, the RHS of (2.8) and (2.7) are directly comparable, and might lead us to expect that the profit to sales ratio in the strategic investment case will be less than in the Cournot case. However, even if this is so, we cannot infer that the equilibrium price will therefore be lower in the strategic investment case. For any given price θ, the Cournot profit to sales ratio is larger, since average costs are at their minimum. It is therefore quite possible that $\theta^* > \theta^c$ even though the inequality is reversed for the respective profit to sales ratios. No general comparison is presented in this paper.[1] However, in the linear model in section III, the Cournot price will always be the higher of the two. It can also be shown in the case of

[1] For a general treatment see Dixon [1984b, chapter 6, Theorem 6.1].

Cobb–Douglas firms and constant elasticity demand, that a sufficient condition for $\theta^c > \theta^*$ is inelastic demand ($\varepsilon_d > -1$). The presence of ε_s in (2.7) reflects the fact that in choosing its capital stock, the firm takes into account not only the downward slope of the demand curve, but also the reduction in (all) firms' outputs as θ falls. In the Cournot case, of course, these outputs are treated as constant.

An implication of the fact that $\theta^* > a_i$ is that firms will employ an inefficient technology, and incur costs in excess of a_i. The reason for this is that the firm is on its short-run cost curve in the market stage. Hence it will only employ least-cost technology if $\theta^* = a_i$. If $\theta^* > a_i$, then the firm will not be on its long-run cost-curve, and will in fact be *undercapitalised*: the firm's output capital ratio $s(\theta^*)$ is higher than the cost-minimising ratio $s(a)$, so that the firm employs an excessively labour intensive technology. Although the firm is maximising profits, the strategic structure of the model—and the resultant asymmetry between the firm's choice of capital and labour—implies that the firm does not employ the least-cost technology.

In order to bring out even more clearly the nature of the distortion, we can telescope the firm's decision into a simple optimisation programme:

$$\text{(2.9)} \qquad \max_{k_i, L_i, x_i} \theta(k_i, k_{-i}) \cdot x_i - w \cdot L_i - r \cdot k_i \qquad \text{subject to} \qquad f(k_i, L_i) - x_i \geqslant 0$$

The firm chooses x_i and L_i freely as in the standard competitive case. The strategic nature of the firm's investment decision is captured by making θ a function of k_i (and k_{-i}). The first-order conditions yield

$$\text{(2.10)} \qquad \frac{w}{r} = \frac{f_L}{f_k - \varepsilon_i \cdot s(\theta)} > \frac{f_L}{f_k}$$

From (2.9) and (2.10) we can see that the dependence of the competitive price in the firm's capital stock reduces the "marginal revenue product" from f_k to $f_k - \varepsilon_i \cdot s(\theta)$, and hence leads to a *lower* capital-labour ratio than required for least-cost production. When choosing k_i, the firm takes into account both its effect on the subgame price, and its effect on costs via the capital-labour ratio. At $\underline{k}^*$, if any firm were to increase its capital stock, the gains from a lower output-capital ratio in terms of reducing average costs would be outweighed by the resultant fall in θ. It should be clear from this simple treatment that the undercapitalisation result is general in this model, and does not depend at all on the assumption of constant returns in A1.

The symmetric industry equilibrium is depicted in Figure 1. The equilibrium price θ^* is determined by the intersection of the industry demand function and the supply function which results from the capital stocks chosen in the strategic stage. The U-shaped industry "short-run" average cost curve is marked AC. The strategic inefficiency due to under capitalisation is represented by the fact that average cost AC* is less than marginal cost in equilibrium. The industry profits $\Sigma k_i^* \cdot \pi(\theta^*)$ are given by the area A. The profit to sales ratio is given by

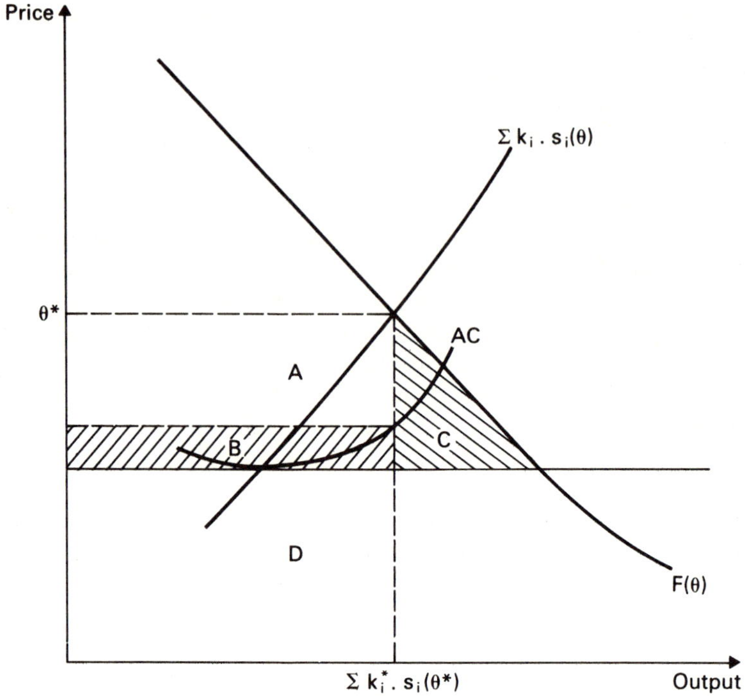

FIGURE 1
Welfare Loss

the ratio of area A to areas A, B, D. We shall now briefly consider the welfare losses in this framework employing the familiar consumer surplus approach, as in the "social costs of monopoly" literature (see Marshall [1920], Harberger [1954], Cowling and Mueller [1978] *inter alia*). Whilst this approach is open to serious criticism, it provides a useful first guide. In this model there will be two sources of lost consumers' surplus. Firstly we have the standard welfare loss given by the "triangle" under the demand curve, area C in the figure. Secondly we have the welfare loss due to strategic inefficiency, which is represented by area B in Figure 1, being the lost profits to shareholders $(AC^* - a) \cdot F(\theta^*)$. It should be noted that this strategic inefficiency is totally different in origin to the X-inefficiency as in Leibenstein [1966] and Comanor and Leibenstein [1969]. In the strategic investment model presented here the inefficiency is due to the dynamic structure of the model, not the fact that the best monopoly profit is a quiet life. In the market stage, the managers minimise costs: the inefficiency stems from the constraint the managers have imposed on themselves by their choice of capital in the strategic stage. In section III below, we show that in a linearised model (Case 2), the welfare loss due to strategic inefficiency may well be larger than the conventional triangle. This is not surprising, since the efficiency loss is $AC^* - a$ multiplied by the entire industry output.

We have now explored the properties of the strategic investment equilibrium. Even if the product market is perfectly competitive—or at least approximately so—the possibility of strategic commitment of capital would lead to prices above least-average cost.

The second important property of the model leads firms to choose under-capitalised technologies that are economically inefficient. It should be noted that this result only occurs because the firm is forced to separate its choice of capital and labour, and cannot choose them simultaneously. As we discuss in Dixon [1984a], were firms able to precommit both factors of production, and hence their capacity, then there would be no strategic factor bias, and the equilibrium of the two stage game would be Cournot. The strategic inefficiency is also related to the nature of the technology. Even in the case where firms precommit only capital, if the technology is Leontief or putty-clay, then in effect output and labour are thereby precommited, so that there will be a Cournot outcome with no strategic inefficiency. We should also note that the undercapitalisation result stems from the particular nature of the market subgame: had we assumed a Cournot equilibrium in the market stage, we would have obtained an overcapitalisation result, as in Brander and Spencer [1983].[2]

III. SOME EXPLICIT SOLUTIONS TO THE MODEL

In order to explore the mechanisms of the model more closely, it is useful to consider some specific functional forms. We will consider two cases. In case 1 we will explore the model in the case of identical firms with Cobb–Douglas technology, and constant elasticity demand. In case 2 we explore the model when firms may be different, but demand and supply functions are "linear". The second case is particularly simple for exploring the welfare loss due to strategic inefficiency. Consideration of these examples also gives us some ideas about existence in the model, since in both cases an equilibrium will exist under fairly weak conditions.

Case 1: Constant Elasticities: Cournot and Bertrand Outcomes as Limiting Cases of the Strategic Investment Model

In the case of identical firms, we recall the simple equilibrium condition (2.7):

$$\frac{\pi(\theta)}{\theta\cdot s(\theta)}=\frac{1}{n(\varepsilon_s-\varepsilon_d)}$$

Since the RHS of the equation is expressed in terms of ε_s and ε_d, we first consider the model when these are parameters. It will be recalled that ε_s is the elasticity of supply-per-unit capital $s(\theta)$ with respect to the market price.

[2] The market stage can be generalised to allow for a wider range of market outcomes. Yarrow [1985] has allowed for a conjectural variations model.

Cobb–Douglas technologies yield constant elasticity supply functions. Formally, if we specialise A5 to:

A1(a): $x = L^{\alpha} \cdot k^{1-\alpha} : \varepsilon_s = \alpha/1-\alpha \qquad (0 < \alpha < 1)$

We also specialise A2 to constant elasticity of demand:

A2(a): $F(p) = p^{-\beta} \qquad (\varepsilon_d = -\beta)$

Under A1(a) and A2(a), the profit to sales ratio will be uniquely determined by the three parameters of the model: n, α and β. Before proceeding to the explicit solution, however, it is necessary to consider whether or not an equilibrium exists: equation (2.8) merely tells us that the first order conditions are satisfied. Under A1–2 we know that there is a unique vector $\underline{k}^*$ which satisfies (2.8), in which all firms capital stocks are the same ($k_i^* = k^*$ for all i). Define ϕ where:

$$(3.1) \qquad \phi = (n-1) \cdot k^*/k_a$$

and k_a is the competitive level of the capital stock ($a = \theta(k_a)$). Given that the other firms choose k^*, firm i will never want to choose its own capital stock so that the price is less than a, so we can restrict our attention to $k_i \leqslant (1-\phi) \cdot k_a$. Under what conditions will $\underline{k}^*$ so defined be an equilibrium? Proposition 1 gives a sufficient condition for the payoff function to be quasi-concave.

Proposition 1 (A1(a), A2(a)): *A unique symmetric equilibrium exists if*

$$\frac{1}{1-\phi} \geqslant \frac{1-\varepsilon_d+2\cdot\varepsilon_s}{2\cdot(\varepsilon_s-\varepsilon_d)}$$

The proof is given in the appendix. A sufficient condition for Proposition 1 to be satisfied is that demand is elastic. If there are more than a few firms, ϕ will be close to unity, so that we can be reasonably assured of existence.

Under A1(a) the profit to sales ratio is given by:

$$(3.2) \qquad \frac{\pi(\theta)}{\theta \cdot s(\theta)} = [1-\alpha]\left[1-\left(\frac{a}{\theta}\right)^{1/1-\alpha}\right]$$

We can now express (2.7) in terms of our parameters and solve for θ^*.

$$(3.3) \qquad \theta^* = a \cdot \left[1 - \frac{1}{n\cdot(\alpha+(1-\alpha)\cdot\beta)}\right]^{\alpha-1}$$

(3.3) is particularly useful if we wish to compare the strategic investment equilibrium with the Cournot equilibrium. Recall that in Dixon [1984a] we interpret the Cournot equilibrium as corresponding to the case where the firm precommits both factors of production, and hence chooses its capacity in the strategic move. In this case, firms will always choose a cost minimising capital labour ratio. Since there are constant returns to scale, the resultant Cournot equilibrium is:

$$(3.4) \qquad \theta^c = a \cdot \left(1 - \frac{1}{n \cdot \beta}\right)^{-1}$$

Comparing (3.4) and (3.3) it can be seen that since $0 < \alpha < 1$, a sufficient condition for the Cournot price θ^c to exceed θ^* is that $\beta \leqslant 1$.

Having computed the equilibrium values $\{k^*, \theta^*\}$ under A1(a) and A2(b), we shall briefly consider how the equilibrium varies with the technological parameter α. When the firm chooses k_i in the strategic move, it chooses the supply function it will have in the market subgame. The parameter α determines the elasticity of the "short run" supply function $s(\theta)$: as $\alpha \to 1$, $\varepsilon_s \to +\infty$; as $\alpha \to 0$, $\varepsilon_s \to 0$. Thus α can be interpreted as representing the flexibility of production in the market stage. With Cobb–Douglas technology the limiting cases of $\alpha = 1$ or $\alpha = 0$ are not in themselves interesting, but they can act as a guide to the intuition for α close to 0 or 1. If $\alpha = 0$, then $x = k$ (for $L > 0$), so that output is totally determined by investment in the strategic move. We would thus expect a Cournot outcome, where the profit to sales ratio is $-1/\varepsilon_d$. If $\alpha = 1$, then $x = L$ ($k > 0$), so that precommitment does not affect the short run supply function, which would be perfectly elastic at $\theta = w$. In this case we would expect the Bertrand case of a zero profit to sales ratio.

The reasoning from these two cases is indeed correct, since from equations (3.3) and (3.4) it follows that:

$$\alpha \to 1 \quad \text{implies} \quad \frac{\theta^*}{a} \to \left[1 - \frac{1}{n}\right]^0 = 1 \qquad (n \geqslant 2) \text{ "Bertrand"}$$

$$\alpha \to 0 \quad \text{implies} \quad \frac{\theta^*}{a} \to \left[1 - \frac{1}{n\beta}\right]^{-1} \qquad (n \cdot \beta > 1) \text{ "Cournot"}$$

(Note that a itself varies with α.) Thus, depending on the elasticity of supply, the markup of price over least cost has the Cournot and the Bertrand values as limiting cases.

More can be said about the relationship with the Cournot case. If firms have constant returns Leontief technology, for example, then the output (or rather capacity) will be tied down in the strategic stage, and hence the Cournot equilibrium will occur. A further interesting property of the Leontief case is that there is no strategic inefficiency since, given its capacity, the firm will not employ labour over and above the minimum technically required, whatever the market price. Indeed, there will be no inefficiency for any technology for which the capacity is determined by the choice of capital stock. For example, if technology is putty-clay, then the capital labour ratio will be efficient, and the strategic investment equilibrium will be the Cournot equilibrium.

Case 2: The Welfare Loss in a Linear Model

In this section we show how the model works out in the linear case, where the supply and demand functions in the market subgame are linear. Linearity of the firm's supply-per-unit-capital function $s(p)$, can be seen as arising from a symmetric Cobb–Douglas technology (where the exponents on capital and labour are both 0.5). This is a special case of assumption A1(a), if we allow for non-identical firms:

A1(b): $x_i = k_i^{0.5} \cdot L_i^{0.5}$

From this specification of the production function we can derive the functions $s(\theta)$, $\pi(\theta)$. These are best expressed using the parameter v, where v is defined as the least-cost or efficient output-capital ratio, so that $s(a) = v$.

$$(3.5) \qquad s(\theta) = \frac{v}{a} \cdot \theta$$

$$(3.6) \qquad \pi(\theta) = \frac{v}{2a}(\theta^2 - a^2)$$

On the demand side we give a special case of A2:

A2(b): $F(p) = \max[0, \bar{p} - p]$

Thus we assume linearity and normalise so that $F' = -1$. Under these assumptions the market stage equilibrium condition implies the simple relation between capital stocks and price:

$$(3.7) \qquad \theta(\underline{k}) = \frac{\bar{p}}{1 + \Sigma k_i \cdot \omega_i} \qquad \text{where} \qquad \omega_i = v_i / a_i$$

Substitution of (3.7) into (3.6) yields the payoff function:

$$(3.8) \qquad U_i(\underline{k}) = \frac{\bar{p}^2}{2} \cdot \frac{\omega_i \cdot k_i}{1 + \Sigma \omega_j \cdot k_j} - r \cdot k_i$$

Thus U_i is strictly concave in k_i in this linear case. Hence an equilibrium exists. It can be shown that the equilibrium price is less than the Cournot price (Dixon [1984b, Theorems 5.1 and 6.1]).

One of the properties of the strategic investment equilibrium is that production is inefficient. The rest of this section of the paper is devoted to deriving explicit terms for this inefficiency in the linear case.

The excessive labour-capital ratio leads to average-costs in excess of minimum average costs a. Hence the strategic-inefficiency in production can be measured by:

$$(3.9) \qquad \text{AC} - a = \frac{(\theta - a)^2}{2\theta}$$

We are now in a position to derive an expression giving the total welfare loss in the strategic investment game as a function of θ^*. There are, we recall, two sources of "lost" consumer's surplus in the strategic investment model, as depicted in Figure 1. First, we have the standard welfare-loss given by the "triangle" under the demand curve, area A.

$$(3.10) \qquad \Delta w_1 = \frac{(\theta - a)^2}{2}$$

Second, we have the additional efficiency loss given by area B. This reflects the consumer surplus lost to shareholders due to average costs exceeding their minimum. From (3.9) this area is given by:

$$(3.11) \qquad \Delta w_2 = F(\theta) \cdot \left[\frac{c(s(\theta))}{s(\theta)} - a \right] = \frac{(\bar{p} - \theta) \cdot (\theta - a)^2}{2\theta}$$

Hence the total welfare-loss $\Delta w = \Delta w_1 + \Delta w_2$ is given by:

$$(3.12) \qquad \Delta w = \frac{(\theta - a)^2}{\theta} \cdot \frac{\bar{p}}{2}$$

It is quite clear that the total welfare loss is strictly monotonic for $\theta \geqslant a$. However, whilst the standard welfare-loss triangle increases with θ, the strategic inefficiency Δw_2 is not monotonic. From (3.11) we can see that the strategic inefficiency is equal to zero both when output is zero ($\theta = \bar{p}$), and when AC $= a$ ($\theta = a$). We could reasonably expect that the welfare loss due to strategic inefficiency might be rather large relative to the standard welfare loss. If we compare (3.10–3), then:

$$\Delta w_2 = -[\Delta w_1 / \varepsilon_d]$$

Thus the consumer surplus lost through strategic inefficiency equals the surplus lost via the triangle divided by the elasticity of demand. For $\varepsilon_d \geqslant -1$, the strategic inefficiency will represent the more important welfare loss. This is not so surprising, since the welfare loss due to strategic inefficiency is the excess cost multiplied by the entire industry output, so that even if the average cost is only slightly in excess of the minimum, it will be considerably magnified. The importance of strategic inefficiency in this model is not peculiar to this specification.

IV. STRATEGIC INVESTMENT AND ENTRY

The main body of this paper has assumed that there is a fixed set of active incumbents in the industry, with no entry or exit. This section provides a simple example of how entry might be modelled, and its welfare implications. It needs to be made quite clear from the outset that this section is more an outline than a detailed formal analysis. The special case considered provides an interesting illustration that is reasonably typical.

There are many ways of treating entry, depending on when entry is allowed.[3] We shall consider the simplest case: we add an extra entry move prior to the

[3] In effect, the treatment presented does not allow for entry after the investment decisions have been taken. This contrasts with models of entry deterrence where entry may occur after the incumbents have made their investment decision (e.g. Dixit [1980]).

strategic stage of the model. Firms incur sunk set-up costs $\mu > 0$. There is an infinite set of identical firms, which make their entry decision in some pre-ordained order. Given the number of firms that decide to enter, a strategic investment equilibrium occurs. No entry occurs after the initial entry move. In evaluating the profits from entry, firms have perfect foresight.

With strictly positive set-up costs and constant returns to scale production, the model is of course the rather special case of natural monopoly (since the industry cost structure is super-additive (see Baumol *et al.* [1982]). Whilst this makes the analysis very simple, the qualitative results are generally valid.

Consider first the social optimum in this industry, which we shall take to be the Ramsey solution, which maximises the consumer surplus subject to the self-financing constraint. The Ramsey solution is the triplet $\{n_r, a_r, k_r\}$, the optimal number of firms, price, and capital stock respectively. Since the industry is a natural monopoly, the analysis is very simple, since we know that $n_r = 1$. Furthermore, it will be socially optimal to produce efficiently, with the output capital ratio v. Since demand is downward sloping, the Ramsey optimal price and capital stock are those which maximise output subject to the finance constraint:

$$(4.1) \qquad \max \quad F(a_r)$$

$$(4.2) \qquad \text{subject to} \qquad k_r \cdot v \cdot (a_r - a) \geqslant \mu$$

$$(4.3) \qquad F(a_r) = k_r \cdot v$$

How does the strategic investment equilibrium with entry compare with the Ramsey optimum? Let us denote this equilibrium by the triplet $\{n^*, K^*, \theta^*\}$, where K^* is the industry capital stock, and $\theta = \theta(K^*)$ (since firms are identical, the equilibrium is symmetric). These values are determined by the equilibrium condition (2.7) between the active incumbents, plus the entry condition. Both of these conditions can be summarised using the "outcome function" $\Omega(n)$, giving profits net of entry costs when there are n firms in the industry. For a broad class of standard models Ω is a uniquely defined, strictly decreasing function of n, and from (2.7) $\Omega \to 0$ as $n \to \infty$. The number of firms n^* is determined by $\Omega(n^*) \geqslant \mu \geqslant \Omega(n^* + 1)$. This will in turn define the equilibrium capital stock in the industry.

Given this skeletal outline, we have enough information to compare the strategic investment equilibrium with the Ramsey optimum. There are four points of contrast which are of interest:

(i) *Excess Entry*: $n^* \geqslant n_r$. Unless entry costs are large, $n^* > n_r$.

To see why, note that if $\Omega(1) > \mu$, there will be more than one firm. Entry in excess of the social optimum will occur unless entry costs are large, where "large" means that $\mu > \Omega(2)$.

(ii) *Inefficiency in Production*: We know from the analysis in section II that the method of producing output will be inefficient, being under-capitalised. This is unchanged by entry, since $\theta^* > a$ for all finite n.

(iii) *Excessive Price*: $\theta^* > a_r$.

This must be so if the incumbents are to cover their entry costs μ. From (i), fixed costs in the industry $n^* \cdot \mu$ are at least as great as in the Ramsey case. But for $\theta > a$, production is inefficient by (ii). For any given price, therefore, industry profits are less than in the efficient Ramsey case (see (4.2)). Hence the equilibrium price θ^* must exceed the Ramsey price.

(iv) *Underinvestment*: $K^* < K_r$. There is less investment in the industry than in the Ramsey case.

This follows from (ii) and (iii). Since $\theta^* > a_r$, industry output is less than optimal. But $s(\theta^*) > v$ from (ii), so that $K^* < K_r$.

In the strategic investment model with entry, there are too many firms which underinvest and are inefficient. In essence there are too many firms producing too little output with too little capital. As should be quite clear from the analysis, the conclusions (i)–(iv) will apply beyond the case of fixed set-up costs plus constant returns technology. However, the case of natural monopoly is rather special.

What happens if firms have the more standard U-shaped long run average cost curves? These can be seen as arising from a diminishing returns to scale production function with strictly positive fixed or sunk costs. All comparisons

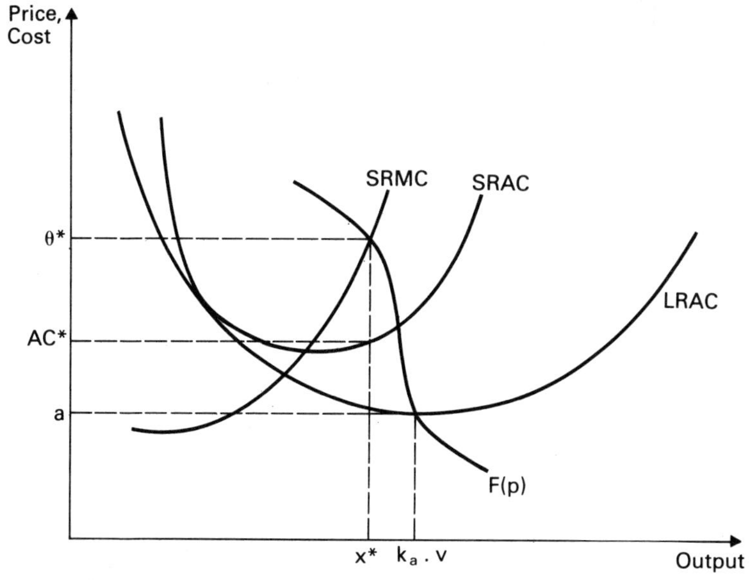

FIGURE 2
Chamberlinian Excess Capacity

(i)–(iii) will still be directly valid. The only important modification concerns comparison (iv). If we ignore the integer problem, in the Ramsey solution each firm will produce at the bottom of its "long run" average cost curve. This implies a certain capital stock for each firm, denoted k_a. However, in the strategic investment equilibrium the zero profit entry condition will mean that firms will produce at below the least cost capacity, as depicted in Figure 2, which depicts a symmetric equilibrium as in Figure 1, except that the LRAC is U-shaped. Thus we can extend (iv) to include the standard "Chamberlinian" undercapacity result. Not only are firms off their LRAC as in the constant returns case, but the output is below the minimum economic scale ($k^* < k_a$). With the introduction of a U-shaped cost function, we have a rather paradoxical result. Given the capital stocks chosen in equilibrium, there is overutilisation of capacity, an excessive output-capital ratio. This is due to strategic inefficiency. The entry condition, however, implies that the capital stock is too small, being less than the "capacity" level k_a.

V. CONCLUSION

There may still be a relationship between concentration and welfare loss even in an industry where conditions in the product market are competitive. Firms can employ such variables as investment to influence the market outcome, and their ability to do so is directly related to their "market share", interpreted as the firm's share in the industry capital stock. This leads to a price which is higher than the price that occurs when investment is not employed strategically, and there is a corresponding welfare loss due to the resultant restriction of output. The strategic use of investment in this way also gives rise to an additional inefficiency in production, since the technology will be too labour intensive. In the simple linear model presented in section III, the welfare loss due to this strategic inefficiency may be larger than the loss due to the price being too high. This suggests that the evaluation of monopoly power needs to go beyond a simple analysis of the conditions in the product market and the actual cost structure of firms, and to take into account such strategic behaviour and the distortions to which it gives rise.

HUW DIXON
Birkbeck College,
London University,
7–15 Gresse Street,
London W1P 1PA,
U.K.

ACCEPTED NOVEMBER 1984

APPENDIX

Proof of Proposition 1

We show that U_i is strictly quasi-concave in k_i. A necessary and sufficient condition for quasi-concavity is that *if* $U_{ki} = 0$ then the second partial U_{kki} is non-positive. Now,

$$U_{ki} = \pi(\theta) + k_i \cdot s(\theta) \cdot \frac{\partial \theta}{\partial k_i} = \pi(\theta) - \frac{1}{\varepsilon_s - \varepsilon_d}(\theta \cdot s(\theta) \cdot \sigma)$$

where

$$\sigma = \frac{K_i}{\Sigma k_j} \qquad (j = 1 \dots n),$$

σ being the ith firm's capital share. If $U_{ki} = 0$, then

$$\frac{\pi(\theta)}{\theta \cdot s(\theta)} = \frac{\sigma}{\varepsilon_s - \varepsilon_d}$$

If we evaluate U_{kki} when $U_{ki} = 0$ we find after some manipulation that:

$$\left.\frac{\partial U_i^2}{\partial k_i^2}\right|_{U_{ki}=0} = -\frac{1}{\varepsilon_s - \varepsilon_d} \cdot \frac{\pi(\theta)}{\Sigma k_j} \cdot \left[\varepsilon_s \cdot 2 \cdot \frac{(1-\sigma)}{\sigma} - \varepsilon_d \cdot \left(\frac{2-\sigma}{\sigma}\right) - 1\right]$$

This will be non-positive if

$$\frac{1}{\sigma} \geqslant \frac{1 - \varepsilon_d + 2 \cdot \varepsilon_s}{2 \cdot (\varepsilon_s - \varepsilon_d)}$$

But $\sigma \leqslant 1 - \phi$ (for profits to be positive).

THE JOURNAL OF INDUSTRIAL ECONOMICS 0022-1821 $2.00
VOLUME XXXIII June 1985 No. 4

PRODUCT DIVERSITY AND MONOPOLISTIC COMPETITION UNDER UNCERTAINTY*

NORMAN J. IRELAND

I. INTRODUCTION

MONOPOLISTIC competition with free entry is of course traditionally characterised by the individual firm producing at the tangency between average revenue and average cost curves. However if output has to be decided *ex ante* of the position of the average revenue curve being revealed, then this description is no longer adequate. In fact two additional factors need to be incorporated. The first is that the firm's attitude towards risk combined with stochastic variations of marginal revenue may imply an adjustment in optimal output. In particular, if the firm is risk averse then the possibility of an extra dollar marginal revenue will not counter-balance the (same probability) possibility of a dollar less marginal revenue. Thus desired output will be less. This result is well known in the theory of the firm, emanating from papers by Sandmo [1971] and Ishii [1977] amongst others.

If, as is likely, the uncertainty relates to demand conditions in the industry as a whole rather than being limited to demand for a particular firm's (differentiated) product, a second factor is also important. If firms are risk averse then the possibility of a positive profit of one dollar will not counter-balance the (same probability) possibility of a loss of one dollar. Thus at expected profit of zero, firms will leave the industry, decreasing the number of products available, and increasing the demand for those remaining. For the individual firm which remains in the industry while uncertainty is imposed on the industry's demand, two effects via demand are seen. One is the increase in demand for the firm's product due to decreased competition and the other is the lower evaluation of demand due to the risk aversion of the firm.

The effect of uncertainty on the output of the individual firm may be ambiguous in a totally general model as the two effects above influence desired output in different directions. Also the market equilibrium nature of the monopolistic competition model implies that if output is reduced in firms within the industry, this increases the incentive for new firms to enter the industry and may indeed mean that the number of firms increases rather than decreases with the onset of uncertainty. Thus both the level of output in an individual firm and the number of firms within the industry may respond with either sign to the introduction of uncertainty, although we can rule out the case where both

* The author is grateful to participants in the meeting of the Industrial Economics/Economic Theory Study Groups, Oxford 1984, and to the editors and referees of this Journal for a number of valuable comments.

increase. In this paper we wish to study and demonstrate these possibilities and investigate their welfare implications.

As we are considering the equilibrium of an industry composed of differentiated but similar products, we will take as our source of uncertainty the level of market demand. Thus next period's demand for all kinds of ice cream is dependent on random weather conditions; next period's demand for all makes of washing machine are dependent on unknown consumer preferences concerning washing machines and other commodities as well as on consumers' incomes. We will not be focussing primarily on uncertainty which arises over a specific firm's share in a given market demand—due for instance to incomplete consumer information, although the model can be interpreted in this way except in the analysis of welfare effects where a rather different approach would be needed.

In section II the model is outlined and basic assumptions are discussed. In section III an industry equilibrium is defined and studied for the "symmetric" case of identical firms. It is argued that, under very general assumptions, incorporating a Nash quantity-setting non-cooperative game augmented by conjectural variations embodied in agents' behaviour, an increase in uncertainty will result in a decrease in a measure of aggregate industry supply. In section IV we take a special case to investigate the composition of this decrease in terms of changes in number of firms (products) and output per firm (product). In section V, welfare aspects are considered and it is shown that, in a non-trivial set of circumstances, uncertainty will *increase* the expected net welfare created by the industry. Section VI summarises the conclusions.

II. THE MODEL

Providing that there are a sufficient number of candidate firms able to enter the industry at zero cost, we can define long run monopolistic competition equilibrium under uncertainty by requiring that the expected utility of a firm within the industry is the same as that obtained by a firm outside the industry, and that each firm conceives its output decisions as maximising its expected utility given its conjecture concerning the response (if any) of industry supply as a whole to such decisions. Each firm faces identical demand and cost conditions (i.e. firms are symmetric) and are affected by the same industry-wide uncertainty over demand. Thus we will define

(i) *Demand*. The price at which a typical (j^{th}) firm can sell its product is p_j given by

$$(1) \qquad p_j = \alpha f(x, z) \qquad f_x \leqslant 0; f_z < 0$$

where α is of the form

$$(2) \qquad \alpha = \mu + \sigma r$$

In (2), r is a random variable with mean zero and variance one. Thus the parameters μ and σ^2 are the mean and variance of α. The function $f(x, z)$ is differentiable with negative partial derivative with respect to a measure of industry supply, z, and non-positive partial derivative with respect to the firm's own output, x. Note that to the extent that firms supply differentiated products, z is not merely the sum of individual firms' outputs. For instance, a one per cent increase in the number of producing firms combined with a one per cent fall in output per firm may well increase z, even though total quantity supplied by the industry is unchanged, due to the greater variety of choice available.

Thus if there are n producing firms

$$(3) \qquad z = g(x, n) \qquad g_x > 0; g_n > 0$$

(ii) *Cost.* We will define

$$(4) \qquad c_j = c(x) \qquad c_x > 0; c(0) > 0$$

as the cost incurred by the typical (j^{th}) firm. We will assume that (4) is sufficiently convex (or not concave) that second-order conditions hold where necessary. Also we will assume that there are no interproduct economies of scale (economies of scope, see Waterson [1983]). Thus each firm will produce at most one product.

(iii) *Entry and Exit.* There are an arbitrarily high number of potential firms. The decision to exit or enter the industry is taken on the basis of the expected utility from participation. If the initial Nash equilibrium of production plans of firms currently in the industry yields a level of expected utility per firm not equal to the level that can be obtained from non-participation, then entry or exit takes place and a new Nash equilibrium of the revised group of participating firms is reached. This process is repeated until the expected utility of participating firms is the same as that of non-participating firms. We will take the latter level as zero without loss of generality. Only when equilibrium is reached does output take place, and only after output has been produced is the actual demand regime (value of α) revealed.

(iv) *Conjectural Variations.* The nature of the Nash equilibrium of participating firms is that each firm maximises its expected utility given other firms' behaviour but assuming a specific response of the rest of the industry to changes in its output. This conjectured response is to the effect that if the firm increases (decreases) its output by one per cent, it believes that total industry supply as measured by the index z increases (decreases) by η per cent, where η is common for all firms and is a constant conjectural elasticity defined by[1]

$$(5) \qquad \eta = \frac{dz}{dx}\frac{x}{z}$$

Of course, the industry's actual response may be very different to that conjectured. In this sense, conjectural variations are not "rational" (see Perry [1982]) unless $\eta = 0$. In this case of competitive pricing (Spence [1976]) or

[1] A similar treatment of a constant elasticity η is used in Ireland [1983a]. Koenker and Perry [1981] use a rather different formulation of conjectural variation.

large group of firms (Dixit and Stiglitz [1977]), the rest of the industry is perceived by a firm to "make room" for increases in its output, so that z is unaffected. More generally we will consider that $0 \leqslant \eta \leqslant \bar{\eta}$, indicating a range of possible conjectural elasticities representing the degree of apparent collusion in the industry (Cubbin [1983]). The value of η which would imply that the industry's behaviour mimicked joint profit maximisation of participating firms would depend on the nature of z, that is the form of (3). Also the value of η may combine conjectures over entry and exit with those over other firms' output responses. In the absence of such conjectures over entry and exit, a pure Nash equilibrium would involve a value for η of $1/n$.

III. THE INDUSTRY EQUILIBRIUM UNDER UNCERTAINTY

Given the assumptions stated in the last section, we require for an industry long-run equilibrium that:

$$E\{V(\pi)\} = 0 \tag{6}$$

and

$$E\{V_\pi(\pi) \cdot \pi_x^*\} = 0 \tag{7}$$

where $V(\cdot)$ is the (typical) firm's utility function which is increasing in profit, π, and also strictly concave to represent the firm's decision-maker's risk aversion. Equation (6) is thus a generalisation of the zero profit condition for free entry and exit. Equation (7) is the marginal utility from the conjectured marginal profit (distinguished as π_x^*) from producing (and selling) an additional unit, and incorporates the conjectural elasticity η. Thus

$$\pi = \alpha f(x, z)x - c(x) \tag{8}$$

and

$$\pi_x^* = \alpha f(x, z)\{1 - \varepsilon - \eta\theta\} - c_x(x) \tag{9}$$

where
$$\varepsilon = -f_x x/f > 0$$
$$\theta = -f_z z/f > 0$$

and η is defined by (5).

If x were fixed then (6) would imply that z is lower under uncertainty than under certainty, since in the former case $E(\pi) > 0$ due to the concavity of $V(\cdot)$, and $\sigma > 0$. Similarly if z were fixed then (7) would imply that output per firm is less under uncertainty as the single competitive firm analysis of Sandmo [1971] would be applicable. Furthermore any increase in uncertainty ($d\sigma > 0$) would imply less z (if x was fixed) and less x (if z was fixed); the latter result provided that the coefficient of absolute risk aversion is non-increasing in income (a commonly accepted proposition) is due to Ishii [1977]. As our model is based on the notion that neither x nor z can be taken as fixed, a comparative analysis of their simultaneous responses to increased uncertainty requires (6) and (7) to be considered simultaneously determining x and z, while (3) then yields the number of active firms n. Obviously the equilibrium (x, z, n) will depend on the amount of uncertainty, specifically on the parameter σ. To facilitate analysis, we write (6) and (7) in the implicit form:

$$\phi(x, z; \sigma) = 0 \tag{6'}$$

$$\psi(x, z; \sigma) = 0 \tag{7'}$$

Total differentiation of the implicit functions (6′) and (7′) yield

$$\begin{pmatrix} \phi_z & \phi_x \\ \psi_z & \psi_x \end{pmatrix} \begin{pmatrix} dz/d\sigma \\ dx/d\sigma \end{pmatrix} = \begin{pmatrix} -\phi_\sigma \\ -\psi_\sigma \end{pmatrix} \tag{10}$$

We will argue that the following sign pattern holds:

$$\begin{pmatrix} - & + \\ - & - \end{pmatrix} \begin{pmatrix} dz/d\sigma \\ dx/d\sigma \end{pmatrix} = \begin{pmatrix} + \\ + \end{pmatrix} \tag{10'}$$

where the + sign for ϕ_x is replaced by a zero value if $\eta = 0$, as then ϕ_x is simply ψ and thus zero. The value of ϕ_z and ψ_z reflect the fact that both expected utility and the expected utility from the marginal unit produced is less if industry supply is greater as price becomes depressed. In fact $\psi_z < 0$ represents an assumption as it is conceivable that the marginal revenue curve could shift up while the average revenue shifted down. In this case it may be that $\psi_z \geqslant 0$, but we will discount this possibility, although in fact our analysis could be extended, via a dynamic stability of equilibrium argument, to incorporate it. We also have $\psi_x < 0$ as a second-order condition if $\eta > 0$ does not affect the sign. On the right hand side, $\phi_\sigma < 0$ because of the concavity of $V(\cdot)$ and $\psi_\sigma < 0$, assuming non-increasing absolute risk aversion, following the argument of Ishii [1977]. Note that the sign pattern is consistent with the cases discussed above where one of x and z is fixed.

By Cramer's rule we have immediately that

$$dz/d\sigma < 0$$

and

$$dx/d\sigma \text{ is ambiguous.}$$

Thus we can state

Proposition 1. A mean-preserving increase in risk (variance of α) will reduce the equilibrium level of an index of industry supply, providing the coefficient of absolute risk aversion of the firm is non-increasing in profit.

Proposition 1 is a result for the industry in Nash equilibrium which is analogous to the Sandmo/Ishii results for the single competitive firm. We will see in the next section that the apparent ambiguity in response of the typical firm's output is confirmed and that both output per firm and number of firms can change in either direction. Proposition 1, however, assures us that at least one of these will decrease with uncertainty.

Before proceeding to a more specific analysis, it should be pointed out that comparative statics of (6) and (7) with respect to μ would yield a negative right-hand-side vector. Then $dz/d\mu > 0$ while $dx/d\mu$ is ambiguous, (although the sign of $dx/d\mu$ is not necessarily opposite to the sign of $dx/d\sigma$). However this yields the result that an upward shift in demand increases the supply of industry services but the source of this increase—whether from increased output per firm or an increase in the number of firms or both—is not determined.

IV. A SPECIFIC CASE

In the introduction, we conjectured that uncertainty might increase output per firm (by reducing the number of firms) or increase the number of firms (by reducing output per firm). In the last section, a fairly general analysis allowed us to conclude that an index of industry supply would always fall in response to increased uncertainty, but the possibility that both output per firm and number of firms do not decrease simultaneously remains. In this section we will show within a simple and tractable example that the following three possibilities can exist for feasible ranges of parameters:

(i) uncertainty leads to fewer firms and lower output per firm in long-run monopolistic competition equilibrium,
(ii) uncertainty leads to less firms and more output per firm in long-run monopolistic competition equilibrium,
(iii) uncertainty leads to more firms and less output per firm in long-run monopolistic competition equilibrium.

Although our example will be far from general, it will suffice to show that these three cases can all easily exist and that (ii) and (iii) are not mere curiosities. A particular reason for demonstrating this is the possibility that uncertainty may change the constituents of industry services so that although these decrease, reducing net welfare, the mix of constituents may improve in terms of efficiency to such an extent that net welfare is increased overall. We will return to this topic in the next section where we will also consider some more general issues in welfare and regulation.

As well as taking a particular welfare function to generate a specific demand system, our analysis will also be simplified by only investigating the effect of the onset of small uncertainty from an initial certainty equilibrium. Thus we compare (6′) and (7′) at $\sigma = 0$ and $\sigma = d\sigma > 0$. When $\sigma = 0$, (6′) and (7′) are solved by x and z which equate π and π_x^* ((8) and (9)) to zero and are independent of firms' utility functions. On the other hand, a slight complication occurs because both (6′) and (7′) have zero derivatives with respect to σ at $\sigma = 0$. The reason for this is that moving from $\sigma = \sigma_1 > 0$ has the same effect as moving from $\sigma = 0$ to $\sigma = -\sigma_1$ if the distribution of r is symmetric and as $\sigma_1 \to 0$ any significance of asymmetry disappears. Thus the functions (6′) and (7′) are flat with respect to σ at $\sigma = 0$. In order to avoid this problem but retain tractability we will expand (6′) and (7′) in second-order Taylor's expansions around $\sigma = 0$, evaluate expectations, and then use an exogenous shift in σ^2 from zero in order to assess the implications of uncertainty for the industry equilibrium. A similar expansion is involved in Ireland [1980] and developed in Aaftink, Ireland and Sertel [1982], and although results are only valid for the effect of the first "small" amount of uncertainty, they are indicative of likely behaviour and can also show where non-ambiguous results are not possible. Our current problem has the additional complication that it is not only the behaviour of individual agents which is affected by the imposition of uncertainty, but also the number of agents.

Second-order expansions of (6) and (7) yield, after taking expectations,

$$EV(\pi) \simeq [V(\pi)] + \frac{1}{2}\left[V_{\pi\pi}(\pi)\left(\frac{\partial\pi}{\partial\alpha}\right)^2\right]\sigma^2 \tag{6''}$$

$$E\{V_\pi(\pi)\pi_x^*\} \simeq [V_\pi(\pi)\pi_x^*] + \left[V_{\pi\pi}(\pi)\frac{\partial\pi_x^*}{\partial\alpha}\frac{\partial\pi}{\partial\alpha}\right]\sigma^2 \tag{7''}$$

where all terms in square brackets are evaluated at $\sigma = 0$ and at the certainty equilibrium values of x and z. Setting (6″) and (7″) to zero and taking comparative statics at $\sigma^2 = 0$ brings us back to a system such as (10), that is,

$$\begin{pmatrix} [V_\pi(\pi)\pi_z] & [V_\pi(\pi)\pi_x] \\ \left[V_\pi(\pi)\dfrac{\partial\pi_x^*}{\partial z}\right] & \left[V_\pi(\pi)\dfrac{\partial\pi_x^*}{\partial x}\right] \end{pmatrix} \begin{pmatrix} dz \\ dx \end{pmatrix} = \begin{pmatrix} \dfrac{1}{2}\left[\dfrac{\partial\pi}{\partial\alpha}\right] \\ \left[\dfrac{\partial\pi_x^*}{\partial\alpha}\right] \end{pmatrix} \left[-V_{\pi\pi}(\pi)\frac{\partial\pi}{\partial\alpha}\right] d\sigma^2 \tag{11}$$

Dividing through (11) by $V_\pi(\pi)$ and defining the coefficient of absolute risk aversion as $A = -V_{\pi\pi}(\pi)/V_\pi(\pi)$ yields, again using [ ] to denote evaluation at $\alpha = \mu$ and the certainty equilibrium,

$$\begin{pmatrix} [\pi_z] & [\pi_x] \\ \left[\dfrac{\partial\pi_x^*}{\partial z}\right] & \left[\dfrac{\partial\pi_x^*}{\partial x}\right] \end{pmatrix} \begin{pmatrix} \left[\dfrac{dz}{d\sigma^2}\right] \\ \left[\dfrac{dx}{d\sigma^2}\right] \end{pmatrix} = \begin{pmatrix} \dfrac{1}{2}\left[\dfrac{\partial\pi}{\partial\alpha}\right] \\ \left[\dfrac{\partial\pi_x^*}{\partial\alpha}\right] \end{pmatrix} \left[A\frac{\partial\pi}{\partial\alpha}\right] \tag{12}$$

The specific demand system we will use is derived from the gross welfare function

$$W = \alpha(z - \tfrac{1}{2}z^2) \tag{13}$$

and the industry services index

$$z = \sum_{i=1}^{n} x_i^\beta \tag{14}$$

Equations (13) and (14) imply a constant elasticity of substitution between products of $1/(1-\beta)$. Then, ignoring income effects, marginal welfare of good

j is the price that consumers are willing to pay for good j, that is

$$(15) \qquad p_j = \alpha(1-z)\beta x_j^{\beta-1} \qquad j = 1, 2, \ldots, n$$

We will assume that cost functions for all firms are identical, and for the typical (j^{th}) firm is equal to $cx_j^{\beta}+C$. The restriction that the exponent on x_j in costs is the same as that on x_j in (14) is purely to allow algebraic solutions; note however that it encompasses (i) the case of homogeneous products ($\beta = 1$) and constant marginal cost, and (ii) the case of heterogeneous products ($\beta < 1$) and diminishing marginal cost. As all x_j will be the same in equilibrium by symmetry, the j subscript may be dropped, giving profit for the typical firm as:

$$(8') \qquad \pi = x^{\beta}\{\alpha(1-z)\beta - c\} - C$$

The certainty equilibrium is defined by (8′) and (9′) set equal to zero, where

$$(9') \qquad \begin{aligned} \pi_x^* &= \beta x^{\beta-1}\{\alpha(1-z)\beta - c\} - x^{\beta}\alpha\beta\eta z/x \\ &= \beta x^{\beta-1}\{\alpha\beta(1-z) - \alpha\eta z - c\} \end{aligned}$$

and $\sigma^2 = 0$ implies $\alpha = \mu$. Note that $\eta > 0$ (that is, non-competitive pricing) is required for second-order conditions. The certainty equilibrium is the solution to (8′) and (9′) and is

$$(16) \qquad z = (\mu\beta - c)/(\mu(\beta+\eta))$$

$$(17) \qquad x^{\beta} = C(\beta+\eta)/(\eta(\mu\beta - c))$$

We use (8′) and (9′) in (12) and obtain, using (16) and (17), and simplifying:

$$(12') \qquad \begin{pmatrix} -\mu & \eta\dfrac{(\mu\beta-c)/x}{\beta+\eta} \\ -\mu(\beta+\eta) & 0 \end{pmatrix} \begin{pmatrix} \dfrac{dz}{d\sigma^2} \\ \dfrac{dx}{d\sigma^2} \end{pmatrix} = \begin{pmatrix} \dfrac{1}{2}\dfrac{\mu\eta+c}{\mu(\beta+\eta)} \\ \dfrac{c}{\mu} \end{pmatrix} [A\partial\pi/\partial\alpha]$$

where $[A\partial\pi/\partial\alpha] > 0$. Using Cramer's rule we have

$$(18) \qquad \frac{dz}{d\sigma^2} = -[A\partial\pi/\partial\alpha]c/\{\mu^2(\beta+\eta)\}$$

$$(19) \qquad \frac{1}{x}\frac{dx}{d\sigma^2} = [A\partial\pi/\partial\alpha]\frac{\frac{1}{2}(\mu\eta - c)}{\mu\eta(\mu\beta - c)}$$

From (14) and the fact that symmetry implies $x_i = x$ for all i:

$$\frac{d\log n}{d\sigma^2} = \frac{d\log z}{d\sigma^2} - \beta\frac{d\log x}{d\sigma^2}$$

Hence we obtain from (18) and (19) by using (16)

$$(20) \qquad \frac{d\log n}{d\sigma^2} = [A\partial\pi/\partial\alpha]\frac{\{-c\eta - \beta(\mu\eta - c)/2\}}{\eta\mu(\mu\beta - c)}$$

Thus we have

Proposition 2. The imposition of uncertainty can give rise to any one of the following three responses of long-run equilibrium:

(i) *the number of firms and output per firm will both fall;*
(ii) *the number of firms will fall but output per firm will rise;*
(iii) *the output per firm will fall but the number of firms will rise.*

We have proved Proposition 2 by using a specific example and small uncertainty. For this example, (19) and (20) hold so that

$$\frac{dx}{d\sigma^2} \gtrless 0 \qquad \text{as} \qquad \eta \gtrless \frac{c}{\mu}$$

$$\frac{dn}{d\sigma^2} \gtrless 0 \qquad \text{as} \qquad \eta \lessgtr \frac{c}{\mu}\frac{\beta\mu}{2c+\beta\mu} = lc/\mu$$

so that case (i) above holds if $lc/\mu < \eta < c/\mu$, case (ii) holds if $\eta \geqslant c/\mu$ and case (iii) holds if $\eta < lc/\mu$.

The fact that the same example can contain all three cases for feasible parameter values demonstrates that no case can be dismissed as obscure or pathological.[2]

V. WELFARE ASPECTS

Under certainty, a rough and ready measure of welfare in a partial equilibrium model would be the sum of consumers' and producers' surpluses. Under uncertainty, however, it would be necessary to deduct that part of producers' surplus or profit which compensates producers for running risks to which they are averse. This is a "deadweight" loss of uncertainty, and if all profits in long run equilibrium are required to be used for such compensation then expected net welfare (ENW) may be described as

$$\text{(21)} \qquad \text{ENW} = E\{W - p\textstyle\sum x\}$$

On the other hand the proportion of profits necessary to compensate producers may be quite small. Two scenarios may illustrate this. First consider that firms' decisions are taken by managers as agents for society. Managers decide what goods to produce (that is, entry and exit) and how much to produce. They are rewarded on the basis of profits—either by a performance-linked income schedule or by reputation which affects their future income streams—but this reward itself is an insignificant part of a firms' profits and losses. The latter is (virtually) fully distributed to consumers who also receive income from other industries, have fully-diversified asset portfolios, and who are

[2] Of course not every welfare-based demand system generates all three possibilities. For instance, among a fairly small set of tractable alternatives, the constant elasticities model (see for instance Koenker and Perry [1981]), where $W = \alpha z^{\theta}$ and z is of the form (14), does *not* permit case (ii) although it does permit cases (i) and (iii).

essentially risk-neutral as a result. A second possibility is that firms are controlled by a small subset of stock holders (a single stock holder for example) who have a small proportion of the total stock but whose holding is a large part of their personal portfolio of assets, and thus they require a positive expected profit as compensation for risk-bearing.[3]

The limit of either case is such that virtually all profit is distributed to risk neutral consumers; firm controllers have the same long run expected utility, and so expected net welfare is

$$(22)\qquad \begin{aligned} \text{ENW} &= E\{W-p\textstyle\sum x+n\pi\} \\ &= E\{W-nc(x)\} \end{aligned}$$

and consumers consider the profit-generating aspects of their (personal) expenditure as insignificant, so that they choose consumption levels to maximise consumers' surplus $W-p\sum x$, given α.

The correct model certainly lies between (21) and (22), but we will confine our attention here to these two polar cases in order to analyse the welfare effects of introducing uncertainty into a monopolistic competition equilibrium.

It will be anticipated that if all profits are "deadweight" loss, and ENW is (21), then, for a very large class of models, uncertainty reduces ENW. In particular if $z = \sum_j x_j^\beta$ then $p_j = W_z \beta x_j^{\beta-1}$, all j, and ENW $= W - W_z z\beta$. Then as W is concave in z, $d\text{ENW}/dz > 0$, so that $d\text{ENW}/d\sigma^2 < 0$ as z declines with the imposition of uncertainty. If, however, there is little deadweight loss from uncertainty it is *a priori* not inconceivable that the changes in the number of firms and output per firm resulting from the imposition of uncertainty may well give rise to increased ENW as defined by (22). In the example of the last section, expected net welfare would then be:

$$(22')\qquad \text{ENW} = \mu(z-\tfrac{1}{2}z^2)-cz-nC$$

as $c(x) = cx^\beta + C$. The optimum $n^0 = 1$ and $z^0 = 1 - c/\mu$ is found from maximising (22′) with respect to n and x given the constraint $n \geqslant 1$. Industry services, supplied in a monopolistic competition long run equilibrium under certainty, given by (16), is less than z^0 as $\beta \leqslant 1$ and $\eta > 0$, and we might assume this undersupply of industry services to hold more generally. The imposition of general demand uncertainty would decrease the industry supply of services and thus tend to reduce welfare by moving to a socially worse position. However this is not the complete story as we have also seen that the number of firms/output per firm mix is likely to be radically changed by uncertainty. We may consider a situation where economies of scale exist and products are fairly homogeneous. Would it then be possible that uncertainty would drive out sufficient firms that those remaining could expand their

[3] The connection between firm behaviour and the asset portfolio of controlling shareholders in relation to mergers is considered in a number of papers including Bradburd [1980] and Ireland [1983b]. (Note however that an additional restriction of an upper bound on s is required for the proof of Proposition 1 of the latter to be correct.)

outputs to take advantage of economies of scale and thereby increase expected welfare because of increased efficiency?

We will attack this question in two ways. First we will investigate a general model but with homogeneous goods. We will show that ENW will increase with uncertainty if and only if output per firm increases with uncertainty. This we will state as Proposition 3. We will then argue that this case can occur by referring to our example of section II. Then we will see how, within this example, the result can be extended to differentiated products provided the conjectural variation elasticity increases in compensation.

If the industry's products are homogeneous, we have $\beta = 1$ and can write

$$z = xn$$

and expected net welfare can be written as

$$\text{ENW} = \mu G(z) - nc(x) \qquad G_z > 0; G_{zz} < 0 \tag{23}$$

Now we have

$$\frac{d\text{ENW}}{d\sigma^2} = \frac{\partial \text{ENW}}{\partial x}\frac{dx}{d\sigma^2} + \frac{\partial \text{ENW}}{\partial n}\frac{dn}{d\sigma^2} \tag{24}$$

and

$$\frac{\partial \text{ENW}}{\partial x} = \mu G_z n - nc_x(x) \tag{25}$$

$$\frac{\partial \text{ENW}}{\partial n} = \mu G_z x - c(x) \tag{26}$$

Now $\mu G_z \equiv p_j$, the price for the homogeneous products, as μG_z is the utility of the marginal unit of the commodity. In zero-profit equilibrium under certainty (26) is thus zero. Also as $\eta > 0$, the (conjectural) profit-maximising output per firm is given by $\mu G_z - c_x(x) + \mu G_{zz}\eta z/x = 0$. Thus as $G_{zz} < 0$, (25) is positive. We then have from (24):

Proposition 3. In long run equilibrium, if products are homogeneous then expected net welfare defined by (22) is decreased by the addition of small uncertainty if output per firm decreases as a result of the uncertainty, and is increased if output per firm is increased.

Note that as products are homogeneous, a Chamberlinian equilibrium under certainty will be characterised by too small an output level compared with the social optimum due to a too-small firm output level. Increasing output per firm improves efficiency (increased economies of scale) and there is no loss of variety from the smaller number of firms as products are homogeneous.

With differentiated products, $\partial\text{ENW}/\partial n \neq 0$ and the result of uncertainty on ENW is a trade-off between the effects of less total supply and less variety on the one hand and increased efficiency from increasing returns to scale on the other. To see this, we can find $d\text{ENW}/d\sigma^2$ for our example. It will be simplest to consider (22′) as a function of z and n. Thus

$$\frac{d\mathrm{ENW}}{d\sigma^2} = (\mu(1-z)-c)\frac{dz}{d\sigma^2} - Cn\frac{d\log n}{d\sigma^2} \tag{25}$$

Some tedious substitution from (16), (17), (18) and (20) yields

$$\frac{d\mathrm{ENW}}{d\sigma^2} = \frac{[A\partial\pi/\partial\alpha]}{\mu^2(\beta+\eta)^2}\{\eta\mu(-c(1-\beta)+\beta(\mu\beta-c)/2) - c(c(1-\beta)+\beta(\mu\beta-c)/2)\}$$

Thus

$$\frac{d\mathrm{ENW}}{d\sigma^2} \gtrless 0 \quad \text{as} \quad \eta \gtrless s\frac{c}{\mu}$$

where

$$s = \frac{c(1-\beta)+\beta(\mu\beta-c)/2}{-c(1-\beta)+\beta(\mu\beta-c)/2}$$

provided that $-c(1-\beta)+\beta(\mu\beta-c)/2 > 0$, that is $\dfrac{c}{\mu} < \dfrac{\beta^2}{2-\beta}$

$$\text{and} \quad \frac{d\mathrm{ENW}}{d\sigma^2} < 0 \quad \text{otherwise.}$$

Obviously if $\beta = 1$ (homogeneous products) then $s = 1$ and $d\mathrm{ENW}/d\sigma^2$ has the sign $dx/d\sigma^2$ (see Proposition 2) thus confirming: Proposition 3. If $\beta < 1$ (differentiated products), then our example also has reducing marginal costs (as β is also the exponent in the cost function). Although η is required to be bigger then $s(c/\mu)$ where $s > 1$ for $\beta < 1$, and thus the parameter range allowing $d\mathrm{ENW}/d\sigma^2$ to be positive is smaller with differentiated products, it is still easy to find combinations of parameter values which do allow this result. For instance $c/\mu = \frac{1}{2}$, $\beta = 0.9$ yields $s = 1.769$ and $\eta > 0.885$ implies $d\mathrm{ENW}/d\sigma^2 > 0$; $c/\mu = 0.2$, $\beta = 0.9$ yields $s = 1.136$ and $\eta > 0.227$ implies $d\mathrm{ENW}/d\sigma^2 > 0$.

Thus there are non-trivial cases when the removal of uncertainty by insuring the price function so that $\alpha \equiv \mu$ is not in the social interest, and these cases prevail where the conjectural variation is large so that the industry is behaving in a fairly "collusive" way even if overt collusion is not taking place. A final point relates to the case of zero marginal cost, that is $c = 0$. The welfare maximum is then $z^0 = 1$ (the bliss point) and $n = 1$. The industry equilibrium given by (16) and (17) still exists as $\eta > 0$ but we then see that $d\mathrm{ENW}/d\sigma^2 > 0$ as $sc/\mu = 0$, and thus $\eta > sc/\mu$, all $\eta > 0$. In this case the level of industry services is the same after the imposition of uncertainty ($dz/d\sigma^2 = 0$ from (18)) and so the only result is a shift in the mix of services so that more benefit is obtained from economies of scale.

VI. CONCLUSION

We have argued that to consider that demand uncertainty leads to lower output per firm or that it leads to fewer participating firms is too simplistic. If simultaneous adjustment to uncertainty is allowed then all we can be confident of is that at least one of these responses will occur. Indeed the same simple example showed the possibility that either output per firm or number of firms could respond positively to the onset of (small) uncertainty.

The possibility of a fall in the provision of industry services being accompanied by a large change in the number of firms to output per firm mix led to the possibility that uncertainty might in fact increase net welfare by virtue of a more efficient mix provided there was little "deadweight" loss from uncertainty. This possibility would be indicated in our example by (i) a high value of β and thus a high value of the elasticity of substitution among products, (ii) low marginal cost compared to fixed cost, (iii) high demand and (iv) high conjectural elasticity. The last two suggest an industry equilibrium with a large number of firms as the high conjectural elasticity will imply fairly low outputs of participating firms. High substitutability plus high fixed cost mean that welfare is improved by moving to a few firms/high output per firm mix, and thus the introduction of uncertainty may achieve a better expected net welfare outcome.

This study is partial equilibrium in character. It does not consider economic problems outside the industry in question and is limited in application. However the need to allow for demand uncertainty in models of monopolistic competition which treat more complex problems such as that of intra-industry trade (see Krugman [1980]) is considerable; it is hoped to extend the analysis of this paper in those directions.

NORMAN J. IRELAND,
Department of Economics,
University of Warwick,
Coventry CV4 7AL,
U.K.

ACCEPTED NOVEMBER 1984

THE JOURNAL OF INDUSTRIAL ECONOMICS 0022-1821 $2.00
Volume XXXIII June 1985 No. 4

WELFARE LOSSES IN OLIGOPOLY AND MONOPOLISTIC COMPETITION

G. K. Yarrow

I. INTRODUCTION

Estimates of the magnitudes of monopoly welfare losses (MWL) appearing in the economics literature have tended to differ quite widely. At one end of the spectrum we find figures of the order of 0.1 % of GNP quoted by Harberger [1954] in his pioneering study, while at the other extreme Cowling and Mueller [1978] have derived estimates of around 10 % of gross corporate product from some of their measures. Two of the major sources of such differences lie in the treatment of (a) the general equilibrium aspects of deviations between prices and marginal costs, and (b) the impact of market power on the cost levels of firms; but, unfortunately, the tendency of writers to adopt rather different analytical frameworks often makes it difficult to accurately assign the variations in the estimates to specific factors.

In the present paper the issue of monopoly welfare loss is considered in the context of a differentiated goods model based upon work on monopolistic competition by Spence [1976] and by Dixit and Stiglitz [1977]. Within a set of common assumptions about demand, the effects of varying cost conditions and differing equilibria on the level of MWL are examined. On this basis, four major factors connected with suboptimal resource allocation can be identified: (a) supernormal profits, (b) product differentiation, (c) suboptimal scale, and (d) factor bias. The first of these needs little explanation: its association with welfare loss has been well explored in structure-conduct-performance theory and is used extensively in applied anti-trust economics. Attention will therefore be focused upon the remaining three, all of which can produce MWL in zero-profit equilibria.

The paper is organised as follows. Section II sets out and discusses the differentiated goods framework which will be used throughout the rest of the analysis. It is also shown how a simple transformation of variables reduces the model to the homogeneous goods case and thereby makes immediately available a number of familiar results from the structure-conduct-performance literature. In Section III the focus is on welfare analysis of monopolistic competition. The results here are essentially restatements of earlier work, although the transformation of variables helps to clarify their foundations. Section IV extends the analysis to incorporate additional decision variables such as advertising, research and development, etc., while section V considers the case where market conditions will not sustain a large number of firms in equilibrium and suboptimal scale effects become important. Factor bias is analysed in section VI and it is shown that its direction and magnitude are strongly affected by the "degree of competitiveness" between firms in their price-output decisions. Finally, section VII outlines a case where firms behave in a joint-profit maximising manner with respect to output choice but competitively with respect to product selection, and a lower bound for the resulting MWL is derived.

The technical analysis throughout the paper is informal: the aim is to pinpoint the central issues by covering a number of areas, rather than by looking in detail at the full implications of any individual piece of analysis.

II. THE COMMON FRAMEWORK

Consumers' preferences are assumed to be represented by a utility function:

$$(1) \qquad U(x, \underline{q}) = x + h\left(\sum_k q_k^\alpha; \alpha\right),$$

where x is the quantity of some numeraire commodity, q_i is the output of variety i of a differentiated product, $0 < \alpha < 1$, $h'(.) > 0$ and $h''(.) < 0$. The inverse demand function of product variety i is therefore given by

$$(2) \qquad p_i = \partial U / \partial q_i = \alpha h'(.) q_i^{\alpha - 1}$$

From the outset it is worth noting certain restrictive features of this specification: (a) income effects in the demands for differentiated goods are zero; (b) demand for every commodity is strictly positive at any finite price vector; (c) the demand functions are symmetric and, *ceteris paribus*, a change in the output of any variety will have the same proportionate effect on the demand for each of the other varieties (that is, there are no "near neighbour" effects).

These limitations are not considered vital for the issues to be tackled below and the demand model has the merit of allowing a straightforward parameterisation of the degree of product differentiation. To see this, consider the elasticities of the price of variety i with respect to other outputs and own output:

$$(3) \qquad -(q_j/p_i)(\partial p_i/\partial q_j) = -\alpha(h'' q_j^\alpha / h') = \alpha e(.) s_j,$$

and

$$(4) \qquad -(q_i/p_i)(\partial p_i/\partial q_i) = 1 - \alpha + \alpha e(.) s_i,$$

where $e(.)$ is the absolute value of the elasticity of $h'(.)$ and $s_i = q_i^\alpha / \Sigma q_k^\alpha$ is a type of market share measure. Thus, α is an obvious measure of the degree of substitutability in demand or product differentiation between the varieties, with *smaller* values of α implying *greater* differentiation and $\alpha = 1$ corresponding to the homogeneous goods case (where the own- and cross-price elasticities are equal).

Following Spence [1980], given the above assumptions, significant simplifications of analysis can be obtained via the substitutions

(5) $z_i = q_i^\alpha$, and $z = \sum_k z_k$

Referring back to the utility function, it is immediately apparent that, from the consumers' viewpoint, these transformed output variables of the firms are perfect substitutes for one another. Henceforth, z_i will be labelled the *utility-output* of firm i, to distinguish it from the physical output level q_i.

If each variety of the differentiated commodity is produced by one, single-product firm, the revenue of the latter is

(6) $p_i q_i = \alpha h'(\,.\,) q_i^\alpha = \alpha h'(\,.\,) z_i = \hat{p}(z) z_i$

where $\hat{p}(z) = \alpha h'(\,.\,)$ will be referred to as the *pseudo inverse demand curve* for the product. Thus, in utility-output space, the firm can be viewed as producing a commodity which is a perfect substitute for the outputs of other firms in the market—the unit "price" for the commodity $\hat{p}$ being a function only of the total output on offer, z. This allows the effects of product differentiation to be incorporated exclusively on the cost sides of the models and thereby makes instantly available a number of insights derived from the familiar homogeneous good analyses.

Turning, then, to cost conditions, it will be assumed initially that the total costs of firm i are given by

(7) $C_i = f + c q_i = f + c z_i^\phi, \qquad \phi = 1/\alpha > 1$

That is, the cost per physical unit of output is a declining function of output, but the average cost curve for utility-output is U-shaped. The unit cost of utility-output is minimised where

(8) $z_i = z(m) = \{[f/c]/[\phi - 1]\}^{1/\phi}$

Adapting traditional terminology, $z(m)$ will be called the minimum efficient scale (m.e.s.) of the firm; the scale of operations here being measured in terms of the variable z_i. The physical output level corresponding to $z(m)$ is

(9) $q(m) = [f/c]/[\phi - 1]$

Note that, as in standard analysis, the minimum efficient scale is an increasing function of the ratio of fixed to (physical) unit variable costs of production. The novel feature of the model is the dependence of m.e.s. on product differentiation. As ϕ increases from 1 (differentiation is increased), $z(m)$ falls, although the two variables will be positively related for sufficiently high levels of product differentiation. On the other hand, from (9), m.e.s. measured in physical output units is always a decreasing function of differentiation.

To summarise then, working in utility-output space we find that the differentiated products model with scale economies in production is equivalent to a homogeneous good model with cost conditions characterised by U-shaped average cost curves.

III. WELFARE LOSS AND MONOPOLISTIC COMPETITION

With free entry the market for the differentiated good will tend to be characterised by a large number of firms/varieties whenever the minimum efficient scale is very small in relation to the size of the market. To be more precise, define the market size $z(s)$ as the quantity of utility-output demanded when price is equal to minimised average cost:

$$(10) \qquad z(s) = p^{-1}(f/z(m) + cz(m)^{\phi-1})$$

Then the regions of parameter space producing monopolistically competitive equilibria are defined by the condition that

$$(11) \qquad z(m) \ll z(s),$$

where $z(m)$ is given by equation (8).

Necessary conditions for the monopolistic competition zero-profit equilibria are that, for each firm in the market, marginal revenue be equal to marginal cost and price be equal to average cost. For Nash quantity setting equilibria these become

$$(12) \qquad p\{1 - s_i e(z)\} = c\phi z_i^{\phi-1}$$

and

$$(13) \qquad pz_i = f + cz_i^{\phi}$$

where $e(z)$, as defined earlier, is the inverse elasticity of $p(.)$ $(= -[z/p][dp/dz])$. But, with a large number of firms in the market, the term $s_i e(z)$ can be neglected. Hence, in utility-output space, (12) and (13) reduce to the conditions: price = marginal cost = average cost. This, of course, is just the familiar long run equilibrium position of the competitive firm.

Working with the transformed output variables makes it clear, therefore, that, from the social welfare perspective, each firm will operate at the optimum scale (cf. Dixit and Stiglitz [1977]), producing utility-output at the minimum unit cost. In the space of physical output, however, the diagrammatic representation would show the equilibrium of the firm occurring at the customary Chamberlinian tangency point, where the downward sloping demand curve for the firm's product touches the negatively sloped average cost curve. The usual excess capacity argument is now revealed to be misleading because of its neglect of consumers' preferences for variety. When these tastes are properly incorporated into the analysis the output level of each firm in the market is socially optimal.

If output per firm is socially optimal it might be tempting to conclude that the monopolistic competition equilibrium is a first-best optimum, but this would be incorrect. The market supply curve of utility-output will be horizontal at a price equal to minimised unit costs (OG) and the equilibrium market output (z^*) will be given by the point at which this line crosses the pseudo

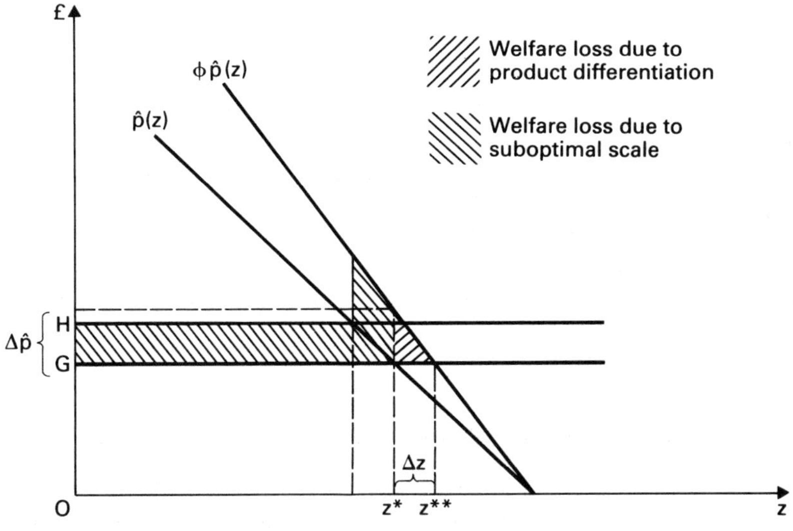

FIGURE 1

demand curve (see Figure 1). Next consider the marginal utility of transformed output. From (1) and (6):

$$(14) \qquad \partial U/\partial z = h'(\,.\,) = \phi\hat{p}$$

The marginal utility curve therefore lies above the pseudo demand curve and the first-best level of market output is given by z^{**} in Figure 1—where marginal utility is equal to marginal cost. Thus, although each firm produces at the socially optimal output level, the monopolistic competition equilibrium implies too few firms in the market. That is, the market is offering insufficient product variety to consumers (see Dixit and Stiglitz [1977]).

The source of the market failure in this case is the assumed absence of price discrimination. If firms could charge a constant price per unit of utility-output to consumers, the marginal utility and demand curves in utility output space would coincide and the resulting equilibrium would be a first-best optimum. But constancy of $\hat{p}$ across customers implies a non-linear pricing scheme for units of physical output.

Welfare loss arising from the lack of price discrimination can be estimated by the area of the shaded triangle shown in Figure 1. When product differentiation is low it is given approximately by

$$(15) \qquad \Delta W = \Delta\hat{p}\Delta z/2 = [\phi - 1]\hat{p}\Delta z/2 = [\phi - 1]^2 R/[2e]$$

where R is the industry's total revenue. This measure can be re-expressed in terms of the firm ($\eta(F)$) and market ($\eta(I)$) demand elasticities for output measured in physical units (given from (4) by setting s_i equal to zero and unity respectively):

(16) $$\Delta W = \eta(I)R/\{2[\eta(F)-1][\eta(F)-\eta(I)]\}$$

As an illustrative calculation, when $e = 1$ and $\phi = 1.1$ (corresponding to firm and market demand elasticities for physical output of 11 and 1 respectively), the welfare loss is about 0.5% of total revenue, which is the sort of magnitude that would be produced by the Harberger approach. Application of the Cowling and Mueller formula, which is based upon firm elasticities of demand only, would give misleading results in this case (low product differentiation, high $\eta(F)$) because it fails to take proper account of the interactions between firms.

IV. EXTENSIONS OF THE MONOPOLISTIC COMPETITION MODEL

Immediate extensions of the welfare propositions outlined above can be obtained for certain specifications of the effects of additional decision variables. Suppose, for example, that

(17) $$U = x + h\left(\sum_k g(v_k)^\alpha q_k^\alpha\right), \qquad g'(.) > 0,$$

where v_i is an output-augmenting variable such as quality of the product, number of brands offered by the firm, number of advertising messages, product improving research and development inputs, etc. Letting $z_i = g(v_i)^\alpha q_i^\alpha$ it can quickly be shown that the revenue of firm i can again be written as $R_i = \hat{p}(z)z_i$. Now suppose that costs are

(18) $$C_i = f + rv_i + cq_i = f + rv_i + cz_i^\phi/g(v_i)$$

Since the variable v_i does not affect revenue the model can be solved sequentially, first finding the level of v_i which minimises the costs of producing a given utility output and then treating profit as a function of utility output only. From (18) the cost minimising condition for choice of v_i is

(19) $$r - cz_i^\phi g'(v_i)/g(v_i)^2 = 0$$

Substituting for v_i from (19) into (18) gives total costs as a function of utility-output only and the analysis can then proceed as before. Thus, if market conditions are such as to sustain a large number of firms, the resulting levels of the product augmenting variable will constitute a constrained social optimum.

The most important implication arising from the addition of output-augmenting variables to the model is the effect on the minimum efficient scale of operations. Equation (18) shows that increases in v_i will, for any output level, increase fixed costs $(f+rv_i)$ and reduce variable costs $(cz_i^\phi/g(v_i))$, thereby tending to increase m.e.s. For example, let

(20) $$C_i = f + rv_i + cv_i^{-\mu} z_i^\phi$$

Then, solving (19) for v_i,

(21) $$v_i = [\mu c/r]^{1/[1+\mu]} z_i^{\phi/[\mu+1]},$$

and hence,

(22) $$C_i = f + k z_i^{\phi/[\mu+1]}$$

Unit costs of utility-output will therefore decline with scale (that is, there is no minimum efficient scale) if

(23) $$\mu > \phi - 1$$

In other words, if products are not highly differentiated, relatively small opportunities for augmentation will yield natural monopoly conditions. In less extreme circumstances, the existence of opportunities for quality improvement, advertising, research and development, etc., will render small numbers of equilibria somewhat more likely. Fewness will, of course, imply deviations from constrained social optima (see section V).

V. FREE ENTRY EQUILIBRIA WITH SMALLER NUMBERS

When minimum efficient scale is a non-trivial fraction of market size the resulting equilibria will tend to exhibit individual market shares which are not negligibly small. In utility-output space the firm's marginal revenue will differ significantly from average revenue, and the latter curve will slope downwards. Ignoring problems connected with the restriction of the number of firms in the market (n) to an integer value, the equilibrium of the firm in utility-output space will be as shown in Figure 2. We now have a true excess capacity result:

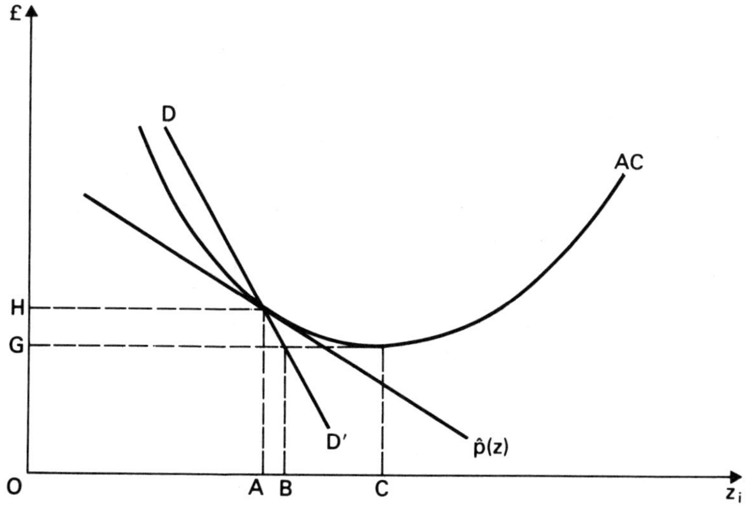

FIGURE 2

the unit cost of producing utility-output (which already incorporates the necessary allowance for consumer preferences for variety) is not minimised. Firms each produce too low an output and the magnitude of the resulting unit cost increase is represented by the distance GH. Translating into the market equilibrium diagram (Figure 1), we find a monopoly welfare loss *relative to the constrained optimum* and due to *suboptimal scale* given by the shaded region indicated.

In Figure 2 the line DD' shows the constant share of the market pseudo-demand curve for the firm. In a symmetric equilibrium it follows that total utility-output should be increased by a fraction AB/OA to take it to its constrained optimum level, while each firm's output would have to increase by a fraction AC/OA ($>AB/OA$) to minimise the costs of producing that output level. Hence, the number of firms/varieties would need to fall by a fraction BC/OA. In other words the equilibrium in this case features too many varieties of the product when judged from a second-best welfare benchmark: there is too much product differentiation. Indeed, if $BC/OA > (z^{**}-z^{*})/z^{*}$ (see Figure 1) the number of products on offer would exceed that appropriate for a first-best result.

A second reason for suboptimal scale is the possibility that the equilibrium may be less "competitive" than that of the Cournot–Nash case. Thus, consider a conjectural variations approach where each firm expects a unit increase in its utility-output will lead to an increase in utility-output of ψ by each of its rivals. When $\psi = 0$ this reduces to the Nash quantity setting equilibrium, but there are reasons for believing that the latter will not always offer an appropriate way to proceed. Suppose, for example, that decisions are sequential: in some first period firms decide whether or not to enter the market at a (sunk) cost of f, and that subsequently those firms which have entered play a price-output game in which their (physical) unit costs of production are equal to c. In practice, price-output games will usually extend over durations of time in which there will be opportunities for several moves, and they can often be approximated by a sequence of repeated one-shot games. Now Nash equilibria of repeated games with limited information can closely resemble collusive solutions of one-period games (Kreps and Wilson [1982]). Hence, we might think of the value of ψ in the simpler, static conjectural variations analysis as being a crude parameterisation of the outcome of extended competition.

Adopting the conjectural approach, (12) and (13) become

$$(24) \qquad p\{1-e\psi-e[1-\psi]/n\} = c\phi z_i^{\phi-1}$$

and

$$(25) \qquad pz_i = f+cz_i^{\phi}$$

Dividing (24) by (25) we find that

$$(26) \qquad z_i = \{[f/c][1-\lambda]/[\phi+\lambda-1]\}^{1/\phi}$$

where $\lambda = e\psi + e[1-\psi]/n$. The proportionate increase in the unit costs of utility output over the minimum level is therefore

$$[\phi - 1]^{1-1/\phi}/\{[\phi + \lambda - 1]^{1-1/\phi}[1-\lambda]^{1/\phi}\} - 1$$

The number of firms (n) is, of course, endogenous and depends upon the values of the various parameters. Suppose that the latter are such as to imply $\lambda = 0.2$, and that $\phi = 1.1$ (the focus is again upon relatively low levels of product differentiation). Then the proportionate increase in unit costs is 10.8%. Ignoring the integer problem, it follows that monopoly welfare loss as a fraction of revenue exceeds 9.2%, which is considerably in excess of the levels calculated in the previous section.

As ψ increases, so that the second period equilibrium becomes "less competitive", n will increase: the prospect of greater returns in the price-output game will attract more firms into the market. Entry will continue until supernormal profit is bid away and we are left with the traditional cartel result: even though profits are zero there will be welfare loss arising from an excessive number of firms and suboptimal scale—the greater expenditures on entry costs implying greater than minimum unit costs (cf. Posner [1975]). Generally, both the welfare loss and excessive product variety will increase as the second-period equilibrium becomes more collusive.

VI. FACTOR BIAS

In the two-stage interpretation of the preceding models the entry cost f was assumed to have no effect on the second-stage marginal costs of the firms. More generally the first-period decisions may well involve expenditures which *do* influence subsequent marginal costs. Thus, if the outlays rv_i in the analysis of section IV are incurred at stage 1 and are not recoverable, the values chosen will affect the parameters of the later competitive game. In considering their initial decisions, therefore, firms will take account of these strategic effects and, in general, we will find that profit maximisation no longer implies cost minimisation (in the sense of selecting the least cost method of producing any given level of utility-output).

The tendency for firms not to employ cost-minimising input combinations in conditions of strategic interdependence leads to a third source of monopoly welfare loss, which will be referred to as factor bias. It should, however, be noted that factor bias will not occur in the extreme case of *pure* monopoly where there are no strategic incentives to vary the input vectors from their cost-minimising values. Oligopoly welfare loss might therefore be a better term for this type of inefficiency.

In order to simplify the analysis it will henceforth be assumed that $r = 1$ and that the pseudo inverse demand curve is iso-elastic:

(27) $$\alpha h'(.) = \beta[.]^{-e}$$

The profit function of firm i thus becomes

$$\Pi_i = \beta[\,.\,]^{-e} z_i - f - v_i - c z_i^{\phi}/g(v_i) \tag{28}$$

Now the first-stage decisions are heavily conditioned by expectations concerning the nature of the later competition. Suppose, as before, the second-stage outcome is parameterised by (constant) conjectural coefficients ψ_{ij}, where ψ_{ij} is the conjectured rate of change of firm j's utility-output with respect to firm i's output. In other words, the first-order condition for profit maximisation by firm i at stage 2 is

$$\beta[\,.\,]^{-e} - e\beta z_i[\,.\,]^{-e-1}\left[1 + \sum_{j \neq i} \psi_{ij}\right] - \phi c z_i^{\phi-1}/g(v_i) = 0 \tag{29}$$

Consider next the first-order conditions for profit maximisation with respect to v_i (the stage 1 decision). Differentiating (28) with respect to v_i, and remembering that v_i is a parameter of the second stage game and that variations in its level will affect outputs according to the equations in (29),

$$\{\beta[\,.\,]^{-e} - e\beta z_i[\,.\,]^{-e-1} - \phi c z_i^{\phi-1}/g(v_i)\}\, dz_i/dv_i - \beta e z_i[\,.\,]^{-e-1} \sum_{j \neq i} dz_j/dv_i - 1 + [c z_i^{\phi}/g(v_i)^2]g'(v_i) = 0 \tag{30}$$

Substituting from (29) this reduces to

$$e\beta z_i[\,.\,]^{-e-1}\left\{\sum_{j \neq i} \psi_{ij} dz_i/dv_i - \sum_{j \neq i} dz_j/dv_i\right\} - 1 + [c z_i^{\phi}/g(v_i)^2]g'(v_i) = 0 \tag{31}$$

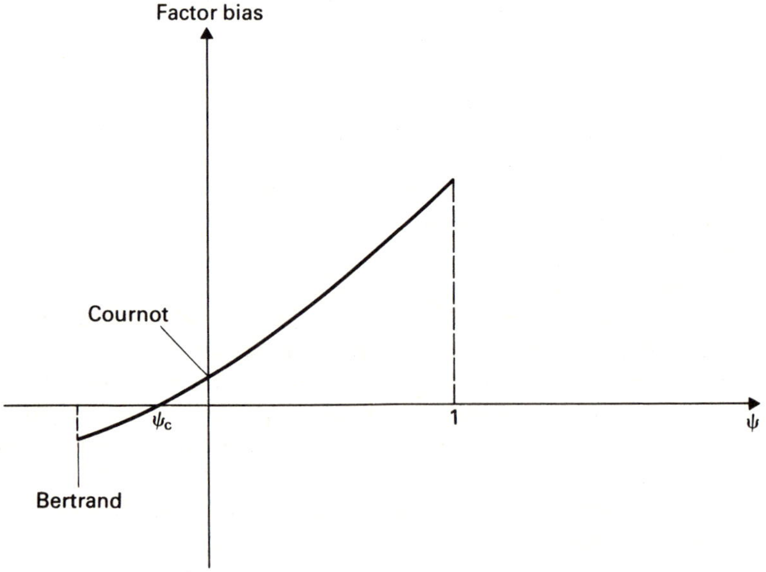

FIGURE 3

If the first term in (31) is zero we have the familiar cost-minimisation condition for the determination of v_i. In general, however, the first term will not be zero: it represents the strategic payoffs from changes in the first-period, non-recoverable expenditure. In the Cournot–Nash case the conjectural coefficients are all zero and the first term will typically (but not invariably) be negative. That is, an increase in v_i will reduce firm i's second-period marginal costs, inducing an accommodating reduction in rivals' outputs at stage 2. Expressed in terms of reaction functions, an increase in v_i will shift firm i's second-period reaction function outwards and, provided that the aggregate, second-period reaction function of rivals is negatively sloped, the equilibrium output of competitors will fall.

The effect of an additional negative term in equation (31) is equivalent in its impact to either a lower first-period marginal cost for the first-period variable or, alternatively, to a higher marginal payoff for that variable. Under normal assumptions it can therefore be expected that the outcome will tend to be a higher, optimal first-period expenditure than would be implied by the cost minimisation condition.

Differentiating the first-order conditions in (29) totally with respect to z_i and using (30),

$$(32) \qquad [dz_i/dv_i] \Big/ \Big[\sum_{j \neq i} dz_j/dv_i\Big] = 1 \Big/ \Big[\sum_{j \neq i} dz_j/dz_i\Big]$$

Hence, when $\psi_{ij} = dz_j/dz_i$, we find that the first expression in (31) is zero. But $\psi_{ij} = dz_j/dz_i$ are the conditions for first-order consistent conjectural equilibrium (CCE) (see Bresnahan [1981]). Thus, if the second-period equilibrium is expected to be of the first-order CCE type, there will be no factor bias.

In the symmetric case, where $\psi_{ij} = \psi$ for all i and j, the magnitude of factor bias, measured by the difference between the optimal v/z ratio and its cost minimising value, can be expressed as a function of ψ. Figure 3 illustrates a typical case. Factor bias is zero at the CCE value of ψ, say ψ_c, which is intermediate between the Bertrand and Cournot values of the conjectural coefficient. As ψ increases (decreases) from ψ_c, the factor bias increases (decreases). Intuitively, the strategic value of higher initial expenditures becomes greater as the second-period equilibrium becomes less competitive: the extra output achieved by virtue of the associated reductions in rivals' output having a higher payoff when the second-period equilibrium is more collusive because of the greater gap between price and marginal cost. At very competitive second-period equilibria (such as Bertrand), factor bias is negative: firms choose lower v/z ratios than are implied by cost minimisation because, although each expects to lose volume relative to its competitors as a result of its own decision, the increase in price cost margins from the lower aggregate output more than compensates.

We are now in a position to examine, informally, the effects of factor bias on welfare. Take first the case when $\psi > \psi_c$. Here there are two counterbalancing

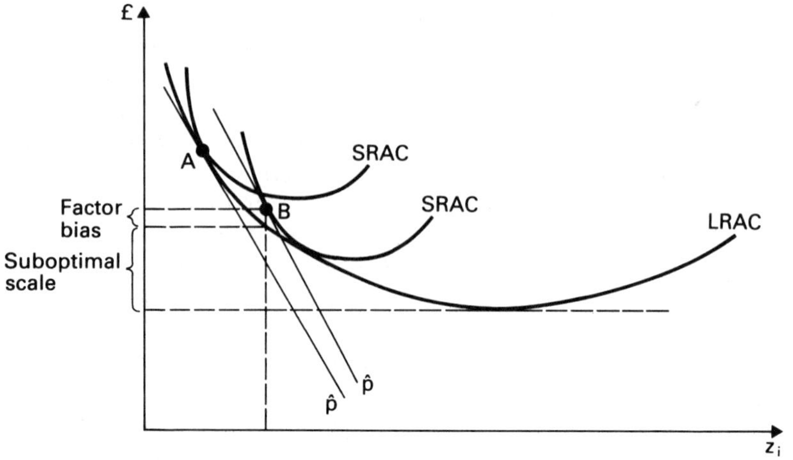

FIGURE 4

effects. Clearly the upward shift in the firms' cost curves resulting from excessive first-period expenditures will imply monopoly welfare losses. But these same increases in expenditures tend to reduce second-period marginal costs and thus imply increased equilibrium output levels for each firm which can offset some of the effects of suboptimal scale. Figure 4 shows a free entry, zero-profit equilibrium at *A* for the case where v_i and z_i are chosen simultaneously, the short run average cost curve showing the relationship between unit costs and utility-output when v_i is fixed at its long run equilibrium value. Now higher first-period expenditures in the sequential case will be associated with an equilibrium position such as *B*. Long run unit costs of producing the given output level are not minimised at this point and there are fewer, but larger, firms in the market as compared with *A*. In both cases, of course, economic profits are zero.

The diagram also shows a breakdown of the difference between market price and the lowest attainable unit cost into an effect due to suboptimal scale (which is lower than in the equivalent, one-stage model) and an effect due to factor bias. In the case illustrated the final outcome exhibits a lower market price (implying higher social welfare) than the equivalent non-sequential model. Although firms are no longer cost minimisers, the ability to sink costs in the first stage has here contributed to a better welfare outcome. The precise welfare results will vary from case to case however, and no claim for generality is being made on behalf of the one illustrated.

When $\psi < \psi_c$ the effect of sequential decisions on monopoly welfare loss is less ambiguous. The ability to sink first-period expenditures will tend to reduce the output level of each firm in equilibrium (increasing the number of firms in the market and raising MWL from the suboptimal scale effect) *and* raise the cost of producing that output level because of factor bias.

VII. FACTOR BIAS: A LIMITING CASE

It has been argued that factor bias tends to be greater the more collusive is the expected solution to the second-stage game and this section will sketch out a solution in a limiting case where firms act as joint maximisers with respect to their price/output decisions. It is assumed that each firm can choose to produce as many products as it likes and that product selection decisions are taken in the first period. Product selection decisions are, however, taken non-cooperatively and it is assumed that the outcome is a Nash equilibrium. The aim will be to place a lower bound on the level of monopoly welfare loss arising from excessive costs in this (admittedly extreme) case.

The costs of firm i are assumed to be given by

$$(33) \qquad C_i = f + bm_i^{\gamma} + cm_i q_i = f + bm_i^{\gamma} + cm_i^{1-\phi} z_i^{\phi},$$

where m_i is the number of products offered by firm i. The expression bm_i^{γ} represents the costs of bringing product varieties on to the market and will be referred to as the product development cost. The term $cm_i q_i$ represents production costs ($m_i q_i$ being the total output of the firm). Note that, to maintain the analytical convenience of symmetry, it is being assumed that firms produce the same number of units of each of their products.

Fixing z_i, the first-order condition for cost minimisation is

$$(34) \qquad \gamma bm_i^{\gamma-1} - c[\phi - 1] m_i^{-\phi} z_i^{\phi} = 0$$

Hence, the conventional long run cost function can be written as

$$(35) \qquad C_i = f + kz_i^{\phi\gamma/[\phi+\gamma-1]},$$

where k is a constant depending upon the cost parameters. The unit cost curve of utility output will therefore have a minimum point when $\phi\gamma > \phi + \gamma - 1$. The corresponding, cost-minimising ratio of product development to production costs is, from (34),

$$(36) \qquad \bar{\theta} = [bm_i^{\gamma}]/[cm_i^{1-\phi} z_i^{\phi}] = [\phi - 1]/\gamma$$

In period 2 the output levels of the firms are chosen to maximise joint profits. Hence,

$$(37) \qquad \beta[1 - e] z^{-e} = \phi cm_i^{1-\phi} z_i^{\phi-1}$$

and

$$(38) \qquad m_i/m_j = z_i/z_j$$

That is, market shares of the firms (in units of transformed output) are proportional to the number of products that each chooses to offer. Thus, in choosing the number of varieties in period 1 against an assumption of given numbers of rivals' products, a firm is directly selecting its market share, although it will recognise that an increase in, say m_i, will also increase the total output of commodities on the market and thereby depress market price. Solving equations (37) and (38) for the firms' outputs:

$$(39) \qquad z_i = \{\beta[1-e]/[\phi c]\}^{1/[\phi+e-1]} m_i M^{-e/[\phi+e-1]}$$

where $M = \Sigma_k m_k$ is the total number of varieties on the market.

In period 1 firm i chooses the profit-maximising value of m_i. The first-order conditions for Nash equilibrium are

$$(40) \qquad \{\beta z^{-e} - c\phi m_i^{1-\phi} z_i^{\phi-1}\} dz_i/dm_i - e\beta z_i z^{-e-1} dz/dm_i - \gamma b m_i^{\gamma-1} + c[\phi-1] m_i^{-\phi} z_i^{\phi} = 0$$

As before, it is the first two terms which produce the deviation from the cost-minimising input combination. From (37), followed by differentiation of (39), they can be written as

$$(41) \qquad \begin{aligned} e\beta z^{-e}\{dz_i/dm_i - [dz/dm_i]/n\} &= e\beta z^{-e}\rho M^{-e/[\phi+e-1]}\{1-1/n\} \\ &= e\beta z^{-e}[z_i/m_i]\{1-1/n\} \\ &= e\phi c\{1-1/n\} m_i^{-\phi} z_i^{\phi}/[1-e], \end{aligned}$$

where $\rho = \{\beta[1-e]/\phi c\}^{1/[\phi+e-1]}$. Substituting back into the condition for the optimal number of products, (40), and rearranging we find that

$$(42) \qquad \theta = [bm_i^{\gamma}]/[cm_i^{1-\phi} z_i^{\phi}] = \{\phi - 1 + e\phi[1-1/n]/[1-e]\}/\gamma$$

Comparing with the cost minimisation condition (36), the ratio of product development costs to production costs has been increased by the third term on the right hand side of (42). For example, if $\phi = 1.1$, $e = 0.5$, $\gamma = 1$, and $n = 5$, the ratio rises from 0.1 to 0.98. That is, cost minimisation implies that product development costs at a given output level are a tenth of production costs, but the strategic advantages of product proliferation in the sequential model indicate that development costs will rise to about the same magnitude as production costs.

It is now straightforward to calculate the proportionate increase in variable costs (that is, total costs less f) at any output level and thereby obtain a lower bound for the ratio of welfare loss to revenue. Let $\bar{m}$ be the cost minimising number of products offered by a firm for a given level of output z. The ratio of variable costs is

$$(43) \qquad \begin{aligned} [bm^{\gamma} + cm^{1-\phi}z^{\phi}]/[b\bar{m}^{\gamma} + c\bar{m}^{1-\phi}z^{\phi}] &= [m/\bar{m}]^{1-\phi}[1+\theta]/[1+\bar{\theta}] \\ &= [\theta/\bar{\theta}]^{[1-\phi]/[\phi+\gamma-1]}[1+\theta]/[1+\bar{\theta}] \end{aligned}$$

from the definitions of θ and $\bar{\theta}$ (see (36)). Thus, for the parameter values specified in the preceding paragraph the proportionate deviation of unit variable costs from their minimum level for the given output is 46.3%. In the absence of market failures elsewhere this number places a lower bound on the magnitude of welfare loss in this particular case.

VIII. CONCLUSIONS

The most important implication of the above analysis is that the magnitude of monopoly welfare loss can be substantial in zero-profit equilibria. In this sense some support is provided for the view that resource misallocations resulting from monopoly power are a significant policy problem, despite the sorts of numbers generated by the Harberger approach.

Large levels of MWL appear to be most likely where market conditions are such that costs are inflated, either via suboptimal scale or non-cost-minimising input choices, as a result of competition for monopoly positions. Thus, relatively "collusive" solutions to price-output subgames produce more intense competition in earlier stages of the game (entry, choice of non-price variables, etc.) leading to a transformation of monopoly rents into costs. Market conditions would be most likely to produce such "substitution of competition" results where the effective number of repetitions of the price-output subgame is large (price and output changes can be made quickly with little cost) while the number of repetitions of earlier subgames is small (for example, sunk costs are more significant). Case by case analysis of individual markets would therefore be in order to establish the precise characteristics of competition in each.

G. K. YARROW,
Hertford College,
Oxford,
U.K.

ACCEPTED NOVEMBER 1984

THE JOURNAL OF INDUSTRIAL ECONOMICS 0022-1821 $2.00
Volume XXXIII June 1985 No. 4

THE SUPPLY OF QUALITY ON A MARKET FOR "EXPERIENCE GOODS"

Thomas von Ungern-Sternberg
Carl Christian von Weizsäcker

I. INTRODUCTION

This paper is concerned with the analysis of markets for experience goods, that is, markets where consumers are imperfectly informed about the quality of the products they buy. Renewed interest in models of this kind was sparked off by Akerlof's seminal article "The Market for Lemons" in 1970.[1] He showed that in certain kinds of markets quality uncertainty on the part of consumers could lead to market failure in the form of an insufficient supply of high quality products, or even market breakdown (no trade takes place at all). The market Akerlof focused on to illustrate his point is the market for second hand cars. This is no accidental choice. The second hand car market is characterized by the fact that most suppliers appear on the market only once. This means that they do not have the possibility to build up reputations or goodwill with the consumers. This restriction is of some importance. The two factors leading to market failure in the presence of imperfectly informed consumers are (1) moral hazard and (2) adverse selection.[2] Moral hazard arises from the fact that if the producers' sales volume is totally independent of the quality of the products they sell, they will maximize profits by supplying only cheap low cost products. Adverse selection arises from the fact that suppliers of the cheapest low quality products will drive from the market any producer who for whatever reason wishes to supply higher quality products. The crucial assumptions giving rise to both of these sources of market failure are: (a) high quality products are more expensive to produce than low quality products, and (b) the sales volume of each supplier is independent of the quality he supplies. (As consumers cannot observe quality, the producer's choice of quality cannot have any influence on his sales volume.)

In most real world situations suppliers stay on the market for considerably longer than one "period". They then have the possibility to build up reputations or goodwill with the consumers. This is due to the following mechanism. While the consumers cannot directly observe a product's quality at the time of purchase, they may try to draw inferences about this quality from the past experience they (or others) have had with this supplier's products. The inferences will be of the kind: "If a producer has supplied good quality in the past,

[1] Akerlof [1970]. The term "experience good" for products whose qualities cannot be observed prior to purchase was created by Nelson, cf., Nelson [1970] and [1974].

[2] Akerlof [1970] focuses mainly on the adverse selection part of the issue. Arrow [1963] concentrates mainly on moral hazard aspects.

he will supply good quality in the future."[3] Under certain circumstances the supplier has an incentive not to disappoint these expectations. The expectations then establish a link between the quality a producer supplied (in the past) and his sales volume (in the present and future). The greater the quality a producer supplies at a given price, the greater the sales volume he can achieve. This reduces the scope for market failure due to moral hazard and/or adverse selection.

Under what circumstances will suppliers have an incentive not to cheat their customers by supplying low quality products? To answer this question one has to study the following trade-off: By cheating his customers and supplying low quality today, the producer can increase his current profits. Via the goodwill mechanism he would also decrease his future profits.[4] In a steady state equilibrium this means: The only way to induce a supplier not to make profits now by cheating the consumers by selling them low quality products is for him to make positive profits in each of the future periods. Future profits (in the sense of variable revenue minus variable costs) are compatible with a situation of free market entry only if the sunk costs of market entry are sufficiently high. Markets with quality uncertainty in which high quality products are supplied must thus in steady state equilibrium be characterized by the following properties. In each of the periods (1) variable revenue must be greater than variable costs, and (2) the *sunk* set-up costs of market entry must be sufficiently high.[5]

The interactions described in the last paragraph are analysed in some detail in Klein and Leffler [1981] and von Ungern-Sternberg and von Weizsäcker [1981]. The essential difference between these two models is as follows: Klein and Leffler assume that their firms act as quantity setters, that is, each firm acts as a price taker and chooses its output level till price equals marginal cost. Ungern-Sternberg and Weizsäcker assume instead that the firm is a quantity taker, that is, total demand and the number of suppliers on the market determine how much each of them can sell at the exogenously given price. Both of the above cited works have one weakness in common. They both study how high the market price has to be for a given quality level to be supplied, or, to put it slightly differently, what quality is forthcoming, when a given price is being charged. Statements about quality supplies are made *for an exogenously given price level*, and statements about the price level are made *for an exogenously given quality level.* This structure of the models means that they are unable to answer one of the questions one is most interested in, namely: *Will the market undersupply or oversupply quality*? To answer questions of this kind *one needs a model in which both the price charged by each producer and the quality he supplies are endogenously*

[3] cf., von Weizsäcker [1980a] and [1980b]. Because of the ubiquity of this kind of expectations formation he refers to it as the "extrapolation principle".

[4] This point is stressed in Farrel [1980], von Weizsäcker [1980a] and [1980b], Klein and Leffler [1981], von Ungern-Sternberg and von Weizsäcker [1981], Shapiro [1983], von Ungern-Sternberg [1984a].

[5] cf., Klein and Leffler [1981] and von Ungern-Sternberg and von Weizsäcker [1981].

determined. The aim of this paper is to fill just this gap. We construct a model with consumer quality uncertainty in which each producer endogenously determines both the price he charges and the quality he supplies. The model is similar to the one developed by Spence [1975] to study the quality choice of a firm in an environment with no uncertainty. As a result of this similarity it is very easy to pinpoint those quality distortions, which are due to imperfect information and the goodwill mechanism, and clearly separate them from those which would occur even in the absence of imperfect information on the part of consumers.

Our main conclusion is that the consumers' inability to observe quality directly does not, in the presence of goodwill, lead to the market undersupplying quality. On the contrary: the quality supplied is closer to what is socially optimal than would be the case in an environment of perfect information. The interactions leading to this result can be briefly summarized as follows. Spence [1975] shows that with fully informed consumers the quality supplied by a monopolist (or any other producer facing a downward-sloping demand curve) is determined by the consumers' valuation of quality of the last unit they buy, that is, the consumers' *marginal valuation of quality*. What is relevant from a social point of view, however, is not this marginal valuation but the additional utility the consumers derive from the extra quality on every one of the units they buy, that is, the consumers' *average valuation of quality*. Thus, if the marginal valuation of quality is lower than the average valuation, quality is undersupplied and in the opposite case it is oversupplied. Only if marginal and average valuation coincide is the "monopolist's" quality choice socially correct.[6]

How will quality uncertainty and the goodwill mechanism affect these results? The producer's choice of quality (and price) now affects two variables: First, *how much* each of his customers will buy from him, and second, *how many* customers he will actually have. The goodwill mechanism determines the number of consumers buying from a given producer. We thus have to ask ourselves: What are the factors determining whether a consumer recommends a given supplier to the other consumers? Surely it is not price alone. A low price producer selling terrible quality will hardly be recommended. Neither is it quality alone. A high quality supplier charging exorbitant prices is just as unlikely to be recommended. *The most reasonable approximation seems to us to say that consumers recommend those products to each other, which they believe to be yielding them the highest surplus*. This assumption leads directly to our results. The effect quality has on total consumer surplus is measured by the average valuation of quality. If a producer were interested only in the number of consumers buying from him his quality choice would therefore be guided only by the consumers' average valuation of quality. If the producer were interested only in the sales volume to each one of his customers, his quality choice would be guided only

[6] cf., Spence [1975, pp. 418–422]. Spence works with the consumers' inverse demand functions, rather than the direct demand functions, which are more convenient for our purposes. These are, however, mere notational differences.

by the consumers' marginal valuation of quality. As the producer is interested in both the total number of customers and the sales volume to each one of them, his quality choice will be guided by some kind of "weighted mean" of the consumers' marginal and average valuation of quality. If the marginal valuation of quality is lower than the average valuation, the quality supplied in a situation of imperfect information will still be lower than the social optimum. It will, however, be somewhat higher than would be the case in a situation of perfect information. A similar argument holds for the case where there would be an oversupply of quality in the presence of perfectly informed consumers. The quality supplied in the presence of imperfect consumer information will still be higher than is socially optimal but somewhat closer to the social optimal.

All of this does not, of course, imply that less information improves the working of the market as a whole. The goodwill mechanism implies that the equilibrium price charged by each producer will be higher, the less informed are the consumers.[7] The basic lesson to learn from this model is thus as follows: In models without a goodwill mechanism, imperfect quality information causes market failure due to an undersupply of high quality products. In markets where the goodwill mechanism does work, imperfect information will still cause market failure. Market failure does not, however, take the form of excessively low quality, but rather of prices above marginal costs. This conclusion might seem somewhat curious at first sight, but it fits everyday observations quite well. Clothing, sport goods, cars, restaurant meals, etc., are all to a certain extent "experience goods". We doubt, however, that cars (for example) would be of higher quality if customers could perfectly observe their various characteristics prior to purchase. It seems much more plausible that increased information would lead to more intensive competition and this would cause the price level to fall.

In the next section of this paper we derive the interactions just described in a formal model. Section III contains some concluding remarks.

II. THE MODEL

We consider a model of a market for an experience good which can be produced in different qualities q.

The assumptions concerning the supply side are:

(i) There are N suppliers i, $i = 1 \dots N$ of this good. Each of them produces according to a per period total cost function $TC_i(x_i, q_i)$ where x_i is the quantity he sells, and q_i the quality he supplies. The producers do *not* (necessarily) all have the same cost functions. All the cost functions do however have the

[7] cf., the works cited in footnote 4.

property that:

$$(1) \qquad \frac{\partial TC_i}{\partial x_i} = c_i(q_i) \qquad \text{with } c_i' > 0 \text{ and } c_i'' > 0 \qquad \nabla i$$

that is, all the per period production functions exhibit constant returns to scale and increasing costs of quality.

(ii) The producers' decision variables are the price they charge and the quality they supply in all the periods they stay on the market. These two determine their (expected) sales volume. The producers act as Nash competitors in their choice of price and quality.

(iii) The discount rate used by all the producers is r. To simplify that notation we introduce

$$R_T = \sum_{t=1}^{T} (1+r)^{-t}$$

The assumptions concerning the demand side are:

(iv) In every period there are Q *identical* new consumers entering in the market. The consumers entering in the market in period t will be called the consumers of generation t. Each generation of consumers stays on the market for $(T+1)$ periods.

(v) Each consumer's demand for the good is decreasing in price and increasing in quality. Demand for a product of quality q sold at a price p is denoted by

$$(2) \qquad x = D(p, q)$$

The associated surplus is denoted by

$$(3) \qquad S = S(p, q) = \int_p^{\infty} D(v, q)\, dv$$

We introduce the common notation

$$\frac{\partial x}{\partial p} = D_1, \qquad \frac{\partial x}{\partial q} = D_2, \qquad \frac{\partial S}{\partial p} = S_1 \quad \text{and} \quad \frac{\partial S}{\partial q} = S_2$$

Note for later use that

$$\frac{\partial x}{\partial q} \bigg/ \frac{\partial x}{\partial p} = \frac{D_1}{D_2}$$

gives us the consumer's *marginal valuation of quality*, that is, the amount he is willing to pay for an increase in the quality of *the last* unit he buys. Similarly

$$\frac{\partial S}{\partial q} \bigg/ \frac{\partial S}{\partial p} = \frac{\partial S}{\partial q} \bigg/ D(p, q) = \frac{S_2}{S_1}$$

gives us the consumer's *average valuation of quality*, that is, the amount he would be willing to pay for an increase in the quality of *all* the units he buys.

The goodwill mechanism in this model works as follows:

(vi) In the first period each consumer randomly[8] visits one producer and samples *one unit of his good*. At the end of the first period each consumer meets a number of other consumers of his generation, and they exchange information about the price and the quality of the products they have sampled. As a result of this exchange of information each consumer then chooses one producer from whom he will buy in the remaining T periods he stays on the market. Each consumer will obviously choose that producer whom he believes to be supplying the "best" product, that is, *the producer whom he believes to be selling the product yielding the greatest surplus*. We assume that the information consumers exchange contains a certain amount of noise, so that *the number of customers who end up buying from any given supplier i is a continuous increasing function of the surplus his product yields.*[9]

Denote by f_i the fraction of a generation who will end up buying from supplier i. Introducing the notation $S_i = S(p_i, q_i)$ we have

$$f_i = f(S_i, S_1, \ldots, S_{i-1}, S_{i+1}, \ldots, S_N) \tag{4}$$

with $\partial f/\partial S_i = f_1 > 0$ and $\partial f/\partial S_j < 0$, $i \neq j$. For consistency we must, of course, have $\sum_{i=1}^{N} f_i = 1$.

(vii) Once the consumers have been allocated to the various suppliers according to the mechanism described above, each of them buys from his supplier according to his demand function $x_i = D(p_i, q_i)$.

Equilibrium

We shall not prove the existence of a unique equilibrium in the model described above, but content ourselves with the analysis of the properties it must exhibit: The sales volume of producer i to any given generation of consumers is

$$V = Q\left[\frac{1}{N} + Tf(S_i, .)x_i\right] \tag{5}$$

The present value of profits he earns on any given generation of consumers is

$$\Pi_i = [p_i - c_i(q_i)]Q\left[\frac{1}{N} + R_T f(S_i, .)x_i\right] \tag{6}$$

[8] Given the information the consumers have, it is rational for them to choose the producer from which they buy this first unit at random. While they may know that the stores charging a higher price sell better quality (on average), this tells them nothing about which producer offers the best price–quality combination.

[9] The structure of the model is similar to many of the "brand choice" models in the management science literature cited. In that literature the transition matrices among different brands are often exogenously specified. We assume that there exists an objective measure of quality, and that the probability of purchase is an increasing function of quality and a decreasing function of price.

Given the Nash assumption, profit maximization implies[10] choosing p_i and q_i such that

$$\frac{\partial \Pi_i}{\partial p_i} = 0 \rightarrow$$

$$(7) \qquad R_T[f_1 S_1 x_i + f(S_i,.)D_1] = -\frac{[1/N + R_T f(S_i,.)x_i]}{[p_i - c_i(q_i)]}$$

$$\frac{\partial \Pi_i}{\partial q_i} = 0 \rightarrow$$

$$(8) \qquad R_T[f_1 S_2 x_i + f(S_i,.)D_2] = \frac{\partial c_i/\partial q_i\,[1/N + R_T f(S_i,.)x_i]}{[p_i - c_i(q_i)]}$$

Taking the quotient of (7) and (8), we obtain

$$(9) \qquad \frac{\partial c_i}{\partial q_i} = \frac{x_i f_1 S_2 + f(S_i,.)D_2}{x_i f_1 S_1 + f(S_i,.)D_1}$$

Define $x_i f_1 = a$ and $f(S_i,.) = b$. Equation (9) can then be rewritten

$$(10) \qquad \frac{\partial c_i}{\partial q_i} = \frac{aS_2 + bD_2}{aS_1 + bD_1} = A$$

where both a and b are strictly positive numbers.

It is shown in the Appendix that

$$(11) \qquad \text{if } \frac{S_2}{S_1} < \frac{D_2}{D_1}, \quad \text{then } \frac{S_2}{S_1} < A < \frac{D_2}{D_1}$$

and

$$(12) \qquad \text{if } \frac{S_2}{S_1} > \frac{D_2}{D_1}, \quad \text{then } \frac{S_2}{S_1} > A > \frac{D_2}{D_1}$$

Equation (9) is the main result of this paper. Let us turn to its interpretation: Recall from the definitions following equation (3) that S_2/S_1 gives the consumers' *average valuation of quality*, that is, it is the *social incentive to produce quality*. A social planner facing the total cost function $TC_i(x_i, q_i)$, will choose his quality level such that

$$(13) \qquad \frac{\partial c_i}{\partial q_i} = \frac{S_2}{S_1}$$

[10] When formulating the problem in this way we are assuming that the producer's profit maximization problem does have an *interior* solution. In particular it must be the case that the new consumers coming on the market each period will not buy from a producer if the price he charges is exorbitantly high. What we are assuming essentially is that it does not pay the producer to charge a very high price and supply the lowest possible quality compatible with the production technology he has chosen. Denote by $p^{\max}$, the maximum price at which consumers are willing to buy the product and by $c_i(\beta_1)$ the marginal cost of producing the lowest possible quality. We are assuming then that the per period profits obtained by selling quality β_1 at a price $p^{\max}$ yields lower per period profits than the interior solution we are discussing.

The socially optimal quality choice, that is, the quality choice satisfying equation (13) will be denoted q_i^s. Similarly D_2/D_1 gives the consumers' *marginal valuation of quality*, that is, it is the private incentive to produce quality in a situation of complete information. A monopolist would then choose his quality level such that

$$\frac{\partial c_i}{\partial q_i} = \frac{D_2}{D_1} \tag{14}$$

The monopolist's quality choice, that is, the quality choice satisfying equation (14) will be denoted q_i^m. Spence [1975] has shown that whenever $D_2/D_1 < S_2/S_1$, the monopolist has an insufficient incentive to produce quality. The quality forthcoming will be too low, that is, $q_i^m < q_i^s$. When $D_2/D_1 > S_2/S_1$, the monopolist has too great an incentive to produce quality. The quality forthcoming will be too high, that is, $q_i^m > q_i^s$.

Equations (9) and (10) and their interpretations (11) and (12) give a supplier's incentive to produce quality in a situation of *imperfect* information. Denote the producer's optimal quality choice by q_i^*. Equation (11) tells us that if in a situation of perfect information there is a private incentive to produce excessively high quality, this incentive will persist in a situation of incomplete information. The incentive will, however, be somewhat lower, that is, $q_i^m < q_i^* < q_i^s$. Similarly equation (12) tells us that if in a situation of perfect information there is an insufficient private incentive to produce quality, again this tendency will persist in a situation of imperfect information. The incentive to produce quality will, however, be somewhat higher, that is, $q_i^s < q_i^* < q_i^m$.

The main conclusion we derive from the above analysis is as follows: *With a functioning goodwill mechanism one cannot say that imperfect consumer information will lead to the market undersupplying quality.* While the market will not, of course, always choose the socially optimal quality level, this fact cannot be ascribed to the information problem *per se*. The same kind of problems arise even in situations of perfect information. The result that imperfect information leads to quality levels closer to the social optimum can be explained as follows: In a situation of imperfect information a producer's choice of quality level affects two variables: First, the surplus he yields to the consumers and thus, via the goodwill mechanism, his total number of customers. And, second, his sales volume to each customer. A social planner is interested only in the first of these effects; a monopolist selling to customers with perfect information only in the second. A supplier selling on a market with imperfect information has to take both factors into account. It is thus hardly surprising that his quality choice will lie somewhere in between the social optimum and the monopolist's.

Further Interpretations

Apart from this main result, the above model has some further interesting properties that one would expect to find in any model of a market for an experience good. Substituting the producer's optimal quality choice q_i^* into (7) we obtain:

$$(15) \qquad [p_i - c_i(q_i^*)] = -\frac{[1/N + R_T f(S_i, .)x_i]}{R_T[f_1 S_1 x_i r f(S_i, .) D_1]}$$

Equation (15) has the following properties:

(i) $[p_i - c_i(q_i^*)] > 0$. As in all models of the goodwill mechanism with quantity taking suppliers, high quality products will be forthcoming only if price is greater than marginal cost, that is, if the producers make positive per period profits. This result together with the preceding analysis shows that imperfect information on the part of consumers does indeed lead to market failure. In the presence of the goodwill mechanism, the market failure does not, however, take the form of low quality, but of excessively high prices (that is, prices above marginal costs).

$$\text{(ii)} \qquad \frac{\partial [p_i - c_i(q_i^*)]}{\partial R_T} < 0$$

The lower R_T, that is the higher the interest rate, the higher will be the price cost margin charged by each producer. Again this is an intuitively plausible result. The greater the interest rate, the greater is the incentive to "cheat" the new customers entering each period by charging a high price, even if this does imply a loss of sales volume in future "repeat purchases".

$$\text{(iii)} \qquad \frac{\partial [p_i - c_i(q_i^*)]}{\partial f_1} < 0$$

The greater f_1, that is the stronger the sales volume reacts to a given increase in the surplus to the consumers, the lower will be the equilibrium price cost margin. In the special case, where $D_2/D_1 = S_2/S_1$, the social incentive to provide quality coincides with the private incentive. We will then of course have $q_i^S = q_i^* = q_i^m$. In such a situation an increase in f_1 will leave the choice of quality unchanged, and lead to a simple reduction in price.[11]

III. CONCLUSION

The analysis can, of course, be extended in several directions. However, it should be clear from the formulation of the problem adopted here that the producer's quality choice depends critically on the exact specification of the repeat purchase function. The specification we have adopted, while certainly somewhat *ad hoc*, is the most plausible first approximation we could think of. However, if price were given a preponderant weight in the goodwill function, this would bias the results in the direction of excessively low quality. The opposite would occur if quality were the main determinant of the total number

[11] Analogous results are derived in a somewhat different framework and discussed in much greater detail in von Ungern-Sternberg and von Weizsäcker [1981] and von Ungern-Sternberg [1984a, chapters 4–6].

of customers. The fact that the price level can usually be exactly observed, but quality only with some noise, does not seem to bias the results against the provision of quality. That, at least, is the result explicitly derived in von Ungern-Sternberg [1984b] in an admittedly somewhat more restrictive framework.

The essential message of our current knowledge of the goodwill mechanism is certainly that the market does have powerful self-correcting mechanisms for "lemons"-type problems which are due to adverse selection and moral hazard. It is imperative that we understand the working of these mechanisms. Such an understanding is a necessary prerequisite for formulating a government's role in helping the consumers with their search for information. As the calls for government intervention to regulate markets are, at least in Germany, getting continuously stronger, the workings of the perhaps too invisible hand of the goodwill mechanisms should be made somewhat more visible by the profession.

ACCEPTED NOVEMBER 1984

THOMAS VON UNGERN-STERNBERG
AND CARL CHRISTIAN VON WEIZSÄCKER,
Department of Economics,
Universität Bern,
Gesellschaftsstr. 27,
Bern 3012,
Switzerland.

APPENDIX

We shall restrict ourselves to proving only one of the four inequalities in (11) and (12). The other three can be proven in the same way:

Theorem: If

$$\frac{S_2}{S_1} < \frac{D_2}{D_1} \tag{A1}$$

and $a > 0$ *and* $b > 0$, *then*

$$\frac{S_2}{S_1} < \frac{aS_2 + bD_2}{aS_1 + bD_1} \tag{A2}$$

Proof: There exists a positive constant α, such that we can write

$$D_2 = \alpha S_2 \tag{A3}$$

As $S_2/S_1 < D_2/D_1$, then there must also exist some positive constant k such that we can write

$$D_1 = \alpha(S_1 - k) \tag{A4}$$

Substituting (A3) and (A4) into (A2) and simplifying, we obtain:

$$\frac{S_2}{S_1} < \frac{S_2(a+\alpha b)}{S_1(a+\alpha b) - \alpha k} \tag{A5}$$

As both α and k are greater than zero, A5 is obviously correct. QED

BIBLIOGRAPHY

AAFTINK, J., IRELAND, N. J. and SERTEL, M. R., 1982, 'On Cournot–Nash Equilibria with Exogenous Uncertainty', Warwick Economic Research Paper No. 210 (July), forthcoming *Journal of Optimisation Theory and Applications*.

AKERLOF, G. A., 1970, 'The Market for Lemons: Qualitative Uncertainty and the Market Mechanism', *The Quarterly Journal of Economics*, 84, 3 (August), pp. 488–500.

ANDERSON, J., 1984, 'Identification of Interactive Behaviour in Air Service Markets: 1973–76', *Journal of Industrial Economics*, 23, 4 (June), pp. 489–508.

APPELBAUM, E., 1979, 'Testing Price Taking Behaviour', *Journal of Econometrics*, 9, pp. 283–294.

APPELBAUM, E., 1982, 'The Estimation of the Degree of Oligopoly Power', *Journal of Econometrics*, 19, pp. 287–299.

AREEDA, P. and TURNER, D. F., 1975, 'Predatory Pricing and Related Practices Under Section 2 of the Sherman Act', *Harvard Law Review*, 88, 4 (February), pp. 697–733.

AREEDA, P. and TURNER, D. F., 1976, 'Scherer on Predatory Pricing: A Reply', *Harvard Law Review*, 89, 5 (March), pp. 891–900.

ARROW, K. J., 1963, 'Uncertainty and the Welfare Economics of Medical Care', *The American Economic Review*, 53, 5 (December), pp. 465–491.

D'ASPREMONT, C. and GERARD-VARET, L., 1979, 'Incentives and Incomplete Information', *Journal of Public Economics*, 11, pp. 25–34.

AUMANN, R. J., 1960, 'Acceptable Points in Games of Perfect Information', *Pacific Journal of Mathematics*, 10, pp. 381–417.

BAKER, J. and BRESNAHAN, T., 1984, 'Estimating the Demand Curve Facing a Single Firm: Estimates for Three Brewing Firms', Research Paper 54, Stanford Workshop on the Economics of Factor Markets.

BAKER, J. and BRESNAHAN, T., 1985, 'The Gains from Merger or Collusion in Product-Differentiated Industries', *Journal of Industrial Economics*, this issue.

BASAR, T. and HO, Y. C., 1974, 'Information Properties of the Nash Solutions of Two Nonzero-sum Games, *Journal of Economic Theory*, 7, 4 (April), pp. 370–387.

BAUMOL, WM. J., 1979, 'Quasi-Permanence of Price Reductions: A Policy for Prevention of Predatory Pricing', *Yale Law Journal*, 89, 1 (November), pp. 1–26.

BAUMOL, WM. J., PANZAR, J. C. and WILLIG, R. D., 1982, *Contestable Markets and the Theory of Industry Structure* (Harcourt, Brace, Jovanovitch, San Diego).

BEATH, J. and ULPH, D., 1984, 'The Welfare Economics of Vertical Products Differentiation', mimeo, University of Bristol.

Beer Marketer's Insights, annual.

BERNHEIM, B. D., 1984, 'Rationalisable Strategic Behaviour', *Econometrica*, 52, 4 (July), pp. 1007–1028.

BIGGADIKE, E. R., 1976, *Corporate Diversification Entry, Strategy and Performance* (Harvard University Press, Cambridge).

BRADBURD, R. M., 1980, 'Conglomerate Power without Market Power: the Effect of Conglomeration on a Risk Averse Quantity Adjusting Firm', *American Economic Review*, 70, 3 (June), pp. 483–488.

BRANDER, J. and SPENCER, B., 1983, 'Strategic Commitment with R & D: the Symmetric Case', *Bell Journal of Economics*, 14, 1 (Spring), pp. 225–235.

BRESNAHAN, T. F., 1980, 'Competition and Collusion in the American Automobile Industry: The 1955 Price War', mimeo, Stanford University.

BRESNAHAN, T. F., 1981, 'Departures from Marginal-Cost Pricing in the American Automobile Industry: Estimates for 1977–1978', *Journal of Econometrics*, 11, pp. 201–227.

BRESNAHAN, T. F., 1981, 'Duopoly Models with Consistent Conjectures', *American Economic Review*, 71, 5 (December), pp. 934–945.

BRESNAHAN, T. F., 1981, 'Competition and Collusion in the American Automobile Industry: The 1955 Price War', mimeo, Stanford University.

BRESNAHAN, T. F., 1982, 'The Oligopoly Solution Concept is Identified', *Economics Letters*, 10, 1, pp. 87–92.

BRODLEY, J. F. and HAY, G. A., 1981, 'Predatory Pricing: Competing Economic Theories and the Evolution of Legal Standards', *Cornell Law Review*, 23, 4 (April), pp. 738–803.

BROWN, D. and HEAL, G., 1979, 'Equity, Efficiency and Increasing Returns', *Review of Economic Studies*, 46, 4 (October), pp. 571–586.

BULOW, J. and PFEIDERER, P., 1983, 'A Note on the Effect of Cost Changes on Prices', *Journal of Political Economy*, 91, 1 (February), pp. 182–185.

CAVES, R. and PUGEL, T., 1980, 'Intraindustry Differences in Conduct and Performance: Viable Strategies in U.S. Manufacturing Industries', Monograph Series in Finance and Economics, N.T.U. Graduate School of Business Administration.

CHAMBERLIN, E. H., 1929, 'Duopoly: Value when Sellers are Few', *Quarterly Journal of Economics*, 43, pp. 63–100.

CHAMBERLIN, E. H., 1933, *The Theory of Monopolistic Competition* (Harvard University Press, Cambridge, Mass.).

CLARKE, R. N., 1983, 'Duopolists Don't Wish to Share Information', *Economics Letters*, 11, pp. 33–36.

CLARKE, R. N., 1983, 'Collusion and the Incentives for Information Sharing', *Bell Journal of Economics*, 14, pp. 383–394.

CLARKE, R., DAVIES, S. and WATERSON, M., 1984, 'The Profitability-Concentration Relation: Market Power or Efficiency?', *Journal of Industrial Economics*, 32, 4 (June), pp. 435–450.

COMANOR, W. and LEIBENSTEIN, H., 1969, 'Allocative Efficiency, X-inefficiency, and the Measurement of Welfare Losses', *Economica*, N.S. 36, 143 (August), pp. 304–309.

COWLING, K. and CUBBIN, J., 1972, 'Hedonic Price Indexes for Cars in the U.K.', *Economic Journal*, 82, 327 (September), pp. 963–978.

COWLING, K. and WATERSON, M., 1976, 'Price Cost Margins and Market Structure', *Economica*, 43, 171, pp. 267–274.

COWLING, K. and MUELLER, D., 1978, 'The Social Costs of Monopoly Power', *Economic Journal*, 88, 352 (December), pp. 727–748.

CRAWFORD, V. and SOBEL, J., 1982, 'Strategic Information Transmission', *Econometrica*, 50, pp. 1431–1451.

CUBBIN, J., 1975, 'Quality Change and Pricing Behaviour in the U.K. Car Industry, 1956–1968', *Economica*, 42, 165 (February), pp. 43–58.

CUBBIN, J., 1983, 'Apparent Collusion and Conjectural Variations in Differentiated Oligopoly', *International Journal of Industrial Organisation*, 1, pp. 155–163.

CYERT, D. and DEGROOT, M., 1973, 'An Analysis of Cooperation and Learning in a Duopoly Context', *American Economic Review*, 63, 1, pp. 24–37.

DANSBY, R. and WILLIG, R., 1979, 'Industry Performance Gradient Indices', *American Economic Review*, 69, 3, pp. 249–260.

DASGUPTA, P. and STIGLITZ, J., 1980, 'Industrial Structure and the Nature of Innovative Activity', *Economic Journal*, 90 (June), pp. 266–293.

DASGUPTA, P., 1982, 'The Theory of Technological Competition', ICERD Discussion Paper No. 82/46 (May), London School of Economics, International Centre for Economics and Related Disciplines.

DASGUPTA, P., 1984, 'The Theory of Technological Competition', in F. Matthewson and J. Stiglitz (eds.), *New Developments in the Analysis of Market Structure* (M.I.T. Press, Boston, Mass.).

DEMSETZ, H., 1974, 'Two Systems of Belief about Monopoly', in Goldschmid *et al.* (eds.), *Industrial Concentration: The New Learning* (Little and Brown, Boston).

DE PALMA, A., GINSBURGH, V., PAPAGEROGIOU, Y. and THISSE, J.-F., 1983, 'The Principle of Minimum Differentiation Holds under Sufficient Heterogeneity', CORE, Discussion Paper, No. 8339, Louvain-la-Neuve.

DICKSON, V., 1983, 'Collusion and Price-Cost Margins', *Economica*, 49, 193 (February), pp. 39–42.

DIXIT, A., 1980, 'The Role of Investment in Entry Deterrence', *Economic Journal*, 90, 357 (March), pp. 95–106.

DIXIT, A., 1982, 'Recent Developments in Oligopoly Theory', *American Economic Review*, 72, 2 (May), papers and proceedings, pp. 12–17.

DIXIT, A. K. and STIGLITZ, J. E., 1977, 'Monopolistic Competition and Optimum Product Diversity', *American Economic Review*, 67, 3 (June), pp. 297–308.

DIXON, H. D., 1984a, 'Cournot and Bertrand Outcomes as Equilibria in a Strategic Metagame with Precommitment', Birkbeck Discussion Paper, No. 166.

DIXON, H. D., 1984b, *Approximate Bertrand Equilibria and Strategic Precommitment*, D. Phil. Thesis, Oxford.

DIXON, H. D., 1985, 'Strategic Investment in an Industry with a Competitive Product Market', *Journal of Industrial Economics*, this issue.

DOLBEAR, F., LAVE, L. and BOWMAN, G., 1968, 'Collusion in Oligopoly: An Experiment on the Effect of Numbers and Information', *Quarterly Journal of Economics*, 82 (May), pp. 240–259.

EASLEY, D., MASSON, R. T. and REYNOLDS, R. J., 1981, 'A Dynamic Analysis of Predatory Pricing with Rational Expectations', Working Paper 250, Cornell University.

EASLEY, D., MASSON, R. T. and REYNOLDS, R. J., 1984, 'Preying for Time: Additional Analysis', mimeo, Cornell University.

EASLEY, D., MASSON, R. T. and REYNOLDS, R. J., 1985, 'Preying for Time', *Journal of Industrial Economics*, this issue.

EATON, B. C. and LIPSEY, R. G., 1975, 'The Principle of Minimum Differentiation Reconsidered: Some New Developments in the Theory of Spatial Competition', *Review of Economic Studies*, 42, 1 (January), pp. 27–49.

EATON, B. C. and LIPSEY, R. G., 1976, 'The Non-Uniqueness of Equilibrium in the Löschian Location Model', *American Economic Review*, 66, 1 (March), pp. 77–93.

EATON, B. C. and LIPSEY, R., 1978, 'Freedom of Entry and the Existence of Price Profit', *Economic Journal*, 80 (September), pp. 455–469.

EATON, B. C. and LIPSEY, R., 1980, 'Exit Barriers and Entry Barriers: The Durability of Capital as a Barrier to Entry', *Bell Journal of Economics*, 11, 2 (Autumn), pp. 721–729.

EATON, B. C. and LIPSEY, R., 1981, 'Capital, Commitment and Entry Equilibrium', *Bell Journal of Economics*, 12, 2 (Autumn), pp. 593–604.

EISENBERG, B. S., 1980, 'Information Exchange Among Competitors: the Issue of Relative Value Scales for Physicians' Services', *Journal of Law and Economics*, 23, 2 (October), pp. 441–460.

EISENSTAT, P., MASSON, R. T. and RODDY, D., 'An Economic Analysis of the Associated Milk Producers, Inc. Monopoly', filed with the court in *U.S. v. Associated Milk Producers, Inc.*, 394 F. Supp. 29 (W.D. Mo. 1975) *aff'd* 534 F.2d 113 (8th Cir., 1976), 628 pp.

ELLISON, R. I. and UHL, K. P., 1964, 'Influence of Beer Brand Identification on Taste Perception', *Journal of Marketing Research* (August), pp. 321–332.

ELZINGA, K. G., 1982, 'The Beer Industry', in Walter Adams (ed.), *The Structure of American Industry* (6th edition, Macmillan, New York).

ENCAOUA, D., GEROSKI, P. and JACQUEMIN, A., 1984, 'Strategic Competition and the Persistence of Dominant Firms: A Survey', in F. Matthewson and J. Stiglitz (eds.), *New Developments and the Analysis of Market Structure* (M.I.T. Press, Boston, Mass.).

FARREL, J., 1980, 'Prices as Signals of Quality', unpublished Ph.D. dissertation.

FISHER, F. M., MCGOWAN, J. J. and GREENWOOD, J. E., 1983, *Folded, Spindled and Mutilated: Economic Analysis and U.S. v. IBM* (M.I.T. Press, Cambridge and London).

FOURAKER, L. and SIEGEL, S., 1963, *Bargaining behavior* (McGraw-Hill, New York).

FRIEDMAN, J. W., 1963, 'Individual Behavior in Oligopolistic Markets: An Experimental Study', *Yale Economic Essays*, 3, pp. 359–417.

FRIEDMAN, J. W., 1969, 'On Experimental Research in Oligopoly', *Review of Economic Studies*, 36, pp. 399–415.

FRIEDMAN, J. W., 1970, 'Equal Profit as a Fair Division', in H. Sauermann (ed.), *Beiträge zur Experimentellen Wirtschaftsforschung*, II (J. C. B. Mohr (Paul Siebeck), Tübingen), pp. 19–32.

FRIEDMAN, J. W., 1971, 'A Non-Cooperative Equilibrium for Supergames', *Review of Economic Studies*, 38, pp. 1–12.

FRIEDMAN, J. W., 1972, 'On the Structure of Oligopoly Models with Differentiated Products', in H. Sauermann (ed.), *Beiträge zur Experimentellen Wirtschaftsforschung*, III (J. C. B. Mohr (Paul Siebeck), Tübingen), pp. 28–63.

FRIEDMAN, J. W., 1977, *Oligopoly and the Theory of Games* (North-Holland Publishing Co., Amsterdam).

FRIEDMAN, J. W., 1983, *Oligopoly Theory* (Cambridge University Press, Cambridge).

FRIEDMAN, J. W. and HOGGART, A. C., 1980, *An Experiment in Non-Cooperative Oligopoly* (JAI Press, Greenwich, Connecticut).

FUDENBERG, D., GILBERT, R. J., STIGLITZ, J. E. and TIROLE, J., 1983, 'Preemption, Leapfrogging and Competition in Patent Races', *European Economic Review*, 22, pp. 3–31, Special Issue on Market Competition, Conflict and Collusion.

FUDENBERG, D. and TIROLE, J., 1984, 'Dynamic Models of Oligopoly', mimeo, Stanford University.

GAL-OR, E., 1982, 'Information Sharing in Oligopoly', University of Pittsburgh, Working Paper.

GEROSKI, P., 1982, 'Interpreting a Correlation Between Profits and Concentration', *Journal of Industrial Economics*, 30, 3 (March), pp. 305–318.

GEROSKI, P., 1982b, 'The Empirical Analysis of Conjectural Variations in Oligopoly', mimeo, Université Catholique de Louvain.

GEROSKI, P., 1983, 'Some Reflections on the Theory and Application of Concentration Indices', *International Journal of Industrial Organization*, 1, pp. 79–94.

GEROSKI, P. and ULPH, A., 1984, 'A Model of the Crude Oil Market in Which Conduct Varies Over Time', mimeo, University of Southampton.

GEROSKI, P. and JACQUEMIN, A., 1984, 'Dominant Firms and Their Alleged Decline', *International Journal of Industrial Organisation*, 2, pp. 1–27.

GEROSKI, P., INGHAM, A. and ULPH, A., 1984, 'Asymmetric Information and Entry: The Case of Learning by Observing', mimeo, University of Southampton.

GILBERT, R. J., 1981, 'Patents, Sleeping Patents and Entry Deterrence', in S. C. Salop (ed.), *Strategy, Predation and Antitrust Analysis*, Federal Trade Commission, pp. 205–269.

GILBERT, R. J. and NEWBERY, D., 1982, 'Pre-emptive Patenting and the Persistence of Monopoly, *American Economic Review*, 72, 3 (June), pp. 514–526.

GILBERT, R. J. and NEWBERY, D., 1984a, 'Uncertain Innovation and the Persistence of Monopoly: Comment', *American Economic Review*, 74, 1 (March), pp. 238–242.

GILBERT, R. J. and NEWBERY, D., 1984b, 'Pre-emptive Patenting and the Persistence of Monopoly: Reply', *American Economic Review*, 74, 1 (March), pp. 251–253.

GOLLOP, F. and ROBERTS, M., 1979, 'Firm Interdependence in Oligopolistic Markets', *Journal of Econometrics*, 10, pp. 313–331.

GREEN, E. J., 1980, 'Non-Cooperative Price Taking in Large Dynamic Markets', *Journal of Economic Theory*, 22, 2 (April), pp. 155–182. Reprinted in A. Mas-Collell (ed.), *Non-Cooperative Approaches to the Theory of Perfect Competition* (Academic Press, 1982), pp. 37–64.

GREEN, E. J. and PORTER, R. H., 1984, 'Noncooperative Collusion under Imperfect Price Information', *Econometrica*, 52, 1 (January), pp. 87–100.

GREER, D. F., 1971, 'Product Differentiation and Concentration in the Brewing Industry', *Journal of Industrial Economics*, 19, 3 (July), pp. 201–219.

GREER, D. F., 1979, 'A Critique of Areeda and Turner's Standards for Predatory Practices', *The Antitrust Bulletin*, XXIV, 2 (Summer), pp. 233–261.

GREER, D. F., 1981, 'The Causes of Concentration in the Brewing Industry', *Quarterly Review of Economics and Business*, 21, 4 (Winter), pp. 87–106.

GROSSMAN, S., 1981, 'Nash Equilibrium and the Industrial Organisation of Market with Large Fixed Costs', *Econometrica*, 49, 5 (September), pp. 1149–1172.

GROSSMAN, G. and SHAPIRO, C., 1984, 'Information Advertising with Differentiated Products', *Review of Economic Studies*, 51, 1 (January), pp. 63–81.

HARBERGER, A., 1954, 'Monopoly and Resource Allocation', *American Economic Review*, Papers and proceedings, 44 (May), pp. 77–87.

HARRIS, C. J. and VICKERS, J. S., 1985, 'Perfect Equilibrium in a Model of a Race', *Review of Economic Studies*, 52, pp. 193–209.

HARRIS, C. J. and VICKERS, J. S., 1985, 'Patent Races and the Persistence of Monopoly', *Journal of Industrial Economics*, this issue.

HARSANYI, J. C., 1967–68, 'Games with Incomplete Information Played by Bayesian Players', *Management Science*, 14, 11 (July), Parts I, II, III, pp. 159–182, 320–334, 486–502.

HART, O. D., 1983, 'Monopolistic Competition in the Spirit of Chamberlin: A General Model', *I.C.E.R.D. Discussion Paper, 83/82*, LSE.

HATTEN, K. J. and SCHENDAL, D. E., 1977, 'Heterogeneity Within an Industry: Firm Conduct in the U.S. Brewing Industry 1952–71', *Journal of Industrial Economics*, 26, 2 (December), pp. 99–114.

HAY, D., 1976, 'Sequential Entry and Entry Deterring Strategies in Spatial Competition', *Oxford Economic Papers*, 28, 2 (July), pp. 240–257.

HAZILLA, M. and KOPP, R. J., 1983, 'Substitution between Energy and Other Factors of Production', *Resources of the Future*.

HOGARTY, T. F. and ELZINGA, K. G., 1972, 'The Demand for Beer', *Review of Economics and Statistics*, 54, 2 (May), pp. 195–198.

HOGGATT, A. C., 1959, 'An Experimental Business Game', *Behavioural Science*, 4, pp. 192–203.

HOGGATT, A. C., 1967, 'Measuring the Cooperativeness of Behaviour in Quantity Variation Duopoly Games', *Behavioural Science*, 12, pp. 109–121.

HOLAHAN, W. L., 1978, 'Cartel Problems: Comment', *American Economic Review*, 68, 5 (December), pp. 942–946.

HOTELLING, H., 1929, 'Stability in Competition', *Economic Journal*, 39 (March), pp. 41–57.

IRELAND, N. J., 1980, 'The Analogy between Parameter Uncertainty and Parameter Changes', *Economics Letters*, 6, pp. 301–308.

IRELAND, N. J., 1983a, 'Monopolistic Competition and a Firm's Product Range', *International Journal of Industrial Organization*, 1, pp. 239–252.

IRELAND, N. J., 1983b, 'A Note on Conglomerate Merger and Behavioural Response to Risk', *Journal of Industrial Economics*, 31, 3 (March), pp. 283–290.

IRELAND, N., 1985, 'Product Diversity and Monopolistic Competition under Uncertainty', *Journal of Industrial Economics*, this issue.

ISHII, Y., 1977, 'On the Theory of the Competitive Firm under Price Uncertainty: A Note', *American Economic Review*, 67, 4 (September), pp. 768–769.

IWATA, G., 1974, 'Measurement of Conjectural Variations in Oligopoly', *Econometrica*, 42, 5 (September), pp. 947–966.

JOSCOW, A., 1983, 'A Welfare Analysis of Industry Product Variety', mimeo, Yale University.

JOSKOW, P. L. and KLEVORICK, A. K., 1979, 'A Framework for Analyzing Predatory Pricing Policy', *Yale Law Journal*, 89, 2 (December), pp. 213–270.

JUST, R. and CHERN, W., 1980, 'Tomatoes, Technology and Oligopoly', *Bell Journal of Economics*, 11, 2 (Autumn), pp. 584–602.

KAMIEN, M. I. and SCHWARTZ, N. L., 1982, *Market Structure and Innovation* (Cambridge University Press, New York and Sydney).

KEITHAHN, C., 1978, 'Staff Report of the Federal Trade Commission', *The Brewing Industry*, December.

KELTON, C. M. L. and KELTON, W. D., 1982, 'Advertising and Intra-industry Brand Shift in the U.S. Brewing Industry', *Journal of Industrial Economics*, 30, 2 (March), pp. 293–303.

KIRMAN, WM. and MASSON, R. T., 1984, 'Capacity Signalling to Deter Entry', unpublished paper, Cornell University.

KLEIN, B. and LEFFLER, K., 1981, 'Non Governmental Enforcement of Contracts: The Role of Marketforces in Assuring Quality', *The Journal of Political Economy*, 88, 4 (August), pp. 615–641.

KOENKER, R. W. and PERRY, M. K., 1981, 'Product Differentiation, Monopolistic Competition and Public Policy', *Bell Journal*, 12, 1 (Spring), pp. 217–231.

KOLLER, R. H., III, 1971, 'The Myth of Predatory Pricing: An Empirical Study', *Antitrust Law and Economics Review*, 4, 4 (Summer), pp. 105–123.

KREPS, D. M., MILGROM, P. and WILSON, R., 1982, 'Rational Cooperation in the Finitely Repeated Prisoners' Dilemma', *Journal of Economic Theory*, 27, pp. 245–252.

KREPS, D. M. and WILSON, R., 1982a, 'Sequential Equilibria', *Econometrica*, 50, pp. 863–894.

KREPS, D. M. and WILSON, R., 1982b, 'Reputation and Imperfect Information', *Journal of Economic Theory*, 27, 2 (August), pp. 253–279.

KREPS, D. M. and SCHEINKMAN, J. A., 1983, 'Quantity Precommitment and Bertrand Competition Yield Cournot Outcomes', *Bell Journal of Economics*, 14, 2 (Autumn), pp. 326–337.

KRUGMAN, P., 1980, 'Scale Economies, Product Differentiation and the Pattern of Trade', *American Economic Review*, 70, 5 (December), pp. 950–959.

LAITNER, J., 1980, 'Rational Duopoly Equilibria', *Quarterly Journal of Economics*, 95, 4 (December), pp. 641–662.

LAMBIN, J., NAERT, P. A. and BULTEY, A., 1975, 'Optimal Marketing Behaviour in Oligopoly', *European Economic Review*, 6, pp. 105–128.

LANCASTER, K., 1975, 'Socially Optimal Product Differentiation', *American Economic Review*, 65, 4 (September), pp. 567–585.

LANCASTER, K., 1979, *Variety, Equity and Efficiency* (Columbia University Press, New York).

LANE, W., 1980, 'Product Differentiation in a Model with Endogenous Sequential Entry', *Bell Journal of Economics*, 11, 1 (Spring), pp. 237–260.

LEE, L.-F. and PORTER, R. H., 1984, 'Switching Regression Models with Imperfect Sample Separation Information—With an Application on Cartel Stability', *Econometrica*, 52, 3 (March), pp. 391–418.

LEE, T. and WILDE, L., 1980, 'Market Structure and Innovation: A Reformulation', *Quarterly Journal of Economics*, 94, 2 (March), pp. 429–436.

LEIBENSTEIN, H., 1966, 'Allocative Efficiency versus X-efficiency', *American Economic Review*, 56 (June), pp. 392–415.

LERNER, A., 1934, 'The Concept of Monopoly and the Measurement of Monopoly Power', *Review of Economic Studies*, 11 (June), pp. 157–175.

LOURY, G., 1979, 'Market Structure and Innovation', *Quarterly Journal of Economics*, 93, 3 (August), pp. 395–410.

LUCE, R. D. and RAIFFA, H., 1966, *Games and Decisions* (Wiley).

MACLEOD, W. B., 1984, 'The Core and Oligopoly Theory', CORE, Louvain-la-Neuve, mimeo (revised version of CORE Discussion Paper No. 8331).

MACLEOD, W. B., NORMAN, G. and THISSE, J.-F., 1984, 'Competition, Collusion and Free Entry in Spatial or Differentiated Product Markets', CORE Discussion Paper No. 8436, Louvain-la-Neuve.

MCCONNELL, J. D., 1968, 'An Experimental Examination of the Price-Quality Relationship', *Journal of Business*, 41 (October), pp. 439–449.

MCGEE, J. S., 1980, 'Predatory Pricing Revisited', *Journal of Law and Economics*, XXIII, 2 (October), pp. 289–330.

MCKINNON, R. I., 1966, 'Stigler's Theory of Oligopoly: A Comment', *Journal of Political Economy*, 74, pp. 281–285.

MADDALA, G. S., 1983, *Limited-Dependent and Qualitative Variables in Econometrics* (Cambridge University Press, Cambridge).

MARRIS, R. AND MUELLER, D. C., 1980, 'The Corporation, Competition and the Invisible Hand', *Journal of Economic Literature*, 18, 1 (March), pp. 32–63.

MARSHALL, A., 1920, *Principles of Economics* (Macmillan (8th Ed.), London).

MEADE, J., 1974, 'The Optimal Balance between Economies of Scale and Variety of Products: An Illustrative Model', *Economica*, 41, 164 (November), pp. 359–367.

MILGROM, P. and ROBERTS, J., 1982a, 'Predation, Reputation, and Entry Deterrence', *Journal of Economic Theory*, 27, 2 (August), pp. 280–312.

MILGROM, P. and ROBERTS, J., 1982b, 'Limit Pricing and Entry under Incomplete Information: An Equilibrium Analysis', *Econometrica*, 50, 2 (March), pp. 443–459.

MUELLER, D., 1981, 'Economies of Scale, Concentration and Collusion', mimeo, F.T.C.

MYERSON, R., 1984, 'Two-Person Bargaining Problems with Incomplete Information', *Econometrica*, 52, pp. 461–487.

NELSON, P., 1970, 'Information and Consumer Behaviour', *The Journal of Political Economy*, 78, 2 (March/April), pp. 311–329.

NELSON, P., 1974, 'Advertising as Information', *The Journal of Political Economy*, 82, 4 (July/August), pp. 729–754.

NERMUTH, M., 1979, *Information Structures in Economics*, Studies in the Theory of Markets with Imperfect Information, Lecture Notes in Economics and Mathematical Systems No. 196 (Springer-Verlag, Berlin).

NOVSHEK, W. and SONNENSCHEIN, H., 1980, 'Small Efficient Scale as a Foundation for Walrasian Equilibrium', *Journal of Economic Theory*, 22, pp. 243–255.

NOVSHEK, W. and SONNENSCHEIN, H., 1982, 'Fulfilled Expectations Cournot Duopoly with Information Acquisition and Release', *Bell Journal of Economics*, 13, pp. 214–218.

OKADA, A., 1980, 'Information Exchange Between Oligopolists', Department of Systems Science, Tokyo Institute of Technology, Research Report B-83, June, 1980.

ORDOVER, J. and WILLIG, R., 1981, 'An Economic Definition of Predation: Pricing and Product Innovation', *Yale Law Review*, 91, 1 (November), pp. 8–53.

ORNSTEIN, S., 1981, 'Antitrust Policy and Market Forces as Determinants of Industry Structure: Case Histories in Beer and Distilled Spirits', *The Antitrust Bulletin*, 26 (Summer), pp. 281–313.

ORR, R. and MACAVOY, P., 1965, 'Price Strategies to Promote Cartel Stability', *Economica*, 44, pp. 186–197.

OSBORNE, D. K., 1976, 'Cartel Problems', *American Economic Review*, 66, 5 (December), pp. 835–844.

PALFREY, T. R., 1982, 'Risk Advantages and Information Acquisition, *Bell Journal of Economics*, 13, pp. 219–224.

PATINKIN, D., 1947, 'Multi-Plant Firms, Cartels, and Imperfect Competition', *Quarterly Journal of Economics*, 61 (February), pp. 173–205.

PEARCE, D. G., 1984, 'Rationalisable Strategic Behaviour and the Problem of Perfection', *Econometrica*, 52, 4 (July), pp. 1029–1050.

PERLOFF, J. and SALOP, S., 1983, 'Equilibrium with Product Differentiation', mimeo.

PERRY, M. K., 1982, 'Oligopoly and Consistent Conjectural Variations', *Bell Journal of Economics*, 13, pp. 197–205.

PHLIPS, L., 1983, *The Economics of Price Discrimination* (Cambridge University Press, Cambridge).

PHLIPS, L. and THISSE, J. F., 1982, *Symposium on Spatial Competition and the Theory of Differentiated Markets, Journal of Industrial Economics*, 31, 1/2 (September, December).

PHLIPS, L. and RICHARD, J.-F., 1984, 'A Dynamic Oligopoly Model with Demand Inertia and Inventories', CORE Discussion Paper No. 84, Université Catholique de Louvain, Louvain-la-Neuve.

PLOTT, C. R., 1982, 'Industrial Organization Theory and Experimental Economics', *Journal of Economic Literature*, 20, pp. 1485–1527.

PORTER, R. H., 1983a, 'Optimal Cartel Trigger Price Strategies', *Journal of Economic Theory*, 29, 2 (April), pp. 313–338.

PORTER, R. H., 1983b, 'A Study of Cartel Stability: The Joint Executive Committee, 1880–1886', *The Bell Journal of Economics*, 14, 2 (Autumn), pp. 301–314.

PORTER, R. H., 1985, 'On the Incidence and Duration of Price Wars', *Journal of Industrial Economics*, this issue.

POSNER, R. A., 1975, 'The Social Costs of Monopoly and Regulation', *Journal of Political Economy*, 83, 4 (August), pp. 807–828.

POSNER, R. A., 1976, *Antitrust Law: An Economic Perspective* (University of Chicago Press, Chicago).

PRESCOTT, E. and VISSCHER, M., 1977, 'Sequential Location among Firms with Foresight', *Bell Journal of Economics*, 8, 2 (Autumn), pp. 378–393.

REES, R., 1984, 'The Theory of Principal and Agent', forthcoming *Bulletin of Economic Research.*

REES, R., 1985, 'Cheating in a Duopoly Supergame', *Journal of Industrial Economics*, this issue.

REINGANUM, J. F., 1981, 'Market Structure and the Diffusion of New Technology', *Bell Journal of Economics*, 12, 2 (Autumn), pp. 618–624.

REINGANUM, J. F., 1983, 'Uncertain Innovation and the Persistence of Monopoly', *American Economic Review*, 73, 4 (September), pp. 741–748.

REINGANUM, J. F., 1984, 'Uncertain Innovation and the Persistence of Monopoly: Reply', *American Economic Review*, 74, 1 (March), pp. 243–246.

ROBERTS, K., 1983, 'Self-Agreed Cartel Rules', mimeo, University of Warwick.

ROBERTS, K., 1985, 'Cartel Behaviour and Adverse Selection', *Journal of Industrial Economics*, this issue.

ROBERTS, M., 1983, 'Testing Oligopolistic Behaviour: An Application of the Variable Profit Function', forthcoming *International Journal of Industrial Organization.*

ROSENTHAL, R. W., 1981, 'Games of Perfect Information, Predatory Pricing and the Chain-Store Paradox', *Journal of Economic Theory*, 25, 1 (August), pp. 92–100.

ROSSE, J. N., 1970, 'Estimating Cost Function Parameters without Using Cost Data', *Econometrica*, 38, 2 (March), pp. 256–275.

ROTHSCHILD, R., 1981, 'Cartel Problems: Note'', *American Economic Review*, 71, 1 (March), pp. 179–181.

SALANT, S. W., SWITZER, S. and REYNOLDS, R. J., 1983, 'Losses from Horizontal Merger: The Effects of an Exogenous Change in Industry Structure in Cournot–Nash Equilibrium', *Quarterly Journal of Economics*, 98, 2 (May), pp. 185–199.

SALOP, S., 1979a, 'Strategic Entry Deterrence', *American Economic Review*, Papers and Proceedings, 69, 2 (May), pp. 335–338.

SALOP, S., 1979b, 'Monopolistic Competition with Outside Goods', *Bell Journal of Economics*, 10, 1 (Spring), pp. 141–156.

SANDMO, A., 1971, 'On the Theory of the Competitive Firm under Price Uncertainty', *American Economic Review*, 61, 1 (March), pp. 65–80.

SATTINGER, M., 1983, 'Value of an Additional Firm in Monopolistic Competition', mimeo.

SAUERMANN, H. and SELTEN, R., 1967, 'Ein Oligopolexperiment', in H. Sauermann (ed.), *Beitrage zür experimentellen Wirtschaftsforschung*, 1, Tübingen, pp. 9–59.

SCHELLING, T., 1960, *The Strategy of Conflict* (Harvard University Press, Cambridge, Mass.).

SCHERER, F. M. *et al.*, 1975, *The Economics of Multi-Plant Operation* (Harvard University Press, Cambridge, Mass.).

SCHERER, F. M., 1976a, 'Predatory Pricing and the Sherman Act: A Comment', *Harvard Law Review*, 89, 5 (March), pp. 868–890.

SCHERER, F. M., 1976b, 'Some Last Words on Predatory Pricing', *Harvard Law Review*, 89, 5 (March), pp. 901–903.

SCHERER, F. M., 1981, *Industrial Market Structure and Economic Performance* (2nd Edition, Rand-McNally, Chicago).

SCHMALENSEE, R. L., 1978, 'A Model of Advertising and Product Quality', *The Journal of Political Economy*, 86, 3 (June), pp. 485–503.

SCHMALENSEE, R., 1978, 'Entry Deterrence in the Ready to Eat Breakfast Cereal Industry', *Bell Journal of Economics*, 9, pp. 305–327.

SCHMALENSEE, R., 1979, 'On the Use of Economic Models in Antitrust: The *ReaLemon* Case', *University of Pennsylvania Law Review*, 127, 4 (April), pp. 994–1050.

SCHWARTZ, M. and REYNOLDS, R. J., 1983, 'Contestable Markets: An Uprising in the Theory of Industry Structure: Comments', *American Economic Review*, 73, 3 (June), pp. 488–490.

SELTEN, R., 1965, 'Spieltheoretische Behandlung eines Oligopolmodells mit Nachfrageträgheit', *Zeitschrift für die gesamte Staatswissenschaft*, 121, pp. 301–324 and 667–689.

SELTEN, R., 1978, 'The Chain Store Paradox', *Theory and Decision*, 9, 2 (April), pp. 127–159.

SELTEN, R., 1979, 'Experimentelle Wirtschaftsforschung', *Reinisch-Westfälische Akademie der Wissenschaften, Vorträge*, 287, pp. 41–72.

SELTEN, R., 1982, 'Einführung in die Theorie der Spiele mit unvollständiger Information', in *Information in der Wirtschaft*, Schriften der Vereins für Socialpolitik, Gesellschaft für Wirtschafts- und Socialwissenschaften, Neue Folge Band 126 (Duncker und Humblot, Berlin), pp. 81–147.

SHAKED, A. and SUTTON, J., 1982, 'Relaxing Price Competition through Product Differentiation', *Review of Economic Studies*, 49, 1 (January), pp. 3–14.

SHAKED, A. and SUTTON, J., 1983a, 'Natural Oligopolies and International Trade', in H. Kierzkowski (ed.), *Monopolistic Competition and International Trade* (Oxford University Press, Oxford).

SHAKED, A. and SUTTON, J., 1983b, 'Natural Oligopolies', *Econometrica*, 51, 5 (September), pp. 1469–1484.

SHAPIRO, C., 1983, 'Premiums for High Quality as Returns to Reputations', *The Quarterly Journal of Economics*, 98, 4 (November), pp. 659–679.

SHUBIK, M., 1982, *Game Theory in the Social Sciences*, Concepts and Solutions (MIT Press, Cambridge, Mass.).

SIMPSON, P. and WATERSON, M., 1984, 'Cartel Problem: The Incentive to Lie about Costs', mimeo, University of Newcastle.

SLADE, M., 1984, 'Conjectures, Firm Characteristics and Market Structure: An Analysis of Vancouver's Gasoline—Price Wars', mimeo, University of British Columbia.

SPENCE, A. M., 1975, 'Monopoly, Quality and Regulation', *Bell Journal of Economics*, 6, 2 (Autumn), pp. 417–429.

SPENCE, A. M., 1976, 'Product Selection, Fixed Costs and Monopolistic Competition', *Review of Economic Studies*, 43, 2 (July), pp. 217–236.

SPENCE, A. M., 1977, 'Entry Capacity, Investment and Oligopolistic Pricing', *Bell Journal of Economics*, 8, 2 (Autumn), pp. 534–544.

SPENCE, A. M., 1978, 'Tacit Co-ordination and Imperfect Information', *Canadian Journal of Economics*, 11, 3 (August), pp. 490–505.

SPENCE, A. M., 1979, 'Investment Strategy and Growth in a New Market', *Bell Journal of Economics*, 10, 1 (Spring), pp. 1–19.

SPENCE, A. M., 1980, 'Notes on Advertising, Economies of Scale, and Entry Barriers', *Quarterly Journal of Economics*, 95, 3 (November), pp. 493–507.

SPILLER, D. and FAVARO, E., 1984, 'The Effects of Entry Regulation on Oligopolistic Interaction: The Uruguayan Banking Sector', *Rand Journal of Economics*, 15, pp. 244–254.

SPULBER, D., 1981, 'Capacity, Output and Sequential Entry', *American Economic Review*, 71, 3 (June), pp. 503–514.

STAHL, K., 1982, 'Differentiated Products, Consumer Search, and Locational Oligopoly', *Journal of Industrial Economics*, 31, 1 (September), pp. 97–113.

STERN, N., 1972, 'The Optimal Size of Market Areas', *Journal of Economic Theory*, 4, 2 (April), pp. 154–173.

STIGLER, G. J., 1964, 'A Theory of Oligopoly', *Journal of Political Economy*, 72, 1 (February), pp. 44–61.

STOECKER, R., 1980, *Experimentelle Untersuchung des Entscheidungsverhaltens im Bertrand-Oligopol* (Pfeffersche Buchhandlung, Bielefeld).

SUMNER, D., 1981, 'Measurement of Monopoly Behaviour: An Application to the Cigarette Industry', *Journal of Political Economy*, 89, 5, pp. 1010–1019.

TELSER, L. G., 1966, 'Cutthroat Competition and the Long Purse', *Journal of Law and Economics*, 9, 2 (October), pp. 259–277.

TELSER, L. G., 1972, *Competition, Collusion and Game Theory* (Aldine-Atherton, Chicago).

ULEN, T. S., 1983, 'Railroad Cartels Before 1887: The Effectiveness of Private Enforcement of Collusion', *Research in Economic History*, 8, pp. 125–144.

VICKREY, W., 1961, 'Counter-speculation, Auctions, and Competitive Sealed Tenders', *Journal of Finance*, 16, pp. 8–37.

VIVES, X., 1983, 'Duopoly Information Equilibrium: Cournot and Bertrand', Department of Economics, University of Pennsylvania.

VON UNGERN-STERNBERG, T., 1984a, *Zur Analyse von Märkten mit unvollständiger Nachfragerinformation* (Springer-Verlag, Berlin-Heidelberg-New York).

VON UNGERN-STERNBERG, T., 1984b, 'Marktschutz und legaler Schutz auf Märkten mit Qualitötsunsicherheit', *Abhandlungen des Vereins für Socialpolitik*.

VON UNGERN-STERNBERG, T. and VON WEIZSÄCKER, C. C., 1981, 'Markstruktur und Marktverhalten bei Qualitätsunsicherheit', *Zeitschrift für Wirtschafts- und Sozialwissenschaften*, 101, pp. 609–626.

von Ungern-Sternberg, T. and von Weizsäcker, C. C., 1985, 'The Supply of Quality on a Market for "Experience Goods"', *Journal of Industrial Economics*, this issue.
von Weizsäcker, C. C., 1980a, 'A Welfare Analysis of Barriers to Entry', *Bell Journal of Economics*, II, 2 (Autumn), pp. 399–420.
von Weizsäcker, C. C., 1980b, 'Barriers to Entry: A Theoretical Treatment' (Springer-Verlag, Berlin-Heidelberg-New York).
Ware, R., 1984, 'Sunk Costs and Strategic Commitment: A Proposed Three-Stage Equilibrium', *Economic Journal*, 94, 374, pp. 370–378.
Waterson, M., 1983, 'Economies of Scope within Market Frameworks', *International Journal of Industrial Economics*, 1, pp. 223–237.
Williamson, O. E., 1977, 'Predatory Pricing: A Strategic and Welfare Analysis', *Yale Law Journal*, 87, 2 (December), pp. 284–340.
Wolinsky, A., 1983, 'Prices as Signals of Product Quality', *Review of Economic Studies*, 50, 4 (October), pp. 647–658.
Wolinsky, A., 1984, 'Product Differentiation with Imperfect Information', *Review of Economic Studies*, 51, 1 (January), pp. 53–61.
Yarrow, G., 1985, 'Welfare Losses in Oligopoly and Monopolistic Competition', *Journal of Industrial Economics*, this issue.

P. W. S. ANDREWS MEMORIAL ESSAY PRIZE—£300

The PWSA Memorial Prize of £300 is awarded annually. Competitors for the prize are asked to submit an essay on a subject of their own choice within the general field of Industrial Economics and Theory of the Firm, broadly interpreted. Entry to the competition is open to anyone under 30 years of age (or over 30, if not more than eight years have elapsed since taking a first degree). The essay, written in English, and not exceeding 10,000 words in length, should be a work of original research by the candidate only, not previously published and not previously awarded any other prize.

The winning essay may, at the discretion of the Editors, be published in *The Journal of Industrial Economics*.

The closing date for entries is 31st December.

Further details are available from:

Miss B. Cox,
University House,
The University of Lancaster,
Bailrigg, Lancaster, LA1 4YX, England.

The General Editor,
Journal of Industrial Economics,
The Institute of Economics and Statistics,
The University of Oxford,
St Cross Building, Manor Road,
Oxford, OX1 3UL, England.

The North American Editor,
Journal of Industrial Economics,
Graduate School of Business Administration,
New York University, 90 Trinity Place,
New York 10006, U.S.A.

THE JOURNAL OF INDUSTRIAL ECONOMICS

Published first in October 1952, the *Journal* has a very wide international circulation, and has established itself as the leading journal in the field of industrial economics. It was founded to promote the analysis of modern industry, particularly the behaviour of firms, and the functioning of markets. More specifically it seeks to bring the tools of modern economic analysis to bear on the analysis of real problems of industrial economies.

Contributions are welcomed covering all the major areas of industrial economics. One such area is the relationship between market structure and market behaviour in the areas of pricing, product differentiation, advertising and the dissemination of information and R&D. Another area focuses more directly on the firm, its objectives, finance, investment and growth. A third area comprises the background environment within which industrial firms operate: the changing structure of industry, public policy on monopoly and restrictive trade practices, regulation, fiscal and monetary policies as they affect firms, and underlying changes in productivity and international competitiveness.

The *Journal* has a tradition of publishing a blend of theory and evidence. Theoretical discussion is welcomed provided that the more abstract theory includes sufficient introduction and other explanation to convey the significance of the material to the general reader who wants to decide whether to follow the analysis through. Empirical analysis, and especially econometric analysis, should include an explanation of the data sources used, of the methods applied and of the underlying theoretical basis of the study. The *Journal* has a particular tradition of case studies of firms and industries, which the Editors would wish to continue. However contributors of such studies are asked to remember that a study will be of interest to the international readership of the *Journal* only if it makes a particular contribution to the methodology of such studies, or if the empirical results are exceptionally interesting.

Alongside articles of more normal length, the Editors are ready to publish shorter notes, especially where these give interim results of important research studies, or where they report significant new empirical results. Books are not reviewed, although books received will be listed, sometimes with a short note: but substantial review articles will be considered.

Information for Contributors

Submissions (*three* copies are required) should be in typescript, double-spaced, and should conform to the style of the *Journal*. Detailed Information for Contributors is available from the General Editor. The submission should include an Abstract, not exceeding 100 words.

Typescripts from North America should be sent to the North American Editor, Journal of Industrial Economics, Graduate School of Economics and Business Administration, New York University, 100 Trinity Place, New York, NY 10006, U.S.A.

Typescripts from *all* other countries should be sent to the General Editor, Journal of Industrial Economics, Institute of Economics and Statistics, University of Oxford, St Cross Building, Manor Road, Oxford OX1 3UL, U.K.

Information for Subscribers

The *Journal* is published four times a year, in September, December, March and June, by Basil Blackwell Ltd., 108 Cowley Road, Oxford OX4 1JF, U.K. Prices are as follows:

	UK	Overseas	USA	Canada
Institutions	£26.50	£33.50	$65.75	$80.50
Individuals	£16.25	£20.35	$35.00	$43.25
Single issue prices for:				
Institutions	£7.20	£8.80	$17.70	$21.50
Individuals	£5.20	£6.40	$12.00	$14.70

CONTRIBUTORS TO THIS NUMBER

P. A. GEROSKI: Department of Economics, University of Southampton, U.K.
L. PHLIPS: C.O.R.E., Université Catholique de Louvain, Belgium, and Editor of this *Journal*.
A. ULPH: Department of Economics, University of Southampton, U.K.
RAY REES: Department of Economics, University College, Cardiff, U.K., and Associate Editor of this *Journal*.
KEVIN ROBERTS: Department of Economics, University of Warwick, U.K.
ROBERT H. PORTER: State University of New York at Stony Brook, U.S.A.
JONATHAN B. BAKER: Department of Economics, Stanford University, U.S.A., and Member of the Bar, District of Columbia.
TIMOTHY F. BRESNAHAN: Department of Economics, Stanford University, U.S.A., and Associate Editor of this *Journal*.
DAVID EASLEY: Department of Economics, Cornell University, New York, U.S.A.
ROBERT T. MASSON: Department of Economics, Cornell University, New York, U.S.A.
ROBERT J. REYNOLDS: ICF, Incorporated.
CHRISTOPHER HARRIS: Nuffield College, University of Oxford, U.K.
JOHN VICKERS: Nuffield College, University of Oxford, U.K., and Associate Editor of this *Journal*.
HUW DIXON: Birkbeck College, University of London, U.K.
NORMAN J. IRELAND: Department of Economics, University of Warwick, U.K.
G. K. YARROW: Hertford College, University of Oxford, U.K., and Editor of this *Journal*.
THOMAS von UNGERN-STERNBERG: Department of Economics, University of Berne, Switzerland.
CARL CHRISTIAN von WEIZSÄCKER: Department of Economics, University of Berne, Switzerland, and Associate Editor of this *Journal*.

US Mailing: Second class postage paid at New York. Postmaster: Send address corrections to: Journal of Industrial Economics, c/o Expediters of the Printed Word Ltd., 515 Madison Avenue, New York, NY 10022 (US Mailing Agent).

Reprints of Back Volumes: Volumes 1–28 of the *Journal* are available (in complete volumes only) from the Kraus Reprint Corporation, Route 100, Millwood, New York 10546, U.S.A. More recent back issues are available from the publisher at the current single issue price.

Microfilm: An agreement for the supply of microfilm copies from Volume 1 onwards has been made with University Microfilms International, Department PR, 30–32 Mortimer Street, London W1N 7RA, England, or 300 North Zeeb Road, Ann Arbor, Michigan 48106, U.S.A.

Set in Monophoto Baskerville by Advanced Filmsetters (Glasgow) Ltd
Printed and Bound in Great Britain by T. J. Press (Padstow) Ltd, Cornwall